# G

# DIRECTORY
## 1996

**Sponsored by Jacksons Landing, Hartlepool,**
the Factory Outlet Shopping Centre
for the North-East.

Developed by
The Guinea Group Limited

# DEAR READER

We hope you enjoy reading this book,
the definitive guide to value for money
shopping in Britain.

We have lots of other exciting books
which we'd like to tell you about.
Send us a card with your name and address
FREEPOST and we will send you information
about how to obtain these books.
Write to: The Good Deal Directory,
FREEPOST SW 6037,
London SW10 9YY.

You do not need to affix a stamp.

# THE
# GOOD
# DEAL
## DIRECTORY
# 1996

**NOELLE WALSH**

First published in 1995 by
**The Good Deal Directory Company Limited**
P.O. Box 4, Lechlade, Glos GL7 3YB

ISBN 0-9526529-0-0

Typeset by Windmill Typesetters, 87-89 Saffron Hill, London EC1N 8QU.
Printed and bound in Great Britain
by Cox & Wyman Ltd, Reading, Berkshire.

# CONTENTS

*Continued overleaf*

# INTRODUCTION

Welcome to this, the third edition of The Good Deal Directory, popularly known as the bargain hunter's Bible. Since it first appeared in September 1993, the Directory has become a household name. It's been favourably reviewed by almost all the well-known, high circulation women's magazines, every national daily newspaper bar The Sun, most of the Sundays and a huge array of local newspapers. It's also been the subject of wide tv and radio coverage, including Good Morning with Anne and Nick, GMTV's Breakfast Show and BBC Radio 4's Woman's Hour.

Part of the reason for this is that the information contained in this book is difficult for an individual to obtain. Even now, four years after I first started researching this area, I sometimes have "difficult" phone calls with factory shop managers who want to know where I found out about them. Others specifically ask me not to write about their factory shop, even when I or one of my readers have been there and want to recommend it as good value for money. They prefer to rely on word of mouth and local advertising. That way, they can control what is said about their outlet so that if, for instance, they sell Marks & Spencer clearance lines, M&S's name won't appear anywhere in the copy. High street shops are still wary of factory outlets and fear that greater public knowledge of their existence might have an adverse effect on their full-price sales.

This book, like the two previous editions, tells you all about the pick of the factory shops, permanent discount outlets, dress agencies, hire shops, designer sales, architectural salvage outlets, food and drinks discounters, secondhand shops and vintage clothes shops in your area.

Each year, there is a major change in the rapidly growing area of discount shopping. Last year, it was the increase in food discounting which brought media attention to the whole area of "bargain" shopping. Food discounting hit the news when foreign supermarket companies from Germany, France and Denmark came into the marketplace offering food and grocery items at prices which were significantly lower than the same or similar items in British supermarkets. Competition proved to be good for the consumer: the net result of the supermarket price war was that food prices across the board dropped in 1994/5.

This year, the great change in discount retailing has again been provoked by foreign competition: this time, from the Americans. Factory outlet centres or "malls" are opening up in Britain at an incredible rate, offering anything up to 48 different factory shops on the one site. The sudden flush of "mall" type centres has been sparked, in part, by their success in the States where there are now 275 such centres with 8,500 shops, and another 160 in the pipeline. But with the chances of further expansion in the States low, successful US factory mall companies began to look elsewhere to establish new businesses. Hence the explosion in Britain.

In June 1994, there were just two factory outlet centres in Britain. By June 1995, there were nine. These are: Hornsea Freeport Shopping Village in East Yorkshire; Clarks Village Factory Shopping in Street, Somerset; Lightwater Village and Factory Shopping in Ripon, North Yorkshire; Merchants Quay at Brighton Marina; Jacksons Landing, Hartlepool Factory Outlet Shopping Mall; Cheshire Oaks Designer Outlet Village near Ellesmere Port, South Wirral; K Village in Cumbria (sister to Clarks Village); Bicester Village, Bicester, Oxfordshire; and Freeport Shopping Village, Fleetwood, Lancashire (sister to Hornsea Freeport).

Although the first two factory outlet centres are in fact British - Hornsea Freeport in East Yorkshire and Clarks Village in Street, Somerset - and each of these has given birth to another centre - Fleetwood in Merseyside and K Village in Cumbria - much of the activity for the future is centred around the "marriages" of British and American companies. These partnerships, spurred on by the

American experience, have a list of "commandments" when it comes to choosing factory centre sites: thou shalt not build near a town centre and upset the very retailers whose stock, albeit not quite so fresh and new, you are selling cheaper than they are; thou shalt give as good a service as if the customer was paying full price; thou shalt have discounts of at least 30%; thou shalt have plenty of parking spaces; thou shalt make shopping fun. Thus, you shouldn't be surprised to see that the addresses of factory shopping centres in this book are more likely to dwell on the motorway junction to which they are nearest than to their post code.

Fears that factory shopping could irretrievably damage full-price shops seem to be contradicted by the American experience, where market share is still less than 2%. American enthusiasts claim that everyone is in a win-win situation: the manufacturer can earn some money from his overruns, cancelled orders, seconds and returns; the retailer can "clean" his rails of slow-moving merchandise and bring in new, exciting lines; and the customer can enjoy the fun of choosing from a new range each time they shop in the high street, while being able to take advantage of the discount opportunities of slightly older stock in the factory shops.

But in America, factory shopping is a way of life. Most consumers understand what it's all about and most retailers accept it as part of the retailing cycle. Here, there is still widespread ignorance of exactly what factory shopping means. According to the little research that has been done in this area, British shoppers expect to save less, shop in a less pleasant environment and be able to choose from fewer current styles in factory shops than do their American counterparts. A British shopper's idea of a factory shop may have been gleaned from a visit to an outlet which is still just a curtained-off corner of the factory. While British manufacturers are increasingly viewing their factory outlets as separate profit centres and an extension of their brand image, there are still sufficient numbers of the old-style factory shops around to convince the intermittent bargain hunter that this is what it's all about.

The Mulberry factory shop at Chilcompton, near Bath, is an example of those which conveys the same image whether in the high street or in the quiet backwater where the factory shop is situated. It has all the style you would expect from the Mulberry name and only the discreetly crossed through price tags indicate its real purpose in selling clearance stock.

The newest factory outlet malls enhance the clean-cut image of factory shopping in the 1990s. Jacksons Landing, in deference to the inclement weather in the north-east, is an indoor factory mall which resembles any smart shopping centre in the country. Like Clarks Village, Bicester Village and Cheshire Oaks,it features a range of well-known brand names in high-street-style-shop settings. All the shops have changing rooms (where applicable), helpful staff, shelves or rails packed with goods usually marked with the original and the reduced price, and take credit cards. The shops maintain their brand image in their sites: thus Joan & David's factory shop at Bicester Village is exactly what you would expect from it - spacious and elegant.

The brand names now available in factory shops is impossible to list here - though they're all in the book. But to give you a flavour: in fashion alone, there's Polo Ralph Lauren, Cerruti, Hobbs, Jaeger, Windsmoor, Joan & David, Osh Kosh b'Gosh, Timberland, Paul Costelloe, Burberry, Mulberry, Levi's, Kurt Geiger, Barbour, Lyle & Scott, Joe Bloggs, Benetton, Laura Ashley, Wallis, Scotch House, Racing Green, Warners, Triumph, Dannimac.

The nine factory shopping villages which I mentioned earlier are not all alike. Jacksons Landing, Clarks Village, Cheshire Oaks, Bicester Village, Freeport Shopping Village and K Village all feature stand-alone shops, each representing one manufacturer or manufacturer/retailer. Merchants Quay at Brighton and Lightwater Valley have a few of these separate shops as well as large outlets selling a wide range of brand names under the one roof. Thus at Lightwater, one huge warehouse might sell a wide range of men's brand name clothes from different manufacturers, a similarly wide range of women's clothes, as well as make-up, luggage, cookware, jewellery, bedlinen and books.

There is one aspect, however, which they all share: they all feature fashion as the main ingredient. The majority of the shops sell women's clothes and accessories (including shoes), with men's clothes a close second and children's clothes lagging lamentably behind. Next comes crystal and glassware with luggage and bags a long way behind. The other areas covered usually feature only one shop in each centre: bedlinen, home accessories, electrical equipment, sports gear, toys. If centres want to attract families - and they obviously do as most of them have children's play areas - they will need to offer more than just the odd clothes and/or toy shop to bring in parents with children.

If you think nine factory shopping centres is a lot, wait until next year. This year's book has expanded by 120 pages, partly due to the growth of such malls. Next year, if planning permission is forthcoming and development money flows in, there will be factory shopping centres at Tewkesbury in  Gloucestershire; Doncaster; Clacton-on-Sea; Kinross in Scotland; Bradford; Sandbach in Cheshire; London's Tobacco Dock; Ebbw Vale in Gwent, to name just a few of the areas targeted as we went to press in August 1995.

Of course, there's a price to pay for factory shopping, even in the glamorous surroundings of the new centres. And the price is higher if you're interested in fashion. Remember, all the stock that's in these factory shops is there because it didn't sell sufficiently quickly in the high street. Perhaps the colour wasn't as popular as all the others that were available in that style; or it didn't look as good on size eights as it did on size fourteens. So if you find something you like in a factory shop, only you want it a size bigger and in black please, the assistant won't just be able to ring the branch down the road and get them to hold one for you. The blue size 10 you've fallen in love with is it - that's all there is left, ever. However, the common belief that most of the stock in factory shops is made up of seconds is a misconception. Nowadays, most stock is made up of overstocks, returns, samples, last season's lines and discontinued lines. At Clarks Village, for instance, 85% of the merchandise is perfect.

It doesn't matter at all - well, it doesn't to me, anyway - that the six crystal wine glasses I bought were the shape of 1992 or that the duvet cover I treasure reflects 1993's popular shades. Or that the jigsaw puzzle I coveted was on sale in high streets last Christmas or the girl's party dress I grabbed was what all the five year olds were wearing last summer. It doesn't even matter to me that the palazzo pants I now wear to death were the triumph of the catwalks aeons ago in fashion's high-speed time frame or the black jacket that turns my slightly casual dress instantly to smart meeting mode is at least two seasons old. But if I wanted to scan the catwalks and look instantly a la mode, factory shopping would not be for me.

Don't let factory shopping malls overshadow the fact that there are scores of other opportunity to buy brand-name bargains at discount prices. Designer sales - where designers allow trusted organisers to sell off their end of season lines and samples - are a marvellous way of adding lustre to your wardrobe at dramatically reduced prices. Here, you can try names which you couldn't possibly afford to buy in the shops. Dress agencies - selling nearly-new outfits from the high street to couture - are another rapidly growing way in which people make their budget stretch. In fact, if you're really clever, you can visit the designer sales, buy a top designer outfit for, say, £100, reduced from £500, wear it once or twice and then sell it on to a dress agency and get your money back.

While the housing market stagnates, our interest in our homes does not, and that's proved by the wide range of options available for those looking for fabrics and curtains. Fabric manufacturers bring out new designs each season and with rolls of fabric taking up so much space, they have to move last year's designs out quickly. Some run their own warehouse sales (Designers Guild, Osborne & Little), some have factory shops (GP & J Baker, Sandersons) and most leading names are available through the host of discounters detailed in this book.

Anyone who is looking to replace curtains and doesn't look first in a secondhand curtain shop has got to have more money than sense. They are THE greatest find for home decorators. Here, you can find fabrics you could never in a million years afford, made up into lined and interlined and sometimes even weighted curtains, some with matching tie-backs and valances. Most of the outlets display the curtains full-length, so you get a much better idea of how they will look than you do by buying fabric and getting them made up yourself. Many also let you take the curtains home, hang them and, if they don't look quite right, return them and get your money back the next day. You can't get fairer than that.

This book also contains details of outlets where you can find paint, tiles, carpet, wallpaper and furniture. But be warned: to a large extent you do get what you paid for. So if, for instance, you buy cheap paint, it may not last as long or look as good for as long as the more expensive brand name. The reason why I don't mention more furniture makers is that everyone knows where they can buy cheap pine or reproduction sideboards or bargain sofas. But unless you can dig around and see the actual wood and the method of making, you don't really know whether you're getting a good deal. You might buy a sofa cheaply but it's unlikely to be as well made as its more expensive counterpart.

The Good Deal Directory isn't about where to find items cheaply. If it was, it would be full of details of markets and car boot sales. What it is about is buying quality goods at prices which are lower than they were originally. Most of the information has been gathered by myself and my team of researchers over the past five or more years; a lot of it is now also supplied by readers of The Good Deal Directory newsletter which appears monthly. I pay for tips: places which readers have visited and believe is good value. My readers tell me what they bought, what else was for sale there, what the discounts were and what the service was like. I couldn't ask for a better team of researchers. If you know of somewhere that isn't in this book and which I subsequently publish, remember I pay £10 for tips. So you could end up enjoying a free book.

Happy bargain hunting! **Noelle Walsh**

# A NOTE ABOUT REGIONS

Within the various chapters, for ease of reference, the UK has been divided into the following regions:

## LONDON
Including Greater London.

## SOUTH EAST
Including Buckinghamshire, Bedfordshire, Hertfordshire, Essex, Kent, East Sussex, West Sussex, Hampshire and the Isle of Wight, Bershire, Surrey.

## SOUTH WEST
Including Cornwall, Devon, Somerset, Dorset, Wiltshire, Avon.

## WALES AND WEST MIDLANDS
Including Clwyd, Gwynedd, Dyfed, Powys, West Glamorgan, Mid Glamorgan, Gloucestershire, Oxfordshire, Warwickshire, West Midlands, Staffordshire, Shropshire, Hereford and Worcester.

## EAST ANGLIA AND EAST MIDLANDS
Including Norfolk, Suffolk, Cambridgeshire, Northamptonshire, Leicestershire, Lincolnshire, Nottinghamshire, Derbyshire.

## NORTH WEST, YORKSHIRE AND HUMBERSIDE
Including Lancashire, Merseyside, Cheshire, Greater Manchester, West Yorkshire, South Yorkshire, Humberside, North Yorkshire.

## NORTH AND SCOTLAND
Including Cumbria, Durham, Cleveland, Tyne and Wear, Northumberland, Dumfries and Galloway, Strathclyde, Lothian, Central, Fife, Tayside, Grampian, Highlands and Islands.

## NORTHERN IRELAND

# WOMENSWEAR

*Permanent Discount Outlets,*
*Factory Shops,*
*Dress Agencies,*
*Hire Shops,*
*Secondhand and Vintage Clothes,*
*Designer Sales*

# LONDON

## Permanent Discount Outlets

### BUTTERFLY

28A PONSONBY PLACE, LONDON SW1
☎ 0171-821 1983. OPEN 11.30 - 6.30 MON - FRI, UNTIL 7.30 ON THUR.
Sells fashion samples obtained through extensive contacts in the industry at wholesale price or less. Stock is from the current season and the following season so that you can be ahead of the fashion - but only if you are a size 10 or 12 as samples are model-sizes only. As well as some British designers, the shop has a lot of French and Italian labels, many of which can be seen in Harrods designer department. There's Dusk, Diana Gee, Caroline Roumer, Character, August Silk, and Frank Usher, as well as silk shirts and skirts from Fenn Wright & Manson.

### CAVENAGH SHIRTS

659 FULHAM ROAD, LONDON SW6 5PY
☎ 0171-371 0528. OPEN 11 - 7 MON - THUR, 10 - 6 FRI, SAT.
MAIL ORDER.
Offers Jermyn Street quality women's and men's shirts at half the normal Jermyn Street price. Made from two-fold cotton poplin or classic cotton Oxford, the shirts are now available by mail order. There is also a full range of similarly competitively priced accessories, including pure silk ties, cuff links, boxer shorts, and Italian calf belts. Everything is manufactured in the UK.

### CORIOLIS

1ST FLOOR, 202/208 REGENTS PARK ROAD, FINCHLEY,
LONDON N3 3HP
☎ 0181-343 2579. OPEN 10 - 5 WED - SAT, 11 - 2 SUN.
Offers stylish Continental women's collections at fantastically reduced prices all year round. For summer, they have crisp linen mixes, sumptuous silks and uncrushable crepes; in winter, beautiful cashmere and virgin wools. Coats, jackets, suits, separates and dresses come in sizes 8-20. Ninety-five percent of the stock is Italian, and

most of the labels are not widely available in this country, though they claim the quality is equivalent to Marella or MaxMara. Stock includes this season's lines.

## DASH SALE SHOP

WOOD GREEN SHOPPING CENTRE, LONDON N22
☎ 0181-889 9560. OPEN 9 - 5.30 MON - FRI, 9 - 6 SAT.
Dash and Alexon ends of ranges and seconds and some Eastex sold here at discount. Also some Ann Harvey outsize stock 16-26. Jackets cost about £60 and skirts £30.

## DESIGNERS SALE STUDIO

241 KING'S ROAD, LONDON SW3 5EL
☎ 0171-351 4171. OPEN 10.30 - 6.30 MON - FRI, 10 - 6 SAT, 12 - 6 SUN.
Catwalk clothes for both women and men at discounts of up to 60%. Perfectly tailored Armani, Bagutta and Apara suits and separates hang alongside pastel shades in chiffon by Genny, together with the essential military pinstripe from Complice. Also available are designer bodies, T-shirts and jeans from Emporio Armani and Dolce e Gabbana as well as accessories by Moschino and Genny and the indispensable Prada handbag. There is a complementary menswear collection on the lower ground floor.

## DISCOUNT DRESSING

39 PADDINGTON STREET, LONDON W1M 3RN
☎ 0171-486 7230. OPEN 10 - 6 SEVEN DAYS A WEEK.
16 SUSSEX RING, WOODSIDE PARK, LONDON N12
☎ 0181-343 8343. OPEN 10 - 6 SEVEN DAYS A WEEK.
Discount Dressing is a veritable Aladdin's Cave of designer bargains. They sell mostly German, Italian and French designer labels at prices at least 50% and up to 90% below those in normal retail outlets, and all items are brand new and perfect. They have a team of buyers all over Europe who purchase stock directly from the manufacturer, therefore by-passing the importers and wholesalers and, of course, their mark-up. They also buy bankrupt stock in this country. Their agreement with their suppliers means that they are not able to advertise brand names for obvious reasons, but they are all well-known for their top quality and style. So confident is Discount Dressing that you will be unable to find the same item cheaper elsewhere, that they offer

to give the outfit to you free of charge should you perform this miracle. Merchandise includes raincoats, dresses, suits, trousers, blouses, evening wear, special occasion outfits and jackets, in sizes 6-24 and in some cases larger. GDD readers can obtain a further 10% discount if they visit the shop taking a copy of this book with them.

## EURO DIRECT

37-39 BEAVOR LANE, HAMMERSMITH, LONDON W6 9AT
☎ 0181-563 2233. OPEN 9 - 5 MON - SAT.
German mail order company, trading under the name Sportive Elegance, which holds clearance sales twice a year at Chelsea Old Town Hall and also has a permanent warehouse in Hammersmith, selling designer fashions at discounts of up to 50%. Outfits are mainly casual, with lots of linen shorts, shirts and waistcoats; silk blouses; leather and suede trousers; cotton and linen trouser suits. Most of the stock is discontinued lines from the catalogue, in sizes 10-18, but there are also some samples in sizes 10 and 12.

## FIRST SPORT

456-458 THE STRAND, LONDON WC2R ORG
☎ 071-839 5161. OPEN 9.30 - 6 MON - SAT, UNTIL 7 ON THUR.
They are so certain that their prices for top brand-name sports shoes are the lowest you will find that they guarantee that if you buy from them and then see the same shoes cheaper elsewhere, they will refund the difference. Brand names on sale at discounts of up to 50% include Nike, Reebok, Puma and Adidas. The shop also sells clothing, bags, T-shirts, skiwear, skis, ski boots and a full range of back packing equipment such as tents, camping tools and accessories. With 60 shops to buy for, they can purchase in bulk and get good deals.

## I KINN

80 GEORGE LANE, SOUTH WOODFORD, LONDON E18 1JJ
☎ 0181-989 2927. OPEN 10 - 5.30 MON - FRI, 10 - 5 SAT & SUN.
Large showroom selling classic store merchandise such as is found in Lewis and House of Fraser groups at bargain prices. There are plenty of ladies jackets, suits, dresses and skirts plus designer clothes from time to time at about half the normal retail price.

# JADE

22 HAMPSTEAD HIGH STREET, LONDON NW3
☎ 0171-794 3889. OPEN 10 - 6 MON - SAT, UNTIL 7 THUR, 11 - 6.30 SUN.
82 GOLDERS GREEN ROAD, LONDON NW
☎ 11 0181-201 9155. OPEN 10 - 6 SEVEN DAYS A WEEK,
UNTIL 6.30 ON THUR.
Italian, French, American and German clothes for women, mostly in
silk, with few designer names. A small selection for men. Evening
dresses cost from £90 upwards and there are skirts, blouses, jackets and
shirts. All perfects. Accessories include scarves, camisoles and ties.

# JOEL & SON

77 CHURCH STREET, LONDON NW8
☎ 0171-724 6895. OPEN 8.30 - 5 MON - SAT.
London's foremost designer fabric store sells offcuts and end of roll
fabrics used by the top catwalk designers and couturiers from St
Laurent and Cerruti to Versace, Christian Lacroix, Pierre Balmain
and Gianfranco Ferre. Prices are not cheap, but the fabric is exceptional; all are heavily discounted. Also carries a wide range of supplies
for bridal wear including embroidered laces, beaded fabrics,
Jacquards, Duchess satins, as well as veils in silk and silk mixes. Good
range of designer lookalike buttons. Mr Joel has been in the business
for nearly 45 years and at the same premises for 12 years.

# KNOTS KNITWEAR

19 JERDAN PLACE FULHAM LONDON SW6 1BE
☎ 0171-385 2252. OPEN TUE,WED AND THUR 10.30 - 4
AND ON SAT 11 - 3 OR BY APPOINTMENT. STUDIO -
☎ 0171-385 9929. OPEN MON - SAT 9 - 6.30 AND UNTIL 7.30 ON THUR.
Knots Knitwear has just opened a new showroom in London selling
goods at wholesale prices. There are silky cottons, alpaca and linens,
jumpers, jackets, skirts and twinsets, and 100% cashmere and silk
scarves, shawls, throws, skirts and dressing gowns. There is a new
studio upstairs with hundreds of Rococo frames all ready-made and
sold at factory prices to the public. There is a print room with a wide
selection of modern and old - fashioned prints from £3. There is also
a Medieval Mirror room and a Gift room with many cards and
presents from under £5.

## LAUREL HERMAN

18A LAMBOLLE PLACE, LONDON NW3 4PG
☎ 0171-586 7925. FAX 0171-586 7926. BY APPOINTMENT ONLY

Established for almost 25 years, and with 2,000 regular clients, this is London's best-kept secret in order to maintain its exclusivity. Housed in a spacious, airy "concealed" Hampstead showroom is an ever-changing melange of 6,000 upmarket designer items (Armani, Escada, MaxMara, Donna Karan, Valentino etc) at a fraction of their original price. Both brand new and "gently-worn" but sourced only from Laurel's own personal contacts who shop the world to answer all requirements for day or evening, however casual or formal. This unique concept is ideal for those who normally hate shopping, need a new look, have figure problems...or just clothesaholics. Many clients work towards the ultimate wardrobe solution i.e.Laurel Herman's Wardrobe That Works, but all advice is totally objective, free of charge and based on personal life, style, shape, personality and budget. (There is a brochure to explain the concept in more detail.) In order to maintain the peaceful, relaxed ambience, appointments are necessary from 10 am Mon - Sat but extending to 11 in the evening twice weekly for busy women. Be warned, customers usually stay three to four hours! The collection is taken twice yearly to Southampton in June and November. Workshops and seminars are available on style-related topics and these are planned for male consultancy, too.

## MACCULLOCK AND WALLIS

25-26 DERING STREET, LONDON W1R OBH
☎ 0171-409 3506. OPEN 9 - 6 MON-FRI, 10.30 - 5 SAT. MAIL ORDER.

Wedding dress pattern specialists both by mail order and through a retail outlet, they sell wedding dress kits which will ensure handy brides-to-be are decked out in ivory silk dupion at a fraction of the cost of the ready-made outfit. There are five different kits available, each priced at £99 including p&p; the standard one takes about 34 hours to make from start to finish and is aimed at the home dress maker. Also sell wholesale and retail fabric. Send for catalogue.

## MORE HAIR EXTENSIONS

9 SEYMOUR MEWS, LONDON W1H 9PH
☎ 0171-487 5977. PHONE FIRST.

Offers you a thicker or longer head of hair in just two or three hours. Available in any style, colour or texture, the extensions are made of finest quality human hair and come in a variety of lengths ranging from six inches to twenty-four inches and can be adapted to suit wavy, straight, Afro-Caribbean, Asian or European hair. The extensions do not come into contact with the scalp, but are moulded to natural hair with a water-resistant fixative which requires a special sovent for removal. They last until they grow out naturally and allow you to swim, curl or style your hair in any way you want. Prices for extensions are about 25% less than you would expect to pay in high street salons and range from about £200 upwards for a session which would cost £300 with other upmarket companies. They should always be fitted by an experienced stylist.

## MORRY'S

39-40 THE BROADWAY, EDMONTON, LONDON N9 0TJ
☎ 0181-807 6747. OPEN 8.30 - 5 MON - SAT, CLOSED AT 1 ON THUR.

Liquidation stock which includes some famous makes and can comprise anything from gardening equipment (shovels, forks and hoses) and household items to eletrical equipment (CDs, radios, TVs, CDi's, radio alarms) and clothing for women, men and children. Everything is at least half the retail price. Phone beforehand to find out what they've got in stock or if you live nearby, drop in frequently.

## NEXT TO NOTHING

UNIT 11, WATERGLADES CENTRE, EALING BROADWAY,
LONDON W5 2ND
☎ 0181-567 2747. OPEN 9.30 - 6 MON - SAT.

Sells perfect surplus stock from Next stores and the Next Directory catalogue - from belts, jewellery and underwear to day and evening wear - at discounts of 50% or more. The ranges are usually last season's and overruns but there is the odd current item if you look carefully. Stock consists of men's, women's and children's clothing, with some homeware and shoes, depending on the branch. Stock is replenished twice a week and there is plenty of it. This branch does not stock homes items and has only a small amount of accessories.

## OGEE

81 SHAFTESBURY AVENUE, LONDON W1
☎ 0171-434 0064. OPEN 9 - 6 MON - SAT, 11 - 3 SUN.
Sells a huge range of hair products and hair styling and beauty equipment (including a wide range of nail products but no make-up) from cheap and cheerful curling tongs at around £4.95 to top of the range professional hair driers at more than £100. You won't find any of the recognisable brands advertised on television here, but what you will find are products which professional hairdressers use - which means they're likely to last a long time and be well-priced. The curling tongs are sold with different barrel widths so you can give yourself a tight or a loose curl. All prices are exclusive of VAT in this shop which is primarily a wholesaler, but which does sell to individual members of the public.

## SCREEN FACE

24 POWIS TERRACE, LONDON W11 1JH
☎ 0171-221 8289. OPEN 9 - 6 MON - SAT.
Stocks the biggest selection of make-up in England and is open to individuals as well as professionals. It sells own brands as well as Cosmetics A La Carte and RCMA - the latter with 80 different foundations - as well as make-up which department stores and chemists don't offer such as line fillers. Also wide selection of squirrel and sable brushes and make-up bags.

## SUNGLASS HUT INTERNATIONAL

KING'S WALK MALL, 122 KING'S ROAD, LONDON SW3
☎ 0171-225 3150. OPEN 10 - 7 MON - SAT, 12 - 6 SUN.
The world's largest retailer of quality sunglasses offers "lowest price guarantee" on famous brands such as Ray-Ban, Oakley, Boole, Armani, SunGear and Georgio Armani.

## SWIMGEAR

11 STATION ROAD, FINCHLEY LONDON N3 2SB
☎ 0181-346 6106. OPEN 9.30 - 5 MON - FRI, UNTIL 8 ON THUR.
MAIL ORDER.

A mail order company which also operates via a retail outlet next to Finchley Central station. They sell discontinued and ends of line ranges of swimwear for women, men and children at between 20%-30% less than normal retail prices. They also stock goggles and flippers in adult sizes . Flippers normally cost about £18.50, but can be bought here for about £8 in black rubber. The catalogues are full colour and carry the names Speedo, Adidas, Hind and Maru, as well as Swimgear's own brand full colour Mark One brochure. Prices are lower than than would be offered at swim meets and retail shops. Examples of prices include Classic Goggles, £2.80, silicone earplugs, £2.05, handpaddles, £6.40, armbands, £4.30. As part of their service, they do not cash your cheque until your full order has been completed. P&p extra, orders over £50 are post free.

## THE BRAND CENTRE

MOLLISON AVENUE, STOCKINGSWATER LANE, BRIMSDOWN, ENFIELD, MIDDLESEX EN3 7PH
☎ 0181-805 8080. OPEN 10 - 8 MON - FRI, 10 - 7 SAT, 12 - 6 SUN.

The fashion equivalent of the US warehouse-style supermarkets in that it offers out-of-town location, plenty of free car parking and brand name goods at discount prices. In the case of The Brand Centre, a 40,000 sq ft warehouse, the brand names range from Mulberry, Timberland, Ally Capellino and Moschino to YSL. As well as clothes for women, men and children, the outlet also sells jewellery, shoes, lingerie, handbags and umbrellas at discounts which average about 25% by working on high turnover and low profit margins. For women, there is Jacques Vert, Ego, Bassini, Jeff Banks, Sara Sturgeon, Fenn Wright & Manson, Benny Ong and Naff Naff.

## THE CLOTH SHOP

290 PORTOBELLO ROAD, LONDON W10
☎ 0181-968 6001. OPEN 10.30 - 6 MON - THUR, 10 - 6 FRI AND SAT.

Discounted fabric from good tweeds and cottons, muslin and calico to Lycra, as well as brand name ends of rolls and sample lengths. Turnover is high and stock changes constantly.

# THE DISCOUNT DESIGNER CLOTHES STORE

14 PROCTOR STREET, HOLBORN, LONDON WC1
☎ 0171-404 4049. OPEN 9 - 5.30 MON - FRI, 10 - 1 SAT.

The Discount Designer Clothes Store sells a range of new outfits which it buys direct from mainly American and Canadian designer wholesalers. You may not recognise many of the labels because they are transatlantic, but the quality is good and they are all current season. Most are perfects with some imperfects and all are half price or less. Labels include Suzelle, Stephanie, Magnolia, Kasper and Joseph Ribkoff. Items on sale include suits, casualwear, special occasion outfits, cotton tops and silk separates. Most of the range is daywear in sizes 10-16, and prices range from £15 to £100. There are no accessories.

# THE MAKE-UP CENTRE

26 BUTE STREET, LONDON SW7 3EX
☎ 0171-584 2188. OPEN 11 - 6.30 MON - FRI, 11 - 5.30 SAT.

Sells own brands of matt eyeshadow, foundation, and blusher which are twice the size of ones you can buy in department stores. Also good sable brushes which are cheaper than those found in artists' shops. Also do makeovers and offer make-up lessons for £60 for one and a half hours. With thirty years experience in the business, they have not only trained the best makeup artists, but made up prime ministers, film stars and tv presenters. Full wedding makeovers from £75

# THE SALVAGE SHOP

34-38 WATLING AVENUE, BURNT OAK, MIDDLESEX HA8 0LR
☎ 0181-952 4353. OPEN 9 - 5.30 MON - SAT.

An Aladdin's cave of "salvaged" stock for the avid bargain hunter, most of which has been the subject of bankruptcy, insurance claims, fire or flood. Regular visitors have found anything from half-price Kenwood Chefs, typewriters and telephones to furniture, kitchen items and designer clothes. Yves St Laurent, Ungaro, MaxMara, Chloe, Agnes B, Mondi, are just some of the labels (though they are often cut out) to appear. Discounts range from 50%-75%. Phone first to check stock.

# VIVM

201 NEW KING'S ROAD, LONDON SW6 4SR
☎ 0171-731 5567. OPEN 10 - 6 MON - SAT, 7 ON WED

A stylish shop at the Parsons Green end of the New King's Road which offers fabulous new designer clothes and accessories at substantial discounts - usually half the original price. The clothes are as impressive as the decor with outfits from Caroline Charles, Maxfield Parrish, Paddy Campbell, Robinson Valentine, Edina Ronay, Ungaro, Sonja Nuttall, Paul Frith' elegant evening wear, Pazuki's waistcoats and silk dressing gowns, Alfred Dunhill and Lesley George. The shop also sells handbags from Lulu Guinness, scarves from Harriet Anstruther and Jan Lindsay, and jewellery from Reema Pachachi, painted shirts from Carole Waller and silk shoes from Orford and Swan. Owner Micola Neville has many contacts in the top end of the fashion industry and is supplied direct from the designer with returned orders, samples and end of season outfits. There are also some menswear gift items from Alfred Dunhill such as ties, braces, cashmere scarves and sweaters - all at half the original price.

# *Factory Shops*

# BODEN WAREHOUSE SHOP

2, 4 & 7, PEMBROKE BUILDINGS, CUMBERLAND PARK, SCRUBS LANE, LONDON NW10
☎ 0181-964 2662. OPEN 10 - 7 FRI, 10 - 5 SAT.

Sale goods and discontinued lines from this well-known mail order company as well as full-price clothes from the current catalogue. Most of the merchandise is smart casual wear for women and men in 100% natural fabric. There is also cricketwear, tennis gear, silk shirts, silk blouses, belts, cufflinks, a small amount of luggage and shoulder bags but no shoes.

## BURBERRY

29-53 CHATHAM PLACE, LONDON E9 6LP
☎ 0181-985 3344. OPEN 12.30 - 6 MON - FRI, 9.30 - 1 SAT
This Burberry factory shop sells the full range of Burberry merchandise, none of which is current. It stocks seconds and overmakes of the famous name raincoats and duffle coats as well as accessories such as the distinctive umbrellas, scarves and handbags. All carry the Burberry label and are about one third of the normal retail price. Childrenswear tends to be thin on the ground, but there are plenty of gift items such as Burberry brand name teas, coffees and marmalade. A large warehouse with clothes set out on dozens of rails, surroundings are relatively spartan and the outlet is often full of tourists.

## IN WEAR FACTORY SHOP

100 GARRATT LANE, WANDSWORTH, LONDON SW18
☎ 0181-871 2155. OPEN 10 - 5 MON - FRI, 10 - 4 SAT.
In Wear for women and Martinique for men at discounts of between 30%-70% for last season's stock, ends of lines and seconds. All the stock is made up of stylishly casual separates.

## NICOLE FARHI OUTLET SHOP

75-83 FAIRFIELD ROAD, BOW, LONDON E3 2QR
☎ 0181-981 3931 EXT 203. OPEN 10 - 3 TUE, WED, SAT,
11 - 6.30 THUR, 10 - 5.30 FRI.
This tiny factory shop in London's East End sells previous season merchandise, samples and seconds from Nicole Farhi and French Connection for women, men and children. Stock varies so do phone first if you have a specific requirement and particularly if you are looking for children's clothes which tend to be very seasonal. There is much more women's than menswear.

## ONE STEP

3 - 5 HIGH STREET, ISLINGTON, LONDON N1
☎ 0171-837 4984. OPEN 9.30 - 6 MON - THUR, 9 - 6 FRI, SAT.
Value for money chain of self-service shoe shops, which are part of the British Shoe Corporation Ltd. This one sells Saxone, Freeman Hardy Willis, Dolcis, Roland Cartier, Hush Puppies and Stone Creek brands at 25%-50% discount. Sizes range up to size 9 ladies, up to size 12 for men and a wide range of children's sizes.

# R P ELLEN

46 CHURCH ROAD, LEYTON, LONDON E10 5JD
☎ 0181 539 6872 OPEN 10 - 4 MON - SAT.

Imports shoes from Italy and Spain. Apart from their regular stock, they have some seconds and sample shoes in small sizes at amazingly low prices. They also stock boots, slippers and men's shoes and trainers. Most of the styles are described as upmarket daywear and glitzy eveningwear, and the choice is enormous, although the full range of sizes is not always available. Prices range from £5 to £40.

# TON SUR TON

35 RIDING HOUSE STREET, LONDON W1 7PT
☎ 0171-637 3473. OPEN 10.30 - 5 MON - FRI.

This European casual wear company which sells tracksuits, sweat-shirts, T-shirts in unusual colours and soft fabrics, has a factory outlet in the heart of London's rag trade area. The company also sells denim, a fitness range, training shoes, rugby shirts, jackets, jeans and accessories. The factory outlet sells samples, returns and perfect garments at at least 50% of their normal retail price, and lower in a number of cases.

# *Dress Agencies*

# ANYTHING GOES

293 WEST END LANE, LONDON NW6
☎ 0171-794 2565. OPEN 11 - 6 MON, 10 - 6 TUE - SAT

Offers upmarket labels and classic styles including Valentino and Chanel, as well as German and continental designers such as Mondi, Escada and MaxMara. The shop is quite big and also sells nearly-new shoes, accessories, jewellery, bags and scarves. There is also a selection of new wool and cashmere coats for £79, usual price £159. Examples of stock include an Escada blouse for £29. Prices range from £15-£200. There is also a bargain area with items under £15.

## BERTIE GOLIGHTLY

48 BEAUCHAMP PLACE, LONDON SW3 1NX
☎ 0171-584 2720. OPEN 10 - 5 MON - SAT.

A mixture of new and nearly-new designer names from Chanel, Ungaro, Guy Laroche and Armani to Yves St Laurent, Valentino and Anouska Hempel. No high street names are stocked. Some of the new merchandise is samples and is therefore likely to be sizes 10 and 12 only. There is a silk room, a special occasion room, a jackets, skirts and day wear room, a ballgown room with a vast selection (with some for hire) and a room for cocktail wear. Prices are reasonable considering the designer label, with Chanel suits going for £350, original retail price over £1,000. Hats, shoes and scarves are also stocked, but no gloves, and new costume jewellery.

## BUTTERFLY,

3 LOWER RICHMOND ROAD, PUTNEY BRIDGE, LONDON SW15
☎ 0181-788 8304. OPEN 10.30 - 6.30 MON - FRI, 10 - 5 SAT.

Selling middle to upper range nearly-new designer clothes, new samples and end of ranges, this shop has been going since 1981. Selection includes Armani, Rifat Ozbek, Chanel, Nicole Farhi, French Connection, Jigsaw and Hobbs. Lots of linen, silks, cashmere, wool and natural fibres. Also some samples and clothes used for modelling, handbags, scarves, new jewellery, purses and handbags.

## CATWALK

42 CHILTERN STREET, LONDON W1M 1PL
☎ 0171-935 1052. 11.15 - 6 MON, FRI, 11.15 - 7 TUE - THUR, 11.15 - 5 SAT.

Nearly-new designer clothes from Chanel to Jaeger, MaxMara to Whistles and including Byblos, Krizia, and Escada. Always has a wide variety of jackets and separates as well as jewellery, hats, shoes, belts, scarves and handbags. For example, Kenzo linen jacket, £55; Armani jacket, £75; Nicole Farhi silk blouse, £32.

## CHANGE OF HABIT

25 ABBEVILLE ROAD, LONDON SW4 9LA
☎ 0181-675 9475. OPEN 11 - 5 MON - FRI, 10 - 6 SAT.

Daywear and evening wear as good as new. Also nearly-new clothes for babies and children up to the age of 10. Described by the proprietor as "everyday clothes for everyday people at realistic prices". As new costs amount to about one quarter of the original price. Very high turnover. Also has mothers-to-be wear and prams, cots and toys.

## CHANGE OF HEART

59A PARK ROAD, LONDON N8
☎ 0181-341 1575. OPEN 10 - 6 MON - SAT, BY APPOINTMENT ON SUNS.

Sells a mixture of designer and good high street labels for women, men and children including labels such as DKNY, Ghost, Betty Jackson, Kenzo, Armani, Jigsaw, Next, Whistles, Paul Smith and Fenn Wright & Manson. Prices vary from £20 for a pair of Armani shorts to £50 for a Nicole Farhi silk two-piece suit.

## CHICERIA

93 WANDSWORTH BRIDGE ROAD, LONDON SW6 2TD
☎ 0171-371 0697. OPEN 10 - 6 MON - FRI, UNTIL 7 ON THUR, 10 - 6 SAT.

Sells a wide range of secondhand clothes from Jigsaw and Hobbs to Georges Rech, MaxMara, Joseph, Paddy Campbell and Edina Ronay. There is also a range of accessories, belts, shoes, hats and costume jewellery, both new and secondhand. All items are less than three years old. Ascot, Henley and party style catered for, although most of the clothes are more suitable for normal daytime wear.

## CHLOE 2

21-23 MONTPELIER VALE, BLACKHEATH VILLAGE, LONDON SE3 OTJ
☎ 0181-318 4300. OPEN 10 - 6 MON - SAT.

Chloe has been trading in top quality, fashion for more than 25 years, specialising in special occasion outfits in sizes 8-22. Chloe 2, on the lower ground floor, stocks thousands of samples and seconds from Chloe's usual supliers, enabling customers to buy top quality clothes at prices which range from 25%-75% off the usual retail price. There is also a small section of top label nearly-new on sale. There are always batch clearance rail for under £40; hats at half price; jewellery from £6; but no shoes.

## DESIGNS

60 ROSSLYN HILL, LONDON  NW3 1ND
☎ 0171-435 0100. OPEN 10 - 5.45 MON - SAT, UNTIL 6.45 ON THUR.

Designs has been established for more than twelve years, selling ladies designer clothes and accessories. Their most sought-after labels include Hermes, Chanel, Donna Karan, Moschino, Ralph Lauren, YSL, Giorgio Armani and Valentino. They only accept perfect merchandise under two years old, and seasonal. They have a rapid turnover and regular customers talk about the spacious, relaxed atmosphere. Designs only take forty percent commission on sale of goods, so prices remain keenly competitive and the most exciting pieces come their way. Prices range from £5 to £500. They have more than 6,000 clients and take in stock from the UK, America and Italy. They also stock a range of girls' clothes from 0 - 8 years.

## DRESS CIRCLE

2 LEVERTON PLACE, LONDON NW5 2PL
☎ 0171 284 3967. OPEN 10 - 6 TUE - SAT, UNTIL 7 ON THUR AND FRI.

Dress Circle is a nearly-new shop for adults which has a children's dress agency at the back called Boomerang. Dress Circle sells good quality secondhand clothing with a strong emphasis on middle of the road high street names such as Next, Hobbs, Jigsaw and Gap. Prices range from £1-£100. There are also shoes, accessories, jewellery, hats and costume jewellery from £2-£30. Stock usually consists of wearable daywear; unusual, trendy separates; period dresses; evening clothes; special occasion outfits such as a silk and linen Nicole Fahri skirt £35; and a good selection of Levi 501's for about £12. Menswear tends to be casual shirts, sweaters and jackets with the occasional Yves St Laurent suit, £75 and jacket £45.

## DYNASTY

12A TURNHAM GREEN TERRACE, LONDON W4
☎ 0181-995 3846. OPEN 10 - 5 TUE - SAT.
63 KENSINGTON CHURCH STREET, LONDON W8
☎ 0171-376 0291. OPEN 10 - 5 TUE - SAT.

Sells good quality secondhand clothes for women. Labels include Edina Ronay, Louis Feraud, Joseph, Moschino, as well as La Perla swimwear. Examples of outfits for sale include an Edina Ronay suit for £175, A Christian Lacroix dress for £99, and a Paul Costelloe dress, £49, La Perla swimsuits from £25-£39; Valentino three-piece, £220, originally £1,000.

## EXCLUSIVO

24 HAMPSTEAD HIGH STREET, HAMPSTEAD, LONDON NW3
☎ 0171-431 8618. OPEN 11.30 - 6 SEVEN DAYS A WEEK.

A small shop stocked high with every kind of label from Jaeger and Windsmoor to YSL, Chanel, Donna Karan and Nicole Farhi. Prices range from £50-£500. For example, Alaia dress £120, as new £450. Specialise in accessories: for example Chanel handbags, £250 usually £750; Prada bags, £85; Moschino bags, from £50. Good range of footwear such as Donna Karan shoes, £89, originally £200; Hermes scarves, £49; Chanel earrings, from £50; Donna Karan earrings, from £29. There are usually about 100 outfits from which to choose.

## FROCK FOLLIES

18 THE GRANGEWAY, GRANGE PARK, LONDON N21 2HG
☎ 0181-360 3447. OPEN 9.30 - 5 TUE - SAT

Recommended by one of The Good Deal Directory readers who says that the owner is so helpful that shopping here is a pleasure. Double-fronted shop with more than 2,000 items in stock including costume jewellery, handbags, swimwear and shoes. Labels include Tom Bowker, Jacques Vert, Basler, Betty Barclay and Betty Jackson.

## HANG UPS

366 FULHAM ROAD, LONDON SW10
☎ 0171-351 0047. OPEN 11 - 6.45 MON - FRI, 10.30 - 6 SAT, 10 - 4 SUNS
(OCCASIONALLY, PHONE FIRST)
Designer labels in the trendier, younger end of the market with
designers such as Gaultier, Aliai, Ghost, Moschino, Hobbs, Whistles,
Escada, Frank Usher and shoes from Pied a Terre and Manolo
Blahnik. Prices range from £1 for a T-shirt to £500 for a Chanel suit.
There is daywear, evening wear, casual clothes, shoes, handbags, as
well as lingerie and a large children's section selling cots, baby seats,
prams, and hand-painted wooden toys.

## HANGERS

120 PITSHANGER LANE, EALING, LONDON W5 1QP
☎ 0181-810 9363. OPEN 10-6 MON - SAT.
Designer names from Jacques Vert, Escada and Louis Feraud to
Windsmoor and Next. Also sells children's clothes.

## HEARTS

64 SOUTH MOLTON STREET, LONDON W1Y 1HH
☎ 0171-493 1331. BY APPOINTMENT ONLY.
Nearly-new designer wedding dresses and samples and after you've
worn it, you can take it back and re-sell it to the shop. Designers
stocked include Catherine Rayner, Beverley Summers, Mirror Mirror
and Hollywood Dreams, and prices start at £500-£1,500, about half
of the original price. They also sell bridesmaids dresses, shoes and
veils, and there is an alteration service. They also make bridesmaids
dresses and pageboy outfits.

## KABOODLE

238 BROMPTON ROAD, LONDON SW3
☎ 01956 873719. OPEN 11 - 6 MON - SAT, CLOSED WED.
New designer dress agency selling unusual clothes. There are skirts,
jackets, coats, trousers, shoes, handbags, dresses, some hats, belts and
a selection of jewellery.

## LA SCALA

39 ELYSTAN STREET, LONDON SW3 3NT
☎ 0171-589 2784. OPEN 10 - 5.30 MON - SAT.

La Scala has been so successful in selling women's nearly-new clothes and accessories since opening in 1993 that, due to popular demand, owner Sandy Reid in summer 1995 acquired large adjacent premises, enabling her to house men's and children's clothes as well as wedding dresses under the same roof. Sandy lived for 14 years in Northern Italy and uses her experience there in her marble-floored shop behind the Conran Shop in Chelsea. There, she sells end of season Italian designer wear and top name nearly-new outfits from Yves Saint Laurent to Chanel. Regular excursions to Italy ensure an interesting and unusual range of clothes and accessories.

## LEVY & FRIEND

47 SLOANE AVENUE, OFF KING'S ROAD, LONDON SW3 3DH
☎ 0171-589 9741. OPEN 11 - 5 TUE- SAT.

Well presented garments in pristine condition are sold in a relaxed atmosphere in this large ground floor shop. Specialising in day wear, the shop offers fashionable, functional, tailored clothing from labels such as MaxMara, Marella, Donna Karan, Valentino, Escada, Margaret Howell and Ferragamo, as well as designer bags, belts, shoes and boots. Established for nine years, the shop has a clientele from around the world and the owners are ready with advice, if needed. Prices range from £20-£300 and credit cards - American Express, Visa, Access and Mastercard - are taken.

## NOT QUITE NEW

159 BRENT STREET, HENDON, LONDON NW4 4DH
☎ 0181-203 4691. OPEN 10 - 4.30 MON - FRI, CLOSED WEDS, 10 - 1 SAT.

Personal service are the key words to this unique boutique which sells beautiful garments in pristine condition. In business for more than 16 years, Not Quite New sells top Italian, French and German designer names including Basler, Louis Feraud, Valentino, Yarell, Mondi, Betty Baclay and Jaeger, as well as shoes and bags of the highest quality. Sizes stocked range from 8-18 and most items cost less than £100. Examples of prices include a Basler dress, £40; Liz Claiborne suit, £50. There is a men's nearly-new outlet just down the road (see Menswear, London, Dress Agencies.)

## PAMELA'S

16 BEAUCHAMP PLACE, LONDON SW3 1MQ
☎ 0171-589 6852. OPEN 10- 5 MON - SAT.
Selection of mostly French and Italian designer labels – Chanel,
Valentino – as well as middle range names such as Jaeger and Country
Casuals. There is plenty to choose from for weddings and balls, as
well as lots of accessories and a good selection of hats.

## PANDORA

16-22 CHEVAL PLACE, LONDON SW7 1ES
☎ 0171-589 5289. OPEN 10-6 MON-SAT AND MOST BANK HOLIDAYS.
Based around the corner from Harrods, this large shop with more
than 5,000 items in stock sells only the top, well-known designer
names: Donna Karan, Emporium Armani, Thierry Mugler, Hardy
Amies, Chanel, Bruce Oldfield, Valentino, Escada, Ghost. They sell
everything to do with a woman's wardrobe but it has to be in good
condition and sport a top label. Also stocks a range of size 16 plus, as
well as handbags, belts, hats and shoes. Shoes have to be mistakes (ie
new) though bags can be older eg crocodile, Hermes, Gucci.
Everything is categorised into daywear, evening wear, trousers, skirts,
etc so it is easy to browse. Examples of price include Louis Feraud
suit, £188 originally £600; Ghost dress, £70, originally £300; Hardy
Amies suit, £165, originally £800.

## PENGUIN SOCIETY

144 WEST END LANE, LONDON NW6 1SD
☎ 0171-625 7778. OPEN 11 - 7.30 MON - FRI, 10. 30 - 5.30 SAT
"Gently worn" designer ladies and mens wear. Designers range from
Valentino and Ghost to Jigsaw and Warehouse in the womens' range
and from Armani to Willy Smith and Boss in the men's. The clothes
stocked cover both casual working day and evening wear, though they
tend towards the former. Prices range from £10 - £200. Twice yearly
sales in Summer and Winter. Clothing styles range from current to
classical. Quick turnover and deposits accepted on items of clothing.

## POPPY OF TWICKENHAM

92 HEATH ROAD, TWICKENHAM, MIDDLESEX TW1
☎ 0181-891 3133. OPEN 10 - 5.30 MON - SAT.
Sells nearly-new Chloe, Portara, MaxMara, Yves St Laurent, Mondi and Betty Barclay. Often has a good selection of party and evening clothes. Caters mainly for the middle market and mostly day wear.

## PZAZZ

153 CHURCH ROAD, CASTELNAU, BARNES, LONDON SW13
☎ 0181-748 1094. OPEN 10 - 5.30 MON - SAT
Features more of the avant garde designers such as Jean Paul Gaultier, Azzedine Alaia and Vivienne Westwood, with some classics from Ungaro, Edina Ronay, Donna Karan, Kenzo, Ralph Lauren and Yves St Laurent. Also J M Davidson bags, and shoes.

## SALOU

6 CHEVAL PLACE, LONDON SW7
☎ 0171-581 2380. OPEN 10 - 5 MON - SAT.
Sells secondhand designer labels such as Giorgio Armani, Valentino, Moschino, Byblos, Christian Lacroix, Chanel and Jean Paul Gaultier.

## SECOND SINNS

34 MORETON ST, PIMLICO, LONDON SW1V 2PD
☎ 0171 834 7485. OPEN 12 - 7 MON - FRI, 10 - 4 SAT.
Rapidly becoming the place to visit for wise Pimlico residents. Its owner hails from the United States, where attitudes to discount dressing are still far more advanced than they are here though that is changing rapidly. She stocks a wide range of new and nearly new designer clothes.

## SECOND THOUGHTS

87 REGENTS PARK ROAD, LONDON NW1
☎ 0171 586 1090 OPEN 10 - 6 MON - SAT.
Top designers include Chanel, St Laurent and Katherine Hamnett. Selection varies from evening and day suits, new couture clothes and dresses. Prices range from £5 - £300, with two bargain baskets with everything under £5. Good shoes and accessories ie; Louis Vuitton bags, Ascot hats. Friendly and leisurely atmosphere, coffee and tea served.

# SHARP

1A HOLLYWOOD ROAD, LONDON SW10
☎ 0171-376 3137. OPEN 10.30 - 6 MON - FRI, 10.30 - 2 SAT, UNTIL 8 ON WED.

Sharp is a charity shop which benefits from its closeness to an area of London which houses people who can still afford to dress in designer clothes - and discard them when they've worn them a few times. Designers include MaxMara, Ungaro and Escada for women, Armani, Paul Smith and Versace for men. All the clothes are in good condition, with prices from £10 to £500.

# SHEILA WARREN-HILL

126 TOTTENHAM LANE LONDON N8
☎ 0181-348 0303. OPEN 10 - 6 MON - SAT.
THE GARDEN FLAT, 63 SHEPHERDS HILL, HIGHGATE, LONDON N6
☎ 0181-348 8282. BY APPOINTMENT ONLY.

Sheila is a lovely, lively character who has recently opened a shop in addition to operating from her garden flat in London's Highgate, offering open house on Sundays when lunch and drinks are served while customers try on couture outfits. Many of her outfits were originally owned by rich and famous personalities. Having worn a dress to a special event, they can't be seen wearing the same outfit twice and so pass it on to Sheila to dispose of discreetly and enable them to recoup some of the costs and buy another dazzling creation for the next outing. The labels are top range - Jasper Conran, Azzedine Alaia, Yves St Laurent, Chanel, Tomasz Starzewski, Place Vendome, Gianfranco Ferre, Escada. The atmosphere is relaxed, with Sheila on hand to dispense advice if wanted. She also sells daywear, designer shoes, swimwear and jewellery. Sheila also has an arrangement with other nearly-new businesses around the country, who take some of her stock, which means that she always has a very good supply. Phone her for details of other shops taking her stock.

## SIGN OF THE TIMES

17 ELYSTAN STREET, LONDON SW3
☎ 0171-589 4774. OPEN 10 - 5.30 MON - SAT.
Sells Jean Muir, YSL, Joseph, Chanel, Yamamoto, Escada, Ralph Lauren and Giorgio Armani among its range of nearly new bargains. Also lots of hats (Frederick Fox, Jilly Forge), handbags and shoes (Manolo Blahnik, Bruno Magli) There's also a small selection of men's clothes, as well as some accessories. Plans to open late one evening.

## THE BEST OF SECONDHAND

42 GOLDERS GREEN ROAD, LONDON NW11
☎ 0181-458 3890. OPEN 9.30 - 5.30 MON - FRI, 9 - 6 SAT, 10 - 5 SUN.
Sells both top designer names such as Frank Usher, Louis Feraud, Escada, Laurel, Mondi and Bruce Oldfield and middle of the range labels such as Jaeger and Marks & Spencer. The shop is known for its suits and special occasion wear, with evening wear, Ascot and mother-of-the-bride outfits. Prices are about one quarter of the original price and sizes range from 8-22. There's also a small selection of children's party dresses and Chester Barry and Dior menswear.

## THE BRIDAL EXCHANGE

19 EDGWAREBURY LANE, EDGWARE, MIDDLESEX
☎ 0181-958 7002. OPEN 9 - 6 MON - SAT, 11 - 3 SUN.
Once-worn wedding dresses from £50-£4,000 from a vast range of designer and couture numbers. Also veils, headdresses and shoes, both new and nearly-new. Some of the stock is ex-hire, some from liquidations, some was bought but never worn and all are about half the original price. All the top wedding dress designer names are here: Ronald Joyce, Hollywood Dreams, Catherine Rayner, Helen Marina, Tatters and Karen Ashton. Headdresses can be made to order by Irresistible. All wedding dresses and accessories can be bought or hired. Also will dress the groom, either from hired clothes or nearly-new, including accessories such as cravats. Grooms who are hiring will be fitted out at the actual showroom of the formal wear hire company and the suit they try on will be the one they wear on the day. Bridesmaids dresses range from £25 and there are also pageboy and mother of the bride outfits.

## THE DESIGNER SALE AND EXCHANGE SHOP

61D LANCASTER ROAD, LONDON W11
☎ 0171-243 2396. OPEN 10 - 6 TUE - SAT, 12 - 6 MON.

Sells samples and seconds from last season – Rifat Ozbek, Pascale Smit, Galliano, Paddy Campbell – as well as nearly new clothes from British and European designers and low-priced fashion suede and leatherwear. Prices range from £10 - £300, with the average about £100. There are also hats, shoes, handbags, scarves, sunglasses (£18-£40), belts (£5-£20) and a small selection of menswear.

## THE DRESS BOX

8-10 CHEVAL PLACE, LONDON SW7
☎ 0171-589 2240. OPEN 10.15 - 6 MON - FRI, 10.30 - 6 SAT.

Operating for more than 50 years, the Dress Box caters for the top end of the market including new and nearly-new couture - YSL, Victor Edelstein, Chanel and Pierre Cardin. Those looking for special occasion wear, evening outfits or ball gowns are well catered for. Among the 500 or so outfits in the shop at any one time are Chanel suits from £750 and Valentino and Ungaro suits from £450. Wonderful collection of YSL suits, some Chanel jackets and suits. Prices range from £150-£1,000 for suits though most outfits cost £200-£400. There is also a collection of about 30 hats from £45-£100 (Philip Somerville, Philip Tracey) and shoes from £5-£90. Alterations service available. There are also Chanel handbags, scarves from £95, costume jewellery, as well as a small selection of menswear.

## THE DRESSER

10 PORCHESTER PLACE LONDON W2 2BS
☎ 0171-724 7212. OPEN 11 - 5.30 MON - SAT.

Secondhand designer women and men's clothes including names such as Yohji Yamamoto, Montana, YSL and Jean Muir at prices ranging from £50-£400. There are lots of separates, some hats and shoes.

# THE WEDDING DRESS EXCHANGE

97 CLAXTON GROVE, FULHAM, LONDON W6 8HB
☎ 0171-385 3940. PHONE FOR AN APPOINTMENT.

Boasts the widest collection of new or once-worn bridal gowns in the country, all for sale at half their original retail price. You could save up to £4,000 on an as-new top designer gown or £750 on a Catherine Rayner. What's more, the agency promises to buy back your dress should you decide you want to sell it again after your big day. All dresses are immaculate and there is a hugh variety to choose from, with prices ranging from £40 to £4,000, and sizes from 8 to 22.

# THE WEDDING SHOP

171 FULHAM ROAD, LONDON SW3
☎ 0171- 838 0171. BY APPOINTMENT ONLY.

Once-worn designer wedding dresses at substantially reduced prices. Customers can buy the quality of workmanship found in a designer wedding dress with its top quality fabric and precise construction and detailing made by designers such as Anouska Hempel, Phillipa Lepley, Tomasz Starzewski, Catherine Walker and Louise Hamlyn-Wright. Prices range from £800 for a new and up and coming designer such as Neil Cunningham to as much as £18,000 for a Christian Lacroix dress which originally cost £30,000. The Wedding Shop is also interested in buying wedding dresses which fit these pre-requisites. A non-refundable fee of £100 is charged when a dress is registered and the owner receives two-thirds of the selling price when the wedding dress is sold.

# UPSTAIRS DOWNSTAIRS

46 CHALCOT ROAD, PRIMROSE HILL, LONDON NW1 8LS
☎ 0171-483 2499. OPEN 10 - 5 TUE - SAT.

One of London's most prestigious dress agencies, Upstairs Downstairs features all the top designer makes in perfect condition on uncluttered rails which makes for unhurried browsing. Evening wear and accessories are for sale as well as day clothes. Customers come from all over the country and clothes from all over the world, where they both enjoy personal attention. Designers include Louis Feraud, Valentino, Escada, Yarell, MaxMara and Cerruti. There is also an alternations service

## WELLINGTONS

1 WELLINGTON PLACE, LONDON NW8
☎ 0171-483 0688. OPEN 11 - 5 MON - SAT.

Stunning selection of YSL, Chanel, Escada, MaxMara, Marella. There's also a bargain basement full of high street names such as Marks & Spencer and Benetton as well as reduced designer clothing. Also sells menswear.

## *Hire Shops*

## BLACKOUT 11

51 ENDELL STREET, COVENT GARDEN, LONDON WC2
☎ 0171-240 5006. OPEN 11 - 7 MON - SAT.

Twenties and upwards gear, plus hats, for sale and to hire at reasonable prices. Specialises in Sixties and Seventies gear.

## BUMPSADAISY

43 THE MARKET, COVENT GARDEN, LONDON WC2E 8HA
☎ 0171-379 9831. OPEN 10 - 5.30 MON - SAT.

Franchised hire shops with large range of special occasion maternity wear, from wedding outfits to ball gowns, to hire and to buy. Hire costs average about £55 for special occasion wear. Phone 0171-379 9831 for details of your local stockist.

## EMPORIUM

330-332 CREEK ROAD, GREENWICH, LONDON SE10
☎ 0181-305 1670. OPEN 10.30 - 6 TUE - SUN.

Vintage clothes shop which also hires out ballgowns.

## FROCK AROUND THE CLOCK

42 VARDENS ROAD, BATTERSEA, LONDON SW11 1RH
☎ 0171-924 1669. BY APPOINTMENT ONLY.

Up-to-the-minute evening designer wear including cocktail dresses, party gear, gloves, handbags, and accessories. All the dresses are made by top British designers and would cost more than £600 each to buy. Sizes range from 8-18. Cost: £50-£70 plus £100 deposit for a 3-day hire. Phone for an appointment.

## HEADY HEIGHTS

LONDON

☎ 0171-350 1417. PHONE FOR AN APPOINTMENT.

Home based business in Battersea hiring couture hats, all of which are handmade and cost more than £300. Jane Lewis, who runs the business, has 75 hats at any one time, suitable for a range of events from weddings and christenings to the races, Henley and knighthoods. Each hat can be altered to fit you personally and there are matching handmade handbags. Jane makes some of the hats herself; others come from Philip Somerville, Rachel Trevor-Morgan and Herald and Heart Hatters, who made all the hats for the hit film, Four Weddings and a Funeral. There is a flat charge for hiring, plus a deposit. Delivery available.

## JO DALBY COSTUME HIRE

4 RAVEY STREET, LONDON EC2

☎ 0171-739 3026. OPEN 10 - 5.30 MON - FRI.

Everything the dedicated dresser-upper or fancy dress party-goer could want from Victorian ladies and Twenties sirens to clowns, cats, harlequins and batmen, wigs, masks, hats and shoes. Cost from £18-£55 for the weekend.

## LOSNERS DRESS HIRE

232 STAMFORD HILL, LONDON N16 6TT

☎ 0181-800 7466. OPEN 9 - 5.30 MON - SAT, UNTIL 7 ON WED, UNTIL 5 ON THUR.

Specialises in top end of the market wedding outfits to hire and to buy. Basic hire costs anything from £100 to £300; you can choose from a huge range that includes new and nearly-new bridal outfits. Labels include Ronald Joyce, Ellis, Hilary Morgan, Margaret Lee. Can also make dresses to order. All the accessories are to buy only and there is a shoe-dyeing service. There are also morning and dinner suits to hire from £40-£70.

## ONE NIGHT STAND

44 PIMLICO ROAD, LONDON SW1

☎ 0171-730 8708. OPEN 10 - 6.30 MON - FRI, 10 - 5 SAT.

More than 1,000 dresses in stock from the middle and upper end of the market. Also hires jewellery, evening bags, capes and jackets. Cost £50-125 for 4 days. Phone for an appointment.

## ROYAL NATIONAL THEATRE

HIRE DEPARTMENT, CHICHESTER HOUSE, 1-3 BRIXTON WAY,
LONDON SW9 6DE
☎ 0171-735 4774. OPEN 10 - 6 MON - FRI BY APPOINTMENT ONLY,
CLOSED 1-2 DAILY.

If the recession hasn't stopped all the fun and you have been invited
to the odd fancy dress party or perhaps you're involved in an amateur
theatrical production, take a look at the Royal National Theatre's collection of costumes for hire. It stocks more than 60,000 original
costumes from Roman togas to leather biker jackets. A warning note,
however: some of the costumes looked better on stage than they do in
the full glare of daylight.

## THE COSTUME STUDIO

6 PENTON GROVE, OFF WHITE LION STREET, LONDON N1
☎ 0171-388 4481/6576. OPEN 9.30 - 6 MON - FRI, 10 -5 SAT.

Between ten and twelve thousand costumes from medieval times to
the 70s. Clients include TV and video companies. Individual hiring
costs from £30-£60 for one week. There are plenty of accessories from
shoes and hats to bags and gloves to complete an outfit.

## THE FASHION CLINIC

180 WANDSWORTH BRIDGE ROAD, LONDON SW6 2HF
☎ 0171-736 4425. OPEN 2 - 7 MON, 10 - 7 TUE, THUR, 10 - 6 FRI,
10 - 5 SAT.

This large corner shop stocks pretty and elegant special occasion wear,
ready to hire for £98-£115 for three nights. Designer labels include
Terence Nolder, Jenny Packham and Antony Price. Everything is for
sale as well. They offer a special wardrobe alteration service with
personal advice on shapes and the potential for that dated outfit
sitting in the cupboard. Daywear is now mostly for sale only.

## THE MERCHANT OF EUROPE

232 PORTOBELLO ROAD, LONDON W11
☎ 0171-221 4203. OPEN 10.30 - 6 MON - SAT.

Period style specialists, selling and hiring out vintage clothing from
the 1880s to the 1970s, particularly leather jackets from the Forties
and Fifties. There is also a large hire section of exquisite period
evening wear. Men can hire unusual stage wear and classic suits.

## TWENTIETH CENTURY FROX

614 FULHAM ROAD, LONDON SW6 5RP
☎ 0171-731 3242. OPEN 10 - 7 MON - FRI, 10 - 5.30 SAT.

Two hundred dresses from those suitable for Ascot to grand ball gowns, to hire or to buy, plus accessories. Costs £60-100 for three days' hire. Cost price if new, less if nearly-new. No appointment necessary.

# Secondhand and Vintage Clothes

## AMERICAN CLASSICS

404 KING'S ROAD, LONDON SW10
☎ 0171-351 5229. OPEN 11 - 7 MON - SAT.

Vintage American clothes from the Forties, Fifties, Sixties and Seventies with matching accessories including boots, belts, buckles for women and men.

## ANNIES

10 CAMDEN PASSAGE, LONDON N1 8DU
☎ 0171-359 0796. OPEN 11 - 5.30 TUE, THUR, FRI, 9 - 5.30 WED, SAT.

Mainly women's clothes from late Victorian times to the Forties, specialising in Twenties beaded garments on ground floor, as well as ball-gowns, silk lingerie, Forties suits and blouses; upstairs are table linen, cushions, curtains and sporting goods.

## BLACKOUT II

51 ENDELL STREET, COVENT GARDEN, LONDON WC2
☎ 0171-240 5006. OPEN 11 - 7 MON - SAT.

Twenties and upwards gear, plus hats, for sale and to hire at reasonable prices. Specialises in Sixties and Seventies gear.

## CENCI

31 MONMOUTH STREET, LONDON WC2
☎ 0171-836 1400. OPEN 10.30 - 7 MON - FRI, 10.30 - 6.30 SAT.

Small shop selling vintage clothing from the Forties to the Seventies from America and Europe. There are about 10,000 items in the shop at any one time, many of which are bought from a factory in Italy devoted to the recycling of old style and quality clothing. As well as 1960s sweaters from £16 to £125, Forties' and Sixties' suits from £75 and a large selection of cashmere, there are also accessories and some shoes.

## CHENIL GALLERY

181-183 KING'S ROAD, LONDON SW3
☎ 0171-352 8581. OPEN 10.30 - 5.30 MON - SAT.

Clothes for women and men from 1800 to the 1950s can be found at Fouthergill & Crawley, Enigma, Pamela Haywood and Persiflages. Forties crepe dress, £25; fitted women's jacket, £25; beaded evening dress, £150; period men's DJs, £35; tails, £50-£75; top hats and gloves also. Some children's clothes. Enigma caters for men with dinner suits from the Twenties to the Sixties, £60, morning suits, cummerbunds, bow ties and cufflinks.

## COBWEBS

60 ISLINGTON PARK STREET, LONDON N1
☎ 0171-359 8090. OPEN 11 - 6 MON - SAT.

Small shop which has been in operation for 14 years, selling second-hand clothes in very English style for men and women, particularly Sixties clothes and accessories. Cotton Forties dresses, £15; long evening dresses from £38; ladies black Fifties jackets, £28; ladies silk blouses, £12.

## CORNUCOPIA

12 UPPER TACHBROOK STREET, LONDON SW1
☎ 0171-828 5752. OPEN 11 - 6 MON - SAT, UNTIL 7 ON WEDS.

Established for more than 25 years, Cornucopia specialises in glamorous evening wear for men and women from the Twenties to modern day. Huge selection of eveningwear, some evening shoes, wedding dresses from the Thirties including some designer samples, silk suits and hats.

## EMPORIUM

330-332 CREEK ROAD, GREENWICH, LONDON SE10
☎ 0181-305 1670. OPEN 10.30 - 6 TUE - SUN.
Sell men's and women's classic clothing from Twenties to Seventies.
Specialise in hats including panamas, trilbies and fashion hats and
have some secondhand hats. Although most of the clothing is
original, they also specialise in reproduction costume jewellery.
Ballgowns can be hired.

## FLIP

125 LONG ACRE, COVENT GARDEN, LONDON WC2E 9PE
☎ 0171-836 4688. OPEN 10 - 7 MON - SAT, 12 - 6 SUN, UNTIL 8 ON
THUR.
Original Levi's and cut-off Levi jeans, waistcoats, hippy shirts, wide
denim flares, denim jackets, £40-£60. Most of the stock is jeans with
some Sixties dresses, short jackets, and coats for both men and
women.

## OXFAM NOLOGO

26 GANTON STREET, LONDON W1
☎ 0171-437 7338. OPEN 11 - 6 MON - SAT.
Famous in the past for its one-off designs made up by fashion
students using donated fabric from top designers, this Oxfam shop
now sells retro clothing for women and men. Women's T-shirts,
£2.99, men's trousers, £4.44 to £5.79.

## PHILIP OF KING'S ROAD

191 KING'S ROAD, LONDON SW3 5ED
☎ 0171-352 4332. OPEN 10 - 6.30 MON - FRI, 10 - 7 SAT.
Specialises in American clothing, both new and secondhand, from
baseball to army surplus, jeans, jackets, baseball boots and 501s. Full
selection of American sports equipment and accessories including
caps and baseball bats.

## ROKIT

225 CAMDEN HIGH STREET, LONDON NW1
☎ 0171-267 3046. OPEN 10 - 6 MON - FRI, 9.30 - 6.30 SAT, SUN.
Mostly Seventies gear, ethnic, colourful and 501 jeans, shoes, hats and
accessories. Vintage Capital E and selvedge seam jeans.

## SPATZ

48 MONMOUTH STREET, COVENT GARDEN, LONDON WC2
☎ 0171-379 0703. OPEN 11.30 - 6.30 MON - SAT.
Mainly Forties and Fifties original clothing and also lace, antique lace
square pillowcases, bedspreads and curtains,

## STEINBERG & TOLKEIN

193 KING'S ROAD, LONDON SW3 5EB
℅ 0171-376 3660. OPEN 10.30 - 7 MON - SAT, 1 - 6 SUN.
Situated on two floors, one floor is devoted totally to jewellery and
houses one of the largest collection of baubles from the Twenties to
the Sixties in the world - from Chanel and Schiaparelli to Trifari. The
other floor sells American vintage and European couture clothing
from the Twenties and Thirties to the Seventies - more than 7,000
pieces. Some of the more interesting items were worn by movie stars
of the Thirties and Forties and the garment is often seen on the
original wearer in photographs around the shop. Popular with those
looking for something unusual for a theme evening or a gala event,
it's also frequented by those searching for an individual look in a style
and quality unmatched even by couture designers today. Prices range
from £6 to £3,000, with a Chanel suit, for example, costing £500, a
Valentino velvet suit, £200. There are also hats, gloves, shoes and fob
watches. There is a small selection of men's clothes.

## THE CAVERN

154 COMMERCIAL STREET, LONDON E1 6NV
☎ 0171-247 1889. OPEN 12 - 6 TUE, WED, THUR, FRI, 12 - 5 SAT.
Sixties and Seventies clothes, shoes, jewellery, lamps, posters, postcards, watches, ninety percent of which is unworn and unused. For
example watches from £20-£150; leather jackets, from £10-£50;
denim flares, from £15-£25; embroidered flares, £25. Watch manufacturers include Secura and Camy. Men's and women's, but few
children's, clothes stocked. Student discounts of at least 10%.

## THE GALLERY OF ANTIQUE COSTUME & TEXTILES

2 CHURCH STREET, LONDON NW8 8ED
☎ 0171-723 9981. OPEN 10 - 5.30 MON - SAT.

Original costumes from Victorian times to the 1940s and waistcoats and fabrics from the early textiles to mid nineteenth century. Cushions from £65-£500; table covers from £100-£400; curtains from £300; Edwardian tea dresses from £45; Twenties and Thirties evening wear from £75 upwards.

## THE GLORIOUS CLOTHING COMPANY

60 UPPER STREET, ISLINGTON, LONDON N1
☎ 0171-704 6312. OPEN 11 - 6.30 MON - SAT.

Mainly selling secondhand period clothing from the Twenties to the Nineties, including feather boas, jewellery and shoes.

## THE MERCHANT OF EUROPE

232 PORTOBELLO ROAD, LONDON W11
☎ 0171-221 4203. OPEN 10.30 - 6.30 MON - SAT.

Period style specialists, selling and hiring out vintage clothing from the 1880s to the 1970s, particularly leather jackets from the Forties and Fifties. There is also a large hire section of exquisite period evening wear. Men can hire unusual stage wear and classic suits.

## THE OBSERVATORY

20 GREENWICH CHURCH STREET, GREENWICH, LONDON SE10
☎ 0181-305 1998. OPEN 10 - 6 EVERY DAY.

Two floors of secondhand clothes from Thirties onwards for women and men. Women's frocks, shoes, hats and jewellery as well as lots of leather, suede and denim garments. Men's suits, jackets and trousers.

# *Designer* Sales

## ANGELA MARBER'S PRIVATE BUY

FIVEMARCH, COOMBE PARK, KINGSTON HILL, SURREY KT2 7JA
☎ 0181-549 8453.

Private Buy arranges for its club members to purchase current and next season's top label European and American samples and stock in the Agent's intimate and friendly showrooms, most of which are in London, ahead of the season at half the cost. Also available at trade price are household linens, fabrics, wallpapers - even holidays. Usually a recommendation-only club; due to this exclusivity, some personal references may be required. Membership costs £30 a year and includes a regular newsletter informing you of future showroom visits.

## DELLA FINCH

☎ 0171 834 9161.

Della organises designer sales, usually at the Rochester Hotel, SW1, selling top name clothes direct from the showroom at wholesale prices. Some are from next season's collections, some this season, and include labels such as Thierry Mugler, YSL and Paul Costelloe, evening wear, smart suits, blouses and swimwear. There's usually a special bargain rail, all priced at about £5. Phone to put your name on the mailing list.

## THE BRITISH DESIGNERS SALE FOR WOMEN

42 YORK MANSIONS, PRINCE OF WALES DRIVE, LONDON SW11 4BP
☎ 0171-228 5314. OPEN 10 - 4 MON - FRI.

The first of what is now a booming industry, the British Designers Sale was started by Debbie Hodges, a former PR, more than 15 years ago. Because of her contacts, it offers top British designer labels - plus a number of top Italian, German and French labels - you won't find at other designer sales, but no names can be mentioned or those publicity-shy designers would not be happy to let Debbie sell their overstocks. Labels are the sort you would expect to find in the designer rooms at Harrods or Harvey Nichols. The women's sales, which are held five times a year in London, are now open to members only, but there is a waiting list, updated once a year in June, on which it is well worth putting your name down. Membership costs £26 per year. If you want to write to Debbie to add your name to the mailing list, please enclose an sae. Debbie has also recently started holding sales in Edinburgh.

## THE DESIGNER ROADSHOW

ORGANISER ELAINE FOSTER
☎ 0171-226 7437.

One of the few designer sales which takes place outside London, the Designer Roadshow usually takes in six or seven venues around the country before ending up in Deep Space Studios, 10A Belmont St, London NW1. Stock is more likely to appeal to the younger end of the market, and there is plenty to appeal to men, too. Cities visited last year include Glasgow, Liverpool, Leeds, Bristol, Brighton, Cardiff, Bath and Manchester and among the sixty designers whose clothes were on sale were Rifat Ozbek, Nick Coleman, Felix Blow, Val Pirou, Jasper Conran, Duffer of St George, Fred Bear hats, Xavier Foley, Sonnentag Mulligan, Copperwheat Blundell, Griffin Laundry, No Such Soul and Komodo. Phone Elaine for more information and to put your name on the mailing list.

## THE DESIGNER WAREHOUSE SALE FOR WOMEN

ROGER DACK LTD, STUDIO 2, SHEPPERTON HOUSE,
83 SHEPPERTON ROAD, LONDON N1 3DF
☎ 0171-704 1064. SALES USUALLY OPEN 10 - 8 FRI, 10 - 6 SAT, 11 - 5 SUN.

The Designer Warehouse Sale for Women is the sister sale to the Warehouse Sale for Men and usually takes place at The Worx, Balfe St, London N1, over a weekend. Labels regularly seen include Bella Freud, Rifat Ozbek, Nicole Farhi, Ally Capellino, Betty Jackson, Sara Sturgeon, Flyte Ostell. Prices are normally about one third of the shop price. Admission is £2. Phone for more details and dates.

## UNICO CORPORATION LTD

SWINSTEAD HALL, SWINSTEAD, NEAR GRANTHAM,
LINCOLNSHIRE
☎ 01476 550016.

Holds regular warehouse clearance sales in London and countrywide with up to 3,000 garments at prices ranging from £9.99. Designers include Louis Feraud, Gianfranco Ferre, Armani, Serge Nancel, Yarell, Fink and a host of top designer names. There are usually current season's collections as well as plenty of last season's collections at even sillier prices. Ring and put your name on their mailing list.

## WINDSMOOR WAREHOUSE

WINDSMOOR HOUSE, 83 LAWRENCE ROAD, TOTTENHAM, LONDONN 15 4EP
☎ 0181-800 8022.
Regular sales are held here (usually four times a year) during which first quality fashion from the Windsmoor, Planet, Precis and Berkertex ranges are sold at discounts of up to 75%. Sometimes, there is also Nautica casualwear for men, Centaur for men and Dannimac rainwear for men and women. Phone or write to be put on the mailing list.

# SOUTH EAST

## *Permanent Discount Outlets*

## ALEXON SALE SHOP

UNIT 2, CHEAPSIDE, LUTON, BEDFORDSHIRE LU1 2PB
☎ (01582) 483422. OPEN 9 - 5.30 MON - SAT.
CHILTERNS SHOPPING CENTRE, HIGH WYCOMBE, BUCKING-HAMSHIRE HP13 5ES
☎ (01494) 464214. OPEN 9 - 5.30 MON - SAT.
Alexon, Eastex and Dash from previous seasons at 40%-70% less than the original price; during sale time in January and June, the reductions are up to 70%. Stock includes separates, skirts, jackets, blouses, and leisurewear. Current stock at 10%-40% discounts. also Ann Harvey casual wear in larger sizes.

## BEAUTIFUL BRIDES

APARTMENT ONE, EASTFIELD LODGE, ANDOVER, HAMPSHIRE
☎ (0374) 936610. MAIL ORDER ONLY.
Brand new wedding gowns from Alfred Angelo, Catherine Rayner, Margaret Lee and Ronald Joyce to order at discounts of 25% off the

recommended retail price. Also bridal underwear and Ivory of Bond Street shoes at discount. If you buy a dress, the discount on the accessories is even greater.

## CHOICE DISCOUNT STORES LIMITED

14-20 RECTORY ROAD, HADLEIGH, BENFLEET, ESSEX SS7 2ND
☎ (01702) 555245. OPEN 9 - 5.30 MON - SAT.
26-28 HIGH STREET, BARKINGSIDE, ILFORD, ESSEX IG6 2DO
☎ 0181-551 2125. OPEN 9 - 5.30 MON - FRI, 9 - 6 SAT, 10 - 4 SUN.
44-46 HIGH STREET, WATFORD, HERTFORDSHIRE WD1 2BR
☎ (01923) 23355. OPEN 9 - 5.30 MON - SAT.
10-11 LADYGATE CENTRE, HIGH STREET, WICKFORD, ESSEX SS12 9AK
☎ (01268) 764893. OPEN 9 - 5.30 MON - THUR, 9 - 6 FRI, SAT.
UNIT 6A, MAYFLOWER RETAIL PARK, GARDINERS LINK,
BASILDON, ESSEX SS14 3AR
☎ (01268) 288331. OPEN 9 - 6 MON, TUE, WED, 9 - 7 THUR, FRI, 9 - 5.30
SAT, 11 - 5 SUN.
14-16 HIGH STREET, GRAYS, ESSEX RM17 6LV
☎ (01375) 385780. OPEN 9 - 5.30 MON - SAT.

Surplus stock including women's, men's and children's fashions from Next plc, Next Directory and other high street fashions, Next Interiors and footwear. You can save up to 50% off normal retail prices for first quality; up to two thirds for seconds. There are no changing rooms but the shop offers refunds if goods are returned in perfect condition within 28 days. There are special sales each January and September. Easy access for wheelchairs and pushchairs. The Watford and Wickford stores are known as Next 2 Choice; the former specialises in ladies and menswear only from Next plc and Next Directory.

## CROMWELL'S MAD HOUSE

28-29 TOWN SQUARE MALL, THE PEACOCKS SHOPPING CENTRE,
WOKING, SURREY GU21 1GB
☎ 0181-903 5888.

Discunted jeans and casualwear, hiking jackets, caps, USA football jackets, Fruit of the Loom T shirts, and a range of Lee Cooper, Wrangler and Lee outfits, mostly for men with somewomenswear. Clothes are normally about 20% less than in the high street as most of the items are either ends of lines or have been bought in bulk and priced to sell quickly. Some of its prices are cheaper than the equivalent items in the high street, others are not such good bargains. There are now 50 branches of this shop - phone 0181 903 5888 for your nearest outlet.

## DASH SALE SHOP

64 HIGH STREET, RAMSGATE, KENT
☎ (01843) 589860. OPEN 9 - 5.30 MON - SAT.
Eastex, Dash and Alexon clothing at reduced prices. Stock is mostly last year's and at least half the original price. There is also Ann Harvey merchandise in sizes 16-26.

## DISCOUNT DRESSING

164 QUEENS ROAD, BUCKHURST HILL, ESSEX
☎ 0181-559 1025. OPEN 10 - 6 SEVEN DAYS A WEEK.
521 CRANBROOK ROAD, GANTS HILL, ILFORD,
☎ 0181-518 3446. OPEN 10 - 6 SEVEN DAYS A WEEK.
Discount Dressing is a veritable Aladdin's Cave of designer bargains. They sell mostly German, Italian and French designer labels at prices at least 50% and up to 90% below those in normal retail outlets, and all items are brand new and perfect. They have a team of buyers all over Europe who purchase stock directly from the manufacturer, therefore by-passing the importers and wholesalers and, of course, their mark-up. They also buy bankrupt stock in this country. Their agreement with their suppliers means that they are not able to advertise brand names for obvious reasons, but they are all well-known for their top quality and style. So confident is Discount Dressing that you will be unable to find the same item cheaper elsewhere, that they offer to give the outfit to you free of charge should you perform this miracle. Merchandise includes raincoats, dresses, suits, trousers, blouses, evening wear, special occasion outfits and jackets, in sizes 6-24 and in some cases larger. GDD readers can obtain a further 10% discount if they visit the shop taking a copy of this book with them. The Gants Hill branch has recently been turned into a clearance centre where you can now buy designer goods from only £5. There is nothing wrong with the items on sale apart from the fact that they are slightly slower sellers, but it gives the company the space to turn over merchandise more quickly in the other shops.

## HANNINGTONS SALE SHOP

9 BRIGHTON SQUARE, BRIGHTON SUSSEX BN1 1HD
☎ (01273) 203785. OPEN 10 - 6 MON - SAT, 11 - 5 SUN.

Formerly the Label Stable, this outlet now serves as the clearance centre of Hanningtons department store, selling old stock including designer labels Rodier and Betty Barclay, and discontinued lines. There are no shoes or handbags.

## IN SECONDS

17 CRESCENT ROAD, WORTHING, WEST SUSSEX
☎ (01903) 820845. OPEN 9.30 - 5 MON - SAT, CLOSED WED.

Large selection of seconds from Marks & Spencer and other department stores for men, women and children. For example, ski pants, £8, originally £35; denim shirt, £8, originally £25; leather jacket trimmed with lambswool, £60, originally £249. Large stock and sizes up to 20 for ladies. The shop also sells handbags, slippers, nightwear and picture frames but no underwear.

## LIMITED EDITION

158 MOULSHAM STREET, CHELMSFORD, ESSEX CM2 OLD
☎ (01245) 494950. OPEN 10 - 3 FIRST THUR OF EACH MONTH.

Ladies separates ranging from £5 to £105 which are ex-showroom samples from three different collections. Because they are showroom samples, they are all size 12 but the fact that they come from different collections means the sizing may vary. The collections are suitable for ages 25 to 60. Factory seconds are also available in a variety of colours and sizes at excellent prices, usually even less than cost - average cost is £30.

## M & G DESIGNER FASHIONS

OLD LONDON ROAD (OLD A23), HICKSTEAD VILLAGE, WEST SUSSEX RH17 5 RL
☎ (01444) 881511. OPEN 10 - 5 MON - SAT AND SOME BANK HOLIDAYS; PHONE FIRST.

A large fashion warehouse selling designer and famous high-street name clothes at discounted prices from 20% to 80% less than the normal retail price. Because they carry many famous high street and designer labels in the 3,400 sq ft outlet, they are unable to advertise these names. Some of the clothes are discontinued lines, others late deliveries, bankrupt stock or cancelled orders. Twice a year, they hold "silly" sales where no garment is over £30. They also hold winter and summer clearance sales. Their range covers everything from T-shirts to ballgowns in sizes 10-28. There is ample parking, free coffee or tea, easy access for wheelchairs and individual changing rooms. They have only recently started selling menswear, mens and ladies shoes. (Follow the signs to Ricebridge and Hickstead Village.)

## MATALAN

UNIT 4B, THE TUNNEL ESTATE, WESTERN AVENUE,
LAKESIDE RETAIL PARK, WEST THURROCK, ESSEX RM16 1HH
☎ (01708) 864350. OPEN 10 - 8 MON - FRI, 9.30 - 5.30 SAT, 10 - 6 SUN.
UNIT 4, RIVERSIDE RETAIL PARK, VICTORIA ROAD, CHELMSFORD,
ESSEX EM2 6LL
☎ (01245) 348787. OPEN 10 - 8 MON - FRI, 9.30 - 5.30 SAT, 11 - 5 SUN.
ROSE KILN LANE, READING, BERKSHIRE RG2 0SN
☎ (01734) 391958. OPEN 10 - 8 MON - FRI, 9.30 - 5.30 SAT, 10 - 6 SUN.
BILTON ROAD, BLETCHLEY, MILTON KEYNES,
BUCKINGHAMSHIRE MK1 1HS
☎ (01908) 373735. OPEN 10 - 8 MON - FRI, 9 - 6 SAT, 10 - 4 SUN.

As the UK's first National Discount Club, Matalan has the buying power to guarantee its members up to 60% discounts on a huge range of brand name clothing, household goods, luggage and toiletries for all the family. Top quality merchandise, current season, no seconds, is offered to its members at exclusive, permanently discounted prices seven days a week. Matalan operates strictly on a membership basis, one of the key factors for its success in offering 20%-60% savings off recommended retail prices. Membership cards are issued through companies, organisations and associations in the vicinity of the stores, and are available to their employees/members. They are valid at any of the 50 Matalan stores in the UK. To find out if your organisation is registered, phone the Matalan hotline on 01772 629447.

# NATIONAL WEDDING INFORMATION SERVICES

121 HIGH STREET, EPPING, ESSEX CM16 4BD
☎ (01992) 576461. OPEN 8.30 - 9.30 MON - FRI, 9 - 5.30 SAT.

Free information on a range of facilities in your area from car hire to bridal wear, florists to discos, hall decoration to marquee hire. Phone them and tell them where your wedding is taking place and they will send you, free, a list of services local to you. Obviously, the quality of the list depends on which locals have registered with the Information Service. Also offers guidelines on wedding procedure and changes in the law.

# ROCOCO

WOODSIDE, ROMANHURST AVENUE, BROMLEY, KENT BR2 OPF
☎ 0181- 460 4041. BY APPOINTMENT ONLY.

Imports Continental designer clothes and shoes and sells for about half the normal retail store price. Merchandise is mainly Italian, French and German - Maurioni and Maurizio and Hoffman, and consists mainly of separates. Also sells Moschino belts, Mondi and Pierre Lawrence shoes. Holds regular sale days in the West End. Sizes go up to size 16.

# RUBERT OF LONDON LIMITED

UNIT 7, STIRLING INDUSTRIAL CENTRE, STIRLING WAY, BOREHAM-WOOD, HERTFORDSHIRE WD6 2BT
☎ 0181-207 2620. OPEN 10 - 4 MON - FRI, 10 - 2 SUN,
CLOSED SATS AND BANK HOLIDAYS.

A friendly, family-run permanent warehouse sale of ladies fashions at prices which are at least 20%-40% below retail price, Rubert specialises in wool and cashmere coats and jackets in sizes 10-20. It also stocks a comprehensive summer selection of separates for all age groups and there is always a small range for sizes 20-24. There are superb blouses, skirts, jackets, trousers, rainwear and much more, all of which are current season's merchandise. There are two changing rooms and parking is easy. To find the outlet, at Stirling Corner roundabout go past Curry's down Stirling Way about 300 yards on the left. Look out for the sign on the car park and go down the alley to Unit 7.

## SCENT TO YOU

17 CHURCH STREET, KINGSTON, SURREY
☎ 0181-974 6231. OPEN 9.30 - 5.30 MON - SAT. MAIL ORDER:
☎ (01494) 712855
10 PEASCOD STREET, WINDSOR, BERKSHIRE.
☎ (01753) 833693. OPEN 9.30 - 5.30 MON - SAT.
Discounted perfume and accessories including body lotions and gels.
The company, which has three branches (see under Womenswear,
North and Scotland) and a mail order service buys in bulk and sells
more cheaply, relying on a high turnover for profit. Discounts range
from 5% to 60%, with greater savings during their twice-yearly sales.
Most of the leading brand names are stocked including Christian
Lacroix, Armani, Charlie, Givenchy, Anais Anais from Cacherel,
Charlie from Revlon, Coco Chanel, Christian Dior, Elizabeth Taylor,
Blue Grass from Elizabeth Arden, Aramis, Lagerfeld. Occasionally,
they also buy in a limited range of skincare lines, gift wrappings and
cards.

## SECOND EDITION

MONTAGUE STREET, WORTHING, WEST SUSSEX PO22 6DS
☎ (01903) 823163. OPEN 9.30 - 5 MON - FRI, 9 - 5.30 SAT.
Second Edition sells a wide range of goods from designer clothes and
children's bedding to lamps, china ornaments, tablecloths and
kitchenware. Some are seconds, some perfects and discounts range
from 25%-50%. They have been known to stock designers such as
Caroline Charles as well as a wide range of high street and chainstore
brand names. Kitchenware includes storage jars, assorted mugs,
kitchen clocks and saucepans. Examples of prices include medium-
sized Swan saucepans without lids, £7.99; table cloths from £1.99.

## SNIPS IN FASHION

234 HIGH STREET, ORPINGTON, KENT BR6 OLS
☎ (01689) 828288. OPEN 9.30 - 5.30 MON - SAT.
Clearance outlet featuring labels such as Basler, le Truc, Mansfield,
Olsen, Hammer, Joy Fun at less than half the original price. Some are
current stock, others samples from showrooms, yet others discontinued lines, seconds or late deliveries. The whole range of clothing is
stocked from ballgowns and coats to jeans and beach wear, but no
accessories.

# T K MAXX

THE GALLERIA SHOPPING CENTRE, COMET WAY,
JUNCTION 3 OFF THE A1, HATFIELD, HERTFORDSHIRE
☎ (01707) 270063. OPEN 10 - 8 MON - FRI, 10 - 6 SAT, 11 - 5 SUN.
173-178 HIGH STREET, BELOW BAR, SOUTHAMPTON
☎ (01703) 631600. OPEN 9 - 5.30 MON - FRI, 9 - 6 SAT, UNTIL 7 ON
THUR.
BROAD STREET MALL, BROAD STREET, READING, BERKSHIRE
☎ (01734) 511117. OPEN 9 - 5.30 MON - FRI, 9 - 6 SAT.
LOWER CONCOURSE, THE PEACOCKS, WOKING, SURREY
☎ (01483) 750263. OPEN MON - FRI, 9.30 - 6 SAT, UNTIL 8 ON THUR.
SAT 9 - 6, SUN 11 - 5.

Based on an American concept, TK Maxx is the first British retailer to
practise "off-price" retailing. This means a centrally located store
which offers famous label goods with up to 60% savings off recommended retail prices. TK Maxx has fashion for the whole family -
women's, men's and childrenswear - accessories, shoes, gifts, kitchenware and home goods. Everything in the store is branded with a choice
of well-known high street names to designer labels, and while a small
percentage mightly be clearly marked past season, the great majority of
items in store are current season, current stock and still with phenomenal savings. There is a huge choice with 50,000 pieces in store with
5,000 new items arriving a week, so it's worth keeping abreast of the
lastest deliveries as turnaround is very fast. One of the ways in which
TK Maxx is able to offer such low prices is by running a very low-cost
operation, so the stores are simple and unfussy with wide aisles,
shopping trolleys and baskets, and a spacious, functional feel to them.
Service is not compromised, however: there are individual changing
rooms, ramps for buggies and wheelchairs, plenty of staff on the shop
floor and all the branches accept all major credit and debit cards.

# *Factory Shops*

## ALAN PAINE KNITWEAR

SCATS COUNTRY STORE, BRIGHTON ROAD, GODALMING, SURREY
☎ (01483) 419962. OPEN 9 - 5 MON - FRI, 8.30 - 4.30 SAT.

Men's and ladies knitwear, made in the factory in Wales (see Womenswear, Wales and West Midlands) and sold here at factory shop prices. Although most of the jumpers and cardigans are made for men and start at size 38" chest, they are as likely to be bought by women. Choose from cotton, cashmere, lambswool, camel hair, merino and merino and silk mix. The factory makes most of its stock for export, and sells to some of the top shops in London. This shop is also supplied by another sister company with men's T-shirts, long-sleeved shirts and cotton trousers and shorts.

## AQUASCUTUM

CLEVELAND ROAD, MAYLANDS WOOD ESTATE, HEMEL HEMPSTEAD, HERTFORDSHIRE HP2 7EY
☎ (01442) 248333. OPEN 10 - 4 MON - FRI, OCCASIONALLY
9 - 1 SAT.

Previous season's stock and seconds for women and men at greatly reduced prices. For women, jackets, suits, blouses, skirts, sweaters, belts, handbags and hats. For men, blazers, suits and silk ties. Examples include half-price ladies silk blouses and 60% off men's suits. Also sell cotton and wools from £3 a metre to cashmere at £43 a metre, most of which are remnants and end of line rolls.

## BERLEI

GROVEBURY ROAD, LEIGHTON BUZZARD, BEDFORDSHIRE LE7 8SH
☎ (01525) 850088. OPEN 9.30 - 5.30 MON - SAT.

Factory shop sells discontinued ranges of its famous-name briefs, bras, suspender belts, thongs, sports bras, Ultra bras, bodies and basques at one-third off the recommended retail price. Seconds in the same items are sold at what the staff say are "silly prices".

## CLAREMONT GARMENTS

26 DOLPHIN ROAD, SHOREHAM-BY-SEA, SUSSEX BN34 6PS
☎ (0273) 461571. OPEN 9 - 4.30 MON - FRI, 9 - 3 SAT.
Sell seconds and discontinued lines of famous chainstore ladies underwear as well as non-chainstore products such as skirts, jeans and swimwear. Ladies panties are reduced from £10 to £4, cami-knickers are one-third of the full retail price.

## DAVID EVANS COLLECTION

BOURNE ROAD, CRAYFORD, KENT DA1 4BP
☎ (01322) 559401. OPEN 9.30 - 5 MON - FRI, 9.30 - 4.30 SAT.
Silk ties, silk fabric, purses, wallets, handbags, photo frames, silk cosmetic bags, woollen shawls and seconds in scarves are all on sale here at incredibly low prices. Silk fabric sold by the metre, dressing table accessories, hairbrush and comb sets. Occasional clearance sales make for even better bargains.

## GOSSARD

GROVEBURY ROAD, LEIGHTON BUZZARD, BEDFORDSHIRE LU7 8SN
☎ (01525) 851122. OPEN 9.3- - 5.30 MON - SAT.
Factory shop sells seconds and discontinued ranges of Gossard underwear including bras, briefs, suspender belts and bodies, but no nightwear or long-line slips at discounted prices. Most of the stock is last year's trade catalogue styles at discounts of between 25%-75%.

## JAEGER FACTORY SHOP

208 LONDON ROAD, BURGESS HILL, WEST SUSSEX RH15 9RD
☎ (01444) 871123. OPEN 12.30 - 4 MON, 9.30 - 4 TUE - FRI, 9.30 - 3.30 SAT.
Classic tailoring from Jaeger, Jaeger Man and Viyella at old-fashioned prices for women and men. Most of the merchandise is last season's stock and some seconds, but you may find the odd gem from this season if you hunt carefully. Some factory shops stock the whole range of Jaeger clothes, some just knitwear; yet others sell goods other than those with the Jaeger label. This shop sells mens and ladies wear, as well as accessories, towels and linens.

# KANGOL

46 CHURCH STREET, LUTON, BEDFORDSHIR LU1 3JG
☎ (01582) 405000. OPEN 10 - 4 MON - FRI, 9 - 12.30 SAT.
Kangol Factory Shop sells end of lines, seconds, samples and some perfect prototypes of their famous caps, berets, felt, woollen and straw hats and special occasion headwear for events such as Henley. There are more than 100 different styles on display for women and men including elaborate hats made from anything from polyester and straw to cotton and silk. Caps start from £3.50 and special occasion hats range from £8-£30.

# MERCHANTS QUAY

BRIGHTON MARINA, BRIGHTON, SUSSEX BN2 5UF
☎ (01273) 693636. FAX 01273 675082.
Ten main factory shops plus twenty-four small factory concessions including The Factory Shop, Edinburgh Crystal, Bookscene and Hornsea Pottery. The concessions include Tom Sayer menswear, Coloroll and Double Two shirts. There are also two "affordable" art galleries, a craft shop, a framing shop, a full-price bridal shop, a multi-complex 8-screen cinema, an Asda superstore, small playground and a variety of eating places.

# MEXX INTERNATIONAL

132-133 FAIRLIE ROAD, SLOUGH TRADING ESTATE, SLOUGH, BERKSHIRE SL1 4PY
☎ (01753) 525450. OPEN 9.30 - 5.30 MON - SAT, 10 - 4 SUN, UNTIL 7 ON THUR.
High street fashion at factory outlet prices for men, women and children. There are usually at least 6,000 items in stock in this 10,000 sq ft outlet, with regular new deliveries, all of which are heavily discounted by between 40%-80%. Seventy-five percent of the stock is Mexx own label from last season, the rest is from concessions including Jane Shilton, Gossard, Debut Sports, Fiorelli, and Charnos. The outlet can be found by turning down off the Slough Farnham Road at Do It All and turning right at the second set of traffic lights.

## MOTOWN JEANS

MOTOWN YARD, THE BREWERY, LONDON ROAD, STANFORD-LE-
HOPE, ESSEX
☎ (01375) 675643. OPEN 9 - 5 MON - FRI, 9 - 1 SAT.
Manufactures denim jeans for retail outlets and sells its own label
jeans at half price in its factory shop. It also sells denim jackets from
a sister factory which it supplies with denim and Motown jeans. All
are perfect and come in ladies, men's and children's sizes. Prices start
at £12 for jeans and £27 for denim jackets.

## STERLING LEATHERS

UNIT A2, SEEDBED CENTRE, COLDHARBOUR ROAD, PINNACLES,
HARLOW, ESSEX CM19 5AF
☎ (01279) 444449. OPEN 9 - 4 MON - FRI, 10 - 12 SAT.
Sterling Leathers manufacture top quality women's and men's leather
and suede garments for many of the best known names at the upper
end of the high street. Their production ranges from full-length coats,
jackets and blousons to waistcoats. Their factory shop at Harlow is a
bargain hunger's paradise which sells garments a good deal cheaper
than normal retail prices. In the vicinity of the factory are a number
of tourist attractions about which details can be provided to shoppers
on request.

## THE FACTORY SHOP (ESSEX) LTD

THE GLOUCESTERS, LUCKYN LANE, PIPPS HILL INDUSTRIAL ESTATE,
BASILDON, ESSEX SS14 3AX
☎ (01268) 520446. OPEN 9 - 5.30 MON - SAT, 10 - 5 SUN.
No-frills factory shop selling seconds, discontinued lines and some
perfect current stock from department and chain store high street
names, as well as direct from the manufacturer. This is not the place
to look for high fashion, but it has an enormous amount of middle of
the range women's, men's and children's clothes, as well as bedlinen,
towels, toys, food, kitchen utensils, disposable cutlery and partyware,
short-dated food, garden furniture, tools, sportswear, china, glass and
barbecues within its 8,000 square feet of selling space. Everything is
sold at between 30% and 50% of the retail price. Parking is easy, the
M25 is near and there's good wheelchair/pushchair access.

## THE FALMER FACTORY SHOP

24 BROOK ROAD, RAYLEIGH, ESSEX SS6 7XE
☎ (01268) 773633. OPEN 9 - 5.30 MON - SAT.
Selected current stock perfects and seconds from the Falmer jeans
range as well as seconds and discontinued garments from leggings and
sweatshirts to jackets and knitwear for men and women. Twice a year,
they also hold clearance sales.

## THE SHOE SHED

ORCHARD ROAD, ROYSTON, HERTFORDSHIRE SG8 5HA
☎ (01763) 241933. OPEN 9 - 5.30 TUE, WED, 9 - 6 THUR, FRI, 9 - 4 SAT, 10
- 2 SUN.
C/O MEXX UK, 132-133 FAIRLIE ROAD, SLOUGH, BERKSHIRE
☎ (01753) 525450. OPEN 9.30 - 5.30 MON - WED, FRI, SAT, 9.30 - 7 THUR,
10 - 4 SUN.
Large factory shop selling a vast range of all types of women's, men's
and children's shoes, all of which are perfects, at up to 30% below
normal high street prices. Ladies sandals cost from £5; ladies shoes
from £7.50. Men's shoes from £10; sports shoes from £10.


# Dress Agencies

## ALWAYS IN VOGUE

1 THE OLD MILL, RIVER ROAD, ARUNDEL, WEST SUSSEX BN18 9NY
☎ (01903) 883192. OPEN 10 - 4 MON - SAT, CLOSED WED AFTER-
NOONS.
Sells only designer clothes - no high street chainstore labels. Labels
range from Planet and Jaeger to designers such as Escada and
Valentino. Many clients shop there for weddings, ladies day at
Ascot and the Goodwood races. Eveningwear, hats and accessories
are also stocked.

## ANCORA DRESS AGENCY

74 CHURCH STREET, WEYBRIDGE, SURREY KT13 8DL
☎ (01932) 855267. OPEN 9.30 - 5.30 MON, TUE, THUR, FRI, 9.30 - 5 WED,
SAT.
Middle to upper range designer outfits from Alexon, Monsoon and
Wallis to Betty Barclay, Mondi, Yarell and Frank Usher.

## BARGAIN BOUTIQUE

SNOW HILL, CRAWLEY DOWN, WEST SUSSEX
☎ (01342) 712022. OPEN 9.15 - 2.15 TUE - SAT.
BB stocks mainly high street names such as Marks & Spencer, Next, BhS, Laura Ashley, as well as labels such as Windsmoor and Jacques Vert. Mainly caters for women and children, though there is a limited selection of menswear. Most of the merchandise is made up of separates, with few suits, and there are some shoes for adults. There is also a sample rail with great bargains at one third of the original price, but no accessories.

## BE-WISE

5 GLOUCESTER PARADE, BLACKFEN ROAD, SIDCUP, KENT DA15 8TS
☎ 0181-859 2658. OPEN 10 - 5 MON - SAT, CLOSED THUR.
Middle market names including Principles, Berkertex, Marks & Spencer and Next as well as the occasional designer label.

## BENJAMIN'S MESS

77 HIGH STREET, ROCHESTER, KENT ME1 1LX
☎ (01634) 817848. OPEN 9 - 5.30 MON - SAT.
This shop sells bankrupt stock, designer seconds and samples as well as nearly-new clothes from Next, Laura Ashley, Benetton, Naff Naff, Levi's, Hobbs and Jigsaw. Half the shop is devoted to childrenswear including designers such as Oilily, Osh Kosh, Little Levi's, Portofini and Laura Ashley. There are also new accessories: hats, jewellery, bags and scarves.

## BON MARCHE

114A NORTHGATE, CANTERBURY, KENT
☎ (01227) 764823. OPEN 9.30 - 5.30 MON - SAT.
A fairly small dress agency in Kent which offers across-the-board labels from Marks & Spencer up to YSL, with plenty of Jaeger, Maxmara, Mondi, Alexon and Caroline Charles. Prices range from £18 for an M&S top quality outfit to £150, though most items are in the £45-£75 price range. Day and evening wear as well as shoes, jewellery, bags, scarves and hats are stocked. The owner says that style is more important than the label and is as likely to stock Dorothy Perkins as Dior. As we were going to press, they were about to start selling nearly-new wedding dresses.

# BROWSERS OF RICHMOND

36 FRIARS STILE ROAD, RICHMOND, SURREY TW10 6QN
☎ 0181-332 0875. OPEN 10 - 6 MON - SAT.
39 HIGH STREET, COBHAM, SURREY KT11 3DP
☎ (0932) 860166. OPEN 9 - 5.30 MON - SAT.

The largest dress agency in Surrey, Browsers is now so successful that last year it expanded to another floor which is bright and fresh. They carry a wide range of top designer labels at realistic and irresistible prices. The owners keep up to date with fashion trends and are experienced at both pricing and merchandising their stock at a realistic level. They have a large volume of stock and a fast turnover and are therefore constantly looking for new stock.

# CACHE-CACHE

10 GREGORIES ROAD, BEACONSFIELD, BUCKINGHAMSHIRE
HP9 1 HQ
☎ (01494) 671727. OPEN 10 - 5 MON - SAT.

Sells blouses, skirts, trousers, knitwear, suits, jackets, dresses, eveningwear, accessories, belts, handbags, hats but no swimwear. All clothes are less than two years old and have been dry cleaned or washed and pressed. Designers include Yarrell, Betty Barclay, Planet and Country Casuals.

# CAMEO

150 HIGH STREET, BERKHAMSTEAD, HERTFORDSHIRE HP4 3AT
☎ (01442) 865791. OPEN 9.30 - 5.15 MON - FRI, 9.30 - 4.45 SAT.

Women's and children's clothes, mostly middle market names such as Marks & Spencer and Next, but with some designer labels. The women's range covers dresses, suits, sweaters, coats, jackets, belts, handbags, trousers, hats, skirts, blouses. Opposite is Mansworld where nearly-new designer men's clothes can be found.

# CANCER RESEARCH GROUP

172 TERMINUS ROAD, EASTBOURNE, EAST SUSSEX BN21 3SB
☎ (01323) 739703. OPEN 9.30 - 4.30 MON - SAT.
7 HIGH STREET, SOUTHEND, ESSEX SS1 1JE
☎ (0170) 2432698. OPEN 9.30 - 4.30 MON - SAT.

Shop specifically aimed at the bridal market which sells or hires from Cinderella-style to Twenties-style wedding dresses in white, cream, ivory or pink; bridal accessories for the bride, pageboys and brides-maids; bridesmaids dresses and pageboy outfits; black and grey morning suits, plus accessories, for the groom, as well as dinner suits; hats for weddings and for Ascot. Prices range from: silk wedding dresses, £150 to hire, £40-£495 to buy; morning suits, £25 to hire, £50 to buy; dinner suits, £16.50 to hire, £35 to buy. The most expensive wedding dress in stock was £795 reduced from £2,500. Most of the stock is either donated or straight from the manufacturer. Labels for wedding dresses cover Annelles Sharp, Laura Ashley, Ellis, Berkertex, Pronuptia, Bow Bells, Charmaine Jones, and Hilary Morgan.

## CHANGES

121 DEEP CUT BRIDGE ROAD, DEEP CUT, CAMBERLEY,
SURREY GU16 6SD
☎ (01252) 834487. OPEN 10 - 5 TUE - SAT.

Designer and high street range of nearly-new ladies wear. Full range from leisure wear to ballgowns. Evening wear a speciality with stock held throughout the year. Accessories include shoes, handbags, and jewellery. Prices range from £5-£100 and stock changes constantly and is only held on sale for six weeks.

## CLOTHES CONNECTION

239 NEW ROAD, PORTSMOUTH, HAMPSHIRE PO2 7QY
☎ (01705) 672711. OPEN 10 - 4 MON - SAT, CLOSED WED.

Clothes Connection is a well-established, friendly dress agency, selling middle market fashions from high street, boutique, Continental and designer labels. They stock everything from beachwear to ballgowns in sizes 8-18. About half the stock is imported French and German secondhand clothing without the labels - but, claims the owner, far superior to the equivalent middle market English styles. Prices range from £8 to £80, about one third of the original cost. New outfits are also available, usually ends of lines, at reduced prices. Owner Heather Lax enthusiastically promotes style and the enjoyment of fashion and takes her message "dress for less" on the road with fortnightly makeover shows at corporate or charity venues. She also hires out hats for all occasions. There is ample parking outside the shop, which is not in a main shopping thoroughfare.

## CLOTHESLINE

58 UNION STREET, MAIDSTONE, KENT
☎ (01622) 758439. OPEN 9.30 - 5 TUE - SAT.
Recommended by a GDD reader, this shop stocks designer labels of
not more than two years in age and in mint condition.

## DEJA VU

1ST FLOOR, 21-23 HIGH STREET, WOBURN SANDS,
BEDFORDSHIRE MK17 8RF
☎ (01908) 584296. OPEN 10 -5 MON - SAT.
Labels such as Jaeger and Armani, plus end of range designer wear
available at high street prices, such as a Jaeger jacket sold at £38, originally retailing at £130. Wide range of clothing available from suits to
special occasion wear and ballgowns. Hats can be hired for all occasions. New and nearly new clothes are sold at a fraction of the original
price. A mail shot operates to tell customers about latest availability.
A friendly style analysis service is also available. Wide range of accessories.

## DEJA VU

OLD SEAL HOUSE, 19 CHURCH STREET, SEAL, NEAR SEVENOAKS,
KENT TN15 ODA
☎ (01732) 762155. OPEN 10 - 4.30 MON - SAT.
In this small, friendly shop, established in 1977, you will find British
and European designers such as Caroline Charles, Paul Costelloe and
Valentino as well as old favourites such as Jaeger, Marks & Spencer,
Liberty and Laura Ashley. The price range is from £10 to £200. There
is also a small range of children's dresses and riding wear, and from
September each year, ski wear for adults and children. After six to
eight weeks, clothes which haven't sold are reduced. An alteration
service is also offered for clothes purchased here.

## DESIGNER NEARLY NEW

105 SANDERSTEAD ROAD, SOUTH CROYDON, SURREY CR2 OPJ
☎ 0181-680 5734. OPEN 10 - 5.30 MON - SAT.
121 STATION ROAD EAST, OXTED, SURREY RH8 OQE
☎ (01883) 717604. OPEN 10 -5 MON - SAT.
Upmarket ladies designer wear such as Escada and Laurel. Top quality
wedding gowns, including Hollywood Dreams and Catherine
Rayner, are less than one year old and all cost more than £1,000 when
new. They can also be returned to the shop, if in good condition, and
sold again, and the vendor will get half the sale price. All other items
are checked for quality and are less than 18 months old.

## DIAMONDS DRESS AGENCY

48 HIGH STREET, STORRINGTON, WEST SUSSEX RH20 4BW
☎ (01903) 746824. OPEN 10 - 5 MON - SAT.
Designer labels such as MaxMara, Yves St Laurent, Escada, Mondi,
Betty Barclay, as well as good high street names, plus accessories.

## DRESS RELEASE

17 NEW ROAD, KINGSTON, SURREY
☎ 0181-549 1438. OPEN 11 - 6 TUE - SAT, CLOSED 1.30 - 2.30.
Tiny shop which sells top quality, nearly new designer clothes and
accessories. There are work suits, casual separates, evening wear,
shoes, jewellery, hats and handbags from middle to upmarket designers: French Connection, Jacques Vert, Jaeger, Planet, Claude
Montana, Rifat Ozbek, Arabella Pollen, Ralph Lauren. There are also
some new samples, without labels, available.

## ENCORE

2A CHURCH STREET, SAFFRON WALDEN, ESSEX
☎ (01799) 524812. OPEN 10 - 4 TUE, WED, FRI, SAT, 10 - 1 MON, THUR.
Well established shop, with little, if any, stock from chain stores. Lots
of German labels such as Escada, Mondi and Gerry Weber, although
British high street names such as Laura Ashley usually sell well.
Arabella Pollen two-piece suit, £75; Laura Ashley dress, £18; half-
price evening wear. Some hats, but no jewellery or shoes.

## FLAIR OF ASHTEAD

11 CRADDOCKS PARADE, CRADDOCKS AVENUE, LOWER ASHTEAD,
SURREY KT21 1QL
☎ (01372) 277207 OPEN 9.30 - 5 MON - SAT.
Nearly new ladies wear with a wide variety of good labels to choose
from ie; Caroline Charles, Jaeger, etc. Strong on seasonal event
clothing as well as wedding outfits. Well established business with
sister shop, Flair of Cobham, ensures value for money and inter-
trading, giving you more opportunity to find the right sizes and
colours. Friendly and well informed, will alter garments and assist in
wardrobe selection, even keeping an eye out for suitable outfits for
regular customers. Some costume jewellery, as well as shoes, handbags
and belts.

## FLAIR OF COBHAM

15 CHURCH STREET, COBHAM, SURREY
☎ (01932) 865825 OPEN 9.30 - 5 MON - SAT.
Nearly new ladies wear with a wide variety of good labels to choose
from ie; Caroline Charles, Jaeger, etc. Strong on seasonal event
clothing as well as wedding outfits. Well established business with
sister shop, Flair of Ashtead, ensures value for money and inter-
trading, giving you more opportunity to find the right sizes and
colours. Friendly and well informed, will alter garments and assist in
wardrobe selection, even keeping an eye out for suitable outfits for
regular customers.

## FROCK FOLLIES

49 HIGH STREET, BECKENHAM, KENT BR3 1DA
☎ 0181-650 9283. OPEN 9.30 - 5.30 MON - SAT.
Middle market labels from Marks & Spencer to Armani and Frank
Usher with some new samples. Specialises in hats, with more than
100 to choose from, as well as swimwear, shoes, hat pins, belts and
scarves. The hats and jewellery are new. Plenty of evening wear, particularly ball gowns, especially from September to Christmas.

## GOOSEBERRY BUSH

2 BARNHAM ROAD, BARNHAM, NR BOGNOR, SUSSEX
☎ (01243) 554552 OPEN 10 - 4 MON - SAT.
Nearly-new largely high street fashions for the mother and child ie Next, Heskia and Mothercare. Stock ranges from a good selection of maternity wear (Blooming Marvellous), to children's cots and high chairs. New items can be found for very reasonable prices. Friendly atmosphere and said to be a particular favourite with grandparents.

## HANG-UPS

1A THE SQUARE, LONG CRENDON, NEAR AYLESBURY,
BUCKINGHAMSHIRE
☎ (01844) 201237. OPEN 9.30 - 4 TUE, THUR, FRI, 9.30 5 SAT.
Good quality high street names such as Country Casuals, Jaeger, Windsmoor, Jacques Vert, Wallis, Bellino and Marks & Spencer. Day wear available in sizes 10-18. A separate studio houses evening wear, some of which is Frank Usher and some from chain stores. Children's wear is also stocked here. Clientele ranges from students to business women. Also has a special rail for men's blazers and suits.

## LITTLE CLASSICS

ODIHAM, NEAR HOOK, HAMPSHIRE
☎ (01256) 764170. PHONE FOR AN APPOINTMENT.
Run by a team of two who work from home in a very friendly atmosphere, this company offers secondhand wedding dresses and sample designer wedding dresses at half the original price. There is plenty of choice, with long or short options, and at least 40 dresses in stock at any one time. Accessories on sale include veils and silk flowers and the duo can also arrange for silk flowers to decorate the church or organise the shoes and cake. There is also an alteration service.

## PANACHE

5 STANFORD SQUARE, WARWICK ST, WORTHING, SUSSEX BN11 3EZ
☎ (01903) 212503. OPEN 10 - 5 MON - SAT.
Two shops in one: Panache sells women's nearly-new at savings of up to 50% on High Street prices; Smarties sells childrenswear up to the age of nine. The adult dress agency stocks a wide range of labels from Marks & Spencer and Viyella to Jacques Vert, MaxMara and Escada. They also sell hats, evening wear, coats, shoes, jackets, handbags and

belts. The children's range from Petite Bateau, Laura Ashley and Oilily to Matrise and Osh Kosh. They do not stock children's sleepwear or underwear.

## PHOENIX

5 CHURCH STREET, COBHAM, SURREY KT11 3EG
☎ (01932) 862147. OPEN 9.30 - 5 MON - SAT.
This black and white cottage devotes 2 floors and 4 rooms to middle to upmarket labels, usually no more than 2 years old, from Marks & Spencer to Escada, Laurel, Mondi, Simon Ellis and Parigi. One whole floor is devoted to evening wear. There's also plenty of accessories from jewellery and hats to belts and shoes, as well as a bargain rail.

## POSH GEAR

29 BILLET LANE, HORNCHURCH, ESSEX RM11 1XP
☎ (01708) 456128. OPEN 10 - 6 MON - SAT OR BY APPOINTMENT.
Home-based business selling brand new samples and a few once-worn designer label wedding dresses at discount prices, as well as samples of designer label outfits. Wedding dresses includes designs by Cupid, Ellis, House of Nicholas, Margaret Lee and Sally B up to size 30 and costing from £50. There are also bridesmaids dresses from £30 and a shoe and handbag dyeing service. Other outfits from smart suits to evening wear, jewellery, shoes and handbags include designs by Serenade, Medici, Finnkarellia in sizes 10-28. There is also a hire service for evening wear, bridal wear, ball gowns and hats.

## REFLECTIONS

7-9 MARINE WALK, HYTHE, KENT CT21 5NW
☎ (01303) 262233. OPEN 10 - 4 MON - SAT, CLOSED WED.
About fifty percent of reflection's stock is second hand, the other fifty percent are German and Italian designer samples. Nearly-new labels include Jaeger, Jobis, Ouiset, Windsmoor, Aquascutum, Country Casuals, Mondi and Betty Barclay. They also sell some manufacturers samples. They will buy on order if they know you, look out for particular requests in nearly nearly-new and phone you if anything suitable comes in, and are very helpful in choosing accessories. Large selection of hats for hire; also good selection of ballgowns.

## RICHE

6A EWELL HOUSE PARADE, EPSOM ROAD, EWELL VILLAGE,
SURREY KT6 1AA
☎ 0181-393 2256. OPEN 9.45 - 5 MON - SAT.

Riche has made its name selling current top quality designer wear at
much reduced prices. The owner is a former model and fashion buyer
and has brought a wealth of experience to this small high street shop,
making it more than just another nearly-new agency. Escada, Yves St
Laurent, Mondi and Krizia are just a few of the regular labels. While
most of the stock is nearly-new, some is ex-fashion show samples and
ends of lines.

## ROUNDABOUT

8 CLIFFE ARCADE, CLIFFE HIGH STREET, LEWES, EAST SUSSEX
☎ (01273) 471325. OPEN 9.30 - 5 MON & TUE, 9.30 - 5 THUR - SAT.

Good quality Jaeger, Marks & Spencer, Windsmoor, Principles, Paul
Costelloe and MaxMara. Prices range from £28 for an Aquascutum
short skirt; £28 for a Paul Costelloe linen shirt; to £90 for an
Aquascutum suit. Also small selection of hats, some jewellery, shoes
and handbags.

## SECOND EDITION

6 WESTMEAD CORNER, CARSHALTON, SURREY SM5 2HZ
☎ 0181-643 8639. OPEN 10 - 4 TUE - SAT.

Mainly high street names such as Marks & Spencer and Next, day
and evening wear, cocktail dresses and ballgowns, are on sale here
There is a separate bridal room stocking, amongst 100 dresses,
designs by Catherine Walker and Ronald Joyce. Prices for wedding
dresses range from £300-£1,000. There are also veils, shoes and headdresses.

## SECONDS OUT

10-14 THE ARCADE, HIGH STREET, COOKHAM, BERKSHIRE SL6 9TA
☎ (01628) 850371. OPEN 9.30 - 5 MON - SAT.

This shop, which has been in operation for nine years, offers middle
to upper range designer labels, including Betty Barclay, Laurel,
Armani, Karl Lagerfeld, Versace and Chanel. There's casual wear and
smart Ascot outfits, as well as evening wear, in this spacious shop. All

the clothes are colour coded by hangers. There is also a selection of brand new clearance stock and never-worn outfits and accessories including up to 60 hats at any one time, shoes and handbags.

## SEQUEL

181 CHESSINGTON ROAD, WEST EWELL, SURREY KT19 9XE
☎ 0181 786 7552. OPEN 10 - 5 MON- SAT, CLOSED WED.
Specialises in upmarket chain store makes including Next, and Laura Ashley, as well as Mondi, Betty Barclay, Paul Costelloe and MaxMara. Nothing is more than two seasons old. On sale in the past have been a Karl Lagerfeld jacket, £79, originally £300; Betty Barclay linen dress, £29, originally £100; Mondi suit, £39, originally £159; Cache D'Or linen two-piece, £79. They also sell hats, new scarves, bags, jewellery and shoes, including secondhand Charles Jourdan, as well as Mexx label clothes, sizes range from 8-18.

## SWITCHGEAR

20 ST LEONARD'S ROAD, WINDSOR, BERKSHIRE SL4 3BU
☎ (01753) 867438. OPEN 9.30 - 5 MON - SAT.
A selection of Escada, Frank Usher, Jaeger and Betty Barclay among other designer names. Merchandise is general wear with some evening outfits. There's also leisure wear, hats, shoes, handbags and belts, with a continuous flow of reductions to two-thirds of the original price.

## TATTERS

23 WEST STREET, RINGWOOD, HAMPSHIRE
☎ (01425) 478511. OPEN 10 - 5 MON - FRI, CLOSED 1 WED, SAT.
As good as new clothes, with many high street names and sizes ranging from 8 to 22. One room is devoted to exclusive designer labels, another to ballgowns and hats and the third to everyday wear. There is also a big selection of ballgowns, general evening wear and seasonal outfits, with labels such as Frank Usher, Jaeger and Peter Barron available. Hats are hired out for Ascot, weddings and funerals. There are two sales, one in January, the other throughout August. Prices range from below £5 to £200.

# THE CHANGING ROOM

50 HIGH STREET, CHALFONT ST GILES, BUCKINHAMSHIRE HP8 4QY
☎ (01494) 875933. OPEN 10 -5 TUE - SAT.

Nearly new clothes ranging from names such as Betty Barclay and
Mondi to Armani and Escada. Generally caters to the upper end of
the market. Clothes sold at 1/3 of the original price and bargains can
always be found. Clothing tends to be very seasonal with a swift
turnover of stock. Wonderful selection of hats and a wide range of
occasion wearin all sizes. A fascinating little shop - not to be missed if
you like hunting for bargains.

# THE CLOTHES LINE

171 HIGH STREET, WINCHESTER, HAMPSHIRE SO23 NBQ
☎ (01962) 868892. OPEN 10 - 4 MON - SAT, CLOSED 1 ON WED.

Designer and high street labels from Next and Laura Ashley to Frank
Usher, Laurel, YSL, Marella and Jacques Vert plus accessories: hats,
costume jewellery and shoes. During February, the owner runs
wedding dress promotions with dresses which would normally cost
£1,000 selling for £600, as well as veils and headdresses at half price.

# THE DESIGNER CLOTHES SHOP

NEAR BATTLE, EAST SUSSEX
☎ (01424) 892409. BY APPOINTMENT.

Works by appointment only from its site near Battle in East Sussex.
It sells top range designers including Chanel, Armani, DKNY,
Valentino, Georgio Armani and Emporio Armani, Moschino,
Thierry Mugler and Versace. Many outfits are samples from catwalk
shows. For example, a Versace outfit which sells in Bond Street for
£1,750 cost £350; normally there is 25%-30% off the retail price.
Also sells accessories: handbags, belts, jewellery, shoes, scarves, but no
hats. Sizes range from 8-14. Regular customers are kept up to date
with new stock via monthly lists. Phone for an appointment.

## THE DRESS AGENCY

5B RECTORY LANE, ASHTEAD, SURREY KT21 2BA
☎ (01372) 271677. OPEN 9 - 5 MON - FRI, UNTIL 3.30 ON WED, & 4 ON
SAT.

Double-fronted shop, half of which is devoted to daywear, the other
of which sells bridal outfits. The daywear includes mostly middle of
the road, good quality names such as Planet, Basler, Jaeger,
Windsmoor and Aquascutum. The bridal section has about 30
wedding dresses at any one time from £100-£600, plus veils, headdresses, and pageboy outfits. They also have ballgowns, jewellery and
occasionally shoes, hats and bags.

## THE DRESS CIRCLE

6 WOOLMEAD WALK, FARNHAM, SURREY GU9
☎ (01252) 716540 OPEN 9.30 - 4.30 MON - SAT.

Renowned designer labels in good condition - Parigi, Betty Barclay,
Louis Feraud - as well as good high street names such as Marks &
Spencer, Laura Ashley, Next and Benetton. Caters for seasonal events
such as Ascot and towards Christmas supplies a wide variety of good
evening wear. Also stocks dozens of hats and some shoes but no
jewellery. Two annual sales in the summer and winter.

## THE DRESS REVIVAL

14 CHESTERFIELD DRIVE, RIVERHEAD, SEVENOAKS, KENT TN13 2EG
☎ (01732) 459538. OPEN 10 - 5 TUE, FRI OR BY APPOINTMENT.

Home-based business selling labels such as Louis Feraud, Mondi,
Laurel, Fink, Yarrell, Jean Claude Mansfield, as well as some Marks &
Spencer and Wallis. There is a selection of shoes, bags, belts and jewellery, some of which are new. Prices range from £1 to £200. Also
operates an evening wear hire service.

## THE STOCK EXCHANGE

1 HIGH STREET, SUNINGHILL, ASCOT, BERKSHIRE SL5 5NQ
☎ (01344) 25420 OPEN 9 - 5.30 MON - FRI, 9 - 4.30 SAT.

Ladies, men's and children's wear available, usually not more than 2
years old. Stock sold at either one third or half price after 4 weeks.
Rapid turnover of clothes. Good sellers include Marks & Spencer and
Laura Ashley in particular.

## THE VANITY BOX

16 CHURCH STREET, DUNSTABLE, BEDFORDSHIRE LU5 4RU
☎ (01582) 600969. OPEN 9.30 -5 MON - SAT, 10 - 4 THUR.
Large shop on two levels which has been in operation for 19 years
selling good as new seasonal ladies wear. Only items up to 2 years old
accepted and 50% of stock is designer wear such as Jaeger, Mondi,
Bianca, Frank Usher, Ted Lapidus and Windsmoor in sizes 10 - 26.
Both day and evening wear are available. The owner also buy in
Danish designer samples and sells them at half price. Hats, shoes and
bags are also stocked. Twice yearly sales usually in July and January.

## TOUCH OF CLASS

8 MARK LANE, EASTBOURNE, SUSSEX BN21 4RJ
☎ (0323) 639890 OPEN 10 - 4.30 MON - SAT.
Designer labels for women and men, including Jaeger, Windsmoor,
Aquascutum, Burberry and Daks. Reduced price wedding outfits. All
garments under 2 years old, some of which were "mistakes" or once-
worn only. Shoes, handbags, hats and other accessories are also on
sale. After 2 months without a sale at the price agreed between vendor
and shop, garments are sold at reduced prices.

# Hire Shops

## BUMPSADAISY

33 WEST STREET, MARLOW, BUCKINGHAMSHIRE SL7 2LS
☎ (01628) 478487. OPEN 10 - 5.30 MON - SAT.
BROMPTON WALK, LAKESIDE SHOPPING COMPLEX, WEST
THURROCK, ESSEX
☎ (01708) 890121. OPEN 10 - 8 MON - THUR, 10 - 9 FRI, 9 - 7.30 SAT.
Franchised hire shops with large range of special occasion maternity
wear, from wedding outfits to ball gowns, to hire and to buy. Hire
costs range from about £15-£85, costing about £55 for special
occasion wear. Sizes range from 8-18 and labels include JoJo,
Blooming, and Touboro. Phone 0171-379 9831 for details of your
local stockist.

## CLOTHES CONNECTION

239 NEW ROAD, PORTSMOUTH, HAMPSHIRE PO2 7QY
☎ (01705) 672711. OPEN 10 - 4 MON - SAT, CLOSED WED.
Clothes Connection is a well-established, friendly dress agency, selling
middle market fashions and some new outfits, usually ends of lines,
at reduced prices. Owner Heather Lax also hires out hats for all occasions. There is ample parking outside the shop, which is not in a main
shopping thoroughfare.

## DEJA VU

1ST FLOOR, 21-23 HIGH STREET, WOBURN SANDS, BEDFORDSHIRE
☎ (01908) 584296. OPEN 10 -5 MON - SAT.
Primarily a dress agency, Deja Vu also hires out hats. There are usually
about 100 from which to choose, starting at £10.

## JUST BETWEEN US

29 HILLSIDE ROAD, ST ALBANS, HERTFORDSHIRE
☎ (01727) 811172. BY APPOINTMENT ONLY.
Offers a choice of evening wear from 150 short and zappy party
dresses to formal ballgowns in sizes 8-18. No accessories. Cost: £50
plus £50 deposit for a flexible number of days. By appointment only,
including evenings.

## POSH GEAR

29 BILLET LANE, HORNCHURCH, ESSEX RM11 1XP
☎ (01708) 456128. OPEN 10 - 6 MON - SAT. OR BY APPOINTMENT.
Home-based business selling brand new samples and some nearly-
new designer label wedding dresses which are also available for hire.
There is also a hire service for evening wear, ball gowns and hats.

## REFLECTIONS

7-9 MARINE WALK, HYTHE, KENT CT21 5NW
☎ (01303) 262233. OPEN 10 - 4 MON - SAT, CLOSED WED.
Dress agency selling designer samples and nearly-new designer outfits
and which also hires out hats and ballgowns.

## SPECIAL OCCASIONS

1 OLD WOKING ROAD, WEST BYFLEET, WEYBRIDGE,
SURREY KT14 6LW
☎ (01932) 354907. OPEN 9.30 - 5.30 MON - SAT. EVENINGS BY
APPOINTMENT.
More than 400 evening dresses for hire from £50-£85 and hats for
hire from £15-£25. Not designer labels. Also express shoe and bag
dyeing service with over 300 colours to choose from.

## TATTERS

23 WEST STREET, RINGWOOD, HAMPSHIRE  BH24 1DY
☎ (01425) 478511. OPEN 10 - 5 MON - FRI, CLOSED 1 WED, SAT.
Dress agency with up to 200 hats at any one time to hire.

## THE DRESS REVIVAL

14 CHESTERFIELD, RIVERHEAD, SEVENOAKS, KENT TN13 2EG
☎ (01732) 459538. OPEN 10 - 5 TUE, FRI OR BY APPOINTMENT.
A home-based dress agency which also operates an evening wear hire
service.

# Secondhand and Vintage Clothes

## CASANOVA CLOTHING

110 HIGH STREET, ROCHESTER, KENT ME1 1JS
☎ (0634) 817300. OPEN 9.30 - 5.30 MON - SAT, 11 - 5.30 SUN.
Casanova Clothing sells anything from mid-market labels to Sixties
and Seventies gear, with lots of leather. Typical prices include waistcoats, £5, to leather jackets, £30. There are ballgowns, suede coats,
overcoats, skirts, bloudes, wedding and bridesmaids dresses.

# SOUTH WEST

## *Permanent Discount Outlets*

### BUSY BEE

20 CHEAP STREET, FROME, SOMERSET BA11 1BN
☎ (01373) 472012. OPEN 9.30 - 5 MON - SAT, CLOSED AT 3 ON THUR.
Sells selected fashion seconds and over-runs from leading high street chain stores and boutiques, but the main thrust of the shop is towards casual wear. Just because this shop sells chainstore surpluses, don't expect it to be chainstore-sized. All the labels are removed before sale from the underwear, ladies and children's clothes and occasional menswear. Seconds usually sell for between half and two thirds of the normal retail price; perfects are discounted by one-third. Also stocks Trutex school wear. Stocks changes all the time.

### CACHET

34 SOUTH STREET, EXETER, DEVON
☎ (01392) 217727. OPEN 10.30 - 4.30 MON - FRI, 10.30 - 4.30 SAT.
This tiny, but full, boutique sells new designer clothes, knitwear and accessories at permanently discounted prices. Some of the stock is from bankrupt businesses and overmakes, but most of it is normal, perfect outfits which are priced to sell quickly as part of the shop's low profit/high turnover philosophy. Akong the labels to be found are Jacqmar, Lecomte, Suzelle, Stephanie, Oui, Cristina Santandrea, Lucia, Gerry Webber, David Emanuel and Rifat Ozbek. Many are less than half price with up to 25% off this season's ranges.

### DARTMOOR EXCHANGE

29 EAST STREET, ASHBURTON, DEVON
☎ (01364) 654272. OPEN 10 - 4.30 TUE - SAT.
Formerly selling secondhand curtains, this shop now sells Continental designer clothes at discount. Stock is obtained from liquidations and clearance operations. Most of the new outfits are French and priced from £75-£300.

## GRACEFUL GOWNS

69 BELL HILL ROAD, ST GEORGE, BRISTOL
☎ (0117) 9557166. OPEN 10.30 - 8 THUR, 10.30 - 5 FRI, SAT OR BY
APPOINTMENT EARLIER IN THE WEEK.

Sells remaindered bridal wear from previous seasons, some of which
sell for as little as £50. Wedding dresses, shoes, veils, headdresses -
dresses from £50-£1,000; bridesmaids' dresses from £20-£150. Labels
include Alfred Angelo, Dreammaker and Moira Lee.

## HANSONS (DISCOUNT) FABRICS

STATION ROAD, STURMINSTER NEWTON, DORSET
☎ (01258) 472698. OPEN 9 - 5.30 MON - SAT, UNTIL 7 ON FRI.

Fashion and curtaining fabric specialists which also sells sewing
machines, haberdashery, craft items, and patterns. It stocks all the
well-known names such as Rose & Hubble, James Hare, Bennett
silks, Liberty and Ibor, and the full range of fabric weights. Lots of
choice for wedding dress fabric: polyester dupion, satin, silk dupion,
taffeta, tuiles, veiling and lining. No making-up service for brides but
lots of bridal pattern books available. If you spend more than £25,
you get a 5% discount; more than £125 and you receive a seven and
a half percent discount; more than £250 and your discount is 10%.

## MATALAN

UNIT 2, HAVEN BANKS, WATER LANE, EXETER, DEVON EX2 8DW
☎ (01392) 413375. OPEN 10 - 8 MON - FRI, 9.30 - 5.30 SAT, 10 - 6 SUN.
UNIT 1, ALDERMOOR WAY, LONGWELL GREEN, BRISTOL BS15 7AD
☎ (0117) 9352828. OPEN 10 - 8 MON - FRI, 9.30 - 5.30 SAT, 10 - 6 SUN.
UNITS 2/3, TURBURY RETAIL PARK, RINGWOOD ROAD, POOLE,
DORSET BH12 3JJ
☎ (01202) 590686. OPEN 10 - 8 MON - FRI, 9 - 6 SAT, 11 - 5 SUN.

As the UK's first National Discount Club, Matalan has the buying
power to guarantee its members up to 60% discounts on a huge range
of brand item clothing, household goods, luggage and toiletries for all
the family. Top quality merchandise, current season, no seconds, is
offered to its members at exclusive, permanently discounted prices
seven days a week. Matalan operates strictly on a membership basis,
one of the key factors for its success in offering 20%-60% savings off
recommended retail prices. Membership cards are issued through
companies, organisations and associations in the vacinity of the

stores, and are available to their employees/members. They are valid at any of the 50 Matalan stores in the UK. To find out if your organisation is registered, phone the Matalan hotline on 01772 629447.

## STONEFLAKE LTD

5 SMITH STREET, ST PETER PORT, GUERNSEY, CHANNEL ISLANDS GY1 2JN
☎ (01481) 720053. FAX (01481) 713808. OPEN 9 - 5.15 MON - SAT. MAIL ORDER AVAILABLE

Family-run business which has operated in Guernsey for more than 80 years serving both locals and tourists alike. In recent years, they have added a mail order service. They have two shops - one a pharmacy and perfumery, the other selling perfumery and cosmetics, and specialise in fragrance bargains from the UK and French companies, in aftershaves, cosmetics, perfumes, toilet waters, soaps and talcs. Being duty-free, and with no VAT, they have competitive prices on standard ranges and by buying excess stocks and ends of lines, they have a large list of extra special offers including ranges no longer sold in the UK. Brand names stocked include YSL, Elizabeth Taylor, Paloma Picasso, Cacharel, Boss, Georgio, Paco Rabane, Gucci, Safari, Elizabeth Arden, Givenchy, Oscar de la Renta, Nina Ricci, and Roc cosmetics. Free postage and packaging on mail orders over £40.

## TK MAXX

THIRD FLOOR, THE GALLERIES, BRISTOL, AVON
☎ (0117) 9304404. OPEN 9 - 5.30 MON - SAT, 7 ON THUR.

Based on an American concept, TK Maxx is the first British retailer to practise "off-price" retailing. This means a centrally located store which offers famous label goods with up to 60% savings off recommended retail prices. TK Maxx has fashion for the whole family - women's, men's and childrenswear - accessories, shoes, gifts, kitchenware and home goods. Everything in the store is branded with a choice of well-known high street names to designer labels, and while a small percentage mightly be clearly marked past season, the great majority of items in store are current season, current stock and still with phenomenal savings. There is a huge choice with 50,000 pieces in store with 5,000 new items arriving a week, so it's worth keeping abreast of the lastest deliveries as turnaround is very fast. One of the ways in which TK Maxx is able to offer such low prices is by running a very low-cost operation, so the stores are simple and unfussy with wide aisles, shopping trolleys and baskets, and a spacious, functional feel to them. Service is not compromised, however: there are individual changing rooms, ramps for buggies and wheelchairs, plenty of staff on the shop floor and all the branches accept all major credit and debit cards.

## TRAGO MILL

REGIONAL SHOPPING CENTRE, NEWTON ABBOT DEVON TQ12 6JD
☎ (01626) 821111. OPEN 9 - 5.30 MON - SAT, 10.30 - 4.30 SUN.
Sells virtually everything from women's, men's and children's wear, gardening equipment and cookwear to wallpaper, carpets and fitted kitchens. Most are branded goods and there is a creche, cafe, pizza bar and petrol station.

## *Factory Shops*

## CLARKS FACTORY SHOP

CLARKS VILLAGE, FARM ROAD, STREET, SOMERSET BA16 OBB
☎ (01458) 843161. OPEN 9 - 6 MON - SAT AND BANK HOLIDAYS, 11 - 5 SUN.
Clarks International operate a chain of factory shops nationally which specialise in selling discontinued lines and slight sub-standards for women, men and children from Clarks, K Shoes and other famous brands. These shops trade under the name of Crockers, K Shoes Factory shop or Clarks Factory Shop and while not all are physically attached to a shoe factory, these shops are treated as factory shops by the company. Customers can expect to find an extensive range of quality shoes, sandals, walking boots, slippers, trainers, handbags, accessories and gifts, while their major outlets such as here at Clarks Village also offer luggage, sports clothing, sports equipment and outdoor clothing. Brands stocked include Clarks, K Shoes, Springer, CICA, Hi-Tec, Puma, Mercury, Dr Martens, Nike, LA Gear, Fila, Mizuno, Slazenger, Weider, Samsonite, Delsey, Antler and Carlton, although not all are sold in every outlet. Discounts are on average

30% off the normal high street price for perfect stock. From November to end of March, weekday and Saturday closing times are 5.30.

## CLARKS VILLAGE FACTORY SHOPPING

FARM ROAD, STREET, SOMERSET BA16 OBB
☎ (01458) 840064. OPEN 9 - 6 MON - SAT, 11 - 5 SUN. TIMES CHANGE WINTER AND SUMMER.

Purpose-built village of brick-built shops with extensive car parking facilities. Restaurant run by Leith's, fast food stands, carousel, indoor play area, outdoor play area. Here, there were at August 1995, 37 shops with more planned: Royal Brierley, Royal Worcester, Denby Pottery, Dartington Crystal, Jumpers, Monsoon/Accessorize, Laura Ashley, Benetton, Crabtree & Evelyn, The Baggage Factory, The Linen Cupboard, The Pier, Wrangler, James Barry, Jaeger, Viyella, Alexon/Eastex/Dash, Fred Perry, Triumph, JoKids, Clarks Factory Shop, Claude Gill Books, Woolea (which also sells Lyle & Scott and Barbour), Rohan, Farah Menswear, Thorntons Chocolates, The Sports Factory, Windsmoor (which also sells Planet, Berkertex, Precis and Genesis), Black & Decker, Liz Claiborne, Hallmark, Remington, The Golf Factory and Esprit.

## CROCKERS

2 EASTOVER, BRIDGWATER, SOMERSET TA6 5AB
☎ (01278) 452617. OPEN 9 - 5.30 MON - SAT.
10A HIGH STREET, BURNHAM-ON-SEA, SOMERSET TA8 1NX
☎ (01278) 794668. OPEN 9 - 5.30 MON - SAT, 11 - 5 SUN, 10 - 5 BANK HOLIDAYS.
112-114 HIGH STREET, STREET, SOMERSET BA16 OEW
☎ (01458) 442055. OPEN 9 - 5.30 MON - SAT AND BANK HOLIDAYS, 11 - 5 SUNS.
UNITS 1 AND 13, WEST SWINDON DISTRICT CENTRE, SWINDON, WILTSHIRE SN5 7DI
☎ (01793) 873662. OPEN 9 - 8 MON - FRI, 9 - 6 SAT, 10 - 4 SUN, 10 - 5 BANK HOLIDAYS.
UNIT 2, SAINSBURYS PRECINCT, QUEENSWAY SHOPPING CENTRE, WORLE, AVON BS22 OBT
☎ (01934) 521693. OPEN 9 - 8 MON - FRI, 9 - 6 SAT, 10.30 - 4.30 SUN, 9 - 5 BANK HOLIDAYS.

Clarks International operate a chain of factory shops nationally which specialise in selling discontinued lines and slight sub-standards for women, men and children from Clarks, K Shoes and other famous brands. These shops trade under the name of Crockers, K Shoes Factory shop or Clarks Factory Shop and while not all are physically attached to a shoe factory, these shops are treated as factory shops by the company. Customers can expect to find an extensive range of quality shoes, sandals, walking boots, slippers, trainers, handbags, accessories and gifts, while their major outlets also offer luggage, sports clothing, sports equipment and outdoor clothing. Brands stocked include Clarks, K Shoes, Springer, CICA, Hi-Tec, Puma, Mercury, Dr Martens, Nike, LA Gear, Fila, Mizuno, Slazenger, Weider, Samsonite, Delsey, Antler and Carlton, although not all are sold in every outlet. Discounts are on average 30% off the normal high street price for perfect stock. The Swindon branch is also a sports and baggage factory shop.

## DENTS

FAIRFIELD ROAD, WARMINSTER, WILTSHIRE BA12 9DL
☎ (01985) 212291. OPEN 10 - 4 THUR - SUN.
The accessories company which produces such covetable gloves, belts, handbags and leather wallets and purses for most of the big department stores has a factory outlet near Salisbury. Most of the stock in this reasonably-sized warehouse shop consists of gloves, sold at at least 50% discount, but there are also some umbrellas, including telescopic, golf and walking umbrellas, handbags, silk ties, leather belts, leather card holders and key fobs. Stock from the discontinued and end of ranges changes constantly. The shop usually closes for the summer between May and September so phone first.

## ESPRIT

CLARKS VILLAGE FACTORY SHOPPING, FARM ROAD, STREET, SOMERSET BA16 OBB
☎ (01458) 840064. OPEN 9 - 6 MON - SAT, 11 - 5 SUN. TIMES CHANGE WINTER AND SUMMER.
Large, two-storey outlet divided into men's and women's wear, with older stock and shoes upstairs. Wide range of clothes from casual trousers and T-shirts, shorts and shirts, to dresses and shoes, all at discounted prices. (Telephone number above is the general Village number.)

# FOX'S MILL SHOP

TONEDALE MILLS, WELLINGTON, SOMERSET TA21 OAW
☎ (01823) 661860. OPEN 2 - 4 MON - FRI.

Cloth for men's and women's suiting, coats and dresses from about £4 a metre for seconds to £19 a metre for wool and cashmere with a full range in between. Cloth can be bought and taken away or the in-situ tailor will make up garments at a fraction of the London charges. The shop sells woollen and worsted cloth, wool and cashmere seconds and perfect quality and there's a bargain basket with fabric at silly prices. The tailor is on site three days a week and will make men's and women's suits, although there is usually a waiting list.

# FRED PERRY SPORTSWEAR UK LTD

UNIT 10, CLARKS VILLAGE, FARM ROAD, STREET,
SOMERSET BA16 OBB
☎ (01458) 841730. OPEN 9 - 6 MON - SAT, 11 - 5 SUN.

Men's and women's ranges of the famous Fred Perry sportswear and leisure clothing: shorts, tennis tops, tracksuits, T-shirts. All price labels show the original and the reduced price, which usually amount to a 30% discount.

# GEORGINA VON ETZDORF

THE AVENUE, ODSTOCK, NEAR SALISBURY, WILTSHIRE
☎ (01722) 326625. OPEN 10 - 6 MON - SAT, 12 - 5 SUN
(CLOSED 1- 2 FOR LUNCH DAILY).

A sweet, little factory shop near Salisbury. Sandwiched between workrooms, it has a limited but exciting range of clothes and lots of wonderful accessories. Her products are not cheap, but the Jacquard scarves, squares and shawls, and the men's silk cravats, ties and Jacquard scarves with cashmere linings are affordable at prices ranging from £20. Everything is half price, which means that the lovely Devore tunic jackets, which cost £385 in the shops are marked down to £181 here. The price tag also tells you what season the outfit is from and whether it is a second. There are men's silk dressing gowns at about £200, Georgette long and short dresses, £170 and £193, wool crepe long gloves, £25, ladies Jacquard print waistcoats, £88, men's silk cravats £21.50, silk ties, from £10, and oddments of fabric. The factory shop is in a tiny lane.

## LAURA ASHLEY

UNIT 5, CLARKS VILLAGE, FARM ROAD, STREET,
SOMERSET BA16 OBB
☎ (01458) 840405. OPEN 9 - 6 MON - SAT AND BANK HOLIDAYS, 11 - 5
SUN.
UNIT 32, GREEN LANES SHOPPING CENTRE, BARNSTAPLE, DEVON
☎ (01271) 329072. OPEN 9 - 5.30 MON - SAT.

Laura Ashley fashion and home furnishings. Most of the merchandise
is made up of perfect carry-overs from the high street shops around
the country, though there are also some discontinued lines. Stock
reflects the normal high street variety, though at least one season later
and with less choice in colours and sizes.

## LIZ CLAIBORNE UK

UNIT 31, CLARK'S VILLAGE, FARM ROAD, STREET,
SOMERSET BA16 OBB
☎ (01458) 447311. OPEN 9 - 6 MON - FRI, 11 - 5 SUN. TIMES VARY
SEASONALLY.

Ends of lines and store returns of Liz Claiborne's famous top quality
styles at reductions of 50%. Stock quantities and sizes vary depending on whether there has recently been a delivery so it's worth either
making frequent visits or phoning beforehand. Silk dresses, about
£50, 100% wool jackets, about £75, half cashmere sweaters, £59.
Hundreds of different styles in a variety of sizes and colours.

## MINEHEAD SHOE CO-OPERATIVE LTD

1 NORTH ROAD, MINEHEAD, SOMERSET TA24 5QW
☎ (01643) 705591. OPEN 8 - 5 MON - FRI, 10 - 1 SAT. MAIL ORDER.

Shoes, including golf and bowling shoes, and leather handbags and
wallets. Wide and large sizes are catered for. Clutch bags, from £8,
sholder bags, £16, belts, £2-£5, everyday bags, £16; ladies wallets, £4-
£10. Mail order available.

# MULBERRY

THE STREET, CHILCOMPTON, SOMERSET
☎ (01761) 232878. OPEN 9 - 5 MON - SAT.

A very popular large, attractive, factory outlet, which sells last season's and seconds of the famous Mulberry leather handbags, briefcases, filofaxes and wallets at discounted prices. Also last season's clothes including a few men's shoes and ties and some ladies shoes from £65 upwards; umbrellas, men's gifts; hand knits; and belts. Discontinued lines are discounted by 30%-40%; current seconds, many of which come direct from the factory, are discounted by 20%.

# SILKEN LADDER

VICTORIA SQUARE, NEAR ROCHE, CORNWALL PL26 8LX
☎ (01726) 891092. OPEN 10.30 - 5 MON - SAT, AND MOST BANK HOLIDAYS.

Silken Ladder design, manufacture and wholesale thousands of blouses in cotton, polycotton and silk lookalike fabrics and in classic designs which sell to more than 400 shops, hotels and choirs around Britain. Its factory shop sells prototypes, samples, ends of lines, over-makes and less than perfect mistakes at appropriately reduced prices. There is an enormous spread of ladies blouses from £3 to £100: plain polycotton tops, cut-work, broderie Anglaise and hand-embroidered in polyester, polycotton, cotton and silk. Sizes range from 10-30. There are also skirts, trousers and shorts and a supporting range of accessories and giftwear, costume jewellery, lingerie and hosiery. Recent expansion and refurbishment has meant that the shop can accommodate more stock both from Silken Ladder and La Scala di Seta as well as Kinloch Anderson (kilt makers to the Queen and the Prince of Wales) skirts and kilted skirts from Scotland, lingerie by Arabella, Debut and Tessa Sanderson leisurewear. There is also an increased slection of larger goods up to size 30. Find it on the A30, 6 miles west of Bodmin and 6 miles north of St Austell, next to a BP petrol station on the north side of the road opposite the Victoria Inn.

# THE FACTORY SHOP

36-37 ROUNDSTONE STREET, TROWBRIDGE, WILTSHIRE BA12 9AN
☎ (01225) 751399. OPEN 9 - 5.30 MON - SAT.
24 MARKET PLACE, WARMINSTER, WILTSHIRE BA12 9AN
☎ (01985) 217532. OPEN 9 - 5.30 MON - FRI, 9 - 5 SAT.
MART ROAD, MINEHEAD, SOMERSET
☎ (01643) 705911. OPEN 9.30 - 5.30 MON - SAT, 11 - 5 SUN.

Wide range on sale includes women's, men's and children's clothing
and footwear; household textiles, toiletries, hardware, luggage,
lighting and bedding, most of which are chainstore and high street
brands at discounts of approximately 30%-50%. There are weekly
deliveries and brands include all the major stars: Coloroll, Wrangler
and Dartington to name just three. Lines are continually changing
and few factory shops offer such a variety under one roof.

# THE SHOE SHED

STATION ROAD, BUDLEIGH, SALTERTON, DEVON EX9 6RU
☎ (01395) 443399. OPEN 8.30 - 5.30 MON - SAT, 10 - 4 SUN.
23 FAIRMILE ROAD, CHRISTCHURCH, DORSET BH23 2LA
☎ (01202) 474123. OPEN 10 - 5 MON - FRI, 9 - 5 SAT, 10 - 4 SUN.
MENDEVILLE ROAD, WYKE REGIS, WEYMOUTH, DORSET DT4 9HW
☎ (01305) 766772. OPEN 8.30 - 5 MON - WED, 8.30 - 8 THUR, FRI, 8.30 -
5.30 SAT, 10 - 4 SUN.

Large factory shop selling a vast range of all types of women's, men's
and children's shoes, all of which are perfects, at up to 30% below
normal high street prices. Ladies sandals cost from £5; ladies shoes
from £7.50. Men's shoes from £10; sports shoes from £10.

# TRIUMPH INTERNATIONAL LTD

ARKWRIGHT ROAD, GROUNDWELL, SWINDON, WILTSHIRE SN2 5BE
☎ (01793) 722200. OPEN 10 - 4 MON - SAT.

Factory shop next to the factory itself selling a wide and ever-
changing range of Triumph lingerie, swimwear and tights which are
last season's stock or discontinued lines. Also men's underwear and
swimwear from the Hom range. Outlets also at Clarks Village in
Street, Somerset and Bicester Village in Bicester, Oxfordshire (see
West Midlands).

## VIYELLA

CLARKS FACTORY SHOPPING VILLAGE, STREET, SOMERSET
☎ (01458) 840064. OPEN 9 - 6 MON - SAT AND BANK HOLIDAYS, 11 - 5 SUN.
Wide range of Viyella ladieswear at discount prices from jackets and blouses to dresses, waistcoats, sweaters and hats.


## *Dress Agencies*

## BUDGET-BOX

24A DITTON ST, ILMINSTER, SOMERSET TA19 0BQ
☎ (01460) 53316. OPEN 9 - 5 MON - WED & FRI, 9 - 1 THUR & SAT.
Designs range from Windsmoor and Jaeger to Marks & Spencer, Next and other high street retailers. There's usually more evening wear towards Christmas, more casual wear in the summer. Very reasonable prices, and open to a bit of bartering. Good value fashionable accessories. Nearly-new childrenswear up to early teens stocked, including school uniforms and labels such as Osh Kosh.


## CAMELEON

74 NEW ST, ST HELIER, JERSEY, CHANNEL ISLANDS
☎ (01534) 22438. OPEN 10 - 4 MON - SAT.
Offers nearly-new and some period fashion for men and women, covering a wide range of labels from well known high street names to Fenn Wright & Manson. As well as daywear and evening wear, there are also hats, jewellery and evening shoes for women. For men, there is nearly new day and evening wear, shoes, hats, waistcoats, shirts and dinner suits. Also offers a hire service.


## CINDERELLA'S WARDROBE

10 CONWAY ST, JERSEY
☎ (01534) 618545. OPEN 10 - 5.30 MON - SAT.
Sells nearly-new and new designer outfits, shoes and accessories. Labels are top quality: Lindka Cierach, Louis Feraud, Escada, Chanel, Byblos and Krizia. New outfits are below cost price. For example, a MaxMara 100% cashmere jacket, £90, as-new price, £400, and shoes for £29, original price £60.

## GEMMA

422 LYMINGTON ROAD, HIGHCLIFFE, CHRISTCHURCH, DORSET
☎ (01425) 276928. OPEN 10 -5 MON - SAT, 10 - 1 WED.
Stocks anything from Marks & Spencer to Ralph Lauren, with a wide
range of shoes and jewellery available. Childrens wear is also stocked
and there is a separate play area for kids. Bargain rail of older stock
sold at half-price; sales in the summer and after Christmas.

## GOLDI

53 WINCHESTER STREET, SALISBURY, WILTSHIRE SP1 1HL
☎ (01722) 421969. OPEN 10 - 5 MON - SAT.
Sells high quality, non-chain store designer nearly-new clothes from
Nicole Farhi, Escada and MaxMara to Valentino, YSL and Dior. Fifty
percent of the stock is new, consisting of either cancelled orders from
this season or last season's outfits at approximately 50% discounts.
The nearly-new items are rarely more than two seasons old.
Accessories include shoes, bags and scarves, new jewellery and secondhand and new belts. Good range of special occasion wear and hats
on one floor, with daywear on a separate floor. Examples of prices
include Nicole Farhi skirt, £38; nearly new long Paul Costelloe skirt,
£54; Jasper Conran suit, £115; silk dresses from £65-£300.

## KARALYNE'S

20 WEST STREET, WILTON, WILTSHIRE
☎ (01722) 742802. OPEN 9.30 - 4 MON - SAT, CLOSED WED.
Tiny but full shop selling nearly-new clothing and accessories for
women and children at bargain prices, including evening and maternity wear. Stocks more than 1,000 items at a time with a constant
flow of new arrivals and very popular "special rails". Permanent half-
price rails added to weekly, plus two "everything half price" sales each
year in February and August. Useful children's play corner for hassle-
free browsing.

## ROUNDAGAIN

5 SUSSEX PLACE, WIDCOMBE PARADE, BATH, AVON BA2 4LA
☎ (01225) 312220 OPEN 10 - 5 MON - SAT.

Nearly new ladies wear, as well as maternity wear. High street names such as Country Casuals, Next, Hobbs and Jigsaw. Some stock clearance items and new designer wear at amazingly discounted prices; for example, £100 outfits selling for £20. Next door to Roundabout which sells childrenswear.

## SELECTIONS

4 RACE HILL, LAUNCESTON, CORNWALL PL15 9BB
☎ (01566) 775471. OPEN 9.30 - 4.30 MON - SAT.

Selections sells quality high street and designer label nearly-new outfits. There is always a wide selection of day clothes, as well as separates, jackets and an excellent choice of evening wear and special occasion outfits. For example, there are usually at least fifty different mother of the bride outfits, some with matching hats. In fact, hats are a minor speciality, with more than three dozen usually in stock, some new and some nearly-new. Prices range from £12-£25. Labels include Planet, Jacques Vert, Ultima, Wallis, Jaeger, Betty Barclay, Berketex, Next and Marks & Spencer. New and nearly-new costume jewellery is also on sale here at prices ranging from £2.50 to £12. There is usually a good selection of sizes up to 24. A small range of men's suits is also stocked, with suits starting at £50.

## THE FROCK EXCHANGE

9 SEAWAY ROAD, PRESTON, PAIGNTON, DEVON JE2 3PG
☎ (01803) 522951. OPEN 10 - 4.45 TUE - SAT, CLOSED 1 - 2.

Women's and menswear with a cross section of clothes from designer labels to high street names and chain stores: Mondi, Jaeger, Jacques Vert, Windsmoor and Alexon. There are also handbags and shoes, but no hats or jewellery. Two-thirds of the shop is taken up with womenswear; one third with men's.

## THE FROCK EXCHANGE

CHEAPSIDE, ST HELIER, JERSEY TQ3 2NY
☎ (01534) 68324. OPEN 10 - 5.30 MON - SAT.

Sells everything from blouses and skirts to ballgowns and bikinis. Labels range from high street to good quality middle market names such as Jaeger and Jacques Vert. When we visited, we saw a Jaeger wool two-piece, £38, a Jacques Vert blouse and skirt, £24, and blouses from £6-£18.

# Secondhand and Vintage Clothes

## GREAT WESTERN ANTIQUES CENTRE

BARTLETT STREET, BATH, BA1 2QZ
☎ (01225) 424243. GROUND FLOOR OPEN 10 - 5 MON, TUE, THUR, FRI,
8.30 - 5 WED, 9.30 - 5.30 SAT. LOWER FLOOR OPEN 7.30 - 4 (WED).
Stalls with linen, lace, period costumes, jewellery, buttons, furniture, secondhand goods, picture frames, carpets, clocks and watches, gramophones and radios, dolls and dollshouses, glass and ceramics.

## THE COLLECTABLE COSTUME

GREAT WESTERN ANTIQUES CENTRE, BARTLETT STREET, AVON
☎ (0225) 428731. OPEN 10 - 5 MON, TUE, THUR, FRI, 9.30 - 5.30 SAT,
8.30 - 5 WED.
Area in Antiques Centre selling pre-Fifties men's and women's costumes and accessories. Accessories including jewellery, hats and fans. Also suitcases from the Twenties from £12 to £60.

# Secondhand Shops

## CAMEO OF COWES

16 BATH ROAD, THE PARADE, COWES, ISLE OF WIGHT
☎ (01983) 297907. OPEN 10 - 5 SEVEN DAYS A WEEK.
Buy and sell unclaimed property from British Airways, Royal Mail, London Transport and police departments. This can include anything from clothes and shoes to umbrellas and jewellery; make-up and perfume to purses and designer items.

## CAMEO SPORT AND LEISURE

92 HIGH STREET, COWES, ISLE OF WIGHT
☎ (01983) 297219. OPEN 10 - 5 SEVEN DAYS A WEEK.
Run by the son of the owner of Cameo of Cowes, this shop also specialises in buying and selling unclaimed lost property and bankrupt stock but with the emphasis on sportswear: tennis rackets, wet suits, surf boards and anything to do with sports generally.

# WALES AND WEST MIDLANDS

## *Permanent Discount Outlets*

### ALEXON SALE SHOP

34 GEORGE STREET, TAMWORTH, STAFFORDSHIRE
☎ (01827) 310041. OPEN 9 - 5.30 MON - SAT.
7 PRIDE HILL GALLERY, SHREWSBURY, SHROPSHIRE SY1 1BU
☎ (01743) 362065. OPEN 9 - 5.30 MON - SAT.
CARDIFF ROAD, HAWTHORN, PONTYPRIDD, MID
GLAMORGAN, WALES
☎ (01443) 480673. OPEN 10 - 5 MON - SAT.

Alexon, Eastex and Dash from last season at 40% less than the original price; during sale time in January and June, the reductions are as much as 70%. Stock includes separates, skirts, jackets, blouses, and leisurewear; there is no underwear or night clothes. The Shrewsbury branch does not carry Dash except for swimwear. The Cardiff road branch is situated at the back of the factory itself and also sells belts, some shoes, and Ann Harvey for sizes 16-26.

### ANN HARVEY

9 GOMOND STREET, MAYLORD ORCHARDS, HEREFORD,
WORCESTERSHIRE HR4 9TF
☎ (01432) 342468. 9 - 5.30 MON - SAT.

Half the shop sells Ann Harvey at full price in sizes 16-26, the other half is a sale shop selling Dash leisurewear for men and women at reductions of between 25%-50%. Stock is usually one year old. There are winter and summer sales during which stock is further reduced.

### DESIGNER DISCOUNT CLUB

ASHBURTON ESTATE, ROSS-ON-WYE, HEREFORDSHIRE HR9 7BW
☎ (0990) 143153. MAIL ORDER.

This designer discount mail order business has just opened up a retail outlet in Ross-on-Wye where members can come and purchase top quality clothes at wholesale prices. The outlet will also feature a selection of well-known German and Italian designers at savings of up to 80%, providing classic, smart clothes for work or daywear and plenty of special occasion wear and evening clothes. Members will also be kept up-to-date by post of special offers.

## FASHION FACTORY

THE MALTINGS, KING STREET, WELLINGTON, TELFORD,
SHROPSHIRE TF1 3AE
☎ (01952) 260489. OPEN 9.30 - 5 MON - SAT, 11 - 5 SUN.
WYRLEYBROOK PARK, VINE LANE, CANNOCK,
STAFFORDSHIRE WS11 3XF.
☎ (0543) 466000. OPEN 9.30 - 5.30 MON - SAT, 11 - 5 SUN.

Sells last season's perfect quality Alexon, Dash, Eastex, Gossard and
Lee Cooper. Among the 30,000 garments in stock at any one time is
anything from lingerie (Berlei and Warners) to raincoats with Dash
T-shirts costing £1.99, and branded jackets costing £23, reduced
from £80. Discounts are in the range of 40%-70%.

## IMPS

69B HIGH STREET, WITNEY, OXFORDSHIRE
☎ (01993) 779875. OPEN 9 - 5 MON - SAT.
40 UPPER HIGH STREET, THAME, OXFORDSHIRE
☎ (01844) 212985. OPEN 9 - 5 MON - SAT.
52 SHEEP STREET, BICESTER, OXFORDSHIRE
☎ (01869) 243455. OPEN 9 - 5 MON - SAT.
26 MARKET PLACE, HENLEY-ON-THAMES, OXFORDSHIRE
☎ (01491) 411530. OPEN 9 - 5 MON - SAT.

High street shops selling popular chainstore seconds. Witney shop
extends over two floors and has plenty of stock from clothes for all the
family to towels, china, trays and flower cachepots. For women, there
are jeans, £11.99, swimwear, £8.99, dressing gowns, £21. There are
also bath towels, £5.99, bath sheets, £11.99, fruit design jugs, £9.99,
plates, £3.50. Stock changes constantly.

## KAREN MILLEN

PINGLE DRIVE, BICESTER, JUNCTION 9 OF M40, OXFORDSHIRE
OX6 7WD
☎ (01869) 325932. OPEN 10 - 6 MON - SAT AND BANK  HOLIDAYS,
11 - 5 SUN.
Top fashion from well known British designer.

## LAURA ASHLEY SALE SHOP

BEAR LANE, NEWTOWN, POWYS, WALES
☎ (01686) 626549. OPEN 9.30 - 5.30 MON, 9 - 5.30 TUE - SAT.
Laura Ashley fashion and home furnishings. Most of the merchandise is made up of perfect carry-overs from the high street shops around the country, though there are also some discontinued lines. Stock reflects the normal high street variety, though at least one season later and with less choice in colours and sizes.

## LOOT

7 GURNEYS LANE, DROITWICH (ADJACENT TO THE MARKET HALL), WORCESTER, WORCESTERSHIRE
☎ (01905) 771708. OPEN 9.30 - 5.15 TUE - SAT.
Loot sells a wide range of goods which are the result of bankruptcy or are ends of lines. Stock changes constantly and can consist of anything from clothes, gifts, china, glass, leatherware, shoes, wrought iron and handcrafted items. The clothes are described as 'boutique' clothes and consist of such labels such as Kasper, Tricoville, Choise and Parigi. Items on sale when we visited included sandwashed silk shirts, £29, new full length overcoats, £118 and china seconds and giftware.

## M C HITCHEN & SONS LTD

299 COVENTRY ROAD, BIRMINGHAM, WEST MIDLANDS B10 0RA
☎ (0121) 772 1637. OPEN 9 - 5.30 MON - SAT.
236 HAWTHORN ROAD, KINGSTANDING, BIRMINGHAM, WEST MIDLANDS B44 8PP
☎ (0121) 373 1276.OPEN 9.15 - 5.30 MON - SAT.
14-16 NORTH STREET, RUGBY, WARWICKSHIRE CV21 2AF
☎ (01788) 565116. OPEN 9.30 - 5.30 MON - WED, 9 - 5.30 THUR - SAT.
Littlewoods sell off their overstocks in a network of shops called M C Hitchen & Sons Ltd. Most of them are in the north of England and offer up to 40% off the catalogue price for clothing and between 50% and 60% off for electrical goods. Littlewoods also run a mobile shop which operates in cities where they don't have a sale shop. For details of further venues for the sales, which usually take place once a month, Contact Jean Banks, c/o Crosby DC, Kershaw avenue, Endbutt Lane, Crosby, Merseyside L70 1AH.

## MAJOR SAVINGS

38 CITY ARCADE, COVENTRY, WEST MIDLANDS CV1 3HW
☎ (01203) 553355. OPEN 9 - 5.30 MON - SAT.

Grattan use a chain of shops in the north and midlands to clear there overstocks. There is a selection of items from those featured in the catalogue, which can consist of anything from children's clothes and toys to bedding, electrical equipment and nursery accessories. Each shop sells a slightly different range, so always ring first to check they stock what you want. All items are discounted between 30% and 50%. Some of the shops are being refitted and renamed as Scoops - although stock will remain the same - so again do ring and check first.

## MANORGROVE

7-9 RHOSDDU ROAD, WREXHAM LL11 1AR
☎ (01978) 266450. OPEN 9 - 5.30 MON - SAT.
567-569 BEARWOOD ROAD, SMETHWICK, WARLEY, BA1 1DA
☎ (0121) 434 3086. OPEN 9 - 5.30 MON - SAT.
15 BRADFORD STREET, WALSALL WS1 1PB
☎ (01922) 611111. OPEN 9 - 5.30 MON - SAT.

Grattan use a chain of shops called Manorgrove or Scoops in the north and midlands to clear their overstocks. There is a selection of items from those featured in the catalogue, which in the catalogue, which can consist of anything from children's clothes and toys to bedding, electrical equipment and nursery accessories. Each shop sells a slightly different range, so always ring first to check they stock what you want. All items are discounted between 30% and 50%. Some of the shops are being refitted and renamed as scoops - although stock will remain the same - so again do ring and check first.

## MATALAN

UNIT 5, THE JOHN ALLEN CENTRE, COWLEY, OXFORD,
OXFORDSHIRE OX4 3JP
☎ (01865) 747400. OPEN 10 - 8 MON - FRI, 9.30 - 5.30 SAT, 10 - 6 SUN.
UNITS A1/A2, GALLAGHER RETAIL PARK, TEWKESBURY ROAD, CHEL-
TENHAM, GLOUCESTERSHIRE GL51 9RR
☎ (01242) 254001. OPEN 10 - 8 MON - FRI, 9.30 - 5.30 SAT, 10 - 6 SUN.
UNIT 1, MEOLE BRACE RETAIL PARK, HEREFORD ROAD, SHREWS-
BURY SY3 9NB
☎ (01743) 363240. OPEN 10 - 8 MON - FRI, 9.30 - 5.30 SAT, 10 - 6 SUN.

UNIT 7, VENTURA SHOPPING CENTRE, VENTURA PARK ROAD, BONE HILL, TAMWORTH, STAFFORDSHIRE B78 3HB
☎ (01827) 50900. OPEN 10 - 8 MON - FRI, 9.30 - 5.30 SAT, 10 - 6 SUN.
FOUNDRY ROAD, MORRISTON, SWANSEA SA6 8DU
☎ (01792) 792229. OPEN 10 - 8 MON - FRI, 9.30 - 5.30 SAT, 10 - 6 SUN.
BIRMINGHAM ROAD, HOWARD STREET, WOLVERHAMPTON, WEST MIDLANDS WV2 2LQ
☎ (01902) 352813. OPEN 10 - 8 MON - FRI, 9.30 - 5.30 SAT, 10 - 6 SUN.
UNIT 4B, CWMBRAN RETAIL PARK CWNBRAN DRIVE, CWNBRAN, GWENT NP44 3JQ
☎ (01633) 866944. OPEN 10 - 8 MON - FRI, 9.30 - 5.30 SAT, 10 - 6 SUN.
UNIT E, MAYBIRD CENTRE, BIRMINGHAM ROAD, STRATFORD-UPON-AVON CV37 OHZ
☎ (01789) 262223. OPEN 10 - 8 MON - FRI, 10 - 5.30 SAT, 10 - 6 SUN.
UNIT 1A & 1B, CAENARFON ROAD, BANGOR LL57 4SU.
☎ (0248 362778). OPEN 10 - 8 MON - FRI, 9.30 - 5.30 SAT, 10 - 8 SUN.
WOLSTANTON RETAIL PARK, WOLSTANTON, NEWCASTLE, STAFFORDSHIRE ST5 1DY
☎ (01782) 711731. OPEN 9.30 - 8 MON - FRI, 9.30 - 6 SAT, 10 - 5.30 SUN.
UNITS 5 & 6, QUEENSVILLE RETAIL PARK, SILKMORE LANE, STAFFORD ST17 4SU
☎ (01785) 226211. OPEN 10 - 8 MON - FRI, 9.30 - 5.30 SAT, 10 - 6 SUN.
UNIT 2, 382-384 NEWPORT ROAD, CARDIFF, WALES CF3 7AE
☎ (01222) 491781. OPEN 10 - 8 MON - FRI, 9 - 6 SAT, 11 - 5 SUN.
UNIT A, LICHFIELD STREET, BURTON-ON-TRENT, STAFFORDSHIRE DE14 3QZ
☎ (01283) 540865.
UNIT 8, GLAMORGAN VALE RETAIL PARK, LLANTRISANT, MID-GLAM-ORGAN, SOUTH WALES CF7 8RP
☎ (01433) 224854. OPEN 10 - 8 MON - FRI, 9 - 6 SAT, 10 - 5 SUN.

As the UK's first National Discount Club, Matalan has the buying power to guarantee its members up to 60% discounts on a huge range of brand name clothing, household goods, luggage and toiletries for all the family. Top quality merchandise, current season, no seconds, is offered to its members at exclusive, permanently discounted prices seven days a week. Matalan operates strictly on a membership basis, one of the key factors for its success in offering 20%-60% savings off recommended retail prices. Membership cards are issued through companies, organisations and associations in the vicinity of the stores, and are available to their employees/members. They are valid at any of the 50 Matalan stores in the UK. To find out if your organisation is registered, phone the Matalan hotline on 01772 629447.

## NEXT TO NOTHING

24-25 WALFRUN CENTRE, WOLVERHAMPTON, WEST
MIDLANDS WV1 3HG
☎ (01902) 29464. OPEN 9 - 5.30 MON - SAT.
104 CORPORATION STREET, BIRMINGHAM, WEST MIDLANDS
☎ (0121) 233 0022. OPEN 9 - 5.15 MON - FRI, 9.30 - 6 SAT.

Sells perfect surplus stock from Next stores and the Next Directory
catalogue - from belts, jewellery and underwear to day and evening
wear - at discounts of 50% or more. The ranges are usually last
season's and overruns but there is the odd current item if you look
carefully. Stock consists of men's, women's and children's clothing,
with some homeware and shoes, depending on the branch. Stock is
replenished twice a week and there is plenty of it.

## PREVIEW

FIRST FLOOR, 8 NEEDLESS ALLEY, OFF NEW STREET, BIRMINGHAM
B2 5AE
☎ (0121) 643 2007. OPEN 9.30 - 5.30 MON - SAT.

Preview is an upmarket designer boutique-showroom: a real find in
the heart of Birmingham's city centre. It stocks current top label
sample collections, all at least one-third off shop prices. Among the
many labels on sale are the best of British, German, Italian and
American collections. Seasonal sales are held four times a year with
75% discounts, and fashion shows and events regularly take place at
the start of each season, combined with cheerful and informative
assistance. Phone to get on their mailing list.

## STUDIO

11 ABBEY ROAD, MALVERN, WORCESTERSHIRE WR14 3ES
☎ (01684) 576253. OPEN 9 - 5.30 MON - SAT.

Finest designer clothes from the Continent at discounts of 50%. The
company's team of buyers search out and secure considerable discounts on top European name ranges which include both this season's
stock and next. The names are well-known but they cannot be
divulged here - suffice it to say that they are excellent labels. All stock
is perfect, and the vast range covers from casual wear to special
occasion outfits. New Studio shop branches were being planned as we
went to press - call for more details.

## THE SALE SHOP

ROSS LABELS LTD, OVERROSS, ROSS ON WYE, HEREFORDSHIRE
HR9 7QJ
☎ (01989) 769000. OPEN 9 - 5.30 MON - SAT, 10 - 5 SUN.

Twenty thousand square feet of selling space, with women's, mens and children's wear from underwear and jeans to good, middle of the road brand name outfits and suits bought direct from the manufacturer. Some of the labels on sale include Alexon, Eastex, Dash, Big Bubble, Fruit of the Loom, Viyella, Wolsey, Elsie Whiteley, Double Two, Telemac and Lyle & Scott. There is also a selection of Norman Linton fashion in larger sizes - up to 46 for men and 22 for women - and Alexa for women in sizes 18-28. Stock is usually one year old, while current merchandise consists of overmakes. Discounts range from 20% to 50%. There is also a Lee Cooper and big kids wear department and Aquascutum clothes are sold at less than normal high street prices.

## TK MAXX

THE POTTERIES SHOPPING CENTRE, HANLEY, STOKE-ON-TRENT, STAFFORDSHIRE.
☎ (01782) 289822. OPEN 9 - 5.30 MON - FRI, UNTIL 8 ON THUR, 9 - 6 SAT.

Based on an American concept, TK Maxx is the first British retailer to practise "off-price" retailing. This means a centrally located store which offers famous label goods with up to 60% savings off recommended retail prices. TK Maxx has fashion for the whole family - women's, men's and childrenswear - accessories, shoes, gifts, kitchenware and home goods. Everything in the store is branded with a choice of well-known high street names to designer labels, and while a small percentage mightly be clearly marked past season, the great majority of items in store are current season, current stock and still with phenomenal savings. There is a huge choice with 50,000 pieces in store with 5,000 new items arriving a week, so it's worth keeping abreast of the lastest deliveries as turnaround is very fast. One of the ways in which TK Maxx is able to offer such low prices is by running a very low-cost operation, so the stores are simple and unfussy with wide aisles, shopping trolleys and baskets, and a spacious, functional feel to them. Service is not compromised, however: there are individual changing rooms, ramps for buggies and wheelchairs, plenty of staff on the shop floor and all the branches accept all major credit and debit cards.

## TOGS

13 HIGH STREET, THAME, OXFORDSHIRE OX9 2BZ
☎ (01844) 215002. OPEN 9.30 - 5 MON - SAT.
36 STURT STREET, ABINGDON, OXFORDSHIRE
☎ (01235) 524989. OPEN 9.30 - 5 MON - SAT.
6 MONNOW STREET, MONMOUTH, WALES
☎ (01600) 772629. OPEN 9.30 - 5 MON - SAT.

Wide range of casual wear for women at competitive prices, including labels such as Falmer, Fruit of the Loom and Jeffrey Rogers. Sizes range from 10 - 18 for women. All items are perfects and current fashion. Prices start from £10.

## TOP MARKS

23 HIGH STREET, MORETON-IN-MARSH, GLOUCESTERSHIRE GL56 OAF
☎ (01608) 651272. OPEN 9 - 5.30 MON - FRI, 9 - 5 SAT.
8 HIGH STREET, CHIPPING NORTON, GLOS
☎ (01608) 642653. OPEN 9 - 5.30 MON - FRI, 9 - 5 SAT.

Sells seconds from leading chain stores for all the family. Most of the stock is made up of men's and women's wear, and there is also children's wear, Most of which are Marks & Spencer seconds, sold at about one third cheaper than M&s. Wide range of stock in various sizes with new stock arriving twice a week, just six weeks after it was first introduced to M&S department stores.

# Factory Shops

## ALAN PAINE KNITWEAR

NEW ROAD, AMMANFORD, DYFED SA18 3ET
☎ (01269) 592316. OPEN 9 - 4 MON - SAT.

Small room in the front of the factory itself selling knitwear manufactured in the factory. Most of the knitwear is for men, but women are as likely to buy the round neck sweaters and cardigans. The smallest size they make is a 38" chest. Chose from lambswool, cotton, camel hair, cashmere, merino and merino and silk mix. The company sells to the top shops in London, although most of their stock is made for export.

# BAIRDWEAR

UNIT 2, CYFARTHA INDUSTRIAL ESTATE, MERTHYR TYDFIL, MID
GLAMORGAN, WALES CF47 8PE
☎ (01685) 383837. OPEN 10 - 4.30 MON - SAT.
SANDFIELDS ESTATE, PURCELL AVENUE, PORT TALBOT, WEST GLAM-
ORGAN, WALES SA12 7UF
☎ (01639) 895038. OPEN 9.30 - 4.30 MON - SAT.
BEDWAS PARK INDUSTRIAL ESTATE, BEDWAS, CAERPHILLY, WALES
NP1 6XH
☎ (01222) 864699. OPEN 9.30 - 4.30 MON - SAT.
UNIT 32, GELLI INDUSTRIAL ESTATE, GELLI, RHONDDA, WALES
CF34 OEU
☎ (01443) 439907. OPEN 9.30 - 4.30 MON - SAT.
NORTH DOCK, LLANELLI, DYFED, WALES SA15 2NF
☎ (01554) 771252. OPEN 9.30 - 4.30 MON - SAT.

Manufactures underwear for a well-known high street chain store, the
factory shops sell seconds and overmakes at as little as one-third of
their normal retail price. Stock includes designer wraps, waist slips,
full slips, camisoles, bras, French knickers, crop tops and designer
nightwear in a wide choice of colours, fabrics and sizes. The staff are
friendly and helpful. For details of the other outlets, phone (01443)
875055.

# BENETTON

BICESTER OUTLET SHOPPING VILLAGE, PINGLE DRIVE, BICESTER,
JUNCTION 9 OF M40, OXFORDSHIRE OX6 7WD
☎ (01869) 323200. OPEN 10 - 6 MON - SAT AND BANK HOLIDAYS, 11 - 5
SUN.

One of 48 shops, with more planned, in this factory shopping village
which opened in June 1995. Billed as Bond Street comes to Bicester,
the shops are very smart indeed, beautifully designed and stocked
with end-of-season designer fashions, mens and childrenswear, tableware, shoes and more, all on permanent sale at prices reduced from
25%-50%, with some reductions up to 75%. Benetton stocks a wide
range of clothes for women, men and children including colourful T-
shirts, sweatshirts, men's button-neck T-shirts, swimwear, jeans,
children's jackets, stretch shorts and all-in-one shorts. Some of the
stock is marked seconds, but it is often difficult to tell why. The
centre also has two restaurants, a small children's play area and free
parking.

# BICESTER OUTLET SHOPPING VILLAGE

PINGLE DRIVE, BICESTER, JUNCTION 9 OF M40, OXFORDSHIRE
OX6 7WD
☎ (01869) 323200. OPEN 10 - 6 MON - SAT AND BANK HOLIDAYS,
11 - 5 SUN.

Factory shopping village comprising 48 different outlets, which opened in June 1995. Billed as Bond Street comes to Bicester, the shops are very smart indeed, beautifully designed and stocked with end-of-season designer fashions, mens and childrenswear, tableware, shoes and more, all on permanent sale at prices reduced from 25%-50%, with some reductions up to 75%. The outlets include: casualwear for all the family from Benetton; witty slogans on T-shirts and nightshirts from the US company, Big Dog; Cerruti women's designer fashions; Clarks footwear; sports shoes from the US company, Converse; glassware and crystal from Edinburgh Crystal; brand name luggage from Equator; casualwear and sportswear from Fred Perry; home furnishings from Hico; women's shoes and fashions from high street shop, Hobbs; men's and women's underwear and swimwear from HOM and Triumph; women's shoes and handbags from Jane Shilton; designer fashion from Karen Millen; younger women's fashions from Jeffrey Rogers; men's and women's fashions from Jigsaw; children clothes for boys and girls from JoKids; women's designer shoes and fashions from Joan & David; country clothing from John Partridge; glassware from John Jenkins; footwear from Kurt Geiger; toys and games from well-known names such as Hasbro, Mattel, Matchbox, Little Tikes at Kids Play Factory; specialist outerwear from Mileta Sport at Tog 24; women's fashions from Monsoon; gifts and homes accessories from Museum Merchandise; silver and stainless cutlery from Oneida; childrenswear from Osh Kosh b'Gosh; casualwear from Pepe Jeans; designer fashions for men and women from Polo Ralph Lauren; candles and candlesticks from Price's Candles; men's and women's fashions from Principles; casualwear and after sailing clothes for men and women from Scandinavian company Red/Green; casualwear from mail order specialists Racing Green; books, CDs and cassettes from Sapphire Books; men's and women's fashions from Scotch House; men's suits, jackets and top designer name shirts from the Moss Bros shop, The Suit Company; top-class tableware and glass from Villeroy & Boch; lingerie from Warners; toiletries and gifts from Woods of Windsor; jeans and casualwear from Wrangler; bedlinen from Descamps; smart women's fashion from Aquascutum; and Helly Hansen. The centre also has two restaurants, a small children's play area and free parking.

## BIG DOG

BICESTER OUTLET SHOPPING VILLAGE, PINGLE DRIVE, BICESTER, JUNCTION 9 OF M40, OXFORDSHIRE OX6 7WD
☎ (01869) 323200. OPEN 10 - 6 MON - SAT AND BANK HOLIDAYS, 11 - 5 SUN.

This is a US company which sells T-shirts, sweatshirts, shorts and nightwear with a slogan for women, men and children. As they are not a well-known name here, it is difficult to tell how good their prices are. All the clothes are unisex and there are also golf balls, golf umbrellas, dogs leads and mouse mats. All the stock is currently on sale in the USA. Examples of prices in June 1995 include sweatshirts, £14.99 reduced from £25; T-shirts, £7.99 reduced from £10; long nightie T-shirts, £18 reduced from £20; men's shorts, £24.99 reduced from £30. The village also has two restaurants, a small children's play area and free parking. The telephone number given here is for the village.

## BURBERRY

YNYSWEN ROAD, TREORCHY, RHONDDA, MID GLAMORGAN, WALES
☎ (0443) 772020. OPEN 9 - 4 MON - THUR, 9 - 2 FRI, 9 - 1.30 SAT.

This Burberry factory shop is quite difficult to find as it is some way up the Rhondda Valley. However, GDD readers have written to tell me it is definitely worth the trip - although rather olde world, it has some good merchandise at extremely good prices. It sells seconds and overmakes of the famous name raincoats and duffle coats as well as accessories such as the distinctive umbrellas, scarves and handbags. All carry the Burberry label and are about one third of the normal retail price. For example, trench coats, £159.95; classic coats, £129.95 which amount to a reduction of two thirds. Childrenswear tends to be thin on the ground, but there are plenty of gift items such as Burberry brand name teas, coffees and marmalade.

## CERRUTI 1881-PARIS

BICESTER OUTLET SHOPPING VILLAGE, PINGLE DRIVE, BICESTER,
JUNCTION 9 OF M40, OXFORDSHIRE OX6 7WD
☎ (01869) 323200. OPEN 10 - 6 MON - SAT AND BANK HOLIDAYS, 11 - 5
SUN.
Cerruti has a very stylish shop with a range of their women's clothes
at discounts of up to 60%. Examples of prices include jackets reduced
from £499 to £299; silk blouses reduced from £159 to £89; linen
dresses reduced from £229 to £115; trousers suits reduced from £625
to £339; trousers reduced from £199 to £99. The centre also has two
restaurants, a small children's play area and free parking.

## CHARNOS

THE OLD SCHOOL BUILDING, OUTCLOUGH ROAD, BRINDLEY
FORD, STOKE-ON-TRENT, STAFFORDSHIRE
☎ (01782) 522529. OPEN 10 - 4 TUE - FRI, 12.30 - 1 SAT.
Famous Charnos lingerie, as well as hosiery and knitwear for women
and men at factory shop prices. Current ladies lingerie is discounted
by 25%, discontinued lingerie by 50%. Knitwear is reduced by one-
third. Some stock is grade B quality. Also sells menswear and childrenswear with lots of baby clothes.

## CLARKS FACTORY SHOP

UNIT 27, BICESTER OUTLET SHOPPING VILLAGE, PINGLE DRIVE,
BICESTER, JUNCTION 9 OF M40, OXFORDSHIRE OX6 7WD
☎ (01869) 325646. OPEN 10 - 6 MON - SAT, 11 - 5 SUN AND BANK
HOLIDAYS.
One of 48 shops, with more planned, in this factory shopping village.
Clarks International operate a chain of factory shops nationally which
specialise in selling discontinued lines and slight sub-standards for
women, men and children from Clarks, K Shoes and other famous
brands. These shops trade under the name of Crockers, K Shoes
Factory shop or Clarks Factory Shop and while not all are physically
attached to a shoe factory, these shops are treated as factory shops by
the company. Customers can expect to find an extensive range of
quality shoes, sandals, walking boots, slippers, trainers, handbags,
accessories and gifts, while their major outlets also offer luggage,
sports clothing, sports equipment and outdoor clothing. Brands
stocked include Clarks, K Shoes, Springer, CICA, Hi-Tec, Puma,

Mercury, Dr Martens, Nike, LA Gear, Fila, Mizuno, Slazenger, Weider, Samsonite, Delsey, Antler and Carlton, although not all are sold in every outlet. Discounts are on average 30% off the normal high street price for perfect stock.

## CONVERSE EUROPE LTD

BICESTER OUTLET SHOPPING VILLAGE, PINGLE DRIVE, BICESTER, JUNCTION 9 OF M40, OXFORDSHIRE OX6 7WD
☎ (01869) 323200. OPEN 10 - 6 MON - SAT AND BANK HOLIDAYS, 11 - 5 SUN.

Converse is the largest sports footwear company in the US and this is its first factory outlet in Europe. Discounts range from 30% to 50% on seconds. Leather chunk shoes, £24.99, reduced from £39.99, plus baseball shoes, canvas plimsolls and a wide range of sports shoes. The village also has two restaurants, a small children's play area and free parking. The telephone number given here is for the village.

## FRED PERRY

UNIT 31, BICESTER OUTLET SHOPPING VILLAGE, PINGLE DRIVE, BICESTER, JUNCTION 9 OF M40, OXFORDSHIRE OX6 7WD
☎ (01869) 325504. OPEN 10 - 6 MON - SAT AND BANK HOLIDAYS, 10 - 4 SUN.

This shop sells men's and women's ranges of the famous Fred Perry sportswear and leisure clothing: shorts, tennis tops, tracksuits, T-shirts. All price labels show the original and the reduced price. Tennis shorts were reduced from £27.99 to £14.99; tracksuits bottoms now from £14.99. When we visited in June 1995, there was a much better selection of menswear than women's, though that may change. The village also has two restaurants, a small children's play area and free parking.

## GOSSARD

10 MAIN ROAD, PONTLLANFRAITH, BLACKWOOD, GWENT NT2P 2DL
☎ (01495) 228171. OPEN 9.30 - 5.30 MON - SAT.

Factory shop sells seconds and discontinued ranges of Gossard under-wear including bras, briefs, suspender belts and bodies, but no night-wear or long-line slips at discounted prices. Most of the stock is last year's trade catalogue styles at discounts of between 25%-75%.

## HOBBS

BICESTER OUTLET SHOPPING VILLAGE, PINGLE DRIVE, BICESTER,
JUNCTION 9 OF M40, OXFORDSHIRE OX6 7WD
☎ (01869) 323200. OPEN 10 - 6 MON - SAT AND BANK HOLIDAYS, 11 - 5
SUN.
Hobbs has a range of clothes for women and a smaller selection of
shoes. For example, long dresses, £82.99 reduced from £118; short
linen dress, £69 reduced from £99; shoes, £39 reduced from £59;
striped linen suits, £37.99 reduced from £52; as well as smart suits,
floral blouses and bodies. The village also has two restaurants, a small
children's play area and free parking.

## HOM

BICESTER OUTLET SHOPPING VILLAGE, PINGLE DRIVE, BICESTER,
JUNCTION 9 OF M40, OXFORDSHIRE OX6 7WD
☎ (01869) 323200. OPEN 10 - 6 MON - SAT AND BANK HOLIDAYS, 11 - 5
SUN.
This shop sells Hom swimwear and underwear for men and Triumph
swimwear, nightwear and lingerie for women. For women, there are
Triumph swimming costumes, tracksuits, Blissy briefs, nightgowns
and bras. The village also has two restaurants, a small children's play
area and free parking. The telephone number given here is for the
village.

## I J DEWHIRST

UNIT 22, THE KINGSWAY, FFORESTFACH INDUSTRIAL ESTATE,
FFORESTFACH, SWANSEA
☎ (01792) 584621. OPEN 9 - 5.30 MON - FRI, 9 - 5 SAT, 11 - 5 SUN.
Wide range of women's, men's and children's clothes including
women's jackets, blouses, skirts and trousers; men's suits, jackets,
shirts, trousers; girl's dresses, blouses, trousers, skirts and jackets and
boy's shirts, trousers and jackets, and much much more.

# JAEGER FACTORY SHOP

42 CHURCH STREET, TAMWORTH, STAFFORDSHIRE B79 7DE
☎ (01827) 52828. OPEN 9.30 - 5.30 MON - SAT.
Classic tailoring at old-fashioned prices. This is a large shop which deals mainly in separates and casual wear from last year's stock. For example skirts, £39, originally £89; jackets, £65, originally £289. Most of the merchandise is last season's or earlier stock and some seconds. There are now 13 Jaeger factory shops, some selling the whole range of Jaeger clothes, some just knitwear; yet others sell goods other than those with the Jaeger label.

# JANE SHILTON PLC

BICESTER OUTLET SHOPPING VILLAGE, PINGLE DRIVE, BICESTER, JUNCTION 9 OF M40, OXFORDSHIRE OX6 7WD
☎ (01869) 323200. OPEN 10 - 6 MON - SAT AND BANK HOLIDAYS, 11 - 5 SUN.
This is Jane Shilton's first stand-alone factory outlet, although her goods do sell in other discount outlets. A card in the window states that this shop only carries merchandise from past seasons' collections or factory seconds. There is a wide range of handbags, suitcases, some women's shoes and travel bags. The village also has two restaurants, a small children's play area and free parking. The telephone number given here is for the village.

# JEFF & ANNABEL'S

35 WARSTONE LANE, WARSTONE LANE, BIRMINGHAM B18 6JQ
☎ (0121) 236 6310. OPEN 9 - 5 MON - SAT, 10.30 - 2.30 SUN AND SOME BANK HOLIDAYS.
Because they make all their own jewellery, they can offer very competitive prices. Specialise in coloured stones and diamond and wedding rings. Also sell quality 9 and 18 carat gold earrings, bracelets, lockets, cufflinks, and charms.

# JEFFREY ROGERS

BICESTER OUTLET SHOPPING VILLAGE, PINGLE DRIVE, BICESTER, JUNCTION 9 OF M40, OXFORDSHIRE OX6 7WD
☎ (01869) 323200. OPEN 10 - 6 MON - SAT AND BANK HOLIDAYS, 11 - 5 SUN.

Jeffrey Rogers stocks fashions for the younger, trendy end of the market including white blouses, £17.99 reduced from £21.99; dresses, £24.99 reduced from £36.99; bodies, £6.99 reduced from £9.99; baggy drawstring waist trousers, £14.99 reduced from £21.99; and sleeveless T-shirts, £5.99 reduced from £9.99. The village also has two restaurants, a small children's play area and free parking. The telephone number given here is for the village.

# JOAN & DAVID

BICESTER OUTLET SHOPPING VILLAGE, PINGLE DRIVE, BICESTER, JUNCTION 9 OF M40, OXFORDSHIRE OX6 7WD
☎ (01869) 323200. OPEN 10 - 6 MON - SAT AND BANK HOLIDAYS, 11 - 5 SUN.

This is a very stylish shop with divine shoes reduced by about 50%, though they are still mostly above the £60 mark. It also sells classic clothes. Examples include green suede shoes, £89 marked down from £170; black lace-ups, £69 marked down from £135; black brocade evening jacket, £229 reduced from £445; grey trousers, £109 from £200; linen collarless jacket, £229 from £395. The mix in the shop is 60% footwear, 25% clothing and 15% accessories. The village also has two restaurants, a small children's play area and free parking. The telephone number given here is for the village.

# KURT GEIGER

BICESTER OUTLET SHOPPING VILLAGE, PINGLE DRIVE, BICESTER, JUNCTION 9 OF M40, OXFORDSHIRE OX6 7WD
☎ (01869) 323200. OPEN 10 - 6 MON - SAT AND BANK HOLIDAYS, 11 - 5 SUN.

This shop sells ladies ranges from Bruno Magli, Charles Jourdan, Via Spiga, Van-Dal, Kurt Geiger and Carvela. All the shoes are set out in easily accessible racks ranged in sizes. The village also has two restaurants, a small children's play area and free parking. The telephone number given here is for the village.

## PEPE JEANS

UNIT 2, BICESTER OUTLET SHOPPING VILLAGE, PINGLE DRIVE,
BICESTER, JUNCTION 9 OF M40, OXFORDSHIRE OX6 7WD
☎ (01869) 325378. OPEN 10 - 6 MON - SAT AND BANK HOLIDAYS,
11 - 5 SUN.

Pepe Jeans sells a wide selection of denim jeans and jackets as well as
coloured jeans and jackets, cords, waistcoats and donkey jackets.
There is a small range of children's jeans from 134cm upwards. All
stock is discontinued or last season's. The village also has two restaurants, a small children's play area and free parking.

## POLO RALPH LAUREN

BICESTER OUTLET SHOPPING VILLAGE, PINGLE DRIVE, BICESTER,
JUNCTION 9 OF M40, OXFORDSHIRE OX6 7WD
☎ (01869) 323200. OPEN 10 - 6 MON - SAT AND BANK HOLIDAYS,
11 - 5 SUN.

Polo Ralph Lauren, the largest shop in the village with the prime spot,
has discounted items by between 35% and 60% for men and women.
The women's range included navy reserve athletic department stretch
shorts, £44; T-shirts, £24; long skirts, £69; smart striped jackets,
£200; wrapover skirts, £69; wide leather belts, £59; and handbags,
£100. At the time of my first visit, it was difficult to tell by how much
each item was reduced, but by my second visit, big signs spelling out
the discount were on display. The village also has two restaurants, a
small children's play area and free parking. The telephone number
given here is for the village.

## PRINCIPLES

BICESTER OUTLET SHOPPING VILLAGE, PINGLE DRIVE, BICESTER,
JUNCTION 9 OF M40, OXFORDSHIRE OX6 7WD
☎ (01869) 323200. OPEN 10 - 6 MON - SAT AND BANK HOLIDAYS,
11 - 5 SUN.

The Principles shop caters for men and women, selling only end of
season lines at lower prices. For women, there are shirts, slip-on shoes,
evening blouses, waistcoats, linen jackets - everything to cater for
both a casual and a smart wardrobe. The village also has two restaurants, a small children's play area and free parking. The telephone
number given here is for the village.

# RED/GREEN

BICESTER OUTLET SHOPPING VILLAGE, PINGLE DRIVE, BICESTER,
JUNCTION 9 OF M40, OXFORDSHIRE OX6 7WD
☎ (01869) 323200. OPEN 10 - 6 MON - SAT AND BANK HOLIDAYS,
11 - 5 SUN.

Red/Green is a Scandinavian compnay and this is their first factory
outlet in the UK. They sell very stylish "post sailing" clothes (though
you don't have to sail to wear them) for men and women, which
looked as if they were high quality. All the clothes are last season's and
discounts are between 30% and 40%. There are sailing clothes, golf
wear, nautical and casual wear, shirts, sweatshirts, apres ski wear,
anoraks, gilets, classic sweaters, sailing shoes and soft bags. The village
also has two restaurants, a small children's play area and free parking.
The telephone number given here is for the village.

# SECONDS OUT

6 GREAT DARKGATE STREET, ABERYSTWYTH, DYFED, WALES
☎ (01970) 611897. OPEN 9.30 - 5 MON - SAT.

Makes clothes for women, men and children, mostly for department
stores. The factory shop sells everything from jeans, £9-£13; jodphurs
and casual trousers to school uniform items and mini chinos, from
£5. Ladies summer trousers, £8.50; denim jackets, £16, usually
£33.99; men's sweaters and waistcoats from £12.

# STEWART SECONDS

12 PIER STREET, ABERSTWYTH, DYFED, WALES
☎ (01970) 611437. OPEN 9 - 5.30 MON - SAT, 11 - 5 SUN IN SUMMER.
14 NOTT SQUARE, CAMARTHEN, DYFED, WALES
☎ (01267) 222294. OPEN 9 - 5.30 MON - SAT.
HARFORD SQUARE, LAMPETER, DYFED, WALES
☎ (01570) 422205. OPEN 9.30 - 5.30 MON - SAT.
52 STEPNEY STREET, LLANELLI, DYFED, WALES
☎ (01554) 776957. OPEN 9 - 5.30 MON - SAT.
Y MAES, PWLLHELI, GWYNEDD, NORTH WALES
☎ (01758) 701130. OPEN 9 - 5.30 MON - SAT.

Branded merchandise from most of the major UK chain stores.
Fashion is usually in season and consists of overcuts, discontinued
lines and cancelled orders, as well as some seconds. Apart from
fashion for women, men and children, there is also household textiles
such as bedding and towels at reduced prices and crockery, glasses and
cutlery at competitive prices.

# THE ABBEY WOOLLEN MILL

MARITIME AND INDUSTRIAL MUSEUM, MARITIME QUARTER,
SWANSEA, WALES SA1 1SN
☎ (01792) 650351. OPEN 10 - 5 TUE - SUN.
Sells pure wool blankets and shawls which have been made on the
premises from raw fleeces as well as knitting wool packs, wraps and
scarves, all at between 30% and 50% cheaper than the same items in
the high street. Every batch is unique and unrepeatable.

# THE FACTORY SHOP

WESTWARD ROAD, CAINSCROSS, STROUD,
GLOUCESTERSHIRE GL5 4JE
☎ (01453) 756655. OPEN 9 - 5 MON - THUR, SAT, 9 - 6 FRI,
11 - 5 SUN AND BANK HOLIDAYS.
115 HIGH STREET, NEWCASTLE-UNDER-LYME, STAFFORDSHIRE
ST5 1PS
☎ (01782) 717364. OPEN 9 - 5.30 MON - SAT.
NEW ROAD, PERSHORE, WORCESTERSHIRE WR10 1BY
☎ (01386) 556467. OPEN 9 - 5 MON - SAT, 10.30 - 4.30 SUN AND BANK
HOLIDAYS.
Wide range on sale includes women's, men's and children's clothing
and footwear; household textiles, toiletries, hardware, luggage,
lighting and bedding, most of which are chainstore and high street
brands at discounts of approximately 30%-50%. There are weekly
deliveries and brands include all the major stars: Coloroll, Wrangler
and Dartington to name just three. Lines are continually changing
and few factory shops offer such a variety under one roof.

# THE FACTORY SHOP

NEWLAND, WITNEY, OXFORDSHIRE OX8 6JG
☎ (01993) 708338. OPEN 10 - 5 MON - SAT.
Part of the Coats Viyella group which makes clothes for many of the
high street department stores, this medium sized factory shop - not
surprisingly - had many recognisable items on sale. Stocks clothes for
all the family. For women, swimwear, lambswool long cardigans with
V-necks or round necks which looked very good value, jackets, skirts,
pyjamas, nightdresses, dressing gowns, opaque tights, blouses, underwear. Stock changes constantly.

## THE SCOTCH HOUSE

BICESTER OUTLET SHOPPING VILLAGE, PINGLE DRIVE, BICESTER,
JUNCTION 9 OF M40, OXFORDSHIRE OX6 7WD
☎ (01869) 323200. OPEN 10 - 6 MON - SAT AND BANK HOLIDAYS,
11 - 5 SUN.

One of 48 shops, with more planned, in this factory shopping village
which opened in June 1995. Billed as Bond Street comes to Bicester,
the shops are very smart indeed, beautifully designed and stocked
with end-of-season designer fashions, mens and childrenswear, tableware, shoes and more, all on permanent sale at prices reduced from
25%-50%, with some reductions up to 75%. This shop stocks the
traditional range of Scotch House clothes for women and men
including tartan skirts, wool jackets, lambswool cardigans, Argyle
socks, serapes, scarves and waistcoats. There are two prices marked
above each display: the Knightsbridge one and the factory village
reduced price. The village also has two restaurants, a small children's
play area and free parking. The telephone number given here is for
the village.

## THE SHOE SHED

CASTLEFIELDS, NEWPORT ROAD, STAFFORD, STAFFORDSHIRE
ST16 1BQ
☎ (01785) 211311. OPEN 10 - 4 SEVEN DAYS A WEEK.

Large factory shop selling a vast range of all types of women's, men's
and children's shoes, all of which are perfects, at up to 30% below
normal high street prices. Ladies sandals cost from £5; shoes from
£7.50. Men's shoes cost from £10; sports shoes from £10.

## TWEEDMILL FACTORY SHOPPING

LLANNERCH PARK, ST ASAPH, CLYWD, (OFF A55), WALES
☎ (01745) 730072. OPEN 10 - 6 SEVEN DAYS A WEEK.

Has a wide range of ladies clothes, both designer and top end of the
high street, and childrenswear, as well as handbags, scarves, blankets
and ties. There are ladiesjackets from Racing Green, Lakeland and a
variety of good quality high street fashion stores. For example,
Lakeland trousers at £29.95, and leather jackets from £79, all of
which represent discounts of up to 60%. Labels on sale include
Feminella, Jersey Masters, Pierre Cardin, Double Two and Barry
Sherr as well as high street names such as Principles.

# V & F PARKER LTD

(ARDEN JEWELLERY), 51 VYSE STREET, OFF GREAT
HAMPTON STREET, BIRMINGHAM, WEST MIDLANDS B18 6HF
☎ (0121) 554 3587. OPEN 9.30 - 5 MON - FRI, 9.30 - 3 SAT.
Part of Birmingham's famous jewellery quarter, V & F Parker are specialists in making rings, bangles and earrings. They are suppliers to jewellers, stocking more than 3,000 lines and hold stocks of major patterns enabling them to make or remake old rings. They also sell loose stones. They claim to be able to sell at "best prices available".

# VELMORE FASHIONS

1-2 JAEGER HOUSE, 141 HOLT ROAD, WREXHAM, CLWYD,
WALES LL13 9DY
☎ (01978) 363456. OPEN 10.30 - 3 MON, WED, FRI.
Overmakes of skirts, jackets and trousers originally made for the most famous high street name at very cheap prices.

# WARNERS

BICESTER OUTLET SHOPPING VILLAGE, PINGLE DRIVE, BICESTER,
JUNCTION 9 OF M40, OXFORDSHIRE OX6 7WD
☎ (01869) 323200. OPEN 10 - 6 MON - SAT AND BANK HOLIDAYS, 11 - 5
SUN.
One of 48 shops, with more planned, in this factory shopping village which opened in June 1995, This shop sells a wide range of women's lingerie, bras, bodies and briefs at discount prices. Above each display is a sign saying what the old and the new price is. For example bikini brief, £6.99 reduced from £17; underwire bra, £14.99 reduced from £33; body, £24.99 reduced from £65. The village also has two restaurants, a small children's play area and free parking. The telephone number given here is for the village.

## Dress Agencies

### ADDITIONS AND IMAGINE BRIDAL WEAR

3A MERE GREEN RD, MERE GREEN, SUTTON COLDFIELD WEST
MIDLANDS B75 5BL
☎ (0121) 308 7765. OPEN 10 - 4 TUE - FRI, 10 - 5 SAT.
A dress agency which also has a full-price bridal shop operating from
the same premises. Nearly-new labels include Mondi, Jaeger, Frank
Usher, Planet and Dorothy Rowley for women only. There are also
some new bought-in lines. Some of the bridal wear is made by the
owner, others are bought in from designers at competitive prices. Also
hires wedding wear and hats, some made to the individual's requirements.

### CHAMELEON DRESS AGENCY

123 EIGN STREET, HEREFORD, HEREFORDSHIRE HR4 ORJ
☎ (01432) 353436. OPEN 10 - 5 MON - SAT.
Very friendly shop, which is light and well stocked. Customers are
encouraged to exchange views - if it doesn't suit, the owner says they
don't sell it to you. Sited near Sainsbury's, it stocks a wide range of
clothes, from Marks & Spencer, Jaeger, Country Casuals, Alexon,
Berketex and Eastex to Yarrell, Nicole Farhi, Bianca, Ralph Lauren
and Joseph. Twice a year, there are special sales. There is plenty of day
wear, wedding outfits and evening wear, as well as accessories. Prices
range from £10 upwards to about £100. A Bianca jacket would sell
for about £45, Jaeger jacket, £55, Nicole Farhi two-piece, £75, Joseph
leggings, £30. There is also a huge selection of hats.

### CLIO OF CHELTENHAM

11 IMPERIAL SQUARE, CHELTENHAM, GLOUCESTERSHIRE GL50 1QB
☎ (01242) 226024. OPEN 9.30 - 5 MON - SAT.
Armani, YSL, Escada, Jean Muir, MaxMara, Valentino, Nicole Farhi
and Jaeger are among some of the nearly-new designer outfits on sale
here. She also sells some hats, belts, jewellery, handbags and good
shoes. Clio has recently added secondhand ridingwear, hunting
clothes and riding equipment for adults and children to her selection.

## DRESS EXCHANGE

1003A ALCESTER ROAD SOUTH (ABOVE THREE COOKS),
THE MAYPOLE, BIRMINGHAM, WEST MIDLANDS B14 5JA
☎ (0121) 474 5707. OPEN 10 - 5 MON - SAT.
Middle to up market designer wear, with accessories to match, at prices ranging from £40-£200. Designers range from Marks & Spencer upwards and include MaxMara, Escada, Ghost, Armani and Valentino. Occasionally stocks wedding dresses and wedding outfits, as well as seasonal event wear. Casual wear is stocked. Quite a good menswear selection.

## ELLE

41A HIGH STREET, COWBRIDGE, SOUTH GLAMORGAN
☎ (01446) 775687. OPEN 10.30 - 5.30 MON - SAT.
Jasper Conran, Escada, Laurel, Mondi, Christian Dior and occasionally Louis Feraud, Jean Paul Gaultier and Armani are on sale at this centrally located shop. There are a lot of separates and good office wear and half-price sales in January and July. There are also some wedding dresses from £200-£600, as well as veils and headdresses. Prices tend to be below £100.

## ENCORE

48-52 ST MARYS ROW, MOSELEY, BIRMINGHAM
☎ (0121) 442 4888. OPEN 9.30 - 5 MON - SAT.
Divided into 2 shops catering mainly for ladies, with a small selection of menswear. One shop is devoted entirely to designer wear, including names such as Betty Barclay, Valentino and Mondi. Frank Usher suits can be found for about £50 - £60. Accessories are also available in this shop to complement the clothes. The second and larger of the two shops, stocks high street names such as Dorothy Perkins, Principles and also new and nearly-new German outfits. Prices are very reasonable, with special prices for imperfect designer wear. Most separates are under £10 and suits sell for between £12-£20. Accessories are also available in the second shop.

# GAINSBOROUGH

12 SWANSEA ROAD, LLANGYFELACH, SWANSEA, WALES SA5 7JD
☎ (01792) 790922. OPEN 10 - 5 MON - SAT.

There is no merchandise from chain stores in this shop, which only stocks top labels such as Mansfield, Jaeger, Jean Muir and Frank Usher, all with savings of between 55-75% off the original price. There is some shop clearance stock, and plenty of day and evening wear and special occasion wear, including ballgowns and hats from which there are more than 200 to choose. There is also an alteration service and discounted dry cleaning. Good range of jewellery, especially earrings.

# GOOD AS NEW

21 NEWBURY STREET, WANTAGE, OXFORDSHIRE OX12 8BU
☎ (01235) 769526 OPEN 9.30 - 5 MON - SAT.

High street, medium sized shop selling ladies designer wear ranging from Marks & Spencer to Armani, though the majority of clothes come from Jaeger, Windsmoor and Planet. All nearly-new clothes are under 2 years old and come in all sizes. Good selection of evening wear including Frank Usher, Jean Allen and Laura Ashley ballgowns. The full range from coats, dresses, separates, evening wear and hats to shoes and handbags is sold.

# JUST JENNIFER

65 GREAT NORWOOD STREET, CHELTENHAM, GLOUCESTERSHIRE
GL50 2BQ
☎ (01242) 512639. OPEN 10.30 - 4.30 TUE - SAT.

Nearly-new outlet with labels such as Windsmoor, MaxMara, Eastex, Berkertex,and Marella, as well as some high street names and evening wear.

# MOONLIGHT VISIONS

21 FRIAR STREET, WORCESTER, WORCESTERSHIRE
☎ (01905) 613792. OPEN 9.30 - 4 MON - SAT, CLOSED THUR.

Nearly-new and new designer clothes at greatly reduced prices as well as designer ballgowns for sale and for hire. The overall feel of the shop is towards smart day wear with some dressy items from Jacques Vert, Windsmoor and Berkertex. Selection of hats, both new and nearly-new, from £5-£30.

## REGINE

71 READING ROAD, HENLEY-ON-THAMES, OXFORDSHIRE
☎ (01491) 572054. OPEN 10 - 4.30 MON - FRI, 10 - 4 SAT.
All top quality design labels, including some high street names.
Amongst the labels on offer are Paul Bianco, Betty Barclay, Jaeger,
Escada, Fink and Louis Feraud. Suits, dresses, skirts, blouses, perfect
condition shoes and a limited range of accessories are all stocked, but
not trousers. A large selection of hats from Frederick Fox downwards
from £12-£30. Everything is below £150.

## SANDS

18 CASTLE ARCADE, CARDIFF, WALES
☎ (01222) 230020. OPEN 9.30 - 5.30 MON - SAT.
Vast array of outfits set within a Victorian arcade in the middle of
Cardiff. Specialises in wedding and Ascot outfits with hats to match.
Designer labels include Jasper Conran, Janice Wainwright, Paul
Costelloe and Jean Muir. They also have a lot of new clearance stock.
Accessories include shoes and umbrellas. Coffee and sherry is on offer
and the atmosphere is lively.

## SCOOP

77 BELL STREET, HENLEY-ON-THAMES, OXFORDSHIRE RG9 2BD
☎ (01491) 572962. OPEN 9.30 - 4 MON - SAT.
Nearly-new ladies wear from designers at the top end of the market,
including Escada, Betty Barclay, Louis Ferraro. Often stocks seasonal
wear for Ascot and Derby Day, as well as cocktail and wedding
outfits. Also has a supply of holidaywear, shoes, hats, jewellery and
other accessories.

## SECOND CHANCE

6A WEST ST, ALDBOURNE, MARLBOROUGH, WILTSHIRE
☎ (01672) 411111. OPEN 10 - 4 TUE - SAT, CLOSED 1 - 2 DAILY.
Small village dress agency which sells "good country clothes as well as
occasional designer clothes" for women and children. Labels include
Windsmoor, Marks & Spencer, Next.

## SECOND THOUGHTS

THE OVEN, 1 HIGH STREET, BODICOTE, OXFORDSHIRE OX15 4BZ
☎ (01295) 263880. OPEN 9.30 - 4 MON - SAT.
Homes-based business based in a converted barn selling labels such as Nicole Farhi, Jaeger and Windsmoor. Also operates a hat hire business with 300-400 hats from which to choose.

## SECOND TIME AROUND

13B PARK STREET, LEAMINGTON SPA, WARWICKSHIRE CV32 4QN
☎ (01926) 889811. OPEN 10 - 5 TUES - SAT.
Offers middle of the range nearly-new clothes, mostly from chain stores and Marks & Spencer. There is also a bargain rail, where clothes which haven't sold after one month are reduced to half price. There is a massive amount of stock, including children's clothes but no menswear. Also offers a bridal service for sale and for hire with up to 80 nearly-new wedding dresses from £20-£400, veils, headdresses and shoes as well as some pageboy outfits.

## SECRETS

71 THE GREEN, KINGS NORTON, BIRMINGHAM, WEST MIDLANDS
☎ (0121) 459 8509. OPEN 10 - 5 TUE - SAT, CLOSED 4 ON WED, SAT.
Two storey shop, one floor with mixed merchandise, the other stocked full of evening wear. Wide range of labels available from Marks & Spencer to Jaeger and Betty Barclay. The selection includes ballgowns and evening wear, wedding outfits, seasonal wear, including some ski wear, dresses, shoes and trousers. There is also some jewellery from the shop's own supplier.

## STOCK EXCHANGE

4 CHURCH STREET, NEWENT, GLOUCESTER
☎ (01531) 821681. OPEN 9 - 4 MON - SAT, CLOSED 1 - 2 DAILY, AND AT 1 ON WED.
Nearly new shop stocking labels from Mondi to Marks & Spencer, Laura Ashley, Next, Wallis and Principles. Also childrenswear.

## THE CHANGING ROOM

11 MERE GREEN RD, SUTTON COLDFIELD, WEST MIDLANDS
☎ (0121) 308 1848. OPEN 10 - 5 MON - SAT.

A very upmarket dress agency selling labels such as Versace, Moschino, Louis Feraud, Georges Rech and Armani. The shop itself is tiny, but it is full to the brim with stock which tends to turn over completely within three days. They do not stock men's or childrenswear, but do carry accessories such as belts and handbags, as well as some new merchandise from last season at reduced prices.

## THE CUCKOO'S NEST

70 SMITH STREET, WARWICK, WARWICKSHIRE CV34 4HU
☎ (01926) 496804. OPEN 9.30 - 5 MON - FRI, 9.30 - 4.30 SAT.

Wide range of ladies clothing from Marks & Spencer to Pierre Cardin, Mondi and Lagerfeld. Prices equally variable, anything from £8 to £250. For example, a Pierre Cardin suit originally retailing at over £500 was sold for £120. Limited stock of evening wear, although there are usually some special occasion outfits. A lot of casual wear, suits and jackets, as well as classical tailored wear. The varied contents of the shop is reflected in the rapid turnover and age range - between 14 and 95 - of those who visit. No garment is more than 2 years old.

## THE HOUSE OF BEAUTIFUL CLOTHES

18 BRIDGE ST, PERSHORE, WORCESTERSHIRE WR10 1AT
☎ (01386) 552121. OPEN 10 - 4.30 MON - SAT, CLOSED THUR.

High class, pristine condition and seasonal garments.Some of the stock is designer label - Basler, Windsmoor, Jaeger, Eastex, Jacques Vert, Country Casuals - and nothing costs over £100. There are also hats, jewellery, shoes and handbags.

## THE PAMELA HOWARD FASHION CONSULTANCY

WOODLAND, BEDWELLS HEATH, BOARS HILL, OXFORD OX1 5JE
☎ (0865) 735735. BY APPOINTMENT ONLY.

Pamela Howard holds successful sales of new and nearly-new designer clothes, shoes and accessories including Armani, Valentino, Jean Muir, Joseph, Chanel, Moschino. Prices range from £1-£500. There is an exciting range of new jewellery also for sale, together with new hats. The Sales have become extremely popular over a number of years, and have been described by regulars as fun and a totally different concept of shopping in a relaxed and friendly atmosphere. A hire service for designer evening wear, ball gowns and outfits for Henley and Ascot is also available. Write or telephone to go on the mailing list, or if you are visiting Oxford, phone and arrange to view the clothes between the Sales.

## TIFFANY CLOTHING AGENCY

14 MARDOL GARDENS, SHREWSBURY, SHROPSHIRE SY1 1PR
☎ (01743) 233542. OPEN 9.30 - 4 TUE - SAT.
Aquascutum, Jaeger, Yarrell, Marks & Spencer, everything carefully arranged by size - tops, bottom, coats, activity clothes, etc. Also sells men's nearly-new outfits, bric a brac, paperback books and curtains.

## TOAD HALL: THE DRESS AGENCY

7 ROTUNDA TERRACE, MONTPELLIER, CHELTENHAM,
GLOUCESTERSHIRE GL50 1SW
☎ (01242) 255214. OPEN 9 - 5.30 MON - SAT.
An extensive range of new and gently-worn clothing for women, including labels such as Chanel, Givenchy, Armani, Caroline Charles, Escada and Nicole Farhi.

## TOP DRAWER

19-20 WOOD STREET, STRATFORD-UPON-AVON, WARWICKSHIRE
CV37 6JF
☎ (01789) 269766. OPEN 10 - 4.30 TUE - SAT.
It's an adventure in itself setting out to find Top Drawer, whose Tudor beams and friendly atmosphere is discreetly tucked away above Bottoms Up. Here, you will find a wide variety of carefully selected as-new ladies clothes and accessories for the discerning woman, with labels such as Escada, MaxMara, Umberto Ginnochietti and many more well-known names at prices to suit most pockets.

# Hire Shops

## ADDITIONS AND IMAGINE BRIDAL WEAR

3A MERE GREEN RD, MERE GREEN, SUTTON COLDFIELD, WEST
MIDLANDS B75 5BL
☎ (0121) 308 7765. OPEN 10 - 4 TUE - FRI, 10 - 5 SAT.
A dress agency which also hires wedding wear and hats, some made
to the individual's requirements. This includes wedding dresses, pet-
ticoats, headdresses, veils, bridesmaid dresses.

## BUMPSADAISY

25 FRIARS STREET, WORCESTER
☎ (01905) 28993. OPEN 10 - 5.30 MON - SAT.
Franchised hire shops with large range of special occasion maternity
wear, from wedding outfits to ball gowns, to hire and to buy. Hire
costs average about £55 for special occasion wear. Phone 0171-379
9831 for details of your local stockist.

## GOWNS GALORE

1 OLD WARWICK ROAD, HOCKLEY HEATH, SOLIHULL, WEST
MIDLANDS B94 6HH
☎ (01564) 783003. OPEN 9 - 5 MON - SAT, UNTIL 8 ON TUE.
Specialises in hiring cocktail dresses and ball gowns from a selection
of 200. Also day suits, mother-of-the-bride and Ascot outfits, as well
as accessories, hats and jewellery to hire. Costs from £39 for three-day
hire. Holds twice-yearly sales of ex-hire gowns in July and January.

## MOONLIGHT VISIONS

21 FRIAR STREET, WORCESTER, WORCESTERSHIRE
☎ (01905) 613792. OPEN 9.30 - 4 MON - SAT, CLOSED THUR.
Nearly-new and new designer clothes at greatly reduced prices as well
as designer ballgowns for sale and for hire.

## SECOND THOUGHTS

THE OVEN, 1 HIGH STREET, BODICOTE, OXFORDSHIRE OX15 4BZ
☎ (01295) 263880. OPEN 9.30 - 4 MON - SAT.
Homes-based business based in a converted barn selling labels such as
Nicole Farhi, Jaeger and Windsmoor. Also operates a hat hire business
with 300-400 hats from which to choose.

## THE BALLROOM

5-6 THE PLAIN, OXFORD OX4 1AS
☎ (01865) 241054 OR ☎ (01865) 202303 FOR MENSWEAR. OPEN
9 - 6 MON - SAT.
Bridal wear, ballgowns, and men's formal wear to hire or to buy. £45
to hire and up to £750 to buy. More than 2,000 ballgowns in stock,
all brides dresses are self-made.

## THE PAMELA HOWARD FASHION CONSUL-TANCY

WOODLAND, BEDWELLS HEATH, BOARS HILL, OXFORD OX1 5JE
☎ (0865) 735735. BY APPOINTMENT ONLY.
Pamela Howard holds successful sales of new and nearly-new designer
clothes, shoes and accessories including Armani, Valentino, Jean
Muir, Joseph, Chanel, Moschino, and operates a hire service for
designer evening wear, ball gowns and outfits for Henley and Ascot.
Write or telephone to go on the mailing list, or if you are visiting
Oxford, phone and arrange to view the clothes.

# EAST ANGLIA AND EAST MIDLANDS

## *Permanent Discount Outlets*

## ALEXON SALE SHOP

ST BENEDICTS SQUARE, LINCOLN, LINCOLNSHIRE
☎ (01522) 545220. OPEN 9 - 5.30 MON - SAT.
THEATRE PLAIN, GREAT YARMOUTH, SUFFOLK
☎ (01493) 332146. OPEN 9 - 5.30 MON - SAT.
Alexon, Eastex and Dash from last season at 40% less than the
original price; during sale time in January and June, the reductions
are as much as 70%. Stock includes separates, skirts, jackets, blouses,
and leisurewear; there is no underwear or night clothes. The Great
Yarmouth shop does not carry Eastex.

## BAGS OF VALUE

7 & 8 MARKET GATE, GREAT YARMOUTH, NORFOLK
☎ (01493) 842014. OPEN 9 - 5.30 MON - SAT.
120 LONDON ROAD, LOWESTOFT, SUFFOLK
☎ (01502) 515234. OPEN 9 - 5.30 MON - SAT.

As these are clearance outlets for the Salisbury shops, stock can vary dramatically. The shop could contain any of the following: handbags and jewellery to gloves, scarves, hosiery and wallets, as well as suitcases, school bags, leather and synthetic handbags, flight and sports bags, umbrellas, gifts, watches and sun glasses. It is unlikely that all will be represented at any one time. However, when they are on sale, it is at well below retail price. Some of the items may be shop soiled, but most are ends of lines or seconds. Discounts are generally between 25% and 50%.

## BLUNTS

128-132 GRAMBY STREET, LEICESTER LE1 1DL
☎ (0116) 2555959. OPEN 8.30 - 6 MON - SAT 10 - 5 SUN.

Women's shoes from the Clark's, K Shoes and Portland ranges at 40% of the normal shop price for discontinued stock, seconds and ends of ranges. Men's and children's shoes are also stocked.

## DIRECT COSMETICS LTD

LONG ROW, OAKHAM, LEICESTER LE15 6LN
☎ (01572) 724477. MAIL ORDER.

Established since 1977, Direct Cosmetics sells branded cosmetics and fragrances such as Max Factor, Elizabeth Arden, Cutex and Revlon, at discounts of up to 80% off the manufacturers recommended retail price. New lists of more than 400 products are issued every four weeks. Discounts are available on orders over £50. Please call for a current list to be sent to you free of charge and without obligation.

## DISCOUNT DRESSING

45 STEEP HILL, LINCOLN, LINCOLNSHIRE LN2 1LU
☎ (01522) 532239. OPEN 10 - 6 MON - SAT AND SELECTED SUNS.

Discount Dressing is a veritable Aladdin's Cave of designer bargains. They sell mostly German, Italian and French designer labels at prices at least 50% and up to 90% below those in normal retail outlets, and all items are brand new and perfect. They have a team of buyers all over Europe who purchase stock directly from the manufacturer, therefore by-passing the importers and wholesalers and, of course, their mark-up. They also buy bankrupt stock in this country. Their agreement with their suppliers means that they are not able to advertise brand names for obvious reasons, but they are all well-known for their top quality and style. So confident is Discount Dressing that you will be unable to find the same item cheaper elsewhere, that they offer to give the outfit to you free of charge should you perform this miracle. Merchandise includes raincoats, dresses, suits, trousers, blouses, evening wear, special occasion outfits and jackets, in sizes 6-24 and in some cases larger. GDD readers can obtain a further 10% discount if they visit the shop taking a copy of this book with them.

## FOREIGN AFFAIRS

32 GUILDHALL ROAD, NORTHAMPTON, NORTHAMPTONSHIRE NN1 1EW
☎ (01604) 602797. OPEN 10 - 6 MON - SAT.

Not a discount shop as such, but a boutique "without the boutique prices" as a GDD reader says. Run by a friendly and helpful Texan lady, she is said to have a real eye for what women want and a good head for the prices they want to pay. Lace bodies, dresses, wedding outfits, holiday fashions from Los Angeles, Dallas, Sydney and London. Beautiful linen suits and embroidered denim shirts.

## LAMBOURNE CLOTHING

CHRISTCHURCH ST, IPSWICH, SUFFOLK
☎ (01473) 250404. OPEN 10 - 4 TUE & WED, 12 - 4 THUR & FRI, AND 10- 1 SAT.

Manufactures and sells own brand, Windsmoor and Country Casuals skirts, trousers and jackets. The clothes, for men and women, are overmakes and seconds and are usually discounted by about 50%. They also make and sell towels.

## M C HITCHEN & SONS LTD

7 HIGH STREET, GRANTHAM, LINCOLNSHIRE NG31 6PN
☎ (01476) 590552. OPEN 9.30 - 5.30 MON, 9 - 5.30 TUE - SAT.

Littlewoods sell off their overstocks in a network called M C Hitchen & Sons Ltd. Most of them are in the north of England and offer up to 40% off the catalogue price for clothing and between 50% and 60% off for electrical goods. Littlewoods also run a mobile shop which operates in cities where they don't have a sale shop. For details of further venues for the sales, which usually take place once a month contact Jean Banks, c/o Crosby DC, Kershaw Avenue, Endbutt Lane, Crosby, Merseyside L70 1AH.

## MANORGROVE

32 LOW STREET, SUTTON-IN-ASHFIELD, NOTTINGHAM, NOTTINGHAMSHIRE NF17 4AB
☎ (01623) 440911. OPEN 9 - 5.30 MON - SAT.

Grattan use a chain of shops called Manorgrove or Scoops in the north and midlands to clear their overstocks. There is a selection of items from those featured in the catalogue, which can consist of anything from children's clothes and toys to bedding, electrical equipment and nursery accessories. Each shop sells a slightly different range, so always ring first to check they stock what you want. All items are discounted by between 30% and 50%. Some of the shops are being refitted and renamed as Scoops - although stock will remain the same - so again do ring and check first.

## MATALAN

UNIT 1, WEEDON ROAD INDUSTRIAL ESTATE, TYNE ROAD, NORTHAMPTON NN5 5BE
☎ (01604) 589119. OPEN 10 - 8 MON - FRI, 9.30 - 5.30 SAT, 10 - 6 SUN.
UNIT 1, PHOENIX RETAIL PARK, PHEONIX PARKWAY, CORBY, NORTHAMPTONSHIRE NN17 5DT
☎ (01536) 408042. OPEN 10 - 8 MON - FRI, 9 - 6 SAT, 11 - 5 SUN.
BLACKFRIARS ROAD, KINGS LYNN, NORFOLK PE30 1RX
☎ (01553) 765696. OPEN 10 - 8 MON - FRI, 9 - 6 SAT, 11 - 5 SUN.
EAST STATION ROAD, PETERBOROUGH, CAMBRIDGESHIRE PE2 8AA
☎ (01733) 341229. OPEN 10 - 8 MON - FRI, 9 - 6 SAT, 11 - 5 SUN.
LINDIS RETAIL PARK, TRITTON ROAD, LINCOLN LN6 7QY
☎ (01522) 696541. OPEN 10 - 8 MON - FRI, 9 - 6 SAT, 11 - 5 SUN.
DUDLEY ROAD, SCUNTHORPE DN16 1BA
☎ (01724) 270958. OPEN 10 - 8 MON - FRI, 9 - 6 SAT, 11 - 5 SUN.

As the UK's first National Discount Club, Matalan has the buying power to guarantee its members up to 60% discounts on a huge range of brand name clothing, household goods, luggage and toiletries for all the family. Top quality merchandise, current season, no seconds, is offered to its members at exclusive, permanently discounted prices seven days a week. Matalan operates strictly on a membership basis, one of the key factors for its success in offering 20%-60% savings off recommended retail prices. Membership cards are issued through companies, organisations and associations in the vicinity of the stores, and are available to their employees/members. They are valid at any of the 50 Matalan stores in the UK. To find out if your organisation is registered, phone the Matalan hotline on 01772 629447.

## STAGE TWO

SAVILLE ROAD, WESTWOOD, PETERBOROUGH, CAMBRIDGESHIRE PE3 7PR
☎ (01733) 263308. OPEN 10 - 8 MON - FRI, 9 - 6 SAT AND BANK HOLIDAYS.
UNIT 3, TRITTON RETAIL PARK, CENTURION ROAD, LINCOLN LN1
☎ (01522) 560303. OPEN 10 - 8 MON - FRI, 9 - 6 SAT, 10 - 4  BANK HOLIDAYS.
The names of the stores which sell discontinued line from Freeman's catalogues. The full range is carried, but stock depends on what has not been sold at full price from the catalogue itself, or has been returned or the packaging is damaged or soiled. Clothing discounts range from about 50% - 65%. There are also household items and electrical equipment. There are branches in Nottingham, Lincoln and Peterborough.

## THE FACTORY SHOP

BARTON BUSINESS CENTRE, BARTON ROAD, BURY ST EDMUNDS, SUFFOLK 1P32 7BQ
☎ (01284) 701578. OPEN 9.30 - 5.30 MON - FRI, 11 - 5 SUN.
Wide range on sale includes women's men's and children's clothing and footwear, luggage, lighting and bedding, most of which are chain store and high street brands - including Colorall, Wrangler, and Dartington - at discounts of between 30%-50%.

## W G BODILEY

2 OVERSTONE ROAD, NORTHAMPTON NN1 3JH
☎ (01604) 37971. OPEN 9.30 - 5.30 MON - FRI, 9.30 - 5 SAT.
The best Continental leather shoes for women and men, as well as
handbags. Ladies shoes start at £29.97 and all the shoes are perfects.
There are two sales a year - in July and January - but throughout the
year there is a special sale rack.

# Factory Shops

## BALLY FACTORY SHOP

HALL ROAD, NORWICH, NORFOLK NR4 6DP
☎ (01603) 760590. OPEN 9.30 - 5.30 MON - FRI, 9 - 5.30 SAT AND MOST
BANK HOLIDAYS - PHONE FIRST.
The Bally factory shop is situated next to the main factory and sells
women's, men's and children's footwear, and accessories for women
and men such as hosiery, socks, scarves, shoe horns and shoe care
products. Also sold are leather handbags, briefcases, suitcovers,
holdalls and overnight cases. Most of the merchandise is rejects, sub-
standard, ends of line or ex-sale stock and is priced from £5-£200,
which is usually at least one-third off the recommended retail price.
There is also a coffee shop which serves morning coffee, light lunches
and afternoon teas, a children's play area, toilet facilities, free parking
and disabled facilities. Within the factory shop, there is also a full
price department which sells all the current styles. A small "museum"
is incorporated within the shop showing the history of shoe-making
since the Roman times and the history of Bally, with examples of
shoes on display. Coach parties are welcome by prior arrangement.
Factory tours are not available.

## BARKER

STATION ROAD, EARLS BARTON, NORTHAMPTON, NORTHAMPTON-
SHIRE NN6 0NT
☎ (01604) 810387. OPEN 9 - 5 MON - FRI, 10 - 4 SAT.
Factory shop selling discontinued lines of shoes at 30% off the retail
price, and rejects at 50% off the normal retail price. Only sells shoes
manufactured by its own factory and these include brogues, smart day
shoes for men and women, but no trainers.

## BARRATT'S SALE SHOP

BARRACK ROAD, KINGSTHORPE HOLLOW, NORTHAMPTON,
NORTHAMPTONSHIRE
☎ (01604) 718632. OPEN 9 - 5.30 MON - SAT.
Reject trainers and ex-window display shoes at factory prices among
a range of perfect shoes, the latter of which are sold at sale prices.

## BECK MILL FACTORY SHOP

33 KINGS ROAD, MELTON MOWBRAY, LEICESTERSHIRE LE13 1QF
☎ (01664) 480147. OPEN 10 - 5 MON - SAT, UNTIL 6 ON FRI, 10 - 4 SUN.
Recommended by a reader, Beck Mill sells designer clothes for
women and men at up to 70% discounts. Brands include Feminella,
Barry Sherrard, Jeffrey Brownleader, Elsie Whiteley, Astraka, Wolsey,
Cavvalini, Dannimac, Roman Originals, Warners, Double Two,
Farah, Lee Cooper, James Barry, Lancers, Nautica, Christian Dior,
Norman Linton, Hathaway, plus many more. Come and see their
exciting selection of top quality brands, which consist of perfects and
seconds at factory shop prices. There is easy parking.

## BIG L FACTORY OUTLET

34 COMMERCIAL STREET, NORTHAMPTON NN1 1PJ
☎ (01604) 603022. OPEN 10 - 5.30 MON & TUE, 9.30 - 5.30 WED - FRI, 9 -
6 SAT, OPEN BANK HOLIDAYS - PHONE FOR TIMES FIRST.
This store retails a large range of Levi jeans, shirts, jackets, sweatshirts
and shirts from a very big outlet. T-shirts cost from £27.99; orange
tab jeans from £23.99; red tab jeans from £29.99; T-shirts from
£9.99; jackets from £35.99; and sweatshirts from £18.99. Most of the
stock is seconds and ends-of-lines.

## BYFORDS

PO BOX 63, ABBEY LANE, LEICESTER, LEICESTERSHIRE LE4 0DX
☎ (0116) 2611135. OPEN 9.30 - 5 MON - SAT.
70 - 74 BELGRAVE GATE, LEICESTER, LEICESTERSHIRE LE1 3GQ
☎ (0116) 2518003. OPEN 9 - 5.30 MON - FRI, 9 - 5 SAT.
FACTORY STREET, SHEPSHED, LEICESTER LE12 9AQ
☎ (01509) 503068. OPEN 10 - 5 MON, 9 - 5 TUE - SAT.
Part of the Coats Viyella group, which makes clothes for - among
others - Marks & Spencer, they have overstocks and clearance lines
which are sold through the 40 factory shops which are also part of the
group. Frequent shoppers at M&S will recognise many of the

garments on sale, despite the lack of the well-known St Michael's label. Womenswear includes dresses, blouses, jumpers, cardigans, trousers, nightwear, underwear, lingerie and hosiery. Menswear includes trousers, shirts, ties, jumpers, cardigans, underwear, nightwear, breathable jackets and hosiery. Children's clothes are not stocked in great quantities, but often includes jackets, trousers, T-shirts and jumpers, dresses and hosiery. The factory shops also offer a 28-day money back guarantee. There are weekly deliveries to constantly update the merchandise.

## CHARNOS

AMBER BUSINESS CENTRE, GREENHILL LANE, RIDDINGS, DERBYSHIRE
☎ (01773) 540408. OPEN 10 - 4 TUE - FRI, 9.30 - 1 SAT.
CORPORATION ROAD, ILKESTON, DERBYSHIRE
☎ (0115) 9440301. OPEN 10 - 4 TUE - FRI, 9.30 - 1 SAT.
NOTTINGHAM ROAD, LONG EATON, NOTTINGHAMSHIRE.
☎ (0115) 9730345. OPEN 10 - 4 TUE - FRI, 9.30 - 1 SAT.
About 25% of the shop is given over to discontinued perfects of the famous Charnos lingerie at discounts of 25%-50%. Current ladies lingerie is discounted by 25%, discontinued lingerie by 50%. The rest of the shop stocks wool, acrylic and cotton knitwear for women and men, and bought-in bedding, towelling and babywear, cards and giftwrap. Some stock is grade B quality.

## COURTAULDS MERIDIAN

HAYDN ROAD, NOTTINGHAMSHIRE MG5 1DH
☎ (0115) 9246100. OPEN 9 - 5 MON - FRI, 9 - 5.30 SAT, 10 - 4 SUN.
Factory shop sells women's underwear, leisure and knitwear as well as men's clothes, children's clothes and nursery soft furnishings and household items. Discounts average 30%. Take time out at the coffee shop - don't worry about parking as there's a car park on site.

## COURTAULDS TEXTILES

ALLENBY INDUSTRIAL ESTATE, CROFTON CLOSE, MONKS ROAD, LINCOLN LN2 5QT
☎ (01522) 539859. OPEN 9 - 5 MON - SAT.
Factory shop in Lincoln selling women's men's and children's clothes, including seconds from other chainstores. Discounts are usually at least 20% and stock changes constantly.

# CROCKERS

111 FRONT STREET, ARNOLD, NOTTINGHAMSHIRE NG5 7ED
☎ (0115) 9674212. OPEN 9 - 6 MON - SAT, 10 - 4 BANK HOLIDAYS.

Clarks International operate a chain of factory shops nationally which specialise in selling discontinued lines and slight sub-standards for women, men and children from Clarks, K Shoes and other famous brands. These shops trade under the name of Crockers, K Shoes Factory shop or Clarks Factory Shop and while not all are physically attached to a shoe factory, these shops are treated as factory shops by the company. Customers can expect to find an extensive range of quality shoes, sandals, walking boots, slippers, trainers, handbags, accessories and gifts, while their major outlets also offer luggage, sports clothing, sports equipment and outdoor clothing. Brands stocked include Clarks, K Shoes, Springer, CICA, Hi-Tec, Puma, Mercury, Dr Martens, Nike, LA Gear, Fila, Mizuno, Slazenger, Weider, Samsonite, Delsey, Antler and Carlton, although not all are sold in every outlet. Discounts are on average 30% off the normal high street price for perfect stock.

# DAVID NIEPER

ORANGE STREET, OFF NOTTINGHAM ROAD, ALFRETON, NOTTING-HAMSHIRE
☎ (01773) 833335. OPEN 9.30 - 3.30 MON - SAT AND BANK HOLIDAYS.

Primarily a company making and selling lingerie, nightwear and leisurewear for the retail trade and the mail order business, there is now a factory shop in the factory. The boutique, within the factory, sells the current range of clothes at full price, while the factory shop sells discontinued lines and those not being sold by the catalogue any more. Mostly perfects, they are all marked with the original and the discount price (usually half-price) and range from nightdresses in pure cotton, silk and satin, to slips and half-slips, lingerie sets, camisoles and French knickers, blouses and leisurewear.

# GLOVERALL PLC

LONDON ROAD, WELLINGBOROUGH, NORTHAMPTONSHIRE
NN8 2QX
☎ (01933) 225183. OPEN 10 - 5 MON - FRI FROM APRIL TO AUG, 10 - 5 TUE - FRI, 10 - 4.30 SAT FROM SEPT TO END MARCH.

The award-winning duffle coat and jacket manufacturer has a factory shop which sells their good quality clothes at less than half the normal retail price. There are woollen mix duffle coats, anoraks, car rugs and scarves on sale here, most of which are obsolete styles, ends of ranges or export rejects. Children's duffle coats start at £20, ladies at £38; reefer jackets cost from £50, down-filled anoraks at £45. All lengths of duffle coats are stocked for men, women and children.

## GYMPHLEX SPORTSWEAR

BOSTON ROAD, HORNCASTLE, LINCOLNSHIRE
☎ (01507) 523243.
Holds a one-day factory shop sale just once a year, usually in early spring. Your chance to buy a huge range of sportswear for all the family: jogging pants, tracksuits, rugby and football shirts, rugby shorts. Some of the stock is seconds, some overmakes. The rest is freshly-made stock which is especially reduced for the sale.

## JAEGER FACTORY SHOP

1 HANSA ROAD, KING'S LYNN, NORFOLK PE30 4HZ
☎ (01553) 691111 EXT. 2143. OPEN 10 - 4.30 MON - FRI, 9 - 3.30 SAT.
39 WATNALL STREET, HUCKNALL, NOTTINGHAMSHIRE NG15 7JR
☎ (0115) 9680500. OPEN 9.45 - 4.45 TUE - FRI, 10 - 1 SAT, CLOSED MON.
NOTTINGHAM ROAD, SOMERCOTES, DERBYSHIRE DE55 4SB
☎ (01773) 727500. OPEN 10 - 4 MON - FRI, 9 - 4 SAT.
C/O RHYN GRIEVE, WOLSLEY ROAD, COALVILLE,
LEICESTERSHIRE LE6 4ES
☎ (0530) 835506. OPEN 10 - 5 TUE - FRI, 10 - 3 SAT.
THE COURTYARD, THE MARKETPLACE, BELPER,
DERBYSHIRE
☎ (01773) 821320. OPEN 10 - 5 TUE - FRI, 10 - 1 SAT.
ARMADA CENTRE, MAYFLOWER STREET, PLYMOUTH PL1 1LE
☎ (01752) 668315. OPEN 9 - 5.30 MON, WED - SAT, 9.30 - 5.30 TUE.
Classic tailoring at old-fashioned prices from Jaeger and Viyella. Most of the merchandise is last season's stock and some seconds, but you may find the odd gem from this season if you hunt carefully. Some of the 13 Jaeger factory shops sell the whole range of Jaeger clothes, some just knitwear; yet others sell goods other than those with the Jaeger label. The King's Lynn shop covers the range of Jaeger clothing for men and women, with some knitwear; the Hucknall and Somercotes shops specialise in knitwear for women and men; the Coalville shop caters for the full range of Jaeger clothing for men and women, and there is some knitwear; and the Belper shop stocks

mainly knitwear, but it does have a small selection of skirts, blouses and jackets, many of which are several seasons old. Prices are at least one third of the original, sometimes a lot less.

## JOHN SMEDLEY LTD

LEA MILLS, LEA BRIDGE, MATLOCK, DERBYSHIRE DE4 5AG
☎ (01629) 534571. OPEN 10 - 4 SEVEN DAYS A WEEK AND MOST BANK HOLIDAYS.
Sells mostly knitwear under the John Smedley own label which are ends of ranges or seconds, as well as some perfects, from £14 to £32. There are cardigans and sweaters for ladies and men in lambswool and marino wool; two ranges of underwear; second skin wear including cropped tops and bodies, and Tootal shirts in perfects and seconds from £8.50 for seconds, £11.50 for perfects. Childrenswear is not stocked.

## LANDS END DIRECT MERCHANT

PILLINGS ROAD, OAKHAM, RUTLAND LE15 6NY
☎ (01572) 722553. OPEN SEVEN DAYS A WEEK, BANK HOLIDAYS.
This US mail order company has its first ever factory outlet alongside its UK headquarters. Modelled on the dozen or so factory shops they operate in and around their US headquarters in Dodgeville, Wisconsin, it's designed to sell warehouse overstocks, obsolete lines and a range of "not quite perfect" products. There will normally be about 3,000 items in the 2,000 sq ft store from jeans to jumpers, leggings to luggage, turtlenecks to trousers. Genuine overstocks are priced at 40% below normal catalogue prices; catalogue returns and near-perfect seconds are reduced by between 20%-70%. All overstock items are guaranteed, first quality Lands' End label products, all of which have been offered previously in their catalogues at regular prices. There is ample free parking, easy wheelchair and pushchair access and changing rooms. However, you cannot buy current catalogue merchandise from the factory shop.

## LORIEN TEXTILES

COOKSON STREET, KIRKBY-IN-ASHFIELD, NOTTINGHAMSHIRE
☎ (01623) 757748. OPEN 9 - 4.30 MON - FRI.
Manufactures nightwear and underwear for women and children,
mostly for Etam and BhS, and sells overmakes and ends of lines in the
factory shop.

## PARK CLOTHING

212 NARBOROUGH ROAD SOUTH, NEAR FOSSE, LEICESTER,
LEICESTERSHIRE LE3 2LD
☎ (0116) 2825047. OPEN 10 - 5 MON - SAT.
Park Clothing is a children's knitwear manufacturer with contracts
with some of the major high street stores. Its factory shop, which is
attached to the factory and warehouse, sells current and previous
season's perfect stock at discounts of up to 50%. As well as children's
knitwear and dresses in wool, cotton, acrylic and mixed fibres for 0-
8 year olds from £8, there is also a range of women's clothes bought
in from other manufacturers. Blouses cost from £7.99-£19.99, and
skirts range from £7.99-£17. There is also a range of teenage clothing
consisting of fashionable tops and dresses.

## ROMBAH WALLACE FACTORY SHOP

14-17 IRONSIDE WAY, NORWICH ROAD, HINGHAM, NORFOLK
☎ (01953) 851106. OPEN 9 - 5 MON - SAT.
Good selection of shoes for women and men at discount (ladies
courts from £18.95 - £60) as well as leather jackets from £99 and
accessories, vanity cases, suitcases and flight bags. Sandals, court
shoes, smart or casual.

## SHEERS LTD

ST MARY'S ST, EYNNESBURY, ST NEOTS, CAMBRIDGESHIRE PE19 2PA
☎ (01480) 473476. OPEN 10 - 12 TUES, WED, 10 - 12 & 2 - 3.30 THUR.
Factory shop selling chainstore seconds in lingerie at up to 50%
discount as well as bought-in children's and babies underwear,
babygros, cot quilts and towels at competitive prices.

## SUNDAES SHOES

THE CHASE, 18 HIGH STREET, MOULTON, SPALDING,
LINCOLNSHIRE PE12 7LF
☎ (0406) 371370. OPEN 9 - 3.30 MON - FRI, SAT BY APPOINTMENT.
Handmade shoes in bright summer colours, top quality materials,
including leather uppers and linings. There are 35 styles for all the
family, with some women's shoes up to size 10, including an award
winning range of Ecco shoes and Hogl courts, plus Sundaes sandals,
from £42.95. Their small, informal factory shop sells the full range of
Sundaes made on the premises and usually has a selection of discontinued styles, colours and slight seconds at bargain prices. Visitors are
always welcome, but do phone first.

## T GROOCOCK & CO LTD

GORDON STREET, ROTHWELL, NORTHAMPTONSHIRE NN14 6EG
☎ (01536) 710444. OPEN 10 - 5 MON - FRI, 9 - 1 SAT.
Factory shop selling high quality women's and men's slightly imperfect and end of line shoes at half price.

## THE FACTORY SHOP

OSMASTON WORKS, OSMASTON ROAD, DERBY,
DERBYSHIRE DE3 8LF
☎ (01332) 360045. OPEN 12 - 4.30 TUE - FRI, 9 - 12 SAT.
Seconds and surplus clothing from the Multifabs factory above the
shop. Workwear and waterproof clothing, thermal outerwear, shirts,
T-shirt, blouses and skirts. Most of the clothes are for men, with some
women's. For example, standard government regulation high visibil-
ity jackets, £35, which would cost £70 in the high street; Fruit of the
Loom sweatshirts, £7.99, which would cost £30 in the high street.
Most are first quality with some seconds and mismakes.

## THE SHOE FACTORY SHOP

TRAFFIC STREET, EAGLE CENTRE, DERBY, DERBYSHIRE NR19 1PR
☎ (01332) 372823. OPEN 9 - 5 MON - SAT.
20 BROAD STREET, NOTTINGHAM
☎ (0115) 924 2390. OPEN 10 - 5 MON - FRI, 9.30 - 5.30 SAT.
CONSTANCE ROAD, LEICESTER
☎ (0116) 249 0114. OPEN 10 - 5 MON - FRI, 9 - 5 SAT.
Women's, men's and children's shoes and accessories which are bought
in from other manufacturers including Spanish, Portuguese and

Italian companies. All are unbranded. The range covers from mocassins to dressy shoes.

## THE SHOE SHED

ELLIS STREET, KIRKBY-IN-ASHFIELD, NOTTINGHAMSHIRE NG17 7AL
☎ (01623) 723083. OPEN 9 - 5 MON - SAT
Large factory shop selling a vast range of all types of women's, men's and children's shoes, all of which are perfects, at up to 30% below normal high street prices. Ladies sandals cost from £5; ladies shoes from £7.50. Men's shoes from £10; sports shoes from £10.

## THE WORKSOP FACTORY SHOP

RAYMOTH LANE, WORKSOP, NOTTINGHAMSHIRE
☎ (01909) 472841. OPEN 9 - 5 MON - SAT, 10 - 4 SUN.
Manufacturers for top chainstores, the factory shop sells over-runs and returns in household textiles, bedding, fashion for all the family, including knitwear and underwear at discount of 20%-40%. The factory shop is 10,000 sq ft and most of the stock is clothing with good availability on colours and sizes.

## VANNERS MILL SHOP

GREGORY STREET, SUDBURY, SUFFOLK CO10 6BB
☎ (01787) 313933. OPEN 9 - 5 MON - FRI, 9 - 12 SAT.
Silk ties, silk fabric, purses, wallets, handbags, photo frames, silk cosmetic bags, woollen shawls and seconds in scarves are all on sale here at incredibly low prices. Occasional clearance sales make for even better bargains.

## WARNERS

DABELL AVENUE, BLENHEIM INDUSTRIAL PARK, BULWELL,
NOTTINGHAMSHIRE NG6 8WA
☎ (0115) 9795796. OPEN 10 - 5 WED, FRI, SAT, 10 - 7 THUR.
Manufacturers of ladies underwear, including the Andante range of all-in-ones, high briefs, suspender belts and wired bras, the factory shop sells overmakes and seconds at up to 50% off normal retail prices. The shop occasionally also sells discounted Christian Dior ties and shirts, boxed and wrapped.

## WHITE & CO (EARLS BARTON) LTD

11 NEW STREET, DAVENTRY, NORTHAMPTONSHIRE NN11 4BP
☎ (01327) 702291. OPEN 10 - 4 TUE, FRI, SAT.
Sells footwear, espcially Dr Martens and Gripfast, boots, motorbike
boots, steel-capped shoes, street fashion footwear and classic welted,
many of which are not available elsewhere in the UK as most are
produced for export. Winner of the Queen's Award for Export in
1990, much of the stock is seconds and ends of lines.

# Dress Agencies

## CASTAWAYS

10 BURTON ROAD, LINCOLN LN1 3LB
☎ (01522) 535495. OPEN 9.30 - 4.30 MON - SAT, CLOSED WEDS.
Cheery corner shop in upper Lincoln which specialises in almost-new
children's clothing, nursery equipment and toys, all of which are
housed downstairs, as well as ladies fashions (Next, Laura Ashley,
Gap), accessories and maternity wear, which can be seen upstairs.

## CHANGE OF A DRESS

294 BROXTOWE LANE, NOTTINGHAM NG8 5NB
☎ (0115) 9291531. 0115 9296888 FAX. OPEN 9.30 - 5 MON - SAT.
This must be the country's most glamorous dress agency. Where else
could you find Chanel, Armani, Moschino and Escada modelled by
the agency's "in house" mannequin, whilst accompanied by their
resident pianist at a grand piano? The owner imports clothing from
Hollywood and has sold garments from Joan Collins, Priscilla Presley
and Zsa Zsa Gabor. The extensive salon is decorated with 15 chandeliers and ornate gilded mirrors, with a coffee lounge for customers'
comfort. Clients travel far and wide to this mecca for the fashion-con-
scious and penny-wise.

## DIANA'S DRESS AGENCY

42 LONDON ROAD, KETTERING, NORTHAMPTONSHIRE NN15 7QA
☎ (01536) 84949. OPEN 10 - 4.30 MON - SAT.
Sells both new and secondhand clothes for women, as well as wedding
dresses. Only famous name labels are stocked, from Windsmoor,

Jaeger, Berkertex and Bellino to Betty Barclay, Mondi and Jacques Vert. For example, red Simon Ellis suit, with hat, which normally retails for £375 plus £65 for the hat, for £150 for the complete outfit. Also Jacques Vert three-piece for £340, normally retailing at £200. There are usually about 1,000 outfits from which to choose including a wide range of hats. Sizes range from 8-28. Wedding dresses include Ronald Joyce, Hilary Morgan and Dante, with headdresses, veils and shoes.

## DINDY'S

HAWSTEAD HOUSE, HAWSTEAD, BURY ST EDMUNDS,
SUFFOLK IP29 5NL
☎ (01284) 388276. OPEN 10 - 4 TUE & THUR, 10 - 1 SAT. CLOSED
DURING STATE SCHOOL HOLIDAYS.
Set in a converted stables, Dindy's sells high quality second hand clothes ranging from Marks & Spencer to Yves St Laurent, Betty Barclay, Escada, Louis Feraud, Tom Bowker, etc. Well respected for evening dresses, cocktail wear and wedding outfits, they also sell a selection of new, top label clothes at less than 50% of the normal retail price. Also a wide range of new gift items such as jewellery, handbags and belts. New jumpers and cardigans can be made to order. Childrens wear is available from 3 years up to teenagers.

## ELEGANT EXCHANGE

24 SHELFORD ROAD, RADCLIFFE-ON-TRENT,
NOTTINGHAMSHIRE NG12 2AG
☎ (0115) 9336086. OPEN 10 - 5 MON - FRI, 9 - 4 SAT.
Sells middle to top range designer labels including names such as Escada, Caroline Charles, Jaeger, Windsmoor, Valentino and MaxMara. Lots of hats for special occasions and some accessories such as shoes, handbags and jewellery.

## GLAD RAGS

24 HIGH STREET, HADLEIGH, IPSWICH, SUFFOLK
☎ (01473) 827768. OPEN 9.30 - 4 TUE, THUR - SAT.
Range of nearly-new outfits includes Monsoon, Gerry Webber, Viyella, Jacques Vert, Betty Barclay, Caroline Charles, Windsmoor and Alexon as well as American, Italian and German designers. Accessories on sale include belts, scarves, hats and shoes. Prices vary

according to design and wear. Childrenswear - both English and Continental for 0-10-year-olds, is sold very quickly.

## GLADRAGS

THE BARN, HUNTS FARM, HILLS ROAD, SAHAM TONEY, WATTON, NORFOLK
☎ (01953) 885210. OPEN 10 - 4 TUE - THUR AND SAT.
Sells women's new and nearly-new outfits, including ballgowns, as well as some new clothes which are Austrian in origin. Labels include Marks & Spencer, MaxMara and Christian Dior; accessories also on sale range from hats and bags to shoes scarves and belts.

## HARPERS

73 ST NICHOLAS ROAD, GREAT YARMOUTH, NORFOLK NR30 1NN
☎ (01493) 855614 OPEN 10 - 5 DAILY, CLOSED 4 THUR & SAT.
Neighbouring shops, one with a more "bargain" feel to it and with lots of items under £20. Emphasis on designer labels at drastically reduced prices ie: Escada suit reduced from £375 to £95, Jean Muir top from £180 to £35. Occasionally, clothes from High Street retailers such as Wallis can be found. Mostly current fashions and designer labels from £30 - £200. Good range of hats, shoes and bags and tailoring ranges in price from £2 - £10. Many of the items are brand new.

## LOUISE OF FINEDON

HIBISCUS HOUSE, 7 HIGH STREET, FINEDON, (OFF A6), NORTHAMPTONSHIRE NN9 5JN
☎ (01933) 680190. OPEN 10 - 5 MON - FRI, 10 - 4, SAT.
Pretty shop which specialises in good quality bridal wear and brides mothers outfits, hats, smart guest wear and evening wear in sizes 8-24. Wedding dress designers inclue Ronald Joyce, Margaret Lee, Benjamin Roberts, Hilary Morgan, Sally Bee, Brides of Paradise and Angelo Dreammaker in sizes 8-30. Prices range form £75-£800. Also veils, headdresses, flowers and shoes, all beautifully presented and an enormous range of hats from £25-£150. Other outfits include designers such as Chanel, Hardob, and Condicco up to size 24 and priced from £55-£500. There are lots of samples at good prices and lots of larger sizes.

## ORCHIDS

3 PARK STREET, TOWCESTER, NORTHAMPTON NH12 6DQ
☎ (01327) 358455. OPEN 9.30 - 5 MON - SAT, AND 7 - 8 WED EVENING.
Sells women's and children's as-new clothes. The ladies wear includes
a range of good quality accessories: belts, tights and stockings, socks,
scarves, costume jewellery and hair accessories. Labels sold include
Marks & Spencer, Jaeger, Betty Barclay, Mondi and Alexon. Nothing
is more than two years old and sizes range from 8-20. Occasionally,
there are free open sessions with a colour consultant who will help to
co-ordinate your wardrobe. The children's range is from birth to
twelve years, with more girl's outfits than boy's, and includes snowsuits and coats, with labels from Marks & Spencer, Mothercare and
Gap to Osh Kosh and Oilily.

## RICH PICKINGS

77A LOW PAVEMENT, CHESTERFIELD, DERBYSHIRE STO 1PB
☎ (01246) 211036. OPEN 10 - 4.30 MON - SAT.
Ladies wear labels from labels such as Windsmor, Planet and
Mansfield to Next and Principles. For example, Condicci two-piece,
with matching hat, £150, originally £400; up to 200 hats, some
costume jewellery, handbags and scarves.

## ROTATIONS

HILL FARM, OUNDLE ROAD, CHESTERTON, PETERBOROUGH,
CAMBRIDGESHIRE PE7 3UH
☎ (01733) 390909. OPEN 9.30 - 4.30 MON - SAT.
Converted barn which sells nearly-new clothes from Marks & 
Spencer upwards, and including Country Casuals, Planet, Betty
Barclay, Valentino, Mondi, Laurel, Escada. sizes range from 8-20 and
there is also a selection of about 30 hats, some jewellery and
handbags.

## SECOND CHANCE

65 CHURCH STREET, SOUTHWELL, NOTTINGHAM,
NOTTINGHAMSHIRE
☎ (01636) 813464. OPEN 10 - 4 TUE, WED, FRI, SAT, CLOSED 12.45 - 2
DAILY.
The shop itself is very small, but there are lots of upmarket, stylish
designers such as Nicole Farhi, Paul Costelloe, Rodier and Jean Muir
in stock, as well as a selection of hats and shoes.

## THE DRESS CIRCLE

125 ST MARY'S ROAD, MARKET HARBOROUGH,
LEICESTERSHIRE LE16 7DT
☎ (01858) 433521. OPEN 10 - 4 TUE - FRI, 10 - 2 SAT.
Good quality ladies wear, with a selection of both designer wear -
Jacques Vert, Planet, Jaeger, Windsmoor - and high street names such
as Marks & Spencer. Mixed selection, including dresses, two-piece
suits and handbags. Hats for hire or to buy. There are two sales a year.

## THE EXCHANGE DRESS AGENCY

9 LEYLAND DRIVE, KINGSTHORPE, NORTHAMPTON NN2 8QA
☎ (01604) 842933. OPEN 10 - 4.30 TUE - SAT.
The Exchange has between 600 and 800 items in stock at any one
time. Labels include Zandra Rhodes, Betty Jackson, Next,
Windsmoor, Marks & Spencer and tends to consist of middle market
smart daywear separates, as well as dresses, evening wear and coats.
Examples of prices range from skirts £5-£30, coats from £15, suits,
£15-£65, blouses £5-£20, trousers from £10, dresses from £10 up to
£70 for a Zandra Rhodes outfit which cost £250 new.

## THE FROCK EXCHANGE

7 HIGH STREET, FENSTANTON, HUNTINGDON, CAMBRIDGESHIRE
PE18 9LH
☎ (01480) 461187. OPEN 9.15 - 5 TUE - FRI, 9.15 - 4 SAT, CLOSED MON.
Good quality separates from Escada and Mondi, Windsmoor and
Mansfield to Nicole Farhi and Joseph at half the initial shop price.
Many come from celebrities anxious not to wear the same outfits too
often. Also a good selection of "wedding guest" outfits or special
occasion wear, including hats. No shoes or handbags. Clothes are no
more than two years old. There's also a men's hire shop and a
ballgown hire service. A new "club house" means you can enjoy a cup
of coffee, watch the tv or read the daily papers.

## THE FROCK EXCHANGE

MAIN STREET, COTTESMORE, NR OAKHAM, RUTLAND LE15 7DJ
☎ (01572) 813247. OPEN 10 - 6 TUE - FRI, 10 - 4 SAT.
Middle market to high quality designer clothes including labels such
as Basler, Escada, Bianca, Jaeger, Louis Feraud, Mondi, Mansfield.

Fairly good selection of hats from £15-£70. Also high quality evening wear and costume jewellery to hire or to buy, sizes 8-24.

## THE UPPINGHAM DRESS AGENCY

2-6 ORANGE STREET, UPPINGHAM, RUTLAND LE15 9SQ
☎ (01572) 823276. OPEN 9 - 5.30 MON - SAT, 12 - 4 SUN.

One of the oldest and possibly the largest dress agency in the country with 10 rooms on three floors packed with quality nearly-new clothing for ladies, men and children. Preference is given to designer labels, but better quality high street names are also stocked. The proprietors are very selective about the condition and all stock is carefully vetted. Names regularly stocked include Laurel, Mondi, Escada, Nicole Farhi, Karl Lagerfeld, Paul Costelloe, Jaeger, Armani and many more. There is an evening wear section, as well as sections for shoes, hats and accessories.

## TWICE AS NICE

209 HIGH STREET, GORLESTON, NEAR GREAT YARMOUTH, NORFOLK NR31 6RR
☎ (01493) 655359. OPEN10 - 4 MON, TUE, THUR, FRI, 11 - 4 SAT.

Smallish shop packed with a wide range of nearly-new clothes covering both the designer label end of the market and the high street department store end, although the latter dominates the merchandise. Some of the top names include Frank Usher, Condicci and Mansfield, but there are plenty of Dorothy Perkins and Marks & Spencer. They also sell handbags, shoes, jewellery and belts. Sizes range from 8-30.

## VOGUE CLOTHING AGENCY

94 EASTGATE, LOUTH, LINCOLNSHIRE LN11 9AA
☎ (01507) 604233. OPEN 10 - 5 MON - SAT, CLOSED THUR..

Trading for 20 years, this shop stocks a wide range of middle to designer good quality women's clothing. Consisting of two floors situated next to Curry's on the main street, it offers day wear, wedding and evening outfits as well as accessories. Labels include Jaeger, Aquascutum, Mondi and Laura Ashley. There is a hire department which stocks cocktail wear, and hat hire from £10.

# *Hire Shops*

## THE DRESS CIRCLE

16 MAIN STREET, EAST BRIDGFORD, NOTTINGHAM,
NOTTINGHAMSHIRE NG13 8PA
☎ (01949) 20861. OPEN 9.30 - 5 MON, WED, FRI, 9.30 - 7 THUR, 9.30 - 4
SAT, CLOSED TUE.
Women's evening wear only to hire or to buy. Ballgowns, cocktail
dresses and evening gowns from £30 up to £75 to hire, including jewellery. Up to 250 different outfits from which to choose.

## THE DRESS CIRCLE

125 ST MARY'S ROAD, MARKET HARBOROUGH,
LEICESTERSHIRE LE16 7DT
☎ (01858) 433521. OPEN 10 - 4 TUE - FRI, 10 - 2 SAT.
Good quality dress agency which also hires out hats.

## THE FROCK EXCHANGE

HIGH STREET, HUNTINGDON, CAMBRIDGESHIRE LE15 7DJ
☎ (01480) 461187. OPEN 9.15 - 5 TUE - SAT, CLOSED MONS.
A dress agency with a choice of more than 300 new ballgowns and
cocktail wear to hire and to buy as well as men's special occasion wear.
Also offers hat hire service.

## THE FROCK EXCHANGE

MAIN STREET, COTTESMORE, NR OAKHAM, RUTLAND PE18 9LH
☎ (01572) 813247. OPEN 10 - 6 TUE - FRI, 10 - 4 SAT.
Primarily a dress agency selling middle market to high quality
designer clothes and also offering a hire service of high quality
evening wear, sizes 8 - 24, and costume jewellery.

## VOGUE CLOTHING AGENCY

94 EASTGATE, LOUTH, LINCOLNSHIRE LN11 9AA
☎ (01507) 604233. OPEN 10 - 5 MON - SAT, CLOSED THUR.
Dress agency which also has a hire department which stocks cocktail
wear, and hat hire from £10.

## *Secondhand and Vintage Clothes*

### GRANDMA'S WARDROBE

NORTHGATE STREET, GREAT YARMOUTH, NORFOLK NR30 1BY
☎ (01493) 856995. OPEN 10.30 - 4.15 MON - SAT, CLOSED TUE, THUR.
Mostly women's secondhand clothes from Victorian period onwards,
specialising in Fifties and also sell hats and accessories.

## *Designer Sales*

### UNICO CORPORATION LTD

SWINSTEAD HALL, SWINSTEAD, NEAR GRANTHAM,
LINCOLNSHIRE
☎ (01476) 550016.
Holds regular warehouse clearance sales with up to 3,000 garments at
prices ranging from £9.99. Designers include Louis Feraud,
Gianfranco Ferre, Armani, Serge Nancel, Yarell, Fink and a host of
top designer names. There are usually current season's collections as
well as plenty of last season's collections at even sillier prices. Ring and
put your name on their mailing list for their countrywide sales.

# NORTH WEST, YORKSHIRE AND HUMBERSIDE

## *Permanent Discount Outlets*

### ALEXON SALE SHOP

25 VICTORIA STREET, CREWE, CHESHIRE CW1 2HF
☎ (01270) 213929. OPEN 9 - 5.30 MON - SAT.
10-14 BRIDGEGATE, ROTHERHAM, SOUTH YORKSHIRE S60 1PQ
☎ (01709) 382491. OPEN 9 - 5.30 MON - SAT.
HORNSEA FREEPORT SHOPPING VILLAGE, HORNSEA, EAST YORK-
SHIRE HU18 1UJ
☎ (01964) 535441. OPEN 10 - 5 SEVEN DAYS A WEEK.

469 LORD STREET, SOUTHPORT, MERSEYSIDE
☎ (01704) 531281. OPEN 9 - 5.30 MON - SAT.
71 BANK HEY STREET, BLACKPOOL, LANCASHIRE
☎ (01253) 22528. OPEN 9 - 5.30 MON - SAT.
Alexon, Eastex and Dash from last season at 40% less than the
original price; during sale time in January and June, the reductions
are 70%. Stock includes separates, skirts, jackets, blouses, and
leisurewear; there is no underwear or night clothes. The Halifax and
Barnsley shops also have a small selection of menswear from Dash,
although the latter does not stock Eastex sale stock.

## BAGS OF VALUE

3D ELLESMERE RETAIL PARK, WALKDEN,
☎ (0161) 799 6476. OPEN 10 - 6 MON - WED, 10 - 7 THUR, FRI, 9 - 6 SAT.
As this is a clearance outlet for the Salisbury shops, stock can vary dramatically. The shop could contain any of the following: handbags and
jewellery to gloves, scarves, hosiery and wallets, as well as suitcases,
school bags, leather and synthetic handbags, flight and sports bags,
umbrellas, gifts, watches and sun glasses. It is unlikely that all will be
represented at any one time. However, when they are on sale, it is at
well below retail price. Some of the items may be shop soiled, but
most are ends of lines or seconds. Discounts are generally between
25% and 50%.

## BARGAIN STREET

BUY WELL SHOPPING CENTRE, THORPE ARCH TRADING ESTATE,
WETHERBY, WEST YORKSHIRE
☎ (01937) 845650. OPEN 9 - 5 MON - FRI, 9.30 - 5.30 SAT, 10.30 - 4.30
SUN.
A wide range of ex-catalogue items from men's, women's and
children's clothes to leisure wear, sports gear, underwear, household
goods, linen, electrical equipment such as tvs, music centres and
vacuum cleaners, and toys. Prices are usually about 50%-70% off the
catalogue prices with extra discounts on certain days. Quality is
variable and stock changes constantly.

## BEANS OF BATLEY

SKOPOS MILLS, BRADFORD ROAD, BATLEY, WEST YORKSHIRE
WF17 6LZ
☎ (01924) 477717. OPEN 9 - 5.30 MON - FRI, 9 - 5.30 SAT, 10 - 5 SUN AND
BANK HOLIDAYS.
Friendly, family-run business on one flat level, 10,000 square feet in
size, which operates as a permanent factory outlet store. There, you
will discover man's and ladies fashions at excellent prices. Beans sell
top of the range quality brands at special prices - names like Viyella
on the women's side and Christian Dior on the men's. Beans offers
both current season stock and previous season's classics, all at up to
50% off high street prices. There is also a coffee shop which offers
snacks and light meals every day. Beans has wonderful motorway connections courtesy of the M1 exit 40, and the M62, exit 27, which is
only minutes away. There is car parking for 600 cars on site.

## BOUNDARY MILL STORES

BURNLEY ROAD, COLNE, LANCASHIRE BB8 8LS
☎ (01282) 865229. OPEN 10 - 6 MON - FRI, 10 - 5 SAT AND BANK
HOLIDAYS, 11 - 5 SUN.
One of the largest clearance stores in Britain, it covers more than
60,000 square feet. As well as a department selling household textiles
at discount prices, some of the top end of the high street designer
labels are on sale here for both women and men. The women's and
men's departments are very extensive - not to mention impressive -
and cover the whole range from casual to evening wear, with reductions of between 30% and 50%. There is also a large shoe and a jeans
department, a lingerie and nightwear department, and a section
where brand name household textiles and bedlinen are sold. Four
times a year, there are special sales at which prices are discounted still
further. Most of the stock is perfect clearance and ends of lines with
the occasional marked seconds. There is a coffee shop and restaurant.

## CASTLE'S CLOTHING

18-20 MARKET HILL, BARNSLEY, YORKSHIRE S70 2QE
☎ (01226) 202903. OPEN 9 - 5.30 MON - SAT.
Two-floor outlet which used to be an Alexon sale shop but which now
stocks full-price ladies clothes as well as discounted brands such as
Elsie Whiteley, Butte Knit suits, Jamie Oliver separates, Eleganze suits

and jackets, Match Set suits and separates, Telemac and Dannimac, Black leisure wear. Items on sale cover the spectrum from skirts and trousers to smart suits, some of which are clearance stock, some seconds. There is no hats, shoes or underwear. Downstairs, the men's shop is mostly full price but there are discounted suits eg Farah.

## CLOVER

2 BRIDGE ROAD, KIRKSTALL, LEEDS, YORKSHIRE LS5 3BL
☎ (0113) 2783331. OPEN 10 - 5.30 MON - WED, 10 - 8 THUR, FRI, 9.30 - 5.30 SAT, 11 - 5 SUN.
Sells a basic range of regular priced stock but two or three times a year receives some of the biggest ranges of German designer samples which are sold at half the retail price. These are usually one-offs and sell out very quickly. Also sells regular branded concession items from well-known British designers. Ring and put your name on the mailing list.

## DESIGNER CLEARANCE

MIDDLETON ROAD, ROYTON, NEAR OLDHAM, LANCASHIRE
OL2 5PA
☎ (0161) 624 4864. OPEN 9.30 - 5.30 MON - SAT.
Sells ends of ranges and last season's stocks from Top Shop to Versace, with the main emphasis on separates and casual to smartwear. Some stock is this season's, but most is last. Designers include Betty Barclay and the American Jessica McLintock as well as a large number of French, German and Italian designers. Examples of prices include Jessica McLintock outfits at between £30-£90.

## FOSC (FACTORY OUTLET SHOPPING CENTRE)

HULL ROAD, YORK, YORKSHIRE YO1 3JA
☎ (01904) 430481. OPEN 10 - 6 MON - SAT, 11 - 5 SUN.
Branded merchandise from more than 50 manufacturers which initially consisted of ends of lines, surplus stock, cancelled orders and slight seconds but is more likely now to be firsts. Some of the best-known high street names are here, including clothing from Courtaulds, selling everything from clothing and books to bedding, towels, children's clothes, small electrical kitchen equiment such as kettles, stereos, batteries and toys at discounts of between 30%-70%. There is also a cafe, free car parking, disabled facilities and no membership is necessary.

## GREAT CLOTHES

84 YORK ROAD, LEEDS, WEST YORKSHIRE LS9 9AA
☎ (0113) 2350303. OPEN 9.30 - 9 MON - FRI, 9.30 - 6 SAT, 11 - 5 SUN.
Clothes for men, women and children from French Connection, Adidas, Pringle, Farah, Puma, Christian Dior to Jacqmar and including all brands of jeans. Levi's costs from £35.99; full-length button-through dress, £12.99. There are also accessories such as socks, shoes, hats, scarves and underwear. All stock is current season and is discounted by 25%-30%.

## HARRIETS

11 MARKET PLACE, KNARESBOROUGH, NORTH YORKSHIRE
☎ (01423) 863375. OPEN 9.3 - 5 MON, WED, THUR, 9.30 - 5.30 FRI, SAT, 1 - 5 SUN.
Clothes which are mostly Marks & Spencer seconds and discontinued lines, but also come from Next, Dorothy Perkins and Littlewoods. For example, a Marks & Spencer jacket which would normally cost £85, for sale at £40; skirts less than £20; and coats and jackets to suit everyone from teenagers upwards in sizes 8-20.

## LABELS FOR LESS

16 PRINCES STREET, HARROGATE, NORTH YORKSHIRE HG1 1NH
☎ (01423) 567436. OPEN 9.15 - 5.15 MON - SAT.
The designer and quality fashion clearance outlet for Harrogate's leading fashion store, Hewletts. At Labels for Less, you will find an extensive range of sensational design houses at a fraction of their original price - all year round. Basler, Betty Barclay, Gerry Weber, Bianca, Fink Separa and Ara are just a few of the names on offer. Big savings in fashion, but no reduction in style is the Labels for Less motto where, in addition to regular discounts of up to 50%, there are often also outstanding seasonal offers. All merchandise has previously been sold at full price within the main Hewletts store and comprises mainly end of season lines. All merchandise is new and the majority of items are from the previous year's collections.

# M C HITCHEN & SONS LTD

C/O CROSBY DC, KERSHAW AVENUE, ENDBUTT LANE, CROSBY, MERSEYSIDE L70 1AH
☎ (0151) 928 6611.
116 ST JAMES STREET, BURNLEY, LANCASHIRE BB11 1NL
☎ (01282) 425615. OPEN 9.30 - 5.30 MON, WED - FRI, 9.30 - 4.30 TUE, 9 - 5.30 SAT.
602-608 ATTERCLIFFE ROAD, SHEFFIELD, SOUTH YORKSHIRE S9 3QS
☎ (0114) 2441611. OPEN 9.30 - 5.30 MON - SAT.
102 DEANSGATE, BOLTON, GREATER MANCHESTER BL1 1 BD
☎ (01204) 384969. OPEN 9.30 - 5.30 MON - WED, 9 - 5.30 THUR - SAT.
185 STAMFORD STREET, ASHTON-UNDER-LYME, GREATER MAN-CHESTER OL6 7PY
☎ (0161) 339 0966. OPEN 9 - 5.30 MON - SAT, UNTIL 5.15 ON THUR.
160 MARINE ROAD, CENTRAL MORECAMBE, LANCASHIRE LA4 4BU
☎ (01524) 412074. OPEN 9.30 - 5.30 MON, 9 - 5.30 TUE - SAT.
C/O LITTLEWOODS SHOPPING CITY, RUNCORN, CHESHIRE
☎ (01928) 717777. OPEN 9 - 5 MON - SAT.
69 - 74 LORD STREET, FLEETWOOD, LANCASHIRE FY7 6DS
☎ (01253) 773418. OPEN 9 - 5.30 MON - SAT.
UNIT 3, MONUMENT BUILDINGS, LONDON ROAD, LIVERPOOL L3 8JY
☎ (0151) 708 6118. OPEN 9 - 5.30 MON - SAT.

Littlewoods sell off their overstocks in a network of shops called M C Hitchen & Sons Ltd. Most of them are in the north of England and offer up to 40% off the catalogue price for clothing and between 50% and 60% off for electrical goods. Littlewoods also run a mobile shop which operates in cties where they don't have a sale shop. For details of further venues for the sales, which usually take place once a month, contact Jean Banks, c/o Crosby DC, Kershaw Avenue, Endbutt Lane, Crosby, Merseyside L70 1AH.

# MANORGROVE

25 TOWN STREET, ARMLEY, LEEDS, WEST YORKSHIRE LS12 1UX
☎ (0113) 263825. OPEN 9.30 - 5 MON - SAT.
121-123 MAIN STREET, BINGLEY BD16 2ND
☎ (01274) 561933. OPEN 9 - 5.30 MON - SAT.
85 THE ROCK, BURY BL9 0BP 0161 797 4112. OPEN 9 - 5.30 MON - SAT.
1 QUEEN STREET, RIPON HG4, 1EG
☎ (01765) 603223. OPEN 9 - 5.30 MON - SAT.
41 BARNSLEY ROAD, SOUTH ELMSALL WF9 2RN
☎ (01977) 642256. OPEN 9 - 5.30 MON - SAT.

Grattan use a chain of shops called Manorgrove or Scoops in the north and midlands to clear their overstocks. There is a selection of items from those featured in the catalogue, which can consist of anything from children's clothes and toys to bedding, electrical equipment and nursery accessories. Each shop sells a slightly different range, so always ring first to check they stock what you want. All items are discounted by between 30% and 50%. Some of the shopsare being refitted and renamed as Scoops - although stock will remain the same - so again do ring and check first.

## MATALAN

HOLME ROAD, BAMBER BRIDGE, PRESTON, LANCASHIRE PR5 6BP
☎ (01772) 627365. OPEN 10 - 8 MON - FRI, 9.30 - 5.30 SAT, 10 - 6 SUN.
UNIT 1, RED ROSE CENTRE, REGENT ROAD, SALFORD M5 3GR
☎ (061) 848 0792. OPEN 10 - 8 MON - FRI, 9.30 - 5.30 SAT, 10 - 6 SUN.
UNIT 29, GREYHOUND RETAIL PARK, SEALAND ROAD, CHESTER CH1 1QG
☎ (01244) 380877. OPEN 10 - 8 MON - FRI, 9.30 - 5.30 SAT, 10 - 6 SUN.
UNIT 13, THE WHEATLEY CENTRE, WHEATLEY HALL ROAD, DONCASTER DN2 4PE
☎ (0302) 760444. OPEN 10 - 8 MON - FRI, 9.30 - 5.30 SAT, 10 - 6 SUN.
UNIT 4B, STADIUM WAY RETAIL PARK, PARKGATE, ROTHERHAM S60 1TG
☎ (01709) 780173. OPEN 10 - 8 MON - FRI, 9.30 - 5.30 SAT, 10 - 6 SUN.
UNIT 10 & 11, CLIFTON MOORE COURT, YORK YO3 4XZ
☎ (01904) 693080. OPEN 10 - 8 MON - FRI, 9 - 5 SAT, 9.30 - 6 SUN.
NEW CHESTER ROAD, BROMBOROUGH, SOUTH WIRRAL L62 7EK
☎ (0151) 343 9494. OPEN 10 - 8 MON - FRI, 10 - 6 SAT, SUN.
SEFTON RETAIL PARK, DUNNINGS BRIDGE ROAD, BOOTLE, MERSEYSIDE L30 6UU
☎ (0151) 525 1190. OPEN 10 - 8 MON - FRI, 9.30 - 5.30 SAT, 10 - 6 SUN.
UNIT 3, ALEXANDRA COURT, OLDHAM, LANCASHIRE OL4 1SG
☎ (0161) 620 6686. OPEN 10 - 8 MON - FRI, 9.30 - 5.30 SAT, 10 - 6 SUN.
WESTOVER STREET, OFF STATION ROAD, SWINTON N27 2AH
☎ (0161) 794 3441. OPEN 10 - 8 MON - FRI, 9 - 6 SAT, 11 - 5 SUN.
UNIT 1, GREENMOUNT RETAIL PARK, PELLON ROAD, HALIFAX HX1 5QN
☎ (01422) 383051. OPEN 10 - 8 MON - FRI, 9 - 5.30 SAT, 11 - 5 SUN.
UNIT 2, CLIFTON RETAIL PARK, CLIFTON ROAD, BLACKPOOL FY4 4US
☎ (01253) 697850. OPEN 10 - 8 MON - FRI, 9 - 6 SAT, 11 - 5 SUN.
UNITS G & H, THE TRIUMPH CENTRE, HUNTS CROSS, LIVERPOOL L24 9GB
☎ (0151) 486 0325. OPEN 10 - 8 MON - FRI, 9 - 6 SAT, 11 - 5 SUN.

WINWICK ROAD, KERFOOT STREET, WARRINGTON,
CHESHIRE WA2 8NU
☎ (01925) 235365. OPEN 10 - 8 MON - FRI, 9 - 6 SAT, 11 - 5 SUN.
TONGE MOOR ROAD, BOLTON, GREATER MANCHESTER BL2 2DJ
☎ (01204) 383733. OPEN 10 - 8 MON - FRI, 9 - 6 SAT, 11 - 5 SUN.
As the UK's first National Discount Club, Matalan has the buying
power to guarantee its members up to 60% discounts on a huge range
of brand name clothing, household goods, luggage and toiletries for
all the family. Top quality merchandise, current season, no seconds, is
offered to its members at exclusive, permanently discounted prices
seven days a week. Matalan operates strictly on a membership basis,
one of the key factors for its success in offering 20%-60% savings off
recommended retail prices. Membership cards are issued through
companies, organisations and associations in the vicinity of the stores,
and are available to their employees/members. They are valid at any
of the 50 Matalan stores in the UK. To find out if your organisation
is registered, phone the Matalan hotline on 01772 629447.

## READMANS LTD

ALFRED HOUSE, SPENCE LANE, HOLBECK, LEEDS, WEST YORKSHIRE
LS12 1EF
☎ (0113) 2444960 DRAPERY. ☎ (0113) 2436355 CASH AND CARRY.
Women's, men's and children's clothing as well as bedding, textiles,
footwear, towels at prices which are cheaper than the high street.

## SCOOPS

79-83 COMMERCIAL STREET, BATLEY, WF17 5EF
☎ (01924) 475454. OPEN 9 - 5.30 MON - SAT.
89-100 NEW STREET, HUDDERSFIELD HD1 2UD
☎ (01484) 543301. OPEN 9 - 5.30 MON - SAT.
INGLEBY ROAD (OPPOSITE GRATTAN), BRADFORD
☎ (01274) 521674. OPEN 10 - 8 TUE - FRI, 10 - 5.30 MON, SAT.
UNIT 9, CROWN POINT, CROWN POINT RETAIL PARK,
HUNSLETT ROAD, LEEDS
☎ (0113) 2341924. OPEN 10 - 5 MON, 10 - 7 TUE - FRI, 9.30 - 6 SAT,
11 - 5 SUN.
SHIRETHORNE CENTRE, 34-43 PROSPECT STREET, HULL HU2 8PX
☎ (01482) 224354. OPEN 9 - 5.30 MON - SAT.
C/O DISCOUNT GIANT, BROTHERS STREET, BLACKBURN BB2 4SY
☎ (01254) 200449. OPEN 8.30 - 6 MON - WED, SAT, 8.30 - 8 THUR,
10 - 4 SUN.

SISSON STREET, OFF OLDHAM ROAD, FAILSWORTH M35 OEJ
☎ (0161) 682 5684. OPEN 8.10 - 8 MON - THUR, 8.30 - 9 FRI, 8.30 - 8 FRI,
10 - 4 SUN.

Grattan use a chain of shops called Manorgrove or Scoops in the north and midlands to clear their overstocks. There is a selection of items from those featured in the catalogue, which can consist of anything from children's clothes and toys to bedding, electrical equipment and nursery accessories. Each shop sells a slightly different range, so always ring first to check they stock what you want. All items are discounted by between 30% and 50%. Some of the shops are being refitted and renamed as Scoops - although stock will remain the same - so again do ring and check first.

## SOMETHING DIFFERENT GROUP

44 LOWER BRIDGE STREET, CHESTER, CHESHIRE CH1 1RS
☎ (01244) 317484. OPEN 9.30 - 5 MON - SAT.

Upmarket ladies clothes, with a lot of day wear from the top end of the high street names such as Alexon, Louis Feraud, Liberty and Jaeger, amongst others. There is a special events room, a hire section for ballgowns and cocktail dresses. Casual wear is also available with some sports wear including ski clothing. There are no annual sales but there is a special couture designer rail. The shop also runs charity shows at hotels. They also sell a new range of clothes called Saraha.

## THE DESIGNER WAREHOUSE

PARADISE MILL, PARK LANE, MACCLESFIELD, CHESHIRE, SK11 6TV
☎ (01625) 511169. OPEN 9.30 - 5.30 MON - SAT.

Top quality Continental designers at discounts of 50%. Summer and winter sales held with even greater discounts. Skirts which would sell for £95 cost about £59; Valentino suit which would normally cost £450, would be £225; Gianfranco Ferre suit which would cost £325 would be £185. No accessories. Sizes range from 8-20.

## TK MAXX

15 PARKER ST, OFF CLAYTON SQUARE, LIVERPOOL, MERSEYSIDE
☎ (0151) 708 9919. OPEN 9 - 6 MON - SAT.

Based on an American concept, TK Maxx is the first British retailer to practise "off-price" retailing. This means a centrally located store which offers famous label goods with up to 60% savings off recommended retail prices. TK Maxx has fashion for the whole family - women's, men's and childrenswear - accessories, shoes, gifts, kitchenware and home goods. Everything in the store is branded with a choice of well-known high street names to designer labels, and while a small percentage mightly be clearly marked past season, the great majority of items in store are current season, current stock and still with phenomenal savings. There is a huge choice with 50,000 pieces in store with 5,000 new items arriving a week, so it's worth keeping abreast of the lastest deliveries as turnaround is very fast. One of the ways in which TK Maxx is able to offer such low prices is by running a very low-cost operation, so the stores are simple and unfussy with wide aisles, shopping trolleys and baskets, and a spacious, functional feel to them. Service is not compromised, however: there are individual changing rooms, ramps for buggies and wheelchairs, plenty of staff on the shop floor and all the branches accept all major credit and debit cards.

## *Factory Shops*

### ACCED LTD

UNIT 29, CHESHIRE OAKS DESIGNER OUTLET VILLAGE, KINSEY ROAD, NEAR ELLESMERE PORT, (JUNCTION 10 OF THE M53) SOUTH WIRRAL L65 9JJ
☎ (0151) 357 1579. OPEN 10 - 6 MON - SAT, 10 - 4 SUN AND BANK HOLIDAYS.

Smart daywear and workwear from this French designer company selling men's and women's fashions as well as a range of accessories to complement the outfits. Special offers are available throughout the year. For women, labels include: Kevin Conrad smart and casual clothes, plus Oz sportswear for men and women.

## AQUASCUTUM

HORNSEA FREEPORT SHOPPING VILLAGE, HORNSEA, EAST
YORKSHIRE HU18 1UT
☎ (01964) 536759. OPEN 10 - 5 SEVEN DAYS A WEEK.

Ends of ranges, last season's stock and cancelled export orders for
women and men from the complete Aquascutum range. The
shopping village has restaurants, play centres, a vintage car collection,
water games, and plenty for the family to enjoy.

## BENETTON

CHESHIRE OAKS OUTLET VILLAGE, KINSEY ROAD, NEAR ELLESMERE
PORT, (JUNCTION 10 OF M53), SOUTH WIRRAL L65 9JJ
☎ (0151) 357 3131. OPEN 10 - 6 MON - SAT, 10 - 4 SUN.

The usual well-known range of Benetton clothes for women and
children. There were lots of seconds here when we visited in May
1995, each garment market with a sticky circle where it is torn or
marked.

## BRIDGE OF YORK

3 MAIN STREET, FULFORD, YORK, YORKSHIRE YO1 4HJ
☎ (01904) 634508. OPEN 8.30 - 5 MON - FRI, 9.30 - 4 SAT.

Makes shirts, blouses, socks and ties for many of the high street
department stores, as well as its own range of perfects which it sells in
the factory shop at discounts of 30%. Cotton and polycotton blouses
cost from £7.95, Viyella ones, £29.95.

## BROOKS MILL

SOUTH LANE, ELLAND, NEAR HALIFAX, WEST YORKSHIRE
☎ (01422) 377337. OPEN 9.30 - 5.30 MON - SAT, 11 - 5.30 SUN.

The clearance outlet for Ponden Mills merchandise - from tablelinen
and quilts, duvets and sheets to bedding and pillowcases, all at appropriately reduced prices. Also clothes for women and men, half of
which is designer wear including such names as Jac Dale and Maggie
of London.

## BURBERRY

WOODROW UNIVERSAL, JUNCTION MILLS, CROSS HILLS, STEETON,
NEAR KEIGHLEY, YORKSHIRE
☎ (01535) 633364. OPEN 1 1- 5 MON - FRI, 10 - 4 SAT.
CORONATION MILLS, ALBION STREET, CASTLEFORD, WEST YORK-
SHIRE
☎ (0197) 7554411. OPEN 10 - 3.45 MON - FRI, 9.30 - 1.15 SAT.

These Burberry factory shops sell overmakes of the famous name
raincoats and duffle coats as well as accessories such as the distinctive
umbrellas, scarves and handbags. They also sell children's duffle coats,
knitwear and shirts, as well as some of the Burberry range of food:
jams, biscuits, tea and chocolate. All carry the Burberry label and are
about one third of the normal retail price.

## CHESHIRE OAKS DESIGNER OUTLET VILLAGE

JUNCTION 10 OF THE M53, NEAR ELLESMERE PORT, SOUTH
WIRRAL L65 9JJ
☎ (0151) 356 7932. OPEN 10 - 6 MON - SAT, 10 - 4 SUN AND BANK
HOLIDAYS.

More than 30 outlets, all selling brand name merchandise at dis-
counted prices, with more outlets in the pipeline. Labels include Paul
Costelloe, Timberland, Nike, Liz Claiborne, Levi's, Scotch House,
Jeffrey Rogers, Fred Perry, Benetton, Kurt Geiger, Equator luggage,
John Partridge countrywear, Edinburgh Crystal, J B Armstrong, Sears
womenswear (Richards, Wallis, Warehouse) trading as Collective,
Principles/Burton, Tie Rack, Viyella, Fruit of the Loom, Catamini
childrenswear, Eminence lingerie, Acced womens and menswear (a
French manufacturer), Dim hosiery and lingerie (including Elbeo,
Pretty Polly, Playtex, Cacherel), Suits You menswear, James Barry,
Sapphire Books, the British Shoe Corporation trading as Famous
Footwear, Remington and JoKids. There is a children's play area, a
Garfunkels restaurant and free car parking. Phase two opens in
November 1995 with 30 more factory shops.

## COLLECTIVE

CHESHIRE OAKS OUTLET VILLAGE, KINSEY ROAD, NEAR ELLESMERE
PORT, SOUTH WIRRAL L65 9JJ
☎ (0151) 357 3249. OPEN 10 - 6 MON - SAT, 10 - 4 SUN.

Collective name for the Wallis, Richards and Warehouse labels. Large
store with each of the three labels taking up about the same amount

of space. Wide range of clothes from summerwear to coats, and with lots of evening wear, all at discount prices. Examples of prices include: Richards silk suede smart jacket, £29 reduced from £46.99, with matching skirt, £19 reduced from £33.99; evening shirts, £40 reduced from £69; macintoshes, £59 reduced from £99.

## DAKS SIMPSON

HORNSEA FREEPORT SHOPPING VILLAGE, HORNSEA,
YORKSHIRE HU18 1UT
☎ (01964) 533268. OPEN 10 - 5 SEVEN DAYS A WEEK, 10 - 6 BANK AND SCHOOL HOLIDAYS.
Sells previous season's stock for women and men as well as any returned merchandise and overmakes. There are good bargains to be had, but stock is very much dependent on what has not sold in the shops. Sizes vary but tend towards the two extremes: 6s, 8s and 10s on the one hand, and 20s and 22s on the other. Ladies jackets, £99, originally £279; blazers, £89, originally £275. Not very many suits for women. The Shopping Village has plenty to entertain the family with playgrounds, an indoor play centre, restaurants, a vintage car collection and butterfly world.

## DALESOX

6 SWADFORD STREET, SKIPTON, NORTH YORKSHIRE BD23 1JA
☎ (01756) 796509. OPEN 9 - 5 SEVEN DAYS A WEEK.
Based in Skipton's main shopping area, Dalesox sells quality hosiery and accessories. Most are perfect ladies, men's and children's socks made for the best high street chainstores and cost about £1-£1.50 a pair, normal retail price up to £4.99. There is lots of design choice from Disney character socks to Christmas pudding socks. There are also ties, ski socks made for famous department stores, unusual design Swedish polyester ties, knickers, boxer shorts, pyjamas and nightshirts. Most of the stock is bought in from other manufacturers, cutting out the middleman.

# DAMART FACTORY CLEARANCE SHOP

UNIT 6A, ALSTON ROAD RETAIL PARK, BYPASS ROUNDABOUT,
BRADFORD ROAD, KEIGHLEY BD21 3NG
☎ (01535) 690648. OPEN 9 - 5.30 MON - SAT, 10 - 4 SUN AND BANK
HOLIDAYS.

Discontinued branded chainstore fashion for women, men and
children, some of which is branded Damart, as well as household
items: kitchen utensils, glassware, towels, tablecloths, brushes, mops
but no electrical equipment. Ladies dress, £27.99, reduced to £9; T-
shirts from £2; toiletries gift sets. Most of the stock is bought in from
other manufacturers and consists of overmakes and discontinued lines
at discounts of 50%. Coffee shop on site.

# DANNIMAC LTD

FACTORY SHOP, LIME MILL, VICTOR STREET, HOLLINWOOD,
OLDHAM, GREATER MANCHESTER
☎ (0161) 681 2060. OPEN 9 - 11 ON FIRST SAT OF EACH MONTH.
FLETCHER STREET, BOLTON, GREATER MANCHESTER BL3 6PR
☎ (01204) 532311. OPEN ONCE A MONTH ONLY. PHONE FOR DETAILS.

Mens and ladies famous-name raincoats, jackets, anoraks, trenchcoats, and macs, as well as, occasionally, waxed and leather jackets at
factory shop prices. Jackets and coats range from £35 to £95. Most
merchandise is either slight seconds or discontinued lines; there is
some current stock, but most is previous seasons.

# DIM

CHESHIRE OAKS OUTLET VILLAGE, KINSEY ROAD, NEAR ELLESMERE
PORT, JUNCTION 10 OF M53, SOUTH WIRRAL L65 9JJ
☎ (0151) 357 2585. OPEN 10 - 6 MON - SAT, 10 - 4 SUN.

Lingerie and underwear shop for women and men selling bras, pants,
briefs, boxer shorts, vests, socks, sweatshirts and tights. Shoppers will
know DIM hosiery, but here there is also Playtex and Cacharel brand
name goods including the Playtex Wonderbra and Cross Your Heart
bra.

# EMINENCE

CHESHIRE OAKS OUTLET VILLAGE, KINSEY ROAD, NEAR ELLESMERE
PORT, (JUNCTION 10 OF M53), SOUTH WIRRAL L65 9JJ
☎ (0151) 357 1562. OPEN 10 - 6 MON - SAT, 10 - 4 SUN.

Eminence Paris is not very well known here and some of the designs
for men and women seemed more suited to the Continental style.
Women's ranges include underwear, swimwear, jodphurs, tracksuits,
and T-shirts. Prices range from £2 - £10.

# FAMOUS FOOTWEAR

CHESHIRE OAKS OUTLET VILLAGE, KINSEY ROAD, NEAR ELLESMERE
PORT, JUNCTION 10 OF M53, SOUTH WIRRAL L65 9JJ
☎ (0151) 357 1512. OPEN 10 - 6 MON - SAT, 10 - 4 SUN.

Wide range of brand names including Dolcis, Roland Cartier,
Saxone, Lotus, K Shoes, Barker, Ava, Miss Selfridge, Cable & Co,
Hush Puppies, Van-Dal, Equity, Ecco and Vagabond all at discount
prices.

# FRED PERRY SPORTSWEAR UK LTD

UNIT 24, CHESHIRE OAKS OUTLET VILLAGE, KINSEY ROAD, NEAR
ELLESMERE PORT, JUNCTION 10 OF M53, SOUTH WIRRAL L65 9JJ
☎ (0151) 357 1383. OPEN 10 - 6 MON - SAT, 10 - 4 SUN AND BANK
HOLIDAYS.

Men's and women's ranges of the famous Fred Perry sportswear and
leisure clothing: shorts, tennis tops, tracksuits, T-shirts. All price
labels show the original and the reduced price, which usually amount
to a 30% discount.

# FREEPORT SHOPPING VILLAGE

ANCHORAGE ROAD, FLEETWOOD, LANCASHIRE
☎ (01253) 877377. OPEN 10 - 6 SEVEN DAYS A WEEK.

Up to 40 shops, a marina, and lots of activities for the family. Shops
include: 424 Superstore (club football gear), Farah menswear, Tom
Sayers menswear, Double Two shirts, Lee jeans, Tick Tock childrenswear, Hallmark cards, Toy World, Sports Unlimited, Honey
fashions, Regatta (outdoor clothing), Jane Shilton, Shoe Sellers,
Warners lingerie, Ponden Mill (home furnishings), Edinburgh
Crystal, Equator luggage, Churchill China and Acorns (dried
flowers).

# FRUIT OF THE LOOM

CHESHIRE OAKS OUTLET VILLAGE, KINSEY ROAD, NEAR ELLESMERE
PORT, JUNCTION 10 OF M53, SOUTH WIRRAL L65 9JJ
☎ (0151) 355 6169. OPEN 10 - 6 MON - SAT, 10 - 4 SUN.
Women's, men's and children's casual wear in the form of T-shirts,
sweatshirts, shorts and tracksuits with the distinctive Fruit of the
Loom logo.

# GOLDEN SHUTTLE MILL SHOP

ALBION ROAD, GREENGATES, BRADFORD BD10 9TQ
☎ (01274) 611161. OPEN 9.30 - 5 MON - SAT, MOST BANK HOLIDAYS.
Men's, women's and children's German designer fashion seconds at
discount prices, plus suitcases, sportsbags, luggage, handbags, purses
and holdalls. Blouses from £11.99-£39.99; jackets from £29.99.
Children's dungarees, from £4.99-£12.99; ladies and men's underwear; boxer shorts and knickers, all discounted. Sales twice a year in
July and January.

# HORNSEA FREEPORT SHOPPING VILLAGE

HORNSEA, EAST YORKSHIRE HU18 1UT
☎ (01964) 534211. OPEN 10 - 5 MON - FRI, 10 - 6 SAT, SUN, BANK
HOLIDAYS.
The original British factory shopping village on the east coast of
Yorkshire comes complete with masses of family entertainment
including Butterfly World, adventure playground, vintage cars, water
games, plus about two dozen shops where you can buy brand name
discounted goods. Labels include Daks Simpson, Edinburgh Crystal,
Laura Ashley, Wrangler, Windsmoor, Planet, Genesis, Berkertex,
Aquascutum, Jersey Pearl, Tom Sayers menswear, Tog 24, Sports
Unlimited, Churchill China and Warners.

# I J DEWHIRST

MIDDLE STREET NORTH, DRIFFIELD, EAST YORKSHIRE
☎ (01377) 256209. OPEN 9 - 5.30 MON - THUR, 9 - 6 FRI, 9 - 5 SAT.
5 WELHAM ROAD, MALTON OPEN 9 - 5.30 MON - FRI, 9 - 5 SAT, 11 - 5
SUN.
Wide range of women's, men's and children's clothes including
women's jackets, blouses, skirts and trousers; men's suits, jackets,
shirts, trousers; girl's dresses, blouses, trousers, skirts and jackets and
boy's shirts, trousers, jackets and much much more.

## JAEGER FACTORY SHOP

GOMERSAL MILLS, CLECKHEATON, YORKSHIRE BD19 4LU
☎ (01274) 852303. OPEN 12.30 - 4.30 MON, 9.30 - 4.30 TUE - FRI, 9.30 -
3.30 SAT.
Classic tailoring from Jaeger and Viyella at old-fashioned prices for
women and men. Most of the merchandise is last season's stock and
some seconds, but you may find the odd gem from this season if you
hunt carefully. Some factory shops the whole range of Jaeger clothes,
some just knitwear; yet others sell goods other than those with the
Jaeger label. This shop sells mens and ladies wear and specialises in
knitwear.

## JEFFREY ROGERS

CHESHIRE OAKS OUTLET VILLAGE, KINSEY ROAD, NEAR ELLESMERE
PORT, JUNCTION 10 OF M53, SOUTH WIRRAL L65 9JJ
☎ (0151) 355 6797. OPEN 10 - 6 MON - SAT, 10 - 4 SUN.
Factory outlet with the emphasis on young street style: from sleeveless mini dresses to drawstring waist trousers, T-shirts, sweaters and
skirts.

## JOHN PARTRIDGE COUNTRY STORE

CHESHIRE OAKS OUTLET VILLAGE, KINSEY ROAD, NEAR ELLESMERE
PORT, (JUNTION 10 OF M53), SOUTH WIRRAL L65 9JJ
☎ (0151) 357 3020. OPEN 10 - 6 MON - SAT, 10 - 4 SUN.
Range of country clothes including waxed jackets, country-style
shirts, bodywarmers, gilets and waxed coats for women and men.
Examples of prices include jackets reduced from £162 to £95; shirts
from £42 to £28; waxed coats from £263 to £184; nylon bodywarmers from £54 to £38.

## JUMPERS

BRIDGE MILL, COWAN BRIDGE, CARNFORTH, LANCASHIRE LA6 2HS
☎ (015242) 72726. OPEN 10 - 4 SEVEN DAYS A WEEK IN SUMMER.
A wide range of sweaters for women and men all at discount prices.
There are also outlets at K Village (see North) and Clarks Village (see
South West).

# K SHOES

UNIT 3, CLIFTON ROAD RETAIL PARK, BLACKPOOL, LANCASHIRE
FY4 4RA
☎ (01253) 699380. OPEN 9.30 - 7.30 MON - FRI AND BANK HOLIDAYS, 9
- 6 SAT, 10 - 4 SUN.
9-11 CHAPEL STREET, SOUTHPORT, MERSEYSIDE PR8 1AE
☎ (01704) 531583. OPEN 9 - 5.30 MON - SAT, 11 - 5 SUN (SUMMER, 11 - 4
SUN IN WINTER) 10 - 5 BANK HOLIDAYS.

Clarks International operate a chain of factory shops nationally which
specialise in selling discontinued lines and slight sub-standards for
women, men and children from Clarks, K Shoes and other famous
brands. These shops trade under the name of Crockers, K Shoes
Factory shop or Clarks Factory Shop and while not all are physically
attached to a shoe factory, these shops are treated as factory shops by
the company. Customers can expect to find an extensive range of
quality shoes, sandals, walking boots, slippers, trainers, handbags,
accessories and gifts, while their major outlets also offer luggage,
sports clothing, sports equipment and outdoor clothing. Brands
stocked include Clarks, K Shoes, Springer, CICA, Hi-Tec, Puma,
Mercury, Dr Martens, Nike, LA Gear, Fila, Mizuno, Slazenger,
Weider, Samsonite, Delsey, Antler and Carlton, although not all are
sold in every outlet. Discounts are on average 30% off the normal
high street price for perfect stock.

# KURT GEIGER

CHESHIRE OAKS OUTLET VILLAGE, KINSEY ROAD, NEAR ELLESMERE
PORT, (JUNCTION 10 OF M53), SOUTH WIRRAL FY4 4RA
☎ (0151) 357 1794. OPEN 10 - 6 MON - SAT, 10 - 4 SUN.

Shoe shop for women and men which sells Charles Jourdan, Cheaney,
Barker, Sweeney's, Bruno Magli, and Carvela ranges. Shoes are laid
out by brand name and in sizes, so it's easy to find your way round.
New ranges are arranged separately. Examples of prices include a pair
of Carvela shoes reduced from £49 to £39 and another blue suede
pair from £65 to £35. There is another Kurt Geiger factory shop at
Bicester Village (see Womenswear and Menswear, Wales and West
Midlands).

## KYME MILL SHOP

NAPIER TERRACE, LAISTER DYKE, BRADFORD, YORKSHIRE BD3 8DD
☎ (01274) 669205. OPEN 9.30 - 5 MON - SAT.
Warehouse clearance lines of women's and menswear - trousers, skirts,
underwear in wool, cotton and polyester, blouses from £8.99 - plus
suitcases from £15.99 and travel bags from £11.99. Most of the stock
is seconds, discontinued with some perfects.

## LAMBERT HOWARTH FOOTWEAR

GAGHILLS MILLS, GAGHILLS ROAD, OFF BURNLEY ROAD EAST,
WATERFOOT, ROSSENDALE, LANCASHIRE BB4 9AS
☎ (01706) 215417. OPEN 10.30 - 5 MON - FRI, 9.30 - 3.30 SAT.
A real mixture of seconds from the factory and perfects from other
sources - footwear, clothes, handbags and towels. The seconds in
footwear are from shoes made for major high street chainstores and
all are at discounted prices. These include slippers, walking boots, flat
shoes and sandals for men, women and children. The perfects in
clothes, towels and bags are two-thirds of the high street prices.

## LAURA ASHLEY

HORNSEA FREEPORT SHOPPING VILLAGE, HORNSEA, EAST
YORKSHIRE HU18 1UT
☎ (01964) 536503. OPEN 10 - 5 MON - FRI, 10 - 6 SAT, SUN.
BOUNDARY MILL STORES, BURNLEY ROAD, COLNE, LANCASHIRE
BB8 8LS
☎ (01282) 860166. OPEN 10 - 6 MON - FRI, 10 - 5 SAT AND BANK
HOLIDAYS, 11 - 5 SUN.
At Hornsea, Laura Ashley fashion is on the ground floor and home
furnishings on the first floor. Most of the merchandise is made up of
perfect carry-overs from the high street shops around the country,
though there are also some discontinued lines. Stock reflects the
normal high street variety, though at least one season later and with
less choice in colours and sizes. The shopping village has restaurants,
play centres, a vintage car collection, water games, and plenty for the
family to do and see. At Boundary Mill Stores, Laura Ashley is one
department in this huge high quality clearance warehouse for men
and women's clothes and home furnishings.

## LEVI'S BIG L FACTORY OUTLET

CHESHIRE OAKS OUTLET VILLAGE, KINSEY ROAD, NEAR ELLESMERE
PORT, JUNCTION 10 OF M53, SOUTH WIRRAL L65 9JJ
☎ (0151) 356 8484. OPEN 10 - 6 MON - SAT, 10 - 4 SUN.
Women's and men's Levi jeans, jackets and shirts but no children's, all
at discount prices.

## LIGHTWATER VILLAGE AND FACTORY SHOPPING

NORTH STAINLEY, RIPON, NORTH YORKSHIRE HG4 3HT
☎ (01765) 635321. OPEN 10 - 5 SEVEN DAYS A WEEK. OPENING TIMES
VARY SEASONALLY.
Lightwater valley theme park is the biggest leisure park in the north
of England; now, some of the property has been converted to factory
shop retailing. You can visit the shopping village free, without visiting
the theme park which makes a charge. There are various factory shops
on site selling brand names such as Windsmoor, Planet, James Barry,
Tula, Jane Shilton, Edinburgh Crystal, Hornsea pottery, Accord
Bedlinen. The pottery shop has plenty of ceramics and kitchen
utensils to choose from, while the crystal shop has glasses, decanters,
giftware and bowls. There are two enormous "warehouses" with
masses of fashion for women and men, bedlinen, duvets, shoes,
perfume, cookware, suitcases and cosmetics. There will eventually be
parking for 4,000 cars and 120 coaches, a market square, coffee
shops, food shops, a wine bar, covered garden centre, visitors farm
and trout pond. Lightwater is 3 miles off the the A1.

## LIZ CLAIBORNE

CHESHIRE OAKS OUTLET VILLAGE, KINSEY ROAD, NEAR ELLESMERE
PORT, (JUNCTION 10 OF M53), SOUTH WIRRAL L65 9JJ
☎ (0151) 357 3271. OPEN 10 - 6 MON - SAT, 10 - 4 SUN.
An American designer who is now becoming more well known here,
Liz Claiborne offers middle of the range, mid-priced smart clothes for
work and weddings, parties and the office. Prices do seem to be
heavily discounted: for example, safari jacket, reduced from £115 to
£35 and matching skirt reduced from £50 to £24; woollen waistcoats
from £124 to £69; smart jackets from £75 to £37. There are also rails
of clothes under £5, under £10 and under £15, as well as handbags.
She has a very large outlet here at Cheshire Oaks, as well as a shop at
Clarks Factory Shopping Village (see Womenswear, South West).

## MADE TO LAST LTD

8 THE CRESCENT, HYDE PARK, LEEDS, NORTH YORKSHIRE LS6 IBH
☎ (0113) 2304983. OPEN 10 - 6 WED, FRI, 11 - 5 SAT. MAIL ORDER.

A workers co-operative making boots and shoes for women, men and children, they have regular stock clearances during which shoes which have been tried on by customers and don't look quite as new are reduced in price by between one third and one half. Their children's shoes took first priz0nto second place. Their children's boots normally cost £36.95, strap shoes, £44.50 and classic men's lace-ups, £56. Send for catalogue. All their styles are also available in a high quality vegetarian material.

## NIKE UK LTD

CHESHIRE OAKS OUTLET VILLAGE, KINSEY ROAD, NEAR ELLESMERE PORT, (JUNCTION 10 OF M53), SOUTH WIRRAL L65 9JJ
☎ (0151) 357 1252. OPEN 10 - 6 MON - SAT, 10 - 4 SUN.

Women's, men's and children's trainers, jackets, T-shirts, sports shirts, shorts, sleeveless T-shirts and tracksuits.

## PACO LIFE IN COLOUR

UNIT 25, CHESHIRE OAKS OUTLET VILLAGE, KINSEY ROAD, NEAR ELLESMERE PORT, JUNCION 10 OF M53, SOUTH WIRRAL L65 9JJ
☎ (0151) 357 3722. OPEN 10 - 6 MON - SAT, 10 - 4 SUN.

Colourful cotton T-shirts, sweaters, cardigans, sweatshirts, leggings, gloves, scarves, shorts, canvas bags, for women and children, all at discounts of about 30%. The children's range is stronger in the age group 9-12 years.

## PAUL COSTELLOE FACTORY SHOP

UNIT 15, CHESHIRE OAKS DESIGNER OUTLET VILLAGE, KINSEY ROAD, NEAR ELLESMERE PORT, (JUNCTION 10 OF M53), SOUTH WIRRAL L65 9JJ
☎ (0151) 357 1681. OPEN 10 - 6 MON - SAT, 10 - 4 SUN.

A wide range of 1,500 garments, consisting of special purchases, seconds, samples and past season stocks at substantial savings on original prices. The comprehensive selection encompasses business and special occasion designs to a more casual range for relaxed weekend wear. There is another factory shop in Dungannon, Northern Ireland.

# PRINCIPLES

CHESHIRE OAKS OUTLET VILLAGE, KINSEY ROAD, NEAR ELLESMERE
PORT, JUNCTION 10 OF M53, SOUTH WIRRAL L65 9JJ
☎ (0151) 357 1033. OPEN 10 - 6 MON - SAT, 10 - 4 SUN.
Wide range of Principles clothes for women, as well as a small range
of Principles for Men items at discounts up to 50%.

# THE FACTORY SHOP

LAWKHOLME LANE, KEIGHLEY, WEST YORKSHIRE BD21 3HW
☎ (01535) 611703. OPEN 9.30 - 5 MON - SAT, 10 - 4 BANK HOLIDAYS.
LANCASTER LEISURE PARK, WYRESDALE ROAD,
LANCASTER, LANCASHIRE LA1 3LA
☎ (01524) 846079. OPEN 10 - 5 MON - SAT, 11 - 5 SUN AND BANK
HOLIDAYS.
5 NORTH STREET, RIPON, NORTH YORKSHIRE HG4 1JY
☎ (01765) 601156. OPEN 9 - 5 MON - SAT, 11 - 4 BANK HOLIDAYS.
HORNSEA FREEPORT SHOPPING VILLAGE, HORNSEA, EAST YORK-
SHIRE
☎ (01964) 534211. OPEN 10 - 5 MON - FRI, 10 - 6 SAT, SUN.
COMMERCIAL STREET, MORLEY, WEST YORKSHIRE LS1 6EX
☎ (0113) 2381240. OPEN 9.30 - 5 MON - FRI, 9 - 5 SAT.
Wide range on sale includes women's, men's and children's clothing
and footwear; household textiles, toiletries, hardware, luggage,
lighting and bedding, most of which are chainstore and high street
brands at discounts of approximately 30%-50%. There are weekly
deliveries and brands include all the major stars: Coloroll, Wrangler
and Dartington to name just three (the Morley branch does not stock
Wrangler). Lines are continually changing and few factory shops offer
such a variety under one roof. The Hornsea branch stock special buys
bought specifically for the Freeport outlet.

# THE SCOTCH HOUSE

CHESHIRE OAKS OUTLET VILLAGE, KINSEY ROAD, NEAR ELLESMERE
PORT, (JUNTION 10 OF M53), SOUTH WIRRAL L65 9JJ
☎ (0151) 357 3203. OPEN 10 - 6 MON - SAT, 10 - 4 SUN.
This outlet sells Pringle and Lyle & Scott for women and men at
discount prices. For example, Lyle & Scott T-shirts, £12.95; definitive tartan skirts, £59.50 to £39.50; cashmere gloves from £15 to
£9.50. There are also coats, jackets, bags, waistcoats.

## THE SHOE FACTORY SHOP

21 WELLOWGATE, GRIMSBY, SOUTH HUMBERSIDE DN32 ORA
☎ (01472) 342415. OPEN 9 - 5 MON - SAT, 9 - 7 THUR.
6/7 OSLO ROAD, SUTTON FIELDS, HULL
☎ (01482) 839292. OPEN 9 - 5 MON - SAT, UNTIL 7 ON THUR AND FRI.
Women's, men's and children's shoes and accessories such as handbags
which are bought in from other manufacturers including Spanish,
Portuguese and Italian companies. All are unbranded. The range
covers from mocassins to dressy shoes. Ladies shoes which would cost
£35 retail are £29.

## THE SHOE SHED

UNITS 10 AND 11, WHEATLEY CENTRE, WHEATLEY HALL ROAD,
DONCASTER, YORKSHIRE
☎ (01302) 341435. OPEN 10 - 6 MON - THUR, 10 - 7 FRI, 9.30 - 5.30 SAT,
11 - 5 SUN.
Large factory shop selling a vast range of all types of women's, men's
and children's shoes, all of which are perfects, at up to 30% below
normal high street prices. Ladies sandals cost from £5; ladies shoes
from £7.50. Men's shoes from £10; sports shoes from £10.

## TIMBERLAND

CHESHIRE OAKS OUTLET VILLAGE, KINSEY ROAD, NEAR ELLESMERE
PORT, JUNCTION 10 OF M53, SOUTH WIRRAL L65 9JJ
☎ (0151) 357 1359. OPEN 10 - 6 MON - SAT, 10 - 4 SUN.
Footwear, clothing and outdoor gear from the well-known
Timberland range. Coats from £50 upwards; jackets from £100; jeans
from £35, shirts from £42. Most of the stock is last season's or discontinued lines, but not seconds. There is no current stock.

## VIYELLA LADIES RETAIL

CHESHIRE OAKS OUTLET VILLAGE, KINSEY ROAD, NEAR ELLESMERE
PORT, (JUNCTION 10 OF M53), SOUTH WIRRAL L65 9JJ
☎ (0151) 357 2627. OPEN 10 - 6 MON - SAT, 10 - 4 SUN.
Wide range of Viyella ladieswear at discount prices from jackets and
blouses to dresses, waistcoats, sweaters and hats. Price reductions
include jackets from £159 to £99; satin blouses from £139 to £69 and
sweaters from £59 to £39.

## WINDSMOOR

HORNSEA FREEPORT SHOPPING VILLAGE, HORNSEA, YORKSHIRE
HU18 1UT
☎ (01964) 536517. OPEN 10 - 5 SEVEN DAYS A WEEK.

The Windsmoor outlet looks just like a shop and sells previous
season's stock as well as any returned merchandise and overmakes
from the Windsmoor, Berkertex evening wear, Genesis and Planet
ranges at discounts of about one third. The Shopping Village has
plenty to entertain the family with playgrounds, an indoor play
centre, restaurants, a vintage car collection and butterfly world.

## WRANGLER

HORNSEA FREEPORT SHOPPING VILLAGE, HORNSEA, YORKSHIRE
HU18 1UT
☎ (01964) 532979. OPEN 10 - 5 MON - SUN.

Previous season's stock as well as returned merchandise and overmakes. Ladies jeans from £18.99, children's from £12.99. The
Shopping Village has plenty to entertain the family with playgrounds,
an indoor play centre, restaurants, a vintage car collection and butterfly world.


# *Dress Agencies*

## ALADDIN'S CAVE

19 QUEEN'S ARCADE, LEEDS LS1 6LF
☎ (0113) 2457903. OPEN 10 - 5 MON - SAT.

Two-storey shop with a dress agency downstairs, and an array of
antique jewellery, silver, and teddy bears on the ground floor. The
nearly-new department sells everything from Marks & Spencer to
designers such as Dolce e Gabbana.

## AS NEW FASHIONS

1 EMSCOTE GROVE, HAUGH SHAW ROAD, HALIFAX, YORKSHIRE
☎ (01422) 365379. OPEN 9.30 - 5 MON - SAT.

Ladies, men's and children's nearly-new clothes all available. Mainly
blouses and skirts from high street stores such as Marks & Spencer,
with 2 designer rails with names such as Betty Barclay, Frank Usher

and Bellino. There is usually a selection of seasonal and sports wear, including ski clothes. Children's school uniforms are stocked, as are accessories. There are no ballgowns and a limited number of cocktail dresses.

## ELITE DRESS AGENCY

1 MARKET STREET, ALTRINCHAM, CHESHIRE
☎ (0161) 928 5424. OPEN 10 -5 MON - SAT.
Mainly ladies wear which is less than one year old, although there are both men's and childrenswear departments. Wide range of clothing including some sports wear. Twice yearly sales at the end of June and December. Labels range from Marks & Spencer to Jaeger and Paul Costelloe. A dress hire section stocks a wide selection of brand new dresses, updated twice a year.

## LABELS

1 MARKET ROW, BARKERS ARCADE, NORTHALLERTON, YORKSHIRE DL7 8LN.
☎ (01609) 779483. OPEN 9.30 - 5 MON - SAT.
Designer nearly-new wear from Pangi, Droopy & Browns, Jaeger, Escada and Windsmoor to Cache D'Or at about half the initial shop price. Two-piece suits, wedding outfits, holiday wear, blazers, evening wear cocktail dresses. Hats to buy and to hire.

## OPPORTUNITIES

13 PROVIDENCE STREET, WAKEFIELD, WEST YORKSHIRE. WF1 3BG
☎ (01924) 290310 OPEN 10 - 5.30 MON - FRI, 9 - 5.30 SAT, UNTIL 7 THUR.
Two floors of nearly-new outfits, from wedding outfits, ball gowns and evening wear to day wear and children's clothes. Occasional bargain baskets. New and secondhand jewellery. Anything from Louis Feraud and Karl Lagerfeld to Marks & Spencer. Easy parking, easy sofas, and coffee and tea served.

## SOPHIE'S CHOICE

19B NORTH LANE, HEADINGLEY, LEEDS, YORKSHIRE
☎ (0113) 2743913. OPEN 10 - 5 MON - SAT, CLOSED WED.
Nearly-new ladies and children's clothes which caters for middle to upmarket labels. Navy blue blazers, £35, originally £200; designer shirts, £14.50, usually £80.

## SPECIAL EVENT

44 LOWER BRIDGE STREET, CHESTER, CHESHIRE
☎ (01244) 340757. OPEN 9.30 - 5 MON - SAT.
Ball gown and cocktail wear, with a large selection of designer dresses from sizes 8-24. Owned by the proprietor of the dress agency called Something Different which specialises in mother of the bride outfits from Armani and Laurel to Mondi and Jaeger.

## THE ELITE DRESS AGENCY

35 KINGS STREET WEST, MANCHESTER M3 2PW
☎ (0161) 8323670. OPEN 10 - 5 MON - SAT.
Three floors of good quality men's, women's and children's clothing, many with a Continental flavour. Among womenswear can be found labels such as Moschino as well as Escada, Betty Barclay to Mondi, with lots of chainstore makes, too. There are lots of hats from which to choose, from £8. There is also a selection of unwanted gifts for sale.

## THE FASHION AGENCY

FIRST FLOOR, 21 QUEEN STREET, BLACKPOOL FY1 1LN
☎ (0253) 28679. OPEN 10.30 - 4.30 MON - SAT.
A spacious showroom above a fashion shop called Femme Fatale. In business for more than 20 years, it offers top end of the market nearly-new outfits and continental separates. A large and constantly changing selection of labels such as YSL, Escada, Chanel and Moschino make this a very popular shop. It caters for all ages and from casual to cocktail wear. It also sells shoes, handbags and jewellery; there is a permanent half-price sale rail.

# Hire Shops

## FOUR SEASONS

154 COLLEGE ROAD, CROSBY, LIVERPOOL L23 3DP
☎ (0151) 924 2863. OPEN 9.30 - 5.30 MON - SAT, CLOSED 1 ON WED, AND 1-2.30 DAILY IN WINTER.
Specialists in hiring and selling hats, Four Seasons has been in business for years and has more than 300 hats from which to choose.

The main business is in hiring hats for all occasions - customers can bring their outfit to find the perfect match, and trimmings can be added from as little as £1.50. Hire fees start from £8 up to £15 for a period of 5 or 6 days. There are also accessories, particularly jewellery, scarves, gloves and handbags. Ex-hire hats are sold off at reasonable prices.

## JUST ONE NIGHT

11 BROOK ST, KNUTSFORD, CHESHIRE WA16 8EB
☎ (01565) 633059. OPEN 10 - 8 TUE & THUR, 10 - 6 MON, FRI, 10 - 4 SAT, 10 - 3 WED. BY APPOINTMENT ONLY
More than 350 designer dresses and gowns to choose from in sizes 8-22, many of which are exclusive to Just One Night. Also an extensive collection of jewellery, evening bags and gloves to hire. Minor alterations can be undertaken for a small extra charge. There are also a few outfits for sale from £70. Hire costs: £85. Shop has its own car park.

## LABELS

1 MARKET ROW, BARKERS ARCADE, NORTHALLERTON, YORKSHIRE DL7 8LN.
☎ (01609) 779483. OPEN 9.30 - 5 MON - SAT.
Two-storey dress agency which also hire out up to 50 hats from £10.

## ONE-NIGHT AFFAIR

1 MARKET STREET, ALTRINCHAM, CHESHIRE WA14 1QE
☎ (0161) 928 8477. OPEN 10 - 5 MON - SAT.
Choose from more than 350 outfits, including cocktail wear, ball gowns, party gear and accessories to hire or to buy. Stock changes frequently. Hire costs £50-£85. No appointment necessary.

## PUMPKIN DRESS HIRE

22 THE FIRST BALCONY, 22 BARTON ARCADE, DEANSGATE, MANCHESTER M3 2BB
☎ (0161) 831 7610. OPEN 10 - 5 MON - SAT, UNTIL 7 ON THUR.
There are more than 2,000 outfits available at any one time at this shop which is well known to Granada TV, whose stars often make use of its hire service. The shop offers a choice of more than 450 garments in evening wear, cocktail wear, ballgowns, wedding outfits and men's

dinner suits. Costs range from £40 for up to one week to amaximum of £95. There is a discount for students of 15% as well as a discount for nurses. Sizes ranges from 8-26 and there are also hats, jewellery and handbags for hire.

## Secondhand and Vintage Clothes

### AFFLECK'S PALACE

52 CHURCH STREET, MANCHESTER M41 PW
☎ (0161) 834 2039. OPEN 10 - 5.15 MON - FRI, 9.30 - 5.30 SAT.
Indoor fashion market specialising in street fashion and alternative fashion. Seventies' fashion including platform shoes. Also jewellery, rubber clothes and hair extensions. Fifties and Sixties nostalgia, new designer clothes and clothes from the Twenties to the present day. Two cafes and two hairdressers, offering hair beading, on site.

### BLOOMERS

CHELTENHAM CRESCENT, HARROGATE, NORTH YORKSHIRE
HG1 1DH
☎ (01423) 569389. OPEN 11 - 5 MON - SAT, CLOSED WED.
Vintage clothes up to the Forties, with Twenties underwear, beaded dresses, accessories and shawls. Also quilts, sheets, pillowcases, fans, lace, tablecloths, hats, men's hats, waistcoats and shirts. For men, there are only hats and waistcoats; for children, christening gowns. Man's bowler hat, from £28 to £38; beaded dresses, £300. Discounts for cash purchases.

### PRIESTLEY'S

1 NORMAN COURT, 11 GRAPE LANE, YORK, NORTH YORKSHIRE
YO1 2HU
☎ (01904) 623114. OPEN 10 - 5 MON - SAT.
1930s-1970s period clothing, particularly tailored clothing, men's and women's tailored jackets, tweeds, blazers, dresses and waistcoats, hats and scarves.

## QUIGGINS CENTRE

12-16 SCHOOL LANE, LIVERPOOL L1 3BT
☎ (0151) 709 2462. OPEN 10 - 6 MON - SAT.

There are thirty different shops at the Quiggins Centre, the second biggest market in Liverpool, selling a variety of goods including theatrical and period costumes, secondhand clothes, furniture, bric-a-brac, jewellery, antiques and a music shop.

## REVIVAL

6 WARNER STREET, ACCRINGTON, LANCASHIRE BB5 1HN
☎ (01254) 382316. OPEN 10.30 - 5 MON - SAT, CLOSED WED.

Vintage clothes from the beginning of the century to the Seventies including suede and leather waistcoats, cheesecloth tops, Biba trousers. Long suede waistcoat, from £6 to £9.50; short one, under £10; Levi jeans, from £9 up to £18; Levi jackets, £10-£35; cocktail dresses from £14-£28; ballgowns from £20-£75; Fifties-style shirts, £6-£12; dinner suits, £24.

# NORTH AND SCOTLAND

*Permanent Discount Outlets*

## CORNICHE PERMANENT SALE SHOP

27 ST MARY'S STREET, EDINBURGH EH1 1DT
☎ (0131) 557 8333. OPEN 10.30 - 5.30 MON - SAT.

Tiny shop selling designer names at discount prices. Merchandise consists of clearance stock from its main retail outlet, as well as special outfits bought in. Designers on sale at discounts of between 40-90% include Christian Lacroix, Montana, Thierry Mugler, Rifat Ozbek, Ghost and Gaultier. On sale in the past have been Gaultier belts, £29, usually £49; leather jacket, £195, usually £295; Gaultier jacket, £75, usually £165; Claude Montana jacket and skirt, £250, usually £541; Vivienne Westwood stripe suit, £295, usually £499. There are also a few hats and some shoes from Dolce e Gabbana. Corniche also has a shop in Jeffrey's Street, which does not sell discounted merchandise.

# INTERNATIONALE

43-51 ARGYLL STREET, GLASGOW G2 8AH
☎ (041) 221 7242. OPEN 9.30 - 6 MON - WED, 9 - 8 THUR, 9 - 6 FRI &
SAT, 12 - 5 SUN.
127 PRINCES STREET, EDINBURGH EH2 4AD
☎ (031) 225 5534. OPEN 9.30 - 6 MON - WED, 9 - 7 THUR, 9 - 6 FRI &
SAT.

Jam packed with fashion bargains from clothes and shoes to belts, bags, jewellery and scarves. Designers are young and top end of the high street, including Jeffrey Rogers, Pinstripe, Crazy, Whatts & Heavy and French Connection.

# MATALAN

16 GOODWOOD SQUARE, TEESSIDE RETAIL PARK, THORNABY,
STOCKTON-ON-TEES TS17 7BW
☎ (01642) 633204. OPEN 10 - 8 MON - FRI, 9.30 - 5.30 SAT, 10 - 6 SUN.
SEAFIELD WAY, SEAFIELD ROAD, EDINBURGH EH15 1TB
☎ (0131) 657 5045. OPEN 10 - 8 MON - FRI, 9.30 - 5.30 SAT, 10 - 6 SUN.
WALNEY ROAD, BARROW LA14 5UU
☎ (01229) 430899. OPEN 10 - 8 MON - FRI, 9.30 - 5.30 SAT, 10 - 6 SUN.
UNIT 2B, METRO CENTRE, RETAIL PARK, GATESHEAD, NEWCASTLE
UPON TYNE NE11 4YD
☎ (0191) 460 0423. OPEN 10 - 7.45 MON - FRI, 10 - 6 SAT, SUN.
UNIT 5, CALEDONIAN CENTRE, NEW ASHTREE STREET, WISHAW
ML2 7UR
☎ (01698) 357075. OPEN 10 - 8 MON - FRI, 9.30 - 5.30 SAT, 10 - 6 SUN.
PLOT 12, DERWENT HOUSE, SOLWAY ROAD, WORKINGTON CA14 3YA
☎ (01900) 870966. OPEN 10 - 8 MON - FRI, 9.30 - 5.30 SAT, 10 - 6 SUN.
UNIT 2, KINGSTONE RETAIL PARK, HULL HU2 2TX
☎ (01482) 586184. OPEN 10 - 8 MON - FRI, 9 - 6 SAT, 11 - 5 SUN.
UNIT 7, GLENCAIRNE RETAIL PARK, KILMARNOCK KA1 4AY
☎ (01563) 573892. OPEN 10 - 8 MON - FRI, 9.30 - 5.30 SAT, 10 - 6 SUN.
UNIT 1 HEWITTS CIRCUS, CLEETHORPES DN35 9QH
☎ (01472) 200255. OPEN 10 - 8 MON - FRI, 9 - 6 SAT, 11 - 5 SUN.

As the UK's first National Discount Club, Matalan has the buying power to guarantee its members up to 60% discounts on a huge range of brand name clothing, household goods, luggage and toiletries for all the family. Top quality merchandise, current season, no seconds, is offered to its members at exclusive, permanently discounted prices seven days a week. Matalan operates strictly on a membership basis, one of the key factors for its success in offering 20%-60% savings off recommended retail prices. Membership cards are issued through companies, organisations and associations in the vicinity of the stores, and are available to their employees/members. They are valid at any of the 50 Matalan stores in the UK. To find out if your organisation is registered, phone the Matalan hotline on 01772 629447.

## NEXT TO NOTHING

83-93 SAUCHIEHALL STREET, GLASGOW GU 3DD
☎ (0141) 332 4056. OPEN 9 - 5.30 MON - WED, 10 - 7 THUR, 9.30 - 6 FRI, 9 - 6 SAT.

Sells perfect surplus stock from Next stores and the Next Directory catalogue - from belts, jewellery and underwear to day and evening wear - at discounts of 50% or more. The ranges are usually last season's and overruns but there is the odd current item if you look carefully. Stock consists of women's, men's and children's clothing, with some homeware and shoes, depending on the branch. Stock is replenished twice a week and there is plenty of it.

## Q MARK

56 BELFORD ROAD, EDINBURGH, SCOTLAND EH4 3BR
☎ (0131) 225 6861. OPEN 9 - 5.30 MON - SAT, 12 - 5 SUN, UNTIL 7 THUR.
BRAIDHOLM ROAD, GIFFNOCK, GLASGOW, SCOTLAND G46 6EB
☎ (0141) 633 3636. OPEN 9 - 6 MON - SAT, UNTIL 8 ON THUR, 12 - 5 SUN.

Scotland's biggest discount clothing warehouse for women, men and children offers top quality fashions at up to 50% off normal high street prices. All garments are good quality seconds, overmakes or cancelled contracts but with their labels cut out. Regular stock deliveries ensure a constant selection of new styles - often recognised in famous chain stores, but always at ridiculously low prices. Q Mark operate a once-a-year membership fee of £5. All prices are subject to VAT and charged at point of sale.

## SCENT TO YOU

UPPER DECK, ST NICHOLAS CENTRE, ABERDEEN, SCOTLAND
☎ (01224) 625340. OPEN 10 - 5 MON - SAT, UNTIL 7 ON THUR. MAIL ORDER: 01494 712855

Discounted perfume and accessories including body lotions and gels. The company, which has three branches (see under Womenswear, South East) and a mail order service buys in bulk and sells more cheaply, relying on a high turnover for profit. Discounts range from 5% to 60%, with greater savings during their twice-yearly sales. Most of the leading brand names are stocked including Christian Lacroix, Armani, Givenchy, Anais Anais from Cacherel, Charlie from Revlon, Coco Chanel, Christian Dior, Elizabeth Taylor, Blue Grass from Elizabeth Arden, Aramis, Lagerfeld. Occasionally, they also buy in a limited range of skincare lines, gift wrappings and cards.

## STATESIDE WHOLESALE CLUB

☎ (01670) 789110. MAIL ORDER ONLY.

Contrary to what it might seem, Stateside Wholesale Club is not an American company. Based in Northumberland, it is a catalogue company along the lines of Betterware - but selling clothes. A trio of catalogues - featuring women's, men's and children's clothes - are left at your home. You can then order the various outfits through the agent who comes to collect the catalogue. The real bargains come if you are an agent, as you can charge whatever price you like for the goods in the catalogue as long as you pay the company a fixed amount for each outfit. The catalogue states the normal retail price for each outfit, but the agent's list states the amount the company wants from the agent for that item. This amount is often half the catalogue price. The company suggests that you sell the outfit at its fixed price plus 20% but if you can get more for it, that's fine and you keep the extra margin. It claims that all the merchandise is perfect, big brand names on sale currently in shops and other catalogues. You have to purchase something in order to get on the mailing list, but once you start receiving catalogues, you can either do a Caura/Cabouchon and sell to friends or use it to buy clothes for yourself and your family at low prices. The women's clothes are of the leggings and T-shirt variety. Brand names include Adidas, LA Gear and Pierre Cardin, but they are mostly in the footwear area.

# THE UNCOLLECTED DRY CLEANING COMPANY

45 GARDEN WALK, METRO CENTRE, GATESHEAD, TYNE & WEAR
☎ (0191) 460 3195. OPEN 10 - 8 MON - SAT.
7 OLD ELDON SQUARE, NEWCASTLE UPON TYNE, NORTHUMBER-
LAND NE1 7JG
☎ (0191) 261 0995. OPEN 9.30 - 5.30 MON - SAT.

It's amazing what people forget they took in for dry cleaning. After three months, most of the big chains clear their uncollected merchandise, which is how they come to be on sale in these two outlets for seemingly amazing prices. These are Aladdin's caves of forgotten clothes from Burberry raincoats to Valentino suits, as well as many more down to earth items. Everything sells for rock-bottom prices; for example, that Burberry raincoat cost £10. Previous bargains in the designer section include a Karl Lagerfeld two-piece evening outfit, size 14, £39 and an Emanuel two-piece suit, £29. Of the two branches, the Metro Centre stocks more of the designer labels, while the Newcastle branch sells a lot of high street names such as Marks & Spencer, Principles and Next, as well an enjoying a uniform section which has been known to stock a Virgin Airways pilot's uniform as well as bus conductors' jackets.

# TK MAXX

LOWER GROUND FLOOR, MONUMENT MALL, NORTHUMBERLAND
STREET, NEWCASTLE-UPON-TYNE, TYNE & WEAR.
☎ (0191) 232 2323. OPEN 9 - 5.30 MON - FRI, UNTIL 8 ON THURS,
9 - 6 SAT.

Based on an American concept, TK Maxx is the first British retailer to practise "off-price" retailing. This means a centrally located store which offers famous label goods with up to 60% savings off recommended retail prices. TK Maxx has fashion for the whole family - women's, men's and childrenswear - accessories, shoes, gifts, kitchenware and home goods. Everything in the store is branded with a choice of well-known high street names to designer labels, and while a small percentage mightly be clearly marked past season, the great majority of items in store are current season, current stock and still with phenomenal savings. There is a huge choice with 50,000 pieces in store with 5,000 new items arriving a week, so it's worth keeping abreast of the lastest deliveries as turnaround is very fast. One of the ways in which TK Maxx is able to offer such low prices is by running a very low-cost operation, so the stores are simple and unfussy with wide aisles, shopping trolleys and baskets, and a spacious, functional feel to them. Service is not compromised, however: there are individual changing rooms, ramps for buggies and wheelchairs, plenty of staff on the shop floor and all the branches accept all major credit and debit cards.

## WORKWEAR COSALT INTERNATIONAL LTD

10 WEST HARBOUR ROAD, GRANTON, EDINBURGH EH5 1PJ
☎ (0131) 552 0011. OPEN 8 - 5 MON - FRI.

Offers a wide selection of leisure and outdoor clothes from Doc Martens and Caterpillar boots to padded jackets and denim shirts, dungarees and donkey jackets. Donkey jackets cost as little as £18, dungarees less than £13, Doc Martens, £35, although VAT has to be added to prices. There are catalogues available for you to order from if what you want isn't in stock.

## *Factory Shops*

## ANTARTEX VILLAGE VISITOR CENTRE

LOMDON INDUSTRIAL ESTATE, ALEXANDRIA,
DUMBARTONSHIRE G83 OTP
☎ (01389) 752393. OPEN 10 - 6 MON - SUN.

Edinburgh woolen mill with a sheepskin factory and craft workshops where you can watch sheepskin jackets being made, pottery and jewellery and glass engraving taking place. Sheepskin jackets costs £199-£375 and there is often a sale in the shop with plenty of baragins.

## BAIRDWEAR RACKE

6-8 COLVILLES PLACE, EAST KILBRIDE, GLASGOW, SCOTLAND
G75 OQS
☎ (01355) 236441. OPEN 10 - 4 MON - THUR, 10 - 12 FRI.
24 ROSYTH ROAD, POLMADIE, GLASGOW
☎ (0141) 429 6611. OPEN 11 - 4 MON - THUR, 9.30 - 12.30 FRI, CLOSED
2.30 - 3.
INCHINNEN INDUSTRIAL ESTATE, ABBOTSBURN, RENFREWSHIRE
☎ (0141) 812 6388. OPEN 9.30 - 4.30 MON - WED, 9.30 - 2.15 THUR, 9.30 -
12.30 FRI.

Manufacturers for a well-known high street chainstore for more than
20 years, Bairdwear has a wide selection of seconds and overmakes in
its factory shops. The East Kilbride shop makes men's shirts and sells
them as well as women's and children's clothes, with some babywear,
as well as towels, sheets and duvets covers. The Abbotsburn shop sells
mainly womenswear with some menswear and lots of babywear. The
Polmadie shop sells women's and children's clothes, some men's, and
household linen and towels, but no duvets.

## BALMOREL MILL

16 CHURCH LANE, GARSTON, AYRSHIRE, SCOTLAND
☎ (01563) 820213. OPEN 9 - 5 MON - SAT, 11 - 4.30 SUN.

Sells cashmere and lambswool knitwear, embroided knitwear and
sportswear, some of which is brand name and some own label, but all
sold at factory direct prices. The emphasis is on sports and
leisurewear. A popular range for women are Alice Collins blouses.
Examples of prices include Farah men's trousers, £23.95, cotton
sweatshirts, £8.50, sweaters, £3.95.

## BEE LINE

NO 6, DARLIETH ROAD, LOMOND INDUSTRIAL ESTATE, ALEXAN-
DRIA, DUNBARTON, SCOTLAND
☎ (01389) 756161. OPEN 10 - 5 TUE - SAT, 12 - 4 SUN.

All major chainstore overmakes for women and children. Stock
depends on the time of year but includes shorts, T-shirts, jogging
pants, dresses, skirts and sweaters, smart separates, some underwear,
all sold at 30% less than normal retail prices. Stock is current and last
season's.

# BELINDA ROBERTSON CASHMERE

22 PALMERSTON PLACE, EDINBURGH EH12 5AL
☎ (0131) 225 1057. OPEN 9 - 5.30 MON - FRI, 10 - 4 SAT, OR BY APPOINT-
MENT.
UNIT 17, LADYLAW CENTRE, HAWICK TD9 7DS
☎ (01450) 377648. OPEN 9 - 4.30 MON - FRI.
Designer and classic knitwear in 100% cashmere for women and
men, as made for leading stores and couture houses worldwide.
Belinda Robertson, who has an international reputation for designing
classics with a twist, and in January, 1993, won the NatWest Export
Award, has a showroom in Edinburgh and a factory shop in Hawick
which offer ends of ranges, samples and over-runs all sold at discount
prices, usually between 25-50% off retail prices. All garments are
designed and manufactured in Scotland. Accessories include capes,
scarves and gloves. London showroom also hosts sample sales twice a
year.

# BIG L

KINGSGATE RETAIL PARK, EAST KILBRIDE, SCOTLAND G74 4UN
☎ (01355) 241413. OPEN 10 - 8 MON - FRI, 9 - 6 SAT, 10 - 5 SUN.
This factory outlet is devoted to selling seconds and ends of lines of
Levi's merchandise, and is well worth a visit. All the clothes, which
includes the full range of shirts, sweatshirts, jackets, jeans, and cords,
are top quality although there may be slight flaws, but please note that
all the tabs are cutt off every item before it gets into the shop. There
is a Fruit of the Loom factory next door, making double the reason
for a visit.

# BURBERRY

KITTY BREWSTER INDUSTRIAL ESTATE, BLYTHE, NORTHUMBER-
LAND
☎ (01670) 352524. OPEN 10 - 3.30 MON - THUR, 10 - 3 FRI, 9.30 - 12.30
SAT.
This Burberry factory shop sells seconds and overmakes of the famous
name raincoats and duffle coats as well as accessories such as the distinctive umbrellas, scarves and handbags. It also sells childrens duffle
coats, knitwear and shirts, as well as some of the Burberry range of
food: jams, biscuits, tea, coffee and chocolate. All carry the Burberry
label and are about one third of the normal retail price.

## CHARLES CLINKARD

JACKSONS LANDING, HARTLEPOOL FACTORY OUTLET SHOPPING
MALL, HARTLEPOOL MARINA, HARTLEPOOL, CLEVELAND TS24 OXN
☎ (01429) 866939. OPEN 10 - 6 MON - FRI, 11 - 5 SUN AND BANK
HOLIDAYS.

Indoor factory shopping centre with twenty-four outlets selling brand
name items including footwear for the family at discounts of between
20% and 30%. Labels include Loake, Camel, Bally, Church's, Ecco,
Gabor, Rohde, Van-Dal, Kickers, Clarks, Dr Martens, K Shoes, Lotus
and Renata plus handbags by Jane Shilton. Men's loafers, £29.99
reduced from £49.99; children's shoes, £9.99, reduced from £16.99;
Elefanten children's shoes, £16.99 reduced from £32.99. Hartlepool
Marina hosts a recreated historic quay and harbours HMS
Trincomalee, the oldest British warship still afloat, and is also the site
of the new Hartlepool Museum with its interactive fighting ships
section and a replica seventeenth century children's play area. There is
free parking adjacent to the centre, a coffee shop, restaurant overlooking the Marina, and baby changing and disabled facilities.

## CLAREMONT GARMENTS

GREENFIELDS ESTATE, WEST AUCKLAND, COUNTY DURHAM
☎ (01388) 661703. OPEN 10 - 4.30 MON - FRI, 10 - 4 SAT.
Manufacturers for Marks & Spencers, this factory shop sells mostly
women's clothes, leisurewear and underwear; no nightwear or
children's clothes. There is also a small selection of men's clothes, but
this may be increasing in the future.

## CLARIDGE MILLS LTD SHOP

RIVERSIDE, NR RIVERSIDE INDUSTRIAL ESTATE, SELKIRK (BETWEEN
PEEBLES AND GALASHIELS), SCOTLAND TD7 5DU
☎ (01750) 20300. OPEN 9 - 4.45 MON - FRI.
Manufactures fashion fabric for some of the top international designers including Ralph Lauren, Donna Karan, Gucci, Valentino, Chanel,
Dior, Perry Ellis, Armani and Worth. The tiny mill shop stocks not
only the fabric but also overmakes of some of the items made from
the material at factory prices. These include capes, blanket jackets and
waistcoats and rugs and carpets in luxury silks and cashmere.

## CROCKERS

UNIT 26, THE FORGE SHOPPING CENTRE, PARKHEAD, GLASGOW, SCOTLAND G31 4EB
☎ (0141) 556 5290. OPEN 9 - 5.30 MON - SAT, 12 - 4.30 SUN AND BANK HOLIDAYS.
Clarks International operate a chain of factory shops nationally which specialise in selling discontinued lines and slight sub-standards for women, men and children from Clarks, K Shoes and other famous brands. These shops trade under the name of Crockers, K Shoes Factory shop or Clarks Factory Shop and while not all are physically attached to a shoe factory, these shops are treated as factory shops by the company. Customers can expect to find an extensive range of quality shoes, sandals, walking boots, slippers, trainers, handbags, accessories and gifts, while their major outlets also offer luggage, sports clothing, sports equipment and outdoor clothing. Brands stocked include Clarks, K Shoes, Springer, CICA, Hi-Tec, Puma, Mercury, Dr Martens, Nike, LA Gear, Fila, Mizuno, Slazenger, Weider, Samsonite, Delsey, Antler and Carlton, although not all are sold in every outlet. Discounts are on average 30% off the normal high street price for perfect stock.

## DANNIMAC LTD

EAST TRADING ESTATE, SOUTHBANK ROAD, CARGO FLEET, MIDDLESBROUGH, CLEVELAND TS3 8BN
☎ (01642) 247794. OPEN 9 - 11 ONE DAY A MONTH ONLY. PHONE FOR DETAILS.
Ladies and mens famous-name raincoats, jackets, anoraks, trenchcoats, and macs, as well as, occasionally, waxed and leather jackets at factory shop prices. Jackets and coats range from £35 to £80. Most merchandise is either slight seconds or discontinued lines; there is some current stock, but most is previous seasons.

## DEWHIRST FACTORY SHOP

MILL HILL, NORTH WEST INDUSTRIAL ESTATE, PETERLEE, COUNTY DURHAM SR8 5AA
☎ (0191) 586 4525. OPEN 9 - 5.30 MON - WED, 9 - 7 THUR, 9 - 6 FRI, 9 - 5 SAT, 11 - 5 SUN.
PENNYWELL INDUSTRIAL ESTATE, PENNYWELL, SUNDERLAND
☎ (0191) 534 7928. OPEN 9 - 5.30 MON - FRI, 9 - 5 SAT, 11 - 5 SUN.

AMSTERDAM ROAD, SUTTON FIELDS INDUSTRIAL ESTATE, HULL
☎ (01482) 820166. OPEN 9 - 5.30 MON - WED, 9 - 7.30 THUR,
9 - 6 FRI, 9 - 5 SAT, 11 - 5 SUN.
WEST COATHAM LANE, DORMANSTOWN INDUSTRIAL ESTATE, DOR-
MANSTOWN, REDCAR
☎ (01642) 474210. OPEN 9 - 5.30 MON - FRI, 9 - 5 SAT, 10.30 - 4.30 SUN.
NEWBIGGIN ROAD, NORTH SEATON INDUSTRIAL ESTATE, ASHING-
TON
☎ (01670) 813493. OPEN 9 - 5.30 MON - FRI, 9 - 5 SAT, 10.30 - 4.30 SUN.
Wide range of women's, men's and children's clothes including
women's jackets, blouses, skirts and trousers; men's suits, jackets,
shirts, trousers; girl's dresses, blouses, trousers, skirts and jackets and
boy's shirts, trousers, jackets and much much more.

## FALMER JEANS LTD

CAPONACRE INDUSTRIAL ESTATE, CAIRN ROAD, CUMNOCK,
AYRESHIRE KA18 1SH
☎ (01290) 421577. OPEN 9.30 - 3.30 MON - THUR, 9.30 - 12.30 FRI, 9 -
11.45 SAT.
Perfects and seconds from the well-known Falmer range including T-
shirts from £6-£10, jeans from £7 for seconds and £14 for perfects.
Mostly for women and men, but a small selection for children.

## GARDINER OF SELKIRK

TWEED MILLS, SELKIRK, SCOTLAND TD7 5DZ
☎ (01750) 20283. OPEN 9 - 5 MON - SAT IN SUMMER, 10 - 4 IN WINTER.
Factory shop making textiles: mixed tweeds at £8 a yard, Shetland
wool at 35p an ounce, men's pyjamas, socks, shirts (£9.95-£10.95),
wool jumpers £20-£25, skirts, £29.95, jackets, £75, scarves, £2.95
and £3.95, tartan rugs at £19.50, woollen rugs, £8.95-£14.95. Best
buys are the tweeds and rugs.

## HAWICK CASHMERE CO LTD

TRINITY MILLS, DUKE STREET, HAWICK, SCOTLAND TD9 9QA
☎ (01450) 372510. OPEN 10 - 5 MON - FRI.
Manufactures cashmere knitwear for top department stores and sells
seconds and ends of lines here at below retail prices. Cashmere and
silk, lambswool, sweaters, scarves, capes, cardigans, dresses, skirts and
gloves. Also bargain baskets of cardigans and sweaters from £15.0

## HONEY

JACKSONS LANDING, HARTLEPOOL FACTORY OUTLET SHOPPING
MALL, HARTLEPOOL MARINA, HARTLEPOOL, CLEVELAND TS24 OXN
☎ (01429) 260488. OPEN 10 - 6 MON - FRI, 11 - 5 SUN AND BANK
HOLIDAYS.

Indoor factory shopping centre with twenty-four outlets selling brand
name items including leisure-oriented women's T-shirts, leggings and
sweaters at discounts of mostly 30%. Motif T-shirts, £8.99 reduced
from £11.99; casual leisure jackets, £14.99 reduced from £19.99;
short-sleeved sweaters, £9.99 reduced from £15.99. Hartlepool
Marina hosts a recreated historic quay and harbours HMS
Trincomalee, the oldest British warship still afloat, and is also the site
of the new Hartlepool Museum with its interactive fighting ships
section and a replica seventeenth century children's play area. There is
free parking adjacent to the centre, a coffee shop, restaurant overlooking the Marina, and baby changing and disabled facilities.

## HOUSE OF HARDY

WILLOW BURN, ALNWICK, NORTHUMBERLAND NE66 2PF
☎ (01665) 602771. OPEN 9 - 5 MON - FRI, 10 - 5 SAT, 1.30 - 5 SUN FROM
APRIL - OCTOBER.

Sells ends of lines for the outdoor type, especially fisherwomen and
men, including waxed jackets, jumpers, fly vests, tops and trousers,
countrywear bags, fishing rods, reels, and lines. There is also a bargain
basement with own brand items on sale at discounts of about 50%.

## JACKSONS LANDING

HARTLEPOOL FACTORY OUTLET SHOPPING MALL, HARTLEPOOL
MARINA, HARTLEPOOL, CLEVELAND TS24 OXN
☎ (01429) 866989 INFORMATION LINE. OPEN 10 - 6 MON - FRI, 11 - 5
SUN AND BANK HOLIDAYS.

Indoor factory shopping centre with twenty-four outlets selling brand
name items from companies such as Edinburgh Crystal, Royal
Brierley, Wrangler and Equator Luggage. Shops such as Clinkards,
Jeli, Bally, Clark's and Kickers footwear, and Jane Shilton handbags;
Jokids sells children'swear; Toy World features many of the leading
brand names such as Tomy, Fisher-Price and Lego; James Barry has a
selection of men's suits, shirts, and jackets; Bookscene sells jigsaws,
stationery, posters; Tog 24 sells leisurewear; Honey offers a range of

affordable knitwear, T-shirts and leggings, including Honey Plus for sizes 18-24; Chas N Whillans, Scottish branded wool specialist, sells famous branded quality lambswool and cashmere including Lyle & Scott and Pringle; Hallmark sells half-price celebration and Christmas cards, wrapping paper, and stuffed toys; and Tom Sayers sells a range of menswear; while Treasure Island sells specialised gifts from Hartlepool. Recent new openings include Benetton and Joe Bloggs. Hartlepool Marina hosts a recreated historic quay and harbours HMS Trincomalee, the oldest British warship still afloat, and is also the site of the new Hartlepool Museum with its interactive fighting ships section and a replica seventeenth century children's play area. There is free parking adjacent to the centre, a coffee shop, restaurant overlooking the Marina, and baby changing and disabled facilities.

## JAEGER FACTORY SHOP

TULLIBODY ROAD, LORNSHILL, ALLOA, SCOTLAND SK10 2EX
☎ (01259) 218985. OPEN 10 - 4 MON - SUN.
15 MUNRO PLACE, BONNYTON INDUSTRIAL ESTATE, KILMARNOCK, SCOTLAND KA1 2NP
☎ (01563) 5265111. OPEN 9 - 12 AND 2 - 4 MON, THUR, 10 - 4 SAT, SUN, 9 - 4 TUE, WED, FRI.

Classic tailoring at old-fashioned prices from Jaeger and Viyella. Most of the merchandise is last season's stock and some seconds. There are now 13 Jaeger factory shops, some selling the whole range of Jaeger clothes, some just knitwear; yet others sell goods other than those with the Jaeger label. This shop has a good range of Viyella skirts, blouses and jackets as well as Jaeger skirts, £39-£59, dresses from £39, and jackets from £89-£129, all usually half price. There is also a wide selection of suits up to size 18.

## JAMES JOHNSTON OF ELGIN

CASHMERE VISITORS CENTRE, NEW MILL, ELGIN SCOTLAND 1V3 2AF
☎ (01343) 554000. OPEN 9 - 5.30 MON - SAT, 11 - 4 SUN JULY AND AUGUST ONLY.

A factory shop with an on site visitors mill, where you can watch raw wool being made into luxurious cashmere from the dyeing and blending, through to the spinning, winding and weaving. Cashmere sweaters sold from £90 - £250, including regular bargain baskets.

## JOCKEY UNDERWEAR FACTORY SHOP

EASTERN AVENUE, TEAM VALLEY TRADING ESTATE, GATESHEAD,
TYNE & WEAR
☎ (0191) 491 0088. OPEN 10 - 4 MON, TUE, THUR, 10 - 2.30 FRI, CLOSED
WED.
Ladies underwear: briefs, ribbed vests, cami-tops, bodies. Up to 17
different types of men's underwear from Y-fronts and boxers to tangas
and hipsters. Although this factory makes underwear, because it is
part of the Courtaulds group, the factory shop also sells Wolsey socks,
Cristy towels, Zorbit babywear, pillows and duvets.

## K SHOES

K VILLAGE, NETHERFIELD, KENDAL, CUMBRIA LA9 7DA
☎ (01539) 721892. OPEN 9.30 - 7 MON - FRI, 9 - 6 SAT, 11 - 5 SUN, 9 - 6
BANK HOLIDAYS.
JAMES STREET, ASKAM-IN-FURNESS, CUMBRIA LA16 7BA
☎ (01229) 462267. OPEN 10 - 5.30 MON - FRI, 9 - 5 SAT, 10 - 5 BANK
HOLIDAYS.
MAIN STREET, SHAP, CUMBRIA CA10 3NL
☎ (01931) 716648. OPEN 9 - 5 MON - SAT, 10 - 5 BANK HOLIDAYS.
Clarks International operate a chain of factory shops nationally which
specialise in selling discontinued lines and slight sub-standards for
women, men and children from Clarks, K Shoes and other famous
brands. These shops trade under the name of Crockers, K Shoes
Factory shop or Clarks Factory Shop and while not all are physically
attached to a shoe factory, these shops are treated as factory shops by
the company. Customers can expect to find an extensive range of
quality shoes, sandals, walking boots, slippers, trainers, handbags,
accessories and gifts, while their major outlets also offer luggage,
sports clothing, sports equipment and outdoor clothing. Brands
stocked include Clarks, K Shoes, Springer, CICA, Hi-Tec, Puma,
Mercury, Dr Martens, Nike, LA Gear, Fila, Mizuno, Slazenger,
Weider, Samsonite, Delsey, Antler and Carlton, although not all are
sold in every outlet. Discounts are on average 30% off the normal
high street price for perfect stock. The Kendal branch is also a sports
factory shop, baggage factory shop and gift shop.

# K VILLAGE FACTORY SHOPPING

KENDAL, NEAR JUNCTION 36 OF M6, CUMBRIA
☎ (01539) 721892. OPEN 9.30 - 7 MON - FRI, 9 - 6 SAT AND BANK
HOLIDAYS, 11 - 5 SUN.

Eight outlets including Crabtree & Evelyn, Denby Pottery,
Dartington Crystal, Farah Menswear, Jumpers, The Baggage Factory,
The Sports Factory and a giant K Shoes factory shop selling a wide
range of labels from Clarks, Laura Ashley, Delsey, Cica, and Antler.
There is also a heritage centre, a 150-seater restaurant, a coffee shop
and free parking.

# KANGOL FACTORY SHOP

CLEATOR MILLS, CLEATOR, CUMBRIA CA23 3DJ
☎ (01946) 810312. OPEN 10 - 4 MON - FRI, 9 - 1 SAT.

Europe's largest manufacturer of headwear has a factory shop selling
hats, scarves, bags and caps as well as Jane Shilton bags, scarves and
belts at about half the shop price. Some are seconds, others obsolete
shades, yet others shop returns. The shop also sells gold sweaters and
shirts, T-shirts and jumpers.

# KILNCRAIGS MILL

PATON & BADLWINS LTD, ALLOA, SCOTLAND
☎ (01259) 723431. OPEN 10 - 4.30 MON - FRI, 10 - 4 SAT.

Sells a range of knitwear from Angora jumpers to tapestries and kits,
as well as Patons wool and discontinued yarns. It also sells garments
from the Coats Viyella group: silk skirts, blouses and ties and
swimwear, nightwear, bedding and towels. Many have been used for
photography for patterns; some are former display garments. The vast
majority, though, are seconds and discontinued lines and are sold at
about half the normal retail price. Tapestries and kits range from £5-
£30; mohair from £6-£10 instead of its normal retail price of £27.50.
Kilncraigs is a working mill with an on-site factory shop.

## LINDSAY ALLAN DESIGNS LTD

BARNPARK DRIVE, OFF LOWER MILL STREET, TILLICOULTRY, CLACK-
MANNANSHIRE, SCOTLAND FK13 6BZ
☎ (01259) 752772. OPEN 8.30 - 5 MON - THUR, 8.30 - 4 FRI.
Designer casualwear for children, women and men at affordable
prices. About 23% of the stock is for women, 2% for men, and all are
designed by an in-house design team and usually sold by Lindsay
Allan's network of agents through Scotland. Guaranteed supply of all
their orders means that they are left each season with a small quantity
from the 100 different designs they offer which can no longer be sold
through the party plan system which Lindsay Allan employs. These
are sold at end of line prices which means discounts of 30%-50%.

## LINTON TWEEDS LTD

SHADDON MILLS, CARLISLE, CUMBRIA CA2 5TZ
☎ (01228) 27569. OPEN 9.30 - 5 MON - SAT, CLOSED SUNS, 10 - 4 BANK
HOLIDAYS. MAIL ORDER.
Eighty percent of Linton Tweeds Ltd's business is for the couture
trade for export and includes fabrics for Chanel, Ann Klein, Ungaro,
Courrege, Bill Blass and Escada. British designers to whom it supplies
fabrics include Windsmoor, Aquascutum, Jaeger and Liberty, and
ranges from fancy yarns to silk and wool crepes. The mill shop has a
large selection of ends of lines and remnants. You have to buy the
fabric when you see it as there are no repeat orders. There is a craft
centre, exhibition section, small museum and restaurant on site with
hands-on display for adults and children, and a car park.

## M C HITCHEN & SONS LTD

19 FAWCETT STREET, SUNDERLAND, TYNE & WEAR SR1 RRH
☎ (0191) 564 0684. OPEN 8.45 - 5.30 MON - SAT.
RAWLINSON STREET, BAROW-IN-FURNESS, CUMBRIA LA14 ABS
☎ (01229) 870668. OPEN 8.45 - 5.15 MON - SAT.
Littlewoods sell off their overstocks in a network of shops called M C
Hitchen & Sons Ltd. Most of them are in the north of England and
offer up to 40% off the catalogue price for clothing anf between 50%
and 60% off for electrical goods. Littlewoods also run a mobile shop
which operates in cities where they don't have a sale shop for details
of further venues for the sales, which useually take place once a
month, contact Jean Banks, c/o Crosby DC, Kershaw Avenue,
Endbutt Lane, Crosby, Merseyside L70 1AH.

## MACGILLIVRAY & CO

BALIVANICH, BENBECULA, WESTERN ISLES, SCOTLAND PA88 5LA
☎ (01870) 602525. OPEN 9.30 - 5 MON - FRI, CLOSED 1 - 2, 9.30 - 4 SAT.
MAIL ORDER.

The MacGillivray Company has been selling handwoven Harris
tweed and hand-knitted sweaters all over the world since 1941.
Usually hand-knitted sweaters in pure new wool cost from £49.50
and 28" (72cm) wide Harris tweed costs £10.50 a yard (£11.55 a
metre). They sometimes hold a stock of special offer fabrics, which
they obtain from various mills throughout Britain. Because these are
surplus stock, cancelled export orders or out of season fabrics, they
can be sold at less than half the original selling price. These can range
from Scottish tweeds, Shetlands, Donegals, dress and fancy fabrics,
suitings and coatings. Send for a brochure.

## PACO LIFE IN COLOUR

SALE SHOP, UNIT 3, PAISLEY HIGH STREET, PAISLEY SHOPPING
CENTRE, PAISLEY, SCOTLAND
☎ (0141) 848 0167. OPEN 9 - 5.30 MON - SAT, UNTIL 7 ON THUR.

Colourful cotton T-shirts, sweaters, cardigans, sweatshirts, leggings,
gloves, scarves, shorts, canvas bags for women and children, all at discounts of about 50%.

## PETER SCOTT

11 BUCCLEUCH STREET, HAWICK, SCOTLAND TD9 OHG
☎ (01450) 372311. OPEN 10 - 5 MON, WED, 9 - 5 TUE, THUR, FRI, 10 - 4
SAT.

Peter Scott is one of the oldest factory shops in the country. It stocks
thousands of sweaters for women and men in almost every conceivable material from cotton and merino wool to cashmere and silk.
Some of the stock is new, some discontinued but there are no seconds.

## SCOTTISH SWEATER STORE

JACKSONS LANDING, HARTLEPOOL FACTORY OUTLET SHOPPING
MALL, HARTLEPOOL MARINA, HARTLEPOOL, CLEVELAND TS24 OXN
☎ (01429) 273994. OPEN 10 - 6 MON - FRI, 11 - 5 SUN AND BANK
HOLIDAYS.

Indoor factory shopping centre with twenty-four outlets selling brand
name items including knitwear for men and women, most of which
is half price. Labels include Pringle and Lyle & Scott. Examples of

prices include Pringle T-shirts, £17.50 reduced from £26.95; Pringle sweaters. £19.95, reduced from £39.95; Hunter Wellington boots, slightly blemished, £24.95 reduced from £37.95; Snowgoose padded gilet, £39.95; ladies reversible Pringle jacket, £45 reduced from £99; John Partridge macintosh, £75 reduced from £172.95; Pringle wool jacket, £75. Hartlepool Marina hosts a recreated historic quay and harbours HMS Trincomalee, the oldest British warship still afloat, and is also the site of the new Hartlepool Museum with its interactive fighting ships section and a replica seventeenth century children's play area. There is free parking adjacent to the centre, a coffee shop, restaurant overlooking the Marina, and baby changing and disabled facilities.

## SHARK SPORTS

NORDSTROM HOUSE, NORTH BROOMHILL, MORPETH, NORTHUMBERLAND NE65 9UJ
☎ (01670) 760365. OPEN 9.30 - 4 MON - FRI, 9.30 - 12 SAT.
Manufactures and sells in the factory shop wetsuits, dry suits, diving suits, cag tops, buoyancy aids, sailing suits, boots, life jackets and gloves, for women, men and children at factory prices. Children's one-piece wetsuits, £40-£45; steamers, £130 and adult wetsuits, £75-£85.

## THE FACTORY SHOP

EMPIRE BUILDING, MAIN STREET, EGREMONT, CUMBRIA CA22 2BD
☎ (01946) 820434. OPEN 9.30 - 5 MON - SAT, 10 - 4 SOME BANK HOLIDAYS.
Wide range on sale includes men's, ladies and children's clothing and footwear; household textiles, toiletries, hardware, luggage, lighting and bedding, most of which are chainstore and high street brands at discounts of approximately 30%-50%. There are weekly deliveries and brands include all the major stars: Coloroll, Wrangler and Dartington to name just three. Lines are continually changing and few factory shops offer such a variety under one roof.

## THE LOCHLEVEN SHOP

TODD & DUNCAN, KINROSS (NEAR M90), SCOTLAND
☎ (01577) 863521. OPEN 9 - 5.30 MON - SAT.
Sells Pringle sweaters and shirts at very competitive retail prices as
well as its own cable cashmere at £70 which includes two-ply
cashmere classic V-necks, crew-necks and roll collars; normal retail
prices for these would normally be about £160. The shop also stocks
lambswool sweaters for between £25-£60; Daks/Simpson skirts and
jackets at competitive prices; Enrico cotton and angora mix skirts and
tops from £12-£40 and other cheaper ranges.

## WRANGLER

JACKSONS LANDING, HARTLEPOOL FACTORY OUTLET SHOPPING
MALL, HARTLEPOOL MARINA, HARTLEPOOL, CLEVELAND TS24 OXN
☎ (01429) 273488. OPEN 10 - 6 MON - FRI, 11 - 5 SUN AND BANK
HOLIDAYS.
Indoor factory shopping centre with twenty-four outlets. Wrangler
sells women's, men' and children's jeans, jackets and waistcoats. For
example, perfect jeans, £32; slight seconds, £18.99; denim shirt,
£14.99; waistcoats, £19.99 reduced from £39.99. Hartlepool Marina
hosts a recreated historic quay and harbours HMS Trincomalee, the
oldest British warship still afloat, and is also the site of the new
Hartlepool Museum with its interactive fighting ships section and a
replica seventeenth century children's play area. There is free parking
adjacent to the centre, a coffee shop, restaurant overlooking the
Marina, and baby changing and disabled facilities.

# *Dress Agencies*

## BEAUTIFUL BRIDES

13-15 ST LEONARDS BRIDGE, CRAIGIE, PERTH, SCOTLAND PH2 0DR
☎ (01738) 443343. OPEN 10 - 4 MON - THURS, 10 - 5 FRI, 9.30 - 4.30 SAT
Designer brides and bridesmaids dresses to hire or to buy both new
and nearly-new at about one third of the original price.

## BLUE MOON

GORDON CHAMBERS, 90 MITCHELL STREET, GLASGOW, SCOTLAND
☎ (0141) 248 4983. OPEN 9.30 - 5 MON - FRI, SAT BY
APPOINTMENT.
Dress agency specialising in wedding dresses and accessories. Up to
200 dresses at any one time ranging in price from £300-£1,000 and
with labels such as Alison Blake, Catherine Rayner, Tracy Connop,
and Andrea Wilkin. Also sells bridesmaids dresses, veils, shoes.

## COCO

11 GRANGE ROAD, DARLINGTON, COUNTY DURHAM DL1 5NA
☎ (01325) 383720. OPEN 10 - 5 MON, TUE, THUR, FRI;
10 - 2 WED, 10 - 4.30 SAT.
Small shop packed with daywear, evening wear and accessories from
every kind of label - Wallis, Next and Laura Ashley to Basler, Escada
and Nicole Farhi. Clothes are immaculate and often mistaken for new
by window shoppers. Sizes are mostly 10-14 with some 16s, and
prices range from £5 to £200. For example, Armani jeans, £45, as
new £90; La Perla dress, £70, as new £275; Moschino shoulder bag,
£40, as new £120.

## DRESS SENSE

44 HANOVER STREET, EDINBURGH EH2 2DR
☎ (0131) 220 1298. OPEN 10.30 - 4.30 TUE - SAT.
Has been in operation for 21 years, run by a mother and daughter
team. Occupying a three-room suite on the top floor of a building in
central Edinburgh, it deals mainly in designer labels, wedding outfits
and evening gowns, with some childrenswear for 3-8-year-olds.
Labels stocked include Basler, Jaeger, Escada and the ubiquitous
M&S. The non-designer clothes are all under £45. Lots of cruise wear
and holiday wear as well as handbags and hats.

## ENCORE

20 FREDERICK ST, SUNDERLAND, TYNE & WEAR SR3 1LT
☎ (0191) 564 2227. OPEN 10- 5 MON - SAT.
Sells designer labels, smart day wear, evening wear, special occasion
wear, wedding outfits, hats and accessories. Labels stocked include
various German labels, Escada, Louis Feraud, Frank Usher, Betty
Barclay, Windsmoor, Planet, Wallis and Next. One of the two rooms

in this outlet specialises in special occasion wear, the other in smart daywear. There is also a hire service for the evening wear only, which costs from £35-£50 a weekend.

## FINE FEATHERS

6 LIBRARY ROAD, KENDAL, CUMBRIA LA9 4QB
☎ (01539) 727241. OPEN 10 - 5 MON - SAT.
Wide range of middle of the market names such as Country Casuals and Lakelands, with mix of in-season styles. Also Jacques Vert, Principles, Next, and Jaeger. More than 2,000 clients sell their as-new clothes here.

## INNOVATIONS

5 ABBOT STREET, PERTH, SCOTLAND PH2 OEB
☎ (01738) 638568. OPEN 10 - 4 MON - SAT, CLOSED WEDS.
Small, friendly shop where customers speak to each other over countless cups of coffee sipped by ladies who come from afar to snap up some of the wonderful clothes which come and go on a daily basis. Prices are kept low to maintain a high turnover. Stocks ballgowns, wedding outfits, business suits and casual/holiday wear, all at less than one third of the original price. Examples of prices include Geiger suit, £120, originally £375; Escada blazer, £200, originally £650; Nicole Farhi dress, £70, originally £295; Armani jeans, £27, originally £85; Options T-shirt, £6, originally £45. There are usually at least 70 different outfits in stock in sizes 8-24, plus lots of costume jewellery, scarves, handbags, and some shoes.

## LABELS OF BARNARDS CASTLE

8 THE BANK, BARNARD CASTLE, COUNTY DURHAM
☎ (01833) 690548 / ☎ (01325) 730271. OPEN 10.30 - 5 MON - SAT, CLOSED THUR.
Sophisticated labels, including ball gowns, in this 300-year old building in this historic market town. Middle of the range outfits from Kenzo, Nicole Farhi, Mondi and Escada to Jean Paul Gaultier. Lots of jewellery, handbags and shoes and some hats. Men's range also now available. Easy parking.

## LYNNE SIM & DAUGHTER

86 CADZOW STREET, HAMILTON, STRATHCLYDE, SCOTLAND
ML3 6DS
☎ (01698) 422265. OPEN 10 - 5.30 MON - SAT.
Nearly-new designer clothes ranging from Chanel, YSL and Escada to
Marella, Mondi, Tom Bowker, Berkertex and Jacques Vert. Also
accessories such as hats, shoes, handbags and belts. Alterations service
available and can make up bridesmaids dresses.

## MARGARET WILLIAMS DRESS AGENCY

21 EAST STREET, WHITBURN, TYNE & WEAR
☎ (0191) 529 2247 OPEN 10 - 4 TUE, THUR, FRI, SAT.
Fairly large shop selling largely designer labels, varying from Frank
Usher, Jean Muir and Mondi to the occasional selection of Marks &
Spencer, Laura Ashley and Next. Stocks both day wear and special
occasion outfits, including hats, costume jewellery and shoes. Also
holds seasonal stock such as shorts and T- shirts.

## NEW TO YOU

1 BOUNDARY ROAD, CURROCK, CARLISLE, CUMBRIA CA2 4HH
☎ (0228) 592669. OPEN 9.30 - 5 MON - FRI, 10 - 4 SAT.
Classic clothing from Louis Feraud, Mansfield, Frank Usher and
Mondi to Kanga, Next and Laura Ashley at anything from one half to
one quarter of the original price. Sizes range from 10-20. Also sells
and hires hats from a range of about 40.

## RE-DRESS

1 PRIESTON ROAD, BRIDGE OF WEIR, SCOTLAND PA11 3AJ
☎ (01505) 615151. OPEN 9.30 - 5.30 MON - SAT.
Sells both new and nearly-new fashion items at bargain prices in the
400 square feet shop. The designers range from high street to top
designers, and often feature Parigi, Betty Barclay, Puccini, and Jacques
Vert. Owner Valerie Lawrence sells everything from blouses, shirts,
suits and dresses to beads, shoes, hats, bags, belts and jewellery. Prices
range from £10 upwards and sizes from 8-18.

## RE-DRESS

43 NEW ROW, OFF GLASGOW ROAD, PERTH, SCOTLAND PH1 5QA
☎ (01738) 444447. OPEN 10 - 4.30 MON - SAT.

Situated in a discreet area in the town of Perth, Re-dress stocks a range of middle to top name nearly-new designer labels and some new clothes. There are wedding outfits and matching accessories at about one third of the original price, as well as evening wear, and a large selection of daywear, shoes and hats. You can choose from labels such as Laurel, Mondi, Louis Feraud, Escada, MaxMara, Paul Costelloe, Caroline Charles, Basler, Geiger, Oui Set, Betty Barclay and Austin Reed. Clearance sales are usually held twice a year.

## REDRESS

31 HIGH STREET, NORTH BERWICK, EAST LOTHIAN EH39 4HH
☎ (01620) 895633. OPEN 10 - 4.30 MON - SAT, CLOSED THUR DURING WINTER.

Friendly atmosphere shop stocking Jaeger, Country Casuals, Frank Usher, Jacques Vert, Laura Ashley, Next, After Six, Bally, Russell & Bromley in sizes 8-30. When available, there is also Hardob, Planet, Wallis, Eastex, Windsmoor, Yarrell, Peter Barron, Parigi, Berkertex, Viyella, Bally, Van Dal, FinnKarelia and many more. There are good prices for quality names and reductions are always available. The shop also sells handbags, shoes, jumpers, evening gowns and a selection of special occasion hats.

## RUMMAGE

5 STEWART STREET, MILNGAVIE, SCOTLAND J62 6BW
☎ (0141) 956 2333. OPEN 10 - 5 MON - SAT.

New and nearly-new designer clothes from Lagerfeld and Dior to Arabella Pollen and Givenchy as well as items from high street chain stores. There are usually at least 200 special occasion outfits available as well as handbags, shoes, costume jewellery and a superb selection of hats which can also be hired. There's also evening wear, ballgowns, bric a brac, china, ornament, glassware and hat boxes.

## SECOND TIME AROUND

5 WALKERGATE, BERWICK-UPON-TWEED, NORTHUMBERLAND
☎ (01289) 307875 10 - 4 MON - SAT.

High quality, nearly new clothes with designers ranging from Jacques
Vert to Marks & Spencer and Laura Ashley. Across the board selection of clothing from casual daywear to wedding outfits. There is
usually a bargain rail with skirts going for as little as £4, and twice
yearly sales in the summer and winter. A varied selection of clothes
can be found year round as the stock is not particularly seasonal.
Accessories can be found: shoes, hats and handbags.

## SELLERS

2 CROWN LANE, OFF CROWN TERRACE, ABERDEEN, SCOTLAND
AB1 2HF
☎ (01224) 582528. OPEN 10.30 - 5 TUE - SAT, UNTIL 7 ON THUR.

Run by a mother and daughter team, this dress agency has been operating for more than eight years. It sells a wide selection of day and
evening wear from Louis Feraud and Paul Costelloe to Mondi and
Jaeger at between one third and one half of the original price as well
as hats, jewellery, accessories and some shoes. Wide selection of
special occasion wear. Stock is a mixture of new and nearly-new as
some designer merchandise is bought in from boutiques' ends of
ranges.

## SHELAGH BUCHANAN

38 BATH STREET, GLASGOW
☎ (0141) 331 1862. OPEN 10 - 4.30 MON - FRI, 9 - 1 SAT.

Sells anything from shoes to ballgowns, and including cocktail
dresses, evening wear, suits, and outfits, bags and accessories.
Designer labels in this outlet at the back of the building which houses
a tailoring alterations service at the front, include Country Casuals,
Mansfield, Tricoville, Frank Usher Jaeger, Mondi, Escada, Jean Muir
and Basler. A Jaeger suit sold for £100, original price £300; a Jean
Muir dress for £100, originally about £300; an Escada jacket £150,
originally £300.

# THE ADDRESS-DESIGNER EXCHANGE

3 ROYAL EXCHANGE COURT, GLASGOW, SCOTLAND G1 3DB
☎ (0141) 221 6898. OPEN 10 - 5 TUE - SAT.

This unique boutique tucked away, yet in the heart of the city centre, specialises in re-selling the top designer fashion - everything from bikins to ballgowns, and accessories, too. Customers are attracted by the promise of quality and style at one third or less of the original cost. Sharp-eyed lovers of style travel from afar to this shop which is full of labels such as Paul Costelloe, Max Mara, Armani, Escada, Rifat Ozbek and others. Stock turns around quickly with new items arriving daily from all over the UK, many from well-known celebrities. Examples of price include: Escada suit, £99, was £490; Armani jacket, £89, was £320; Arabella Pollen top, £99, was £650; MaxMara blouse, £45, was £185; Gucci bag, £39, was £180; Hermes scarf, £35, was £130.

# *Hire Shops*

## ENCORE

20 FREDERICK ST, SUNDERLAND, TYNE & WEAR SR3 1LT
☎ (0191) 564 2227. OPEN 10- 5 MON - SAT.

Dress agency which also has a hire service for evening wear only which costs from £35-£55.

## NEW TO YOU

1 BOUNDARY ROAD, CURROCK, CARLISLE, CUMBRIA CA2 4HH
☎ (0228) 592669. OPEN 9.30 - 5 MON - FRI, 10 - 4 SAT.

Dress agency which also hires out hats from a range of about 40 for £14 plus £12 deposit.

## RUMMAGE

5 STEWART STREET, MILNGAVIE, SCOTLAND J62 6BW
☎ (0141) 956 2333. OPEN 10 - 5 MON - SAT.

Dress agency which also hires out hats from a superb selection.

# Secondhand and Vintage Clothes

## ATTICA

2 OLD GEORGE YARD, BIGG MARKET, NEWCASTLE-UPON-TYNE
NE1 1EZ
☎ (0191) 261 4062. OPEN 10.30 - 5.30 MON - SAT.

Two floors of vintage clothes from Twenties to Seventies with most of
the stock coming from the Sixties and Seventies. Blouses, lots of
suede, Sixties mini-skirts and dresses, jewellery, hats and shoes as well
as men's formalwear including dinner suits. Also mid-century decor,
furniture and china ornaments.

## HAND IN HAND

3 NORTH WEST, CIRCUS PLACE, EDINBURGH EH3 6ST
☎ (0131) 226 3598. OPEN 10 - 5.30 TUE - SAT.

From Victorian costume pieces to classic Thirties wear and underwear, jewellery and accessories, Victorian household linen from £50-
£150, and Thirties dresses from £20-£300. Period wedding dresses,
veils, headdresses, original waxed garlands and shoes, hankies,
parasols and shawls also available. All items are restored original,
dated pieces. Mostly for women and children only, although there
are some morning suits, old waistcoats and linen shirts and kilts.

## PUTTING ON THE RITZ

THE VICTORIAN VILLAGE, 57 WEST REGENT STREET, GLASGOW
☎ (0141) 332 0808 OR 9808. OPEN 10 - 5 MON - SAT.

Retro jewellery, marcasite and Fifties silver, nightwear, Paisley shawls,
vintage dinner suits and tuxedos, Thirties and Forties sportswear,
riding boots, stetsons, 1930s USA football outfits. Jewellery from £5,
dinner suits from £15.

## SARATOGA TRUNK

57 WEST REGENT STREET, GLASGOW, SCOTLAND G2 2AE
☎ (0141) 331 2707. OPEN 10.30 - 5 MON - FRI, 10.30 - 5 SAT.

Old-fashioned and antique clothing, Paisley shawls, embroidered
shawls, wedding dresses from the Forties and Fifties, and Christening
robes. Victorian to 1950s daywear, evening wear and underwear.
Accessories including costume jewellery. Patchwork, lace curtains,
bedlinen and table covers.

## STARRY STARRY NIGHT

19 DOWNSIDE LANE, GLASGOW G12 9BZ
☎ (0141) 337 1837. OPEN 10 - 5.30 MON - SAT.
Retro gear, espcially evening gowns, menswear, including morning
coats, tails and striped blazers from Victorian through the Twenties
and Thirties to the Seventies. Morning suits, £30, dinner suits, £30,
leather jackets, £15-£20, evening gowns, £10 upwards, waistcoats,
collarless shirts and bow ties.


# *Designer Sales*

## THE BRITISH DESIGNERS SALE FOR WOMEN AND MEN

42 YORK MANSIONS, PRINCE OF WALES DRIVE, LONDON SW11 4BP
☎ 0171-228 5314. OPEN 10 - 4 MON - FRI.
The first of what is now a booming industry, the British Designers
Sale was started by Debbie Hodges, a former PR, more than 15 years
ago, and she has recently started running Sales in Edinburgh. Because
of her contacts, it offers top British designer labels - plus a number of
top Italian, German and French labels - you won't find at other
designer sales, but no names can be mentioned or those publicity-shy
designers would not be happy to let Debbie sell their overstocks.
Labels are the sort you would expect to find in the designer rooms at
Harrods or Harvey Nichols. Membership costs £26 per year. If you
want to write to Debbie to add your name to the mailing list, please
enclose an sae.

# NORTHERN IRELAND

## Permanent Discount Outlets

### TK MAXX

FIRST FLOOR, CASTLE COURT SHOPPING CENTRE, BELFAST,
NORTHERN IRELAND OPEN 9 - 5.30 MON - WED, 9 - 9 THUR, 9 - 8 FRI,
9 - 6 SAT.

Based on an American concept, TK Maxx is the first British retailer
to practise "off-price" retailing. This means a centrally located store
which offers famous label goods with up to 60% savings off recommended retail prices. TK Maxx has fashion for the whole family -
women's, men's and childrenswear - accessories, shoes, gifts, kitchenware and home goods. Everything in the store is branded with a
choice of well-known high street names to designer labels, and while
a small percentage mightly be clearly marked past season, the great
majority of items in store are current season, current stock and still
with phenomenal savings. There is a huge choice with 50,000 pieces
in store with 5,000 new items arriving a week, so it's worth keeping
abreast of the lastest deliveries as turnaround is very fast. One of the
ways in which TK Maxx is able to offer such low prices is by running
a very low-cost operation, so the stores are simple and unfussy with
wide aisles, shopping trolleys and baskets, and a spacious, functional
feel to them. Service is not compromised, however: there are individual changing rooms, ramps for buggies and wheelchairs, plenty of
staff on the shop floor and all the branches accept all major credit and
debit cards.

## Factory Shops

### BAIRDWEAR RACKE

CLANDEBOYE ROAD, BANGOR, NORTHERN IRELAND
☎ (01247) 270415. OPEN 9.30 - 4.30 MON - FRI, 9 - 4 SAT.
ANN STREET, NEWTOWNARDS, NORTHERN IRELAND
☎ (01247) 819502. OPEN 10 - 4.30 MON - SAT.

Manufacturers for a well-known high street chainstore for more than
20 years, Bairdwear has a wide selection of seconds and overmakes in

its factory shops for women, men and children. This can cover anything from underwear to jackets, coats and blouses but stock changes constantly. There is also sometimes a range of bedding and household linens.

## DESMOND & SONS LTD

THE MAIN STREET, CLAUDY, LONDONDERRY BT47 3SD
☎ (01504) 338441. OPEN 10 - 5 MON - SAT.
KEVLIN ROAD, OMAGH
☎ (01662) 241560. OPEN 10 - 5 MON - SAT.
MILL STREET, ENNISKILLEN
☎ (01365) 325467. OPEN 10 - 5 MON - SAT.
BALLYQUINN ROAD, DUNGIVEN
☎ (01504) 742068. OPEN 10 - 5 MON - SAT.
31 GARVAGH ROAD, SWATRAGH
☎ (01648) 401639. OPEN 10 - 5 MON - SAT.

Large range of women's, men's and childrenswear including trousers, nightwear and knitwear. Most of the stock is seconds and is sold at discounts of one third. They also buy in some imperfects of household items such as hand towels and bath towels which are sold at competitive prices.

## JEREMIAH AMBLER (ULSTER) LTD

BARN MILLS, TAYLOR AVENUE, CARRICKFERGUS, COUNTY ANTRIM BT38 7HQ
☎ (01960) 361011. OPEN 11 - 1 AND 2 - 4 MON - FRI.

Hand-knitting wools, especially mohair, at 30%- 50% less than retail.

## LEE APPAREL (UK) LTD

16 COMBER ROAD, NEWTOWNARDS, COUNTY DOWN BT23 4HY
☎ (01247) 800200. OPEN 10 - 5.15 MON, TUE, WED, SAT, 10 - 8.15 THUR, FRI.

Women's, men's and children's Lee Jardine jeans, jackets, T-shirts and sweatshirts at up to 50% savings. Also childrenswear, Adidas sportswear and casual ladieswear at competitive prices.

## LOTUS LTD

34 BRIDGE STREET, BANBRIDGE, COUNTY DOWN BT32 3ND
☎ (01820) 622480. OPEN 9 - 5.30 MON - SAT.

All sizes and styles of Lotus shoes - from smart fashion shoes to walking shoes - at discounted prices for discontinued lines and rejects.

Prices from £12.99-£34.99 for women's shoes. Lotus manufactures for well-known chain stores.

## NECTAR BEAUTY SHOPS LTD

95A BELFAST ROAD, CARRICKFERGUS, COUNTRY ANTRIM BT38 8XX
☎ (01960) 351580. OPEN 10 - 5.30 THUR, FRI, 10 - 2 SAT. MAIL ORDER AVAILABLE.
Wide range of Nectar cruelty-free toiletries and cosmetics, perfume, skincare, baby lotions, creams and powder, men's products such as aftershave, shaving foam, at 20% discount. Mail order not available at discount.

## OCTOPUS SPORTSWEAR MFG LTD

UNIT 1, DUBLIN ROAD INDUSTRIAL ESTATE, STRABANE BT82 9ES
☎ (01504) 882320. OPEN 8.30 - 5 THUR, 9 - 1 FRI.
Manufacture own-brand sportswear: shorts, jerseys, socks, pants, hooded tops, sweatshirts and sell seconds and clearance lines at discounts of up 50%-75%.

## PAUL COSTELLOE

PARKMOUNT, 1 MOY ROAD, DUNGANNON, COUNTY TYRONE
BT71 6BS
☎ (01868) 753867. OPEN 10 - 6 MON - SAT.
A wide range of 1,500 garments, consisting of special purchases, seconds, samples and past season stocks at substantial savings on original prices. The comprehensive selection encompasses business and special occasion designs to a more casual range for relaxed weekend wear. There is another factory shop at Cheshire Oaks (see womenwear, North West).

## RELIABLE HOSIERY AT CV CARPETS

THE FACTORY SHOP, 41 HIGH BANGOR ROAD, DONAGHADEE
BT21 OPD
☎ (01247) 888842. OPEN 10 - 5 MON - SAT.
SHAERF DRIVE, SARACEN, LURGAN, COUNTY ANTRIM
☎ (01762) 329253. OPEN 10.30 - 4.30 MON - FRI.
RELIABLE HOSIERY AT CV HOME FURNISHINGS,
36 MAGHERALANE ROAD, RANDALSTOWN, COUNTY ANTRIM
☎ (01849) 473341. OPEN 10 - 5 MON - THUR, 10 - 1 FRI.
Slightly imperfect ladies, men's and children's wear. The emphasis is

on casualwear such as weatherproof golfing suits and coats, shirts, trousers, knitwear, dress shirts, silk ties, Flix swimwear, socks. For women, there are jackets, skirts from £9.99; dresses, Flix swimwear, silk blouses from £9.99; linen-look coats, £39.99. There's also a small department of ladies lingerie from Triumph and Warner. For children, there is a good variety including party dresses. All the clothes are from well-known chain stores and sold at half the usual price. Recent additions include bedding made for one of the top bedding names: duvet covers, £29.99 for a double; double flat sheets, £11.99; matching curtains, £19.99-£24.99.

## SARACEN

SHAERF DRIVE, LURGAN, NORTHERN IRELAND
☎ (01762) 329253. OPEN 10.30 - 4.30 MON - FRI.
Women's, men's and children's clothes and knitwear at factory shop prices, many of which are top brand names. For women, there are dresses, blouses, jumpers, cardigans, trousers, nightwear, underwear, lingerie and hosiery.

## WARNERS (UK) LTD

MOUNT STREET, DROMORE, COUNTY DOWN
☎ (01846) 692466. OPEN 11 - 4 TUE - SAT, 1 - 7 THUR.
Warners famous lingerie at reduced prices. Underwear, nightwear, hosiery and some sweaters and jackets are about one third cheaper than the high street shop price. They also sell outfits for men such as shirts and ties, T-shirts and socks at reductions of about 40%.

## *Dress Agencies*

## CANCER RESEARCH GROUP

50 HIGH STREET, NEWTOWNARDS, COUNTY DOWN BT23 3HZ
☎ (01247) 820268.
Shop specifically aimed at the bridal market which sells or hires from Cinderella-style to Twenties-style wedding dresses in white, cream, ivory or pink; bridal accessories for the bride, pageboys and brides-maids; bridesmaids dresses and pageboy outfits; black and grey morning suits, plus accessories, for the groom, as well as dinner suits;

hats for weddings and for Ascot. Prices range from: silk wedding dresses, £150 to hire, £40-£495 to buy; morning suits, £25 to hire, £50 to buy; dinner suits, £16.50 to hire, £35 to buy. The most expensive wedding dress in stock was £795 reduced from £2,500. Most of the stock is either donated or straight from the manufacturer. Labels for wedding dresses cover Annelles Sharp, Laura Ashley, Ellis, Berkertex, Pronuptia, Bow Bells, Charmaine Jones, and Hilary Morgan.

# MENSWEAR

*Permanent Discount Outlets,*

*Factory Shops,*

*Dress Agencies,*

*Hire Shops,*

*Secondhand and Vintage Clothes*

*Designer Sales*

# LONDON

## *Permanent Discount Outlets*

### CAVENAGH SHIRTS

659 FULHAM ROAD, LONDON SW6 5PY
☎ 0171-371 0528. OPEN 11 - 7 MON - THUR, 10 - 6 FRI, SAT. MAIL ORDER.

Offers Jermyn Street quality men's and women's shirts at half the normal Jermyn Street price. Made from two-fold cotton poplin or classic cotton Oxford, the shirts are now available by mail order. There is also a full range of similarly competitively priced accessories, including pure silk ties, cuff links, boxer shorts, and Italian calf belts. Everything is manufactured in the UK.

### CHARLES TYRWHITT SHIRTS

298-300 MUNSTER ROAD, LONDON SW6 6YX
☎ 0171-386 9900. OPEN 9 - 5.30 MON - FRI. MAIL ORDER.

Traditional, top quality Jermyn-Street-type shirts at M & S prices. Selling only through mail order, overheads are low and the price is kept down by a policy of high volume and low margins. The comparison with Jermyn Street comes not just from the cut of the shirts, but also from the fact they share the same fabric: longstaple Egyptian cotton, which produces a soft, silky finish which washes well and is hard-wearing. If you buy 4 shirts, you get the 5th free. If you buy 4 pairs of Boxer shorts, you get one pair free. All shirts come with brass collar stiffeners. The mail order catalogue now also includes waistcoats in a range of silk and wool, £39.50; collar shirts with stiff collars in two-fold poplin, £39; cufflinks, £5-£60; a range of box ties in silk; and felt and silk braces, £26.

### DESIGNERS FOR LESS

203 UXBRIDGE ROAD, LONDON W13 9AA
☎ 0181-579 5954. OPEN 9.30 - 6 MON - SAT.

High street shop, established since 1973, which sells factory seconds, ends of ranges, samples and previous season's stock in a range of men's clothes. Their main attractions are suits from Germany, although the labels have to be removed from their best contacts' merchandise. However, the normal retail price for such suits is in the region of £300 while Designers for Less price is £95-£145. In stock in the past have been Meyer trousers, £25, normally £49.50-£59.50; Karl Helmold shirts, from £19.50, usually from £45-£90; suits from Mario Barutti, Becon, Baumler and Greiff. Silk Dior ties, Hom and Lanvin, £18, usual price £42. A wide range of sizes is stocked - jockey to giant up to size 60". There is also an extensive dresswear hire department.

## DESIGNERS SALE STUDIO

241 KING'S ROAD, LONDON SW3 SEL
☎ 0171-351 4171. OPEN 10.30 - 6.30 MON - FRI, 10 - 6 SAT, 12 - 6 SUN.
Catwalk clothes for both women and men at discounts of up to 60%. There is a menswear collection of perfect, new clothes on the lower ground floor with designs from Emporio Armani and Henry Cottons, shirts by Alea and belts and ties by Prada.

## FIRST SPORT

456-458 THE STRAND, LONDON WC2R ORG
☎ 071-839 5161. OPEN 9.30 - 6 MON - SAT, UNTIL 7 ON THUR.
They are so certain that their prices for top brand-name sports shoes are the lowest you will find that they guarantee that if you buy from them and then see the same shoes cheaper elsewhere, they will refund the difference. Brand names on sale at discounts of up to 50% include Nike, Reebok, Puma and Adidas. The shop also sells clothing, bags, T-shirts, skiwear, skis, ski boots and a full range of back packing equipment such as tents, camping tools and accessories. With 60 shops to buy for, they can purchase in bulk and get good deals.

## GEORGIANA GRIMSTON

72 MALTINGS PLACE, BAGLEYS LANE, LONDON SW6 2BY
☎ 0171-736 9966. BY APPOINTMENT ONLY.
Georgiana supplies top-grade, Savile-Row made bespoke suits at half the normal price. You can receive a visit from Georgiana to choose the cloth, and a full fitting service from the tailors, but pay only half the usual bill because of her low overheads. Georgiana works in partnership with a tailor who used to work for both Huntsman and Henry Poole. Prices start at £750 to include VAT, and you can buy morning coats, approx £800, waistcoats (to your own design), and wedding trousers, from £195.

# JADE

22 HAMPSTEAD HIGH STREET, LONDON NW3
☎ 0171-794 3889. OPEN 10 - 6 MON - SAT, UNTIL 7 THUR,
11 - 6.30 SUN.
82 GOLDERS GREEN ROAD, LONDON NW11
☎ 0181-201 9155. OPEN 10 - 6 SEVEN DAYS A WEEK, UNTIL 6.30 ON
THUR.
Italian, French, American and German clothes for women, mostly in
silk, with a small selection for men.

# MORRY'S

39-40 THE BROADWAY, EDMONTON, LONDON N9 OTJ
☎ 0181-807 6747. OPEN 8.30 - 5 MON - SAT, CLOSED AT 1 ON THUR.
Liquidation stock which includes some famous makes and can
comprise anything from gardening equipment (shovels, forks and
hoses) and household items to eletrical equipment (CDs, radios, TVs,
CDi's, radio alarms) and clothing for men, women and children.
Everything is at least half the retail price. Phone beforehand to find
out what they've got in stock or if you live nearby, drop in frequently.

# MOSS BROS

27 KING STREET, COVENT GARDEN, LONDON SC2 E8J
☎ 0171-240 4567.
Moss Bros only permanent own-label ex-hire department. Morning
suits, £160; top hats, from £30; dinner suits, £104; kilts, £150; white
tuxedos, £79; shirts, £5; black trousers, £25.

# NEXT TO NOTHING

UNIT 11, WATERGLADES CENTRE, EALING BROADWAY,
LONDON W5 2ND
☎ 0181-567 2747. OPEN 9.30 - 6 MON - SAT.
Sells perfect surplus stock from Next stores and the Next Directory
catalogue - from belts and underwear to day and evening wear - at discounts of 50% or more. The ranges are usually last season's and
overruns but there is the odd current item if you look carefully. Stock
consists of men's, women's and children's clothing, with some
homeware and shoes, depending on the branch. Stock is replenished
twice a week and there is plenty of it. This branch does not stock
homes items and has only a small amount of accessories.

## PAUL SMITH SALE SHOP

23 AVERY ROW, LONDON W1
☎ 0171-493 1287. OPEN 10.30 - 6.30 MON - FRI, 10 - 7 THUR,
10 - 6 SAT.
Offers year-round seconds and ends of lines in the heart of London's
West End. This sale shop has stock from last season, so it is always a
season behind, and sells at discounts of 40%-50%. There are lots of
bargain bins and a wide selection of accessories from belts and
cologne to cuff links. As with all permanent sale shops, stock varies,
so more than one visit may be necessary.

## SHIPTON & HENEAGE

117 QUEENSTOWN ROAD, LONDON SW8 3RH
☎ 071-738 8484. OPEN 9 - 6 MON - FRI, 10 - 2 SAT.
MAIL ORDER.
Traditional men's shoes, loafers, half brogues, Oxfords, and monks-
boots at up to 30% discount on shop prices. Any style can be ordered
from the catalogue and because there is no retail outlet, prices are low.
Or make an appointment for them to visit you at your office.

## STOCKHOUSE

101-105 GOSWELL ROAD, LONDON EC1V 7ER
☎ 0171-253 5761. OPEN 9 - 5 MON - FRI, 9 - 1.30 SUN, CLOSED SATS.
Formerly known as Goldsmith & Company, in late 1994 Stockhouse
expanded from a purely wholesale warehouse into a trade discount
centre for branded menswear that is also open to the public. It stocks
more than 3,500 men's suits, from stylish business suits, formal dresswear and comfortable lounge suits to famous brand men's shirts, silk
ties, blazers, sports jackets, waxed jackets, overcoats, designer
swimwear, underwear, socks and branded sportswear. Sizes range
from 36" chest to 54". By purchasing cancelled orders and broken
ranges from famous manufacturers at clearing prices, they are able to
offer famous brands at greatly reduced prices without compromising
on quality or style.

## SUNGLASS HUT INTERNATIONAL

KING'S WALK MALL, 122 KING'S ROAD, LONDON SW3
☎ 0171-225 3150. OPEN 10 - 7 MON - SAT, 12 - 6 SUN.
The world's largest retailer of quality sunglasses offers "lowest price guarantee" on famous brands such as Ray-Ban, Oakley, Boole, Armani, SunGear and Georgio Armani.

## SWIMGEAR

11 STATION ROAD, FINCHLEY, LONDON N3 2SB
0181-346 6106. OPEN 9.30 - 5 MON - FRI, UNTIL 8 ON THUR. MAIL ORDER.
A mail order company which also operates via a retail outlet next to Finchley Central station. They sell discontinued and ends of line ranges of swimwear for men, women and children at between 20%-30% less than normal retail prices. They also stock goggles and flippers in adult sizes. Flippers normally cost about £18.50, but can be bought here for about £8 in black rubber. The catalogues are full colour and carry the names Speedo, Adidas, Hind and Maru, as well as Swimgear's own brand full colour Mark One brochure. Prices are lower than than would be offered at swim meets and retail shops. Examples of prices include Classic Goggles, £2.80, silicone earplugs, £2.05, handpaddles, £6.40, armbands, £4.30. As part of their service, they do not cash your cheque until your full order has been completed. P&p extra, orders over £50 are post free.

## THE BRAND CENTRE

MOLLISON AVENUE, STOCKINGSWATER LANE, EN3 7PH
BRIMSDOWN, ENFIELD, MIDDLESEX
☎ 0181-805 8080. OPEN 10 - 8 MON - FRI, 10 - 7 SAT, 12 - 6 SUN.
The fashion equivalent of the US warehouse-style supermarkets in that it offers out-of-town location, plenty of free car parking and brand name goods at discount prices. In the case of The Brand Centre, a 40,000 sq ft warehouse, the brand names range from Mulberry, Timberland, Ally Capellino and Moschino to YSL at discounts which average about 25% by working on high turnover and low profit margins. For men, the choice of suits is very wide from designers such as Jasper Conran, Versace, YSL, Jaeger, Baumer and Pierre Cardin at prices from £200-£650.

# THE SALVAGE SHOP

34-38 WATLING AVENUE, BURNT OAK, MIDDLESEX HA8 OLR
☎ 0181-952 4353. OPEN 9 - 5.30 MON - SAT.
An Aladdin's cave of "salvaged" stock for the avid bargain hunter,
most of which has been the subject of bankruptcy, insurance claims,
fire or flood. Regular visitors have found anything from half-price
Kenwood Chefs, typewriters and telephones to furniture, kitchen
items and designer clothes. Yves St Laurent, Ungaro, MaxMara,
Chloe, Agnes B, Mondi, are just some of the labels (though they are
often cut out) to appear. Reasonable selection of men's clothes.
Discounts range from 50%-75%. Phone first to check stock.

# TIMOTHY EVEREST

32 ELDER STREET, LONDON E1 6BT
☎ 0171-377 5770. OPEN 9.30 - 6 MON - FRI, 10 - 4 SAT.
Having trained at Tommy Nutter in Savile Row, Timothy now offers
bespoke tailoring at accessible prices. A suit selling in Savile Row for
between £1,00-£1,700 can be made from £650. There are two types
of bespoke suit: city suits starting at £500, and the full bespoke suit
starting at £650. Jackets, trousers, shirts, overcoats and silk ties can
also be bought. Everything is made on the premises of this unusual
eighteenth century building.

# VIVM

201 NEW KING'S ROAD, LONDON SW6 4SR
☎ 0171-731 5567. OPEN 10 - 6 MON - SAT, 7 ON WED.
A stylish shop at the Parsons Green end of the New Kings Road
which offers fabulous new designer clothes and accessories at substantial discounts - usually half the original price. Mostly catering for
women, there are nevertheless some menswear gift items from Alfred
Dunhill such as ties, braces, cashmere scarves and sweaters.

# WALLERS

21-24 NEWPORT COURT, CHARING CROSS ROAD,
LONDON WC2H 7JS
☎ 0171-437 1665. OPEN 9 - 5.30 MON - FRI, 9 - 4.30 SAT.
Wallers is a family firm established at the same address for more than
70 years. They specialise in famous name suits, sports jackets, blazers,
trousers, coats and morning and evening dress wear at greatly reduced

prices. Well known to tv and film designers, who appreciate the value of choice, their Chinatown shop looks small on the outside but inside is a rabbit warren, full to the brim. Wallers clothes have been seen in Inspector Morse, Minder, Yes Minister, The Bill, Between The Lines and many other screen productions. There are usually at least 2,000 items in stock at any one time, in all sizes, most of which is ends of ranges, cancelled orders, seconds (clearly marked as such) or bought as a result of liquidations. Examples of prices include suits, £99.50, usual price £225; jackets, £49.50, usual price £125; trousers, £25, usual price £59.50; raincoats and overcoats, from £79.50; dinner suits, from £129.50; three-piece morning suits, from £145.

## Factory Shops

### BODEN WAREHOUSE SHOP

2, 4 & 7, PEMBROKE BUILDINGS, CUMBERLAND PARK, SCRUBS LANE, LONDON NW10
☎ 0181-964 2662. OPEN 10 - 7 FRI, 10 - 5 SAT.
Sale goods and discontinued lines from this well-known mail order company as well as full-price clothes from the current catalogue. Most of the merchandise is smart casual wear for women and men in 100% natural fabric. There is also cricketwear, tennis gear, silk shirts, silk blouses, belts, cufflinks, a small amount of luggage and shoulder bags but no shoes.

### BURBERRY

29-53 CHATHAM PLACE, HACKNEY, LONDON E9 6LP
☎ 0181-985 3344. OPEN 12 - 6 MON - FRI, 9 - 3 SAT.
This Burberry factory shop sells the full range of Burberry merchandise, none of which is current stock. There are seconds and overmakes of the famous name raincoats and duffle coats as well as accessories such as the distinctive umbrellas, scarves and handbags. All carry the Burberry label and are about one third of the normal retail price. Childrenswear tends to be thin on the ground, but there are plenty of gift items such as Burberry brand name teas, coffees, chocolate and marmalade. A large warehouse with clothes set out on dozens of rails, surroundings are relatively spartan.

## IN WEAR FACTORY SHOP

100 GARRATT LANE, WANDSWORTH, LONDON SW18
☎ 0181-871 2155. OPEN 10 - 5 MON - FRI, 10 - 4 SAT.
Martinique for men and In Wear for women at discounts of between
30%-70% for last season's stock, ends of lines and seconds. All the
stock is made up of stylishly casual separates.

## NICOLE FARHI OUTLET SHOP

75-83 FAIRFIELD ROAD, BOW, LONDON E3 2QR
☎ 0181-981 3931. OPEN 10 - 3 TUE, WED, SAT, 11 - 6.30 THUR,
10 - 5.30 FRI.
This tiny factory shop in London's East End sells previous season
merchandise, samples and seconds from Nicole Farhi and French
Connection for men, women and children, although the womenswear far outweighs the men's.

## ONE STEP

3 - 5 HIGH STREET, ISLINGTON, LONDON N1
☎ 0171-837 4984. OPEN 9.30 - 6 MON - THUR, 9 - 6 FRI, SAT.
Value for money chain of shoe shops, which are part of the British
Shoe Corporation Ltd. This one sells Saxone, Freeman Hardy Willis,
Dolcis, Roland Cartier, Hush Puppies and Stone Creek brands at up
to 50% discount. Sizes range up to size 9 ladies, up to size 12 for men
and a wide range of children's sizes.

## R P ELLEN

46 CHURCH ROAD, LEYTON, LONDON E10 5JD
☎ 0181 539 6872 OPEN 10 -4 MON - SAT.
Import shoes from Italy and Spain. Apart from their regular stock,
they have some seconds and sample shoes in small sizes at amazingly
low prices. They also stock boots, slippers and men's shoes and
trainers. Most of the styles are described as upmarket daywear and
glitzy eveningwear, and the choice is enormous, although the full
range of sizes is not always available. Prices range from £5 to £40.

## TON SUR TON

35 RIDING HOUSE STREET, LONDON W1 7PT
☎ 0171-637 3473. OPEN 10.30 - 5 MON - FRI.

This European casual wear company which sells tracksuits, sweat-shirts, T-shirts in unusual colours and soft fabrics, has a factory outlet in the heart of London's rag trade area. The company also sells denim, a fitness range, training shoes, rugby shirts, jackets, jeans and accessories. The factory outlet sells samples, returns and perfect garments at at least 50% of their normal retail price, and lower in a number of cases.

## *Dress Agencies*

## BERTIE WOOSTER

284 FULHAM ROAD, LONDON SW10 9EW
☎ 0171-352 5662. OPEN 10 - 7 MON - FRI, 9.30 - 5.30 SAT.

High street shop with two floors of the finest quality secondhand and new clothes and good luggage. New clothes are excellent quality at low prices - suits cost £195 - and there is a made to measure service. Secondhand clothes are of the quality rarely seen outside bespoke tailoring and includes suits, ties, shirts, blazers, waistcoats, and hankies at extremely attractive prices. Now also sells new and made to measure clothes including bespoke morning coats, full backed waistcoats, morning coat trousers and bespoke dinner and sports jackets.

## CHANGE OF HEART

59A PARK ROAD, LONDON N8
☎ 0181-341 1575. OPEN 10 - 6 MON - SAT, BY APPOINTMENT ON SUNS.

Sells a mixture of designer and good high street labels for men, women and children including labels such as Armani, Next, Paul Smith, DKNY, Ghost, Betty Jackson, Kenzo, Jigsaw, Whistles and Fenn Wright & Manson. Prices vary from £20 for a pair of Armani shorts to £50 for a Nicole Farhi silk two-piece suit.

## L'HOMME DESIGNER EXCHANGE

50 BLANDFORD STREET, LONDON W1H 3HD
☎ 0171-224 3266. OPEN 11 - 6 MON & FRI, 11 - 7 TUE, WED, THUR, 11 - 5 SAT.
This shop sells designer menswear from the outrageous to the classic for the beach, the office, the nightclub and special evenings out. Designers in stock vary, but usually include Versace (couture jackets from £180) and Armani (suits from £180), Boss (suits and coats from £140) and Gaultier. All stock is less than two years old.

## LA SCALA

39 ELYSTAN STREET, LONDON SW3 3NT
☎ 0171-589 2784. OPEN 10 - 5.30 MON - SAT.
La Scala has been so successful in selling women's nearly-new clothes and accessories since opening in 1993 that, due to popular demand, owner Sandy Reid in summer 1995 acquired large adjacent premises, enabling her to house men's and children's clothes as well as wedding dresses under the same roof. Sandy lived for 14 years in Northern Italy and uses her experience there in her marble-floored shop behind the Conran Shop in Chelsea.

## PENGUIN SOCIETY

144 WEST END LANE, LONDON NW6 1SD
☎ 0171-625 7778. OPEN 11.OO - 7.30 MON - FRI,
SAT 10.30 - 5.30
"Gently worn" designer ladies and mens wear. Designers range from Valentino and Ghost to Jigsaw and Warehouse in the womens' range and from Armani to Willy Smith and Boss in the men's. The clothes stocked cover both casual working day and evening wear, though they tend towards the former. Prices range from £10 - £200. Twice yearly sales in Summer and Winter. Clothing styles range from current to classical. Quick turnover and deposits accepted on items of clothing.

## SHARP

1A HOLLYWOOD ROAD, LONDON SW10 9HS
☎ 0171-376 3137. OPEN 10.30 - 6 MON - FRI, 10.30 - 2 SAT, UNTIL 8 ON WED.
Sharp is a charity shop which benefits from its closeness to an area of London which houses people who can still afford to dress in designer

clothes - and discard them when they've worn them a few times. Designers include Armani, Paul Smith and Versace for men, MaxMara, Ungaro and Escada for women. All the clothes are in good condition, with prices from £10 to £500.

## SIGN OF THE TIMES

17 ELYSTAN STREET, LONDON SW3
☎ 0171-589 4774. OPEN 10 - 5.30 MON - SAT.
Women's dress agency which also sells a small selection of men's clothes, as well as some accessories.

## THE BEST OF SECONDHAND

42 GOLDERS GREEN ROAD, LONDON NW11
☎ 0181-458 3890. OPEN 9.30 - 5.30 MON - FRI, 9.30 - 6 SAT, 10 - 5 SUN.
Primarily a dress agency for women with some childrenswear, there is also a selection of Chester Barry and Dior menswear.

## THE BRIDAL EXCHANGE

19 EDGWAREBURY LANE, EDGWARE, MIDDLESEX
☎ 0181-958 7002. OPEN 9 - 6 MON - SAT, 11 - 3 SUN.
Once-worn wedding dresses and groom's outfits to buy or to hire. Some of the stock is ex-hire, some from liquidations, some was bought but never worn and all are about half the original price. Grooms who are hiring will be fitted out at the actual showroom of the formal wear hire company and the suit they try on will be the one they wear on the day. There are also pageboy outfits.

## THE DESIGNER SALE AND EXCHANGE SHOP

61D LANCASTER ROAD, LONDON W11
☎ 0171-243 2396. OPEN 10 - 6 TUE - SAT, 12 - 6 MON.
Sells samples and seconds from last season – Rifat Ozbek, Pascale Smit, Galliano, Paddy Campbell – as well as nearly new clothes from British and European designers, mainly for women although there is usually a small selection for men.

## THE DRESS BOX

8-10 CHEVAL PLACE, LONDON SW7
☎ 0171-589 2240. OPEN 10.15 - 6 MON - FRI, 10.30 - 6 SAT.
This upmarket ladies dress agency, which has been in operation for more than 50 years, specialises in couture garments and also has a small selection of menswear.

## THE DRESSER

10 PORCHESTER PLACE, LONDON W2
☎ 0171-724 7212. OPEN 10 - 6 MON - SAT.
Secondhand designer men's and women's clothes including names such as Paul Smith, Jasper Conran, Armani, Gaultier and Comme des Garcons at prices ranging from £30-£400.

## WELLINGTONS

1 WELLINGTON PLACE, LONDON NW8
☎ 0171-483 0688. OPEN 11 - 5 MON - SAT.
Women's dress agency which also sells menswear. Armani, Boss, Kenzo, Versace, Montana. For example, Montana dinner suit, £128; suits from £68-£128; shirts £12-£38; ties from £4-£22.

# *Hire Shops*

## DESIGNERS FOR LESS

203 UXBRIDGE ROAD, LONDON W13 9AA
☎ 0181-579 5954. OPEN 9.30 - 6 MON - SAT.
High street shop, established since 1973, which sells factory seconds, ends of ranges, samples and previous season's stock in a range of men's clothes. Their main attractions are suits from Germany, but there is also an extensive dresswear hire department.

## JO DALBY COSTUME HIRE

4 RAVEY STREET, LONDON EC2
☎ 0171-739 3026. OPEN 10 - 5.30 MON - FRI.
Everything the dedicated dresser-upper or fancy dress party-goer could want from Victorian ladies and Twenties sirens to clowns, cats, harlequins and batmen, wigs, masks, hats and shoes. Cost from £24-55 for the weekend.

## LIPMANS HIRE DEPARTMENT

22 CHARING CROSS RD, LONDON WC2
☎ 0171 240 2310. OPEN 9 -8 MON - FRI, 10 - 6 WEEKENDS.
Hires and sells ex-hire outfits. For example, dinner suits which would normally cost £150 to buy are £95 while those which have seen more wear cost from £50. They also hire out dinner suits and top and tails from £27.95 to £41.

## LOSNERS DRESS HIRE

232 STAMFORD HILL, LONDON N16 6TT
☎ 0181-800 7466. OPEN 9 - 5.30 MON - SAT, UNTIL 7 ON WED, UNTIL 5 ON THUR.
Specialises in top end of the market wedding outfits to hire and to buy from wedding dresses to morning suits from £40-£70 a week.

## ROYAL NATIONAL THEATRE

HIRE DEPARTMENT, CHICHESTER HOUSE, 1-3 BRIXTON WAY, LONDON SW9 6DE
☎ 0171-735 4774. OPEN 10 - 6 MON - FRI BY APPOINTMENT ONLY, CLOSED 1-2 DAILY.
If the recession hasn't stopped all the fun and you have been invited to the odd fancy dress party or perhaps you're involved in an amateur theatrical production, take a look at the Royal National Theatre's collection of costumes for hire. It stocks more than 60,000 original costumes from Roman togas to leather biker jackets. A warning note, however: some of the costumes looked better on stage than they do in the full glare of daylight.

## THE COSTUME STUDIO

6 PENTON GROVE, OFF WHITE LION STREET, LONDON N1
☎ 0171-388 4481/6576. OPEN 9.30 - 6 MON - FRI, 10 -5 SAT.
Between ten and twelve thousand costumes from medieval times to the 70s. Clients include TV and video companies. Individual hiring costs from £30-£60 for one week. There are plenty of accessories from shoes and hats to bags and gloves to complete an outfit.

# THE MERCHANT OF EUROPE

232 PORTOBELLO ROAD, LONDON W11
☎ 0171-221 4203. OPEN 10.30 - 6.30 MON - SAT.

Period style specialists, selling and hiring out vintage clothing from the 1880s to the 1970s, particularly leather jackets from the Forties and Fifties. There is also a large hire section of exquisite period evening wear. Men can hire unusual stage wear and classic suits.

## Secondhand and Vintage Clothes

# AMERICAN CLASSICS

404 KING'S ROAD, LONDON SW10
☎ 0171-351 5229. OPEN 11 - 7 MON - SAT.

Vintage American clothes from the Forties, Fifties, Sixties and Seventies with matching accessories including boots, belts, buckles for women and men.

# CENCI

31 MONMOUTH STREET, LONDON WC2
☎ 0171-836 1400. OPEN 10.30 - 7 MON - FRI, 10.30 - 6.30 SAT.

Vintage clothing from the Forties to the Seventies from America and Europe. There are about 8,000 items in the shop at any one time, many of which are bought from a factory in Italy devoted to the recycling of old style and quality clothing. As well as 1960s sweaters from £16 to £125, Forties' and Sixties' suits from £75 and a large selection of cashmere, there are also accessories and some shoes.

# CHENIL GALLERY

181-183 KING'S ROAD, LONDON SW3
☎ 0171-352 8581. OPEN 10.30 - 5.30 MON - SAT.

Clothes for women and men from 1800 to the 1950s from Fouthergill & Crawley, Enigma, Pamela Haywood and Persiflages. Forties crepe dress, £25; fitted women's jacket, £25; beaded evening dress, £150; period men's DJs, £35; tails, £50-£75; top hats and gloves also. Some children's clothes. Enigma caters for men with dinner suits from the Twenties to the Sixties, £60, morning suits, cummerbunds, bow ties and cufflinks.

## COBWEBS

60 ISLINGTON PARK STREET, LONDON N1
☎ 0171-359 8090. OPEN 11 - 6 MON - SAT.
Small shop which has been in operation for 14 years, selling second-hand clothes in very English style for men and women, particularly Sixties clothes and accessories. Men's waistcoats, £15; men's jackets and coats, £48-£60; men's tweeds, £28; men's shirts, £10.

## EMPORIUM

330-332 CREEK ROAD, GREENWICH, LONDON SE10
☎ 0181-305 1670. OPEN 10.30 - 6 TUE - SUN.
Sell men's and women's classic clothing from Twenties to Seventies. Specialise in hats including panamas, trilbies and fashion hats and have some secondhand hats.

## FLIP

125 LONG ACRE, COVENT GARDEN, LONDON WC2E 9PE
☎ 0171-836 4688. OPEN 10 - 7 MON - SAT, 12 - 6 SUN, UNTIL 8 ON THUR.
Original Levi's and cut-off Levi jeans, waistcoats, hippy shirts, wide denim flares, denim jackets, £40-£60. Most of the stock is jeans with some Sixties dresses, short jackets, and coats for both men and women.

## OXFAM NOLOGO

26 GANTON STREET, LONDON W1
☎ 0171-437 7338. OPEN 11 - 6 MON - SAT.
Famous in the past for its one-off designs made up by fashion students using donated fabric from top designers, this Oxfam shop now sells retro clothing for men and women.

## PHILIP OF KING'S ROAD

191 KING'S ROAD, LONDON SW3 5ED
☎ 0171-352 4332. OPEN 10 - 6.30 MON - FRI, 10 - 7 SAT.
Specialises in American clothing, both new and secondhand, from baseball to army surplus, jeans, jackets, baseball boots and 501s. Full selection of American sports equipment and accessories including caps and baseball bats.

## STEINBERG & TOLKEIN

193 KING'S ROAD, LONDON SW3 5EB
☎ 0171-376 3660. OPEN 10.30 - 7 MON - SAT, 1 - 6 SUN.

Situated on two floors, one floor is devoted totally to jewellery, the other floor to American vintage and European couture clothing from the Twenties and Thirties to the Seventies. Some of the more interesting items were worn by movie stars of the Thirties and Forties and the garment is often seen on the original wearer in photographs around the shop. Popular with those looking for something unusual for a theme evening, it's also frequented by those searching for an individual look in a style and quality unmatched even by couture designers today. There is a small selection of men's clothes.

## THE CAVERN

154 COMMERCIAL STREET, LONDON E1 6NV
☎ 0171-247 1889. OPEN 12 - 6 TUE, WED, THUR, FRI,
12 - 5 SAT.

Sixties and Seventies clothes, shoes, jewellery, lamps, posters, postcards, watches, ninety percent of which is unworn and unused. For example watches from £20-£150; leather jackets, from £10-£50; denim flares, from £15-£25; embroidered flares, £25. Watch manufacturers include Secura and Camy. Men's and women's, but few children's, clothes stocked. Student discounts of at least 10%.

## THE MERCHANT OF EUROPE

232 PORTOBELLO ROAD, LONDON W11
☎ 0171-221 4203. OPEN 10.30 - 6.30 MON - SAT.

Period style specialists, selling and hiring out vintage clothing from the 1880s to the 1970s, particularly leather jackets from the Forties and Fifties. There is also a large hire section of exquisite period evening wear. Men can hire unusual stage wear and classic suits.

## THE OBSERVATORY

20 GREENWICH CHURCH STREET, GREENWICH,
LONDON SE10
☎ 0181-305 1998. OPEN 10 - 6 EVERY DAY.

Two floors of secondhand clothes from Thirties onwards for men and women. Women's frocks, shoes, hats and jewellery as well as lots of leather, suede and denim garments. Men's suits, jackets and trousers.

# *Designer Sales*

## BRITISH DESIGNERS SALE FOR MEN

DEBBIE HODGES, 42 YORK MANSIONS, PRINCE OF WALES DRIVE,
LONDON SW11 4BP
☎ 0171-228 5314.

The first of what is now a booming industry, the British Designers
Sale was started by Debbie Hodges, formerly in PR, more than 15
years ago. Because of her contacts, it offers the sort of top British
designer labels - plus a number of top Italian, French and German
labels - you won't find at other designer sales. However, no names can
be mentioned or those publicity-shy designers would not be happy to
let Debbie sell their overstocks. Labels are the quality found in the
designer rooms at Harrods or Harvey Nichols. Although the women's
sales, which are held five times a year in London, are so oversub-
scribed that there is a waiting list, the men's sales are still open to
members of the public. Please enclose an sae when writing to Debbie
to be put on the mailing list. Debbie has recently also started holding
sales in Edinburgh.

## THE DESIGNER ROADSHOW

ORGANISER: ELAINE FOSTER
☎ 0171-226 7437.

One of the few designer sales which takes place outside London, the
Designer Roadshow usually takes in six or seven venues around the
country before ending up in Deep Space Studios, 10A Belmont St,
London NW1. Stock is more likely to appeal to the younger end of
the market, and there is plenty to appeal to men, too. Cities visited
last year include Glasgow, Liverpool, Leeds, Bristol, Brighton,
Cardiff, Bath and Manchester and among the sixty designers whose
clothes were on sale were Rifat Ozbek, Nick Coleman, Felix Blow, Val
Pirou, Jasper Conran, Duffer of St George, Fred Bear hats, Xavier
Foley, Sonnentag Mulligan, Copperwheat Blundell, Griffin Laundry,
No Such Soul and Komodo. Phone Elaine for more information and
to put your name on the mailing list.

# THE DESIGNER WAREHOUSE SALE FOR MEN

ROGER DACK LTD, STUDIO 2, SHEPPERTON HOUSE,
83 SHEPPERTON ROAD, LONDON N1 3DF
☎ 071-704 1064. 10 - 8 FRI, 10 - 6 SAT, 11 - 5 SUN.
The Designer Warehouse Sale for Men is the sister sale to the
Warehouse Sale for Women and usually takes place at The Worx,
Balfe St, London N1, over a weekend. Labels regularly seen include
Dexter Wong and Roger Dack to Colin Harvey and Niegl Hall. Prices
are normally about one third of the shop price. Admission is £2.
Phone for more details and dates.

# WINDSMOOR WAREHOUSE

WINDSMOOR HOUSE, 83 LAWRENCE ROAD, TOTTENHAM,
LONDON N15
☎ 0181-800 8022.
Regular sales are held here during which first quality fashion from
the Windsmoor, Planet, Precis and Berkertex ranges are sold at discounts of up to 75%. Sometimes, there is also Nautica casualwear
for men, Centaur for men and Dannimac rainwear for men and
women. Phone or write to be put on the mailing list.

# SOUTH EAST

## *Permanent Discount Outlets*

# CHOICE DISCOUNT STORES LIMITED

14-20 RECTORY ROAD, HADLEIGH, BENFLEET, ESSEX SS7 2ND
☎ (01702) 555245. OPEN 9 - 5.30 MON - SAT.
26-28 HIGH STREET, BARKINGSIDE, ILFORD, ESSEX
IG6 2DO
☎ 0181-551 2125. OPEN 9 - 5.30 MON - FRI, 9 - 6 SAT,
10 - 4 SUN.
44-46 HIGH STREET, WATFORD, HERTFORDSHIRE
WD1 2BR
☎ (01923) 23355. OPEN 9 - 5.30 MON - SAT.
10-11 LADYGATE CENTRE, HIGH STREET, WICKFORD, ESSEX SS12 9AK
☎ (01268) 764893. OPEN 9 - 5.30 MON - THUR, 9 - 6 FRI, SAT.
UNIT 6A, MAYFLOWER RETAIL PARK, GARDINERS LINK, BASILDON,
ESSEX SS14 3AR
☎ (01268) 288331. OPEN 9 - 6 MON, TUE, WED, 9 - 7 THUR, FRI, 9 - 5.30
SAT, 11 - 5 SUN.

14-16 HIGH STREET, GRAYS, ESSEX RM17 6LV
☎ (01375) 385780. OPEN 9 - 5.30 MON - SAT.
Surplus stock including men's, women's and children's fashions from Next plc, Next Directory and other high street fashions, Next Interiors and footwear. You can save up to 50% off normal retail prices for first quality; up to two thirds for seconds. There are no changing rooms but the shop offers refunds if goods are returned in perfect condition within 28 days. There are special sales each January and September. Easy access for wheelchairs and pushchairs. The Watford and Wickford stores are known as Next 2 Choice; the former specialises in ladies and menswear only from Next plc and Next Directory.

## CROMWELL'S MAD HOUSE

28-29 TOWN SQUARE MALL, THE PEACOCKS SHOPPING CENTRE, WOKING, SURREY GU21 1GB
☎ 0181-903 5888.
Discounted jeans and casual wear, hiking jackets, USA football,jackets, Fruit of the Loom T-shirts, and a range of Lee Cooper, Wrangler and Lee outfits, mostly for men, with some womenswear. Clothes are normally about 20% less than in the high street, as most of the items are either ends of lines or have been bought in bulk and priced to sell quickly. Some of its prices are cheeper than the equivalent items in the high street; others are not such good bargains. There are now 50 branches of this shop - phone 0181 903 5888 for your nearest outlet.

## HIGH & MIGHTY

4 MARKET STREET, WINCHESTER, HAMPSHIRE
☎ (01962) 842685. OPEN 10 - 4.30 MON - SAT.
High & Mighty, outfitters to big and tall men, has opened a discount shop in Winchester. All stock is previous seasons and in perfect condition. Merchandise comprises everything from casual jackets and trousers to smart suits, shirts and sweaters. Trousers in the tall range go up to 37" leg, 32"-46" waist; jackets up to 40"-48"chest. In the king size range, jackets go from 46"-60" chest and trousers from 42"-60" waist. Examples of prices include trousers £15; shirts £15; and suits from £70-£100; discounts are generally about 50% off normal retail shop prices.

# M & G DESIGNER FASHIONS

OLD LONDON ROAD (OLD A23), HICKSTEAD VILLAGE, WEST SUSSEX RH17 5 RL
☎ (01444) 881511. OPEN 10 - 5 MON - SAT AND SOME BANK HOLIDAYS; PHONE FIRST.

A large fashion warehouse selling designer and famous high-street name clothes and shoes for men and women at discounted prices from 20% to 80% less than the normal retail price. The men's range is relatively recent and now also includes shoes and some accessories. Because they carry many famous high street and designer labels in the 3,400 sq ft outlet, they are unable to advertise these names. Some of the clothes are discontinued lines, others late deliveries, bankrupt stock or cancelled orders. Twice a year, they hold "silly" sales where no garment is over £30. They also hold winter and summer clearance sales. There is ample parking, free coffee or tea, easy access for wheelchairs and individual changing rooms. (Follow the signs to Hickstead Village.)

# MATALAN

UNIT 4B, THE TUNNEL ESTATE, WESTERN AVENUE,RM16 1HH LAKESIDE RETAIL PARK, WEST THURROCK, ESSEX
☎ (01708) 864350. OPEN 10 - 8 MON - FRI, 9.30 - 5.30 SAT, 10 - 6 SUN.
UNIT 4, RIVERSIDE RETAIL PARK, VICTORIA ROAD, CHELMSFORD, ESSEX EM2 6LL
☎ (01245) 348787. OPEN 10 - 8 MON - FRI, 9.30 - 5.30 SAT, 11 - 5 SUN.
ROSE KILN LANE, READING, BERKSHIRE RG2 OSN
☎ (01734) 391958. OPEN 10 - 8 MON - FRI, 9.30 - 5.30 SAT, 10 - 6 SUN.
BILTON ROAD, BLETCHLEY, MILTON KEYNES, BUCKINGHAMSHIRE MK1 1HS
☎ (01908) 373735. OPEN 10 - 8 MON - FRI, 9 - 6 SAT, 10 - 4 SUN.

As the UK's first National Discount Club, Matalan has the buying power to guarantee its members up to 60% discounts on a huge range of brand name clothing, household goods, luggage and toiletries for all the family. Top quality merchandise, current season, no seconds, is offered to its members at exclusive, permanently discounted prices seven days a week. Matalan operates strictly on a membership basis, one of the key factors for its success in offering 20%-60% savings off recommended retail prices. Membership cards are issued through companies, organisations and associations in the vicinity of the stores, and are available to their employees/members. They are valid at any of the 50 Matalan stores in the UK. To find out if your organisation is registered, phone the Matalan hotline on 01772 629447.

# T K MAXX

THE GALLERIA SHOPPING CENTRE, COMET WAY,
JUNCTION 3 OFF THE A1, HATFIELD, HERTFORDSHIRE
☎ (01707) 270063. OPEN 10 - 8 MON - FRI, 10 - 6 SAT,
11 - 5 SUN.
173-178 HIGH STREET, BELOW BAR, SOUTHAMPTON
☎ (01703) 631600. OPEN 9 - 5.30 MON - FRI, 9 - 6 SAT, UNTIL 7 ON THUR.
BROAD STREET MALL, BROAD STREET, READING,
BERKSHIRE
☎ (01734) 511117. OPEN 9 - 5.30 MON - FRI, 9 - 6 SAT.
LOWER CONCOURSE, THE PEACOCKS, WOKING, SURREY,
☎ (01483) 750263. OPEN 9 - 6 MON - FRI, UNTIL 8 ON THURS,
9 - 6 SAT, 11 - 5 SUN.

Based on an American concept, TK Maxx is the first British retailer to practise "off-price" retailing. This means a centrally located store which offers famous label goods with up to 60% savings off recommended retail prices. TK Maxx has fashion for the whole family - men's, women's and childrenswear - accessories, shoes, gifts, kitchenware and home goods. Everything in the store is branded with a choice of well-known high street names to designer labels, and while a small percentage mightly be clearly marked past season, the great majority of items in store are current season, current stock and still with phenomenal savings. There is a huge choice with 50,000 pieces in store with 5,000 new items arriving a week, so it's worth keeping abreast of the lastest deliveries as turnaround is very fast. One of the ways in which TK Maxx is able to offer such low prices is by running a very low-cost operation, so the stores are simple and unfussy with wide aisles, shopping trolleys and baskets, and a spacious, functional feel to them. Service is not compromised, however: there are individual changing rooms, ramps for buggies and wheelchairs, plenty of staff on the shop floor and all the branches accept all major credit and debit cards.

# *Factory Shops*

## ALAN PAINE KNITWEAR

SCATS COUNTRY STORE, BRIGHTON ROAD, GODALMING, SURREY
☎ (01483) 419962. OPEN 9 - 5 MON - FRI, 8.30 - 4.30 SAT.

Men's and ladies knitwear, made in the factory in Wales (see Menswear, Wales and West Midlands) and sold here at factory shop prices. Choose from cotton, cashmere, lambswool, camel hair, merino and merino and silk mix. The factory makes most of its stock for export, and sells to some of the top shops in London. This shop is also supplied by another sister company with men's T-shirts, long-sleeved shirts and cotton trousers and shorts.

## AQUASCUTUM

CLEVELAND ROAD, MAYLANDS WOOD ESTATE, HEMEL HEMPSTEAD, HERTFORDSHIRE HP2 7EY
☎ (01442) 248333. OPEN 10 - 4 MON - FRI,
OCCASIONALLY 9 - 1 SAT.

Previous season's stock and seconds for women and men at greatly reduced prices. For men, blazers, suits and silk ties. Examples include 60% off men's suits and half-price ladies silk blouses.

## DAVID EVANS COLLECTION

BOURNE ROAD, CRAYFORD, KENT DA1 4BP
☎ (01322) 559401. OPEN 9.30 - 5 MON - FRI, 9.30 - 4.30 SAT.

Silk ties, silk fabric, wallets, photo frames and seconds in scarves are all on sale here at incredibly low prices. Also silk dressing gowns, visitors books, silk waistcoats and cravats. Occasional clearance sales make for even better bargains.

## JAEGER FACTORY SHOP

208 LONDON ROAD, BURGESS HILL, WEST SUSSEX RH15 9RD
☎ (01444) 871123. OPEN 9.30 - 4 TUE - FRI, 9.30 - 3.30 SAT.

Classic tailoring from Jaeger, Jaeger Man and Viyella at old-fashioned prices for men and women. Most of the merchandise is last season's stock and some seconds, but you may find the odd gem from this season if you hunt carefully. Some factory shops the whole range of Jaeger clothes, some just knitwear; yet others sell goods other than those with the Jaeger label. This shop sells mens and ladies wear, as well as accessories, towels and linens.

## KANGOL

46 CHURCH STREET, LUTON, BEDFORDSHIRE LU1 3JG
☎ (01582) 405000. OPEN 10 - 4 MON - FRI, 9 - 12.30 SAT.
Kangol Factory Shop sells end of lines, seconds, samples and some perfect prototypes of their famous caps, berets, felt, woollen and straw hats and special occasion headwear for events such as Henley. There are more than 100 different styles on display for men and women including elaborate hats made from anything from polyester and straw to cotton and silk. Caps start from £3.50 and special occasion hats range from £8-£30.

## MERCHANTS QUAY

BRIGHTON MARINA, BRIGHTON, SUSSEX BN2 5UF
☎ (01273) 693636. FAX (01273) 675082.
Ten main factory shop plus twenty-four small factory concessions including The Factory Shop, Edinburgh Crystal, Bookscene and Hornsea Pottery. The concessions include Tom Sayer menswear, Coloroll and Double Two shirts. There are also two "affordable" art galleries, a craft shop, a framing shop, a full-price bridal shop, a multi-complex 8-screen cinema, an Asda superstore, small playground and a variety of eating places.

## MEXX INTERNATIONAL

132-133 FAIRLIE ROAD, SLOUGH TRADING ESTATE, SLOUGH, BERKSHIRE SL1 4PY
☎ (01753) 525450. OPEN 9.30 - 5.30 MON - SAT, 10 - 4 SUN, UNTIL 7 ON THUR.
High street fashion at factory outlet prices for men, women and children. There are usually at least 6,000 items in stock, with regular new deliveries, all of which are heavily discounted by between 40%-80%. Seventy-five percent of the stock is Mexx own label from last season, the rest is from concessions including Debut Sports and Fiorelli. The outlet can be found by turning down off the Slough Farnham Road at Do It All and turning right at the second set of traffic lights.

## MICHELSONS

STAPLEHURST ROAD, SITTINGBOURNE, KENT ME10 2NH
☎ (01795) 426821. OPEN 9 - 4 MON - THUR, 9 - 12 FRI.

Michelsons, one of the largest tie manufacturers in Europe, has a small factory shop attached to the factory selling silk neckties, cufflinks, bowties, handkerchiefs, scarves and cravats. All the stock is current or last season's or ends of lines and is discounted by at least 30%. There is a choice of more than 1,000 ties in silk from £6.99-£16.99; plus silver and gold plated cufflinks from £18.99.

## MOTOWN JEANS

MOTOWN YARD, THE BREWERY, LONDON ROAD,
STANFORD-LE-HOPE, ESSEX
☎ (01375) 675643. OPEN 9 - 5 MON - FRI, 9 - 1 SAT.

Manufactures denim jeans and jackets for retail outlets and sells its own label jeans at half price in its factory shop. It also sells denim jackets from a sister factory which it supplies with denim and Motown jeans. All are perfect and come in men's, ladies and children's sizes. Prices start at £12 for jeans, £27 for denim jackets.

## STERLING LEATHERS

UNIT A2, SEEDBED CENTRE, COLDHARBOUR ROAD,
PINNACLES, HARLOW, ESSEX CM19 5AF
☎ (01279) 444449. OPEN 9 - 4 MON - FRI, 10 - 12 SAT.

Sterling Leathers manufacture top quality men's and women's leather and suede garments for many of the best known names at the upper end of the high street. Their production ranges from full-length coats, jackets and blousons to waistcoats. Their factory shop at Harlow is a bargain hunger's paradise which sells garments a good deal cheaper than normal retail prices. In the vicinity of the factory are a number of tourist attractions about which details can be provided to shoppers on request.

# THE FACTORY SHOP (ESSEX) LTD

THE GLOUCESTERS, LUCKYN LANE, PIPPS HILL INDUSTRIAL ESTATE,
BASILDON, ESSEX SS14 3AX
☎ (01268) 520446. OPEN 9 - 5.30 MON - SAT, 10 - 5 SUN.

No-frills factory shop selling seconds, discontinued lines and some
perfect current stock from department and chain store high street
names, as well as direct from the manufacturer. This is not the place
to look for high fashion, but it has an enormous amount of middle of
the range men's, women's and children's clothes, as well as bedlinen,
towels, toys, food, kitchen utensils, disposable cutlery and partyware,
short-dated food, garden furniture, tools, sportswear, china, glass and
barbecues within its 8,000 square feet of selling space. Everything is
sold at between 30% and 50% of the retail price. Parking is easy, the
M25 is near and there's good wheelchair/pushchair access.

# THE FALMER FACTORY SHOP

24 BROOK ROAD, RAYLEIGH, ESSEX SS6 7XE
☎ (01268) 773633. OPEN 9 - 5.30 MON - SAT.

Selected current stock perfects and seconds from the Falmer jeans
range as well as seconds and discontinued garments from leggings and
sweatshirts to jackets and knitwear for men and women. Twice a year,
they also hold clearance sales.

# THE SHOE SHED

ORCHARD ROAD, ROYSTON, HERTFORDSHIRE SG8 5HA
☎ (01763) 241933. OPEN 9 - 5.30 TUE, WED, 9 - 6 THUR, FRI, 9 - 4 SAT, 10
- 2 SUN.
C/O MEXX UK, 132-133 FAIRLIE ROAD, SLOUGH,
BERKSHIRE
☎ (01753) 525450. OPEN 9.30 - 5.30 MON - WED, FRI, SAT, 9.30 - 7 THUR,
10 - 4 SUN.

Large factory shop selling a vast range of all types of men's, women's
and children's shoes, all of which are perfects, at up to 30%
below normal high street prices. Men's shoes from £10; sports shoes
from £10.

## *Dress Agencies*

### BARGAIN BOUTIQUE

SNOW HILL, CRAWLEY DOWN, WEST SUSSEX
☎ (01342) 712022. OPEN 9.15 - 2.15 TUE - SAT.
BB caters mainly for women and children, though there is a limited selection of menswear. Most of the merchandise is made up of separates, with a few suits, and there are some shoes for adults. For women, it stocks mainly high street names such as Marks & Spencer, Next, BhS, Laura Ashley, as well as labels such as Windsmoor and Jacques Vert. There is also a sample rail with great bargains at one third of the original price, but no accessories.

### BENJAMIN'S MESS

77 HIGH STREET, ROCHESTER, KENT ME1 1LX
☎ (01634) 817848. OPEN 9 - 5.30 MON - SAT.
This shop sells women's and children's clothes with a small men's section.

### CANCER RESEARCH GROUP

172 TERMINUS ROAD, EASTBOURNE, EAST SUSSEX BN21 3SB
☎ (01323) 739703. OPEN 9.30 - 4.30 MON - SAT.
7 HIGH STREET, SOUTHEND, ESSEX SS1 1JE
☎ (01702) 432698.
Shop specifically aimed at the wedding market which sells or hires pageboy outfits; black and grey morning suits, plus accessories, for the groom, as well as dinner suits. Prices range from: morning suits, £25 to hire, £50 to buy; dinner suits, £16.50 to hire, £35 to buy. Most of the stock is either donated or straight from the manufacturer.

### HANG-UPS

1A THE SQUARE, LONG CRENDON, NEAR AYLESBURY, BUCKING-HAMSHIRE
☎ (01844) 201237. OPEN 9.30 - 4 TUE, THUR, FRI, 9.30 5 SAT.
Mainly caters for women, but there is a special rail for men which usually houses suits and blazers.

## MANSWORLD

177 HIGH STREET, BERKHAMSTED, HERTFORDSHIRE HP4 3HP
☎ (0442) 864740. OPEN 9.30 -5.30 MON - FRI, 9.30 -5 SAT.

Ex-hire outfits for sale - for example, dinner suits from £40-£75.
Labels range from Marks & Spencer and Jaeger to Boss and Bruno
Kirsch. Dinner suits, morning suits, tail coats, kilts and pageyboy
outfits, with accessories, for hire. Annual sales in January and July.

## THE STOCK EXCHANGE

1 HIGH STREET, SUNINGHILL, ASCOT, BERKSHIRE SL5 5NQ
☎ (01344) 25420 . OPEN 9 - 5.30 MON - FRI, 9 - 4.30 SAT.

Mens, ladies and children's wear available, usually not more than 2
years old. Stock sold at either one third or half price after 4 weeks.
Rapid turnover of clothes.

## TOUCH OF CLASS

8 MARK LANE, EASTBOURNE, SUSSEX
☎ (01323) 639890 OPEN 10 - 4.30 MON - SAT.

Designer labels for men and women, including Jaeger, Windsmoor,
Aquascutum, Burberry and Daks. Reduced price wedding outfits. All
garments under 2 years old, some of which were "mistakes" or once-
worn only. Shoes and other accessories are also on sale.

# *Secondhand and Vintage Clothes*

## CASANOVA CLOTHING

110 HIGH STREET, ROCHESTER, KENT ME1 1JS
☎ (01634) 817300. OPEN 9.30 - 5.30 MON - SAT, 11 - 5.30 SUN.

Rather like an upmarket charity shop, Casanova Clothing sells
anything from mid-market labels to Sixties and Seventies gear, with
lots of leather. Typical prices include waistcoats, £5, to leather jackets,
£30.

# SOUTH WEST

## *Permanent Discount Outlets*

### MATALAN

UNIT 2, HAVEN BANKS, WATER LANE, EXETER, DEVON EX2 8DW
☎ (01392) 413375. OPEN 10 - 8 MON - FRI, 9.30 - 5.30 SAT,
10 - 6 SUN.
UNIT 1, ALDERMOOR WAY, LONGWELL GREEN,
BRISTOL BS15 7AD
☎ (0117) 9352828. OPEN 10 - 8 MON - FRI, 9.30 - 5.30 SAT,
10 - 6 SUN.
UNITS 2/3, TURBARY RETAIL PARK, RINGWOOD ROAD, POOLE,
DORSET BH12 3JJ
☎ (01202) 590686. OPEN 10 - 8 MON - FRI, 9 - 6 SAT, 11 - 5 SUN.
As the UK's first National Discount Club, Matalan has the buying
power to guarantee its members up to 60% discounts on a huge range
of brand name clothing, household goods, luggage and toiletries for
all the family. Top quality merchandise, current season, no seconds, is
offered to its members at exclusive, permanently discounted prices
seven days a week. Matalan operates strictly on a membership basis,
one of the key factors for its success in offering 20%-60% savings off
recommended retail prices. Membership cards are issued through
companies, organisations and associations in the vicinity of the stores,
and are available to their employees/members. They are valid at any
of the 50 Matalan stores in the UK. To find out if your organisation
is registered, phone the Matalan hotline on 01772 629447.

### MINEHEAD SHOE CO-OPERATIVE LTD

1 NORTH ROAD, MINEHEAD, SOMERSET TA24 5QW
☎ (01643) 705591. OPEN 8 - 5 MON - FRI, 10 - 1 SAT.
MAIL ORDER.
Shoes, including golf and bowling shoes, and leather handbags and
wallets. Wide and large sizes are catered for. Mail order available.

## SUMMERLAND FACTORY SHOP

ROUGE BOUILLION, ST HELIER, JERSEY
☎ (01534) 33511. OPEN 9 - 6 MON - FRI, 9 - 4.30 SAT.

Sell's mostly men's clothes bought direct from the manufacturer, althought about ten percent of its customers are women who buy the ladies sweaters, shoes and boots. The men's range includes underwear, ties, trousers, donkey jackets, coats, suits and short jackets and labels include Wolsey, Baumler, Pierre Balmain and Pierre Cardin, at discounts of up to 50%. All stock is this season's and perfect apart from one rail of seconds which is clearly marked.

## TK MAXX

THIRD FLOOR, THE GALLERIES, BRISTOL.
☎ (0117) 9304404. OPEN 9 - 5.30 MON - SAT, 7 ON THUR.

Based on an American concept, TK Maxx is the first British retailer to practise "off-price" retailing. This means a centrally located store which offers famous label goods with up to 60% savings off recommended retail prices. TK Maxx has fashion for the whole family - men's, women's and childrenswear - accessories, shoes, gifts, kitchenware and home goods. Everything in the store is branded with a choice of well-known high street names to designer labels, and while a small percentage mightly be clearly marked past season, the great majority of items in store are current season, current stock and still with phenomenal savings. There is a huge choice with 50,000 pieces in store with 5,000 new items arriving a week, so it's worth keeping abreast of the lastest deliveries as turnaround is very fast. One of the ways in which TK Maxx is able to offer such low prices is by running a very low-cost operation, so the stores are simple and unfussy with wide aisles, shopping trolleys and baskets, and a spacious, functional feel to them. Service is not compromised, however: there are individual changing rooms, ramps for buggies and wheelchairs, plenty of staff on the shop floor and all the branches accept all major credit and debit cards.

# TRAGO MILL

REGIONAL SHOPPING CENTRE, NEWTON ABBOT DEVON TQ12 6JD
☎ (01626) 821111. OPEN 9 - 5.30 MON - SAT, 10.30 - 4.30 SUN.
Sells virtually everything from men's women's and children's wear, gardening equipment and cookwear to wallpaper, carpets and fitted kitchens. Most are branded goods and there is a creche, cafe, pizza bar and petrol station.

# *Factory Shops*

## CLARKS FACTORY SHOP

CLARKS VILLAGE, FARM ROAD, STREET, SOMERSET BA16 OBB
☎ (01458) 843161. OPEN 9 - 6 MON - SAT AND BANK
HOLIDAYS, 11 - 5 SUN.
Clarks International operate a chain of factory shops nationally which specialise in selling discontinued lines and slight sub-standards for men, women and children from Clarks, K Shoes and other famous brands. These shops trade under the name of Crockers, K Shoes Factory shop or Clarks Factory Shop and while not all are physically attached to a shoe factory, these shops are treated as factory shops by the company. Customers can expect to find an extensive range of quality shoes, sandals, walking boots, slippers, trainers, handbags, accessories and gifts, while their major outlets such as here at Clarks Village also offer luggage, sports clothing, sports equipment and outdoor clothing. Brands stocked include Clarks, K Shoes, Springer, CICA, Hi-Tec, Puma, Mercury, Dr Martens, Nike, LA Gear, Fila, Mizuno, Slazenger, Weider, Samsonite, Delsey, Antler and Carlton, although not all are sold in every outlet. Discounts are on average 30% off the normal high street price for perfect stock. From November to end of March, weekday and Saturday closing times are 5.30.

# CLARKS VILLAGE FACTORY SHOPPING

FARM ROAD, STREET, SOMERSET BA16 OBB
☎ (01458) 840064. OPEN 9 - 6 MON - SAT, 11 - 5 SUN. TIMES CHANGE
WINTER AND SUMMER.

Purpose-built village of brick-built shops with extensive car parking
facilities. Restaurant run by Leith's, fast food stands, carousel, indoor
play area, outdoor play area. Here, there were at August 1995, 37
shops with more planned. For men: Jumpers, Benetton, The Baggage
Factory, Wrangler, James Barry, Jaeger, Fred Perry, Triumph/Hom,
Clarks Factory Shop, Claude Gill Books, Woolea (which also sells
Lyle & Scott and Barbour), Rohan, Farah Menswear, Thorntons
Chocolates, The Sports Factory, Black & Decker, Hallmark,
Remington, The Golf Factory and Esprit.

# CROCKERS

2 EASTOVER, BRIDGWATER, SOMERSET TA6 5AB
☎ (01278) 452617. OPEN 9 - 5.30 MON - SAT.
10A HIGH STREET, BURNHAM-ON-SEA, SOMERSET TA8 1NX
☎ (01278) 794668. OPEN 9 - 5.30 MON - SAT, 11 - 5 SUN, 10 - 5 BANK
HOLIDAYS.
112-114 HIGH STREET, STREET, SOMERSET BA16 OEW
☎ (01458) 442055. OPEN 9 - 5.30 MON - SAT AND BANK
HOLIDAYS, 11 - 5 SUNS.
UNITS 1 AND 13, WEST SWINDON DISTRICT CENTRE, SWINDON,
WILTSHIRE SN5 7DI
☎ (01793) 873662. OPEN 9 - 8 MON - FRI, 9 - 6 SAT, 10 - 4 SUN, 10 - 5
BANK HOLIDAYS.
UNIT 2, SAINSBURYS PRECINCT, QUEENSWAY
SHOPPING CENTRE, WORLE, AVON BS22 OBT
☎ (01934) 521693. OPEN 9 - 8 MON - FRI, 9 - 6 SAT,
10.30 - 4.30 SUN, 9 - 5 BANK HOLIDAYS.

Clarks International operate a chain of factory shops nationally which
specialise in selling discontinued lines and slight sub-standards for
men, women and children from Clarks, K Shoes and other famous
brands. These shops trade under the name of Crockers, K Shoes
Factory shop or Clarks Factory Shop and while not all are physically
attached to a shoe factory, these shops are treated as factory shops by
the company. Customers can expect to find an extensive range of
quality shoes, sandals, walking boots, slippers, trainers, handbags,
accessories and gifts, while their major outlets also offer luggage,

sports clothing, sports equipment and outdoor clothing. Brands stocked include Clarks, K Shoes, Springer, CICA, Hi-Tec, Puma, Mercury, Dr Martens, Nike, LA Gear, Fila, Mizuno, Slazenger, Weider, Samsonite, Delsey, Antler and Carlton, although not all are sold in every outlet. Discounts are on average 30% off the normal high street price for perfect stock. The Swindon branch is also a sports factory shop and baggage factory shop.

## DENTS

FAIRFIELD ROAD, WARMINSTER, WILTSHIRE BA12 9DL
☎ (01985) 212291. OPEN 10 - 4 THUR - SUN.

The accessories company which produces such covetable gloves, belts, handbags and leather wallets and purses for most of the big department stores has a factory outlet near Salisbury. Most of the stock in this reasonably-sized warehouse shop consists of gloves, sold at at least 50% discount, but there are also some umbrellas, including telescopic, golf and walking umbrellas, silk ties, leather belts, leather card holders and key fobs. Stock from the discontinued and end of ranges changes constantly. The shop usually closes for the summer between May and September so phone first.

## ESPRIT

CLARKS VILLAGE FACTORY SHOPPING, FARM ROAD, STREET, SOMERSET BA16 OBB
☎ (01458) 840064. OPEN 9 - 6 MON - SAT, 11 - 5 SUN. TIMES CHANGE WINTER AND SUMMER.

Large, two-storey outlet divided into men's and women's wear, with older stock and shoes upstairs. Wide range of clothes from casual trousers and T-shirts, shorts and shirts, to dresses and shoes, all at discounted prices. (Telephone number above is the general Village number.)

## FOX & CHAVE

FOX HOUSE, LOCKS CROSS, NESTON, WILTSHIRE SN13 9TB
☎ (01225) 812058. BY APPOINTMENT ONLY.

Fox & Chave, who are wholesalers of the largest Italian silk tie collection in the UK, are now offering the public the chance to purchase from their complete range and receive 50% discount on the recommended retail price with the opening of their new showroom. Phone Paul or Tania Banyard for an appointment and a chance to pay just £10 for a hand-made Italian silk tie.

## FRED PERRY SPORTSWEAR UK LTD

UNIT 10, CLARKS VILLAGE, FARM ROAD, STREET,
SOMERSET BA16 0BB
☎ (01458) 841730. OPEN 9 - 6 MON - SAT, 11 - 5 SUN.

Men's and women's ranges of the famous Fred Perry sportswear and leisure clothing: shorts, tennis tops, tracksuits, T-shirts. All price labels show the original and the reduced price, which usually amount to a 30% discount.

## GEORGINA VON ETZDORF

THE AVENUE, ODSTOCK, NEAR SALISBURY, WILTSHIRE
☎ (01722) 326625. OPEN 10 - 6 MON - SAT, 12 - 5 SUN
(CLOSED 1- 2 FOR LUNCH DAILY)

A sweet, little factory shop near Salisbury. sandwiched between workrooms, it has a limited but exciting range of clothes and lots of wonderful accessories. Her products are not cheap, but the men's silk cravats, ties and jacquard silk scarves with cashmere linings are affordable at prices ranging from £20. Everthing is half price, and the price tag also tells you what season the outfit is from and whether it is a second. There are men's silk dressing gowns at about £200, men's silk cravats, £21.50, silk ties, from £10, and oddments of fabric. The factory shop is in a tiny lane.

# MORLANDS SHEEPSKIN

NORTHOVER, BETWEEN GLASTONBURY & STREET,
GLASTONBURY, SOMERSET
☎ (01458) 835042. OPEN 9.30 - 5 MON - SAT.

Manufacturers in the same area for 120 years, Morlands has a factory
shop in Glastonbury, near Clark's village on the A29. It sells traditional sheepskin coats from £199, boots, suede waistcoats from
£39.99, hats, moccasins, rugs, slippers, £19.99 and gloves, mostly for
men with some children's sizes. Most are seconds or overstock.

# MULBERRY

THE STREET, CHILCOMPTON, SOMERSET
☎ (01761) 232878. OPEN 9 - 5 MON - SAT.

A very popular large, attractive, factory outlet, which sells last season's
and seconds of the famous Mulberry leather bags, briefcases, filofaxes
and wallets at discounted prices. Also last season's clothes including a
few men's shoes and ties and men's gift ranges. Discontinued lines are
discounted by 30%-40%; current seconds, many of which come
direct from the factory, are discounted by 20%.

# SHOE SHED

STATION ROAD, BUDLEIGH, SALTERTON, DEVON EX9 6RU
☎ (01395) 443399. OPEN 8.30 - 5.30 MON - SAT, 10 - 4 SUN.
23 FAIRMILE ROAD, CHRISTCHURCH, DORSET BH23 2LA
☎ (01202) 474123. OPEN 10 - 5 MON - FRI, 9 - 5 SAT, 10 - 4 SUN.
MENDEVILLE ROAD, WYKE REGIS, WEYMOUTH, DORSET DT4 9HW
☎ (01305) 766772. OPEN 8.30 - 5 MON - WED, 8.30 - 8 THUR, FRI, 8.30 -
5.30 SAT, 10 - 4 SUN.

Large factory shop selling a vast range of all types of men's, women's
and children's shoes, all of which are perfects, at up to 30% below
normal high street prices. Men's shoes from £10; sports shoes from
£10. Ladies sandals cost from £5; ladies shoes from £7.50.

## THE FACTORY SHOP

36-37 ROUNDSTONE STREET, TROWBRIDGE, WILTSHIRE BA12 9AN
☎ (01225) 751399. OPEN 9 - 5.30 MON - SAT.
24 MARKET PLACE, WARMINSTER, WILTSHIRE BA12 9AN
☎ (01985) 217532. OPEN 9 - 5.30 MON - FRI, 9 - 5 SAT.
MART ROAD, MINEHEAD, SOMERSET
☎ (01643) 705911. OPEN 9.30 - 5.30 MON - SAT, 11 - 5 SUN.

Wide range on sale includes men's, ladies and children's clothing and footwear; household textiles, toiletries, hardware, luggage, lighting and bedding, most of which are chainstore and high street brands at discounts of approximately 30%-50%. There are weekly deliveries and brands include all the major stars: Coloroll, Wrangler and Dartington to name just three. Lines are continually changing and few factory shops offer such a variety under one roof.

# Dress Agencies

## CAMELEON

74 NEW ST, ST HELIER, JERSEY, CHANNEL ISLANDS
☎ (01534) 22438. OPEN 10 - 4 MON - SAT.

Offers nearly-new and some period fashion for men and women, covering a wide range of labels from well known high street names to Fenn Wright & Manson. For men, there is nearly new day and evening wear, shoes, hats, waistcoats, shirts and dinner suits. Also offers a hire service.

## SELECTIONS

4 RACE HILL, LAUNCESTON, CORNWALL PL15 9BB
☎ (01566) 775471. OPEN 9.30 - 4.30 MON - SAT.

Women's dress agency which also sells a small range of men's suits, starting at £50.

## THE FROCK EXCHANGE

9 SEAWAY ROAD, PRESTON, PAIGNTON, DEVON TQ3 2NY
☎ (01803) 522951. OPEN 10 - 4.45 TUE - SAT, CLOSED 1 - 2.

Women's and menswear with a cross section of clothes from designer labels to high street names and chain stores: Louis Feraud, Marks & Spencer, YSL, Christian Dior, Hodges and Dunns. Suits range from £18-£60, and there are hundreds of ties, some shoes from Barkers and Church's, morning suits, blazers, flannels and grey suits. One-third of the shop is taken up with menswear; two thirds with women's.

# WALES AND WEST MIDLANDS

*Permanent Discount Outlets*

## IMPS

69B HIGH STREET, WITNEY, OXFORDSHIRE
☎ (01993) 779875. OPEN 9 - 5 MON - SAT.
40 UPPER HIGH STREET, THAME, OXFORDSHIRE
☎ (01844) 212985. OPEN 9 - 5 MON - SAT.
52 SHEEP STREET, BICESTER, OXFORDSHIRE
☎ (01869) 243455. OPEN 9 - 5 MON - SAT.
26 MARKET PLACE, HENLEY-ON-THAMES, OXFORDSHIRE
☎ (01491) 411530. OPEN 9 - 5 MON - SAT.

High street shops selling popular chainstore seconds. Witney shop extends over two floors and has plenty of stock from clothes for all the family to towels, china, trays and flower cachepots. For men there are shirts, £8-£12, Y-fronts, £1.50, boxer shorts, £2.99, socks, £1.50, pyjamas, £11.99, zipper cardigans, £15, four-button collar T-shirts, £6.99, Wax Jax, £59.95, cord trousers, £15. Stock changes constantly.

## M C HITCHEN & SONS LTD

299 COVENTRY ROAD, BIRMINGHAM, WEST MIDLANDS B10 0RA
☎ (0121) 772 1637. OPEN 9 - 5.30 MON - SAT.
236 HAWTHORN ROAD, KINGSTANDING, BIRMINGHAM, WEST MIDLANDS B44 8PP
☎ (0121) 373 1276.OPEN 9.15 - 5.30 MON - SAT.
14-16 NORTH STREET, RUGBY, WARWICKSHIRE CV21 2AF
☎ (01788) 565116. OPEN 9.30 - 5.30 MON - WED,
9 - 5.30 THUR - SAT.

Littlewoods sell off their overstocks in a network of shops called M C Hitchen & Sons Ltd. Most of them are in the North of England and offer up to 40% off the catalogue price for clothing and between 50% and 60% off for electrical goods. Littlwoods also run a mobile shop which operates in cities where they don't have a sale shop. For details of further venues for the sales, which usually take place once a month, contact Jean Banks, c/o Crosby DC, Kershaw Avenue, Endbutt Lane, Crosby, Merseyside L70 1AH.

# MATALAN

UNIT 5, THE JOHN ALLEN CENTRE, COWLEY, OXFORD, OXFORDSHIRE OX4 3JP
☎ (01865) 747400. OPEN 10 - 8 MON - FRI, 9.30 - 5.30 SAT, 10 - 6 SUN.
UNITS A1/A2, GALLAGHER RETAIL PARK, TEWKESBURY ROAD, CHELTENHAM, GLOUCESTERSHIRE GL51 9RR
☎ (01242) 254001. OPEN 10 - 8 MON - FRI, 9.30 - 5.30 SAT, 10 - 6 SUN.
UNIT 1, MEOLE BRACE RETAIL PARK, HEREFORD ROAD, SHREWSBURY SY3 9NB
☎ (01743) 363240. OPEN 10 - 8 MON - FRI, 9.30 - 5.30 SAT, 10 - 6 SUN.
UNIT 7, VENTURA SHOPPING CENTRE, VENTURA PARK ROAD, BONE HILL, TAMWORTH, STAFFORDSHIRE B78 3HB
☎ (01827) 50900. OPEN 10 - 8 MON - FRI, 9.30 - 5.30 SAT, 10 - 6 SUN.
FOUNDRY ROAD, MORRISTON, SWANSEA SA6 8DU
☎ (01792) 792229. OPEN 10 - 8 MON - FRI, 9.30 - 5.30 SAT, 10 - 6 SUN.
BIRMINGHAM ROAD, HOWARD STREET, WOLVERHAMPTON, WEST MIDLANDS WV2 2LQ
☎ (01902) 352813. OPEN 10 - 8 MON - FRI, 9.30 - 5.30 SAT, 10 - 6 SUN.
UNIT 4B, CWMBRAN RETAIL PARK CWMBRAN DRIVE, CWMBRAN, GWENT NP44 3JQ
☎ (01633) 866944. OPEN 10 - 8 MON - FRI, 9.30 - 5.30 SAT, 10 - 6 SUN.
UNIT E, MAYBIRD CENTRE, BIRMINGHAM ROAD, STRATFORD-UPON-AVON CV37 OHZ
☎ (01789) 262223. OPEN 10 - 8 MON - FRI, 10 - 5.30 SAT, 10 - 6 SUN.
UNIT 1A & 1B, CAENARFON ROAD, BANGOR LL57 4SU.
☎ (0248) 362778. OPEN 10 - 8 MON - FRI, 9.30 - 5.30 SAT, 10 - 8 SUN.

WOLSTANTON RETAIL PARK, WOLSTANTON, NEWCASTLE,
STAFFORDSHIRE ST5 1DY
☎ (01782) 711731. OPEN 9.30 - 8 MON - FRI, 9.30 - 6 SAT,
10 - 5.30 SUN.
UNITS 5 & 6, QUEENSVILLE RETAIL PARK, SILKMORE LANE,
STAFFORD ST17 4SU
☎ (01785) 226211. OPEN 10 - 8 MON - FRI, 9.30 - 5.30 SAT,
10 - 6 SUN.
UNIT 2, 382-384 NEWPORT ROAD, CARDIFF, WALES CF3 7AE
☎ (01222) 491781. OPEN 10 - 8 MON - FRI, 9 - 6 SAT, 11 - 5 SUN.
UNIT A, LICHFIELD STREET, BURTON-ON-TRENT, STAFFORDSHIRE
DE14 3QZ
☎ (01283) 540865.
UNIT 8, GLAMORGAN VALE RETAIL PARK, LLANTRISANT, MID-GLAM-
ORGAN, SOUTH WALES CF7 8RP
☎ (01433) 224854. OPEN 10 - 8 MON - FRI, 9 - 6 SAT, 10 - 5 SUN.
As the UK's first National Discount Club, Matalan has the buying
power to guarantee its members up to 60% discounts on a huge range
of brand name clothing, household goods, luggage and toiletries for
all the family. Top quality merchandise, current season, no seconds, is
offered to its members at exclusive, permanently discounted prices
seven days a week. Matalan operates strictly on a membership basis,
one of the key factors for its success in offering 20%-60% savings off
recommended retail prices. Membership cards are issued through
companies, organisations and associations in the vicinity of the stores,
and are available to their employees/members. They are valid at any
of the 50 Matalan stores in the UK. To find out if your organisation
is registered, phone the Matalan hotline on 01772 629447.

## NEXT TO NOTHING
24-25 WALFRUN CENTRE, WOLVERHAMPTON, WEST
MIDLANDS WV1 3HG
☎ (01902) 29464. OPEN 9 - 5.30 MON - SAT.
104 CORPORATION STREET, BIRMINGHAM, WEST
MIDLANDS
☎ (0121) 233 0022. OPEN 9 - 5.15 MON - FR, 9.30 - 6 SAT.
Sells perfect surplus stock from Next stores and the Next Directory
catalogue at discounts of 50% or more. The ranges are usually last
season's and overruns but there is the odd current item if you look
carefully. Stock consists of men's, women's and children's clothing,
with some homeware and shoes, depending on the branch. Stock is
replenished twice a week and there is plenty of it.

## THE FACTORY SHOP

NEW ROAD, PERSHORE, WORCESTERSHIRE WR10 1BT
☎ (01386) 556467. OPEN 9 - 5 MON - SAT, 10.30 - 4.30 SUN.

Sells clothes, childrenswear, some leisurewear and has a designer clothes section upstairs, as well as household goods, bags, suitcases, electrical goods, kitchenware, shoes, toiletries, suitcases, china, lighting. Most stock is seconds or clearance lines from well-known chain stores and department stores.

## THE FASHION FACTORY

THE MALTINGS, KING STREET, WELLINGTON, TELFORD,
SHROPSHIRE TF1 3AE
☎ (01952) 260489. OPEN 9 - 5.30 MON - SAT, 11 - 5 SUN.
WYRLEYBROOK PARK, VINE LANE, CANNOCK,
STAFFORDSHIRE WS11 3XF.
☎ (01543) 466000. OPEN 9.30 - 5.30 MON - SAT, 11 - 5 SUN.

Sells last season's perfect quality Alexon, Dash, Eastex, Gossard and Lee Cooper. Among the 30,000 garments in stock at any one time is anything from lingerie to raincoats with Dash T-shirts costing £1.99, and branded jackets costing £23, reduced from £80. Discounts are in the range of 40%-70%.

## THE SALE SHOP

ROSS LABELS LTD, OVERROSS, ROSS ON WYE,
HEREFORDSHIRE HR9 7QJ
☎ (01989) 769000. OPEN 9.30 - 5.30 MON - FRI, 9 - 5.30 SAT,
10 - 5 SUN.

Twenty thousand square feet of selling space with men's, ladies and childrens wear from underwear and jeans to good, middle of the road brand name outfits and suits bought direct from the manufacturer. Some of the labels on sale include Alexon, Eastex, Dash, Big Bubble, Fruit of the Loom, Viyella, Wolsey, Elsie Whiteley, Double Two, Telemac and Lyle & Scott. There is also a selection of Norman Linton fashion in larger sizes - up to 46 for men and 22 for women. Also silk ties and waistcoats, James Barry suits from £115 and Double Two shirts from £10-£30. Stock is usually one year old, while current merchandise consists of overmakes. Discounts range from 20% to 50%. There is also a Lee Cooper and big kids wear department and Aquascutum clothes are sold at less than normal high street prices.

# TK MAXX

THE POTTERIES SHOPPING CENTRE, HANLEY,
STOKE-ON-TRENT, STAFFORDSHIRE.
☎ (01782) 289822. OPEN 9 - 5.30 MON - FRI, UNTIL 8 ON THURS,
9 - 6 SAT,

Based on an American concept, TK Maxx is the first British retailer to practise "off-price" retailing. This means a centrally located store which offers famous label goods with up to 60% savings off recommended retail prices. TK Maxx has fashion for the whole family - men's, women's and childrenswear - accessories, shoes, gifts, kitchenware and home goods. Everything in the store is branded with a choice of well-known high street names to designer labels, and while a small percentage mightly be clearly marked past season, the great majority of items in store are current season, current stock and still with phenomenal savings. There is a huge choice with 50,000 pieces in store with 5,000 new items arriving a week, so it's worth keeping abreast of the lastest deliveries as turnaround is very fast. One of the ways in which TK Maxx is able to offer such low prices is by running a very low-cost operation, so the stores are simple and unfussy with wide aisles, shopping trolleys and baskets, and a spacious, functional feel to them. Service is not compromised, however: there are individual changing rooms, ramps for buggies and wheelchairs, plenty of staff on the shop floor and all the branches accept all major credit and debit cards.

# TOP MARKS

23 HIGH STREET, MORETON-IN-MARSH, GLOUCESTERSHIRE
GL56 OAF
☎ (01608) 651272. OPEN 9 - 5.30 MON - FRI, 9 - 5 SAT.
8 HIGH STREET, CHIPPING NORTON, GLOS
☎ (01608) 642653. OPEN 9 - 5.30 MON - FRI, 9 - 5 SAT.

Sells seconds from leading chain stores for all the family. Most of the stock is made up of men's and women's wear, and there is also children's wear, most of which are Marks & Spencer seconds, sold at about one third cheaper than M&S. Wide range of stock in various sizes with new stock arriving twice a week, just six weeks after it was first introduced to M&S department stores.

# *Factory Shops*

## ALAN PAINE KNITWEAR

NEW ROAD, AMMANFORD, DYFED SA18 3ET
☎ (01269) 592316. OPEN 9 - 4 MON - SAT.

Small room in the front of the factory itself selling knitwear manufactured in the factory. The smallest size they make is a 38" chest. Chose from lambswool, cotton, camel hair, cashmere, merino and merino and silk mix. The company sells to the top shops in London, although most of their stock is made for export.

## BENETTON

BICESTER OUTLET SHOPPING VILLAGE, PINGLE DRIVE, BICESTER,
JUNCTION 9 OF M40, OXFORDSHIRE OX6 7WD
☎ (01869) 323200. OPEN 10 - 6 MON - SAT AND BANK
HOLIDAYS, 11 - 5 SUN.

One of 48 shops, with more planned, in this factory shopping village which opened in June 1995. Benetton stocks a wide range of clothes for men, women and children including colourful T-shirts, sweatshirts, men's button-neck T-shirts, swimwear, jeans, children's jackets, stretch short and all-in-one shorts. Some of the stock is marked seconds, but it is often difficult to tell why. The centre also has two restaurants, a small children's play area and free parking.

## BICESTER OUTLET SHOPPING VILLAGE

PINGLE DRIVE, BICESTER, JUNCTION 9 OF M40,
OXFORDSHIRE OX6 7WD
☎ (01869) 323200. OPEN 10 - 6 MON - SAT AND BANK
HOLIDAYS, 11 - 5 SUN.

Factory shopping village comprising 48 different outlets, which opened in June 1995. Billed as Bond Street comes to Bicester, the shops are very smart indeed, beautifully designed and stocked with end-of-season designer fashions, mens and childrenswear, tableware, shoes and more, all on permanent sale at prices reduced from 25%-50%, with some reductions up to 75%. Outlets for men include: casualwear from Benetton; witty slogans on T-shirts and nightshirts from the US company, Big Dog; Clarks footwear; sports shoes from the US company, Converse; brand name luggage from Equator; casualwear and sportswear from Fred Perry; men's underwear and swimwear from HOM; country clothing from John Partridge; glassware from John Jenkins; footwear from Kurt Geiger; specialist outerwear from Mileta Sport at Tog 24; casualwear from Pepe Jeans; designer fashions from Polo Ralph Lauren; candles and candlesticks from Price's Candles; men's fashions from Principles; casualwear and after sailing clothes for men and women from Scandinavian company Red/Green; casualwear from mail order specialists Racing Green; books, CDs and cassettes from Sapphire Books; men's fashions from Scotch House; men's suits, jackets and top designer name shirts from the Moss Bros shop, The Suit Company; jeans and casualwear from Wrangler. The centre also has two restaurants, a small children's play area and free parking.

## BIG DOG

BICESTER OUTLET SHOPPING VILLAGE, PINGLE DRIVE, BICESTER, JUNCTION 9 OF M40, OXFORDSHIRE OX6 7WD
☎ (01869) 323200. OPEN 10 - 6 MON - SAT AND BANK HOLIDAYS, 11 - 5 SUN.

This is a US company which sells T-shirts, sweatshirts, shorts and nightwear with a slogan for men, women and children. As they are not a well-known name here, it is difficult to tell how good their prices are. All the clothes are unisex and there are also golf balls, golf umbrellas, dogs leads and mouse mats. All the stock is currently on sale in the USA. Examples of prices in June 1995 include sweatshirts, £14.99 reduced from £25; T-shirts, £7.99 reduced from £10; long nightie T-shirts, £18 reduced from £20; men's shorts, £24.99 reduced from £30. The village also has two restaurants, a small children's play area and free parking. The telephone number given here is for the village.

## BURBERRY

YNYSWEN ROAD, TREOCHY, RHONDDA, MID GLAMORGAN, WALES
☎ (01443) 772020. OPEN 9 - 4 MON - THUR, 9 - 2 FRI,
9 - 1.30 SAT.

This Burberry factory shop is quite difficult to find as it is some way up the Rhondda Valley. However, GDD readers have written to tell me it is definitely worth the trip - although rather olde world, it has some good merchandise at extremely good prices. It sells seconds and overmakes of the famous name raincoats and duffle coats as well as accessories such as the distinctive umbrellas, scarves and handbags. All carry the Burberry label and are about one third of the normal retail price. For example, trench coats, £159.95; classic coats, £129.95 which amount to a reduction of two thirds. Childrenswear tends to be thin on the ground, but there are plenty of gift items such as Burberry brand name teas, coffees and marmalade.

## CLARKS FACTORY SHOP

UNIT 27, BICESTER OUTLET SHOPPING VILLAGE, PINGLE DRIVE, BICESTER, JUNCTION 9 OF M40, OXFORDSHIRE OX6 7WD
☎ (01869) 325646. OPEN 10 - 6 MON - SAT, 11 - 5 SUN AND BANK HOLIDAYS.

One of 48 shops, with more planned, in this factory shopping village. Clarks International operate a chain of factory shops nationally which specialise in selling discontinued lines and slight sub-standards for men, women and children from Clarks, K Shoes and other famous brands. These shops trade under the name of Crockers, K Shoes Factory shop or Clarks Factory Shop and while not all are physically attached to a shoe factory, these shops are treated as factory shops by the company. Customers can expect to find an extensive range of quality shoes, sandals, walking boots, slippers, trainers, handbags, accessories and gifts, while their major outlets also offer luggage, sports clothing, sports equipment and outdoor clothing. Brands stocked include Clarks, K Shoes, Springer, CICA, Hi-Tec, Puma, Mercury, Dr Martens, Nike, LA Gear, Fila, Mizuno, Slazenger, Weider, Samsonite, Delsey, Antler and Carlton, although not all are sold in every outlet. Discounts are on average 30% off the normal high street price for perfect stock.

## CONVERSE EUROPE LTD

BICESTER OUTLET SHOPPING VILLAGE, PINGLE DRIVE, BICESTER,
JUNCTION 9 OF M40, OXFORDSHIRE OX6 7WD
☎ (01869) 323200. OPEN 10 - 6 MON - SAT AND BANK
HOLIDAYS, 11 - 5 SUN.

One of 48 shops, with more planned, in this factory shopping village
which opened in June 1995. Converse is the largest sports footwear
company in the US and this is its first factory outlet in Europe.
Discounts ranged from 30% to 50% on seconds. Leather chunk
shoes, £24.99, reduced from £39.99, plus baseball shoes, canvas plimsolls and a wide range of sports shoes. The village also has two restaurants, a small children's play area and free parking. The telephone
number given here is for the village.

## FRED PERRY

UNIT 31, BICESTER OUTLET SHOPPING VILLAGE, PINGLE DRIVE,
BICESTER, JUNCTION 9 OF M40, OXFORDSHIRE OX6 7WD
☎ (01869) 325504. OPEN 10 - 6 MON - SAT AND BANK
HOLIDAYS, 10 - 4 SUN.

This shop sells men's and women's ranges of the famous Fred Perry
sportswear and leisure clothing: shorts, tennis tops, tracksuits, T-
shirts. All price labels show the original and the reduced price, which
is usually about 30%. Tennis shorts were reduced from £27.99 to
£14.99; tracksuits bottoms now from £14.99. When we visited in
June 1995, there was a much better selection of menswear than
women's, though that may change. The village also has two restaurants, a small children's play area and free parking.

## HOM

BICESTER OUTLET SHOPPING VILLAGE, PINGLE DRIVE, BICESTER,
JUNCTION 9 OF M40, OXFORDSHIRE OX6 7WD
☎ (01869) 323200. OPEN 10 - 6 MON - SAT AND BANK
HOLIDAYS, 11 - 5 SUN.

This shop sells Hom swimwear and underwear for men and Triumph
swimwear, nightwear and lingerie for women. For men, there are
colourful leisure shirts, £25, reduced from £58; silk ties, £20, down
from £40; swimming trunks, £10; work shirts, £30, reduced from
£59. The village also has two restaurants, a small children's play area
and free parking. The telephone number given here is for the village.

# I J DEWHIRST

UNIT 22, THE KINGSWAY, FFORESTFACH INDUSTRIAL ESTATE,
FFORESTFACH, SWANSEA
☎ (01792) 584621. OPEN 9 - 5.30 MON - FRI, 9 - 5 SAT,
11 - 5 SUN.
Wide range of men's, children's and women's clothes including men's
suits, jackets, shirts, trousers; girl's dresses, blouses, trousers, skirts and
jackets and boy's shirts, trousers and jackets; women's jackets, blouses,
skirts and trousers, and much much more.

## JAEGER SALE SHOP

42-43 CHURCH STREET, TAMWORTH, STAFFORDSHIRE B79 7DE
☎ (01827) 52828. OPEN 9.30 - 5.30 MON - SAT.
Classic tailoring at old-fashioned prices. This is a large shop which
deals mainly in separates and casual wear from last year's stock. For
example skirts, £39, originally £89; jackets, £65, originally £289.
Most of the merchandise is last season's or earlier stock and some
seconds. There are now 13 Jaeger factory shops, some selling the
whole range of Jaeger clothes, some just knitwear; yet others sell
goods other than those with the Jaeger label.

## KURT GEIGER

BICESTER OUTLET SHOPPING VILLAGE, PINGLE DRIVE, BICESTER,
JUNCTION 9 OF M40, OXFORDSHIRE OX6 7WD
☎ (01869) 323200. OPEN 10 - 6 MON - SAT AND BANK
HOLIDAYS, 11 - 5 SUN.
This shop sells men's ranges from Kurt Geiger, Bruno Magli,
Sweeneys, Cheaney, Charles Jourdan and Grenson. All the shoes are
set out in easily accessible racks ranged in sizes. The village also has
two restaurants, a small children's play area and free parking. The telephone number given here is for the village.

## PEPE JEANS

BICESTER OUTLET SHOPPING VILLAGE, PINGLE DRIVE, BICESTER,
JUNCTION 9 OF M40, OXFORDSHIRE OX6 7WD
☎ (01869) 323200. OPEN 10 - 6 MON - SAT AND BANK
HOLIDAYS, 11 - 5 SUN.
Pepe Jeans sells a wide selection of denim jeans and jackets as well as
coloured jeans and jackets, as well as cords, waistcoats and donkey
jackets. The village also has two restaurants, a small children's play
area and free parking.

## POLO RALPH LAUREN

BICESTER OUTLET SHOPPING VILLAGE, PINGLE DRIVE, BICESTER,
JUNCTION 9 OF M40, OXFORDSHIRE OX6 7WD
☎ (01869) 323200. OPEN 10 - 6 MON - SAT AND BANK
HOLIDAYS, 11 - 5 SUN.
Polo Ralph Lauren, the largest shop in the village with the prime spot,
has discounted items by between 35% and 60% for men and women.
Cagoules cost £85; wool jackets, £54; Polo T-shirts, £44; rugby shirts,
£39; trousers, £44; jeans, £39; ties, £29; striped jackets, £199, as well
as socks, dressing gowns, footballs and tennis balls. At the time of my
first visit, it was difficult to tell by how much each item was reduced,
but by my second visit, big signs spelling out the discount were on
display. The village also has two restaurants, a small children's play area
and free parking. The telephone number given here is for the village.

## PRINCIPLES

BICESTER OUTLET SHOPPING VILLAGE, PINGLE DRIVE, BICESTER,
JUNCTION 9 OF M40, OXFORDSHIRE OX6 7WD
☎ (01869) 323200. OPEN 10 - 6 MON - SAT AND BANK
HOLIDAYS, 11 - 5 SUN.
The Principles shop caters for men and women, selling only end of
season lines at lower prices. For men there are trousers, shirts, jackets,
denim shirts, T-shirts and shorts - not as big a selection as for women
but enough to cater for both a casual and a smart wardrobe. The
village also has two restaurants, a small children's play area and free
parking. The telephone number given here is for the village.

## RED/GREEN

BICESTER OUTLET SHOPPING VILLAGE, PINGLE DRIVE, BICESTER,
JUNCTION 9 OF M40, OXFORDSHIRE OX6 7WD
☎ (01869) 323200. OPEN 10 - 6 MON - SAT AND BANK
HOLIDAYS, 11 - 5 SUN.

Red/Green is a Scandinavian compnay and this is their first factory
outlet in the UK. They sell very stylish "post sailing" clothes (though
you don't have to sail to wear them) for men and women, which
looked as if they were high quality. All the clothes are last season's and
discounts are between 30% and 40%. There are sailing clothes, golf
wear, nautical and casual wear, shirts, sweatshirts, apres ski wear,
anoraks, gilets, classic sweaters, sailing shoes and soft bags. The village
also has two restaurants, a small children's play area and free parking.
The telephone number given here is for the village.

## SECONDS OUT

6 GREAT DARKGATE STREET, ABERYSTWYTH, DYFED, WALES
☎ (01970) 611897. OPEN 9.30 - 5 MON - SAT.

Makes clothes for men, women and children, mostly for department
stores. The factory shop sells everything from jeans, £9-£13; jodphurs
and casual trousers to school uniform items and mini chinos, from
£5. Ladies summer trousers, £8.50; denim jackets, £16, usually
£33.99; men's sweaters and waistcoats from £12.

## SHOE SHED

CASTLEFIELDS, NEWPORT ROAD, STAFFORD,
STAFFORDSHIRE ST16 1BQ
☎ (0785) 211311. OPEN 10 - 4 SEVEN DAYS A WEEK.

Large factory shop selling a vast range of all types of men's, women's
and children's shoes, all of which are perfects, at up to 30% below
normal high street prices. Ladies sandals cost from £5; ladies shoes
from £7.50. Men's shoes from £10; sports shoes from £10.

## STEWART SECONDS

12 PIER STREET, ABERSTWYTH, DYFED, WALES
☎ (01970) 611437. OPEN 9 - 5.30 MON - SAT, 11 - 5 SUN IN SUMMER.
14 NOTT SQUARE, CAMARTHEN, DYFED, WALES
☎ (01267) 222294. OPEN 9 - 5.30 MON - SAT.
HARFORD SQUARE, LAMPETER, DYFED, WALES
☎ (01570) 422205. OPEN 9.30 - 5.30 MON - SAT.
52 STEPNEY STREET, LLANELLI, DYFED, WALES
☎ (01554) 776957. OPEN 9 - 5.30 MON - SAT.
Y MAES, PWLLHELI, GWYNEDD, NORTH WALES
☎ (01758) 701130. OPEN 9 - 5.30 MON - SAT.

Branded merchandise from most of the major UK chain stores. Fashion is usually in season and consists of overcuts, discontinued lines and cancelled orders, as well as some seconds. Apart from fashion for men, women and children, there is also household textiles such as bedding and towels and crockery, glasses and cutlery, all at half the retail store price.

## THE FACTORY SHOP

WESTWARD ROAD, CAINSCROSS, STROUD, GL5 4JE
GLOUCESTERSHIRE
☎ (01453) 756655. OPEN 9 - 5 MON - THUR, SAT, 9 - 6 FRI,
11 - 5 SUN AND BANK HOLIDAYS.
115 HIGH STREET, NEWCASTLE-UNDER-LYME,
STAFFORDSHIRE ST5 1PS
☎ (01782) 717364. OPEN 9 - 5.30 MON - SAT.
NEW ROAD, PERSHORE, WORCESTERSHIRE WR10 1BY
☎ (01386) 556467. OPEN 9 - 5 MON - SAT, 10.30 - 4.30 SUN AND BANK
HOLIDAYS.

Wide range on sale includes men's, ladies and children's clothing and footwear; household textiles, toiletries, hardware, luggage, lighting and bedding, most of which are chainstore and high street brands at discounts of approximately 30%-50%. There are weekly deliveries and brands include all the major stars: Coloroll, Wrangler and Dartington to name just three. Lines are continually changing and few factory shops offer such a variety under one roof.

## THE FACTORY SHOP

NEWLAND, WITNEY, OXFORDSHIRE
☎ (01993) 708338. OPEN 10 - 5 MON - SAT.

Part of the Coats Viyella group which makes clothes for many of the
high street department stores, this medium sized factory shop - not
surprisingly - had many recognisable items on sale. Stocks clothes for
all the family. For men, there are cord trousers, smart trousers, jackets
including quilted ones, Peter England shirts, underwear, socks. Stock
changes constantly.

## THE SCOTCH HOUSE

BICESTER OUTLET SHOPPING VILLAGE, PINGLE DRIVE, BICESTER,
JUNCTION 9 OF M40, OXFORDSHIRE OX6 7WD
☎ (01869) 323200. OPEN 10 - 6 MON - SAT AND BANK
HOLIDAYS, 11 - 5 SUN.

One of 48 shops, with more planned, in this factory shopping village
which opened in June 1995. Billed as Bond Street comes to Bicester,
the shops are very smart indeed, beautifully designed and stocked
with end-of-season designer fashions, mens and childrenswear, tableware, shoes and more, all on permanent sale at prices reduced from
25%-50%, with some reductions up to 75%. This shop stocks the
traditional range of Scotch House clothes for men and women
including wool jackets, lambswool cardigans, Argyle socks, scarves
and waistcoats. There are two prices marked above each display: the
Knightsbridge one and the factory village reduced price. The village
also has two restaurants, a small children's play area and free parking.
The telephone number given here is for the village.

## THE SUIT COMPANY

BICESTER OUTLET SHOPPING VILLAGE, PINGLE DRIVE, BICESTER,
JUNCTION 9 OF M40, OXFORDSHIRE OX6 7WD
☎ (01869) 323200. OPEN 10 - 6 MON - SAT AND BANK
HOLIDAYS, 11 - 5 SUN.

This shop is part of the Moss Bros group and every item has a large
price tag with the old and the new price. For example, three-button
T-shirts, £9.95, reduced from £14.95; casual trousers, £14.95,
reduced from £25.95; cotton shirts, £19.95 usually £25.95; pure silk
casual jackets, £19.95, usually £39.95; YSL shirts, £24.95, usually
£29.95; Pierre Cardin pyjamas, £19.95 usually £29.95; macs, £69.50,

usually £89.50; also leather gloves, belts, ties, work shirts, suits, jackets. The village also has two restaurants, a small children's play area and free parking. The telephone number given here is for the village.

## TOG 24

BICESTER OUTLET SHOPPING VILLAGE, PINGLE DRIVE, BICESTER, JUNCTION 9 OF M40, OXFORDSHIRE OX6 7WD
☎ (01869) 323200. OPEN 10 - 6 MON - SAT AND BANK HOLIDAYS, 11 - 5 SUN.

Tog 24 sells specialist outdoor clothing: golf suits, golf gilets, T-shirts, Gore-Tex weatherproof breathable jackets, weatherproof anoraks, marginal seconds in jackets and hiking boots. Discounts are mostly about 30%. The village also has two restaurants, a small children's play area and free parking. The telephone number given here is for the village.

## TWEEDMILL FACTORY SHOPPING

LLANNERCH PARK, ST ASAPH, CLYWD, (OFF A55), WALES
☎ (01745) 730072. OPEN 10 - 6 SEVEN DAYS A WEEK.

Has a wide range of clothes, both designer and top end of the high street, as well as ties, accessories and blankets. Labels on sale include Pierre Cardin, Double Two and Barry Sherrard as well as high street names such as Principles. Double Two shirts cost £20 for two.

## VELMORE FASHIONS

1-2 JAEGER HOUSE, 141 HOLT ROAD, WREXHAM, CLWYD, WALES LL13 9DY
☎ (01978) 363456. OPEN 10.30 - 3 MON, WED, FRI.

Overmakes of skirts, jackets and trousers originally made for the most famous high street name at very cheap prices.

## *Dress Agencies*

### DRESS EXCHANGE

1003A ALCESTER ROAD SOUTH (ABOVE THREE COOKS), THE
MAYPOLE, BIRMINGHAM, WEST MIDLANDS B14 5AJ
☎ (0121) 474 5707. OPEN 10 - 5 MON - SAT.
Middle to up market women's designer wear, with quite a good
menswear selection. Jackets from Boss and Armani from £30, Ralph
Lauren shirts, £7.99.

### THE MEN'S ROOM

2ND FLOOR, 30 HIGH STREET, COWBRIDGE, SOUTH
GLAMORGAN, WALES CF7 7AG
☎ (01446) 772211. OPEN 10 - 5.30 MON - SAT, CLOSED 1 ON WEDS.
Top men's designer new and nearly-new clothes from Boss, Dunhill,
Paul Smith and Gieves & Hawkes to Armani, John Richmond,
Valentino and Ralph Lauren. This two-roomed shop devotes half of
its space to special occasion wear - morning and dinner suits (most of
which are handmade, bespoke), tails and top hats, spats and gaiters -
and the other half to trousers, coats, suits, jodphurs, shoes and shirts.
Approximately 40% of the stock in the shop is new and sold at
discount.

### TIFFANY CLOTHING AGENCY

14 MARDOL GARDENS, SHREWSBURY, SHROPSHIRE SY1 1PR
☎ (01743) 233542. OPEN 9.30 - 4 TUE - SAT.
Aquascutum, Jaeger, Yarrell, Marks & Spencer, everything carefully
arranged by size - tops, bottom, coats, activity clothes, etc. Also sells
men's nearly-new outfits, bric a brac, paperback books and curtains.

# EAST ANGLIA AND EAST MIDLANDS

## *Permanent Discount Outlets*

### BLUNTS

128-132 GRAMBY STREET, LEICESTER LE1 1DL
☎ (0116) 2555959. OPEN 8.30 - 6 MON - SAT 10 - 4 SUN.

Men's shoes from the Clark's, K Shoes and Portland ranges at 40% of the normal shop price for discontinued stock, seconds and ends of ranges. Women's and children's shoes are also stocked.

### LAMBOURNE CLOTHING

CHRISTCHURCH ST, IPSWICH, SUFFOLK
☎ (01473) 250404. OPEN 10 - 4 TUE & WED, 12 - 4 THUR & FRI, AND 10- 1 SAT.

Manufactures and sells own brand, Windsmoor and Counrty Casuals skirts, trousers, and jackets, the clothes for men and women are usually discounted by about 50%. They also make and sell towels.

### M C HITCHEN & SONS LTD

7 HIGH STREET, GRANTHAM, LINCOLNSHIRE NG31 6PN
☎ (01476) 590552. OPEN 9.30 - 5.30 MON, 9 - 5.30 TUE - SAT.

Littlewoods sell off their overstocks in a network of shops called M C Hitchen & Sons Ltd. Most of them are in the North of England and offer up to 40% off the catalogue price for clothing and between 50% and 60% off for electrical goods. Littlewoods also run a mobile shop which operates in cities where they don't have a sale shop.. For details of further venues for the sales, which usually take place once a month, contact Jean Banks, c/o Crosby DC, Kershaw Avenue, Endbutt Lane, Crosby, Merseyside L70 1AH.

# MATALAN

UNIT 1, WEEDON ROAD INDUSTRIAL ESTATE, TYNE ROAD,
NORTHAMPTON NN5 5BE
☎ (01604) 589119. OPEN 10 - 8 MON - FRI, 9.30 - 5.30 SAT,
10 - 6 SUN.
UNIT 1, PHOENIX RETAIL PARK, PHEONIX PARKWAY, CORBY,
NORTHAMPTONSHIRE NN17 5DT
☎ (01536) 408042. OPEN 10 - 8 MON - FRI, 9 - 6 SAT, 11 - 5 SUN.
BLACKFRIARS ROAD, KINGS LYNN, NORFOLK PE30 1RX
☎ (01553) 765696. OPEN 10 - 8 MON - FRI, 9 - 6 SAT, 11 - 5 SUN.
EAST STATION ROAD, PETERBOROUGH, CAMBRIDGESHIRE PE2 8AA
☎ (01733) 341229. OPEN 10 - 8 MON - FRI, 9 - 6 SAT, 11 - 5 SUN.
LINDIS RETAIL PARK, TRITTON ROAD, LINCOLN LN6 7QY
☎ (01522) 696541. OPEN 10 - 8 MON - FRI, 9 - 6 SAT, 11 - 5 SUN.
DUDLEY ROAD, SCUNTHORPE DN16 1BA
☎ (01724) 270958. OPEN 10 - 8 MON - FRI, 9 - 6 SAT, 11 - 5 SUN.
As the UK's first National Discount Club, Matalan has the buying
power to guarantee its members up to 60% discounts on a huge range
of brand name clothing, household goods, luggage and toiletries for
all the family. Top quality merchandise, current season, no seconds, is
offered to its members at exclusive, permanently discounted prices
seven days a week. Matalan operates strictly on a membership basis,
one of the key factors for its success in offering 20%-60% savings off
recommended retail prices. Membership cards are issued through
companies, organisations and associations in the vicinity of the stores,
and are available to their employees/members. They are valid at any
of the 50 Matalan stores in the UK. To find out if your organisation
is registered, phone the Matalan hotline on 01772 629447.

# MAX SHOES

46 BELVOIR STREET, LEICESTER LE2 3AG
☎ (0116) 2705050. OPEN 9 - 5.30 MON-SAT.
Sells clearance lines of English-made top quality men's all-leather
shoes. Often, there are brand names, but the shop will not divulge
these beforehand. Shoes which cost £60 in high street retail outlets
cost from £20-£35 here.

## STAGE TWO

SAVILLE ROAD, WESTWOOD, PETERBOROUGH, CAMBRIDGESHIRE
PE3 7PR
☎ (01733) 263308. OPEN 10 - 8 MON - FRI, 9 - 6 SAT, AND BANK
HOLIDAYS.
UNIT 3, TRITTON RETAIL PARK, CENTURION ROAD, LINCOLN LN1
☎ (01733) 263308. OPEN 10 - 8 MON - FRI, 9 - 6 SAT, 10 - 4 BANK
HOLIDAYS.
The names of the stores which sell discontinued lines from Freeman's
catalogues. The full range is carried, but stock depends on what has
not been sold at full price from the catalogue itself, or has been
returned or the packaging is damaged or soiled. Clothing discounts
range from about 50%-65%. There are also household items and
electrical equipment. There are branches in Nottingham, Lincoln and
Peterborough.

## THE FACTORY SHOP

BARTON BUSINESS CENTRE, BARTON ROAD, BURY ST EDMUNDS,
SUFFOLK 1P32 7BQ
☎ (01284) 701578. OPEN 9.30 - 5.30 MON - FRI, 11 - 5 SUN.
Wide range on sale includes men's, women's and children's clothing
and footwear, luggage, lighting and bedding, most of which are chain
store and high street brands - including Coloroll, Wrangler Factory
Shops and Dartington - at discounts of between 30%-50%.

## W G BODILEY

2 OVERSTONE ROAD, NORTHAMPTON NN1 3JH
☎ (01604) 37971. OPEN 9.30 - 5.30 MON - FRI, 9.30 - 5 SAT.
The best Continental leather shoes for women and men, as well as
handbags. Ladies shoes start at £29.97 and all the shoes are perfects.
There are two sales a year - in July and January - but throughout the
year there is a special sale rack.

## BALLY FACTORY SHOP

HALL ROAD, NORWICH, NORFOLK NR4 6DP
☎ (01603) 760590. OPEN 9.30 - 5.30 MON - FRI, 9 - 5.30 SAT AND MOST
BANK HOLIDAYS - PHONE FIRST.
The Bally factory shop is situated next to the main factory and sells
women's, men's and children's footwear, and accessories for women
and men such as hosiery, socks, scarves, shoe horns and shoe care
products. Also sold are leather handbags, briefcases, suitcovers,

holdalls and overnight cases. Most of the merchandise is rejects, sub-standard, ends of line of ex-sale stock and is priced from £5-£200, which is usually at least one-third off the recommended retail price. There is also a coffee shop which serves morning coffee, light lunches and afternoon teas, a children's play area, toilet facilities, free parking and disabled facilities. Within the factory shop, there is also a full price department which sells all the current styles. A small "museum" is incorporated within the shop showing the history of shoe-making since the Roman times and the history of Bally, with examples of shoes on display. Coach parties are welcome by prior arrangement. Factory tours are not available.

## BARKER

STATION ROAD, EARLS BARTON, NORTHAMPTON, NORTHAMPTON-SHIRE NN6 ONT
☎ (01604) 810387. OPEN 9 - 5 MON - FRI, 10 - 4 SAT.
Factory shop selling discontinued lines of shoes at 30% off the retail price, and rejects at 50% off the normal retail price. Only sells shoes manufactured by its own factory and these include brogues, smart day shoes for men and women, but no trainers. There are men's high grade, traditional shoes which sell to top stores and moccasins.

## BARRATT'S SALE SHOP

BARRACK ROAD, KINGSTHORPE HOLLOW, NORTHAMPTON, NORTHAMPTONSHIRE
☎ (01604) 718632. OPEN 9 - 5.30 MON - SAT.
Reject trainers and ex-window display shoes at factory prices among a range of perfect shoes, the latter of which are sold at sale prices.

## BECK MILL FACTORY SHOP

33 KINGS ROAD, MELTON MOWBRAY, LEICESTERSHIRE LE13 1QF
☎ (01664) 480147. OPEN 10 - 5 MON - SAT, UNTIL 6 ON FRI, 10 - 4 SUN.
Recommended by a reader, Beck Mill sells designer clothes for men and women at up to 70% discounts. Brands include Feminella, Barry Sherrard, Jeffrey Brownleader, Elsie Whiteley, Astraka, Wolsey, Cavvalini, Dannimac, Roman Originals, Warners, Double Two, Farah, Lee Cooper, James Barry, Lancers, Nautica, Christian Dior, Norman Linton, Hathaway, plus many more. Come and see their

exciting selection of top quality brands, which consist of perfects and seconds at factory shop prices. There is easy parking.

## BIG L FACTORY OUTLET

34 COMMERCIAL STREET, NORTHAMPTON NN1 1PJ
☎ (01604) 603022. OPEN 10 - 5.30 MON, TUE,
9.30 - 5.30 WED - FRI, 9 - 6 SAT, OPEN BANK HOLIDAYS - PHONE FOR TIMES FIRST.
This store retails a large range of Levi jeans, shirts, jackets, sweatshirts and shirts from a very big outlet. T-shirts cost from £27.99; orange tab jeans from £23.99; red tab jeans from £29.99; T-shirts from £9.99; jackets from £35.99; and sweatshirts from £18.99. Most of the stock is seconds and ends-of-lines.

## BYFORDS

PO BOX 63, ABBEY LANE, LEICESTER, LEICESTERSHIRE LE4 ODX
☎ (0116) 2611135. OPEN 9.30 - 5 MON - SAT.
70 - 74 BELGRAVE GATE, LEICESTER, LEICESTERSHIRE LE1 3GQ
☎ (0116) 2518003. OPEN 9 - 5.30 MON - FRI, 9 - 5 SAT.
FACTORY STREET, SHEPSHED, LEICESTER LE12 9AQ
☎ (01509) 503068. OPEN 10 - 5 MON, 9 - 5 TUE - SAT.
Part of the Coats Viyella group, which makes clothes for - among others - Marks & Spencer, they have overstocks and clearance lines which are sold through the 40 factory shops which are also part of the group. Frequent shoppers at M&S will recognise many of the garments on sale, despite the lack of the well-known St Michael's label. Menswear includes trousers, shirts, ties, jumpers, cardigans, underwear, nightwear, breathable jackets and hosiery. The factory shops also offer a 28-day money back guarantee. There are weekly deliveries to constantly update the merchandise.

## CHARNOS

THE OLD SCHOOL BUILDING, OUTCLOUGH ROAD,
BRINDLEY FORD, STOKE-ON-TRENT, STAFFORDSHIRE
☎ (01782) 522529. OPEN 10 - 4 TUE - FRI, 12.30 - 1 SAT.
Famous Charnos lingerie, as well as hosiery and knitwear for men and women at factory shop prices. Current ladies lingerie is discounted by 25%, discontinued lingerie by 50%. Knitwear is reduced by one-third. Some stock is grade B quality. Also sells menswear and childrenswear with lots of baby clothes.

## CHARNOS

AMBER BUSINESS CENTRE, GREENHILL LANE, RIDDINGS, DER-
BYSHIRE
☎ (01773) 540408. OPEN 10 - 4 TUE - FRI, 9.30 - 1 SAT.
CORPORATION ROAD, ILKESTON, DERBYSHIRE
☎ (0115) 9440301. OPEN 10 - 4 TUE - FRI, 9.30 - 1 SAT.
Although about 25% of the shop is given over to discontinued
perfects of the famous Charnos lingerie at discounts of 25%-50%, the
rest of the shop stocks wool, acrylic and cotton knitwear for men and
women at factory shop prices.

## CHARNOS

NOTTINGHAM ROAD, LONGEATON, NOTTINGHAMSHIRE
☎ (0115) 9730345. OPEN 10 - 4 TUE - FRI, 9.30 - 1 SAT.
Famous Charnos lingerie, as well as hosiery and knitwear for men and
women at factory shop prices. Current ladies lingerie is discounted by
25%, discontinued lingerie by 50%. Knitwear is reduced by one-
third. Some stock is grade B quality. Also sells menswear and childrenswear with lots of baby clothes.

## COURTAULDS MERIDIAN

HAYDN ROAD, NOTTINGHAMSHIRE
☎ (0115) 9246100. OPEN 9 - 5 MON - FRI, 9 - 5.30 SAT,
10 - 4 SUN.
Factory shop sells men's shirts and trousers as well as women's clothes,
children's clothes and nursery soft furnishings and household items.
Discounts average 30%. Take time out at the coffee shop and don't
worry about parking as there's a car park on site.

## COURTAULDS TEXTILES

ALLENBY INDUSTRIAL ESTATE, CROFTON CLOSE, MONKS ROAD,
LINCOLN LN2 5QT
☎ (01522) 539859. OPEN 9 - 5 MON - SAT.
Factory shop in Lincoln selling men's, women's and children's clothes,
including seconds from other chainstores. Discounts are usually at
least 20% and stock changes constantly.

# CROCKERS

111 FRONT STREET, ARNOLD, NOTTINGHAMSHIRE NG5 7ED
☎ (0115) 9674212. OPEN 9 - 6 MON - SAT, 10 - 4 BANK HOLIDAYS.

Clarks International operate a chain of factory shops nationally which specialise in selling discontinued lines and slight sub-standards for men, women and children from Clarks, K Shoes and other famous brands. These shops trade under the name of Crockers, K Shoes Factory shop or Clarks Factory Shop and while not all are physically attached to a shoe factory, these shops are treated as factory shops by the company. Customers can expect to find an extensive range of quality shoes, sandals, walking boots, slippers, trainers, handbags, accessories and gifts, while their major outlets also offer luggage, sports clothing, sports equipment and outdoor clothing. Brands stocked include Clarks, K Shoes, Springer, CICA, Hi-Tec, Puma, Mercury, Dr Martens, Nike, LA Gear, Fila, Mizuno, Slazenger, Weider, Samsonite, Delsey, Antler and Carlton, although not all are sold in every outlet. Discounts are on average 30% off the normal high street price for perfect stock.

# GLOVERALL PLC

LONDON ROAD, WELLINGBOROUGH,
NORTHAMPTONSHIRE
☎ (01933) 225183. OPEN 10 - 5 MON - FRI, CLOSED MON IN WINTER.

The award-winning duffle coat and jacket manufacturer has a factory shop which sells their good quality clothes at less than half the normal retail price. There are woollen mix duffle coats, anoraks, car rugs and scarves on sale here, most of which are obsolete styles, end of ranges or export rejects. Children's duffle coats start at £20, ladies at £38, reefer jackets costs from £50, down-filled anoraks at £45. All lengths of duffle coats are stocked for men, women and children.

# GYMPHLEX SPORTSWEAR

BOSTON ROAD, HORNCASTLE, LINCOLNSHIRE
☎ (01507) 523243.

Holds a one day factory shop sale just once a year, usually in early spring. Your chance to buy a huge range of sportswear for all the family: jogging pants, tracksuits, rugby and football shirts, rugby shorts. Some of the stock is seconds, some overmakes. The rest is freshly-made stock which is especially reduced for the sale.

# JAEGER FACTORY SHOP

1 HANSA ROAD, KING'S LYNN, NORFOLK PE30 4HZ
☎ (01553) 691111 EXT. 2143. OPEN 10 - 4.30 MON - FRI,
9 - 3.30 SAT.
39 WATNALL STREET, HUCKNALL, NOTTINGHAMSHIRE NG15 7JR
☎ (0115) 9680500. OPEN 9.45 - 4.45 TUE - FRI, 10 - 1 SAT, CLOSED MON.
NOTTINGHAM ROAD, SOMERCOTES, DERBYSHIRE DE55 4SB
☎ (01773) 727500. OPEN 10 - 4 MON - FRI, 9 - 4 SAT.
C/O RHYN GRIEVE, WOLSLEY ROAD, COALVILLE,
LEICESTERSHIRE LE6 4ES
☎ (01530) 835506. OPEN 10 - 5 TUE - FRI, 10 - 3 SAT.
THE COURTYARD, THE MARKETPLACE, BELPER,
DERBYSHIRE 01773 821320. OPEN 10 - 5 TUE - FRI, 10 - 1 SAT.
ARMADA CENTRE, MAYFLOWER STREET, PLYMOUTH
PL1 1LE
☎ (01752) 668315. OPEN 9 - 5.30 MON, WED - SAT,
9.30 - 5.30 TUE.

Jaeger operate a three-tier retail service: first, their top high street shops, after which unsold items go to their sale shops and thereafter to the factory shops. The factory shops still offer classic tailoring at old-fashioned prices. Most of the merchandise is last season's stock and some seconds, but you may find the odd gem from this season if you hunt carefully. There are now 13 Jaeger factory shops, some selling the whole range of Jaeger clothes, some just knitwear; yet others sell goods other than those with the Jaeger label. The King's Lynn shop covers the range of Jaeger clothing for men and women, with some knitwear; the Hucknall and Somercotes shops specialise in knitwear for women and men; the Coalville shop caters for the full range of Jaeger clothing for men and women, and there is some knitwear; and the Belper shop stocks mainly knitwear, but it does have a small selection of skirts, blouses and jackets, many of which are several seasons old. Prices are at least one third of the original, sometimes a lot less.

## JOHN SMEDLEY LTD

LEA MILLS, LEA BRIDGE, MATLOCK, DERBYSHIRE DE4 5AG
☎ (01629) 534571. OPEN 10 - 4 MON - SAT AND MOST BANK
HOLIDAYS.

Sells mostly knitwear under the John Smedley own label which are
ends of ranges or seconds, as well as some perfects, from £14 to £32.
There are cardigans and sweaters for men and women in lambswool
and marino wool; two ranges of underwear; second skin wear including cropped tops and bodies; and Tootal shirts in perfects and seconds
from £8.50 for seconds, £11.50 for perfects. Childrenswear is not
stocked.

## LANDS END DIRECT MERCHANT

PILLINGS ROAD, OAKHAM, RUTLAND LE15 6NY
☎ (01572) 722553. OPEN SEVEN DAYS A WEEK, BANK HOLIDAYS.

This US mail order company has its first ever factory outlet alongside
its UK headquarters. Modelled on the dozen or so factory shops they
operate in and around their US headquarters in Dodgeville,
Wisconsin, it's designed to sell warehouse overstocks, obsolete lines
and a range of "not quite perfect" products. There will normally be
about 3,000 items in the 2,000 sq ft store from jeans to jumpers,
leggings to luggage, turtlenecks to trousers. Genuine overstocks are
priced at 40% below normal catalogue prices; catalogue returns and
near-perfect seconds are reduced by between 20%-70%. All overstock
items are guaranteed, first quality Lands' End label products, all of
which have been offered previously in their catalogues at regular
prices. There is ample free parking, easy wheelchair and pushchair
access and changing rooms. However, you cannot buy current catalogue merchandise from the factory shop.

## PIGGLY WIGGLY

178 KETTERING ROAD, NORTHAMPTON,
NORTHAMPTONSHIRE MM1 4BH
☎ (01604) 32798. OPEN 10 - 5 MON, TUE, 9.30 - 5.30 WED - SAT.

Outdoor shoes for men (but women also wear them) at discount
prices. Walking boots and Dr Martens costs from £33 - £120 with a
saving of about £50 on seconds. Shoes which normally retail from
£40-£58 cost £25, although seconds cost from £15 and seconds boots
from £20.

## ROMBAH WALLACE FACTORY SHOP

14-17 IRONSIDE WAY, NORWICH ROAD, HINGHAM, NORFOLK
☎ (01953) 851106. OPEN 9 - 5 MON - SAT.
Good selection of shoes for women and men at discount (ladies courts from £18.95 - £60) as well as leather jackets from £99 and accessories, vanity cases, suitcases and flight bags. Sandals, court shoes, smart or casual.

## T GROOCOCK & CO LTD

GORDON STREET, ROTHWELL, NORTHAMPTONSHIRE NN14 6EG
☎ (01536) 710444. OPEN 10 - 5 MON - FRI, 9 - 1 SAT.
Factory shop selling high quality men's and women's slightly imperfect and end of line shoes at half price.

## THE FACTORY SHOP

SOUTH GREEN, EAST DEREHAM, NORFOLK
☎ (01362) 691868. OPEN 9 - 5 MON - SAT, 10 - 4 BANK HOLIDAYS.
THE FACTORY SHOP, NEWBOLD FOOTWEAR, BROOK STREET, SILEBY, LEICESTERSHIRE LE12 7RF
☎ (01509) 813514. OPEN 9 - 5 MON - SAT.
Wide range on sale includes men's, ladies and children's clothing and footwear; household textiles, toiletries, hardware, luggage, lighting and bedding, most of which are chainstore and high street brands at discounts of approximately 30%-50%. There are weekly deliveries and brands include all the major stars: Coloroll, Wrangler and Dartington to name just three. Lines are continually changing and few factory shops offer such a variety under one roof.

## THE FACTORY SHOP

OSMASTON WORKS, OSMASTON ROAD, DERBY,
DERBYSHIRE DE3 8LF
☎ (01332) 360045. OPEN 12 - 4.30 TUE - FRI, 9 - 12 SAT.
Seconds and surplus clothing from the Multifabs factory above the shop. Workwear and waterproof clothing, thermal outerwear, shirts, T-shirt, blouses and skirts. Most of the clothes are for men, with some women's. For example, standard government regulation high visibility jackets, £35, which would cost £70 in the high street; Fruit of the Loom sweatshirts, £7.99, which would cost £30 in the high street. Most are first quality with some seconds and mismakes.

# THE SHOE FACTORY SHOP

TRAFFIC STREET, EAGLE CENTRE, DERBY, DERBYSHIRE NR19 1PR
☎ (01332) 372823. OPEN 9 - 5 MON - SAT.
20 BROAD STREET, NOTTINGHAM
☎ (0115) 924 2390. OPEN 10 - 5 MON - FRI, 9.30 - 5.30 SAT.
CONSTANCE ROAD, LEICESTER
☎ (0116) 249 0114. OPEN 10 - 5 MON - FRI, 9 - 5 SAT.
Men's, women's and children's shoes and accessories which are bought in from other manufacturers including Spanish, Portuguese and Italian companies. All are unbranded. The range covers from mocassins to dressy shoes.

# THE SHOE SHED

ELLIS STREET, KIRKBY-IN-ASHFIELD, NOTTINGHAMSHIRE NG17 7AL
☎ (01623) 723083. OPEN 9 - 5 MON - SAT.
Large factory shop selling a vast range of all types of men's, women's and children's shoes, all of which are perfects, at up to 30% below normal high street prices. Men's shoes from £10; sports shoes from £10. Ladies sandals cost from £5; ladies shoes from £7.50.

# THE WORKSOP FACTORY SHOP

RAYMOTH LANE, WORKSOP, NOTTINGHAMSHIRE
☎ (01909) 472841. OPEN 9 - 5 MON - SAT, 10 - 4 SUN.
Manufacturers for top chainstores, the factory shop sells over-runs and returns in household textiles, bedding, fashion for all the family, including knitwear and underwear at discount of 20%-40%. The factory shop is 10,000 sq ft and most of the stock is clothing with good availability on colours and sizes.

# WHITE & CO (EARLS BARTON) LTD

11 NEW STREET, DAVENTRY, NORTHAMPTONSHIRE NN11 4BP
☎ (0327) 702291. OPEN 10 - 4 TUE, FRI, SAT.
Sells footwear, espcially Dr Martens and Gripfast, boots, motorbike boots, steel-capped shoes, street fashion footwear and classic welted, many of which are not available elsewhere in the UK as most are produced for export. Winner of the Queen's Award for Export in 1990, much of the stock is seconds and ends of lines.

## *Dress Agencies*

## THE UPPINGHAM DRESS AGENCY

2-6 ORANGE STREET, UPPINGHAM, RUTLAND LE15 9SQ
☎ (01572) 823276. OPEN 9 - 5.30 MON - SAT, 12 - 4 SUN.
One of the oldest and possibly the largest dress agency in the country
with 10 rooms on three floors packed with quality nearly-new
clothing for men, women and children. Preference is given to
designer labels, but better quality high street names are also stocked.
The proprietors are very selective about the condition and all stock is
carefully vetted.

## *Hire Shops*

## THE FROCK EXCHANGE

HIGH STREET, HUNTINGDON, CAMBRIDGESHIRE PE18 9LH
☎ (01480) 461187. OPEN 9.15 - 5 TUE - SAT, CLOSED MONS.
A dress agency with men's special occasion wear and dinner suits (but
no morning suits) to hire as well as new ballgowns and cocktail wear
to hire and to buy.

# NORTH WEST, YORKSHIRE AND HUMBERSIDE

## *Permanent Discount Outlets*

## BARGAIN STREET

BUY WELL SHOPPING CENTRE, THORPE ARCH TRADING ESTATE,
WETHERBY, WEST YORKSHIRE
☎ (01937) 845650. OPEN 9 - 5 MON - FRI, 9.30 - 5.30 SAT, 10.30 - 4.30
SUN.
A wide range of ex-catalogue items from men's, women's and
children's clothes to leisure wear, sports gear, underwear, household
goods, linen, electrical equipment such as tvs, music centres and

vacuum cleaners, and toys. Prices are usually about 50%-70% off the catalogue prices with extra discounts on certain days. Quality is variable and stock changes constantly.

## BEANS OF BATLEY

SKOPOS MILLS, BRADFORD ROAD, BATLEY, WEST
YORKSHIRE WF17 6LZ
☎ (01924) 477717. OPEN 9 - 5.30 MON - FRI, 9 - 5.30 SAT, 10 - 5 SUN AND
BANK HOLIDAYS.
Friendly, family-run business on one flat level, 10,000 square feet in size, which operates as a permanent factory outlet store. There, you will discover man's and ladies fashions at excellent prices. Beans sell top of the range quality brands at special prices - names like Viyella on the women's side and Christian Dior on the men's. Beans offers both current season stock and previous season's classics, all at up to 50% off high street prices. There is also a coffee shop which offers snacks and light meals every day. Beans has wonderful motorway connections courtesy of the M1 exit 40, and the M62, exit 27, is only minutes away. There is car parking for 600 cars on site.

## BOUNDARY MILL STORES

BURNLEY ROAD, COLNE, LANCASHIRE BB8 8LS
☎ (01282) 865229. OPEN 10 - 6 MON - FRI, 10 - 5 SAT AND BANK
HOLIDAYS, 11 - 5 SUNS.
One of the largest clearance stores in Britain, it covers more than 60,000 square feet. As well as a department selling household textiles at discount prices, some of the top end of the high street designer labels are on sale here for both women and men. The women's and men's departments are very extensive - not to mention impressive - and cover the whole range from casual to evening wear, with reductions of between 30% and 50%. There is also a large shoe and a jeans department, a lingerie and nightwear department, and a section where brand name household textiles and bedlinen are sold. Four times a year, there are special sales at which prices are discounted still further. Most of the stock is perfect clearance and ends of lines with the occasional marked seconds. There is a coffee shop and restaurant.

# FOSC (FACTORY OUTLET SHOPPING CENTRE)

HULL ROAD, YORK, YORKSHIRE YO1 3JA
☎ (01904) 430481. OPEN 10 - 6 SEVEN DAYS A WEEK.

Branded merchandise from more than 50 manufacturers which initially consisted of ends of lines, surplus stock, cancelled orders and slight seconds but is more likely now to be firsts. Some of the best-known high street names are here, including clothing from Courtaulds, selling everything from clothing and books to bedding, towels, children's clothes, small eletrical kitchen equiment such as kettles, stereos, batteries and toys at discounts of between 30%-70%. There is also a cafe, free car parking, disabled facilities and no membership is necessary.

# GREAT CLOTHES

84 YORK ROAD, LEEDS, WEST YORKSHIRE
☎ (0113) 2350303. OPEN 9.30 - 9 MON - FRI, 9.30 - 6 SAT, 11 - 5 SUN.

Clothes for men, women and children from French Connection, Adidas, Pringle, Farah, Puma, Christian Dior to Jacqmar and including all brands of jeans. Levi's costs from £35.99. There are also accessories such as socks, shoes, hats, scarves and underwear. All stock is current season and is discounted by 25%-30%.

# M C HITCHEN & SONS LTD

C/O CROSBY DC, KERSHAW AVENUE, ENDBUTT LANE, CROSBY, MERSEYSIDE L70 1AH
☎ (0151) 928 6611.
116 ST JAMES STREET, BURNLEY, LANCASHIRE BB11 1NL
☎ (01282) 425615. OPEN 9.30 - 5.30 MON, WED - FRI,
9.30 - 4.30 TUE, 9 - 5.30 SAT.
602-608 ATTERCLIFFE ROAD, SHEFFIELD, SOUTH
YORKSHIRE S9 3QS
☎ (0114) 2441611. OPEN 9.30 - 5.30 MON - SAT.
102 DEANSGATE, BOLTON, GREATER MANCHESTER
BL1 1 BD
☎ (01204) 384969. OPEN 9.30 - 5.30 MON - WED,
9 - 5.30 THUR - SAT.
185 STAMFORD STREET, ASHTON-UNDER-LYME, GREATER MAN254
CHESTER OL6 7PY
☎ (0161) 339 0966. OPEN 9 - 5.30 MON - SAT, UNTIL 5.15 ON THUR.
160 MARINE ROAD, CENTRAL MORECAMBE,
LANCASHIRE LA4 4BU
☎ (01524) 412074. OPEN 9.30 - 5.30 MON, 9 - 5.30 TUE - SAT.

C/O LITTLEWOODS SHOPPING CITY, RUNCORN, CHESHIRE
☎ (01928) 717777. OPEN 9 - 5 MON - SAT.
69 - 74 LORD STREET, FLEETWOOD, LANCASHIRE FY7 6DS
☎ (01253) 773418. OPEN 9 - 5.30 MON - SAT.
UNIT 3, MONUMENT BUILDINGS, LONDON ROAD,
LIVERPOOL L3 8JY
☎ (0151) 708 6118. OPEN 9 - 5.30 MON - SAT.

Littlewoods sell off their overstocks in a network of shops called M C Hitchen & Sons Ltd. Most of them are in the North of England and offer up to 40% off the catalogue price for clothing and between 50% and 60% off for electrical goods. Littlwoods also run a mobile shop which operates in cities where they don't have a sale shop. For details of further venues for the sales, which useually take place once a month, contact Jean Banks, c/o Crosby DC, Kershaw Avenue, Endbutt Lane, Crosby, Merseyside L70 1AH.

## MATALAN

HOLME ROAD, BAMBER BRIDGE, PRESTON, LANCASHIRE PR5 6BP
☎ (01772) 627365. OPEN 10 - 8 MON - FRI, 9.30 - 5.30 SAT,
10 - 6 SUN.
UNIT 1, RED ROSE CENTRE, REGENT ROAD, SALFORD
M5 3GR
☎ (061) 848 0792. OPEN 10 - 8 MON - FRI, 9.30 - 5.30 SAT,
10 - 6 SUN.
UNIT 29, GREYHOUND RETAIL PARK, SEALAND ROAD, CHESTER CH1
1QG
☎ (01244) 380877. OPEN 10 - 8 MON - FRI, 9.30 - 5.30 SAT,
10 - 6 SUN.
UNIT 13, THE WHEATLEY CENTRE, WHEATLEY HALL ROAD, DON-
CASTER DN2 4PE
☎ (0302) 760444. OPEN 10 - 8 MON - FRI, 9.30 - 5.30 SAT,
10 - 6 SUN.
UNIT 4B, STADIUM WAY RETAIL PARK, PARKGATE,
ROTHERHAM S60 1TG
☎ (01709) 780173. OPEN 10 - 8 MON - FRI, 9.30 - 5.30 SAT,
10 - 6 SUN.
UNIT 10 & 11, CLIFTON MOORE COURT, YORK YO3 4XZ
☎ (01904) 693080. OPEN 10 - 8 MON - FRI, 9 - 5 SAT,
9.30 - 6 SUN.
NEW CHESTER ROAD, BROMBOROUGH, SOUTH WIRRAL L62 7EK
☎ (0151) 343 9494. OPEN 10 - 8 MON - FRI, 10 - 6 SAT, SUN.

SEFTON RETAIL PARK, DUNNINGS BRIDGE ROAD, BOOTLE, MERSEY-
SIDE L30 6UU
☎ (0151) 525 1190. OPEN 10 - 8 MON - FRI, 9.30 - 5.30 SAT,
10 - 6 SUN.
UNIT 3, ALEXANDRA COURT, OLDHAM, LANCASHIRE
OL4 1SG
☎ (0161) 620 6686. OPEN 10 - 8 MON - FRI, 9.30 - 5.30 SAT,
10 - 6 SUN.
WESTOVER STREET, OFF STATION ROAD, SWINTON
N27 2AH
☎ (0161) 794 3441. OPEN 10 - 8 MON - FRI, 9 - 6 SAT, 11 - 5 SUN.
UNIT 1, GREENMOUNT RETAIL PARK, PELLON ROAD,
HALIFAX HX1 5QN
☎ (01422) 383051. OPEN 10 - 8 MON - FRI, 9 - 5.30 SAT,
11 - 5 SUN.
UNIT 2, CLIFTON RETAIL PARK, CLIFTON ROAD,
BLACKPOOL FY4 4US
☎ (01253) 697850. OPEN 10 - 8 MON - FRI, 9 - 6 SAT, 11 - 5 SUN.
UNITS G & H, THE TRIUMPH CENTRE, HUNTS CROSS,
LIVERPOOL L24 9GB
☎ (0151) 486 0325. OPEN 10 - 8 MON - FRI, 9 - 6 SAT, 11 - 5 SUN.
WINWICK ROAD, KERFOOT STREET, WARRINGTON, CHESHIRE WA2
8NU
☎ (01925) 235365. OPEN 10 - 8 MON - FRI, 9 - 6 SAT, 11 - 5 SUN.
TONGE MOOR ROAD, BOLTON, GREATER  MANCHESTER BL2 2DJ
☎ (01204) 383733. OPEN 10 - 8 MON - FRI, 9 - 6 SAT, 11 - 5 SUN.
UNIT 13, THE WHEATLEY CENTRE, WHEATLEY HALL ROAD, DON-
CASTER DN2 4PE
☎ (01302) 760444. OPEN 10 - 8 MON - FRI, 9 - 6 SAT, 11 - 5 SUN.

As the UK's first National Discount Club, Matalan has the buying
power to guarantee its members up to 60% discounts on a huge range
of brand name clothing, household goods, luggage and toiletries for
all the family. Top quality merchandise, current season, no seconds, is
offered to its members at exclusive, permanently discounted prices
seven days a week. Matalan operates strictly on a membership basis,
one of the key factors for its success in offering 20%-60% savings off
recommended retail prices. Membership cards are issued through
companies, organisations and associations in the vicinity of the stores,
and are available to their employees/members. They are valid at any
of the 50 Matalan stores in the UK. To find out if your organisation
is registered, phone the Matalan hotline on 01772 629447.

## READMANS LTD

ALFRED HOUSE, SPENCE LANE, HOLBECK, LEEDS, WEST YORKSHIRE
LS12 1EF
☎ (0113) 2444960 DRAPERY
☎ (0113) 2436355 CASH AND CARRY.
Mainly men's, women's and children's clothing as well as bedding,
textiles, footwear, towels at prices which are cheaper than the high
street.

## TK MAXX

15 PARKER ST, OFF CLAYTON SQUARE, LIVERPOOL, MERSEYSIDE
☎ (0151) 708 9919. OPEN 9 - 6 MON - SAT
Based on an American concept, TK Maxx is the first British retailer
to practise "off-price" retailing. This means a centrally located store
which offers famous label goods with up to 60% savings off recommended retail prices. TK Maxx has fashion for the whole family -
men's, women's and childrenswear - accessories, shoes, gifts, kitchenware and home goods. Everything in the store is branded with a
choice of well-known high street names to designer labels, and while
a small percentage mightly be clearly marked past season, the great
majority of items in store are current season, current stock and still
with phenomenal savings. There is a huge choice with 50,000 pieces
in store with 5,000 new items arriving a week, so it's worth keeping
abreast of the lastest deliveries as turnaround is very fast. One of the
ways in which TK Maxx is able to offer such low prices is by running
a very low-cost operation, so the stores are simple and unfussy with
wide aisles, shopping trolleys and baskets, and a spacious, functional
feel to them. Service is not compromised, however: there are individual changing rooms, ramps for buggies and wheelchairs, plenty of
staff on the shop floor and all the branches accept all major credit and
debit cards.

# Factory Shops

## ACCED LTD

UNIT 29, CHESHIRE OAKS DESIGNER OUTLET VILLAGE, KINSEY ROAD, NEAR ELLESMERE PORT, L65 9JJ
(JUNCTION 10 OF THE M53), SOUTH WIRRAL
☎ (0151) 357 1579. OPEN 10 - 6 MON, TUE, WED, SAT, 10 - 8 THUR, FRI, 11 - 5 SUN AND BANK HOLIDAYS.

Smart daywear and workwear from this French designer company selling men's and women's fashions as well as a range of accessories to complement the outfits. Special offers are available throughout the year. Menswear labels include: Luc Saint Auban's sporting jackets and suits; Carnet De Vol for casually smart dressing; John Stevens' casual jackets, shirts and knitwear plus Oz sportswear for men and women.

## AQUASCUTUM

HORNSEA FREEPORT SHOPPING VILLAGE, HORNSEA, EAST YORKSHIRE HU18 1UT
☎ (01964) 536759. OPEN 10 - 5 SEVEN DAYS A WEEK.

Ends of ranges, last season's stock and cancelled export orders for men and women from the complete Aquascutum range. The shopping village has restaurants, play centres, a vintage car collection, water games, and plenty for the family to enjoy.

## BLACK DYKE MILL SHOP

BLACK DYKE MILLS COMPLEX, QUEENSBURY, BRADFORD, YORKSHIRE BD13 1QA
☎ (01274) 882271. OPEN 9 - 5 MON, TUE, THUR, FRI, 9 - 12 WED, CLOSED SAT, SUN.

Manufactures men's suitings and a small selection of ladies fabric. Seconds, quality worsted and mohair suit lengths, trouser lengths and one metre fents. Suit lengths from £15-£45. Trousers lengths from £6; skirt lengths from £2.50. Can recommend tailors in your area (or nearby). Closed Mill holidays so please ring before travelling far.

# BRIDGE OF YORK

3 MAIN STREET, FULFORD, YORK, NORTH YORKSHIRE YO1 4HJ
☎ (01904) 634508. OPEN 8.30 - 5 MON - FRI, 9.30 - 4 SAT.

Makes shirts, blouses, socks and ties for many of the high street department stores, as well as its own range of perfects which it sells in the factory shop at discounts of 30%. Cotton and polycotton blouses cost from £7.95, Viyella ones, £29.95. Also makes extra long sleeved shirts for the taller man from £10-£24.95.

# BROOKS MILL

SOUTH LANE, ELLAND, NEAR HALIFAX, WEST YORKSHIRE HX5 OHQ
☎ (01422) 377337. OPEN 9.30 - 5.30 MON - SAT, 11 - 5.30 SUN.

Clearance outlet for Ponden Mills merchandise from tablelinens and quilts, duvets and sheets, bedding and pillowcases all at appropriately reduced prices. Also clothes for men and women, half of which is designer wear including names such as Jac Dale and Maggie of London.

# BURBERRY

WOODROW UNIVERSAL, JUNCTION MILLS, CROSS HILLS, NEAR KEIGHLEY, YORKSHIRE BD20 7SE
☎ (01535) 633364. OPEN 11 - 5 MON - FRI, 10 - 4 SAT.
CORONATION MILLS, ALBION STREET, CASTLEFORD, WEST YORK-SHIRE
☎ (0197) 755 4411. OPEN 10 - 3.45 MON - FRI, 9.30 - 1.15 SAT.

These Burberry factory shops sell seconds and overmakes of the famous name raincoats and duffle coats as well as accessories such as the distinctive umbrellas, scarves and handbags. They also sell children's duffle coats, knitwear and shirts, as well as some of the Burberry range of food: jams, biscuits, tea and chocolate. All carry the Burberry label and are about one third of the normal retail price.

# CHESHIRE OAKS DESIGNER OUTLET VILLAGE

JUNCTION 10 OF THE M53, NEAR ELLESMERE PORT, SOUTH WIRRAL L65 9JJ
☎ (0151) 356 7932. OPEN 10 - 6 MON - SAT, 10 - 4 SUN AND BANK HOLIDAYS.

More than 30 outlets, all selling brand name merchandise at discounted prices, with more outlets in the pipeline. Labels for men include Timberland, Nike, Levi's, Scotch House, Fred Perry, Benetton, Kurt Geiger, Equator luggage, John Partridge countrywear, J B Armstrong, Principles/Burton, Tie Rack, Fruit of the Loom, Acced menswear (a French manufacturer), Suits You menswear, James Barry, Sapphire Books, the British Shoe Corporation trading as Famous Footwear and Remington. There is a children's play area, a Garfunkels restaurant and free car parking. Phase two opens in November 1995 with 30 more factory shops.

## DAKS SIMPSON

HORNSEA FREEPORT SHOPPING VILLAGE, HORNSEA, YORKSHIRE HU18 1UT
☎ (01964) 533268. OPEN 10 - 5 SEVEN DAYS A WEEK.
Sells previous season's stock for women and men as well as any returned merchandise and overmakes. There are good bargains to be had, but stock is very much dependent on what has not sold in the shops. Sizes vary but tend towards the two extremes: 6s, 8s and 10s on the one hand, and 20s and 22s on the other. Men's blazers, £99, originally £275; cords, £29, originally £89; good selection of men's suits, £129, originally £300. The Shopping Village has plenty to entertain the family with playgrounds, an indoor play centre, restaurants, a vintage car collection and butterfly world.

## DALESOX

6 SWADFORD STREET, SKIPTON, NORTH YORKSHIRE BD23 1JA
☎ (01756) 796509. OPEN 9 - 5 SEVEN DAYS A WEEK.
Based in Skipton's main shopping area, Dalesox sells quality hosiery and accessories. Most are perfect men's, ladies and children's socks made for the best high street chainstores and cost about £1-£1.50 a pair, normal retail price up to £4.99. There is lots of design choice from Disney character socks to Christmas pudding socks. There are also ties, ski socks, unusual design Swedish polyester ties, knickers, boxer shorts, pyjamas and nightshirts. Most of the stock is bought in from other manufacturers, cutting out the middleman.

## DAMART FACTORY CLEARANCE SHOP

UNIT 6A, ALSTON ROAD RETAIL PARK, BYPASS ROUNDABOUT,
BRADFORD ROAD, KEIGHLEY BD21 3NG
☎ (01535) 690648. OPEN 9 - 5.30 MON - SAT, 10 - 4 SUN AND BANK
HOLIDAYS.

Discontinued branded chainstore fashion for women, men and
children, some of which is branded Damart, as well as household
items: kitchen utensils, glassware, towels, tablecloths, brushes, mops
but no electrical equipment. Men's trousers, £19.99, reduced to £4;
men's boxer shorts, £6, reduced to £1; men's briefs, from 50p, T-
shirts, from £2. Most of the stock is bought in from other manufacturers and consists of overmakes and discontinued lines at discounts
of 50%. Coffee shop on site.

## DANNIMAC LTD

FACTORY SHOP, LIME MILL, VICTOR STREET, HOLLINWOOD,
OLDHAM, GREATER MANCHESTER
☎ (0161) 681 2060. OPEN 9 - 11 ON FIRST SAT OF EACH MONTH
FLETCHER STREET, BOLTON, GREATER MANCHESTER
BL3 6PR
☎ (01204) 532311. OPEN ONCE A MONTH ONLY. PHONE FOR DETAILS.
EAST TRADING ESTATE, SOUTHBANK ROAD, CARGO FLEET, MID-
DLESBROUGH, CLEVELAND TS3 8BH
☎ (01642) 247794. OPEN 9 - 11 ONE DAY A MONTH ONLY. PHONE FOR
DETAILS OF SALES.

Mens and ladies famous-name raincoats, jackets, anoraks, trenchcoats, and macs, as well as, occasionally, waxed and leather jackets at
factory shop prices. Jackets and coats range from £35 to £95. Most
merchandise is either slight seconds or discontinued lines; there is
some current stock, but most is previous seasons.

## DIM

CHESHIRE OAKS OUTLET VILLAGE, KINSEY ROAD, NEAR ELLESMERE
PORT, JUNCTION 10 OF M53, SOUTH WIRRAL L65 9JJ
☎ (0151) 357 2585. OPEN 10 - 6 MON - SAT, 10 - 4 SUN.

Lingerie and underwear shop for men and women selling briefs,
boxer shorts, vests, socks and sweatshirts.

## EMINENCE

CHESHIRE OAKS OUTLET VILLAGE, KINSEY ROAD, NEAR ELLESMERE
PORT, SOUTH WIRRAL L65 9JJ
☎ (0151) 357 1562. OPEN 10 - 6 MON - SAT, 10 - 4 SUN.
Eminence Paris is not very well known here and some of the designs
for men and women seemed more suited to the Continental style.
However, there were lots of men's boxer shorts, underwear, swimwear,
tracksuits and T-shirts. Prices range from £2 - £10.

## FAMOUS FOOTWEAR

CHESHIRE OAKS OUTLET VILLAGE, KINSEY ROAD, NEAR ELLESMERE
PORT, JUNCTION 10 OF M53, SOUTH WIRRAL L65 9JJ
☎ (0151) 357 1512. OPEN 10 - 6 MON - SAT, 10 - 4 SUN.
Wide range of brand names including Dolcis, Roland Cartier,
Saxone, Lotus, K Shoes, Barker, Ava, Miss Selfridge, Cable & Co,
Hush Puppies, Van-Dal, Equity, Ecco and Vagabond all at discount
prices.

## FRED PERRY SPORTSWEAR UK LTD

UNIT 24, CHESHIRE OAKS OUTLET VILLAGE, KINSEY ROAD, NEAR
ELLESMERE PORT, JUNCTION 10 OF M53, SOUTH WIRRAL L65 9JJ
☎ (0151) 357 1383. OPEN 10 - 6 MON - SAT, 10 - 4 SUN AND BANK
HOLIDAYS.
Men's and women's ranges of the famous Fred Perry sportswear and
leisure clothing: shorts, tennis tops, tracksuits, T-shirts. All price
labels show the original and the reduced price, which usually amount
to a 30% discount.

## FREEPORT SHOPPING VILLAGE

ANCHORAGE ROAD, FLEETWOOD, LANCASHIRE
☎ (01253) 877377. OPEN 10 - 6 SEVEN DAYS A WEEK.
Up to 40 shops, a marina, and lots of activities for the family. Shops
for men include: 424 Superstore (club football gear), Farah menswear,
Tom Sayers menswear, Double Two shirts, Lee jeans, Sports
Unlimited, Regatta (outdoor clothing), Shoe Sellers, Equator luggage.

# FRUIT OF THE LOOM

CHESHIRE OAKS OUTLET VILLAGE, KINSEY ROAD, NEAR ELLESMERE
PORT, JUNCTION 10 OF M53, SOUTH WIRRAL L65 9JJ
☎ (0151) 355 6169. OPEN 10 - 6 MON - SAT, 10 - 4 SUN.

Men's, women's and children's casual wear in the form of T-shirts,
sweatshirts, shorts and tracksuits with the distinctive Fruit of the
Loom logo.

# GOLDEN SHUTTLE MILL SHOP

ALBION ROAD, GREENGATES, BRADFORD BD10 9TQ
☎ (01274) 611161. OPEN 9.30 - 5 MON - SAT.

Men's, women's and children's fashions at discount prices, plus suitcases, sportsbags, and holdalls. Suits from £59.99-£89.99; shirts from
£5.50-£17.99; sports jackets from £49.99.

# I J DEWHIRST

42 MIDDLE STREET NORTH, DRIFFIELD, EAST YORKSHIRE
☎ (01377) 256209. OPEN 9 - 5.30 MON - FRI, 9 - 5 SAT.
5 WELHAM ROAD, MALTON OPEN 9 - 5.30 MON - FRI, 9 - 5 SAT,
11 - 5 SUN.

Wide range of men's, women's and children's clothes including men's
suits, jackets, shirts, trousers; women's jackets, blouses, skirts and
trousers; girl's dresses, blouses, trousers, skirts and jackets and boy's
shirts, trousers and jackets and much much more.

# JAEGER FACTORY SHOP

GOMERSAL MILLS, CLECKHEATON, YORKSHIRE BD19 4LU
☎ (01274) 852303. OPEN 12.30 - 4.30 MON, 9.30 - 4.30 TUE - FRI,
9 - 12.30 SAT.

Classic tailoring from Jaeger and Viyella at old-fashioned prices for
menand women. Most of the merchandise is last season's stock and
some seconds, but you may find the odd gem from this season if you
hunt carefully. Some factory shops the whole range of Jaeger clothes,
some just knitwear; yet others sell goods other than those with the
Jaeger label. This shop sells mens and ladies wear, and specialises in
knitwear.

# JAMES BARRY

CHESHIRE OAKS OUTLET VILLAGE, KINSEY ROAD, NEAR ELLESMERE PORT, SOUTH WIRRAL L65 9JJ
☎ (0151) 357 1416. OPEN 10 - 6 MON - SAT, 10 - 4 SUN.
Range of men's suits, jackets, socks, belts, briefs and shirts from the James Barry, Wolsey and Double Two range of brand names. Double Two shirts from £12.99; suits reduced from £175 to £115; casual shirts, £14.99 or two for £25; trousers reduced from £44.95 to £29.95. There is also an outlet at Clarks Factory Shopping Village (see Menswear, South West)

# JOHN PARTRIDGE COUNTRY STORE

CHESHIRE OAKS OUTLET VILLAGE, KINSEY ROAD, NEAR ELLESMERE PORT, SOUTH WIRRAL L65 9JJ
☎ (0151) 357 3020. OPEN 10 - 6 MON - SAT, 10 - 4 SUN.
Range of country clothes including waxed jackets, country-style shirts, bodywarmers, gilets and waxed coats for men and women. Examples of prices include jackets reduced from £162 to £95; shirts from £42 to £28; waxed coats from £263 to £184; nylon bodywarmers from £54 to £38.

# JUMPERS

BRIDGE MILL, COWAN BRIDGE, CARNFORTH, LANCASHIRE LA6 2HS
☎ (01524) 272726. OPEN 10 - 4 SEVEN DAYS A WEEK IN SUMMER.
A wide range of sweaters for men and women all at discount prices. There are also outlets at Hornsea Freeport (see North West), K Village (see North) and Clarks Village (see South West).

# K SHOES

UNIT 3, CLIFTON ROAD RETAIL PARK, BLACKPOOL, LANCASHIRE FY4 4RA
☎ (01253) 699380. OPEN 9.30 - 7.30 MON - FRI AND BANK HOLIDAYS, 9 - 6 SAT, 10 - 4 SUN.
9-11 CHAPEL STREET, SOUTHPORT, MERSEYSIDE PR8 1AE
☎ (01704) 531583. OPEN 9 - 5.30 MON - SAT, 11 - 5 SUN
(SUMMER, 11 - 4 SUN IN WINTER) 10 - 5 BANK HOLIDAYS.
Clarks International operate a chain of factory shops nationally which specialise in selling discontinued lines and slight sub-standards for men, women and children from Clarks, K Shoes and other famous brands. These shops trade under the name of Crockers, K Shoes

Factory shop or Clarks Factory Shop and while not all are physically attached to a shoe factory, these shops are treated as factory shops by the company. Customers can expect to find an extensive range of quality shoes, sandals, walking boots, slippers, trainers, handbags, accessories and gifts, while their major outlets also offer luggage, sports clothing, sports equipment and outdoor clothing. Brands stocked include Clarks, K Shoes, Springer, CICA, Hi-Tec, Puma, Mercury, Dr Martens, Nike, LA Gear, Fila, Mizuno, Slazenger, Weider, Samsonite, Delsey, Antler and Carlton, although not all are sold in every outlet. Discounts are on average 30% off the normal high street price for perfect stock.

## KURT GEIGER

CHESHIRE OAKS OUTLET VILLAGE, KINSEY ROAD, NEAR ELLESMERE PORT, (JUNCTION 10 OF M53), SOUTH WIRRAL L65 9JJ
☎ (0151) 357 1794. OPEN 10 - 6 MON - SAT, 10 - 4 SUN.
Shoe shop for men and women which sells Charles Jourdan, Cheaney, Barker, Sweeney's, Bruno Magli, and Carvela ranges. Shoes are laid out by brand name and in sizes, so it's easy to find your way round. New ranges are arranged separately. Examples of prices include a pair of Carvela shoes reduced from £49 to £39 and another blue suede pair from £65 to £35. There is another Kurt Geiger factory shop at Bicester Village (see Womenswear and Menswear, Wales and West Midlands).

## KYME MILL SHOP

NAPIER TERRACE, LAISTER DYKE, BRADFORD, YORKSHIRE BD3 8DD
☎ (01274) 669205. OPEN 9.30 - 5 MON - SAT.
Warehouse clearance lines of men's and womenswear - trousers, underwear in wool, cotton and polyester, men's suits, from £59.99, dress suits from £99.99, smart shirts from £4.99, ties from £2.99 - plus suitcases from £15.99 and travel bags from £11.99.

## LAMBERT HOWARTH FOOTWEAR

GAGHILLS MILLS, GAGHILLS ROAD, OFF BURNLEY ROAD EAST, WATERFOOT, ROSSENDALE, LANCASHIRE BB4 9AS
☎ (01706) 215417. OPEN 10.30 - 5 MON - FRI, 9.30 - 3.30 SAT.
A real mixture of seconds from the factory and perfects from other sources - footwear, clothes, handbags and towels. The seconds in

footwear are from shoes made for well-known high street chainstores and all are at discounted prices. These include slippers, walking boots, flat shoes and sandals for men, women and children. The perfects in clothes, towel and bags are two-thirds of the high street prices.

## LEVI'S BIG L FACTORY OUTLET

CHESHIRE OAKS OUTLET VILLAGE, KINSEY ROAD, NEAR ELLESMERE PORT, JUNCTION 10 OF M53, SOUTH WIRRAL L65 9JJ
☎ (0151) 356 8484. OPEN 10 - 6 MON - SAT, 10 - 4 SUN.
Men's and women's Levi jeans, jackets and shirts but no children's, all at discount prices.

## LIGHTWATER VILLAGE AND FACTORY SHOPPING

NORTH STAINLEY, RIPON, NORTH YORKSHIRE HG4 3HT
☎ (01765) 635321. OPEN 10 - 5 SEVEN DAYS A WEEK. OPENING TIMES VARY SEASONALLY.
Lightwater valley theme park is the biggest leisure park in the North of England; now, some of the property has been converted to factory shop retailing. You can visit the shopping village free, without visiting the theme park which makes a charge. There are various factory shops on site selling brand names such as Windsmoor, Planet, James Barry, Tula, Jane Shilton, Edinburgh Crystal, Hornsea pottery. The pottery shop has plenty of ceramics and kitchen utensils to choose from, while the crystal shop has glasses, decanters, giftware and bowls. There are two enormous "warehouses" with masses of fashion for women and men, bedlinen, duvets, shoes, perfume, cookware, suitcases and cosmetics. There will eventually be parking for 4,000 cars and 120 coaches, a market square, coffee shops, food shops, a wine bar, covered garden centre, visitors farm and trout pond. Lightwater is 3 miles off the A1.

## MILETA

STATION LANE, HECKMONDWIKE, WEST YORKSHIRE
☎ (01924) 409311. OPEN 10 - 5 MON - THUR, 10 - 4 FRI, SAT.
Manufacturer of specialist outdoor clothing with lots of seconds and overmakes: golf suits, golf gilets, T-shirts, Gore-Tex weatherproof breathable jackets, weatherproof anoraks, marginal seconds in jackets and hiking boots.

# NIKE UK LTD

CHESHIRE OAKS OUTLET VILLAGE, KINSEY ROAD, NEAR ELLESMERE
PORT, (JUNCTION 10 OF M53), SOUTH WIRRAL L65 9JJ
☎ (0151) 357 1252. OPEN 10 - 6 MON - SAT, 10 - 4 SUN.
Men's, women's and children's trainers, jackets, T-shirts, sports shirts,
shorts, sleeveless T-shirts and tracksuits.

# PRINCIPLES

CHESHIRE OAKS OUTLET VILLAGE, KINSEY ROAD, NEAR ELLESMERE
PORT, JUNCTION 10 OF M53, SOUTH WIRRAL L65 9JJ
☎ (0151) 357 1033. OPEN 10 - 6 MON - SAT, 10 - 4 SUN.
Small range of Principles for Men items, plus a wide range of
Principles clothes for women at discounts up to 50%.

# SUITS YOU

CHESHIRE OAKS OUTLET VILLAGE, KINSEY ROAD, NEAR ELLESMERE
PORT, SOUTH WIRRAL L65 9JJ
☎ (0151) 355 6701. OPEN 10 - 6 MON - SAT, 10 - 4 SUN.
Most of the suits and jackets here are sold under the Suits You label,
although there were some Van Kollen jackets and Pierre Cardin suits.
A large sign at the door tells you the sorts of discounts you can expect.
For example, a suit which would have cost £149 is for sale at £100,
or you can buy two for £175.

# THE FACTORY SHOP

LAWKHOLME LANE, KEIGHLEY, WEST YORKSHIRE BD21 3HW
☎ (01535) 611703. OPEN 9.30 - 5 MON - SAT, 10 - 4 BANK HOLIDAYS.
LANCASTER LEISURE PARK, WYRESDALE ROAD, LANCASTER,
LANCASHIRE LA1 3LA
☎ (01524) 846079. OPEN 10 - 5 MON - SAT, 11 - 5 SUN AND BANK
HOLIDAYS.
5 NORTH STREET, RIPON, NORTH YORKSHIRE HG4 1JY
☎ (01765) 601156. OPEN 9 - 5 MON - SAT, 11 - 4 BANK HOLIDAYS.
HORNSEA FREEPORT SHOPPING VILLAGE, HORNSEA, EAST
YORKSHIRE
☎ (01964) 534211. OPEN 10 - 5 MON - FRI, 10 - 6 SAT, SUN.
COMMERCIAL STREET, MORLEY, WEST YORKSHIRE LS1 6EX
☎ (0113) 2381240. OPEN 9.30 - 5 MON - FRI, 9 - 5 SAT.
Wide range on sale includes men's, ladies and children's clothing and
footwear; household textiles, toiletries, hardware, luggage, lighting
and bedding, most of which are chainstore and high street brands at

discounts of approximately 30%-50%. There are weekly deliveries and brands include all the major stars: Coloroll, Wrangler and Dartington to name just three (the Morley branch does not stock Wrangler). Lines are continually changing and few factory shops offer such a variety under one roof. The Hornsea branch stock special buys bought specifically for the Freeport outlet.

## THE SCOTCH HOUSE

CHESHIRE OAKS OUTLET VILLAGE, KINSEY ROAD, NEAR ELLESMERE PORT, SOUTH WIRRAL L65 9JJ
☎ (0151) 357 3203. OPEN 10 - 6 MON - SAT, 10 - 4 SUN.
This outlet sells Pringle and Lyle & Scott for men and women at discount prices. For example, men's lambswool sweaters reduced from £69.50 to £39.50; Lyle & Scott T-shirts, £12.95. There are also coats, jackets, bags, waistcoats.

## THE SHOE FACTORY SHOP

21 WELLOWGATE, GRIMSBY, SOUTH HUMBERSIDE DN32 ORA
☎ (01472) 342415. OPEN 9 - 5 MON - SAT, 9 - 7 THUR.
6/7 OSLO ROAD, SUTTON FIELDS, HULL
☎ (01482) 839292. OPEN 9 - 5 MON - SAT, UNTIL 7 ON THUR AND FRI.
Men's, women's and children's shoes and accessories which are bought in from other manufacturers including Spanish, Portuguese and Italian companies. All are unbranded. The range covers from mocassins to dressy shoes.

## THE SHOE SHED

UNITS 10 AND 11, WHEATLEY CENTRE, WHEATLEY HALL ROAD, DONCASTER, YORKSHIRE
☎ (0302) 341435. OPEN 10 - 6 MON - THUR, 10 - 7 FRI, 9.30 - 5.30 SAT, 11 - 5 SUN.
Large factory shop selling a vast range of all types of men's, women's and children's shoes, all of which are perfects, at up to 30% below normal high street prices. Men's shoes from £10; sports shoes from £10.

## TIE RACK

CHESHIRE OAKS OUTLET VILLAGE, KINSEY ROAD, NEAR ELLESMERE PORT, (JUNCTION 10 OF M53), SOUTH WIRRAL L65 9JJ
☎ (0151) 355 6166. OPEN 10 - 6 MON - SAT, 10 - 4 SUN.
Usual range of Tie Rack items including silk boxer shorts, ties, socks, and waistcoats, all at reduced prices. For example, silk boxers from £15.99 to £9.99; silk ties, from £9.99 to £6.99; socks £3.99 to £2.50.

## TIMBERLAND

CHESHIRE OAKS OUTLET VILLAGE, KINSEY ROAD, NEAR ELLESMERE PORT, JUNCTION 10 OF M53, SOUTH WIRRAL L65 9JJ
☎ (0151) 357 1359. OPEN 10 - 6 MON - SAT, 10 - 4 SUN.
Footwear, clothing and outdoor gear from the well-known Timberland range. Coats from £50 upwards; jackets from £100; jeans from £35, shirts from £42. Most of the stock is last season's or dis-contined lines, but not seconds. There is no current stock.

## WRANGLER

HORNSEA FREEPORT SHOPPING VILLAGE, HORNSEA,
YORKSHIRE HU18 1UT
☎ (01964) 532979. OPEN 10 - 5 MON - SUN.
Previous season's stock as well as any returned merchandise and over-makes. Men's jeans from £18.99, children's from £12.99. The Shopping Village has plenty to entertain the family with playgrounds, an indoor play centre, restaurants, a vintage car collection and but-terfly world.

# *Dress Agencies*

## AS NEW FASHIONS

1 EMSCOTE GROVE, HAUGH SHAW ROAD, HALIFAX, WEST
YORKSHIRE
☎ (01422) 365379. OPEN 9.30 - 5 MON - SAT.
Ladies, men's and children's nearly-new clothes all available. Men's suits are generally Marks & Spencer, although Simon suits, among others, are occasionally stocked, as well as dinner suits at Christmas time. There is usually a selection of seasonal and sports wear, includ-ing ski clothes.

## ELITE DRESS AGENCY

1 MARKET STREET, ALTRINCHAM, CHESHIRE WA14 1QE
☎ (0161) 928 5424. OPEN 10 - 5 MON - SAT.
Mainly ladies wear which is less than one year old, although there are both men's and childrenswear departments. Wide range of clothing including some sports wear. Twice yearly sales at the end of June and December.

## THE ELITE DRESS AGENCY

35 KINGS STREET WEST, MANCHESTER M3 2PW
☎ (0161) 8323670. OPEN 10 - 5 MON - SAT.
Three floors of good quality men's, women's and children's clothing, many with a Continental flavour. For men, there are lots of Italian designer suits from £50-£150 and including Boss and Armani.

## *Hire Shops*

## GREAT CLOTHES

84 YORK ROAD, LEEDS, WEST YORKSHIRE
☎ (0113) 2350303. OPEN 9.30 - 9 MON - FRI, 9.30 - 6 SAT, 11 - 5 SUN.
Clothes shop which also operates a hire service for formal men's and boyswear. Everything from outfits for two-year-olds to clothes for men with a 54" chest. Top hat and tails, with cravat or tie, from £34.99; evening jackets or tuxedos, from £29.99; full kilt wear, £54.99.

## PUMPKINS

22 THE FIRST BALCONY, BARTON ARCADE, DEANSGATE,
MANCHESTER, GREATER MANCHESTER M3 2BB
☎ (0161) 831 7610. OPEN 10 - 5 MON - SAT, UNTIL 7 ON THUR.
There are more than 2,000 outfits available at any one time at this shop which is well known to Granada TV, whose stars often make use of its hire service. The shop offers a choice of more than 450 garments in evening wear, and men's dinner suits. Costs range from £40 for up to one week to a maximum of £95. There is a discount for students of 15% as well as a discount for nurses.

## *Secondhand and Vintage Clothes*

### BLOOMERS

CHELTENHAM CRESCENT, HARROGATE, NORTH
YORKSHIRE HG1 1DH
☎ (01423) 569389. OPEN 11 - 5 MON - SAT, CLOSED WED.
Vintage clothes up to the Forties, with Twenties underwear, beaded
dresses, accessories and shawls. Also quilts, sheets, pillowcases, fans,
lace, tablecloths, hats, men's hats, waistcoats and shirts.

### QUIGGINS CENTRE

12-16 SCHOOL LANE, LIVERPOOL L1 3BT
☎ (0151) 709 2462. OPEN 10 - 6 MON - SAT.
There are thirty different shops at the Quiggins Centre, the second
biggest market in Liverpool, selling a variety of goods including theatrical and period costumes, secondhand clothes, furniture, bric-a-
brac, jewellery, antiques and a music shop.

### REVIVAL

6 WARNER STREET, ACCRINGTON, LANCASHIRE BB5 1HN
☎ (01254) 382316. OPEN 10.30 - 5 MON - SAT, CLOSED WED.
Vintage clothes from the beginning of the century to the Seventies
including suede and leather waistcoats, cheesecloth tops, Biba
trousers. Long suede waistcoat, from £6 to £9.50; short one, under
£10; Levi jeans, from £9 up to £18; Levi jackets, £10-£35; Fifties-
style shirts, £6-£12; dinner suits, £24.

# NORTH AND SCOTLAND

## *Permanent Discount Outlet*

### CORNICHE PERMANENT SALE SHOP

27 ST MARY'S STREET, EDINBURGH EH1 1DT
☎ (0131) 557 8333. OPEN 10.30 - 5.30 MON - SAT.
Sells designer names at discount prices. Merchandise consists of clearance stock from its main retail outlet, as well as special outfits bought

in. Designers on sale at discounts of between 40-90% include Gaultier, Red or Dead and Fujiwara. On sale in the past have been Kenzo silk suits, £250; Fujiwara jackets, £185, usually £299; Gaultier jackets, £175, usually £295. Corniche also has a shop in Jeffrey's Street, which does not sell discounted merchandise.

## CORSTON SINCLAIR LTD

INDUSTRIAL PROTECTIVE CLOTHING, 36 GLENBURN ROAD, COLLEGE MILTON NORTH, EAST KILBRIDE, SCOTLAND G74 5BB
☎ (01355) 222273.

Designer trainers from Reebok, Nike, Dunlop and Inter trainers as well as protective clothing (safety helmets, safety footwear, overalls), sports and leisure items: jeans, shorts, sweatshirts, socks and underwear.

## MATALAN

16 GOODWOOD SQUARE, TEESSIDE RETAIL PARK, THORNABY, STOCKTON-ON-TEES TS17 7BW
☎ (01642) 633204. OPEN 10 - 8 MON - FRI, 9.30 - 5.30 SAT, 10 - 6 SUN.
SEAFIELD WAY, SEAFIELD ROAD, EDINBURGH EH15 1TB
☎ (0131) 657 5045. OPEN 10 - 8 MON - FRI, 9.30 - 5.30 SAT, 10 - 6 SUN.
WALNEY ROAD, BARROW LA14 5UU
☎ (01229) 430899. OPEN 10 - 8 MON - FRI, 9.30 - 5.30 SAT, 10 - 6 SUN.
UNIT 2B, METRO CENTRE, RETAIL PARK, GATESHEAD, NEWCASTLE UPON TYNE NE11 4YD
☎ (0191) 460 0423. OPEN 10 - 7.45 MON - FRI, 10 - 6 SAT, SUN.
UNIT 5, CALEDONIAN CENTRE, NEW ASHTREE STREET, WISHAW ML2 7UR
☎ (01698) 357075. OPEN 10 - 8 MON - FRI, 9.30 - 5.30 SAT, 10 - 6 SUN.
PLOT 12, DERWENT HOUSE, SOLWAY ROAD, WORKINGTON CA14 3YA
☎ (01900) 870966. OPEN 10 - 8 MON - FRI, 9.30 - 5.30 SAT, 10 - 6 SUN
UNIT 2, KINGSTONE RETAIL PARK, HULL HU2 2TX
☎ (01482) 586184. OPEN 10 - 8 MON - FRI, 9 - 6 SAT, 11 - 5 SUN.
UNIT 7, GLENCAIRNE RETAIL PARK, KILMARNOCK KA1 4AY
☎ (01563) 573892. OPEN 10 - 8 MON - FRI, 9.30 - 5.30 SAT, 10 - 6 SUN.
UNIT 1 HEWITTS CIRCUS, CLEETHORPES DN35 9QH
☎ (01472) 200255. OPEN 10 - 8 MON - FRI, 9 - 6 SAT, 11 - 5 SUN.

As the UK's first National Discount Club, Matalan has the buying power to guarantee its members up to 60% discounts on a huge range of brand name clothing, household goods, luggage and toiletries for all the family. Top quality merchandise, current season, no seconds, is offered to its members at exclusive, permanently discounted prices seven days a week. Matalan operates strictly on a membership basis, one of the key factors for its success in offering 20%-60% savings off recommended retail prices. Membership cards are issued through companies, organisations and associations in the vicinity of the stores, and are available to their employees/members. They are valid at any of the 50 Matalan stores in the UK. To find out if your organisation is registered, phone the Matalan hotline on 01772 629447.

## NEXT TO NOTHING

83-93 SAUCHIEHALL STREET, GLASGOW GU 3DD
☎ (0141) 332 4056. OPEN 9 - 5.30 MON - WED, 10 - 7 THUR, 9.30 - 6 FRI, 9 - 6 SAT.

Sells perfect surplus stock from Next stores and the Next Directory catalogue - from belts, jewellery and underwear to day and evening wear - at discounts of 50% or more. The ranges are usually last season's and overruns but there is the odd current item if you look carefully. Stock consists of men's, women's and children's clothing, with some homeware and shoes, depending on the branch. Stock is replenished twice a week and there is plenty of it.

## Q MARK

56 BELFORD ROAD, EDINBURGH, SCOTLAND EH4 3BR
☎ (0131) 225 6861. OPEN 9 - 5.30 MON - SAT, 12 - 5 SUN, UNTIL 7 THUR.
BRAIDHOLM ROAD, GIFFNOCK, GLASGOW, SCOTLAND G46 6EB
☎ (0141) 633 3636. OPEN 9 - 6 MON - SAT, UNTIL 8 ON THUR, 12 - 5 SUN.

Scotland's biggest discount clothing warehouse for men, women and children offers top quality fashions at up to 50% off normal high street prices. All garments are good quality seconds, overmakes or cancelled contracts but with their labels cut out. Regular stock deliveries ensure a constant selection of new styles - often recognised in famous chain stores, but always at ridiculously low prices. Q Mark operate a once-a-year membership fee of £5. All prices are subject to VAT and charged at point of sale.

## STATESIDE WHOLESALE CLUB

☎ (01670) 789110. MAIL ORDER ONLY.

Contrary to what it might seem, Stateside Wholesale Club is not an American company. Based in Northumberland, it is a catalogue company along the lines of Betterware - but selling clothes. A trio of catalogues - featuring men's, women's and children's clothes - are left at your home. You can then order the various outfits through the agent who comes to collect the catalogue. The real bargains come if you are an agent, as you can charge whatever price you like for the goods in the catalogue as long as you pay the company a fixed amount for each outfit. The catalogue states the normal retail price for each outfit, but the agent's list states the amount the company wants from the agent for that item. This amount is often half the catalogue price. The company suggests that you sell the outfit at its fixed price plus 20% but if you can get more for it, that's fine and you keep the extra margin. It claims that all the merchandise is perfect, big brand names on sale currently in shops and other catalogues. You have to purchase something in order to get on the mailing list, but once you start receiving catalogues, you can either do a Caura/Cabouchon and sell to friends or use it to buy clothes for yourself and your family at low prices. The men's clothes are of the casual shirts and leisurewear variety. Brand names include Adidas, LA Gear and Pierre Cardin, but they are mostly in the footwear area.

## THE UNCOLLECTED DRY CLEANING COMPANY

45 GARDEN WALK, METRO CENTRE, GATESHEAD, TYNE & WEAR
☎ (0191) 460 3195. OPEN 10 - 8 MON - SAT.
7 OLD ELDON SQUARE, NEWCASTLE UPON TYNE, NORTHUMBER-
LAND NE1 7JG
☎ (0191) 261 0995. OPEN 9.30 - 5.30 MON - SAT.

It's amazing what people forget they took in for dry cleaning. After three months, most of the big chains clear their uncollected merchandise, which is how they come to be on sale in these two outlets for seemingly amazing prices. These are Aladdin's caves of forgotten clothes from Burberry raincoats to Valentino suits, as well as many more down to earth items. Everything sells for rock-bottom prices; for example, that Burberry raincoat cost £10. Previous bargains in the designer section include a Karl Lagerfeld two-piece evening outfit, size 14, £39 and an Emanuel two-piece suit, £29. Of the two branches, the Metro Centre stocks more of the designer labels, while the Newcastle branch sells a lot of high street names such as Marks & Spencer, Principles and Next, as well an enjoying a uniform section which has been known to stock a Virgin Airways pilot's uniform as well as bus conductors' jackets.

## TK MAXX

LOWER GROUND FLOOR, MONUMENT MALL,
NORTHUMBERLAND STREET, NEWCASTLE-UPON-TYNE, TYNE & WEAR.
☎ (0191) 233 2323. OPEN 9 - 5.30 MON - FRI, UNTIL 8 ON THURS, 9 - 6 SAT.

Based on an American concept, TK Maxx is the first British retailer to practise "off-price" retailing. This means a centrally located store which offers famous label goods with up to 60% savings off recommended retail prices. TK Maxx has fashion for the whole family - men's, women's and childrenswear - accessories, shoes, gifts, kitchenware and home goods. Everything in the store is branded with a choice of well-known high street names to designer labels, and while a small percentage mightly be clearly marked past season, the great majority of items in store are current season, current stock and still with phenomenal savings. There is a huge choice with 50,000 pieces in store with 5,000 new items arriving a week, so it's worth keeping abreast of the lastest deliveries as turnaround is very fast. One of the ways in which TK Maxx is able to offer such low prices is by running a very low-cost operation, so the stores are simple and unfussy with wide aisles, shopping trolleys and baskets, and a spacious, functional feel to them. Service is not compromised, however: there are individual changing rooms, ramps for buggies and wheelchairs, plenty of staff on the shop floor and all the branches accept all major credit and debit cards.

## WORKWEAR COSALT INTERNATIONAL LTD

10 WEST HARBOUR ROAD, GRANTON, EDINBURGH EH5 1PJ
☎ (0131) 552 0011. OPEN 8 - 5 MON - FRI.

Offers a wide selection of leisure and outdoor clothes from Doc Martens and Caterpillar boots to padded jackets and denim shirts, dungarees and donkey jackets. Donkey jackets cost as little as £18, dungarees less than £13, Doc Martens, £35, although VAT has to be added to prices. There are catalogues available for you to order from if what you want isn't in stock.

## Factory Shops
### ANTARTEX VILLAGE VISITOR CENTRE
LOMDON INDUSTRIAL ESTATE, ALEXANDRIA, DUMBARTONSHIRE
G83 OTP
☎ (01389) 752393. OPEN 10 - 6 MON - SUN.
Edinburgh Woollen Mill with a sheepskin factory and craft workshops where you can watch sheepskinjackets being made, pottery and jewellery and glass engraving taking place. Sheepskin jackets costs £199-£375 and there is often a sale in the shop with plenty of bargains.

### BAIRDWEAR RACKE
6-8 COLVILLES PLACE, EAST KILBRIDE, GLASGOW, SCOTLAND
G75 OQS
☎ (01355) 236441. OPEN 10 - 4 MON - THUR, 10 - 12 FRI.
24 ROSYTH ROAD, POLMADIE, GLASGOW
☎ (0141) 429 6611. OPEN 11 - 4 MON - THUR, 9.30 - 12.30 FRI, CLOSED 2.30 - 3.
INCHINNEN INDUSTRIAL ESTATE, ABBOTSBURN, RENFREWSHIRE
☎ (0141) 812 6388. OPEN 9.30 - 4.30 MON - WED, 9.30 - 2.15 THUR, 9.30 - 12.30 FRI.
Manufacturers for a well-known high street chainstore for more than 20 years, Bairdwear has a wide selection of seconds and overmakes in its factory shops. The East Kilbride shop makes men's shirts and sells them as well as women's and children's clothes, with some babywear, as well as towels, sheets and duvets covers. The Abbotsburn shop sells mainly womenswear with some menswear and lots of babywear. The Polmadie shop sells women's and children's clothes, some men's, and household linen and towels, but no duvets.

## BALMOREL MILL

16 CHURCH LANE, GARSTON, AYRSHIRE, SCOTLAND
☎ (01563) 820213. OPEN 9 - 5 MON - SAT, 11 - 4.30 SUN.

Sells cashmere and lambswool knitwear, emboidered knitwear and sportswear, some of which is brand name and some own label, but all sold at factory direct prices. The emphasis is on sports and leisurewear. Examples of prices include Farah men's trousers, £23.95, cotton sweatshirts, £8.50, sweater, £3.95. There are Kangol hats for men and Lyle & Scott sports and knitwear.

## BARBOUR LTD

CUSTOMER SERVICE BUILDING, BEDE INDUSTRIAL ESTATE, SIMONSIDE, JARROW, TYNE & WEAR NE34 QPD
☎ (0191) 455 4444. OPEN 10 - 5 TUES, WED, FRI, 9 - 6 THUR, 9 - 12 SAT.

The famous waterproof waxed jackets and outdoor wear, all of which are seconds or discontinued lines, at discounts of 10%-25%. Jackets comes in fifteen different styles from short to full-length and in various colours, but you may not find the style, colour and size you want as quantities vary. There are also shooting jackets, tweed hats and caps, linings for coats, bags, waxed trousers, waders and some children's waxed jackets.

## BELINDA ROBERTSON CASHMERE

22 PALMERSTON PLACE, EDINBURGH EH12 5AL
☎ (0131) 225 1057. OPEN 9 - 5.30 MON - FRI, 10 - 4 SAT, OR BY APPOINTMENT.
UNIT 17, LADYLAW CENTRE, HAWICK TD9 7DS
☎ (01450) 77648. OPEN 9 - 5 MON - FRI.

Designer and classic knitwear in 100% cashmere for men and women, as made for leading stores and couture houses worldwide. Belinda Robertson, who has an international reputation for designing classics with a twist, and in January, 1993, won the NatWest Export Award, has a showroom in Edinburgh and a factory shop in Hawick which offer ends of ranges, samples and over-runs all sold at discount prices, usually between 25-50% off retail prices. All garments are designed and manufactured in Scotland. Accessories include capes, scarves and gloves.

## BIG L

KINGSGATE RETAIL PARK, EAST KILBRIDE, SCOTLAND G74 4UN
☎ (01355) 241413. OPEN 10 - 8 MON - FRI, 9 - 6 SAT, 10 - 5 SUN.
This factory outlet is devoted to selling seconds and ends of lines of
Levi's merchandise, and is well worth a visit. All the clothes which
includes the full range of shirts, sweatshirts, jackets, jeans, and cords,
are top quality although there may be slight flaws, but please note that
all the tabs cut off every item before it gets to the shop. There is a
Fruit of the Loom factory shop next door, making double the reason
for a visit.

## BURBERRY

KITTY BREWSTER INDUSTRIAL ESTATE, BLYTHE,
NORTHUMBERLAND NE24 4RG
☎ (01670) 352524. OPEN 10 - 3.30 MON - THUR, 10 - 3 FRI, 9.30 - 12.30
SAT.
This Burberry factory shop sells seconds and overmakes of the famous
name raincoats and duffle coats as well as accessories such as the distinctive umbrellas, scarves and handbags. It also sells childrens duffle
coats, knitwear and shirts, as well as some of the Burberry range of
food: jams, biscuits, tea, coffee and chocolate. All carry the Burberry
label and are about one third of the normal retail price.

## CHARLES CLINKARD

JACKSONS LANDING, HARTLEPOOL FACTORY OUTLET SHOPPING
MALL, HARTLEPOOL MARINA, HARTLEPOOL, CLEVELAND TS24 OXN
☎ (01429) 866939. OPEN 10 - 6 MON - FRI, 11 - 5 SUN AND BANK
HOLIDAYS.
Indoor factory shopping centre with twenty-four outlets selling brand
name items including footwear for the family at discounts of between
20% and 30%. Labels include Loake, Camel, Bally, Church's, Ecco,
Gabor, Rohde, Van-Dal, Kickers, Clarks, Dr Martens, K Shoes, Lotus
and Renata plus handbags by Jane Shilton. Men's loafers, £29.99
reduced from £49.99; children's shoes, £9.99, reduced from £16.99;
Elefanten children's shoes, £16.99 reduced from £32.99. Hartlepool
Marina hosts a recreated historic quay and harbours HMS
Trincomalee, the oldest British warship still afloat, and is also the site
of the new Hartlepool Museum with its interactive fighting ships

section and a replica seventeenth century children's play area. There is free parking adjacent to the centre, a coffee shop, restaurant over-looking the Marina, and baby changing and disabled facilities.

## CROCKERS

UNIT 26, THE FORGE SHOPPING CENTRE, PARKHEAD, GLASGOW, SCOTLAND G31 4EB
☎ (0141) 556 5290. OPEN 9 - 5.30 MON - SAT, 12 - 4.30 SUN AND BANK HOLIDAYS.
Clarks International operate a chain of factory shops nationally which specialise in selling discontinued lines and slight sub-standards for men, women and children from Clarks, K Shoes and other famous brands. These shops trade under the name of Crockers, K Shoes Factory shop or Clarks Factory Shop and while not all are physically attached to a shoe factory, these shops are treated as factory shops by the company. Customers can expect to find an extensive range of quality shoes, sandals, walking boots, slippers, trainers, handbags, accessories and gifts, while their major outlets also offer luggage, sports clothing, sports equipment and outdoor clothing. Brands stocked include Clarks, K Shoes, Springer, CICA, Hi-Tec, Puma, Mercury, Dr Martens, Nike, LA Gear, Fila, Mizuno, Slazenger, Weider, Samsonite, Delsey, Antler and Carlton, although not all are sold in every outlet. Discounts are on average 30% off the normal high street price for perfect stock.

## DEWHIRST FACTORY SHOP

MILL HILL, NORTH WEST INDUSTRIAL ESTATE, PETERLEE, COUNTY DURHAM SR8 5AA
☎ (0191) 586 4525. OPEN 9 - 5.30 MON - WED, 9 - 7 THUR, 9 - 6 FRI, 9 - 5 SAT, 11 - 5 SUN.
PENNYWELL INDUSTRIAL ESTATE, PENNYWELL, SUNDERLAND
☎ (0191) 534 7928. OPEN 9  5.30 MON - FRI, 9 - 5 SAT, 11 - 5 SUN.
AMSTERDAM ROAD, SUTTON FIELDS INDUSTRIAL ESTATE, HULL
☎ (01482) 820166. OPEN 9 - 5.30 MON - WED, 9 - 7.30 THUR, 9 - 6 FRI, 9 - 5 SAT, 11 - 5 SUN.
WEST COATHAM LANE, DORMANSTOWN INDUSTRIAL ESTATE, DORMANSTOWN, REDCAR
☎ (01642) 474210. OPEN 9 - 5.30 MON - FRI, 9 - 5 SAT, 10.30 - 4.30 SUN.
NEWBIGGIN ROAD, NORTH SEATON INDUSTRIAL ESTATE, ASHINGTON
☎ (01670) 813493. OPEN 9 - 5.30 MON - FRI, 9 - 5 SAT, 10.30 - 4.30 SUN.

Wide range of men's, women's and children's clothes including men's suits, jackets, shirts, trousers; women's jackets, blouses, skirts and trousers; girl's dresses, blouses, trousers, skirts and jackets and boy's shirts, trousers, jackets and much much more.

## FALMER JEANS LTD

CAPONACRE INDUSTRIAL ESTATE, CAIRN ROAD, CUMNOCK, AYRSHIRE KA18 1SH
☎ (0290) 421577. OPEN 9.30 - 3.30 MON - THUR, 9.30 - 12.30 FRI, 9 - 11.45 SAT.
Perfects and seconds from the well-known Falmer range including T-shirts from £6- £10, jeans from £7 for seconds and £14 for perfects. Mostly for men and women, but a small selection for children.

## HOUSE OF HARDY

WILLOW BURN, ALNWICK, NORTHUMBERLAND NE66 2PF
☎ (01665) 602771. OPEN 9 - 5 MON - FRI, 10 - 5 SAT, 1.30 - 5 SUN FROM APRIL - OCTOBER.
Sells ends of lines for the outdoor type, especially fishermen and women, including waxed jackets, jumpers, fly vests, tops and trousers, countrywear bags, fishing rods, reels, and lines. There is also a bargain basement with own brand items on sale at discounts of about 50%.

## JACKSONS LANDING

HARTLEPOOL FACTORY OUTLET SHOPPING MALL, HARTLEPOOL MARINA, HARTLEPOOL, CLEVELAND TS24 OXN
☎ (01429) 866989 INFORMATION LINE. OPEN 10 - 6 MON - FRI, 11 - 5 SUN AND BANK HOLIDAYS.
Indoor factory shopping centre with twenty-four outlets selling a range of brand name items. Clinkards Sell Bally, Clark's and Kickers footwear; James Barry has a selection of men's suits, shirts, and jackets; Bookscene sells jigsaws, stationary, posters; Tog 24 sells leisurewear; Chas N Whillans, Scottish branded wool specialist, sells famous branded quality lambswool and cashmere including Lyle & Scott and Pringle; Hallmark sells half-price celebration and Christmas cards, wrapping paper, stuffed toys; and Tom Sayers sells a range of menswear; while Teasure Island sells specialised gifts from Hartlepool. Recent new openings include Benetton and Joe Bloggs. Hartlepool Marina hosts a recreated historic quay and harbours HMS

Trincomalee, the oldest British warship still afloat, and is also the site of the new Hartlepool Museum with its interactive fighting ships section and a replica seventeenth century children's play area. There is free parking adjacent to the centre, a coffee shop, restaurant overlooking the Marina, and baby changing and disabled facilities.

## JAEGER FACTORY SHOP

TULLIBODY ROAD, LORNSHILL, ALLOA, SCOTLAND SK10 2EX
☎ (01259) 218985. OPEN 10 - 4 MON - SUN.
15 MUNRO PLACE, BONNYTON INDUSTRIAL ESTATE, KILMARNOCK, SCOTLAND KA1 2NP
☎ (01563) 5265111. OPEN 9 - 12 AND 2 - 4 MON, THUR, 10 - 4 SAT, SUN, 9 - 4 TUE, WED, FRI.
Classic tailoring at old-fashioned prices. Most of the merchandise is last season's stock and some seconds. There are now 13 Jaeger factory shops, some selling the whole range of Jaeger clothes, some just knitwear; yet others sell goods other than those with the Jaeger label.

## JAMES BARRY

JACKSONS LANDING, HARTLEPOOL FACTORY OUTLET SHOPPING MALL, HARTLEPOOL MARINA, HARTLEPOOL, CLEVELAND TS24 OXN
☎ (01429) 860364. OPEN 10 - 6 MON - FRI, 11 - 5 SUN AND BANK HOLIDAYS.
Indoor factory shopping centre with twenty-four outlets selling brand name items including smart menswear. James Barry sells Double Two casual shirts, two for £25; Lancers trousers, £29.95 reduced from £44.95; double Two plain work shirts, two for £20; single breasted suits, £115 reduced from £175; dinner suits, £125; jackets, £59.50 reduced from £130; and belts, £4.95 reduced from £5.95. Hartlepool Marina hosts a recreated historic quay and harbours HMS Trincomalee, the oldest British warship still afloat, and is also the site of the new Hartlepool Museum with its interactive fighting ships section and a replica seventeenth century children's play area. There is free parking adjacent to the centre, a coffee shop, restaurant overlooking the Marina, and baby changing and disabled facilities.

## JAMES JOHNSTON OF ELGIN

CASHMERE VISITORS CENTRE, NEW MILL, ELGIN,
SCOTLAND 1V3 2AF
☎ (01343) 554000. OPEN 9 - 5.30 MON - SAT, 11 - 4 SUN JULY AND
AUGUST ONLY.
A factory shop with an on site visitors mill, where you can watch raw
wool being made into luxurious cashmere from the dying and
blending through to the spinning, winding and weaving. Cashmere
sweaters sold from £90 - £250, including regular bargain baskets.

## JOCKEY UNDERWEAR FACTORY SHOP

EASTERN AVENUE, TEAM VALLEY TRADING ESTATE, GATESHEAD,
TYNE & WEAR
☎ (0191) 491 0088. OPEN 10 - 4 MON, TUE, THUR, 10 - 2.30 FRI, CLOSED
WED.
Up to 17 different types of men's underwear from Y-fronts and boxers
to tangas and hipsters. Also ladies underwear: briefs, ribbed vests,
cami-tops, bodies. Although this factory makes underwear, because it
is part of the Courtaulds group, the factory shop also sells Wolsey
socks, Cristy towels, Zorbit babywear, pillows and duvets.

## K SHOES

K VILLAGE, NETHERFIELD, KENDAL, CUMBRIA LA9 7DA
☎ (01539) 721892. OPEN 9.30 - 7 MON - FRI, 9 - 5 SAT, 11 - 5 SUN,
9 - 6 BANK HOLIDAYS.
JAMES STREET, ASKAM-IN-FURNESS, CUMBRIA LA16 7BA
☎ (01229) 462267. OPEN 10 - 5.30 MON - FRI, 9 - 5 SAT, 10 - 5 BANK
HOLIDAYS.
MAIN STREET, SHAP, CUMBRIA CA10 3NL
☎ (01931) 716648. OPEN 9 - 5 MON - SAT, 10 - 5 BANK HOLIDAYS.
Clarks International operate a chain of factory shops nationally which
specialise in selling discontinued lines and slight sub-standards for
men, women and children from Clarks, K Shoes and other famous
brands. These shops trade under the name of Crockers, K Shoes
Factory shop or Clarks Factory Shop and while not all are physically
attached to a shoe factory, these shops are treated as factory shops by
the company. Customers can expect to find an extensive range of
quality shoes, sandals, walking boots, slippers, trainers, handbags,
accessories and gifts, while their major outlets also offer luggage,
sports clothing, sports equipment and outdoor clothing. Brands

stocked include Clarks, K Shoes, Springer, CICA, Hi-Tec, Puma, Mercury, Dr Martens, Nike, LA Gear, Fila, Mizuno, Slazenger, Weider, Samsonite, Delsey, Antler and Carlton, although not all are sold in every outlet. Discounts are on average 30% off the normal high street price for perfect stock. The Kendal branch is also a sports factory shop, baggage factory shop and gift shop.

## K VILLAGE FACTORY SHOPPING

KENDAL, NEAR JUNCTION 36 OF M6, CUMBRIA
☎ (01539) 721892. OPEN 9.30 - 7 MON - FRI, 9 - 6 SAT AND BANK HOLIDAYS, 11 - 5 SUN.
Eight outlets including Farah Menswear, Jumpers, The Baggage Factory, The Sports Factory and a giant K Shoes factory shop selling a wide range of labels from Clarks, Delsey, Cica, and Antler. There is also a heritage centre, a 150-seater restaurant, a coffee shop and free parking.

## KANGOL FACTORY SHOP

CLEATOR MILLS, CLEATOR, CUMBRIA CA23 3DJ
☎ (01946) 810312. OPEN 10 - 4 MON - FRI, 9 - 1 SAT.
Europe's largest manufacturer of headwear has a factory shop selling hats, scarves, bags and caps as well as Jane Shilton bags, scarves and belts at about half the shop price. Some are seconds, others obsolete shades, yet others shop returns. The shop also sells sweaters and shirts, T-shirts and jumpers.

## M C HITCHEN & SONS LTD

19 FAWCETT STREET, SUNDERLAND, TYNE & WEAR SR1 RRH
☎ (0191) 564 0684. OPEN 8.45 - 5.30 MON - SAT.
RAWLINSON STREET, BAROW-IN-FURNESS, CUMBRIA LA14 ABS
☎ (01229) 870668. OPEN 8.45 - 5.15 MON - SAT.
Littlewoods sell off their overstocks in a network of shops called M C Hitchen & Sons Ltd. Most of them are in the North of England and offer up to 40% off the catalogue price for clothing and between 50% and 60% off for electrical goods. Littlwoods also run a mobile shop which operates in cities where they don't have a sale shop.. For details of further venues for the sales, which usually take place once a month, contact Jean Banks, c/o Crosby DC, Kershaw Avenue, Endbutt Lane, Crosby, Merseyside L70 1AH.

# MACGILLIVRAY & CO

BALIVANICH, BENBECULA, WESTERN ISLES, SCOTLAND PA88 5LA
☎ (01870) 602525. OPEN 9.30 - 5 MON - FRI, CLOSED 1 - 2, 9.30 - 4 SAT.
MAIL ORDER.

The MacGillivray Company has been selling handwoven Harris tweed and hand-knitted sweaters all over the world since 1941. Usually hand-knitted sweaters in pure new wool cost from £49.50 and 28" (72cm) wide Harris tweed costs £10.50 a yard (£11.55 a metre). They sometimes hold a stock of special offer fabrics, which they obtain from various mills throughout Britain. Because these are surplus stock, cancelled export orders or out of season fabrics, they can be sold at less than half the original selling price. These can range from Scottish tweeds, Shetlands, Donegals, dress and fancy fabrics, suitings and coatings. Send for a brochure.

# PETER SCOTT

11 BUCCLEUCH STREET, HAWICK, SCOTLAND TD9 OHG
☎ (01450) 372311. OPEN 10 - 5 MON, WED, 9 - 5 TUE, THUR, FRI, 10 - 4 SAT.

Peter Scott is one of the oldest factory shops in the country. It stocks thousands of sweaters for men and women in almost every conceivable material from cotton and merino wool to cashmere and silk. Some of the stock is new, some discontinued but there are no seconds.

# SCOTTISH SWEATER STORE

JACKSONS LANDING, HARTLEPOOL FACTORY OUTLET SHOPPING MALL, HARTLEPOOL MARINA, HARTLEPOOL, CLEVELAND TS24 OXN
☎ (01429) 273994. OPEN 10 - 6 MON - FRI, 11 - 5 SUN AND BANK HOLIDAYS.

Indoor factory shopping centre with twenty-four outlets selling brand name items including knitwear for men and women, most of which is half price. Labels include Pringle and Lyle & Scott. Examples of prices include Lyle & Scott short-sleeved T-shirt, £9.95, reduced from £21.95; Pringle T-shirts, £17.50 reduced from £26.95; Pringle sweaters. £19.95, reduced from £39.95; Hunter Wellington boots, slightly blemished, £24.95 reduced from £37.95; Pringle tartan shirts, £19.95; MacAlan sweaters, £29.95 reduced from £39.95; Chas N Whillans sweater £29.95 reduced from £39.95; John Partridge macintosh, £75 reduced from £172.95; men's wool waistcoats, £25 reduced from £50. Hartlepool Marina hosts a recreated historic quay and harbours HMS Trincomalee, the oldest British warship still afloat, and is also the site of the new Hartlepool Museum with its interactive fighting ships section and a replica seventeenth century children's play area. There is free parking adjacent to the centre, a coffee shop, restaurant overlooking the Marina, and baby changing and disabled facilities.

## SHARK SPORTS

NORDSTROM HOUSE, NORTH BROOMHILL, MORPETH,
NORTHUMBERLAND NE65 9UJ
☎ (01670) 760365. OPEN 9.30 - 4 MON - FRI, 9.30 - 12 SAT.
Manufactures and sells in the factory shop wetsuits, dry suits, diving suits, cag tops, buoyancy aids, sailing suits, boots, life jackets and gloves, for men, women and children at factory prices. Children's one-piece wetsuits, £40-£45; steamers, £130 and adult wetsuits, £75-£85.

## THE FACTORY SHOP

EMPIRE BUILDING, MAIN STREET, EGREMONT, CUMBRIA CA22 2BD
☎ (01946) 820434. OPEN 9.30 - 5 MON - SAT, 10 - 4 BANK HOLIDAYS.
Wide range on sale includes men's, ladies and children's clothing and footwear; household textiles, toiletries, hardware, luggage, lighting and bedding, most of which are chainstore and high street brands at discounts of approximately 30%-50%. There are weekly deliveries and brands include all the major stars: Coloroll, Wrangler and Dartington to name just three. Lines are continually changing and few factory shops offer such a variety under one roof.

## THE LOCHLEVEN MILL SHOP

TODD & DUNCAN, KINROSS (NEAR M90), SCOTLAND
☎ (01577) 863521. OPEN 9 - 5.30 MON - SAT.
Sells Pringle sweaters and shirts at very competitive retail prices as well as its own cable cashmere at £70 which includes two-ply cashmere classic V-necks, crew-necks and roll collars; normal retail prices for these would normally be about £160. The shop also stocks lambswool sweaters for between £25-£60; Daks/Simpson skirts and jackets at competitive prices; Enrico cotton and angora mix skirts and tops from £12-£40 and other cheaper ranges.

# TOG 24

JACKSONS LANDING, HARTLEPOOL FACTORY OUTLET SHOPPING
MALL, HARTLEPOOL MARINA, HARTLEPOOL, CLEVELAND TS24 OXN
☎ (01429) 866103. OPEN 10 - 6 MON - FRI, 11 - 5 SUN AND BANK
HOLIDAYS.

Indoor factory shopping centre with twenty-four outlets selling brand
name items including leisure and sportswear, including some
children's items. There are anoraks, lumberjack shirts, thick socks,
hiking boots, thick gloves and hats, travel bags. Examples of price
include linen tops, £20, reduced from £35; jackets with Teflon pro-
tection, £99 reduced from £129.95; Top Mark leather hiking boots,
£29, reduced from £39; water proof jackets, £10, reduced from £15;
and children's hiking jackets, age 4, £25 reduced from £35.
Hartlepool Marina hosts a historic quay and harbours HMS
Trincomalee, the oldest British warship still afloat, and is also the site
of the new Hartlepool Museum with its interactive fighting ships
section and a replica seventeenth century children's play area. There is
free parking adjacent to the centre, a coffee shop, restaurant overlooking the Marina, and baby changing and disabled facilities.

# TOM SAYERS CLOTHING CO

JACKSONS LANDING, HARTLEPOOL FACTORY OUTLET SHOPPING
MALL, HARTLEPOOL MARINA, HARTLEPOOL, CLEVELAND TS24 OXN
☎ (01429) 861439. OPEN 10 - 6 MON - FRI, 11 - 5 SUN AND BANK
HOLIDAYS.

Indoor factory shopping centre with twenty-four outlets selling brand
name items including sweaters and casual shirts for men. For
example, long-sleeved cotton shirt, £16.99 reduced from £24.99;
ribbed cardigan, £21.99 reduced from £35.99; V-neck sweater,
£19.99 reduced from £29.99; trousers, £17.99 reduced from £31.99;
cord trousers, £17.99 reduced from £31.99; fine cord long-sleeved
shirt, £17.99 reduced from £26.99.

## WRANGLER

JACKSONS LANDING, HARTLEPOOL FACTORY OUTLET SHOPPING
MALL, HARTLEPOOL MARINA, HARTLEPOOL, CLEVELAND TS24 OXN
☎ (01429) 273488. OPEN 10 - 6 MON - FRI, 11 - 5 SUN AND BANK
HOLIDAYS.

Indoor factory shopping centre with twenty-four outlets selling brand
name items including women', men's and children's jeans, jackets,
shirts, sweatshirts, hooded jackets and waistcoats. For example,
perfect jeans, £32; slight seconds, £18.99; denim shirt, £14.99. The
children's items are mostly for 10-15 year olds.

## *Dress Agencies*

## LABELS OF BARNARDS CASTLE

8 THE BANK, BARNARD CASTLE, COUNTY DURHAM
☎ (01833) 690548/ ☎ (01325) 730271. OPEN 10.30 - 5 MON - SAT, CLOSED
THUR.

Sophisticated labels, including ball gowns in this 300-year-old
building in this historic market town. Men's range also now available.
Smart and casual clothes including Cerruti, Hugo Boss, Versace jeans,
£20, Emporio Armani suits, £90, Byblos; plus ties from £3 up to £15
for a Moschino tie. Easy parking.

## *Hire Shops*

## McCALLS OF THE ROYAL MILE

11 THE HIGH STREET, EDINBURGH EH1 1SR
☎ (0131) 557 3979. OPEN 9 - 5.30 MON - WED, SAT, 9 - 7.30 THUR, FRI,
12 - 4 SUN.

Hire and sell men's formal wear, whether a dinner suit or the full
regalia. Kilt, shoes, bow tie, socks, sporran costs £28.50 plus £5 for
the shirt; men's formal dinner suit, £20. Also hires morning suits,
jackets, waistcoats, trousers, shirts and cravat or tie, £40; boys outfits,
£25, but not girls or ladies. However, does sell women's outfits at full
retail price.

# Secondhand and Vintage Clothes

## ATTICA

2 OLD GEORGE YARD, BIGG MARKET, NEWCASTLE-UPON-TYNE
NE1 1EZ
☎ (0191) 261 4062. OPEN 10.30 - 5.30 MON - SAT.
Two floors of vintage clothes from Twenties to Seventies with most of
the stock coming from the Sixties and Seventies. Lots of suede, Sixties
gear, jewellery, hats and shoes as well as men's formalwear including
dinner suits. Also mid-century decor, furniture and china ornaments.

## PUTTING ON THE RITZ

THE VICTORIAN VILLAGE, 57 WEST REGENT STREET, GLASGOW
☎ (0141) 332 0808. OPEN 10 - 5 MON - SAT.
Retro jewellery, marcasite and Fifties silver, nightwear, Paisley shawls,
vintage dinner suits and tuxedos, Thirties and Forties sportswear,
riding boots, stetsons, 1930s USA football outfits. Jewellery from £5,
dinner suits from £15.

## STARRY STARRY NIGHT

19 DOWNSIDE LANE, GLASGOW G12 9B2
☎ (0141) 337 1837. OPEN 10 - 5.30 MON - SAT.
Retro gear, espcially evening gowns, menswear, including morning
coats, tails and striped blazers from Victorian through the Twenties
and Thirties to the Seventies. Morning suits, £30, dinner suits, £30,
leather jackets, £15-£20, waistcoats, collarless shirts and bow ties.

# NORTHERN IRELAND

## *Permanent Discount Outlets*

### TK MAXX

FIRST FLOOR, CASTLE COURT SHOPPING CENTRE, BELFAST, NORTHERN IRELAND OPEN 9 - 5.30 MON - WED, 9 - 9 THUR, 9 - 8 FRI, 9 - 6 SAT.

Based on an American concept, TK Maxx is the first British retailer to practise "off-price" retailing. This means a centrally located store which offers famous label goods with up to 60% savings off recommended retail prices. TK Maxx has fashion for the whole family - men's, women's and childrenswear - accessories, shoes, gifts, kitchenware and home goods. Everything in the store is branded with a choice of well-known high street names to designer labels, and while a small percentage mightly be clearly marked past season, the great majority of items in store are current season, current stock and still with phenomenal savings. There is a huge choice with 50,000 pieces in store with 5,000 new items arriving a week, so it's worth keeping abreast of the lastest deliveries as turnaround is very fast. One of the ways in which TK Maxx is able to offer such low prices is by running a very low-cost operation, so the stores are simple and unfussy with wide aisles, shopping trolleys and baskets, and a spacious, functional feel to them. Service is not compromised, however: there are individual changing rooms, ramps for buggies and wheelchairs, plenty of staff on the shop floor and all the branches accept all major credit and debit cards.

# Factory Shops

## BAIRDWEAR RACKE

CLANDEBOYE ROAD, BANGOR, NORTHERN IRELAND
☎ (01247) 270415. OPEN 9.30 - 4.30 MON - FRI, 9 - 4 SAT.
ANN STREET, NEWTOWNARDS, NORTHERN IRELAND
☎ (01247) 819502. OPEN 10 - 4.30 MON - SAT.

Manufacturers for a well-known high street chainstore for more than 20 years, Bairdwear has a wide selection of seconds and overmakes in its factory shops for men, women and children. This can cover anything from underwear to jackets, coats and blouses but stock changes constantly. There is also sometimes a range of bedding and household linens.

## CV CARPETS

MAYDOWN INDUSTRIAL ESTATE, CAMPSIE,
LONDONDERRY ☎ (01504) 860838. OPEN 10 - 5 MON - THUR,
10 - 1 FRI.

Branded menswear at factory shop prices.

## DESMOND & SONS LTD

THE MAIN STREET, CLAUDY, LONDONDERRY BT47 3SD
☎ (01504) 338441. OPEN 10 - 5 MON - SAT.
KEVLIN ROAD, OMAGH 01662 241560. OPEN 10 - 5 MON - SAT.
MILL STREET, ENNISKILLEN
☎ (01365) 325467. OPEN 10 - 5 MON - SAT.
BALLYQUINN ROAD, DUNGIVEN
☎ (01504) 742068. OPEN 10 - 5 MON - SAT.
31 GARVAGH ROAD, SWATRAGH
☎ (01648) 401639. OPEN 10 - 5 MON - SAT.

Large range of men's, women's and childrenswear including trousers, nightwear and knitwear. Most of the stock is seconds and is sold at discounts of one third. They also buy in some imperfects of household items such as handtowels and bath towels which are sold at competitive prices.

# LEE APPAREL (UK) LTD

16 COMBER ROAD, NEWTOWNARDS, COUNTY DOWN BT23 4HY
☎ (01247) 800200. OPEN 10 - 5.15 MON, TUE, WED, SAT, 10 - 8.15 THUR,
FRI.
Men's, women's and children's Lee jeans, jackets, T-shirts, hats, and
sweatshirts at up to 50% savings. Also childrenswear, Adidas sportswear and casual ladieswear at competitive prices.

# LOTUS LTD

34 BRIDGE STREET, BANBRIDGE, COUNTY DOWN BT32 3ND
☎ (01820) 622480. OPEN 9 - 5.30 MON - SAT, CLOSED 1 - 2 THUR.
All sizes and styles of Lotus shoes - from smart fashion shoes to
walking shoes - at discounted prices for discontinued lines and rejects.
Prcies from £19.99-£49.99 for men's shoes. Lotus manufactures for
well-known chain stores.

# OCTOPUS SPORTSWEAR MFG LTD

UNIT 1, DUBLIN ROAD INDUSTRIAL ESTATE, STRABANE  BT82 9EA
☎ (01504) 882320. OPEN 9 - 5 MON - FRI, 9 - 1 SAT.
Manufacture own-brand sportswear: shorts, jerseys, socks, pants,
hooded tops, sweatshirts and sell seconds and clearance lines at discounts of up 50%-75%.

# RELIABLE HOSIERY AT CV CARPETS

THE FACTORY SHOP, 41 HIGH BANGOR ROAD
DONAGHADEE BT21 0PD
☎ (01247) 888842. OPEN 10 - 5 MON - SAT.
SHAERF DRIVE, SARACEN, LURGAN, COUNTY ANTRIM
☎ (01762) 329253. OPEN 10.30 - 4.30 MON - FRI.
RELIABLE HOSIERY AT CV HOME FURNISHINGS
36 MAGHERALANE ROAD, RANDALSTOWN, COUNTY ANTRIM
☎ (01849) 473341. OPEN 10 - 5 MON - THUR, 10 - 1 FRI.
Slightly imperfect ladies, men's and children's wear. The emphasis is
on casualwear such as weatherproof golfing suits and coats, shirts,
trousers, knitwear, dress shirts, silk ties, Flix swimwear, socks.

## SARACEN

SHAERF DRIVE, LURGAN, NORTHERN IRELAND
☎ (01762) 329253. OPEN 10.30 - 4.30 MON - FRI.

Women's, men's and children's clothes and knitwear at factory shop prices, many of which are top brand names. For men, there are trousers, shirts, ties, jumpers, cardigans, underwear, nightwear, hosiery and breathable jackets.

## WARNERS (UK) LTD

MOUNT STREET, DROMORE, COUNTY DOWN
☎ (01846) 692466. OPEN 11 - 4 TUE - SAT, 1 - 7 THUR.

Warners famous lingerie at reduced prices. They also sell outfits for men such as shirts and ties, T-shirts and socks at reductions of about 40%.

# *Dress Agencies*

## CANCER RESEARCH GROUP

50 HIGH STREET, NEWTOWNARDS, COUNTY DOWN BT23 3HZ
☎ (01247) 820268.

Shop specifically aimed at the wedding market which sells or hires pageboy outfits; black and grey morning suits, plus accessories, for the groom, as well as dinner suits. Prices range from: morning suits, £25 to hire, £50 to buy; dinner suits, £16.50 to hire, £35 to buy. Most of the stock is either donated or straight from the manufacturer.

# CHILDREN

*Permanent Discount Outlets,*

*Factory Shops,*

*Secondhand Clothes, Equipment and Toys,*

*Hire Shops*

# LONDON

## *Permanent Discount Outlets*

### BABYCARE LTD

74 HIGH STREET, ACTON, LONDON W3 6LE
☎ 0181-993 8542. OPEN 10. - 5 MON - SAT.
Baby feeding equipment, premature baby clothes, nursery equipment including prams, cots and pushchairs from Mamas & Papas and Silver Cross, car seats and cot blankets at prices which are lower than those in department stores. All are brand new and bought direct from the manufacturer, but the company has a policy of high turnover/low profit margins. For example, MacClarens Duette, £155, usually £185. The bedding and Moses baskets are manufactured by Babycare.

### LETTERBOX LIBRARY

2ND FLOOR, LEROY HOUSE, 436 ESSEX ROAD, LONDON N1 3QP
☎ 0171-226 1633. OPEN 10 - 5 MON - THUR OR BY APPOINTMENT.
MAIL ORDER.
Run by a women's co-operative, Letterbox offers non-sexist, non racits, multi-cultural books, as well as those about the environment and disabilty for children up to the age of 14. Books are sold at discounts of between 10%-25%. Send for catalogue.

### MORRY'S

39-40 THE BROADWAY, EDMONTON, LONDON N9 OTJ
☎ 0181-807 6747. OPEN 8.30 - 5 MON - SAT, CLOSED AT 1 ON THUR.
Liquidation stock which includes some famous makes and can comprise anything from gardening equipment (shovels, forks and hoses) and household items to eletrical equipment (CDs, radios, TVs, CDi's, radio alarms) and clothing for children, men and women. Everything is at least half the retail price. Phone beforehand to find out what they've got in stock or if you live nearby, drop in frequently.

## NEXT TO NOTHING

UNIT 11, WATERGLADES CENTRE, EALING BROADWAY,
LONDON W5 2ND
☎ 0181-567 2747. OPEN 9.30 - 6 MON - SAT.

Sells perfect surplus stock from Next stores and the Next Directory catalogue - from belts, jewellery and underwear to day and evening wear - at discounts of 50% or more. The ranges are usually last season's and overruns but there is the odd current item if you look carefully. Stock consists of children's, men's and women's clothing, with some homeware and shoes, depending on the branch. Stock is replenished twice a week and there is plenty of it. Childrenswear is usually the smallest section but discounts are good.

## SWIMGEAR

11 STATION ROAD, FINCHLEY, LONDON N3 2SB
☎ 0181-346 6106. OPEN 9.30 - 5 MON - FRI, UNTIL 8 ON THUR.
MAIL ORDER.

A mail order company which also operates via a retail outlet next to Finchley Central station. They sell discontinued and ends of line ranges of swimwear for children, men and women at between 20%-30% less than normal retail prices. They also stock goggles and flippers in adult sizes. Flippers normally cost about £18.50, but can be bought here for about £8 in black rubber. The catalogues are full colour and carry the names Speedo, Adidas, Hind and Maru, as well as Swimgear's own brand full colour Mark One brochure. Prices are lower than than would be offered at swim meets and retail shops. Examples of prices include Classic Goggles, £2.80, silicone earplugs, £2.05, handpaddles, £6.40, armbands, £4.30. As part of their service, they do not cash your cheque until your full order has been completed. P&p extra, orders over £50 are post free.

## TUTTI FRUTTI DISCOUNT STORE

156-158 RYE LANE, PECKHAM, LONDON SE15 4NB
☎ 0171-732 9933. OPEN 9 - 5.30 MON - SAT. MAIL ORDER.

Nursery equipment shop which offers bigger discounts the more you buy and particularly if you pay cash. There are often special offers - buggies from £20, cots for £100. They stock all leading makes, as well as babywear, shoes, baby accessories, bedding, bath sets, textiles, feeding equipment, and have a repair service and a mail order facility. There are baby changing facilities in the shop and toys to play with.

# *Factory Shops*

## NICOLE FARHI OUTLET SHOP

75-83 FAIRFIELD ROAD, BOW, LONDON E3 2QR
☎ 0181-981 3931. OPEN 10 - 3 TUE, WED, SAT, 11 - 6.30 THUR,
10 - 5.30 FRI.

This tiny factory shop in London's East End sells previous season merchandise, samples and seconds from Nicole Farhi and French Connection for children, men and women. Phone first to check stock levels as the childrenswear tends to be very patchy and seasonal.

## ONE STEP

3 - 5 HIGH STREET, ISLINGTON, LONDON N1
☎ 0171-837 4984. OPEN 9.30 - 6 MON - THUR, 9 - 6 FRI, SAT.

Value for money chain of shoe shops, which are part of the British Shoe Corporation Ltd. This one sells Saxone, Freeman Hardy Willis, Dolcis, Roland Cartier, Hush Puppies and Stone Creek brands at up to 50% discount. Sizes range up to size 9 ladies, up to size 12 for men and a wide range of children's sizes.

## TON SUR TON

35 RIDING HOUSE STREET, LONDON W1 7PT
☎ 0171-637 3473. OPEN 10.30 - 5 MON - FRI.

This European casual wear company which sells tracksuits, sweat-shirts, T-shirts in unusual colours and soft fabrics, has a factory outlet in the heart of London's rag trade area. The company also sells denim, a fitness range, training shoes, rugby shirts, jackets, jeans and accessories. The factory outlet sells samples, returns and perfect garments at at least 50% of their normal retail price, and lower in a number of cases. The children's range isn't extensive but covers sweatshirts, Puffa jackets, jeans and babywear.

## Dress Agencies

### CHANGE OF HABIT

25 ABBEVILLE ROAD, LONDON SW4 9LA
☎ 0181-675 9475. OPEN 11 - 5 MON - FRI, 10 - 6 SAT.
Daywear and evening wear as good as new. Also nearly-new clothes for babies and children up to the age of 10. Described by the proprietor as "everyday clothes for everyday people at exceptional realistic prices". As new costs amount to about one quarter of the original price. Very high turnover. Also has mothers-to-be wear and prams and cots.

### CHANGE OF HEART

59A PARK ROAD, LONDON N8
☎ 0181-341 1575. OPEN 10 - 6 MON - SAT, BY APPOINTMENT ON SUNS.
Sells a mixture of designer and good high street labels for children, women and men.

### CHEEKY MONKEYS

202 KENSINGTON PARK ROAD, LONDON W11 1NR
☎ 0171-792 9022. OPEN 9.30 - 5.30 MON - FRI, 10 - 5.30 SAT.
A mixture of secondhand and new. Secondhand babies and children's clothes and equipment including prams, high chairs, stair gates, car seats, baby bouncers. Nearly-new children's clothes include Oilily and OshKosh. Also, new toys, Start-Rite shoes professionally fitted, gifts, stickers, books, tapes, Playdoh, Tomy goods, safety products and hairdressing for just £6.

### DESIGNS

60 ROSSLYN HILL, LONDON NW3 1ND
☎ 0171-435 0100. OPEN 10 - 5.45 MON - SAT, UNTIL 6.45 ON THUR.
Designs has been established for twelve years, selling ladies designer clothes and accessories. They now also sell a range of girls' clothes for the age range 0-8. David Charles party dresses, £35, originally £130, for example. They only accept perfect merchandise under two years old, and seasonal. They have a rapid turnover and regular customers talk about the spacious, relaxed atmosphere. Designs only take forty percent commission on sale of goods, so prices remain keenly competitive and the most exciting pieces come their way.

## DRESS CIRCLE

2 LEVERTON PLACE, LONDON NW5 2PL
☎ 0171 284 3967. OPEN 10 - 6 TUE - SAT, UNTIL 7 ON THUR AND FRI.
Dress Circle is a nearly-new shop for adults which has a children's dress agency at the back called Boomerang.

## HANG UPS

366 FULHAM ROAD, LONDON SW10
☎ 0171-351 0047. OPEN 11 - 6.45 MON - FRI, 10.30 - 6 SAT, 10 - 4 SUNS (OCCASIONALLY, PHONE FIRST).
Designer labels in the trendier, younger end of the market as well as a large children's section selling cots, baby seats, prams, and hand-painted wooden toys.

## HANGERS

120 PITSHANGER LANE, EALING, LONDON W5 1QP
☎ 0181-810 9363. OPEN 10 - 6 MON - SAT.
Designer names from Jacques Vert, Escada and Louis Feraud to Windsmoor and Next. Also sells children's clothes.

## JUST OUTGROWN

99 DEVONSHIRE ROAD, CHISWICK, LONDON W4
☎ 0181-995 5405. OPEN 10 - 4 MON - FRI, 10 - 1 SAT.
Secondhand children's clothes and equipment with seasonal bargain rails. for ages from birth to twelve years.

## LA SCALA

39 ELYSTAN STREET, LONDON SW3 3NT
☎ 0171-589 2784. OPEN 10 - 5.30 MON - SAT.
La Scala has been so successful in selling women's nearly-new clothes and accessories since opening in 1993 that, due to popular demand, owner Sandy Reid in summer 1995 acquired large adjacent premises, enabling her to house men's and children's clothes as well as wedding dresses under the same roof. Sandy lived for 14 years in Northern Italy and uses her experience there in her marble-floored shop behind the Conran Shop in Chelsea.

## RAINBOW

249 & 253 ARCHWAY ROAD, LONDON N6 5BS
☎ 0181-340 8003. OPEN 10.30 - 5 MON, 10.30 - 5.30 TUE - SAT.

Number 249 sells secondhand items, while 253 is new merchandise. Nearly-new consists of a wide range of well-known baby and children's clothes - from Osh Kosh and Oilily to Baby Gap and Marks & Spencer - as well as good condition baby equipment from cots and high chairs to car seats and playpens. They also sell secondhand toys (Galt and Fisher-Price), including a lot of traditional wooden toys such as Brio wooden trains, and books. The new shop sells a wide range of children's clothes, mainly in natural fabrics, and the imported items are discounted by about twelve and a half percent. There are twice-yearly sales in January and July when prices are discounted further.

## SCARECROW

131 WALHAM GREEN COURT, MOORE PARK ROAD, LONDON SW6 2DG
☎ 0171-381 1023. OPEN 10 - 5 TUE - FRI, 9.30 - 1 SAT.

London's biggest and probably best-known children's dress agency, Scarecrow offers two floors of hardly-worn clothes including popular designer labels which cater for all ages from babyhood to 16 years. As well as the more traditional rompers, smocked dresses and velvet-collared coats, there are dinner jackets and party frocks alongside jeans, checked shirts and sweatshirts. There is also an extensive range of sports clothes which include karate suits, ski wear, riding and sailing gear, plus the appropriate footwear. When the cost of bringing up a child has been estimated at somewhere in the region of a staggering £140,000., it's no wonder that parents adept at judging quality and value have found their way to Scarecrow.

## SWALLOWS & AMAZONS

91 NIGHTINGALE LANE, LONDON SW12 8NX
☎ 0181-673 0275. OPEN 10 - 5 MON - SAT.

Probably the largest good-as-new children's shop in London, S & A has a ground floor full of quality clothes for 0-12 year olds: OshKosh, Oilily, Jean Le Bourget, Mexx etc, as well as a large basement with toys, books, and baby equipment. They carry some new playpens, high chairs and buggies due to demand, but at competitive prices.

The stock is constantly changing and they pride themselves on keeping standards high, but prices low - from 90p to £99. There is also children's hairdressing (with videos) on most afternoons and Saturday mornings (appointments necessary) and a play area. Friendly, helpful staff. There are sales usualy in July/August and January/February during which items are reduced by a further 50%.

## THE BABY GROWS

173 ST JOHN'S HILL, WANDSWORTH, LONDON SW11
☎ 0171 924 4711. OPEN 9.30 - 5 MON - FRI, 10 - 4 SAT.
Sells new and nearly-new nursery equipment and toys, with a small selection of clothing. Prices are usually at least half the normal retail price, depending on the condition of the item, and clothes include designers such as Osh Kosh, Next, Gap and many high street stores.

## THE BEST OF SECONDHAND

42 GOLDERS GREEN ROAD, LONDON NW11
☎ 0181-458 3890. OPEN 9.30 - 5.30 MON - FRI, 9.30 - 6 SAT, 10 - 5 SUN.
Primarily, a dress agency selling top designer names and middle of the range labels, there is now also a small selection of children's party dresses.

## THE BRIDAL EXCHANGE

19 EDGWAREBURY LANE, EDGWARE, MIDDLESEX
☎ 0181-958 7002. OPEN 9 - 6 MON - SAT, 11 - 3 SUN.
Bridal dress agency which also sells and hires children's bridesmaid dresses and pageboy outfits. Some of the stock is ex-hire, some from liquidations, some was bought but never worn and all are about half the original price.

## WINKIE JANE

184 MUNSTER ROAD, FULHAM, LONDON SW6 6AU
☎ 0171-384 1762. OPEN 9 - 5.30 MON - FRI, 10 - 5.304 SAT.
Good quality nearly-new children's clothing in this very child-friendly shop with its big double doors for easy access with buggies and a toy box for children to play with while parent browse. There is on-street parking right outside and the clothes are well presented and unclut-tered. Stock constantly changes and includes designers such as Oilily,

Jacardi, Chicaloo, OshKosh, David Charles and Heather Brown. Age range covered is 0-10. There is also as-new baby equipment: high chairs, buggies, prams and Moses baskets as well as some new range of Baby Dior samples and Damask nightwear at half the original price.

## *Hire Shops*

### BABY AWAY NURSERY HIRE

56A DOLLIS PARK, FINCHLEY, LONDON NZ 1BS
☎ 0181-343 3552. PHONE FIRST.
Part of the British Equipment Hirers Association (BEHA), which has more than 100 members countrywide. A range of equipment can be hired from high chairs, cots and travel cots to baby car seats and buggies. Some members also hire out party equipment including child-sized tables and chairs. BEHA run an advice line which will try and answer any queries you have regarding hiring services for children. Phone the Babyline on 0831 310355.

### BABY EQUIPMENT HIRERS ASSOCIATION

☎ (0831) 310355.
Expecting a visit from grandchildren or friends with young babies? Save them the bother of bringing cots and high chairs with them - hire the equipment instead. The BEHA has more than 100 members countrywide who can provide you with a travel cot, high chair, buggy, back pack or almost anything a parent of young children might want. Phone (tel no above) to find your nearest BEHA member.

### CHELSEA BABY EQUIPMENT HIRE

83 BURNTWOOD LANE, EARLSFIELD, LONDON SW17 OAJ
☎ 0181-994 8124. BY APPOINTMENT ONLY.
Delivery and collection hire service for children's and nursery equipment including cots, prams, pushchairs, high chairs and car seats.

## CHILDREN'S PARTY HIRE

STANMORE, MIDDLESEX

☎ 0181-952 8130 & ☎ 0181-952 2544. PHONE FOR DETAILS.

Offers everything you need for a successful celebration - except for the entertainer! Based in the Stanmore, Middlesex area, a small charge is made for delivery. Examples of prices include three tables and 14 chairs, £6, six tables and and 26 chairs, £10. also offers small-scale adult party hire. A colleague also also offers a variety of different cake tins - shaped with Disney Characters and popular dolls for hire. Telephone for more more details on 0181-952 2544.

## HARLEQUIN BABY HIRE

ISLINGTON, LONDON N 5

☎ 0171-704 0625. PHONE FOR BROCHURE.

Hires out baby equipment from prams and pushchairs to high chairs and car seats. Phone for brochure.

## NURSERY HIRE CO

24 WHITEHALL GARDENS, LONDON W4 3LT

☎ 0181-995 5332. PHONE FIRST.

## THE NAPPY EXPRESS,

128 HIGH ROAD, SOUTHGATE, LONDON N11 1PG

☎ 0181-361 4040. PHONE FIRST.

## KIDDYHIRE

32 GRANGE GARDENS, PINNER, MIDDLESEX HA5 5QE

☎ 0181-868 4368. PHONE FIRST.

## TOTS 'N' TODDLERS

68 BEACON DRIVE, SEAFORD, EAST SUSSEX BN25 2JX

☎ 01323 890962. PHONE FIRST.

All the above are part of the British Equipment Hirers Association (BEHA), which has more than 100 members countrywide. A range of equipment can be hired from high chairs, cots and travel cots to baby car seats and buggies. Some members also hire out party equipment including child-sized tables and chairs. BEHA run an advice line which will try and answer any queries you have regarding hiring services for children. Phone the Babyline on 0831 310355.

## *Secondhand and Vintage Clothes*

### CHENIL GALLERY

181-183 KING'S ROAD, LONDON SW3
☎ 0171-352 8581. OPEN 10.30 - 5.30 MON - SAT.
Clothes for women and men from 1800 to the 1950s with some children's clothes.


# SOUTH EAST

## *Permanent Discount Outlets*

### BABYCARE LTD

2 NEWMARKET SQUARE, TOWN CENTRE, BASINGSTOKE, HAMPSHIRE
☎ (01256) 330728. OPEN 9.30 - 5.15 MON - SAT.
Baby feeding equipment, premature baby clothes, nursery equipment including prams, cots and pushchairs from Mamas & Papas and Silver Cross, car seats and cot blankets at prices which are lower than those in department stores. All are brand new and bought direct from the manufacturer, but the company has a policy of high turnover/low profit margins. For example, MacClarens Duette, £155, usually £185. The bedding and Moses baskets are manufactured by Babycare.

### CHOICE DISCOUNT STORES LIMITED

14-20 RECTORY ROAD, HADLEIGH, BENFLEET, ESSEX SS7 2ND
☎ (01702) 555245. OPEN 9 - 5.30 MON - SAT.
26-28 HIGH STREET, BARKINGSIDE, ILFORD, ESSEX IG6 2DO
☎ 0181-551 2125. OPEN 9 - 5.30 MON - FRI, 9 - 6 SAT, 10 - 4 SUN.
44-46 HIGH STREET, WATFORD, HERTFORDSHIRE WD1 2BR
☎ (01923) 23355. OPEN 9 - 5.30 MON - SAT.
10-11 LADYGATE CENTRE, HIGH STREET, WICKFORD, ESSEX SS12 9AK
☎ (01268) 764893. OPEN 9 - 5.30 MON - THUR, 9 - 6 FRI, SAT.
UNIT 6A, MAYFLOWER RETAIL PARK, GARDINERS LINK, BASILDON, ESSEX SS14 3AR
☎ (01268) 288331. OPEN 9 - 6 MON, TUE, WED, 9 - 7 THUR, FRI, 9 - 5.30 SAT, 11 - 5 SUN.

14-16 HIGH STREET, GRAYS, ESSEX RM17 6LV
☎ (01375) 385780. OPEN 9 - 5.30 MON - SAT.
Surplus stock including children's, men's and women's fashions from
Next plc, Next Directory and other high street fashions, Next
Interiors and footwear. You can save up to 50% off normal retail
prices for first quality; up to two thirds for seconds. There are no
changing rooms but the shop offers refunds if goods are returned in
perfect condition within 28 days. There are special sales each January
and September. Easy access for wheelchairs and pushchairs. The
Watford and Wickford stores are known as Next 2 Choice; the former
specialises in ladies and menswear only from Next plc and Next
Directory.

# MATALAN

UNIT 4B, THE TUNNEL ESTATE, WESTERN AVENUE, LAKESIDE
RETAIL PARK, WEST THURROCK, ESSEX RM16 1HH
☎ (01708) 864350. OPEN 10 - 8 MON - FRI, 9.30 - 5.30 SAT, 10 - 6 SUN.
UNIT 4, RIVERSIDE RETAIL PARK, VICTORIA ROAD, CHELMSFORD,
ESSEX EM2 6LL
☎ (01245) 348787. OPEN 10 - 8 MON - FRI, 9.30 - 5.30 SAT, 11 - 5 SUN.
ROSE KILN LANE, READING, BERKSHIRE RG2 0SN
☎ (01734) 391958. OPEN 10 - 8 MON - FRI, 9.30 - 5.30 SAT, 10 - 6 SUN.
BILTON ROAD, BLETCHLEY, MILTON KEYNES, BUCKINGHAMSHIRE
MK1 1HS
☎ (01908) 373735. OPEN 10 - 8 MON - FRI, 9 - 6 SAT, 10 - 4 SUN.
As the UK's first National Discount Club, Matalan has the buying
power to guarantee its members up to 60% discounts on a huge range
of brand name clothing, household goods, luggage and toiletries for
all the family. Top quality merchandise, current season, no seconds, is
offered to its members at exclusive, permanently discounted prices
seven days a week. Matalan operates strictly on a membership basis,
one of the key factors for its success in offering 20%-60% savings off
recommended retail prices. Membership cards are issued through
companies, organisations and associations in the vicinity of the stores,
and are available to their employees/members. They are valid at any
of the 50 Matalan stores in the UK. To find out if your organisation
is registered, phone the Matalan hotline on 01772 629447.

# NIPPERS

MANSERS, NIZELS LANE, HILDENBOROUGH, KENT TN11 8NX
☎ (01732) 832253. FAX (01732) 833658. OPENING HOURS VARY SO
PHONE FIRST.
CHALKPIT FARM, SCHOOL LANE, BEKESBOURNE, CANTERBURY,
KENT CT4 5EU
☎ (01227) 832006. FAX (01227) 831496.
CODDIMOOR FARM, WHADDON, MILTON KEYNES,
BUCKINGHAMSHIRE MK17 0IR
☎ (01908) 504506. FAX (01908) 505636.
WHITES FARM, BURES ROAD, WHITE COLNE, COLCHESTER, ESSEX
CO6 2QF
☎ (01787) 228000. FAX (01787) 228560.
THE WAFFRONS, WOODSTOCK LANE SOUTH, CHESSINGTON,
SURREY KT9 1UF
☎ 0181-398 3114. FAX 0181-398 7553. OPEN 10 - 4 TUE, WED, FRI, SAT,
2 - 8 THUR, 2 - 4 SUN.

Nippers, the nursery equipment and toy specialists, started with a
very clever and simple idea and have now built it up to create an
award-winning chain of franchises. The company operates from converted barns on farms around the country, offering easy parking, no
queues, and personal service. This is on top of competitive prices on
prams, cots, pushchairs, car seats, outdoor play equipment and toys.
Prices are low partly because they operate from farms, with none of
the overheads of traditional retail outlets, and party because the successful growth of a number of branches means it can now buy in bulk
and negotiate good deals. Customers can try out the merchandise and
the children can see the animals, mostly sheep, chickens and pigs.
Familiar brand names are on sale at all the branches, including Britax,
Maclaren and Bebe Confort, Fisher-Price and Little Tikes. You can
try out the car seats in your car and there is usually a pram/pushchair
repair service on site.

# T K MAXX

THE GALLERIA SHOPPING CENTRE, COMET WAY, JUNCTION 3 OFF
THE A1, HATFIELD, HERTFORDSHIRE
☎ (01707) 270063. OPEN 10 - 8 MON - FRI, 10 - 6 SAT, 11 - 5 SUN.
173-178 HIGH STREET, BELOW BAR, SOUTHAMPTON
☎ (01703) 631600. OPEN 9 - 5.30 MON - FRI, 9 - 6 SAT, UNTIL 7 ON
THUR.
BROAD STREET MALL, BROAD STREET, READING, BERKSHIRE
☎ (01734) 511117. OPEN 9 - 5.30 MON - FRI, 9 - 6 SAT.
LOWER CONCOURSE, THE PEACOCKS, SURREY
☎ (01683) 750263. OPEN 9.30 - 6 MON - FRI, UNTIL 8 ON THURS,
9 - 6 SAT, 11 - 5 SUN.

Based on an American concept, TK Maxx is the first British retailer
to practise "off-price" retailing. This means a centrally located store
which offers famous label goods with up to 60% savings off recommended retail prices. TK Maxx has fashion for the whole family -
children's, men's and womenswear - accessories, shoes, gifts, kitchenware and home goods. Everything in the store is branded with a
choice of well-known high street names to designer labels, and while
a small percentage mightly be clearly marked past season, the great
majority of items in store are current season, current stock and still
with phenomenal savings. There is a huge choice with 50,000 pieces
in store with 5,000 new items arriving a week, so it's worth keeping
abreast of the lastest deliveries as turnaround is very fast. One of the
ways in which TK Maxx is able to offer such low prices is by running
a very low-cost operation, so the stores are simple and unfussy with
wide aisles, shopping trolleys and baskets, and a spacious, functional
feel to them. Service is not compromised, however: there are individual changing rooms, ramps for buggies and wheelchairs, plenty of
staff on the shop floor and all the branches accept all major credit and
debit cards.

# TOYTIME

MEOPHAM BANK FARM, LEIGH ROAD, HILDENBOROUGH, NEAR
TONBRIDGE, KENT TN11 9AQ
☎ (01732) 833695/832416. OPEN 9 - 12 AND 7.30 - 8.30 TUE, 9 - 12 THUR,
9 - 4 SAT.

Sells both new and secondhand toys - anything from a rattle to a
climbing frame. The stock is always changing as you can get immediate cash for your used toys in good condition. There is a huge selec-

tion in three barns including bikes, trikes, doll's prams, doll's houses, trampolines, slides, sandpits, to mention just a few. In addition, party bag fillers and baby toys abound. All the outdoor equipment (as well as Brio) is new and is sold at discounted prices. Climbing frames and swings are on display outside (and some animals) and advice is given, when required.

## Factory Shops

### MEXX INTERNATIONAL

132-133 FAIRLIE ROAD, SLOUGH TRADING ESTATE, SLOUGH, BERKSHIRE SL1 4PY
☎ (01753) 525450. OPEN 9.30 - 5.30 MON - SAT, 10 - 4 SUN, UNTIL 7 ON THUR.

High street fashion at factory outlet prices for men, women and children. On sale are Mini Mexx for 0-2 year olds, Boy Kid and Girl Kid for 2-8 year olds, Boy Teen and Girl Teen for 8-16 year olds. There are usually at least 6,000 items in stock, with regular new deliveries, all of which are heavily discounted by between 40%-80%. The outlet can be found by turning down off the Slough Farnham Road at Do It All and turning right at the second set of traffic lights. There is children's satellite tv on site, a playhouse area and refreshments.

### MOTOWN JEANS

MOTOWN YARD, THE BREWERY, LONDON ROAD, STANFORD-LE-HOPE, ESSEX
☎ (01375) 675643. OPEN 9 - 5 MON - FRI, 9 - 1 SAT.

Manufactures denim jeans for retail outlets and sells its own label jeans at half price in its factory shop. It also sells denim jackets from a sister factory which it supplies with denim and Motown jeans. All are perfect and come in children's, ladies and men's sizes. Prices start at £10 for children's jeans.

## THE FACTORY SHOP (ESSEX) LTD

THE GLOUCESTERS, LUCKYN LANE, PIPPS HILL INDUSTRIAL ESTATE, BASILDON, ESSEX SS14 3AX

☎ (01268) 520446. OPEN 9 - 5.30 MON - SAT, 10 - 5 SUN.

No-frills factory shop selling seconds, discontinued lines and some perfect current stock from department and chain store high street names, as well as direct from the manufacturer. This is not the place to look for high fashion, but it has an enormous amount of middle of the range children's, men's and women's clothes, as well as bedlinen, towels, toys, food, kitchen utensils, disposable cutlery and partyware, short-dated food, garden furniture, tools, sportswear, china, glass and barbecues within its 8,000 square feet of selling space. Everything is sold at between 30% and 50% of the retail price. Parking is easy, the M25 is near and there's good wheelchair/pushchair access.

## THE SHOE SHED

ORCHARD ROAD, ROYSTON, HERTFORDSHIRE SG8 5HA

☎ (01763) 241933. OPEN 9 - 5.30 TUE, WED, 9 - 6 THUR, FRI, 9 - 4 SAT, 10 - 2 SUN.

C/O MEXX UK, 132-133 FAIRLIE ROAD, SLOUGH, BERKSHIRE

☎ (01753) 525450. OPEN 9.30 - 5.30 MON - WED, FRI, SAT, 9.30 - 7 THUR, 10 - 4 SUN.

Large factory shop selling a vast range of all types of children's, men's, and women's shoes, all of which are perfects, at up to 30% below normal high street prices.

## *Dress Agencies*

## ANCORA BAMBINI

27 CHURCH STREET, WEYBRIDGE, SURREY

☎ (01932) 857665. OPEN 9.30 - 5 MON - SAT.

Up the road from the women's dress agency, Ancora Bambini sells middle of the road to designer labels for children aged from birth to 10 years, including Next, Gap, Oilily and Jacardi.

## BARGAIN BOUTIQUE

SNOW HILL, CRAWLEY DOWN, WEST SUSSEX
☎ (01342) 712022. OPEN 9.15 - 2.15 TUE - SAT.
BB stocks mainly high street names such as Marks & Spencer, Next, BhS, Laura Ashley, as well as labels such as Windsmoor and Jacques Vert. Mainly caters for women and children, though there is a limited selection of menswear. Most of the merchandise is made up of separates, with few suits, and there are some shoes for adults.

## BENJAMIN'S MESS

77 HIGH STREET, ROCHESTER, KENT ME1 1LX
☎ (01634) 817848. OPEN 9 - 5.30 MON - SAT.
Half this shop is devoted to childrenswear including designers such as Oilily, Osh Kosh, Little Levi's, Portofini and Laura Ashley.

## CAMEO

150 HIGH STREET, BERKHAMSTEAD, HERTFORDSHIRE HP4 3AT
☎ (01442) 865791. OPEN 9.30 - 5.15 MON - FRI, 9.30 - 4.45 SAT.
Children's and women's clothes, mostly middle market names such as Marks & Spencer and Next, but with some designer labels. About one-third of the shop is devoted to childrenswear with coats, dresses, skirts, jackets, trousers, sweaters for boys and girls.

## CANCER RESEARCH GROUP

172 TERMINUS ROAD, EASTBOURNE, EAST SUSSEX BN21 3SB
☎ (01323) 739703. OPEN 9.30 - 4.30 MON - SAT.
7 HIGH STREET, SOUTHEND, ESSEX SS1 1JE
☎ (01702) 432698. OPEN 9.30 - 4.30 MON - SAT.
Shop specifically aimed at the bridal market which sells or hires bridesmaids dresses and pageboy outfits, with accessories. Most of the stock is either donated or straight from the manufacturer.

## DAISY DAISY

33 NORTH ROAD, BRIGHTON, EAST SUSSEX BN1 1YB
☎ (01273) 689108. OPEN 10 - 5 MON - SAT.
Most of the stock is designer label nearly-new outfits as well as some high street names for children at between one quarter and one half of the original price. Labels include Oilily, OshKosh and Nipper as well as well-known French and Italian designers. High street names

featured include Laura Ashley, Gap and Benetton. There are also plenty of accessories including shoes, hats, socks, tights and swimwear and occasionally bridesmaids dresses and christening gowns. The selection for newborn babies is large and there's a playroom, nappy changing are and toilet.

## DEJA VU

OLD SEAL HOUSE, 19 CHURCH STREET, SEAL, NEAR SEVENOAKS, KENT TN15 ODA
☎ (01732) 762155. OPEN 10 - 4.30 MON - SAT.
Adult dress agency which also sells a small range of children's dresses and riding wear, and from September each year, ski wear for adults and children.

## GOOSEBERRY BUSH

2 BARNHAM ROAD, BARNHAM, NR BOGNOR, SUSSEX
☎ (01243) 554552 OPEN 10 - 4 MON - SAT.
Nearly-new largely high street fashions for the mother and child ie Next, Heskia and Mothercare. Stock ranges from a good selection of maternity wear (Blooming Marvellous), to children's cots and high chairs. New items can be found for very reasonable prices. Friendly atmosphere and said to be a particular favourite with grandparents.

## KID2KID

2 THE HIGH STREET, COOKHAM, BERKSHIRE SL6 1SQ
☎ (01628) 477710. OPEN 10 - 5 MON - SAT.
Nearly-new designer clothes for children 0-10 years. Some of the most popular designer labels include Oilily, Cacheral, Ozona, Jean Bourget, Poivre Blanc, and Oshkosh, although quality items from Next, Marks & Spencer and Laura Ashley are also on sale. Prices range from £5 to £30, normally at least one-third of the original price. Own range of new children's clothes also available.

## PANACHE

5 STANFORD SQUARE, WARWICK ST, WORTHING, SUSSEX BN11 3EZ
☎ (01903) 212503. OPEN 10 - 5 MON - SAT.
Two shops in one: Smarties sells childrenswear up to the age of nine,
Panache sells women's nearly-new at savings of up to 50% on High
Street prices. The children's range from Petite Bateau, Laura Ashley
and Oilily to Matrise and Osh Kosh. They do not stock children's
sleepwear or underwear.

## THE STOCK EXCHANGE

1 HIGH STREET, SUNINGHILL, ASCOT, BERKSHIRE SL5 5NQ
☎ (0344) 25420 . OPEN 9 - 5.30 MON - FRI, 9 - 4.30 SAT.
Children's, women's and menswear available, usually not more than 2
years old. Stock sold at either one third or half price after 4 weeks.
Rapid turnover of clothes. Good sellers include Marks & Spencer and
Laura Ashley in particular.

## *Hire Shops*

## A & A BABY ACCESSORY HIRE

28 SWEPSTONE CLOSE, LOWER EARLY, READING,
BERKSHIRE RG6 3EE
☎ (01734) 669200. PHONE FIRST.

## ABACUS BABY HIRE

VALE FARM, WESTCOTT, DORKING, SURREY RH4 3LP
☎ (01306) 882242. PHONE FIRST.
6 NIGHTINGALE CRESCENT, WEST HORSLEY, SURREY
☎ (01486) 55142. PHONE FIRST.

## ABC HIRE

(CROYDON, SURREY)
☎ 0181-656 1342. PHONE FIRST.

## BABES AND BUMPS

1 GILBY GREEN, NEAR SAFFRON WALDEN, NEWPORT, ESSEX
CB11 3RS
☎ (01799) 541978. PHONE FIRST.

## BABY & CHILD EQUIPMENT HIRE

212 FINCHAMPSTEAD, WOKINGHAM, BERKSHIRE RG11 3HV
☎ (01734) 781463. PHONE FIRST.

## BABYRENT (FRIMLEY)

80 PEVENSEY WAY, FRIMLEY, CAMBERLEY, SURREY GU16 5UX
☎ (01252) 835638. PHONE FIRST.

## BABYWARE HIRE

678 GALLEYWOOD ROAD, CHELMSFORD, ESSEX CM2 8BY
☎ (01245) 251666. PHONE FIRST.

## BABYWISE HIRE

THE BAYS QUEENSWAY, HAYLING ISLAND, HAMPSHIRE PO11 0LY
☎ (01705) 468385. PHONE FIRST.

## BUGGIES PLUS,

127 SMARTS LANE, LOUGHTON, ESSEX IG10 4BP
☎ 0181-508 8248. PHONE FIRST.

## KIDDYHIRE

6 COOPER ROAD, CROYDON, SURREY CR0 4DL
☎ 0181-681 6443. PHONE FIRST.

## KID EQUIP

☎ (01737) 360448. PHONE FIRST.

## KINDERHIRE

31 KENNEDY AVENUE, EAST GRINSTEAD, WEST SUSSEX RH19 2DH
☎ (01342) 322964. PHONE FIRST.

## KINDERHIRE

9 MAY TREE CLOSE, BADGER FARM, WINCHESTER,
HAMPSHIRE SO22 4JB
☎ (01962) 863692. PHONE FIRST.

## LIBERTY TRAVELLING TOTS

54 FOREDOWN DRIVE, PORTSLADE, SUSSEX BN41 2BE
☎ (01273) 422890. PHONE FIRST.

## MOTHER GOOSE NURSERY HIRE

39 LINGFIELD AVENUE, KINGSTON UPON THAMES, SURREY KT1 2TL
☎ 0181-541 1681. PHONE FIRST.

## NURSERY & TODDLER SERVICES

67 PLANTATION ROAD, LEIGHTON BUZZARD, BEDFORDSHIRE
LU7 7HJ
☎ (01525) 378938. PHONE FIRST.

## NURSERY HIRE

25 NECTON ROAD, WHEATHAMPSTEAD, HERTFORDSHIRE AL4 8AT
☎ (01582) 833904. PHONE FIRST.

## NURSERY NEEDS

(BIGGIN HILL, KENT)
☎ (01959) 540930. PHONE FIRST.

## RASCALS BABY EQUIPMENT HIRE

16 PAYNE ROAD, WOOTTON, BEDFORDSHIRE
MK43 9PJ
☎ (01234) 766931. PHONE FIRST.

## ROBINA BABY & NURSERY EQUIPMENT

10 DOWNSWAY, SHOREHAM BY SEA, WEST SUSSEX BN34 5GH
☎ (01273) 453548. PHONE FIRST.

## ROCKABI

14 LOTHAIR ROAD, STOPSLEY, LUTON, BEDFORDSHIRE LV2 7XB
☎ (01582) 455261. PHONE FIRST.

## ROCK-A-BYE

SUFFOLK HOUSE, THE GREEN, WOODBURN GREEN,
BUCKINGHAMSHIRE HP10 0EU
☎ (01628) 523159. PHONE FIRST.

## TINKERS

17 OLD OAK AVENUE, CHIPSTEAD, SURREY CR5 3PG
☎ (01737) 553761. PHONE FIRST.

All the above are part of the British Equipment Hirers Association (BEHA), which has more than 100 members countrywide. A range of equipment can be hired from high chairs, cots and travel cots to baby car seats and buggies. Some members also hire out party equipment including child-sized tables and chairs. BEHA run an advice line which will try and answer any queries you have regarding hiring services for children. Phone the Babyline on 0831 310355.

# SOUTH WEST

## *Permanent Discount Outlets*

## BABYCARE LTD

113A DORCHESTER ROAD, WEYMOUTH, DORSET
☎ (01305) 788095. OPEN 9.30 - 5.30 MON - SAT, CLOSED WED.

Baby feeding equipment, premature baby clothes, nursery equipment including prams, cots and pushchairs from Mamas & Papas and Silver Cross, car seats and cot blankets at prices which are lower than those in department stores. All are brand new and bought direct from the manufacturer, but the company has a policy of high turnover/low profit margins. For example, MacClarens Duette, £155, usually £185. The bedding and Moses baskets are manufactured by Babycare.

## BUSY BEE

20 CHEAP STREET, FROME, SOMERSET
☎ (01373) 472012. OPEN 9.30 - 5 MON - SAT, CLOSED AT 4 ON THUR.
Sells selected fashion seconds and over-runs from leading high street chain stores and boutiques as well as some designer names, but the main thrust of the shop is towards casual wear. Just because this shop sells chainstore surpluses, don't expect it to be chainstore-sized. All the labels are removed before sale from the underwear, ladies and children's clothes and occasional menswear. Seconds usually sell for between half and two thirds of the normal retail price; perfects are discounted by one-third. Also stocks Trutex school wear. Stocks changes all the time.

## MATALAN

UNIT 2, HAVEN BANKS, WATER LANE, EXETER, DEVON EX2 8DW
☎ (01392) 413375. OPEN 10 - 8 MON - FRI, 9.30 - 5.30 SAT, 10 - 6 SUN.
UNIT 1, ALDERMOOR WAY, LONGWELL GREEN, BRISTOL BS15 7AD
☎ (0117) 9352828. OPEN 10 - 8 MON - FRI, 9.30 - 5.30 SAT, 10 - 6 SUN.
UNITS 2/3, TURBARY RETAIL PARK, RINGWOOD ROAD, POOLE, DORSET BH12 3JJ
☎ (01202) 590686. OPEN 10 - 8 MON - FRI, 9 - 6 SAT, 11 - 5 SUN.
As the UK's first National Discount Club, Matalan has the buying power to guarantee its members up to 60% discounts on a huge range of brand name clothing, household goods, luggage and toiletries for all the family. Top quality merchandise, current season, no seconds, is offered to its members at exclusive, permanently discounted prices seven days a week. Matalan operates strictly on a membership basis, one of the key factors for its success in offering 20%-60% savings off recommended retail prices. Membership cards are issued through companies, organisations and associations in the vicinity of the stores, and are available to their employees/members. They are valid at any of the 50 Matalan stores in the UK. To find out if your organisation is registered, phone the Matalan hotline on 01772 629447.

# TK MAXX

THIRD FLOOR, THE GALLERIES, BRISTOL, AVON
☎ (0117) 9304404. OPEN 9 - 5.30 MON - SAT, 7 ON THUR.

Based on an American concept, TK Maxx is the first British retailer to practise "off-price" retailing. This means a centrally located store which offers famous label goods with up to 60% savings off recommended retail prices. TK Maxx has fashion for the whole family - children's, men's and womenswear - accessories, shoes, gifts, kitchenware and home goods. Everything in the store is branded with a choice of well-known high street names to designer labels, and while a small percentage mightly be clearly marked past season, the great majority of items in store are current season, current stock and still with phenomenal savings. There is a huge choice with 50,000 pieces in store with 5,000 new items arriving a week, so it's worth keeping abreast of the lastest deliveries as turnaround is very fast. One of the ways in which TK Maxx is able to offer such low prices is by running a very low-cost operation, so the stores are simple and unfussy with wide aisles, shopping trolleys and baskets, and a spacious, functional feel to them. Service is not compromised, however: there are individual changing rooms, ramps for buggies and wheelchairs, plenty of staff on the shop floor and all the branches accept all major credit and debit cards.

# TRAGO MILL

REGIONAL SHOPPING CENTRE, NEWTON ABBOT, DEVON TQ12 6JD
☎ (01626) 821111. OPEN 9 - 5.30 MON - SAT, 10.30 - 4.30 SUN.

Sells virtually everything from children's, women's and men's wear, gardening equipment and cookwear to wallpaper, carpets and fitted kitchens. Most are branded goods and there is a creche, cafe, pizza bar and petrol station.

# *Factory Shops*

## CLARKS FACTORY SHOP

CLARKS VILLAGE, FARM ROAD, STREET, SOMERSET BA16 OBB
☎ (01458) 843161. OPEN 9 - 6 MON - SAT AND BANK HOLIDAYS,
11 - 5 SUN.

Clarks International operate a chain of factory shops nationally which specialise in selling discontinued lines and slight sub-standards for children, women and men from Clarks, K Shoes and other famous brands. These shops trade under the name of Crockers, K Shoes Factory shop or Clarks Factory Shop and while not all are physically attached to a shoe factory, these shops are treated as factory shops by the company. Customers can expect to find an extensive range of quality shoes, sandals, walking boots, slippers, trainers, handbags, accessories and gifts, while their major outlets such as at here at Clarks Village also offer luggage, sports clothing, sports equipment and outdoor clothing. Brands stocked include Clarks, K Shoes, Springer, CICA, Hi-Tec, Puma, Mercury, Dr Martens, Nike, LA Gear, Fila, Mizuno, Slazenger, Weider, Samsonite, Delsey, Antler and Carlton, although not all are sold in every outlet. Discounts are on average 30% off the normal high street price for perfect stock. From November to end of March, weekday and Saturday closing times are 5.30.

## CLARKS VILLAGE FACTORY SHOPPING

FARM ROAD, STREET, SOMERSET BA16 OBB
☎ (01458) 840064. OPEN 9 - 6 MON - SAT, 11 - 5 SUN. TIMES CHANGE
WINTER AND SUMMER.

Purpose-built village of brick-built shops with extensive car parking facilities. Restaurant run by Leith's, fast food stands, carousel, indoor play area, outdoor play area. Here, there were at August 1995, 37 shops with more planned. For children: Laura Ashley, Benetton, The Baggage Factory, The Linen Cupboard, Wrangler, JoKids, Clarks Factory Shop, Claude Gill Books, Thorntons Chocolates, The Sports Factory, Hallmark and Remington.

## CROCKERS

2 EASTOVER, BRIDGWATER, SOMERSET TA6 5AB
☎ (01278) 452617. OPEN 9 - 5.30 MON - SAT.
10A HIGH STREET, BURNHAM-ON-SEA, SOMERSET TA8 1NX
☎ (01278) 794668. OPEN 9 - 5.30 MON - SAT, 11 - 5 SUN, 10 - 5 BANK
HOLIDAYS.
112-114 HIGH STREET, STREET, SOMERSET BA16 OEW
☎ (01458) 442055. OPEN 9 - 5.30 MON - SAT AND BANK  HOLIDAYS,
11 - 5 SUNS.
UNITS 1 AND 13, WEST SWINDON DISTRICT CENTRE, SWINDON,
WILTSHIRE SN5 7DI
☎ (01793) 873662. OPEN 9 - 8 MON - FRI, 9 - 6 SAT, 10 - 4 SUN,
10 - 5 BANK HOLIDAYS.
UNIT 2, SAINSBURYS PRECINCT, QUEENSWAY SHOPPING CENTRE,
WORLE, AVON BS22 OBT
☎ (01934) 521693. OPEN 9 - 8 MON - FRI, 9 - 6 SAT,
10.30 - 4.30 SUN, 9 - 5 BANK HOLIDAYS.

Clarks International operate a chain of factory shops nationally which specialise in selling discontinued lines and slight sub-standards for children, women and men from Clarks, K Shoes and other famous brands. These shops trade under the name of Crockers, K Shoes Factory shop or Clarks Factory Shop and while not all are physically attached to a shoe factory, these shops are treated as factory shops by the company. Customers can expect to find an extensive range of quality shoes, sandals, walking boots, slippers, trainers, handbags, accessories and gifts, while their major outlets also offer luggage, sports clothing, sports equipment and outdoor clothing. Brands stocked include Clarks, K Shoes, Springer, CICA, Hi-Tec, Puma, Mercury, Dr Martens, Nike, LA Gear, Fila, Mizuno, Slazenger, Weider, Samsonite, Delsey, Antler and Carlton, although not all are sold in every outlet. Discounts are on average 30% off the normal high street price for perfect stock. The Swindon branch is also a sports factory shop and baggage factory shop.

## KIDS' STUFF

10 HENSMANS HILL, CLIFTON, BRISTOL, BS8 4PE
☎ (0117) 9734980. OPEN 9 - 5 MON - FRI, 9.30 - 5.30 SAT.
In operation for more than 17 years, Kids' Stuff sells high quality children's clothes (no coats or underwear), most of which is in 100% cotton, for babies to 12-year-olds. Sited under the factory where the clothes are made, the factory shop sells over-runs, discontinued lines and ex-catalogue items at up to 50% discount.

## THE FACTORY SHOP

36-37 ROUNDSTONE STREET, TROWBRIDGE, WILTSHIRE BA12 9AN
☎ (01225) 751399. OPEN 9 - 5.30 MON - SAT.
24 MARKET PLACE, WARMINSTER, WILTSHIRE BA12 9AN
☎ (01985) 217532. OPEN 9 - 5.30 MON - FRI, 9 - 5 SAT.
MART ROAD, MINEHEAD, SOMERSET
☎ (01643) 705911. OPEN 9.30 - 5.30 MON - SAT, 11 - 5 SUN.
Wide range on sale includes children's, men's and women's clothing and footwear; household textiles, toiletries, hardware, luggage, lighting and bedding, most of which are chainstore and high street brands at discounts of approximately 30%-50%. There are weekly deliveries and brands include all the major stars: Coloroll, Wrangler and Dartington to name just three. Lines are continually changing and few factory shops offer such a variety under one roof.

## THE SHOE SHED

STATION ROAD, BUDLEIGH, SALTERTON, DEVON EX9 6RU
☎ (01395) 443399. OPEN 8.30 - 5.30 MON - SAT, 10 - 4 SUN.
23 FAIRMILE ROAD, CHRISTCHURCH, DORSET BH23 2LA
☎ (01202) 474123. OPEN 10 - 5 MON - FRI, 9 - 5 SAT, 10 - 4 SUN.
MENDEVILLE ROAD, WYKE REGIS, WEYMOUTH, DORSET DT4 9HW
☎ (01305) 766772. OPEN 8.30 - 5 MON - WED, 8.30 - 8 THUR, FRI, 8.30 - 5.30 SAT, 10 - 4 SUN.
Large factory shop selling a vast range of all types of children's, men's and women's shoes, all of which are perfects, at up to 30% below normal high street prices. Ladies sandals cost from £5; ladies shoes from £7.50. Men's shoes from £10; sports shoes from £10.

# Dress Agencies

## BUDGET-BOX

24A DITTON ST, ILMINSTER, SOMERSET TA19 OBQ
☎ (01460) 53316. OPEN 9 - 5 MON - WED & FRI, 9 - 1 THUR & SAT.
Nearly-new childrenswear up to early teens stocked, including school uniforms and labels such as Osh Kosh.

## CHILD'S PLAY

28 ALBION STREET, EXMOUTH, DEVON EX8 1JJ
☎ (01395) 276975. OPEN 10 - 4 MON, TUE, THUR-SAT, 10 - 1 WED, CLOSED 1 - 2 DAILY.
Secondhand and new baby equipment and clothes for ages 0 - 6 years. Babygros cost from 50p to £2.99; prams from £5 to £100.

## GEMMA

422 LYMINGTON ROAD, HIGHCLIFFE, CHRISTCHURCH, DORSET
☎ (01425) 276928. OPEN 10 -5 MON - SAT, 10 - 1 WED.
Adult dress agency which also stocks childrens wear; there is a separate play area for kids. Bargain rail of older stock sold at half-price; sales in the summer and after Christmas.

## KARALYNE'S

20 WEST STREET, WILTON, WILTSHIRE
☎ (0722) 742802. OPEN 9.30 - 4, MON - SAT, CLOSED WED.
Tiny but full shop selling nearly-new clothing and accessories for women and children at bargain prices, including evening and maternity wear. Stocks more than 1,000 items at a time with a constant flow of new arrivals. Very popular "special rails" selling top makes of shoes, handbags and belts. Permanent half-price rails added to weekly, plus two "everything half price" sales each year in February and August. Useful children's play corner for hassle-free browsing.

## MAGIK ROUNDABOUT

153 FISHERTON STREET, SALISBURY, WILTSHIRE SP2 7RP
☎ (01722) 415331. OPEN 9 - 5.30 MON - SAT.
Children's dress agency selling nearly-new babywear and children's clothes up to the age of 12 years, as well as baby equipment such as

prams, pushchairs, high chairs, baths and cots. Prams cost from £50-£200, coach prams from £75. There is also a small range of maternity wear and cot and pram linen.

## MUMS AND TOTS

2 & 4 SOUTH STREET, WILTON, NEAR SALISBURY, WILTSHIRE ST2 OJS
☎ (01722) 744582. OPEN 9.30 - 4 MON - WED, 9.30 - 5 THUR - SAT.

Nearly-new nursery equipment and bedding including prams and pushchairs are sold in this shop which also sells full-price children's clothes and soft toys.

## ROUNDABOUT

2 SUSSEX PLACE, WIDCOMBE, AV0N
☎ (01225) 316696. OPEN 9.30 - 5 MON - SAT.

Side by side shops, Roundabout and RoundAgain, one selling nearly-new and sample childrenswear from Oilily to Cakewalk at discounts of about 45%, the other, RoundAgain, selling womenswear such as Jaeger and Gap. Roundabout has half-price brand new samples from Cakewalk, Oilily, Hunza and Irene Rene as well as nearly-new Laura Ashley, Gap, Next and Petit Bateau. There are also new pure silk christening gowns, £25-£30 which would normally cost £100; party dresses, £8-£20, boys smart jackets and ties, party shoes and occasionally bridesmaids dresses, £25.

# *Hire Shops*

## ABACUS BABY EQUIPMENT HIRE

89 SEABOURNE ROAD, SOUTHBOURNE, BOURNEMOUTH,
DORSET BH8 9BJ
☎ (01202) 429829. PHONE FIRST.

## BABE-EQUIP

9 LEAT STREET, TIVERTON, DEVON EX16 5LG
☎ (01884) 257938. PHONE FIRST.

## BABY HIRE

35 LANGDON ROAD, BRADWORTHY, HOLSWORTHY, DEVON
EX22 7SF
☎ (01409) 241314. PHONE FIRST.

## HUSH-A-BYE HIRE

16 WHITCHURCH AVENUE, EXETER, DEVON EX2 5NU
☎ (01392) 57636. PHONE FIRST.

## JUST FOR YOU

9 TREMLETT MEWS, WORLE, WESTON SUPER MARE, AVON BS22 OYL
☎ (01934) 510092. PHONE FIRST.

## KINDER CARE

159 COWICK STREET, ST THOMAS, EXETER, DEVON EX4 1AS
☎ (01392) 435888. PHONE FIRST.

## LITTLE ONES NURSERY HIRE

24 PRESTBURY, YATE, BRISTOL, AVON BS17 4LB
☎ (01454) 325004. PHONE FIRST.

## TRAVEL TOTS

2 BROADLEAS, KING EDWARD ROAD, MINEHEAD,
SOMERSET TA24 5JB
☎ (01643) 706213. PHONE FIRST.

All the above are part of the British Equipment Hirers Association (BEHA), which has more than 100 members countrywide. A range of equipment can be hired from high chairs, cots and travel cots to baby car seats and buggies. Some members also hire out party equipment including child-sized tables and chairs. BEHA run an advice line which will try and answer any queries you have regarding hiring services for children. Phone the Babyline on 0831 310355.

## MUMS AND TOTS

2 & 4 SOUTH STREET, WILTON, NEAR SALISBURY, WILTSHIRE ST2 OJS
☎ (01722) 744582. OPEN 9.30 - 4 MON - WED, 9.30 - 5 THUR - SAT.

Nearly-new nursery equipment and bedding including prams and pushchairs are hired out in this shop which also sells brand new children's clothes and toys.

# WALES AND WEST MIDLANDS

## *Permanent Discount Outlets*

### IMPS

69B HIGH STREET, WITNEY, OXFORDSHIRE
☎ (01993) 779875. OPEN 9 - 5 MON - SAT.
40 UPPER HIGH STREET, THAME, OXFORDSHIRE
☎ (01844) 212985. OPEN 9 - 5 MON - SAT.
52 SHEEP STREET, BICESTER, OXFORDSHIRE
☎ (01869) 243455. OPEN 9 - 5 MON - SAT.
26 MARKET PLACE, HENLEY-ON-THAMES, OXFORDSHIRE
☎ (01491) 411530. OPEN 9 - 5 MON - SAT.

High street shops selling popular chainstore seconds. The Witney shop extends over two floors and has plenty of stock from clothes for all the family to towels, china, trays and flower cachepots. For children, vests and knickers, 75p, socks, 75p, jeans, £6.99, pyjamas, £6.99, smocked dresses, £8.99, denim shirts, £5 for ages 2/3, taffeta party dresses for ages 5/6, £10, velvet party dresses for age 2, £6, long jumpers, £6.99, Mickey Mouse tracksuits for age 7, £11.99, floral trousers for age 8, £8.99. Stock changes constantly.

### M C HITCHEN & SONS LTD

299 COVENTRY ROAD, BIRMINGHAM, WEST MIDLANDS B10 0RA
☎ (0121) 772 1637. OPEN 9 - 5.30 MON - SAT.
236 HAWTHORN ROAD, KINGSTANDING, BIRMINGHAM, WEST MIDLANDS B44 8PP
☎ (0121) 373 1276.OPEN 9.15 - 5.30 MON - SAT.
14-16 NORTH STREET, RUGBY, WARWICKSHIRE CV21 2AF
☎ (01788) 565116. OPEN 9.30 - 5.30 MON - WED, 9 - 5.30 THUR - SAT.

Littlewoods sell off their overstocks in a network of shops called M C Hitchen & Sons Ltd. Most of them are in the North of England and offer up to 40% off the catalogue price for clothing and between 50% and 60% off for electrical goods. Littlwoods also run a mobile shop which operates in cities where they don't have a sale shop. For details of further venues for the sales, which usually take place once a month, contact Jean Banks, c/o Crosby DC, Kershaw Avenue, Endbutt Lane, Crosby, Merseyside L70 1AH.

# MATALAN

UNIT 5, THE JOHN ALLEN CENTRE, COWLEY, OXFORD,
OXFORDSHIRE OX4 3JP
☎ (01865) 747400. OPEN 10 - 8 MON - FRI, 9.30 - 5.30 SAT, 10 - 6 SUN.
UNITS A1/A2, GALLAGHER RETAIL PARK, TEWKESBURY ROAD,
CHELTENHAM, GLOUCESTERSHIRE GL51 9RR
☎ (01242) 254001. OPEN 10 - 8 MON - FRI, 9.30 - 5.30 SAT, 10 - 6 SUN.
UNIT 1, MEOLE BRACE RETAIL PARK, HEREFORD ROAD,
SHREWSBURY SY3 9NB
☎ (01743) 363240. OPEN 10 - 8 MON - FRI, 9.30 - 5.30 SAT, 10 - 6 SUN.
UNIT 7, VENTURA SHOPPING CENTRE, VENTURA PARK ROAD, BONE
HILL, TAMWORTH, STAFFORDSHIRE B78 3HB
☎ (01827) 50900. OPEN 10 - 8 MON - FRI, 9.30 - 5.30 SAT, 10 - 6 SUN.
FOUNDRY ROAD, MORRISTON, SWANSEA SA6 8DU
☎ (01792) 792229. OPEN 10 - 8 MON - FRI, 9.30 - 5.30 SAT, 10 - 6 SUN.
BIRMINGHAM ROAD, HOWARD STREET,
WOLVERHAMPTON, WEST MIDLANDS WV2 2LQ
☎ (01902) 352813. OPEN 10 - 8 MON - FRI, 9.30 - 5.30 SAT, 10 - 6 SUN.
UNIT 4B, CWMBRAN RETAIL PARK CWNBRAN DRIVE, CWNBRAN,
GWENT NP44 3JQ
☎ (01633) 866944. OPEN 10 - 8 MON - FRI, 9.30 - 5.30 SAT, 10 - 6 SUN.
UNIT E, MAYBIRD CENTRE, BIRMINGHAM ROAD, STRATFORD-
UPON-AVON CV37 OHZ
☎ (01789) 262223. OPEN 10 - 8 MON - FRI, 10 - 5.30 SAT, 10 - 6 SUN.
UNIT 1A & 1B, CAENARFON ROAD, BANGOR LL57 4SU
☎ (01248) 362778. OPEN 10 - 8 MON - FRI, 9.30 - 5.30 SAT, 10 - 8 SUN.
WOLSTANTON RETAIL PARK, WOLSTANTON, NEWCASTLE,
STAFFORDSHIRE ST5 1DY
☎ (01782) 711731. OPEN 9.30 - 8 MON - FRI, 9.30 - 6 SAT, 10 - 5.30 SUN.
UNITS 5 & 6, QUEENSVILLE RETAIL PARK, SILKMORE LANE,
STAFFORD ST17 4SU
☎ (01785) 226211. OPEN 10 - 8 MON - FRI, 9.30 - 5.30 SAT, 10 - 6 SUN.
UNIT 2, 382-384 NEWPORT ROAD, CARDIFF, WALES CF3 7AE
☎ (01222) 491781. OPEN 10 - 8 MON - FRI, 9 - 6 SAT, 11 - 5 SUN.
UNIT A, LICHFIELD STREET, BURTON-ON-TRENT, STAFFORDSHIRE
DE14 3QZ
☎ (01283) 540865.
UNIT 8, GLAMORGAN VALE RETAIL PARK, LLANTRISANT, MID
GLAMORGAN, SOUTH WALES CF7 8RP
☎ (01433) 224854. OPEN 10 - 8 MON - FRI, 9 - 6 SAT, 10 - 5 SUN.

As the UK's first National Discount Club, Matalan has the buying
power to guarantee its members up to 60% discounts on a huge range
of brand name clothing, household goods, luggage and toiletries for
all the family. Top quality merchandise, current season, no seconds, is

offered to its members at exclusive, permanently discounted prices seven days a week. Matalan operates strictly on a membership basis, one of the key factors for its success in offering 20%-60% savings off recommended retail prices. Membership cards are issued through companies, organisations and associations in the vicinity of the stores, and are available to their employees/members. They are valid at any of the 50 Matalan stores in the UK. To find out if your organisation is registered, phone the Matalan hotline on 01772 629447.

## NEXT TO NOTHING

24-25 WALFRUN CENTRE, WOLVERHAMPTON, WEST MIDLANDS WV1 3HG
☎ (01902) 29464. OPEN 9 - 5.30 MON - SAT.
104 CORPORATION STREET, BIRMINGHAM, WEST MIDLANDS
☎ (0121) 233 0022. OPEN 9 - 5.15 MON - FR, 9.30 - 6 SAT.
Sells perfect surplus stock from Next stores and the Next Directory catalogue - from belts, jewellery and underwear to day and evening wear - at discounts of 50% or more. The ranges are usually last season's and overruns but there is the odd current item if you look carefully. Stock consists of children's, men's and women's clothing, with some homeware and shoes, depending on the branch. Stock is replenished twice a week and there is plenty of it. Childrenswear range is not as extensive as the women's and men's.

## NIPPERS

FIELDS FARM, MARTON, NEAR RUGBY, WARWICKSHIRE CV23 9RS
☎ (01926) 633100. FAX 01926 633007. OPENING HOURS VARY SO PHONE FIRST.
ORCHARD COTTAGE FARM, CROOME ROAD, DEFFORD, WORCESTER WR8 9AS
☎ (01386) 750888. FAX (01386) 750333.
Nippers, the nursery equipment and toy specialists, started with a very clever and simple idea and have now built it up to create an award-winning chain of franchises. The company operates from converted barns on farms around the country, offering easy parking, no queues, and personal service. This is on top of competitive prices on prams, cots, pushchairs, car seats, outdoor play equipment and toys. Prices are low partly because they operate from farms, with none of the overheads of traditional retail outlets, and party because the suc-

cessful growth of a number of branches means it can now buy in bulk and negotiate good deals. Customers can try out the merchandise and the children can see the animals, mostly sheep, chickens and pigs. Familiar brand names are on sale at all the branches, including Britax, Maclaren and Bebe Confort, Fisher-Price and Little Tikes. You can try out the car seats in your car and there is usually a pram/pushchair repair service on site.

## NURSERY TO LEISURE

35 SANDWELL CENTRE, QUEENS SQUARE, WEST BROMWICH, W. MIDLANDS
☎ (0121) 525 5162. OPEN 9 - 5.30 MON - SAT, CLOSED WED.
Has a shop and a mail order arm called Prams Direct. The shop stocks reconditioned Maclaren prams from £130 and pushchairs from £23 as well as factory seconds; Silver Cross, Tomy, Mamas & Papas and Britax and aims to be very competitive. It has very occasional reconditioned items and some manufacturers seconds.

## THE FACTORY SHOP

NEW ROAD, PERSHORE, WORCESTERSHIRE WR10 1BT
☎ (01386) 556467. OPEN 9 - 5 MON - SAT, 10.30 - 4.30 SUN.
Sells clothes, household goods, bags, suitcases, electrical goods, kitchenware, shoes, toiletries, suitcases, china, lighting, childrenswear, some leisurewear and has a designer clothes section upstairs. Most stock is seconds or clearance lines from well-known chain stores and department stores.

## THE RED HOUSE

WINDRUSH PARK, WITNEY, OXFORDSHIRE OX8 5YF
☎ (01993) 771144. MAIL ORDER.
An excellent catalogue of children's books, The Red House covers both educational matters, from learning to read to history, and practical activity books as well as fiction. The books are a mixture of hardback and paperback from a variety of different publishers, and good savings are to be made.

## THE SALE SHOP

ROSS LABELS LTD, OVERROSS, ROSS ON WYE, HEREFORDSHIRE
HR9 7QJ
☎ (01989) 769000. OPEN 9 - 5.30 MON - SAT, 10 - 5 SUN.

Twenty thousand square feet of selling space, with children's, women's and menswear from underwear and jeans to good, middle of the road brand name outfits and suits bought direct from the manufacturer. Some of the labels on sale include Alexon, Eastex, Dash, Big Bubble, Fruit of the Loom, Viyella, Wolsey, Elsie Whiteley, Double Two, Telemac and Lyle & Scott. Stock is usually one year old, while current merchandise consists of overmakes. Discounts range from 20% to 50%. There is also a Lee Cooper and big kids wear department and Aquascutum clothes are sold at less than normal high street prices.

## TK MAXX

THE POTTERIES SHOPPING CENTRE, HANLEY, STOKE-ON-TRENT, STAFFORDSHIRE.
☎ (01782) 289822. OPEN MON - FRI 9 - 5.30 UNTIL 8 ON THURS, 9 - 6 SAT.

Based on an American concept, TK Maxx is the first British retailer to practise "off-price" retailing. This means a centrally located store which offers famous label goods with up to 60% savings off recommended retail prices. TK Maxx has fashion for the whole family - children's, men's and womenswear - accessories, shoes, gifts, kitchenware and home goods. Everything in the store is branded with a choice of well-known high street names to designer labels, and while a small percentage mightly be clearly marked past season, the great majority of items in store are current season, current stock and still with phenomenal savings. There is a huge choice with 50,000 pieces in store with 5,000 new items arriving a week, so it's worth keeping abreast of the lastest deliveries as turnaround is very fast. One of the ways in which TK Maxx is able to offer such low prices is by running a very low-cost operation, so the stores are simple and unfussy with wide aisles, shopping trolleys and baskets, and a spacious, functional feel to them. Service is not compromised, however: there are individual changing rooms, ramps for buggies and wheelchairs, plenty of staff on the shop floor and all the branches accept all major credit and debit cards.

## TOP MARKS

23 HIGH STREET, MORETON-IN-MARSH, GLOUCESTERSHIRE
GL56 OAF
☎ (01608) 651272. OPEN 9 - 5.30 MON - FRI, 9 - 5 SAT.
8 HIGH STREET, CHIPPING NORTON, GLOS
☎ (01608) 642653. OPEN 9 - 5.30 MON - FRI, 9 - 5 SAT.

Sells seconds from leading chain stores for all the family. Most of the
stock is made up of men' and women's wear, and there is also childrenswear, most of which are Marks & Spencer seconds, sold at about
one third cheaper than M&s. Wide range of stock in various sizes
with new stock arriving twice a week, just six weeks after it was first
introduced to M&S department stores.

# *Factory Shops*

## BENETTON

BICESTER OUTLET SHOPPING VILLAGE, PINGLE DRIVE, BICESTER,
JUNCTION 9 OF M40, OXFORDSHIRE OX6 7WD
☎ (01869) 323200. OPEN 10 - 6 MON - SAT AND BANK HOLIDAYS,
11 - 5 SUN.

One of 48 shops, with more planned, in this factory shopping village
which opened in June 1995. Benetton stocks a wide range of clothes
for children, men and women including colourful T-shirts, sweatshirts, swimwear, jeans, children's jackets, stretch short and all-in-one
shorts. Some of the stock is marked seconds, but it is often difficult
to tell why. The centre also has two restaurants, a small children's play
area and free parking. The telephone number given here is for the
village.

## BICESTER OUTLET SHOPPING VILLAGE

PINGLE DRIVE, BICESTER, JUNCTION 9 OF M40, OXFORDSHIRE
OX6 7WD
☎ (01869) 323200. OPEN 10 - 6 MON - SAT AND BANK HOLIDAYS,
11 - 5 SUN.

Factory shopping village comprising 48 different outlets, which
opened in June 1995. Billed as Bond Street comes to Bicester, the
shops are very smart indeed, beautifully designed and stocked with
end-of-season designer fashions, mens and childrenswear, tableware,

shoes and more, all on permanent sale at prices reduced from 25%-50%, with some reductions up to 75%. Outlets for children include: casualwear from Benetton; witty slogans on T-shirts and nightshirts from the US company, Big Dog; Clarks footwear; sports shoes from the US company, Converse; children clothes for boys and girls from JoKids; toys and games from well-known names such as Hasbro, Mattel, Matchbox, Little Tikes at Kids Play Factory; specialist outerwear from Mileta Sport at Tog 24; childrenswear from Osh Kosh b'Gosh; casualwear from Pepe Jeans; books, CDs and cassettes from Sapphire Books. The centre also has two restaurants, a small children's play area and free parking.

## BIG DOG

BICESTER OUTLET SHOPPING VILLAGE, PINGLE DRIVE, BICESTER, JUNCTION 9 OF M40, OXFORDSHIRE OX6 7WD
☎ (01869) 323200. OPEN 10 - 6 MON - SAT AND BANK HOLIDAYS, 11 - 5 SUN.

This is a US company which sells T-shirts, sweatshirts, shorts and nightwear with a slogan for children, women and men. As they are not a well-known name here, it is difficult to tell how good their prices are. All the clothes are unisex and there are also golf balls, golf umbrellas, dogs leads and mouse mats. All the stock is currently on sale in the USA.

## CLARKS FACTORY SHOP

UNIT 27, BICESTER OUTLET SHOPPING VILLAGE, PINGLE DRIVE, BICESTER, JUNCTION 9 OF M40, OXFORDSHIRE OX6 7WD
☎ (01869) 325646. OPEN 10 - 6 MON - SAT, 11 - 5 SUN AND BANK HOLIDAYS.

One of 48 shops, with more planned, in this factory shopping village. Clarks International operate a chain of factory shops nationally which specialise in selling discontinued lines and slight sub-standards for children, women and men from Clarks, K Shoes and other famous brands. These shops trade under the name of Crockers, K Shoes Factory shop or Clarks Factory Shop and while not all are physically attached to a shoe factory, these shops are treated as factory shops by the company. Customers can expect to find an extensive range of quality shoes, sandals, walking boots, slippers, trainers, handbags, accessories and gifts, while their major outlets also offer luggage, sports clothing, sports equipment and outdoor clothing. Brands stocked include Clarks, K Shoes, Springer, CICA, Hi-Tec, Puma, Mercury, Dr Martens, Nike, LA Gear, Fila, Mizuno, Slazenger, Weider, Samsonite, Delsey, Antler and Carlton, although not all are sold in every outlet. Discounts are on average 30% off the normal high street price for perfect stock.

## I J DEWHIRST

UNIT 22, THE KINGSWAY, FFORESTFACH INDUSTRIAL ESTATE, FFORESTFACH, SWANSEA
☎ (01792) 584621. OPEN 9 - 5.30 MON - FRI, 9 - 5 SAT, 11 - 5 SUN.
Wide range of children's, men's and women's clothes including girl's dresses, blouses, trousers, skirts and jackets and boy's shirts, trousers and jackets; men's suits, jackets, shirts, trousers; women's jackets, blouses, skirts and trousers, and much much more.

## JOKIDS

BICESTER OUTLET SHOPPING VILLAGE, PINGLE DRIVE, BICESTER, JUNCTION 9 OF M40, OXFORDSHIRE OX6 7WD
☎ (01869) 323200. OPEN 10 - 6 MON - SAT AND BANK HOLIDAYS, 11 - 5 SUN.
One of 48 shops, with more planned, in this factory shopping village which opened in June 1995. This shop sells pretty party dresses for girls, at reductions of up to 50%, all-in-one smocked playsuits, T-shirts, denim shirts, denim dresses, sunhats, shorts, and umbrellas. The village also has two restaurants, a small children's play area and free parking. The telephone number given here is for the village.

## KIDS PLAY FACTORY

BICESTER OUTLET SHOPPING VILLAGE, PINGLE DRIVE, BICESTER, JUNCTION 9 OF M40, OXFORDSHIRE OX6 7WD
☎ (01869) 323200. OPEN 10 - 6 MON - SAT AND BANK HOLIDAYS, 11 - 5 SUN.
This shop sells a wide range of well-known children's brand names: Little Tikes, Tomy, Matchbox, Lego, The First Years, Hasbro, Disney, Playskool, Texas Instruments and Fisher-Price. There are also some reconditioned toys such as Suzuki bikes and Sandblaster trucks, stuffed toys, rattles and bicycles. The village also has two restaurants, a small children's play area and free parking. The telephone number given here is for the village.

## LYNDY FACTORY SHOP

WATLING STREET, CANNOCK, STAFFORDSHIRE WS11 3NB
☎ (01543) 454427. OPEN 9 - 5 MON - SAT, 10 - 4 SUNS, BANK HOLIDAYS.
Wide range of children's outdoor and indoor play equipment and
bicycles. There are trikes from as little as £9.99, children's bicycles,
racing cycles, scooters, as well as slides, climbing frames, play mats,
swim armbands, sand pits, play sand, goal posts, basket ball sets, play
houses and pools, baby swings, trampolines, and water trays. Adult
equipment includes exercise benches and exercise cycles, car roof
boxes, camping trailers, boats and garden accessories.

## OSH KOSH B'GOSH

BICESTER OUTLET SHOPPING VILLAGE, PINGLE DRIVE, BICESTER,
JUNCTION 9 OF M40, OXFORDSHIRE OX6 7WD
☎ (01869) 323200. OPEN 10 - 6 MON - SAT AND BANK HOLIDAYS,
11 - 5 SUN.
One of 48 shops, with more planned, in this factory shopping village
which opened in June 1995. This shop has a big sign at the back
saying everything sold on the premises is the genuine article and sold
at discounts of 30%. It caters for infants to 12-year-olds selling, for
example, the trademark striped all-in-one jeans (age 18 months),
£17.14, reduced from £24.49; T-shirts (30 months), £5.74, reduced
from £11.50; jackets (age 2), £13.29, reduced from £18.99; plus
cardigans, pyjamas, sailor hats and lots of infant wear. The village also
has two restaurants, a small children's play area and free parking. The
telephone number given here is for the village.

## PEPE JEANS

BICESTER OUTLET SHOPPING VILLAGE, PINGLE DRIVE, BICESTER,
JUNCTION 9 OF M40, OXFORDSHIRE OX6 7WD
☎ (01869) 323200. OPEN 10 - 6 MON - SAT AND BANK HOLIDAYS,
11 - 5 SUN.
One of 48 shops, with more planned, in this factory shopping village
which opened in June 1995. Pepe Jeans sells a wide selection of denim
jeans and jackets as well as coloured jeans and jackets, as well as cords,
waistcoats and donkey jackets. There is a small range of children's
jeans from 134cm upwards. The village also has two restaurants, a
small children's play area and free parking.

## PURPLE FISH

THE GATE HOUSE, CHALFORD INDUSTRIAL ESTATE, CHALFORD, STROUD, GLOUCESTERSHIRE GL6 8NT
☎ (01453) 885010. OPEN 9.30 - 5.30 MON - SAT. MAIL ORDER ON
☎ (01453) 882820.
This mail order children's shoe company now has a trade counter at their warehouse in Stroud. All the shoes are designed by Purple Fish and made in Spain, mostly in leather, though there are some canvas shoes. There are desert boots, clogs, back to school shoes, trainers, toggle boots and Velcro boots. Sizes range up to adult size 8 and there are also adults shoes in the same style as the children's.

## SECONDS OUT

6 GREAT DARKGATE STREET, ABERYSTWYTH, DYFED, WALES
☎ (01970) 611897. OPEN 9.30 - 5 MON - SAT.
Makes clothes for children, men and women, mostly for department stores. The factory shop sells everything from jeans, £9-£13; jodphurs and casual trousers to school uniform items and mini chinos, from £5.

## STEWART SECONDS

12 PIER STREET, ABERSTWYTH, DYFED, WALES
☎ (01970) 611437. OPEN 9 - 5.30 MON - SAT, 11 - 5 SUN IN SUMMER.
14 NOTT SQUARE, CAMARTHEN, DYFED, WALES
☎ (01267) 222294. OPEN 9 - 5.30 MON - SAT.
HARFORD SQUARE, LAMPETER, DYFED, WALES
☎ (01570) 422205. OPEN 9.30 - 5.30 MON - SAT.
52 STEPNEY STREET, LLANELLI, DYFED, WALES
☎ (01554) 776957. OPEN 9 - 5.30 MON - SAT.
Y MAES, PWLLHELI, GWYNEDD, NORTH WALES
☎ (01758) 701130. OPEN 9 - 5.30 MON - SAT.
Branded merchandise from most of the major UK chain stores, all well-known high street department store names. Fashion is usually in season and consists of overcuts, discontinued lines and cancelled orders, as well as some seconds. Apart from fashion for women, men and children, there is also household textiles such as bedding and towels at reduced prices and crockery, glasses and cutlery at competitive prices.

# THE FACTORY SHOP

WESTWARD ROAD, CAINSCROSS, STROUD, GLOUCESTERSHIRE
GL5 4JE
☎ (01453) 756655. OPEN 9 - 5 MON - THUR, SAT, 9 - 6 FRI, 11 - 5 SUN
AND BANK HOLIDAYS.
115 HIGH STREET, NEWCASTLE-UNDER-LYME, STAFFORDSHIRE
ST5 1PS
☎ (01782) 717364. OPEN 9 - 5.30 MON - SAT.
NEW ROAD, PERSHORE, WORCESTERSHIRE WR10 1BY
☎ (01386) 556467. OPEN 9 - 5 MON - SAT, 10.30 - 4.30 SUN AND BANK
HOLIDAYS.
Wide range on sale includes children's, women's and men's clothing
and footwear; household textiles, toiletries, hardware, luggage,
lighting and bedding, most of which are chainstore and high street
brands at discounts of approximately 30%-50%. There are weekly
deliveries and brands include all the major stars: Coloroll, Wrangler
and Dartington to name just three. Lines are continually changing
and few factory shops offer such a variety under one roof.

# THE FACTORY SHOP

NEWLAND, WITNEY, OXFORDSHIRE
☎ (01993) 708338. OPEN 10 - 5 MON - SAT.
Part of the Coats Viyella group which makes clothes for many of the
high street department stores, this medium sized factory shop - not
surprisingly - had many recognisable items on sale. Stocks clothes for
all the family. For children, vests and knickers, 99p each; school
jumpers, £3.99; denim dresses for 10-12 year olds, £9.99; woollen
waistcoats for boys; hat and scarf sets, £1.99; luxury sleepsuits, £3.99.
Stock changes constantly.

# THE SHOE SHED

CASTLEFIELDS, NEWPORT ROAD, STAFFORD, STAFFORDSHIRE
ST16 1BQ
☎ (01785) 211311. OPEN 10 - 4 SEVEN DAYS A WEEK.
Large factory shop selling a vast range of all types of children's,
women's and men's shoes, all of which are perfects, at up to 30%
below normal high street prices.

## TP ACTIVITY TOYS FACTORY SHOP

SEVERN ROAD, STOURPORT-ON-SEVERN, WORCESTER,
WORCESTERSHIRE DY13 9EX
☎ (01299) 827728. 9 - 5 MON - FRI, 9 - 4.30 SAT.
A full range of outdoor and indoor play equipment from swings and
climbing frames to sand trays and tree houses, some of which are discounted at certain times of the year as they are used as display items
and aren't as pristine. There is usually one big factory site sale every
year as well, which is well worth going to. This usually takes place in
October or November. Discounts for firsts are 5%-10% and for
seconds 20%-25% on outdoor items only. Site shop has Galt, Tomy
and masses of toys and games, but not at discounted prices.

## TWEEDMILL FACTORY SHOPPING

LLANNERCH PARK, ST ASAPH, CLYWD, (OFF A55), WALES
☎ (01745) 730072. OPEN 10 - 6 SEVEN DAYS A WEEK.
Has a wide range of clothes, both designer and top end of the high
street, and childrenswear at discounts of up to 60%.

## *Dress Agencies*

## CLIO OF CHELTENHAM

11 IMPERIAL SQUARE, CHELTENHAM, GLOUCESTERSHIRE GL50 1QB
☎ (01242) 226024. OPEN 9.30 - 5 MON - SAT.
Primarily a dress agency for women, Clio has recently added chil-
drenwear to her selection. She also sells secondhand hunting and
riding wear and riding equipment for adults and children.

## LITTLE GEMS

20 COTEN END, WARWICKSHIRE CV34 4NP
☎ (01926) 408248. OPEN 10 - 5 MON - FRI, 10.30 - 4 SAT.
Stocks nearly-new clothes, equipment and some toys for babies to
twelve-year-olds. Labels include Oilily, Jean le Bourget, Chicaloo,
Laura Ashley and Start Smart. Equipment ranges from high chairs
and playpens to prams, buggies and Moses baskets, usually at less
than half the normal retail price. There is also some maternity wear.

## SECOND CHANCE

6A WEST ST, ALDBOURNE, MARLBOROUGH, WILTSHIRE
☎ (01672) 411111. OPEN 10 - 4 TUE - SAT, CLOSED 1 - 2 DAILY.
Small village dress agency which sells "good country clothes as well as
occasional designer clothes" for women and children. Labels include
Windsmoor, Marks & Spencer, Next.

## STOCK EXCHANGE

4 CHURCH STREET, NEWENT, GLOUCESTER
☎ (01531) 821681. OPEN 9 - 4 MON - SAT, CLOSED 1 - 2 DAILY,
AND AT 1 ON WED.
Nearly new shop which also childrenswear from babygros to clothes
for 14-year-olds.

# Hire Shops

## ABC NURSERY HIRE

CONEY HALL, COLLETS GREEN, POWICK, WORCESTERSHIRE
WR2 4SB
☎ (01905) 830456. PHONE FIRST.

## ANGLESEY NURSERY & TOY HIRE

10 GORWEL DEG, RHOSTREHWFA, LLANGEFNI, GWYNEDD LL77 7JL
☎ (01248) 723181. PHONE FIRST.

## BABY BOOM

96 NUFFIELD ROAD, COVENTRY, WEST MIDLANDS CV6 7HW
☎ (01203) 666527. PHONE FIRST.

## BABY BORROWS

4 ST JAMES VIEW, WANTAGE, OXFORDSHIRE OX12 OHT
☎ (01235) 868851. PHONE FIRST.

## BABY HIRE

WYCHWOOD, NORTH BROOK ROAD, COVENTRY, WARWICKSHIRE
CV6 2AJ
☎ (01203) 334787. PHONE FIRST.

## BABY LINES

SUNNYRIDGE, LUSTON, LEOMINSTER, HEREFORDSHIRE HR6 OEB
☎ (015680) 612357. PHONE FIRST.

## CHUCKLES BABY HIRE

THE GRANARY, HALF KEY COURT, MALVERN, WORCESTERSHIRE
WR14 1UP
☎ (01886) 833594. PHONE FIRST.

## HOME AND AWAY

50 ELM GROVE, BROMSGROVE, WORCESTERSHIRE B61 OEJ

☎ (01527) 875188. PHONE FIRST.

## IMPS BABY EQUIPMENT HIRE

18 ST MARY'S ROAD, BEARWOOD, WARLEY, WEST
MIDLANDS B67 5DG

☎ (0121) 420 3266. PHONE FIRST.

## IMPS NURSERY HIRE

3 MAIN STREET, STAPENHILL, BURTON ON TRENT, STAFFORDSHIRE
DE15 9AP

☎ (01238) 511822. PHONE FIRST.

## IMPS NURSERY HIRE

CHURCH FARM, NEW CHURCH, BURTON ON TRENT, STAFFORD-
SHIRE DE13 8RJ

☎ (01283) 75372. PHONE FIRST.

## KIDDICARE

24 OAKDENE ROAD, HEMEL HEMPSTEAD, HERTFORDSHIRE HP3 9TS

☎ (01442) 214559. PHONE FIRST.

## KINDERHIRE LTD

7 BEDINGSTONE DRIVE, STAFFORD, PENKRIDGE, STAFFORDSHIRE
ST19 5TE

☎ (01785) 715060. PHONE FIRST.

## LITTLE GEMS

20 COTEN END, WARWICKSHIRE CV34 4NP

☎ (01926) 408248. OPEN 10 - 5 MON - FRI, 10.30 - 4 SAT.

Nearly-new clothes and equipment for babies to twelve year olds with
a hire service also offered.

## LITTLE MONKEYS

4 HOLLOWFIELDS CLOSE, REDDITCH, WORCESTERSHIRE B98 7NR

☎ (01527) 550988. PHONE FIRST.

## MERCIA SAFEY CENTRE

3 SLADE HILL, HAMPTON MAGNA, NEAR WARWICK, WARWICKSHIRE
CV35 8JA

☎ (01926) 411388. PHONE FIRST.

## MOLD NURSERY HIRE

HAWTHORNS, LLYN-Y-PANDY LANE, MOLD, CLWYD CH7 5JF

☎ (01352) 740250. PHONE FIRST.

## NOW AND THEN

1 LLYS TUDUR, PARK VIEW, RHYL, CLWYD LL18 4AX

☎ (01745) 332530. PHONE FIRST.

## THURSDAYS CHILD

3 OAKWOOD CLOSE, ESSINGTON, WOLVERHAMPTON, WEST
MIDLANDS WV11 2DQ
☎ (01922) 402010. PHONE FIRST.

## TOGS FOR TOTS

LONGACRE HOUSE, NESSCLIFFE, SHREWSBURY, SHROPSHIRE SY4 1BJ
☎ (01743) 81335. PHONE FIRST.

All the above are part of the British Equipment Hirers Association
(BEHA), which has more than 100 members countrywide. A range of
equipment can be hired from high chairs, cots and travel cots to baby
car seats and buggies. Some members also hire out party equipment
including child-sized tables and chairs. BEHA run an advice line
which will try and answer any queries you have regarding hiring
services for children. Phone the Babyline on 0831 310355.

## SMALL TALK EQUIPMENT HIRE

204 OLD BATH ROAD, CHELTENHAM, GLOUCESTERSHIRE GL53 9EQ
☎ (01242) 231902. OPEN EVERY DAY.

Bouncy castles for children's parties; "storks" accouncement boards
and "party" signs. Cots, highchairs, buggies, car seats, safety gates and
toys. All items are bought new specially for hire. Small talk is a
member of the BEHA (British Equipment Hirers Association).

# Secondhand Shops

## KIDS STOCK AND EXCHANGE

UNIT 2, WELLINGTON ROAD, RHYL, CLWYD, NORTH WALE
LL18 1BD
☎ (01745) 330115. OPEN 10 - 5 MON - SAT.

Sells nearly-new baby equipment and also hires out. There are
buggies, stair gates, parasols, raincovers, sterilising equipment, Moses
baskets - and everything parents of young children could want,
including items with famous brand names such as Cosatto. No
children's clothes are stocked.

## LILLIPUT AND JACK IN THE BOX

63 AVON CRESCENT, STRATFORD-UPON-AVON, WARWICKSHIRE
☎ (01789) 267991. OPEN 10 - 4 TUE - SAT.
Children's toys, secondhand clothes, and baby equipment from 0 - 10 years as well as some maternity wear.

# EAST ANGLIA AND EAST MIDLANDS

## *Permanent Discount Outlets*

### BLUNTS

128-132 GRAMBY STREET, LEICESTER LE1 1DL
☎ (0116) 2555959. OPEN 8.30 - 6 MON - SAT 10 - 5 SUN.
Children's shoes from the Clark's, K Shoes and Portland ranges at 40% of the normal shop price for discontinued stock, seconds and ends of ranges. Women's and men's shoes are also stocked. Unbranded children's sale shoes range from £4.99 - £20.

### M C HITCHEN & SONS LTD

7 HIGH STREET, GRANTHAM, LINCOLNSHIRE NG31 6PN
☎ (01476) 590552. OPEN 9.30 - 5.30 MON, 9 - 5.30 TUE - SAT.
Littlewoods sell off their overstocks in a network of shops called M C Hitchen & Sons Ltd. Most of them are in the North of England and offer up to 40% off the catalogue price for clothing and between 50% and 60% off for electrical goods. Littlwoods also run a mobile shop which operates in cities where they don't have a sale shop. For details of further venues for the sales, which usually take place once a month, contact Jean Banks, c/o Crosby DC, Kershaw Avenue, Endbutt Lane, Crosby, Merseyside L70 1AH.

### MATALAN

UNIT 1, WEEDON ROAD INDUSTRIAL ESTATE, TYNE ROAD, NORTHAMPTON NN5 5BE
☎ (01604) 589119. OPEN 10 - 8 MON - FRI, 9.30 - 5.30 SAT, 10 - 6 SUN.
UNIT 1, PHOENIX RETAIL PARK, PHEONIX PARKWAY, CORBY, NORTHAMPTONSHIRE NN17 5DT
☎ (01536) 408042. OPEN 10 - 8 MON - FRI, 9 - 6 SAT, 11 - 5 SUN.

BLACKFRIARS ROAD, KINGS LYNN, NORFOLK PE30 1RX
☎ (01553) 765696. OPEN 10 - 8 MON - FRI, 9 - 6 SAT, 11 - 5 SUN.
EAST STATION ROAD, PETERBOROUGH, CAMBRIDGESHIRE PE2 8AA
☎ (01733) 341229. OPEN 10 - 8 MON - FRI, 9 - 6 SAT, 11 - 5 SUN.
LINDIS RETAIL PARK, TRITTON ROAD, LINCOLN LN6 7QY
☎ (01522) 696541. OPEN 10 - 8 MON - FRI, 9 - 6 SAT, 11 - 5 SUN.
DUDLEY ROAD, SCUNTHORPE DN16 1BA
☎ (01724) 270958. OPEN 10 - 8 MON - FRI, 9 - 6 SAT, 11 - 5 SUN.

As the UK's first National Discount Club, Matalan has the buying power to guarantee its members up to 60% discounts on a huge range of brand name clothing, household goods, luggage and toiletries for all the family. Top quality merchandise, current season, no seconds, is offered to its members at exclusive, permanently discounted prices seven days a week. Matalan operates strictly on a membership basis, one of the key factors for its success in offering 20%-60% savings off recommended retail prices. Membership cards are issued through companies, organisations and associations in the vicinity of the stores, and are available to their employees/members. They are valid at any of the 50 Matalan stores in the UK. To find out if your organisation is registered, phone the Matalan hotline on 01772 629447.

## MRS PICKERING'S DOLLS' CLOTHES

THE PINES, DECOY ROAD, POTTER HEIGHAM, GREAT YARMOUTH, NORFOLK NR29 5LX
☎ (01692) 670407. OPEN 9 - 5 MONDAY - FRIDAY. MAIL ORDER.

A wide selection of dolls' clothes which, Mrs Pickering claims, won't fall to bit straight away, are easy to put on and take off and, especially for smaller children, will help them learn how to use various methods of fastening. All the popular dolls are catered for - including Tiny Tears, Timmy, Katie, Action Man, Sindy, Barbie, Paul, Ken, Skipper and Stacie, as well as Teddies. Special outfits can be made on request. Prices range from 40p for a Barbie-sized skirt, £3 for a wedding dress, £2.25 for a Tiny Tears-sized dress, £1.25 for a nappy. Please send a stamped, addressed envelope for a catalogue, and say you read this in The Good Deal Directory.

# NIPPERS

HALL FARM, FLAWBOROUGH, NOTTINGHAM NG13 9PA
☎ (01949) 851244. FAX 01949 851335. OPENING HOURS VARY SO
PHONE FIRST.
THE MANOR, TUR LANGTON, LEICESTERSHIRE LE8 OPJ
☎ (01858) 545434. FAX (01858) 545774.
HALL FARM, POCKTHORPE ROAD, GREAT MELTON, NEAR
NORWICH, NORFOLK NR9 3BW
☎ (01603) 811711. FAX (01603) 812628. OPENING HOURS VARY SO
PHONE FIRST.

Nippers, the nursery equipment and toy specialists, started with a very clever and simple idea and have now built it up to create an award-winning chain of franchises. The company operates from converted barns on farms around the country, offering easy parking, no queues, and personal service. This is on top of competitive prices on prams, cots, pushchairs, car seats, outdoor play equipment and toys. Prices are low partly because they operate from farms, with none of the overheads of traditional retail outlets, and party because the successful growth of a number of branches means it can now buy in bulk and negotiate good deals. Customers can try out the merchandise and the children can see the animals, mostly sheep, chickens and pigs. Familiar brand names are on sale at all the branches, including Britax, Maclaren and Bebe Confort, Fisher-Price and Little Tikes. You can try out the car seats in your car and there is usually a pram/pushchair repair service on site.

# STAGE TWO

SAVILLE ROAD, WESTWOOD, PETERBOROUGH, CAMBRIDGESHIRE
PE3 7PR
☎ (01733) 263308. OPEN 10 - 8 MON - FRI, 9 - 6 SAT AND BANK
HOLIDAYS.
UNIT 3, TRITTON RETAIL PARK, CENTURION ROAD LINCOLN, LN1
☎ (01522) 560303 OPEN 10 - 8 MON - FRI, 9 - 6 SAT, 10 - 4 BANK
HOLIDAYS.

The names of the stores which sell discontinued line from Freeman's catalogues. The full range is carried, but stock depends on what has not been sold at full price from the catalogue itself, or has been returned or the packaging is damaged or soiled. Clothing discounts range from about 50% - 65%. There are also household items and electrical equipment.

## THE FACTORY SHOP

BARTON BUSINESS CENTRE, BARTON ROAD, BURY ST EDMUNDS,
SUFFOLK 1P32 7BQ
☎ (01284) 701578. OPEN 9.30 - 5.30 MON - FRI, 11 - 5 SUN.

Wide range on sale include children's men's and women's clothing and
footwear, luggage, lighting and bedding, most of which are chain
store and high street brands - including Coloroll, Wrangler and
Dartington - at discounts of between 30%-50%.

# Factory Shops

## A & J CARTER LTD

LONDON ROAD, OADBY, LEICESTER, LEICESTERSHIRE
☎ (0116) 2712939. OPEN 1.30 - 4.30 MON, TUE, 9 - 12 AND 1.30 - 4.30
WED, 1.30 - 4.30 THUR, 9 - 12 FRI AND SAT.

Manufacturers for top children's brand names and top London department stores, they specialise in clothes for infants, children and
teenagers. Summerwear includes jersey sundresses, T-shirts and
skirts/shorts sets, pyjamas, babygros, leggings. Sundresses cost £5.99 in
stripes, dots and plain jersey; skirt and top sets, £5.99; T-shirts, £2.99.

## BALLY FACTORY SHOP

HALL ROAD, NORWICH, NORFOLK NR4 6DP
☎ (01603) 760590. OPEN 9.30 - 5.30 MON - FRI, 9 - 5.30 SAT AND MOST
BANK HOLIDAYS - PHONE FIRST.

The Bally factory shop is situated next to the main factory and sells
women's, men's and children's footwear, and accessories for women
and men such as hosiery, socks, scarves, shoe horns and shoe care
products. Also sold are leather handbags, briefcases, suitcovers,
holdalls and overnight cases. Most of the merchandise is rejects, sub-
standard, ends of line of ex-sale stock and is priced from £5-£200,
which is usually at least one-third off the recommended retail price.
There is also a coffee shop which serves morning coffee, light lunches
and afternoon teas, a children's play area, toilet facilities, free parking
and disabled facilities. Within the factory shop, there is also a full
price department which sells all the current styles. A small "museum"
is incorporated within the shop showing the history of shoe-making

since the Roman times and the history of Bally, with examples of shoes on display. Coach parties are welcome by prior arrangement. Factory tours are not available.

## BARRATT'S SALE SHOP

BARRACK ROAD, KINGSTHORPE HOLLOW, NORTHAMPTON, NORTHAMPTONSHIRE
☎ (01604) 718632. OPEN 9 - 5.30 MON - SAT.

Reject trainers and ex-window display shoes at factory prices among a range of perfect shoes, the latter of which are sold at sale prices.

## BYFORDS

PO BOX 63, ABBEY LANE, LEICESTER, LEICESTERSHIRE
☎ (0116) 2611135. OPEN 9.30 - 5 MON - SAT.
70 - 74 BELGRAVE GATE, LEICESTER, LEICESTERSHIRE LE1 3GQ
☎ (0116) 2518003. OPEN 9 - 5.30 MON - FRI, 9 - 5 SAT.
FACTORY STREET, SHEPSHED, LEICESTER LE12 9AQ
☎ (01509) 503068. OPEN 10 - 5 MON, 9 - 5 TUE - SAT.

Part of the Coats Viyella group, which makes clothes for - among others - Marks & Spencer, they have overstocks and clearance lines which are sold through the 40 factory shops which are also part of the group. Frequent shoppers at M&S will recognise many of the garments on sale, despite the lack of the well-known St Michael's label. Children's clothes are not stocked in great quantities, but can include jackets, trousers, T-shirts and jumpers, dresses and hosiery. The factory shops also offer a 28-day money back guarantee. There are weekly deliveries to constantly update the merchandise.

## CHARNOS

AMBER BUSINESS CENTRE, GREENHILL LANE, RIDDINGS, DERBYSHIRE
☎ (01773) 540408. OPEN 10 - 4 TUE - FRI, 9.30 - 1 SAT.
CORPORATION ROAD, ILKESTON, DERBYSHIRE
☎ (0115) 9440301. OPEN 10 - 4 TUE - FRI, 9.30 - 1 SAT.
NOTTINGHAM ROAD, LONGEATON, NOTTINGHAMSHIRE
☎ (0115) 9730345. OPEN 10 - 4 TUE - FRI, 9.30 - 1 SAT.

Although about 25% of the shop is given over to discontinued perfects of the famous Charnos lingerie at discounts of 25%-50%, the rest of the shop stocks bought-in bedding, towelling and babywear at very competitive prices. Some stock is grade B quality.

## COURTAULDS CHILDRENSWEAR

NIX HILL, ALFRETON, DERBYSHIRE DE55 7FQ
☎ (01773) 833421. OPEN 9 - 5 MON - SAT.
Sells extensive range of casual wear for girls and boys from birth to
twelve years, men's and women's clothes, as well as seconds and
bought-in-stock in bedding, towels, duvets and pillows at discounts
of 30%-50%. About half the stock is perfect, the other half seconds.
Children's wear includes tights and underwear from £1.25, cord
trousers, knitwear, coats, thermal socks from 99p to £1.25, sweatshirts, from £9.99, joggers from £11.99, and shirts from £6.99.

## COURTAULDS MERIDIAN

HAYDN ROAD, NOTTINGHAMSHIRE MG5 1DH
☎ (0115) 9246100. OPEN 9 - 5 MON - FRI, 9 - 5.30 SAT, 10 - 4 SUN.
Factory shop sells a large range of children's clothes from twelve
months to about 7 or 8 years including underwear, socks, knitwear,
jeans, trousers, skirts, dresses, leisurewear, and coats for boys and girls.
They also sell the Zobit baby range for the nursery; cot quilts, pram
quilts, duvets, curtains and lamp shades. There is also some bedding
with Peter Pan and Mr Blobby designs. Discounts average 30%. Take
time out at the coffee shop and don't worry about parking as there's a
car park on site.

## COURTAULDS TEXTILES

ALLENBY INDUSTRIAL ESTATE, CROFTON CLOSE, MONKS ROAD,
LINCOLN LN2 5QT
☎ (01522) 539859. OPEN 9 - 5 MON - SAT.
Factory shop in Lincoln selling children's women's and men's clothes,
including seconds from other chainstores. Discounts are usually at
least 20% and stock changes constantly.

## CROCKERS

111 FRONT STREET, ARNOLD, NOTTINGHAMSHIRE NG5 7ED
☎ (0115) 9674212. OPEN 9 - 6 MON - SAT, 10 - 4 SUN,
10 - 5 BANK HOLIDAYS.
Clarks International operate a chain of factory shops nationally which
specialise in selling discontinued lines and slight sub-standards for
children, women and men from Clarks, K Shoes and other famous
brands. These shops trade under the name of Crockers, K Shoes

Factory shop or Clarks Factory Shop and while not all are physically attached to a shoe factory, these shops are treated as factory shops by the company. Customers can expect to find an extensive range of quality shoes, sandals, walking boots, slippers, trainers, handbags, accessories and gifts, while their major outlets also offer luggage, sports clothing, sports equipment and outdoor clothing. Brands stocked include Clarks, K Shoes, Springer, CICA, Hi-Tec, Puma, Mercury, Dr Martens, Nike, LA Gear, Fila, Mizuno, Slazenger, Weider, Samsonite, Delsey, Antler and Carlton, although not all are sold in every outlet. Discounts are on average 30% off the normal high street price for perfect stock.

## DAVENPORT STANNARD KNITWEAR LTD

NORTHOLME ROAD, LOUTH, LINCOLNSHIRE LN11 OHR
☎ (01507) 601951. OPEN 9 - 12 LAST SAT OF EACH MONTH ONLY.
Opens its factory shop to the public one morning a month only, selling brand name baby and toddler wear which is manufactured for well-known children's high street stores. The factory shop offers vast savings on high street prices for baby clothes up to the age of four years, and also on a small selection of ladies sweaters.

## GLOVERALL PLC

LONDON ROAD, WELLINGBOROUGH, NORTHAMPTONSHIRE
☎ (01933) 225183. OPEN 10 - 5 MON - FRI, CLOSED MON IN WINTER.
The award-winning duffle coat and jacket manufacturer has a factory shop which sells their good quality clothes at less than half the normal retail price. There are woollen mix duffle coats, anoraks, car rugs and scarves on sale here, most of which are obsolete styles, end of ranges or export rejects. Chidren's duffle coats start at £20, ladies at £38, reefer jackets cost from £50, down-filled anoraks at £45. All lengths of duffle coats are stocked for children, men and women.

## GYMPHLEX SPORTSWEAR

BOSTON ROAD, HORNCASTLE, LINCOLNSHIRE
☎ (01507) 523243.

Holds a one-day factory shop sale just once a year, usually in early spring. Your chance to buy a huge range of sportswear for all the family: jogging pants, tracksuits, rugby and football shirts, rugby shorts. Some of the stock is seconds, some overmakes. The rest is freshly-made stock which is especially reduced for the sale.

## LORIEN TEXTILES

COOKSON STREET, KIRKBY-IN-ASHFIELD, NOTTINGHAMSHIRE
☎ (01623) 757748. OPEN 9 - 4.30 MON - FRI.

Manufactures nightwear and underwear for children and women, mostly for Etam and BhS, and sells overmakes and ends of lines in the factory shop.

## PARK CLOTHING

212 NARBOROUGH ROAD SOUTH, NEAR FOSSE, LEICESTER,
LEICESTERSHIRE LE3 2LD
☎ (0116) 2825047. OPEN 10 - 5 MON - SAT.

Park Clothing is a children's knitwear manufacturer with contracts with some of the major high street stores. Its factory shop, which is attached to the factory and warehouse, sells current and previous season's perfect stock at discounts of up to 50%. As well as children's knitwear and dresses in wool, cotton, acrylic and mixed fibres for 0-8 year olds from £8, there is also a range of women's clothes bought in from other manufacturers. Blouses cost from £7.99-£19.99, and skirts range from £7.99-£17. There is also a range of teenage clothing consisting of fashionable tops and dresses.

## SHEERS LTD

ST MARY'S ST, EYNNESBURY, ST NEOTS, CAMBRIDGESHIRE PE19 2PA
☎ (01480) 473476. OPEN 10 - 12 TUES, WED, 10 - 12 & 2 - 3.30 THUR.

Factory shop selling chainstore seconds in lingerie at up to 50% discount as well as bought-in children's and babies underwear, babygros, cot quilts and towels at competitive prices.

## START-RITE

8 HIGH STREET, KING'S LYNN, NORFOLK P30 1EJ
☎ (01553) 760786. OPEN 9 - 5.30 MON - SAT.
The children's shoe experts have a large factory shop selling clearance lines at discounts of one third, and rejects at discounts of fifty percent. They don't stock the full range - it's a matter of choosing from what's available.

## THE FACTORY SHOP

SOUTH GREEN, EAST DEREHAM, NORFOLK NR19 1PR
☎ (01362) 691868. OPEN 9 - 5 MON - SAT, 10 - 4 SOME BANK HOLIDAYS.
THE FACTORY SHOP, NEWBOLD FOOTWEAR, BROOK STREET, SILEBY, LEICESTERSHIRE LE12 7RF
☎ (01509) 813514. OPEN 9 - 5 MON - SAT.
Wide range on sale includes children's, men's and women's clothing and footwear; household textiles, toiletries, hardware, luggage, lighting and bedding, most of which are chainstore and high street brands at discounts of approximately 30%-50%. There are weekly deliveries and brands include all the major stars: Coloroll, Wrangler and Dartington to name just three. Lines are continually changing and few factory shops offer such a variety under one roof.

## THE SHOE FACTORY SHOP

TRAFFIC STREET, EAGLE CENTRE, DERBY, DERBYSHIRE
☎ (01332) 372823. OPEN 9 - 5 MON - SAT.
20 BROAD STREET, NOTTINGHAM
☎ (0115) 924 2390. OPEN 10 - 5 MON - FRI, 9.30 - 5.30 SAT.
CONSTANCE ROAD, LEICESTER
☎ (0116) 249 0114. OPEN 10 - 5 MON - FRI, 9 - 5 SAT.
Children's, women's and men's shoes and accessories which are bought in from other manufacturers including Spanish, Portuguese and Italian companies. All are unbranded. The range covers from mocassins to dressy shoes.

## THE SHOE SHED

ELLIS STREET, KIRKBY-IN-ASHFIELD, NOTTINGHAMSHIRE NG17 7AL
☎ (01623) 723083. OPEN 9 - 5 MON - SAT.
Large factory shop selling a vast range of all types of children's, men's and women's shoes, all of which are perfects, at up to 30% below normal high street prices.

# THE WORKSOP FACTORY SHOP

RAYMOTH LANE, WORKSOP, NOTTINGHAMSHIRE
☎ (01909) 472841. OPEN 9 - 5 MON - SAT, 10 - 4 SUN.

Manufacturers for top chainstores, the factory shop sells over-runs and returns in household textiles, bedding, fashion for all the family, including knitwear and underwear at discount of 20%-40%. The factory shop is 10,000 sq ft and most of the stock is clothing with good availability on colours and sizes. There is general babywear and children's clothes up to the age of nine or ten including underwear, coats, mits, helmets, towels, baby baskets, babygros, as well as the Zorbit baby range of pretty bedding, cot quilts and nursery accessories such as lampshades.

# *Dress Agencies*

## CASTAWAYS

10 BURTON ROAD, LINCOLN LN1 3LB
☎ (01522) 546035. OPEN 9.30 - 4.30 MON - SAT, CLOSED WEDS.

Cheery corner shop in upper Lincoln which specialises in almost-new children's clothing, nursery equipment and toys, as well as ladies fashions, accessories and maternity wear.

## DINDY'S

HAWSTEAD HOUSE, HAWSTEAD, BURY ST EDMUNDS, SUFFOLK
IP29 5NL
☎ (01284) 388276. OPEN 10 - 4 TUE & THUR, 10 - 1 SAT. CLOSED DURING STATE SCHOOL HOLIDAYS.

Set in a converted stables, Dindy's sells high quality second hand clothes for ladies as well as a range of children's clothes from three years up to teenagers. Children's partywear ranges from Liberty to David Charles from £18-£30, plus jackets and ties for boys.

## GLAD RAGS

24 HIGH STREET, HADLEIGH, IPSWICH, SUFFOLK
☎ (01473) 827768. OPEN 9.30 - 4 TUE, THUR - SAT.

Range of nearly-new outfits for women as well as childrenswear both English and Continental for 0-10 year olds.

## ORCHIDS

3 PARK STREET, TOWCESTER, NORTHAMPTON NH12 6DQ
☎ (01327) 358455. OPEN 9.30 - 5 MON - SAT, AND 7 - 8 WED EVENING.
Sells women's and children's as-new clothes. The children's range is from birth to twelve years, with more girl's outfits than boy's, and includes snowsuits and coats, with labels from Marks & Spencer, Mothercare and Gap to Osh Kosh and Oilily.

## THE UPPINGHAM DRESS AGENCY

2-6 ORANGE STREET, UPPINGHAM, RUTLAND LE15 9SQ
☎ (01572) 823276. OPEN 9 - 5.30 MON - SAT, 12 - 4 SUN.
One of the oldest and possibly the largest dress agency in the country with 10 rooms on three floors packed with quality nearly-new clothing for children, men and women. Preference is given to designer labels, but better quality high street names are also stocked. The proprietors are very selective about the condition and all stock is carefully vetted.

# Hire Shops

## ABBEY NURSERY HIRE

183C DUFFIELD ROAD, DARLEY ABBEY, DERB, DERBYSHIRE DE22 1JB
☎ (01332) 558766. PHONE FIRST.

## ABSOLUTE BEGINNERS

162 RADCLIFFE ROAD, WEST BRIDGFORD, NOTTINGHAM,
NOTTINGHAMSHIRE NG2 5HF
☎ (0115) 9818135. PHONE FIRST.

## NIKKIS NURSERY HIRE

1 RECTORY FARM COTTAGE, ROOKERY ROAD, STRETTON OAKHAM,
RUTLAND LE15 7RA
☎ (01780) 410359. PHONE FIRST.

## NURSERY HIRE

FIELD COTTAGE, MARCH LANE, FELIXSTOWE, SUFFOLK IP11 9RW
☎ (01394) 282351. PHONE FIRST.

## PLAYSAFE NURSERY HIRE

14 BELMONT DRIVE, COALVILLE, LEICESTERSHIRE LE67 3LQ
☎ (01530) 831119. PHONE FIRST.
2A SWANNINGTON ROAD, RAVENSTONE, LEICESTERSHIRE LE67 3NE
☎ (01530) 813136. PHONE FIRST.

## TINY TRAVELLERS B.E. HIRE

54 ANDREW GOODALL CLOSE, TOFTWOOD, DEREHAM, NORFOLK
NR19 1SR
☎ (01362) 697150. PHONE FIRST.

All the above are part of the British Equipment Hirers Association
(BEHA), which has more than 100 members countrywide. BEHA
run an advice line which will try and answer any queries you have
regarding hiring services for children. Phone the Babyline on 0831
310355.

## BABY RENT

14 THE BOLTONS, SOUTH WOOTTON, KING'S LYNN, NORFOLK
PE30 3NG
☎ (01553) 674200. OPEN WEEKDAY EVES, SOME MORNINGS, SAT
MORNINGS, PHONE FIRST.

Hires out nursery equipment from prams and pushchairs to cots, car
seats and high chairs. Hire periods can be from weekends to six
months and start at £5.

## CUDDLES NURSERY HIRE

1A PARKWAY, WESTON FAVELL, NORTHAMPTON,
NORTHAMPTONSHIRE NN3 3PS
☎ (0604 4) 11233. OPEN MON - SAT BY APPOINTMENT.

Specialises in car seats, enabling the parent to try the child in the car
seat first, and emphasising the safety angle. Minimum hire is for six
months and costs from £9.50 to £19.50 depending on the model.
Cuddles also hires out travel cots, christening wear, high chairs,
pushchairs and backpacks. Minimum hire is for four nights. The
customer has to pick up the items. Cuddles also sells a full range of
nursery equipment, either new or former hire, and a range of broderie
Anglaise and satin christening wear from £15-£45.

# NORTH WEST, YORKSHIRE AND HUMBERSIDE

## *Permanent Discount Outlets*

### BARGAIN STREET

BUY WELL SHOPPING CENTRE, THORPE ARCH TRADING ESTATE, WETHERBY, WEST YORKSHIRE
☎ (01937) 845650. OPEN 9 - 5 MON - FRI, 9.30 - 5.30 SAT, 10.30 - 4.30 SUN.
A wide range of ex-catalogue items from men's, women's and children's clothes to leisure wear, sports gear, underwear, household goods, linen, electrical equipment such as tvs, music centres and vacuum cleaners, and toys. Prices are usually about 50%-70% off the catalogue prices with extra discounts on certain days. Quality is variable and stock changes constantly.

### FINSLEY MILL SHOP

FINSLEY GATE, BURNLEY, LANCASHIRE
☎ (01282) 425641. OPEN 9.30 - 5 MON - FRI, 9 - 4 SAT.
Sells high street brand name children's shoes at discounts of up to 50% from toddlers' size upwards. Slippers, trainers, Wellingtons, school and party shoes are on sale here, as well as a small range of clothes from time to time; all this season's stock. Also some pottery.

### GREAT CLOTHES

84 YORK ROAD, LEEDS, WEST YORKSHIRE
☎ (0113) 2350303. OPEN 9.30 - 9 MON - FRI, 9.30 - 6 SAT, 11 - 5 SUN.
Clothes for men, women and children from French Connection, Adidas, Pringle, Farah, Puma, Christian Dior to Jacqmar and including all brands of jeans. Levi's costs from £35.99; full-length button-through dress, £12.99. There are also accessories such as socks, shoes, hats, scarves and underwear. All stock is current season and is discounted by 25%-30%.

# M C HITCHEN & SONS LTD

C/O CROSBY DC, KERSHAW AVENUE, ENDBUTT LANE, CROSBY,
MERSEYSIDE L70 1AH
☎ (0151) 928 6611.
116 ST JAMES STREET, BURNLEY, LANCASHIRE BB11 1NL
☎ (01282) 425615. OPEN 9.30 - 5.30 MON, WED - FRI, 9.30 - 4.30 TUE,
9 - 5.30 SAT.
602-608 ATTERCLIFFE ROAD, SHEFFIELD, SOUTH YORKSHIRE S9 3QS
☎ (0114) 2441611. OPEN 9.30 - 5.30 MON - SAT.
102 DEANSGATE, BOLTON, GREATER MANCHESTER BL1 1 BD
☎ (01204) 384969. OPEN 9.30 - 5.30 MON - WED, 9 - 5.30 THUR - SAT.
185 STAMFORD STREET, ASHTON-UNDER-LYME, GREATER
MANCHESTER OL6 7PY
☎ (0161) 339 0966. OPEN 9 - 5.30 MON - SAT, UNTIL 5.15 ON THUR.
160 MARINE ROAD, CENTRAL MORECAMBE, LANCASHIRE LA4 4BU
☎ (01524) 412074. OPEN 9.30 - 5.30 MON, 9 - 5.30 TUE - SAT.
C/O LITTLEWOODS SHOPPING CITY, RUNCORN, CHESHIRE
☎ (01928) 717777. OPEN 9 - 5 MON - SAT.
69 - 74 LORD STREET, FLEETWOOD, LANCASHIRE FY7 6DS
☎ (01253) 773418. OPEN 9 - 5.30 MON - SAT.
UNIT 3, MONUMENT BUILDINGS, LONDON ROAD, LIVERPOOL
L3 8JY
☎ (0151) 708 6118. OPEN 9 - 5.30 MON - SAT.

Littlewoods sell off their overstocks in a network of shops called M C
Hitchen & Sons Ltd. Most of them are in the North of England and
offer up to 40% off the catalogue price for clothing and between 50%
and 60% off for electrical goods. Littlwoods also run a mobile shop
which operates in cities where they don't have a sale shop. For details
of further venues for the sales, which usually take place once a month,
contact Jean Banks, c/o Crosby DC, Kershaw Avenue, Endbutt Lane,
Crosby, Merseyside L70 1AH.

# MATALAN

HOLME ROAD, BAMBER BRIDGE, PRESTON, LANCASHIRE PR5 6BP
☎ (01772) 627365. OPEN 10 - 8 MON - FRI, 9.30 - 5.30 SAT, 10 - 6 SUN.
UNIT 1, RED ROSE CENTRE, REGENT ROAD, SALFORD M5 3GR
☎ (061) 848 0792. OPEN 10 - 8 MON - FRI, 9.30 - 5.30 SAT, 10 - 6 SUN.
UNIT 29, GREYHOUND RETAIL PARK, SEALAND ROAD, CHESTER
CH1 1QG
☎ (01244) 380877. OPEN 10 - 8 MON - FRI, 9.30 - 5.30 SAT, 10 - 6 SUN.
UNIT 13, THE WHEATLEY CENTRE, WHEATLEY HALL ROAD,
DONCASTER DN2 4PE
☎ (0302) 760444. OPEN 10 - 8 MON - FRI, 9.30 - 5.30 SAT, 10 - 6 SUN.

UNIT 4B, STADIUM WAY RETAIL PARK, PARKGATE, ROTHERHAM
S60 1TG
☎ (01709) 780173. OPEN 10 - 8 MON - FRI, 9.30 - 5.30 SAT, 10 - 6 SUN.
UNIT 10 & 11, CLIFTON MOORE COURT, YORK YO3 4XZ
☎ (01904) 693080. OPEN 10 - 8 MON - FRI, 9 - 5 SAT, 9.30 - 6 SUN.
NEW CHESTER ROAD, BROMBOROUGH, SOUTH WIRRAL L62 7EK
☎ (0151) 343 9494. OPEN 10 - 8 MON - FRI, 10 - 6 SAT, SUN.
SEFTON RETAIL PARK, DUNNINGS BRIDGE ROAD, BOOTLE,
MERSEYSIDE L30 6UU
☎ (0151) 525 1190. OPEN 10 - 8 MON - FRI, 9.30 - 5.30 SAT, 10 - 6 SUN.
UNIT 3, ALEXANDRA COURT, OLDHAM, LANCASHIRE OL4 1SG
☎ (0161) 620 6686. OPEN 10 - 8 MON - FRI, 9.30 - 5.30 SAT, 10 - 6 SUN.
WESTOVER STREET, OFF STATION ROAD, SWINTON N27 2AH
☎ (0161) 794 3441. OPEN 10 - 8 MON - FRI, 9 - 6 SAT, 11 - 5 SUN.
UNIT 1, GREENMOUNT RETAIL PARK, PELLON ROAD, HALIFAX
HX1 5QN
☎ (01422) 383051. OPEN 10 - 8 MON - FRI, 9 - 5.30 SAT, 11 - 5 SUN.
UNIT 2, CLIFTON RETAIL PARK, CLIFTON ROAD, BLACKPOOL
FY4 4US
☎ (01253) 697850. OPEN 10 - 8 MON - FRI, 9 - 6 SAT, 11 - 5 SUN.
UNITS G & H, THE TRIUMPH CENTRE, HUNTS CROSS,
LIVERPOOL L24 9GB
☎ (0151) 486 0325. OPEN 10 - 8 MON - FRI, 9 - 6 SAT, 11 - 5 SUN.
WINWICK ROAD, KERFOOT STREET, WARRINGTON, CHESHIRE
WA2 8NU
☎ (01925) 235365. OPEN 10 - 8 MON - FRI, 9 - 6 SAT, 11 - 5 SUN.
TONGE MOOR ROAD, BOLTON, GREATER MANCHESTER BL2 2DJ
☎ (01204) 383733. OPEN 10 - 8 MON - FRI, 9 - 6 SAT, 11 - 5 SUN.
☎ (051) 525 1190. OPEN 10 - 8 MON - FRI, 9.30 - 5.30 SAT, 10 - 6 SUN.
UNIT 3, ALEXANDRA COURT, OLDHAM, LANCASHIRE OL4 1SG
☎ (061) 620 6686. OPEN 10 - 8 MON - FRI, 9.30 - 5.30 SAT, 10 - 6 SUN.
UNIT 2, KINGSTONE RETAIL PARK, HULL HU2 2TX
☎ (01482) 586184. OPEN 10 - 8 MON - FRI, 9.30 - 5.30 SAT, 10 - 6 SUN.
UNIT 13, THE WHEATLEY CENTRE, WHEATLEY HALL ROAD,
DONCASTER DN2 4PE
☎ (01302) 760444. OPEN 10 - 8 MON - FRI, 9 - 6 SAT, 11 - 5 SUN.

As the UK's first National Discount Club, Matalan has the buying
power to guarantee its members up to 60% discounts on a huge range
of brand name clothing, household goods, luggage and toiletries for
all the family. Top quality merchandise, current season, no seconds, is
offered to its members at exclusive, permanently discounted prices
seven days a week. Matalan operates strictly on a membership basis,
one of the key factors for its success in offering 20%-60% savings off

recommended retail prices. Membership cards are issued through companies, organisations and associations in the vicinity of the stores, and are available to their employees/members. They are valid at any of the 50 Matalan stores in the UK. To find out if your organisation is registered, phone the Matalan hotline on 01772 629447.

## MR BABY

4 ST JOHN'S ROAD, HUDDERSFIELD, WEST YORKSHIRE
☎ (01484) 515381. OPEN 9 - 5.30 MON - SAT.
Sells reconditioned, seconds and former showroom models of the Mamas & Papas range, as well as full price infant clothes and nursery equipment from other manufacturers. It sometimes has discounted pram samples from Maclaren and Silver Cross, reduced by about £40, as well as everything for the nursery. Infant clothes include Baby-Mini and Petit Bateau.

## NIPPERS

RECTORY FARM, MIDDLE STREET, NAFFERTON, DRIFFIELD, HUMBERSIDE YO25 OJS
☎ (01377) 240689. FAX (01377) 240687. OPENING HOURS VARY SO PHONE FIRST.
Nippers, the nursery equipment and toy specialists, started with a very clever and simple idea and have now built it up to create an award-winning chain of franchises. The company operates from converted barns on farms around the country, offering easy parking, no queues, and personal service. This is on top of competitive prices on prams, cots, pushchairs, car seats, outdoor play equipment and toys. Prices are low partly because they operate from farms, with none of the overheads of traditional retail outlets, and party because the successful growth of a number of branches means it can now buy in bulk and negotiate good deals. Customers can try out the merchandise and the children can see the animals, mostly sheep, chickens and pigs. Familiar brand names are on sale at all the branches, including Britax, Maclaren and Bebe Confort, Fisher-Price and Little Tikes. You can try out the car seats in your car and there is usually a pram/pushchair repair service on site.

## READMANS LTD

ALFRED HOUSE, SPENCE LANE, HOLBECK, LEEDS, WEST YORKSHIRE
LS12 1EF
☎ (0113) 2444960 DRAPERY.
☎ (0113) 2436355 CASH AND CARRY.
Mainly children's, men's and women's clothing as well as bedding,
textiles, footwear, towels at prices which are cheaper than the high
street.

## TK MAXX

15 PARKER ST, OFF CLAYTON SQUARE, LIVERPOOL, MERSEYSIDE
☎ (0151) 708 9919. OPEN 9 - 6 MON - SAT.
Based on an American concept, TK Maxx is the first British retailer
to practise "off-price" retailing. This means a centrally located store
which offers famous label goods with up to 60% savings off recommended retail prices. TK Maxx has fashion for the whole family -
children's, men's and womenswear - accessories, shoes, gifts, kitchenware and home goods. Everything in the store is branded with a
choice of well-known high street names to designer labels, and while
a small percentage mightly be clearly marked past season, the great
majority of items in store are current season, current stock and still
with phenomenal savings. There is a huge choice with 50,000 pieces
in store with 5,000 new items arriving a week, so it's worth keeping
abreast of the lastest deliveries as turnaround is very fast. One of the
ways in which TK Maxx is able to offer such low prices is by running
a very low-cost operation, so the stores are simple and unfussy with
wide aisles, shopping trolleys and baskets, and a spacious, functional
feel to them. Service is not compromised, however: there are individual changing rooms, ramps for buggies and wheelchairs, plenty of
staff on the shop floor and all the branches accept all major credit and
debit cards.

# Factory Shops

## BABYWORLD

HALLAM MILL, HALLAM STREET, HEAVILEY, STOCKPORT, CHESHIRE
☎ (0161) 477 9999. OPEN 9.30 - 5 MON - SAT.
WARWICK MILL, OLDHAM ROAD, MIDDLETON
☎ (0161) 653 7117. OPEN 9 - 5 MON - SAT.

Cots, prams, pushchairs and car seats to nursery bedding. The bedding is made at the factory in Middleton and is thus sold at rock-bottom prices. There are cot sheets, pram sheets, cot quilts, bumper sets, changing bags, foot muffs, curtains, lamp shades, nappy stackers and cot tidies. The company is also a main agent for Mamas & Papas, MacLaren, Chicco, Bebe Confort, Cosatto and Cumfifolda and many more nursery equipment makers and try to ensure the prices of their cots, prams etc, are kept very competitive.

## BENETTON

CHESHIRE OAKS OUTLET VILLAGE, KINSEY ROAD, NEAR ELLESMERE PORT, (JUNCTION 10 OF M53), SOUTH WIRRAL L65 9JJ
☎ (0151) 357 3131. OPEN 10 - 6 MON - SAT, 10 - 4 SUN.

The usual well-known range of Benetton clothes for children and women sold in this factory shopping centre. There were lots of seconds here when we visited in May 1995, each garment market with a sticky circle where the garment was torn or marked.

## BURBERRY

WOODROW UNIVERSAL, JUNCTION MILLS, CROSS HILLS, NEAR KEIGHLEY, YORKSHIRE BD20 7SE
☎ (01535) 633364. OPEN 11 - 5 MON - FRI, 10 - 4 SAT.
CORONATION MILLS, ALBION STREET, CASTLEFORD, WEST YORKSHIRE
☎ (0197) 755 4411. OPEN 10 - 3.45 MON - FRI, 9.30 - 1.15 SAT.

These Burberry factory shops sell seconds and overmakes of the famous name raincoats and duffle coats as well as accessories such as the distinctive umbrellas, scarves and handbags. They also sell children's duffle coats, knitwear and shirts, as well as some of the Burberry range of food: jams, biscuits, tea and chocolate. All carry the Burberry label and are about one third of the normal retail price.

## CATAMINI

CHESHIRE OAKS OUTLET VILLAGE, KINSEY ROAD, NEAR ELLESMERE
PORT, JUNCTION 10 OF M53, SOUTH WIRRAL L65 9JJ
☎ (0151) 357 1521. OPEN 10 - 6 MON - SAT, 10 - 4 SUN.

A wide range of beautiful baby's and children's clothes from the
famous Babymini range. Those who have bought this label will know
that it is not cheap and even in the factory shop, prices are still sufficiently high to make you catch your breath. However, the range is
unusual and very attractive.

## CHESHIRE OAKS DESIGNER OUTLET VILLAGE

JUNCTION 10 OF THE M53, NEAR ELLESMERE PORT, SOUTH WIRRAL
L65 9JJ
☎ (0151) 356 7932. OPEN 10 - 6 MON - SAT, 10 - 4 SUN AND BANK
HOLIDAYS.

More than 30 outlets, all selling brand name merchandise at discounted prices, with more outlets in the pipeline. Labels for teenagers
and children include Levi's, Jeffrey Rogers, Benetton, Kurt Geiger,
Equator luggage, Sears womenswear (Richards, Wallis, Warehouse)
trading as Collective, Principles/Burton, Fruit of the Loom, Catamini
childrenswear, the British Shoe Corporation trading as Famous
Footwear, and JoKids. There is a children's play area, a Garfunkels
restaurant and free car parking. Phase two opens in November 1995
with 30 more factory shops.

## COURTAULDS TEXTILES

WIGAN PIER COMPLEX, TRENCHERFIELD MILL, WIGAN,
LANCASHIRE WN3 4ES
☎ (01942) 239531. OPEN 9.15 - 4.30 MON - FRI, 10 - 3.30 SAT.

Stocks only bedding and textiles. It carries the Zorbit baby range; cot
and pram quilts, sheets and blankets, curtains and lampshades. Also
children's bedding manufactured for Marks & Spencer, including
single bed sets with Mickey Mouse, Lion King, Sonic the Hedgehog
and dinosaur designs.

# DALESOX

6 SWADFORD STREET, SKIPTON, NORTH YORKSHIRE BD23 1JA
☎ (01756) 796509. OPEN 9 - 5 SEVEN DAYS A WEEK.
Based in Skipton's main shopping area, Dalesox sells quality hosiery
and accessories. Most are perfect children's, men's and ladies socks
made for the best high street chainstores and cost about £1-£1.50 a
pair, normal retail price up to £4.99. There is lots of design choice
from Disney character socks to Christmas pudding socks. There are
also ties, ski socks, unusual design Swedish polyester ties, knickers,
boxer shorts, pyjamas and nightshirts. Most of the stock is bought in
from other manufacturers, cutting out the middleman.

# DAMART FACTORY CLEARANCE SHOP

UNIT 6A, ALSTON ROAD RETAIL PARK, BYPASS ROUNDABOUT,
BRADFORD ROAD, KEIGHLEY BD21 3NG
☎ (01535) 690648. OPEN 9 - 5.30 MON - SAT, 10 - 4 SUN AND BANK
HOLIDAYS.
Discontinued branded chainstore fashion for children, men and
women, some of which is branded Damart, as well as household
items: kitchen utensils, glassware, towels, tablecloths, brushes, mops
but no electrical equipment. Most of the stock is bought in from
other manufacturers and consists of overmakes and discontinued lines
at discounts of 50%. Coffee shop on site.

# FAMOUS FOOTWEAR

CHESHIRE OAKS OUTLET VILLAGE, KINSEY ROAD, NEAR ELLESMERE
PORT, JUNCTION 10 OF M53, SOUTH WIRRAL L65 9JJ
☎ (0151) 357 1512. OPEN 10 - 6 MON - SAT, 10 - 4 SUN.
Wide range of brand names including Dolcis, Roland Cartier,
Saxone, Lotus, K Shoes, Barker, Ava, Miss Selfridge, Cable & Co,
Hush Puppies, Van-Dal, Equity, Ecco and Vagabond all at discount
prices.

## FOSC (FACTORY OUTLET SHOPPING CENTRE)

HULL ROAD, YORK, YORKSHIRE YO1 3JA
☎ (01904) 430481. OPEN 10 - 6 SEVEN DAYS A WEEK.
Branded merchandise from more than 50 manufacturers which initially consisted of ends of lines, surplus stock, cancelled orders and slight seconds but is more likely now to be firsts. Some of the best-known high street names are here, including clothing from Courtaulds, children's clothes and toys at discounts of between 30%-70%. There is also a cafe, free car parking, disabled facilities and no membership is necessary.

## FREEPORT SHOPPING VILLAGE

ANCHORAGE ROAD, FLEETWOOD, LANCASHIRE
☎ (01253) 877377. OPEN 10 - 6 SEVEN DAYS A WEEK.
Up to 40 shops, a marina, and lots of activities for the family. Shops for children include: 424 Superstore (club football gear), Lee jeans, Tick Tock childrenswear, Hallmark cards, Toy World, Sports Unlimited and Shoe Sellers.

## FRUIT OF THE LOOM

CHESHIRE OAKS OUTLET VILLAGE, KINSEY ROAD, NEAR ELLESMERE PORT, JUNCTION 10 OF M53, SOUTH WIRRAL L65 9JJ
☎ (0151) 355 6169. OPEN 10 - 6 MON - SAT, 10 - 4 SUN.
Children's, men's and women's casual wear in the form of T-shirt, sweatshirts, shorts and tracksuits with the distinctive Fruit of the Loom logo.

## GOLDEN SHUTTLE MILL SHOP

ALBION ROAD, GREENGATES, BRADFORD BD10 9TQ
☎ (01274) 611161. OPEN 9.30 - 5 MON - SAT.
Children's, men's and women's fashions at discount prices, plus suitcases, sportsbags, and holdalls.

## I J DEWHIRST

MIDDLE STREET NORTH, DRIFFIELD, EAST YORKSHIRE
☎ (01377) 256209. OPEN 9 - 5.30 MON - THUR, 9 - 6 FRI, 9 - 5 SAT.
5 WELHAM ROAD, MALTON OPEN 9 - 5.30 MON - FRI, 9 - 5 SAT, 11 - 5 SUN.
Wide range of children's, men's and women's clothes including girl's dresses, blouses, trousers, skirts and jackets and boy's shirts, trousers

and jackets; men's suits, jackets, shirts, trousers; women's jackets, blouses, skirts and trousers, and much much more.

## JOKIDS

CHESHIRE OAKS OUTLET VILLAGE, KINSEY ROAD, NEAR ELLESMERE PORT, (JUNCTION 10 OF M53), SOUTH WIRRAL L65 9JJ
☎ (0151) 357 1404. OPEN 10 - 6 MON - SAT, 10 - 4 SUN.
JoKids is the factory shop trading name for Jeffrey Ohrenstein which sells unusual and attractive clothes for children aged from birth to ten years. The girls dresses range from denim dresses to pretty party dresses reduced from £31.99 to £17.99; there are also cotton jeans, check shirts, denim shorts, and T-shirts and some jackets. There is also a JoKids at Clarks Factory Shopping Village (see Children, South West) and Jacksons Landing (see Children, North and Scotland)

## K SHOES

UNIT 3, CLIFTON ROAD RETAIL PARK, BLACKPOOL, LANCASHIRE FY4 4RA
☎ (01253) 699380. OPEN 9.30 - 7.30 MON - FRI AND BANK HOLIDAYS, 9 - 6 SAT, 10 - 4 SUN.
9-11 CHAPEL STREET, SOUTHPORT, MERSEYSIDE PR8 1AE
☎ (01704) 531583. OPEN 9 - 5.30 MON - SAT, 11 - 5 SUN
(SUMMER, 11 - 4 SUN IN WINTER) 10 - 5 BANK HOLIDAYS.
Clarks International operate a chain of factory shops nationally which specialise in selling discontinued lines and slight sub-standards for children, women and men from Clarks, K Shoes and other famous brands. These shops trade under the name of Crockers, K Shoes Factory shop or Clarks Factory Shop and while not all are physically attached to a shoe factory, these shops are treated as factory shops by the company. Customers can expect to find an extensive range of quality shoes, sandals, walking boots, slippers, trainers, handbags, accessories and gifts, while their major outlets also offer luggage, sports clothing, sports equipment and outdoor clothing. Brands stocked include Clarks, K Shoes, Springer, CICA, Hi-Tec, Puma, Mercury, Dr Martens, Nike, LA Gear, Fila, Mizuno, Slazenger, Weider, Samsonite, Delsey, Antler and Carlton, although not all are sold in every outlet. Discounts are on average 30% off the normal high street price for perfect stock.

# LAMBERT HOWARTH FOOTWEAR

GAGHILLS MILLS, GAGHILLS ROAD, OFF BURNLEY ROAD EAST,
WATERFOOT, ROSSENDALE, LANCASHIRE BB4 9AS
☎ (01706) 215417. OPEN 10 - 5 MON - FRI, 9.30 - 3.30 SAT.

A real mixture of seconds from the factory and perfects from other
sources - footwear, clothes, handbags and towels. The seconds in
footwear are from shoes made for well-known high street chainstores
and all are at discounted prices. These include slippers, walking boots,
flat shoes and sandals for men, women and children.

# MADE TO LAST LTD

8 THE CRESCENT, HYDE PARK, LEEDS LS6 2NW
☎ (01532) 304983. OPEN 10-6 WED, FRI & 11-5 SAT. MAIL ORDER.

A workers co-operative making boots and shoes for women, men and
children, they have regular stock clearances during which shoes which
have been tried on by customers and don't look quite as new are
reduced in price by between one third and one half. Their children's
shoes took first prize in the 1993 Shoe and Sock Awards, beating
industry giants Start-Rite into second place. Their children's boots
normally cost £36.95, strap shoes, £44.50 and classic men's lace-ups,
£56. Send for catalogue. All their styles are also available in a high
quality vegetarian material.

# NIKE UK LTD

CHESHIRE OAKS OUTLET VILLAGE, KINSEY ROAD, NEAR ELLESMERE
PORT, SOUTH WIRRAL L65 9JJ
☎ (0151) 357 1252. OPEN 10 - 6 MON - SAT, 10 - 4 SUN.

Children's, men's and women's trainers, jackets, T-shirts, sports shirts,
shorts, sleeveless T-shirts and tracksuits.

# PACO LIFE IN COLOUR

UNIT 25, CHESHIRE OAKS OUTLET VILLAGE, KINSEY ROAD, NEAR
ELLESMERE PORT, JUNCION 10 OF M53, SOUTH WIRRAL L65 9JJ
☎ (0151) 357 3722. OPEN 10 - 6 MON - SAT, 10 - 4 SUN.

Colourful cotton T-shirts, sweaters, cardigans, sweatshirts, leggings,
gloves, scarves, shorts, canvas bags for women and children, all at discounts of about 30%. The children's range is stronger in the age
group 9-12 years.

## SILVER CROSS

WESTSIDE RETAIL PARK, GUISELEY, LEEDS, YORKSHIRE LS20 9NE
☎ (01943) 870950. OPEN 10 - 6 MON - WED, FRI, 10 - 8 THUR, 9 - 6 SAT,
10 - 5 SUN.

Factory shop has special deals on last season's colours in their own
brand and carry some ends of lines and discontinued lines in Silver
Cross. Prams with last year's colours could cost £209.90 instead of
£257.90. A discontinued model in a pram would be reduced from
£265 to £199. Pushchair which was £134.90 reduced to £109.90.

## THE FACTORY SHOP

LAWKHOLME LANE, KEIGHLEY, WEST YORKSHIRE BD21 3HW
☎ (01535) 611703. OPEN 9.30 - 5 MON - SAT, 10 - 4 BANK HOLIDAYS.
LANCASTER LEISURE PARK, WYRESDALE ROAD, LANCASTER,
LANCASHIRE LA1 3LA
☎ (01524) 846079. OPEN 10 - 5 MON - SAT, 11 - 5 SUN AND BANK
HOLIDAYS.
5 NORTH STREET, RIPON, NORTH YORKSHIRE HG4 1JY
☎ (01765) 601156. OPEN 9 - 5 MON - SAT, 11 - 4 BANK HOLIDAYS.
HORNSEA FREEPORT SHOPPING VILLAGE, HORNSEA, EAST
YORKSHIRE
☎ (01964) 534211. OPEN 10 - 5 MON - FRI, 10 - 6 SAT, SUN.
COMMERCIAL STREET, MORLEY, WEST YORKSHIRE LS1 6EX
☎ (0113) 2381240. OPEN 9.30 - 5 MON - FRI, 9 - 5 SAT.

Wide range on sale includes children's, men's and women's clothing
and footwear; household textiles, toiletries, hardware, luggage,
lighting and bedding, most of which are chainstore and high street
brands at discounts of approximately 30%-50%. There are weekly
deliveries and brands include all the major stars: Coloroll, Wrangler
and Dartington to name just three (the Morley branch does not stock
Wrangler). Lines are continually changing and few factory shops offer
such a variety under one roof. The Hornsea branch stock special buys
bought specifically for the Freeport outlet.

## THE SHOE FACTORY SHOP

21 WELLOWGATE, GRIMSBY, SOUTH HUMBERSIDE DN32 0RA
☎ (01472) 342415. OPEN 9 - 5 MON - SAT, 9 - 7 THUR.
6/7 OSLO ROAD, SUTTON FIELDS, HULL
☎ (01482) 839292. OPEN 9 - 5 MON - SAT, UNTIL 7 ON THUR AND FRI.

Children's, women's and men's shoes and accessories such as handbags
which are bought in from other manufacturers including Spanish,

Portuguese and Italian companies. All are unbranded. The range covers from mocassins to dressy shoes. Children's shoes from size 6 to adult size 5 from £10 upwards. Slippers start at baby size 4 from £3.50 - £6.50 to junior size 2.

## THE SHOE SHED

UNITS 10 AND 11, WHEATLEY CENTRE, WHEATLEY HALL ROAD, DONCASTER, SOUTH YORKSHIRE
☎ (01302) 341435. OPEN 10 - 6 MON - THUR, 10 - 7 FRI, 9.30 - 5.30 SAT, 11 - 5 SUN.
Large factory shop selling a vast range of all types of children's, men's and women's shoes, all of which are perfects, at up to 30% below normal high street prices. Ladies sandals cost from £5; ladies shoes from £7.50. Men's shoes from £10; sports shoes from £10.

## WRANGLER

HORNSEA FREEPORT SHOPPING VILLAGE, HORNSEA, YORKSHIRE HU18 1UT
☎ (01964) 532979. OPEN 10 - 5 MON - SUN.
Previous season's stock as well as any returned merchandise and over-makes. Children's jeans from £12.99, adults from £18.99. The Shopping Village has plenty to entertain the family with playgrounds, an indoor play centre, restaurants, a vintage car collection and butterfly world.

# *Dress Agencies*

## AS NEW FASHIONS

1 EMSCOTE GROVE, HAUGH SHAW ROAD, HALIFAX, YORKSHIRE
☎ (01422) 365379. OPEN 9.30 - 5 MON - SAT.
Ladies, men's and children's nearly-new clothes all available. Children's school uniforms are stocked, as are accessories.

## ELITE DRESS AGENCY

1 MARKET STREET, ALTRINCHAM, CHESHIRE WA14 1QE
☎ (0161) 928 5424. OPEN 10 -5 MON - SAT.

Mainly ladies wear which is less than one year old, although there are both men's and childrenswear departments. Wide range of clothing including some sports wear. Twice yearly sales at the end of June and December.

## EVERYTHING BUT THE BABY

19 KNARESBOROUGH RD, HARROGATE, NORTH YORKSHIRE
HG2 7SR
☎ (01423) 888292. OPEN 10 - 4 MON - SAT, 1 CLOSED WED.

Sells a wide range of nearly-new babywear from birth to five years, as well as baby equipment, bedding, toys and maternity wear. There is an extensive range of pushchairs from £15-£200. All the equipment is fully checked and the clothes range from Mothercare and Ladybird to OshKosh, Oilily and some French designers.

## OPPORTUNITIES

13 PROVIDENCE STREET, WAKEFIELD, WEST YORKSHIRE WF1 3BG
☎ (0924) 290310 OPEN 10 - 5.30 MON - FRI, 9 - 5.30 SAT, UNTIL 7 THUR.

Two floors of nearly-new outfits, from wedding outfits, ball gowns and evening wear to day wear and children's clothes. Occasional bargain baskets, and new and secondhand jewellery. Easy parking, easy sofas, and coffee and tea served.

## SOPHIE'S CHOICE

19B NORTH LANE, HEADINGLEY, LEEDS, YORKSHIRE
☎ (0532) 743913. OPEN 10 - 5 MON - SAT, CLOSED WED.

Nearly-new children's and women's clothes which caters for middle to upmarket labels. Navy blue blazers, £35, originally £200; designer shirts, £14.50, usually £80.

## THE ELITE DRESS AGENCY

35 KINGS STREET WEST, MANCHESTER M3 2PW
☎ (0161) 8323670. OPEN 10 - 5 MON - SAT.

Three floors of good quality men's, women's and children's clothing, many with a Continental flavour. Children can find a selection of quality clothing. There is also a selection of unwanted gifts for sale.

## YOYO

61 EASTGATE, BEVERLEY, NORTH HUMBERSIDE HU17 0DR
☎ (01482) 861713. OPEN 9.30 - 3 MON - SAT.

YoYo sell good quality, nearly-new childrenswear at prices from one quarter to one third of the original cost. The labels range from Marks & Spencer, Debenhams and BhS to Oilily, Patrizia Wigan, Tick Tock, Babi-Mini, Clayeaux and Absorba. Most items are under £10 and generally you can clothe a child for the price of one week's family allowance. Age range from birth to about 10 years.

## *Hire Shops*

## BABY DAYS

27 DOWER PARK, ESRICK, YORK, NORTH YORKSHIRE YO4 6JN
☎ (01904) 728158. PHONE FIRST.

## BABY EQUIPMENT HIRE

1 PEEBLES CLOSE, LITTLE SUTTON, SOUTH WIRRAL, LANCASHIRE
L66 4JX
☎ (0151) 348 0620. PHONE FIRST.

## BOUNCING BABIES

167 TOTTINGTON ROAD, HARWOOD, BOLTON, LANCASHIRE
BL2 4DF
☎ (01204) 302762. PHONE FIRST.

## CHESHIRE BABY HIRE

9 RYDAL CLOSE, HOLMES CHAPEL, CHESHIRE CW4 7JR
☎ (01477) 533414. PHONE FIRST.
BROADWAY FARM, TWEMLOW, NEAR HOLMES CHAPEL, CHESHIRE
☎ (01477) 71237. PHONE FIRST.

## DEJA VU

134 NORTHENDEN ROAD, SALE MOOR, CHESHIRE M33 3HE
☎ (0161) 969 5495. PHONE FIRST.

## HICCUPS

38 HEATHER LEE AVENUE, DORE, SHEFFIELD, SOUTH YORKSHIRE
S17 3DL
☎ (0114) 2366054. PHONE FIRST.

# HIRE IT FOR BABY

PARTRIDGE HILL FARM, AUSTERFIELD, DONCASTER, SOUTH
YORKSHIRE DN10 6HA
☎ (01302) 711873. PHONE FIRST.

# JACK AND JILL

38 PARKWAYS GROVE, LEEDS, WEST YORKSHIRE LS26 8TP
☎ (01532) 828323. PHONE FIRST.
85 SANDHILL OVAL, ALWOODLEY, LEEDS, WEST YORKSHIRE LS17 8EF
☎ (0113) 2683712. PHONE FIRST.
566 WAKEFIELD ROAD, HUDDERSFIELD, WEST YORKSHIRE HD5 8PU
☎ (01484) 530486. PHONE FIRST.
1 WEST PARK DRIVE, WEST PARK, LEEDS, WEST YORKSHIRE LS16 5AS
☎ (01532) 785560. PHONE FIRST.
5 CARLTON LANE, GUISELEY, LEEDS, WEST YORKSHIRE LS20 2DB
☎ (01943) 877637.

# KIDDYHIRE

1 WHIN GROVE, BOLTON LE SANDS, LANCASTER,
LANCASHIRE LA5 8DD
☎ (01524) 734136. PHONE FIRST.

# KIDDYHIRE

4 WESTFIELD GROVE, WAKEFIELD, WEST YORKSHIRE WF1 2RS
☎ (01924) 365732. PHONE FIRST.

# MOTHER GOOSE NURSERY EQUIPMENT

1 WHITWELL TERRACE, MELMERBY, RIPON, NORTH YORKSHIRE
HG4 5HQ
☎ (01765) 640443. PHONE FIRST.

# NORTH WEST BABY HIRE

1 SIDE AVENUE, ATTRINGHAM, CHESHIRE WA14 3AP
☎ (0161) 941 4916. PHONE FIRST.

# NURSERY NEEDS

43 PIKEPURSE LANE, RICHMOND, NORTH YORKSHIRE DL10 4PS
☎ (01748) 824524. PHONE FIRST.

# NURSERY TIMES HIRE

19 EDINBURGH PLACE, LEEDS, WEST YORKSHIRE LS25 2LN
☎ (0113) 2875321. PHONE FIRST.

All the above are part of the British Equipment Hirers Association
(BEHA), which has more than 100 members countrywide. A range of
equipment can be hired from high chairs, cots and travel cots to baby
car seats and buggies. Some members also hire out party equipment
including child-sized tables and chairs. BEHA run an advice line

which will try and answer any queries you have regarding hiring services for children. Phone the Babyline on 0831 310355.

## GREAT CLOTHES

84 YORK ROAD, LEEDS, WEST YORKSHIRE
☎ (0113) 2350303. OPEN 9.30 - 9 MON - FRI, 9.30 - 6 SAT, 11 - 5 SUN.
Clothes shop which also operates a hire service for formal men's and boyswear. Everything from outfits for two-year-olds to clothes for men with a 54"chest. Top hat and tails, cravat or tie, from £34.99; evening jackets or tuxedos, from £29.99; full kilt wear, £54.99.

## RAINBOW

STATION ROAD, OAKWORTH, KEIGHLEY, WEST YORKSHIRE
BD22 0DU
☎ (01535) 644433. OPEN 9 - 5 MON - SAT.
20 DOCK RAY STREET, COLNE, LANCASHIRE BB8 GHT
☎ (01282) 869141. OOPEN 9 - 4.30 MON, WED - FRI, 9 - 5 SAT.
Retail shops which also hire out baby equipment from wooden cots and car seats to pushchairs, bouncy castle and baby monitors. A wooden cot cost £15 to hire for 1 month, plus a £10 refundable deposit. There is no minimum time limit. The Colne outlet does not hire bouncy castles.

# NORTH AND SCOTLAND

## *Permanent Discount Outlets*

## MATALAN

16 GOODWOOD SQUARE, TEESSIDE RETAIL PARK, THORNABY, STOCKTON-ON-TEES TS17 7BW
☎ (01642) 633204. OPEN 10 - 8 MON - FRI, 9.30 - 5.30 SAT, 10 - 6 SUN.
SEAFIELD WAY, SEAFIELD ROAD, EDINBURGH EH15 1TB
☎ (0131) 657 5045. OPEN 10 - 8 MON - FRI, 9.30 - 5.30 SAT, 10 - 6 SUN.
WALNEY ROAD, BARROW LA14 5UU
☎ (01229) 430899. OPEN 10 - 8 MON - FRI, 9.30 - 5.30 SAT, 10 - 6 SUN.
UNIT 2B, METRO CENTRE, RETAIL PARK, GATESHEAD, NEWCASTLE UPON TYNE NE11 4YD
☎ (0191) 460 0423. OPEN 10 - 7.45 MON - FRI, 10 - 6 SAT, SUN.

UNIT 5, CALEDONIAN CENTRE, NEW ASHTREE STREET, WISHAW ML2 7UR
☎ (01698) 357075. OPEN 10 - 8 MON - FRI, 9.30 - 5.30 SAT, 10 - 6 SUN.
PLOT 12, DERWENT HOUSE, SOLWAY ROAD, WORKINGTON CA14 3YA
☎ (01900) 870966. OPEN 10 - 8 MON - FRI, 9.30 - 5.30 SAT, 10 - 6 SUN
UNIT 2, KINGSTONE RETAIL PARK, HULL HU2 2TX
☎ (01482) 586184. OPEN 10 - 8 MON - FRI, 9 - 6 SAT, 11 - 5 SUN.
UNIT 7, GLENCAIRNE RETAIL PARK, KILMARNOCK KA1 4AY
☎ (01563) 573892. OPEN 10 - 8 MON - FRI, 9.30 - 5.30 SAT, 10 - 6 SUN.
UNIT 1 HEWITTS CIRCUS, CLEETHORPES DN35 9QH
☎ (01472) 200255. OPEN 10 - 8 MON - FRI, 9 - 6 SAT, 11 - 5 SUN.

As the UK's first National Discount Club, Matalan has the buying power to guarantee its members up to 60% discounts on a huge range of brand name clothing, household goods, luggage and toiletries for all the family. Top quality merchandise, current season, no seconds, is offered to its members at exclusive, permanently discounted prices seven days a week. Matalan operates strictly on a membership basis, one of the key factors for its success in offering 20%-60% savings off recommended retail prices. Membership cards are issued through companies, organisations and associations in the vicinity of the stores, and are available to their employees/members. They are valid at any of the 50 Matalan stores in the UK. To find out if your organisation is registered, phone the Matalan hotline on 01772 629447.

## NEXT TO NOTHING

83-93 SAUCHIEHALL STREET, GLASGOW GU 3DD
☎ (0141) 332 4056. OPEN 9 - 5.30 MON - WED, 10 - 7 THUR, 9.30 - 6 FRI, 9 - 6 SAT.

Sells perfect surplus stock from Next stores and the Next Directory catalogue - from belts, jewellery and underwear to day and evening wear - at discounts of 50% or more. The ranges are usually last season's and overruns but there is the odd current item if you look carefully. Stock consists of children's, men's and women's clothing, with some homeware and shoes, depending on the branch. Stock is replenished twice a week and there is plenty of it. Childrenswear range is not extensive but well priced.

## Q MARK

56 BELFORD ROAD, EDINBURGH, SCOTLAND EH4 3BR
☎ (0131) 225 6861. OPEN 9 - 5.30 MON - SAT, 12 - 5 SUN, UNTIL 7 THUR.
BRAIDHOLM ROAD, GIFFNOCK, GLASGOW, SCOTLAND G46 6EB
☎ (0141) 633 3636. OPEN 9 - 6 MON - SAT, UNTIL 8 ON THUR, 12 - 5
SUN.

Scotland's biggest discount clothing warehouse for children, men and
women offers top quality fashions at up to 50% off normal high street
prices. All garments are good quality seconds, overmakes or cancelled
contracts but with their labels cut out. Regular stock deliveries ensure
a constant selection of new styles - often recognised in famous chain
stores, but always at ridiculously low prices. Q Mark operate a once-
a-year membership fee of £5. All prices are subject to VAT and
charged at point of sale.

## STATESIDE WHOLESALE CLUB

☎ (01670) 789110. MAIL ORDER ONLY.

Contrary to what it might seem, Stateside Wholesale Club is not an
American company. Based in Northumberland, it is a catalogue
company along the lines of Betterware - but selling clothes. A trio of
catalogues - featuring men's, women's and children's clothes - are left
at your home. You can then order the various outfits through the
agent who comes to collect the catalogue. The real bargains come if
you are an agent, as you can charge whatever price you like for the
goods in the catalogue as long as you pay the company a fixed amount
for each outfit. The catalogue states the normal retail price for each
outfit, but the agent's list states the amount the company wants from
the agent for that item. This amount is often half the catalogue price.
The company suggests that you sell the outfit at its fixed price plus
20% but if you can get more for it, that's fine and you keep the extra
margin. It claims that all the merchandise is perfect, big brand names
on sale currently in shops and other catalogues. You have to purchase
something in order to get on the mailing list, but once you start
receiving catalogues, you can either do a Caura/Cabouchon and sell
to friends or use it to buy clothes for yourself and your family at low
prices. The children's clothes are of the leggings and T-shirt variety.
Brand names include Adidas, LA Gear and Pierre Cardin, but they are
mostly in the footwear area.

# TK MAXX

LOWER GROUND FLOOR, MONUMENT MALL, NORTHUMBERLAND
STREET, NEWCASTLE-UPON-TYNE, TYNE & WEAR.
☎ (0191) 233 2323. OPEN 9 - 5.30 MON - FRI, UNTIL 8 ON THUR,
9 - 6 SAT.

Based on an American concept, TK Maxx is the first British retailer to
practise "off-price" retailing. This means a centrally located store
which offers famous label goods with up to 60% savings off recommended retail prices. TK Maxx has fashion for the whole family -
children's, men's and womenswear - accessories, shoes, gifts, kitchenware and home goods. Everything in the store is branded with a choice
of well-known high street names to designer labels, and while a small
percentage mightly be clearly marked past season, the great majority of
items in store are current season, current stock and still with phenomenal savings. There is a huge choice with 50,000 pieces in store with
5,000 new items arriving a week, so it's worth keeping abreast of the
lastest deliveries as turnaround is very fast. One of the ways in which
TK Maxx is able to offer such low prices is by running a very low-cost
operation, so the stores are simple and unfussy with wide aisles,
shopping trolleys and baskets, and a spacious, functional feel to them.
Service is not compromised, however: there are individual changing
rooms, ramps for buggies and wheelchairs, plenty of staff on the shop
floor and all the branches accept all major credit and debit cards.

# Factory Shops

# BABYGRO LTD

HAYFIELD INDUSTRIAL ESTATE, KIRKCALDY, FIFE, SCOTLAND
KY2 5DN
☎ (01592) 261177. OPEN 8 - 5 MON - THUR, 8 - 1 FRI.
GATESIDE INDUSTRIAL ESTATE, OLD PERTH ROAD, COWDEN BEATH
☎ (01383) 511105. OPEN 9.30 - 4.30 TUE, WED, THUR,
CLOSED 1.30 - 2.30 DAILY.

Babywear for 0-5 year olds: all-in-ones, playsuits, shorts, T-shirts,
vests, shirts, pyjamas, and rompers at factory shop prices. Pyjamas for
a 4-year-old cost £6.99 compared with £12.99 for the same pair in a
high street store. Also does a line of adult leisurewear. Factory sales
take place three times a year and are advertised locally.

## BAIRDWEAR RACKE

6-8 COLVILLES PLACE, EAST KILBRIDE, GLASGOW, SCOTLAND
G75 OQS
☎ (01355) 236441. OPEN 10 - 4 MON - THUR, 10 - 12 FRI.
24 ROSYTH ROAD, POLMADIE, GLASGOW
☎ (0141) 429 6611. OPEN 11 - 4 MON - THUR, 9.30 - 12.30 FRI,
CLOSED 2.30 - 3.
INCHINNEN INDUSTRIAL ESTATE, ABBOTSBURN, RENFREWSHIRE
☎ (0141) 812 6388. OPEN 9.30 - 4.30 MON - WED, 9.30 - 2.15 THUR,
9.30 - 12.30 FRI.
Manufacturers for a well-known high street chainstore for more than
20 years, Bairdwear has a wide selection of seconds and overmakes in
its factory shops. The East Kilbride shop makes men's shirts and sells
them as well as women's and children's clothes, with some babywear,
as well as towels, sheets and duvets covers. The Abbotsburn shop sells
mainly womenswear with some menswear and lots of babywear. The
Polmadie shop sells women's and children's clothes, some men's, and
household linen and towels, but no duvets.

## BALMOREL MILL

16 CHURCH LANE, GARSTON, AYRSHIRE, SCOTLAND
☎ (01563) 820213. OPEN 9 - 5 MON - SAT, 11 - 4.30 SUN.
Sells cashmere and lambswool knitwear, embroidered knitwear and
sportswear, some of which is brand name and some own label, but all
sold at factory direct prices. The emphasis is on sports and
leisurewear. Children's embroidered sweatshirts and other plain
designs start from £5.50.

## BEE LINE

NO 6, DARLIETH ROAD, LOMOND INDUSTRIAL ESTATE, ALEXAN-
DRIA, DUNBARTON, SCOTLAND
☎ (01389) 756161. OPEN 10 - 5 TUE - SAT, 12 - 4 SUN.
All major chainstore overmakes for children and ladies. Stock depends
on the time of year but includes shorts, T-shirts, jogging pants,
dresses, skirts and sweaters, smart separates, some underwear, all sold
at 30% less than normal retail prices. Stock is current and last
season's.

# CHARLES CLINKARD

JACKSONS LANDING, HARTLEPOOL FACTORY OUTLET SHOPPING
MALL, HARTLEPOOL MARINA, HARTLEPOOL, CLEVELAND TS24 OXN
☎ (01429) 866939. OPEN 10 - 6 MON - FRI, 11 - 5 SUN AND BANK
HOLIDAYS.

Indoor factory shopping centre with twenty-four outlets selling brand
name items including footwear for the family at discounts of between
20% and 30%. Labels include Loake, Camel, Bally, Church's, Ecco,
Gabor, Rohde, Van-Dal, Kickers, Clarks, Dr Martens, K Shoes, Lotus
and Renata plus handbags by Jane Shilton. Children's shoes, £9.99,
reduced from £16.99; Elefanten children's shoes, £16.99 reduced
from £32.99. Hartlepool Marina hosts a recreated historic quay and
harbours HMS Trincomalee, the oldest British warship still afloat,
and is also the site of the new Hartlepool Museum with its interactive
fighting ships section and a replica seventeenth century children's play
area. There is free parking adjacent to the centre, a coffee shop,
restaurant overlooking the Marina, and baby changing and disabled
facilities.

# CROCKERS

UNIT 26, THE FORGE SHOPPING CENTRE, PARKHEAD, GLASGOW,
SCOTLAND G31 4EB
☎ (0141) 556 5290. OPEN 9 - 5.30 MON - SAT, 12 - 4.30 SUN AND BANK
HOLIDAYS.

Clarks International operate a chain of factory shops nationally which
specialise in selling discontinued lines and slight sub-standards for
children, women and men from Clarks, K Shoes and other famous
brands. These shops trade under the name of Crockers, K Shoes
Factory shop or Clarks Factory Shop and while not all are physically
attached to a shoe factory, these shops are treated as factory shops by
the company. Customers can expect to find an extensive range of
quality shoes, sandals, walking boots, slippers, trainers, handbags,
accessories and gifts, while their major outlets also offer luggage,
sports clothing, sports equipment and outdoor clothing. Brands
stocked include Clarks, K Shoes, Springer, CICA, Hi-Tec, Puma,
Mercury, Dr Martens, Nike, LA Gear, Fila, Mizuno, Slazenger,
Weider, Samsonite, Delsey, Antler and Carlton, although not all are
sold in every outlet. Discounts are on average 30% off the normal
high street price for perfect stock.

# DEWHIRST FACTORY SHOP

MILL HILL, NORTH WEST INDUSTRIAL ESTATE, PETERLEE, COUNTY
DURHAM SR8 5AA
☎ (0191) 586 4525. OPEN 9 - 5.30 MON - WED, 9 - 7 THUR, 9 - 6 FRI,
9 - 5 SAT, 11 - 5 SUN.
PENNYWELL INDUSTRIAL ESTATE, PENNYWELL, SUNDERLAND
☎ (0191) 534 7928. OPEN 9 - 5.30 MON - FRI, 9 - 5 SAT, 11 - 5 SUN.
AMSTERDAM ROAD, SUTTON FIELDS INDUSTRIAL ESTATE, HULL
☎ (01482) 820166. OPEN 9 - 5.30 MON - WED, 9 - 7.30 THUR, 9 - 6 FRI,
9 - 5 SAT, 11 - 5 SUN.
WEST COATHAM LANE, DORMANSTOWN INDUSTRIAL ESTATE,
DORMANSTOWN, REDCAR
☎ (01642) 474210. OPEN 9 - 5.30 MON - FRI, 9 - 5 SAT, 10.30 - 4.30 SUN.
NEWBIGGIN ROAD, NORTH SEATON INDUSTRIAL ESTATE,
ASHINGTON
☎ (01670) 813493. OPEN 9 - 5.30 MON - FRI, 9 - 5 SAT, 10.30 - 4.30 SUN.
Wide range of children's, men's and women's clothes including girl's
dresses, blouses, trousers, skirts and jackets and boy's shirts, trousers,
jackets; men's suits, jackets, and much much more.

# JACKSONS LANDING

HARTLEPOOL FACTORY OUTLET SHOPPING MALL, HARTLEPOOL
MARINA, HARTLEPOOL, CLEVELAND TS24 OXN
☎ (01429) 866989 INFORMATION LINE. OPEN 10 - 6 MON - FRI, 11 - 5
SUN AND BANK HOLIDAYS.
Indoor factory shopping centre with twenty-four outlets selling a
range of brand name items. Shops selling children's items include
Clinkards, which sells Bally, Clark's and Kickers footwear; Jokids sells
childrenswear, Toy World features many of the leading brand names
such as Tomy, Fisher-Price and Lego; Bookscene sells jigsaws, stationary, posters; Tog 24 sells leisurewear, including a few children's outfits;
Hallmark sells half-price celebration and Christmas cards, wrapping
paper, stuffed toys. Recent new openings include Benetton and Joe
Bloggs. Hartlepool Marina hosts a recreated historic quay and
harbours HMS Trincomalee, the oldest British warship still afloat,
and is also the site of the new Hartlepool Museum with its interactive
fighting ships section and a replica seventeenth century children's play
area. There is free parking adjacent to the centre, a coffee shop,
restaurant overlooking the Marina, and baby changing and disabled
facilities.

# JOCKEY UNDERWEAR FACTORY SHOP

EASTERN AVENUE, TEAM VALLEY TRADING ESTATE, GATESHEAD,
TYNE & WEAR
☎ (0191) 491 0088. OPEN 10 - 4 MON, TUE, THUR, 10 - 2.30 FRI, CLOSED
WED.

Manufacturers underwear and sells ladies and gents in its factory
shop. Because it is part of the Courtaulds group, the factory shop also
sells Wolsey socks, Cristy towels, Zorbit babywear, pillows and
duvets.

# JOKIDS

JACKSONS LANDING, HARTLEPOOL FACTORY OUTLET SHOPPING
MALL, HARTLEPOOL MARINA, HARTLEPOOL, CLEVELAND TS24 0XN
☎ (01429) 862638. OPEN 10 - 6 MON - FRI, 11 - 5 SUN AND BANK
HOLIDAYS.

Indoor factory shopping centre with twenty-four outlets selling brand
name items including pretty dresses and a selection of casual wear for
boys. There are lots of party dresses here at about half price, plus T-
shirts for both sexes, shorts, dungarees and hats, as well as a seconds
rail of mixed items with the reason for them being seconds written on
the ticket. Examples of prices include party dresses for age 2 years,
£35.50 reduced from £45.50; blue Chambray dress with parrot motif
for age 7 years, £31.99; cotton pique T-shirt for newborn, £4.99 for
two; hairbands, £2.99 reduced from £4.50; set of three T-shirts for
ages 3/4, £4.99 reduced from £7.99; sleeveless denim dress for age 5,
£10.99 reduced from £14.99; cotton denim shirts, £8.99. Hartlepool
Marina hosts a recreated historic quay and harbours HMS
Trincomalee, the oldest British warship still afloat, and is also the site
of the new Hartlepool Museum with its interactive fighting ships
section and a replica seventeenth century children's play area. There is
free parking adjacent to the centre, a coffee shop, restaurant overlooking the Marina, and baby changing and disabled facilities.

# K SHOES

K VILLAGE, NETHERFIELD, KENDAL, CUMBRIA LA9 7DA
☎ (01539) 721892. OPEN 9.30 - 7 MON - FRI, 9 - 5 SAT, 11 - 5 SUN,
9 - 6 BANK HOLIDAYS.
JAMES STREET, ASKAM-IN-FURNESS, CUMBRIA LA16 7BA
☎ (01229) 462267. OPEN 10 - 5.30 MON - FRI, 9 - 5 SAT, 10 - 5 BANK
HOLIDAYS. MAIN STREET, SHAP, CUMBRIA CA10 3NL
☎ (01931) 716648. OPEN 9 - 5 MON - SAT, 10 - 5 BANK HOLIDAYS.

Clarks International operate a chain of factory shops nationally which specialise in selling discontinued lines and slight sub-standards for children, women and men from Clarks, K Shoes and other famous brands. These shops trade under the name of Crockers, K Shoes Factory shop or Clarks Factory Shop and while not all are physically attached to a shoe factory, these shops are treated as factory shops by the company. Customers can expect to find an extensive range of quality shoes, sandals, walking boots, slippers, trainers, handbags, accessories and gifts, while their major outlets also offer luggage, sports clothing, sports equipment and outdoor clothing. Brands stocked include Clarks, K Shoes, Springer, CICA, Hi-Tec, Puma, Mercury, Dr Martens, Nike, LA Gear, Fila, Mizuno, Slazenger, Weider, Samsonite, Delsey, Antler and Carlton, although not all are sold in every outlet. Discounts are on average 30% off the normal high street price for perfect stock. The Kendal branch is also a sports factory shop, baggage factory shop and gift shop.

# LINDSAY ALLAN DESIGNS LTD

BARNPARK DRIVE, OFF LOWER MILL STREET, TILLICOULTRY,
CLACKMANNANSHIRE, SCOTLAND FK13 6BZ
☎ (01259) 752772. OPEN 8.30 - 5 MON - THUR, 8.30 - 4 FRI.

Designer casualwear for children, women and men at affordable prices. About 75% of the stock is for children and all are designed by an in-house design team and usually sold by Lindsay Allan's network of agents through Scotland. Guaranteed supply of all their orders means that they are left each season with a small quantity from the 100 different designs they offer which can no longer be sold through the party plan system which Lindsay Allan employs. They are therefore sold at end of line prices which means discounts of 30%-50%.

## M C HITCHEN & SONS LTD

19 FAWCETT STREET, SUNDERLAND, TYNE & WEAR SR1 RRH
☎ (0191) 564 0684. OPEN 8.45 - 5.30 MON - SAT.
RAWLINSON STREET, BAROW-IN-FURNESS, CUMBRIA LA14 ABS
☎ (01229) 870668. OPEN 8.45 - 5.15 MON - SAT.
Littlewoods sell off their overstocks in a network of shops called M C
Hitchen & Sons Ltd. Most of them are in the North of England and
offer up to 40% off the catalogue price for clothing and between 50%
and 60% off for electrical goods. Littlwoods also run a mobile shop
which operates in cities where they don't have a sale shop. For details
of further venues for the sales, which usually take place once a month,
contact Jean Banks, c/o Crosby DC, Kershaw Avenue, Endbutt Lane,
Crosby, Merseyside L70 1AH.

## PACO LIFE IN COLOUR

SALE SHOP, UNIT 3, PAISLEY HIGH STREET, PAISLEY SHOPPING
CENTRE, PAISLEY, SCOTLAND
☎ (0141) 848 0167. OPEN 9 - 5.30 MON - SAT, UNTIL 7 ON THUR.
Colourful cotton T-shirts, sweaters, cardigans, sweatshirts, leggings,
gloves, scarves, shorts, canvas bags for women and children, all at discounts of about 50%.

## PRAXIS

9-13 NETHERDALE ROAD, NETHERTON INDUSTRIAL ESTATE,
NETHERTON, WISHAW, SCOTLAND
☎ (01698) 357231. OPEN 10 - 4 MON - THUR, 10 - 12 FRI,
CLOSED 1 - 2 DAILY.
Manufactures schoolwear for boys and girls, mostly for BhS, and sells
overmakes and seconds in its factory shop.

## SHARK SPORTS

NORDSTROM HOUSE, NORTH BROOMHILL, MORPETH,
NORTHUMBERLAND NE65 9UJ
☎ (01670) 760365. OPEN 9.30 - 4 MON - FRI, 9.30 - 12 SAT.
Manufactures and sells in the factory shop wetsuits, dry suits, diving
suits, cag tops, buoyancy aids, sailing suits, boots, life jackets and
gloves, for children, men and women at factory prices. Children's
one-piece wetsuits, £40-£45.

## THE FACTORY SHOP

EMPIRE BUILDING, MAIN STREET, EGREMONT, CUMBRIA CA22 2BD
☎ (01946) 820434. OPEN 9.30 - 5 MON - SAT, 10 - 4 BANK HOLIDAYS.
Wide range on sale includes men's, ladies and children's clothing and
footwear; household textiles, toiletries, hardware, luggage, lighting
and bedding, most of which are chainstore and high street brands at
discounts of approximately 30%-50%. There are weekly deliveries
and brands include all the major stars: Coloroll, Wrangler and
Dartington to name just three. Lines are continually changing and
few factory shops offer such a variety under one roof.

## TOY WORLD FACTORY OUTLETS LTD

JACKSONS LANDING, HARTLEPOOL FACTORY OUTLET SHOPPING
MALL, HARTLEPOOL MARINA, HARTLEPOOL, CLEVELAND TS24 OXN
☎ (01429) 273488. OPEN 10 - 6 MON - FRI, 11 - 5 SUN AND BANK
HOLIDAYS.
Indoor factory shopping centre with twenty-four outlets selling brand
name items including a wide range of toys with well-known brand
names. For example, when we visited in June 1995, My First Barbie
(Mattel), £5.99, was reduced from £7.99; Sweet Secrets jewellery box
dollshouse, £9.99 from £19.99; Disney's Aladdin Once Upon A Time
playset, £4.99 from £9.99; Playskool magic teaset, £9.99 from
£19.75; Barbie 26-piece teaset, £4.99 from £9.99; Lego cafe, £14.99
from £19.99; Duplo zoo, £49.99 from £59.99; Rupert hand puppet,
£4.99 from £7.99; Sylvanian Families post office, £9.99 from £15.99;
Fisher-Price pull-along plane, £5.99 from £7.99; Safe & Sound
rechargeable mobile baby monitor, £28.99 from £49.99. Hartlepool
Marina hosts a recreated historic quay and harbours HMS
Trincomalee, the oldest British warship still afloat, and is also the site
of the new Hartlepool Museum with its interactive fighting ships
section and a replica seventeenth century children's play area. There is
free parking adjacent to the centre, a coffee shop, restaurant overlooking the Marina, and baby changing and disabled facilities.

## WRANGLER

JACKSONS LANDING, HARTLEPOOL FACTORY OUTLET SHOPPING
MALL, HARTLEPOOL MARINA, HARTLEPOOL, CLEVELAND TS24 OXN
☎ (01429) 273488. OPEN 10 - 6 MON - FRI, 11 - 5 SUN AND BANK
HOLIDAYS.

Indoor factory shopping centre with twenty-four outlets selling brand
name items including women's, men's and children's jeans, jackets,
shirts, sweatshirts, hooded jackets and waistcoats. For example,
perfect jeans, £32; slight seconds, £18.99; denim shirt, £14.99; waistcoats, £19.99 reduced from £39.99.


## *Dress Agencies*

## DRESS SENSE

44 HANOVER STREET, EDINBURGH EH2 2DR
☎ (0131) 220 1298. OPEN 10.30 - 4.30 TUE - SAT.

Has been in operation for 20 years, run by a mother and daughter
team. Occupying a three-room suite on the top floor of a building in
central Edinburgh, it deals mainly in designer labels, wedding outfits
and evening gowns, with some childrenswear for 3-8-year-olds.

## TURNABOUT

32 PRIORY PLACE, CRAIGIE, PERTH, SCOTLAND
☎ (01738) 630916. OPEN 9.30 5 MON - FRI, 10 - 4 SAT.

Sells a range of nearly-new clothes from babies up to 10-year-olds and
including labels such as Osh Kosh, as well as new clothes made on the
premises. There are usually some bridesmaids/flower girl dresses and
christening gowns, but no shoes. The shop also sells second hand
nursery equipment from high chairs and cots to buggies, playpens
and car seats, as well as offering a hire service.

## *Hire Shops*

### ABC BABY EQUIPMENT HIRE

9 WOODBURN AVENUE, KILWINNING, AYRSHIRE KA13 7DB
☎ (01294) 552549. PHONE FIRST.

### A & E COOPER

MARHABA, SUNNYBANK ROAD, ST OLA, ORKNEY, KW15 1TP
☎ (01856) 874065. PHONE FIRST.

### BABY BABY EQUIPMENT HIRE

5 CAMMO BRAE, EDINBURGH, SCOTLAND EH4 8ET
☎ (0131) 339 5215. PHONE FIRST.

### BABY EQUIPMENT HIRE

23 WILLOW GROVE, PITCORTHIE, DUNFERMLINE, FIFE, SCOTLAND
KY11 5BB
☎ (01383) 720711. PHONE FIRST.

### BABY NEST

222 MARSHALL WALLIS ROAD, SOUTH SHIELDS, TYNE & WEAR
NE33 5PW
☎ (0191) 455 9937. PHONE FIRST.

### BABY WORLD

84 NORTH BRIDGE STREET, BATHGATE, WEST LOTHIAN EH48 1DE
☎ (01506) 56318. PHONE FIRST.

### BOBTAILS

ROSE COTTAGE, KESSOCK, INVERNESS, SCOTLAND IV1 1XG
☎ (01463) 731739. PHONE FIRST.

### BUCKSTONE BABY HIRE

22 BUCKSTONE CIRCLE, EDINBURGH, SCOTLAND EH10 6XB
☎ (0131) 445 2825. PHONE FIRST.

### COT CO

45 COPTLEIGH, HOUGHTON LE SPRING, TYNE & WEAR DH5 8JE
☎ (0191) 512 0242. PHONE FIRST.

### KIDS STUFF

5 LOVAINE TERRACE, BERWICK-ON-TWEED, NORTHUMBERLAND
TD15 1LA
☎ (01289) 307208. PHONE FIRST.

### ROCK-A-BYE BABY

8 ACADEMY GARDENS, GAINFORD, DURHAM DL2 3EN
☎ (01325) 730773. PHONE FIRST.

### ROCK-A-BYE BABY

25 LARUN BEAT, YARM, CLEVELAND TS15 9HP
☎ (01642) 785352. PHONE FIRST.

## SHUFFLES

MORVEN, FERNTOWER ROAD, CRIEFF, PERTHSHIRE PH7 3BX
☎ (01764) 654835. PHONE FIRST.

## TINY TOTS HIRE

KIRKLAND FARM, LESWALT, BY STRANRAER, WIGTOWNSHIRE
☎ (01776) 870214. PHONE FIRST.
WESTFIELD, 1 WILLOWDENE CRES, STRANRAER, WIGTOWNSHIRE
DG9 OHE
☎ (01776) 703894. PHONE FIRST.

All the above are part of the British Equipment Hirers Association
(BEHA), which has more than 100 members countrywide. A range of
equipment can be hired from high chairs, cots and travel cots to baby
car seats and buggies. Some members also hire out party equipment
including child-sized tables and chairs. BEHA run an advice line
which will try and answer any queries you have regarding hiring
services for children. Phone the Babyline on 0831 310355.

## BABY BABY EQUIPMENT HIRE

45 GLENDEVON PLACE, EDINBURGH EH12 5UH
☎ 0131-337 7016. OPEN SEVEN DAYS A WEEK, PHONE FIRST.

A member of the Baby Equipment Hirers Association, a nationwide
referral service with its own code of conduct, hires out all types of
equipment from prams to cots. Travel cots cost from £10 for one
week's hire, high chairs £15 for a fortnight. No minimum time necessary, although it is obviously cheaper to hire for a longer period. For
example, hiring a car seat for one week costs £10 but for three months
the cost would only be £30. Equipment is not sold off and there is no
membership fee. There is a standard delivery charge of £5 within the
city and a collection charge of £2-£5 depending on where the
customer lives.

## KIT FOR KIDS

99 SERPENTINE ROAD, KENDAL, CUMBRIA
☎ (01539) 731103.

Caters mostly for short term requirements, hiring out travel cots, high chairs, buggies, baby bouncers, playpens and car seats, all the equipment needed for children 0-8 years old. Car seats cost £8 per week, travel cots, £10. Deposits of between £10-£30 are required. Local deliveries are free; those up to 20 miles away are charged according to mileage. There is a high turnover of merchandise and most ex-hire equipment is sold off at regular periods.

# NORTHERN IRELAND

## *Permanent Discount Outlets*

## TK MAXX

FIRST FLOOR, CASTLE COURT SHOPPING CENTRE, BELFAST, NORTHERN IRELAND OPEN 9 - 5.30 MON - WED, 9 - 9 THUR, 9 - 8 FRI, 9 - 6 SAT.

Based on an American concept, TK Maxx is the first British retailer to practise "off-price" retailing. This means a centrally located store which offers famous label goods with up to 60% savings off recommended retail prices. TK Maxx has fashion for the whole family - children's, men's and womenswear - accessories, shoes, gifts, kitchenware and home goods. Everything in the store is branded with a choice of well-known high street names to designer labels, and while a small percentage mightly be clearly marked past season, the great majority of items in store are current season, current stock and still with phenomenal savings. There is a huge choice with 50,000 pieces in store with 5,000 new items arriving a week, so it's worth keeping abreast of the lastest deliveries as turnaround is very fast. One of the ways in which TK Maxx is able to offer such low prices is by running a very low-cost operation, so the stores are simple and unfussy with wide aisles, shopping trolleys and baskets, and a spacious, functional feel to them. Service is not compromised, however: there are individual changing rooms, ramps for buggies and wheelchairs, plenty of staff on the shop floor and all the branches accept all major credit and debit cards.

# *Factory Shops*

## BAIRDWEAR RACKE

CLANDEBOYE ROAD, BANGOR, NORTHERN IRELAND
☎ (01247) 270415. OPEN 9.30 - 4.30 MON - FRI, 9 - 4 SAT.
ANN STREET, NEWTOWNARDS, NORTHERN IRELAND
☎ (01247) 819502. OPEN 10 - 4.30 MON - SAT.
Manufacturers for a well-known high street chainstore for more than
20 years, Bairdwear has a wide selection of seconds and overmakes in
its factory shops for children, men and women. This can cover
anything from underwear to jackets, coats and blouses but stock
changes constantly. There is also sometimes a range of bedding and
household linens.

## DESMOND & SONS LTD

THE MAIN STREET, CLAUDY, LONDONDERRY BT47 3SD
☎ (01504) 338441. OPEN 10 - 5 MON - SAT.
KEVLIN ROAD, OMAGH
☎ (01662) 241560. OPEN 10 - 5 MON - SAT.
MILL STREET, ENNISKILLEN
☎ (01365) 325467. OPEN 10 - 5 MON - SAT.
BALLYQUINN ROAD, DUNGIVEN
☎ (01504) 742068. OPEN 10 - 5 MON - SAT.
31 GARVAGH ROAD, SWATRAGH
☎ (01648) 401639. OPEN 10 - 5 MON - SAT.
Large range of and children's, men's and womenswear including
trousers, nightwear and knitwear. Most of the stock is seconds and is
sold at discounts of one third. They also buy in some imperfects of
household items such as handtowels and bath towels which are sold
at competitive prices.

## ELIZABETH ALEXANDRA

MOYBRICK ROAD, DROMARA, COUNTY DOWN BT25 2BT
☎ (01238) 532519. OPEN 8.15 - 5.15 MON - THUR, 8.15 - 1.15 FRI.
Seconds and ends of lines of mainly childrenswear. Discounts of
between 25% and 50%.

## LEE APPAREL (UK) LTD

16 COMBER ROAD, NEWTOWNARDS, COUNTY DOWN BT23 4HY
☎ (01247) 819000. OPEN 10 - 5.15 MON, TUE, WED, SAT,
10 - 8.15 THUR, FRI.

Children's, men's and women's Lee Jardine jeans, jackets, T-shirts and sweatshirts at up to 50% savings. Also childrenswear, Adidas sportswear and casual ladieswear at competitive prices.

## OCTOPUS SPORTSWEAR MFG LTD

UNIT 1, DUBLIN ROAD INDUSTRIAL ESTATE, STRABANE BT82 9ES
☎ (01504) 882320. OPEN 8.30 - 5 THUR, 9 - 1 FRI.

Manufacture own-brand sportswear: shorts, jerseys, socks, pants, hooded tops, sweatshirts and sell seconds and clearance lines at discounts of up 50%-75%.

## RELIABLE HOSIERY AT CV CARPETS

THE FACTORY SHOP, 41 HIGH BANGOR ROAD, DONAGHADEE
BT21 OPD
☎ (01247) 888842. OPEN 10 - 5 MON - SAT.
SHAERF DRIVE, SARACEN, LURGAN, COUNTY ANTRIM
☎ (01762) 329253. OPEN 10.30 - 4.30 MON - FRI.
RELIABLE HOSIERY AT CV HOME FURNISHINGS,
36 MAGHERALANE ROAD, RANDALSTOWN, COUNTY ANTRIM
☎ (01849) 473341. OPEN 10 - 5 MON - THUR, 10 - 1 FRI.

Slightly imperfect children's, men's and womenswear. The emphasis is on casualwear with a good variety of children's clothes including party dresses. All the clothes are from well-known chain stores and sold at half the usual price.

## SARACEN

SHAERF DRIVE, LURGAN, NORTHERN IRELAND
☎ (01762) 329253. OPEN 10.30 - 4.30 MON - FRI.

Women's, men's and children's clothes and knitwear at factory shop prices, many of which are top brand names. For children, there are jackets and trousers, T-shirts and jumpers.

# Dress Agencies

## CANCER RESEARCH GROUP

50 HIGH STREET, NEWTOWNARDS, COUNTY DOWN BT23 3HZ
☎ (01247) 820268.
Shop specifically aimed at the bridal market which sells or hires
bridesmaids dresses and pageboy outfits, with accessories. Most of the
stock is either donated or straight from the manufacturer.

# Hire Shops

## ECONOMY BABY HIRE

67 CLONTONACALLY ROAD, CASTLEREAGH, BELFAST, COUNTY
DOWN BT6 9SJ
☎ (01232) 448657. PHONE FIRST.
Part of the British Equipment Hirers Association (BEHA), which has
more than 100 members countrywide. A range of equipment can be
hired from high chairs, cots and travel cots to baby car seats and
buggies. Some members also hire out party equipment including
child-sized tables and chairs. BEHA run an advice line which will try
and answer any queries you have regarding hiring services for
children. Phone the Babyline on 0831 310355.

# HOUSEHOLD AND GIFTWARE

Including

China, Glass, Cutlery, Towels,
Bedding, Sheets, Linen

*Permanent Discount Outlets,*

*Factory Shops,*

*Sales*

# LONDON

## *Permanent Discount Outlets*

## BUYERS & SELLERS

120-122 LADBROKE GROVE, LONDON W10 5NE
☎ 0171- 229 1947/8468. OPEN 9 - 5 MON - SAT, CLOSED 2.30 ON THUR.

Buyers & Sellers has been in business for more than 40 years, selling brand name domestic equipment at bargain prices. Everything from fridges and freezers, ovens and microwaves, hobs and vacuum cleaners, washing machines and dishwashers, tumble dryers and cookers, all new and guaranteed and in perfect working order. They also sell many ends of lines at bargain prices and can obtain almost any make and model. Nationwide delivery service. Telephone orders taken. Advice line and free leaflets are part of the service.

## DAVID RICHARDS & SONS

12 NEW CAVENDISH STREET, LONDON WIM 7LJ
☎ 0171- 935 3206. OPEN 9.30 - 5.30 MON - FRI.

David Richards & Sons are really wholesalers, but they are pleased to help retail customers from their showroom. Their shop is stacked high with solid silver, antique silver and silver picture frames, trays, cutlery, boxes, grape scissors, dishes and punch bowls. Service is well informed and courteous, and prices are much more reasonable than comparable prices in the high street. This is due to the fact that because the shop wholesales in Britain and Europe, it buys enormous quantities and is thus able to pass on bulk-buying savings to customers.

## DISCOUNT COOKERS

97 RUSHEY GREEN, CATFORD, LONDON SE6
☎ 0181-297 1044.

New and reconditioned models from New World, Whirlpool, Canon with more than 2,000 new cookers in stock at any one time. Because they buy in bulk to supply their five south-east London shops, they can offer competitive prices - although they say that the more expensive the cooker you buy, the better the discount. They also stock between 400-500 reconditioned cookers at prices from £100 upwards

- which works out at between 25%-50% cheaper than when new - as well as some new ex-display models. All the cookers come with a six month guarantee and there is free delivery within the M25 area. Countrywide delivery is by courier.

## DOWEL & LLOYD AUCTIONEERS

118 PUTNEY BRIDGE ROAD, LONDON SW15
☎ 0181-788 7777. TIMES VARY.

Unclaimed goods from the Metropolitan Police are auctioned every two weeks on Thursdays. The auction starts at 9.30 and continues until all the goods are sold, so it's worth staying until the end. Viewing the previous day from 9.30-6. Goods range from jewellery to bikes, cups and saucers to double beds. Furniture auction every other Saturday from 10; viewing the previous day from 9.30-7.30. Furniture is laid out in room sets and sells everything from pictures and china to carpets and pine chests. It costs £60 a year to be put on the mailing list.

## KNOTS KNITWEAR

19 JERDAN PLACE, FULHAM, LONDON SW6 1BE
☎ 0171-385 2252. OPEN TUE,WED AND THUR 10.30 - 4 AND ON SAT
11 - 3 OR BY APPOINTMENT.
STUDIO - ☎ 0171-385 9929. OPEN MON - SAT 9 - 6.30 AND
UNTIL 7.30 ON THUR..

Knots Knitwear has just opened a new showroom in London selling goods at wholesale prices. There are silky cottons, alpaca and linens, jumpers, jackets, skirts and twinsets, and 100% cashmere and silk scarves, shawls, throws, skirts and dressing gowns. There is a new studio upstairs where they claim to have hundreds of Rococo frames all ready-made and are sold at factory prices to the public. There is a print room with a wide selection of modern and old - fashioned prints from £3. There is also a Medieval Mirror room and a Gift room with many cards and presents from under £5.

## MORRY'S

39-40 THE BROADWAY, EDMONTON, LONDON N9 OTJ
☎ 0181-807 6747. OPEN 8.30 - 5 MON - SAT, CLOSED AT 1 ON THUR.
Liquidation stock which includes some famous makes and can
comprise anything from gardening equipment (shovels, forks and
hoses) and household items to electrical equipment (CDs, radios,
CDi's, TVs, radio alarms) and clothing for women, men and
children. Everything is at least half the retail price. Phone beforehand
to find out what they've got in stock or if you live nearby, drop in
frequently.

## ROGER LASCELLES

29 CARNWATH ROAD, LONDON SW6 3HR
☎ 0171- 731 0072. OPEN 9 - 5 MON - FRI.
Makes an inspiring selection of clocks from tickers in a tin to traditional stlyes which replicate covetable antiques. There are wall clocks,
table ones, kitchen ranges, mantel clocks and even tin clocks with
nursery rhyme designs, all with quartz battery movement. At his
factory in London, there are usually seconds and ends of lines available at about half the retail price. For example, mantle clocks from
£20. Stock levels vary dramatically throughout the year, so always
check first by phone.

## S & B EVANS

7A EZRA STREET, LONDON E2 7RH
☎ 0171-729 6635. 9 - 1.30 FIRST SUN EACH MONTH.
Although most of their business is contract work with top interior
design shops and garden shows, they do sell seconds from the kiln at
half price from 60p to £250, but only for half a day each month. The
rest of the time, the shop is full-priced. Their stock ranges from
domestic ware and flower pots to terracotta ware, mugs and jugs,
bowls and lemon squeezers.

## THE CANDLE SHOP

50 NEW KING'S ROAD, LONDON SW6 4LS
☎ 0171-736 0740. OPEN 9 - 6 MON - SAT.
Warehouse outlet servicing the shop in Covent Garden's Piazza,
which sells candles at what they claim are the lowest prices in the
country. You can buy anything from bulk boxes of two hundred 8"

cream candles to church candles at wholesale prices, as well as floating, scented and novelty candles. Candle-making supplies are also available. Mail order catalogue on request.

## THE SALVAGE SHOP

34-38 WATLING AVENUE, BURNT OAK, MIDDLESEX HA8 0LR
☎ 0181-952 4353. OPEN 9 - 5.30 MON - SAT.
An Aladdin's cave of "salvaged" stock for the avid bargain hunter, most of which has been the subject of bankruptcy, insurance claims, fire or flood. Regular visitors have found anything from half-price Kenwood Chefs, typewriters and telephones to furniture, kitchen items and designer clothes. Yves St Laurent, Ungaro, MaxMara, Chloe, Agnes B, Mondi, are just some of the labels (though they are often cut out) to appear. Discounts range from 50%-75%. Phone first to check stock.

## TRACEY EDWARDS

LONDON SE1
☎ 0171-370 7850. MAIL ORDER OR BY APPOINTMENT.
Home-based business selling top-quality linen and Egyptian cotton sheets and pillowcases. A pair of hemstitched super king-sized sheets (305x320) costs £395; an equivalent pair in a well known department store costs £900; double sheets are £260 compared with about £520. A pair of king size two-row corded sheets costs £328 as opposed to £695; singles cost £175 compared with £300, and doubles £215. Egyptian cotton pillowcases cost £9.50 each, compared with £29 in a department store. Two-row corded linen pillowcases cost £28 each. P&P extra.

# Factory Shops

## PRICE'S PATENT CANDLE CO

100 YORK ROAD, LONDON SW11 3RU
☎ 0171-228 3345. OPEN 9.30 - 5.30 MON - SAT.
Factory shop selling the famous Price's candles at discounts of between 10% and 25%. The Christmas factory shop sale with its dec-

orations is legendary and well worth going to. Price's also has an outlet at Bicester Outlet Shopping Village (see Household, Wales and West Midlands).

## VILLEROY & BOCH (UK) LIMITED

267 MERTON ROAD, LONDON SW18 5JS
☎ 0181-870 4168. OPEN 10 - 5 MON - SAT, 11 - 5 SUN.
The UK's main factory outlet for Villeroy & Boch (see West Midlands for other outlet) carries an exclusive range of tableware, crystal and cutlery from Europe's largest tableware manufacturer. Convenient parking and pleasant surroundings make for a pleasurable and unhurried shopping experience. A varied and constantly changing stock, including seconds, hotelware and discontinued lines, on sale at excellent reductions, always makes for a worthwhile visit.

# *Designer Sales*

## HOMES & GARDENS CHRISTMAS GRAND SALE

ORGANISER: ROBERT TORRANCE, PO BOX 427, LONDON SW10 9XE
☎ 0171-351 3088. OPEN 9.30 - 5.30 MON - FRI.
The annual Homes & Gardens Chrismas Grand Sale takes place in London, with over 120 different small companies selling their merchandise to the public. Quality is high and covers everything from dried flowers to bath accessories, Amish quilts to silverware, wooden toys to hand-painted kitchenware, often at discount because they are ends of lines. Book tickets in advance through a coupon in Homes & Gardens magazine in the months running up to the sale, with a proportion of the revenue going to charity. There is also a Homes & Gardens Summer Grand Sale held near Harrogate, Yorkshire every June and a Spring Grand Sale is planned for Edinburgh in March 1996.

# SOUTH EAST
## Permanent Discount Outlets

### ALLDERS

CLEARANCE CENTRE, 78-82 HIGH STREET, SUTTON, SURREY M1 1ES
☎ 0181-770 9770. OPEN 9 - 5.30 MON - FRI, 9 - 6 SAT.

Allders department store has a special clearance centre in its old shop just down the road from Sutton station. Operating under the name of Clearance Centre, rather than Allders, the centre sells lighting, carpets, rugs, fashion items, dishwashers, beds, sofas and a host of other products, all at the sort of discounts you'd expect from end-of-line stock. Don't confuse the discount centre with the Allders store in the St. Nicholas Shopping Centre.

### FLOWER SMITHS

SMITH END FARM, SMITH END LANE, BARLEY, NEAR ROYSTON, HERTFORDSHIRE SG8 8LL
☎ (01763) 848545. OPEN 10 - 5 SUN.

Open on Sundays only between 1st October and 31st March, selling English dried flowers, exotic plant material, baskets and floristry sundries as well as arrangements. A large selection of Christmas decorations using nuts, spices, fruits, cones and church candles are also available. All at up to 75% less than high street prices. For example a 9ft long spruce-style garland, £5.95 undecorated, from £9.95 decorated. Mini terracotta pots filled with roses cost 95p. In the summer, weddings (bouquets, hair decorations, combs, hats and headdresses) and garden parties are catered for by appointment.

### SECOND EDITION

MONTAGUE STREET, WORTHING, WEST SUSSEX PO22 6DS
☎ (01903) 823163. OPEN 9.30 - 5 MON - FRI, 9 - 5.30 SAT.

Second Edition sells a wide range of goods from designer clothes and children's bedding to lamps, china ornaments, tablecloths and kitchenware. Some are seconds, some perfects and discounts range from 25%-50%. They have been known to stock designers such as Caroline Charles as well as a wide range of high street and chainstore brand names. Kitchenware includes storage jars, assorted mugs, kitchen clocks and saucepans. Examples of prices include medium-sized Swan saucepans without lids, £7.99; table cloths from £1.99.

## SILVER EDITIONS

PO BOX 16, CHALFONT ST GILES, BUCKINGHAMSHIRE HP8 4AU
☎ (01494) 876206. FAX 01494 876227. MAIL ORDER.

Specialises in selling fine English sterling silver and silver-plated gifts and cutlery at wholesale prices, often half the sum for the same items in high street shops. Their catalogue features an exceptionally wide range of gifts and cutlery at prices from £2.50 to several thousand pounds. Canteens of cutlery, photo frames, desk sets, serving pieces and children's christening gifts are just a few of the categories on offer. The catalogue also carries the complete range of Hagerty silver cleaning products. Write to the address above for a copy of the catalogue.

## SPOILS

253-254 LAKESIDE SHOPPING CENTRE, WEST THURROCK, ESSEX RM20 2ZQ
☎ (01708) 890298. OPEN 10 - 8 MON - THUR, 10 - 9 FRI, 9 - 7.30 SAT, 11 - 5 SUN.
UNIT 10, THE DRUMMOND CENTRE, CROYDON, SURREY
☎ 0181- 688 8717. OPEN 9 - 5.30 MON - SAT.
52 HEAD STREET, THE CULVER STREET, COLCHESTER, ESSEX CO1 1PB
☎ (01206) 763411. OPEN 9 - 5.30 MON - SAT, 9.30 - 5.30 THUR.
323-324 DUKES WALK, CHEQUERS CENTRE, KING STREET, MAIDSTONE, KENT ME15 6AS
☎ (01622) 678916. OPEN 9 - 5.30 MON - SAT, 9.30 - 5.30 TUE.
145 HIGH STREET, SOUTHEND, ESSEX SS1 1LL
☎ (01702) 352733. OPEN 9 - 5.30 MON - SAT.
UNIT D, THE MARLOWES CENTRE, HEMEL HEMPSTEAD, HERTFORDSHIRE
☎ (01442) 235018. OPEN 9 - 5.30 MON - SAT, UNTIL 8 ON THUR.
UNIT 54B, EASTGATE CENTRE, BASILDON, ESSEX SS14 1AE
☎ (01268) 520827. OPEN 9 - 5.30 MON - FRI, 9 - 6 SAT.
UNIT 22, LIBERTY 2, ROMFORD, ESSEX RM1 3EE
☎ (01708) 751413. OPEN 9 - 5.30 MON - SAT.
UNIT F7-11, THE MARLANDS, SOUTHAMPTON, HAMPSHIRE SO14 7SJ
☎ (01703) 332019. OPEN 9 - 5.30 MON - SAT.
4A CORN EXCHANGE, BISHOPS STORTFORD, HERTFORDSHIRE CM23 3AJ
☎ (01279) 652210. OPEN 9 - 5.30 MON - SAT.

85, 86 & PART 87, COUNTY MALL, CRAWLEY, WEST SUSSEX
☎ (01293) 539941. OPEN 9 - 5.30 MON - WED, 9 - 8 THUR, 9 - 6 FRI, SAT.
UNIT S16, THE BENTALL CENTRE, KINGSTON-UPON-THAMES,
SURREY
☎ 0181-974 9303. OPEN 9 - 6 MON - WED & FRI, SAT , 9 - 9 THUR,
11 - 5 SUN.

General domestic glassware, non-stick bakeware, kitchen gadgets, ceramic oven-to-tableware, textiles, cutting boards, aluminium non-stick cookware, bakeware, plastic kitchenware, plastic storage, woodware, coffee pots/makers, furniture, mirrors and picture frames. Rather than being discounted, all the merchandise is very competitively priced - in fact, the company carry out competitors' checks frequently in order to monitor pricing. With 29 branches, the company is able to buy in bulk and thus negotiate very good prices.

## T K MAXX

THE GALLERIA SHOPPING CENTRE, COMET WAY, JUNCTION 3 OFF
THE A1, HATFIELD, HERTFORDSHIRE
☎ (01707) 270063. OPEN 10 - 8 MON - FRI, 10 - 6 SAT, 11 - 5 SUN.
173-178 HIGH STREET, BELOW BAR, SOUTHAMPTON
☎ (01703) 631600. OPEN 9 - 5.30 MON - FRI, 9 - 6 SAT, UNTIL 7 ON
THUR.
BROAD STREET MALL, BROAD STREET, READING, BERKSHIRE
☎ (01734) 511117. OPEN 9 - 5.30 MON - FRI, 9 - 6 SAT.
LOWER CONCOURSE, THE PEACOCKS, WOKING, SURREY
☎ (01483) 750263. OPEN 9.30 - 6 MON - FRI, UNTIL 8 ON THURS,
9 - 6 SAT, 11 - 5 SUN.

Based on an American concept, TK Maxx is the first British retailer to practise "off-price" retailing. This means a centrally located store which offers famous label goods with up to 60% savings off recommended retail prices. TK Maxx has fashion for the whole family - women's, men's and childrenswear - accessories, shoes, gifts, kitchenware and home goods. Everything in the store is branded with a choice of well-known high street names to designer labels, and while a small percentage might be clearly marked past season, the great majority of items in store are current season, current stock and still with phenomenal savings. There is a huge choice with 50,000 pieces in store with 5,000 new items arriving a week, so it's worth keeping abreast of the latest deliveries as turnaround is very fast. One of the ways in which TK Maxx is able to offer such low prices is by running a very low-cost operation, so the stores are simple and unfussy with wide aisles, shopping trolleys and baskets, and a spacious, functional feel to them. Service is not compromised, however: there are individual changing rooms, ramps for buggies and wheelchairs, plenty of staff on the shop floor and all the branches accept all major credit and debit cards.

## *Factory Shops*

### GENEVIEVE

THE GALLERY 13 VICTORIA STREET, ENGLEFIELD GREEN, SURREY TW20 OQY
☎ (01784) 430516. OPEN 10 - 6 MON - SAT.

A ceramicist of handpainted items with bright floral and foliage designs, Genevieve Neilson is now manufacturing and retailing from the same outlet. At the back is the workshop; at the front, the shop where she sells her own and other individual's products at factory direct prices. Among items on sale are handpainted cushions, candlesticks, clocks, chairs, handblown glass imported from Spain and France, hand-painted furniture, soft toys, bears and rabbits.

### HEIRLOOMS LTD

2 ARUN BUSINESS PARK, BOGNOR REGIS, WEST SUSSEX PO22 9SX
☎ (01243) 820252. OPEN TWICE A MONTH, USUALLY 10 - 5 ON THE FIRST FRIDAY AND SOME SUNS AND BANK HOLIDAYS. PHONE FIRST FOR A LIST OF OPEN DAY DATES.

Sleep like a king, dine like a lord or lounge like a lady....the Heirlooms factory shop is brimming with luxury at affordable prices, the majority of which are made on the premises. Elegant and exceptionally high quality bed linens in Egyptian cotton, pure linen and the finest polycotton percale, in four sizes up to super-king are sold in this 800 sq ft outlet. There's also table linens using classic hem stitching or handmade laces, a cornucopia of gifts with exquisite laces and embroideries, and handmade christening and baby wear. Also seconds in sterling silver and silverplated frames and sterling silver clocks, all in boxes. Normally only found in the most exclusive shops, homes and palaces all over the world, here you can buy ends of lines and slight seconds at between 30% and 65% off the recommended retail price. This busy exporting company only opens the factory shop about twice a month, so check before making what will be a worthwhile journey.

## KENWOOD ELECTRICAL FACTORY SHOP

NEW LANE, HAVANT, HAMPSHIRE
☎ (01705) 476000. OPEN 9 - 4 MON - THUR, 9 - 12 FRI, SAT. MAIL ORDER.

Wide range of Kenwood items from food processors, coffee makers and deep fat fryers to kitchen scales, irons, can openers, juice extractors, hair dryers, shavers and toasters at factory prices. This usually means 20%-25% off the normal retail price. They are in perfect working order, but may be cosmetically slightly imperfect or box damaged. All come with a one year's guarantee. Any new attachments bought at the factory shop are not available at discount.

## LEIGH LIGHTING COMPANY

1593 LONDON ROAD, LEIGH ON SEA, ESSEX SS9 2SG
☎ (01702) 77633. OPEN 9 - 5 MON - FRI, 9 - 5.30 SAT. MAIL ORDER.

Thousands of lighting fixtures at between 20-50% below normal retail prices. Selling to both the commercial and domestic market, they offer recessed lights, table lamps, chandeliers, wall lights and outdoor security lighting, all of which are bought direct from the manufacturer. Their pack, which is given on a month loan basis for a fully refundable deposit of £15, offers big disounts - up to 40%. Full installation and rewiring available countrywide.

## MERCHANTS QUAY

BRIGHTON MARINA, BRIGHTON, SUSSEX BN2 5UF
☎ (01273) 693636. FAX (01273) 675082.

Ten main factory shops plus twenty-four small factory concessions including The Factory Shop, Edinburgh Crystal, Bookscene and Hornsea Pottery. The concessions include Tom Sayer menswear, Coloroll and Double Two shirts. There are also two "affordable" art galleries, a craft shop, a framing shop, a full-price bridal shop, a multi-complex 8-screen cinema, an Asda superstore, small playground and a variety of eating places.

# NAZEING GLASS

NAZEING NEW ROAD, BROXBOURNE, HERTFORDSHIRE EM10 6SU
☎ (0992) 464485. OPEN 9.30 - 4.30 MON - FRI, 9.30 - 3 SAT.

A large factory shop measuring almost 2,000 sq ft selling seconds, overmakes and ends of lines from a range of cut glass decanters, rose bowls, vases, jugs engraved to order, as well as champagne flutes, liqueur and cocktail glasses at factory shop prices, which in practice means 20%-40% off. There are 20 different suites of wine glass in 7 different sizes.

# RYE POTTERY

77 FERRY ROAD, RYE, EAST SUSSEX TN31 7DJ
☎ (01797) 223363. OPEN 9 - 5 MON - SAT, CLOSED 12 - 2 DAILY.

There is always a selection of seconds available in distinctive hand-decorated designs. No two items of this 'majolica' or 'delft' decorated pottery are the same, which is why it is still popular with the Royal Family. Choose from Chaucer figures, American folk heroes, Scenes from Alice or Pastoral Primitives; seconds are usually two-thirds of retail price.

# THE FACTORY SHOP

UNIT 4C, THE GLOUCESTERS, LUCKYN LANE, BASILDON, ESSEX SS14 3AX
☎ (01268) 520446. OPEN 9 - 5.30 MON - SAT, 10 - 5 SUN.

Large warehouse carrying a wide range of almost everything you can imagine: china, glass, bedding, hardware, toys, clothes, cosmetics, cards, disposable partyware, seasonal goods such as Christmas decorations, garden furniture, fans and gardening equipment at discounts of about 30%. Most of the merchandise is overmakes, bankrupt stock, discontinued lines and clearances. Stock changes daily and there are always bargains to be found. There is easy wheelchair access and coach parties are welcome.

## Secondhand Shops

### THE CHINA MATCHING EXCHANGE

29 GREENHILL ROAD, CAMBERLEY, SURREY GU15 1HE
☎ (01276) 64587. OPEN 10.30 - 5 TUE - FRI. MAIL ORDER.
Operates by mail order, although there is a collection and delivery service which operates from an antique centre at Bracknell. They deal in discontinued patterns of twentieth century English china tableware.

# SOUTH WEST

## Permanent Discount Outlets

### COOKMATE KITCHEN SHOP

7 CATHERINE STREET, SALISBURY, WILTSHIRE SP1 2DF
☎ (01722) 331133. OPEN 9 - 5.30 MON - SAT.
Cookmate now incorporates The Pot Bank who are specialists in discontinued and seconds of china, selling Johnsons, Burleigh and Grindley as well as some perfects.

### EXETER SURPLUS

BAKERS YARD, ALPHIN BROOK ROAD, MARSH BARTON, EXETER
☎ (01392) 496731. OPEN 8.30 - 5 MON - SAT, 10 - 4 SUN.
Operates from a 16,000 square foot warehouse, buying good quality, used goods from government departments, schools and the armed forces , among others. Their merchandise includes anything from a World War Two helmet, camping equipment, saucepans, cutlery, gardening tools, Irish linen and woollen blankets to office furniture, catering equipment, shelving, nuts and bolts, leather and bolts of cloth. There are usually more than 20,000 different lines in stock; examples of prices includes brand new Irish linen sheets for £6.99; down and feather sleeping bags, from £15, usually about £100; marquees for £400, usual price £2,500.

# HYBURY CHINA

HIGHER FARM BARN, MILBORNE WICK, SHERBORNE, DORSET
DT9 4PW

☎ (01963) 250500. ☎ (01963) 250335. MAIL ORDER.

Sells pure white, famous-make fine English bone china seconds as
well as a range of pieces with delicate design detail at very compete-
tive prices. All items are dishwasher safe, usable in the microwave, and
available by mail order. The white bona china is ideal for hand
painting. There are two types: the classic which is perfectly plain and
the traditional which is plain with a wavered edge. The china comes
from the major English bone china companies prior to being stamped
by the manufacturer. A perfect bone china dinner plate would
normally cost £14-£18; Hybury offer their dinner plates from £3.50.

# THE DOWNTON TRADING COMPANY

THE OLD MANSION HOUSE, 3 THE HIGH STREET, DOWNTON,
NR SALISBURY, WILTSHIRE SP5 3PG

☎ (01725) 510676. OPEN 9.30 - 5 MON - SAT.

An ingenious new way of shopping:Bryn Parry, cartoonist and frame
maker to the White House, has opened a new shop selling other top-
name company's seconds, overmakes, discounted and discontinued
lines. The number of companies changes constantly but there are
usually about 40 or 50 selling different goods in the shop at any one
time, with a changeover of stock every three months. When I visited
there were hand-painted porcelain boxes; hand lacquered tablemats,
trays and wastepaper baskets; tapestry stools; limited editiond, paint-
ings and prints; drawing room china; seconds in high quality photograph frames, clocks, cartoon frames, and greetings cards from Bryn
Parry; Oleographs; designer fabric nursery bags; and silk ties and
braces; as well as candles, leather goods, table lamps and shades,
drawing room furniture, plant pot holders, silver for the dining room
table, American soft toys, conservatory furniture and accessories,
kitchen pottery, leather-bound photograph albums, bulletin boards,
Christmas decorations (in season), crystal glass and Victorian paint-
ings. Everything is colour coded in four categories so you can tell
wether you're buying a second, discounted, overmake or a perfect but
discontinued line, and prices reflect that. The shop is situated in the
centre of the village at Downton next to the Tannery.

# TK MAXX

THIRD FLOOR, THE GALLERIES, BRISTOL, AVON
☎ (0117) 9304404. OPEN 9 - 5.30 MON - SAT, 7 ON THUR.

Based on an American concept, TK Maxx is the first British retailer to practise "off-price" retailing. This means a centrally located store which offers famous label goods with up to 60% savings off recommended retail prices. TK Maxx has fashion for the whole family - women's, men's and childrenswear - accessories, shoes, gifts, kitchenware and home goods. Everything in the store is branded with a choice of well-known high street names to designer labels, and while a small percentage mightly be clearly marked past season, the great majority of items in store are current season, current stock and still with phenomenal savings. There is a huge choice with 50,000 pieces in store with 5,000 new items arriving a week, so it's worth keeping abreast of the latest deliveries as turnaround is very fast. One of the ways in which TK Maxx is able to offer such low prices is by running a very low-cost operation, so the stores are simple and unfussy with wide aisles, shopping trolleys and baskets, and a spacious, functional feel to them. Service is not compromised, however: there are individual changing rooms, ramps for buggies and wheelchairs, plenty of staff on the shop floor and all the branches accept all major credit and debit cards.

# TRAGO MILL

REGIONAL SHOPPING CENTRE, NEWTON ABBOT DEVON TQ12 6JD
☎ (01626) 821111. OPEN 9 - 5.30 MON - SAT, 10.30 - 4.30 SUN.

Sells virtually everything from children's, women's and men's wear, gardening equipment and cookwear to wallpaper, carpets and fitted kitchens. Most are branded goods and there is a creche, cafe, pizza bar and petrol station.

# *Factory Shops*

## ART CANDLES

DUNMERE ROAD, BODMIN, CORNWALL PL31 2QN
☎ (01208) 73258. OPEN 10 - 6 MON - FRI, 10 - 5 SAT, 11 - 6 SUN IN
SUMMER AND BANK HOLIDAYS.

A family business with a factory outlet selling candles and candle-holders of every shape and design from beeswax to scented, figurative holders to pottery. They specialise in marbled candles, and there are also 3ft high stalagmite candles, owl, tortoise and Buddha-shaped candles. There are tubs of seconds at even cheaper prices.

## CLARKS VILLAGE FACTORY SHOPPING

FARM ROAD, STREET, SOMERSET BA16 OBB
☎ (01458) 840064. OPEN 9 - 6 MON - SAT, 11 - 5 SUN. TIMES CHANGE
WINTER AND SUMMER.

Purpose-built village of brick-built shops with extensive car parking facilities. Restaurant run by Leith's, fast food stands, carousel, indoor play area, outdoor play area. Here, there are at August 1995, 37 shops with more planned. For the household: Royal Brierley, Royal Worcester, Denby Pottery, Dartington Crystal, Crabtree & Evelyn, The Linen Cupboard, The Pier, Wrangler, Black & Decker and Remington.

## DARTINGTON CRYSTAL

LINDEN CLOSE, SCHOOL LANE, TORRINGTON, DEVON EX38 7AN
☎ (01805) 622321.OPEN 9.30 - 5 MON - SAT, 10.30 - 4.30 SUN. MAIL
ORDER.

A factory shop selling an across-the-board selection of Dartington crystal seconds at 20%-30% discounts, as well as some perfects at full price. Range includes wine suites, sherry glasses, tankards, decanters, clear and wavered glass, fruit and salad bowls, cookie jars and perfume atomisers. Wedgwood, Denby and Portmeirion perfects are also avail-able, as well as silk flowers and a massive range of china giftware, cutlery, locally-made food and Colony candles, all at competitive rather than discounted prices.

# DARTMOUTH POTTERY

WARFLEET, DARTMOUTH, DEVON TQ6 9BY
☎ (01803) 832258. OPEN 10 - 5 MON - SAT.
Discontinued lines and some perfects of Dartmouth pottery at varied
discounts. Always some special offers on; prices range from 50p to
£15. On sale are vases, planters, tableware, mugs, plates, cups, money
boxes.

# GLASS HOUSE OF MARBLES

POTTERY ROAD, BOVEY TRACEY, DEVON TQ13 9DE
☎ (01626) 835358. OPEN 9 - 5 SEVEN DAYS A WEEK IN SUMMER.
Factory shop selling seconds and firsts of Teign Valley glass including
handblown decorative glasses and vases, ceramics, speciality marbles,
pub games, figurines, jewellery and gifts. There are also two ranges of
pottery on site and some garden furniture, wrought iron and wicker-
ware. There is a museum and a restaurant on site.

# POOLE POTTERY LTD

POOLE, THE QUAY, DORSET BH15 1RF
☎ (01202) 666200. OPEN 9 - 5.30 MON - SAT, 10 - 5.30 SUN.
Factory shop selling seconds in terracotta, Stuart Crystal (some of
which are perfects), Dartington Crystal and Colony candles at discounts of about 30%. The Poole Pottery selection includes their most
popular ranges: Dorset Fruit in four variations (orange, plum apple
and pear), the Vineyard range and Vincent, the sunflower range, all
with matching textiles. Giftware includes the famous blue dolphins,
large storage jars, bread crocks and butter boxes. There is also a gift
shop, craft village, museum, cafe and restaurant.

# ROYAL BRIERLEY CRYSTAL

CLARKS VILLAGE, FARM ROAD, STREET, SOMERSET BA16 OBB
☎ (01458) 840039. OPEN 9 - 6 MON - SAT AND BANK HOLIDAYS,
11 - 5 SUN.
Royal Brierley crystal seconds and Poole Pottery at very good prices,
with up to 50% off retail. Opening times are half an hour earlier on
weekdays and Saturdays from November to end March.

## THE FACTORY SHOP

36-37 ROUNDSTONE STREET, TROWBRIDGE, WILTSHIRE BA12 9AN
☎ (01225) 751399. OPEN 9 - 5.30 MON - SAT.
24 MARKET PLACE, WARMINSTER, WILTSHIRE BA12 9AN
☎ (01985) 217532. OPEN 9 - 5.30 MON - FRI, 9 - 5 SAT.
MART ROAD, MINEHEAD, SOMERSET
☎ (01643) 705911. OPEN 9.30 - 5.30 MON - SAT, 11 - 5 SUN.

Wide range on sale includes men's, ladies and children's clothing and footwear; household textiles, toiletries, hardware, luggage, lighting and bedding, most of which are chainstore and high street brands at discounts of approximately 30%-50%. There are weekly deliveries and brands include all the major stars: Coloroll, Wrangler Factory shops and Dartington to name just three. Lines are continually changing and few factory shops offer such a variety under one roof. The Minehead shop does not sell furniture.

# WALES AND WEST MIDLANDS

## *Permanent Discount Outlets*

## CHINA MATCH

ST PIRRAN, LEA END, ALVECHURCH, BIRMINGHAM WEST
MIDLANDS B48 7AX
☎ (0121) 445 1169. MAIL ORDER.

Sells and buys china which is mostly out of production, and works mostly by mail order.

## CHINA SEARCH

THE OLD FORGE, TAINTERS HILL, KENILWORTH, WARWICKSHIRE
CV8 2GL
☎ (01926) 512402/59311.

Looks for discontinued china for people who have broken a precious item. The most popular requests are for Wedgewood, Royal Doulton, Royal Worcester, Denby, Hornsea and Poole. They also buy and sell tablewear. Please send a stamped addressed envelope.

## DISCOUNT CHINA

HIGH STREET, BOURTON-ON-THE-WATER, NEAR CHELTENHAM,
GLOUCESTERSHIRE GL54 2AP
☎ (01451) 820662. OPEN 7 - 5 SEVEN DAYS A WEEK.
Retailers of china and cookware direct from the factories of
Staffordshire and suppliers to the catering industry. Supplies are
sourced from different manufacturers so varies according to what is
available at the time, but includes china fancies, beakers, cookware,
planters, Portmeirion cookware and dinner sets.

## G R PRATLEY & SONS

THE SHAMBLES, WORCESTER WR1 2RG
☎ (01905) 22678. OPEN 9 - 5.30 MON - SAT, CLOSES AT 1 ON THUR.
A family business which specialises in bone china and earthenwear,
selling famous designer names at 15% lower than normal retail prices.
Manufacturers include Wedgewood, Royal Worcester, and Spode and
individual pieces as well as sets can be bought. They also stock reproduction furniture, good quality country style furniture, rugs and
Chinese carpets which start at £70.

## IMPS

69B HIGH STREET, WITNEY, OXFORDSHIRE
☎ (01993) 779875. OPEN 9 - 5 MON - SAT.
40 UPPER HIGH STREET, THAME, OXFORDSHIRE
☎ (01844) 212985. OPEN 9 - 5 MON - SAT.
52 SHEEP STREET, BICESTER, OXFORDSHIRE
☎ (01869) 243455. OPEN 9 - 5 MON - SAT.
26 MARKET PLACE, HENLEY-ON-THAMES, OXFORDSHIRE
☎ (01491) 411530. OPEN 9 - 5 MON - SAT.
High street shops selling popular chainstore seconds. Witney shop
extends over two floors and has plenty of stock from clothes for all the
family to towels, china, trays and flower cachepots. There are also
bath towels, £5.99, bath sheets, £11.99, fruit design jugs, £9.99,
plates, £3.50. Stock changes constantly.

## LOOT

7 GURNEYS LANE, DROITWICH (ADJACENT TO THE MARKET HALL), WORCESTER, WORCESTERSHIRE
☎ (01905) 771708. OPEN 9.30 - 5.15 TUE - SAT.

Loot sells a wide range of goods which are the result of bankruptcy or are ends of lines. Stock changes constantly and can consist of anything from clothes, gifts, china, glass, leatherware, shoes, wrought iron and handcrafted items. The clothes are described as 'boutique' clothes and consist of such labels such as Kasper, Tricoville, Choise and Parige. Items on sale when we visited included sandwashed silk shirts, £29, new full length overcoats, £118, and china seconds and giftware.

## SPOILS

UNIT U56B/C, U57, PHASE V, MERRY HILL CENTRE, PEDMORE ROAD, BRIERLEY HILL, DUDLEY, WEST MIDLANDS DY5 1SY
☎ (01384) 76969. OPEN 10 - 8 MON - FRI, 10 - 9 THUR, 9 - 7 SAT, 11 - 5 SUN.

General domestic glassware, non-stick bakeware, kitchen gadgets (but no electricals), ceramic oven-to-tableware, textiles, cutting boards, aluminium non-stick cookware, bakeware, plastic kitchenware, plastic storage, woodware, coffee pots/makers, furniture, mirrors and picture frames. Rather than being discounted, all the merchandise is very competitively priced - in fact, the company carry out competitors' checks frequently in order to monitor pricing. With 29 branches, the company is able to buy in bulk and thus negotiate very good prices.

## THE ABBEY WOOLLEN MILLS

MUSEUM SQUARE, MARITIME QUARTER, SWANSEA SA1 1SN
☎ (01792) 650351. OPEN 10 - 5 TUE - SUN, CLOSED MON EXCEPT FOR BANK HOLIDAYS.

Housed in the Swansea maritime and industrial museum because its products are woven on the restored nineteeth century looms housed in the museum. The Mills specialise in pure wool shawls, rugs and blankets, which are sold at discounts of one third off the normal retail price, with occasional seconds selling at half price. Scarves start at £4.99, picnic rugs from £14-£20, blankets measuring 100"x94" cost £40, smaller blankets measuring 60" x 90" cost £26. Savings can be as much as 50% off retail price.

# THE FACTORY SHOP

WESTWARD ROAD, CAINSCROSS, STROUD,
GLOUCESTERSHIRE GL5 4JE
☎ (01453) 756655. OPEN 9 - 5 MON - THUR, SAT, 9 - 6 FRI,
11 - 5 SUN AND BANK HOLIDAYS.
115 HIGH STREET, NEWCASTLE-UNDER-LYME, STAFFORDSHIRE
ST5 1PS
☎ (01782) 717364. OPEN 9 - 5.30 MON - SAT.
NEW ROAD, PERSHORE, WORCESTERSHIRE WR10 1BY
☎ (01386) 556467. OPEN 9 - 5 MON - SAT, 10.30 - 4.30 SUN AND BANK
HOLIDAYS.

Wide range on sale includes women's, men's and children's clothing
and footwear; household textiles, toiletries, hardware, luggage,
lighting and bedding, most of which are chainstore and high street
brands at discounts of approximately 30%-50%. There are weekly
deliveries and brands include all the major stars: Coloroll, Wrangler
and Dartington to name just three. Lines are continually changing
and few factory shops offer such a variety under one roof.

# TK MAXX

THE POTTERIES SHOPPING CENTRE, HANLEY, STOKE-ON-TRENT,
STAFFORDSHIRE.
☎ (01782) 289822. OPEN 9 - 5.30 MON - FRI, UNTIL 8 ON THURS,
9 - 6 SAT.

Based on an American concept, TK Maxx is the first British retailer
to practise "off-price" retailing. This means a centrally located store
which offers famous label goods with up to 60% savings off recommended retail prices. TK Maxx has fashion for the whole family -
women's, men's and childrenswear - accessories, shoes, gifts, kitchenware and home goods. Everything in the store is branded with a
choice of well-known high street names to designer labels, and while
a small percentage mightly be clearly marked past season, the great
majority of items in store are current season, current stock and still
with phenomenal savings. There is a huge choice with 50,000 pieces
in store with 5,000 new items arriving a week, so it's worth keeping
abreast of the latest deliveries as turnaround is very fast. One of the
ways in which TK Maxx is able to offer such low prices is by running
a very low-cost operation, so the stores are simple and unfussy with
wide aisles, shopping trolleys and baskets, and a spacious, functional
feel to them. Service is not compromised, however: there are individ-

ual changing rooms, ramps for buggies and wheelchairs, plenty of staff on the shop floor and all the branches accept all major credit and debit cards.

## *Factory Shops*

## ARTHUR PRICE OF ENGLAND

BRITANNIA WAY, BRITTANIA ENTERPRISE PARK, LICHFIELD, STAFFORDSHIRE
☎ (01543) 257775. OPEN 9 - 5 MON - FRI, 9 - 1 SAT.
This factory shop in Lichfield sells seconds, discontinued lines and shop-soiled samples of silver-plated and stainless steel cutlery. There are sets as well as loose items on sale at half price or less. Also on sale is giftware consisting of candelabras, cruet sets, tea services, tankards and trays, most at half price. There are usually two sales a year - in October and March - when there is an extra 20%-25% off.

## AYNSLEY CHINA

SUTHERLAND ROAD, LONGTON, STOKE-ON-TRENT, STAFFORDSHIRE ST3 1HS
☎ (01782) 593536. OPEN 9 - 5.30 MON - SAT, 10 - 4 SUN FROM APRIL - SEPT ONLY. MAIL ORDER.
UNIT 3, THE FACTORY SHOP, POTTERIES SHOPPING CENTRE, QUADRANT ROAD/BRYAN STREET, HANLEY, STAFFORDSHIRE ST1 1RZ
☎ (01782) 204108. OPEN 9 - 5.30 MON - SAT.
The chance to buy beautiful china at affordable prices. All of Aynsley's giftware and tableware is stocked at factory shop prices, plus there is a selection of seconds and discontinued lines. The giftware range includes handmade china flowers and jewellery, china and Portland clocks, Master Craft figurines and tableware, table lamps and textiles - place mats, cutlery and crockery.

## BICESTER OUTLET SHOPPING VILLAGE

PINGLE DRIVE, BICESTER, JUNCTION 9 OF M40, OXFORDSHIRE
OX6 7WD
☎ (01869) 323200. OPEN 10 - 6 MON - SAT AND BANK HOLIDAYS,
11 - 5 SUN.

Factory shopping village comprising 48 different outlets, which opened in June 1995. Billed as Bond Street comes to Bicester, the shops are very smart indeed, beautifully designed and stocked with end-of-season designer fashions, mens and childrenswear, tableware, shoes and more, all on permanent sale at prices reduced from 25%-50%, with some reductions up to 75%. Outlets which stock items for the home include: glassware and crystal from Edinburgh Crystal; brand name luggage from Equator; home furnishings, bedlinen, cushions, duvet covers and sheets from Hico; glassware from John Jenkins; gifts and homes accessories from Museum Merchandise; silver and stainless cutlery from Oneida; candles and candlesticks from Price's Candles; books, CDs and cassettes from Sapphire Books; top-class tableware and glass from Villeroy & Boch; toiletries and gifts from Woods of Windsor; bedlinen from Descamps. The village also has two restaurants, a small children's play area and free parking.

## BLAKENEY ART POTTERY

WOLFE STREET, STOKE-ON-TRENT, STAFFORDSHIRE ST4 4DA
☎ (01782) 47244. 9 - 4.30 MON - THUR, 9 - 3.30 FRI. MAIL ORDER.

Large range of decorative ware, floral art, kitchenware, vases, jugs, bowls and a Victorian range, all of which are handmade and hand decorated. Because all the items are made on the premises to be sold to retail outlets, they are sold to individual customers at factory direct prices.

## DESCAMPS

PINGLE DRIVE, BICESTER, JUNCTION 9 OF M40, OXFORDSHIRE
OX6 7WD
☎ (01869) 323636. OPEN 10 - 6 MON - SAT AND BANK HOLIDAYS,
11 - 5 SUN.

Beautiful bedlinen and towels from this top quality manufacturer.

# EARLY'S OF WITNEY

MILL STREET, BURFORD ROAD, WITNEY, OXFORDSHIRE OX8 5EB
☎ (01993) 703131. OPEN 10 - 4 MON - FRI, 9 - 2 SAT.

Blankets in pure new Merino wool, traditional cellular blankets, new designs in cotton blankets, and in a myriad selection of colours, economy priced acrylic blankets, baby blankets, handmade patchwork quilted bedspreads, the famous Witney Point blankets, white cotton embroidered bedlinen, printed duvet covers, quilts, cot sheets, pram blankets, table cloths, towels, teacloths, tissue box covers, crochet toppers at factory prices. Stock is made in the next door factory and depends on what has been ordered from there. There are also some seconds, but most of the goods are perfects. Great place to shop for new bedlinen and bedspreads. There were some exceptional bargains in slightly marked bedspreads and some clearance items when we visited.

# EDINBURGH CRYSTAL

BICESTER OUTLET SHOPPING VILLAGE, PINGLE DRIVE, BICESTER, JUNCTION 9 OF M40, OXFORDSHIRE OX6 7WD
☎ (01869) 323200. OPEN 10 - 6 MON - SAT AND BANK HOLIDAYS, 11 - 5 SUN.

One of 48 shops, with more planned, in this factory shopping village which opened in June 1995. Billed as Bond Street comes to Bicester, the shops are very smart indeed, beautifully designed and stocked with end-of-season designer fashions, mens and childrenswear, tableware, shoes and more, all on permanent sale at prices reduced from 25%-50%, with some reductions up to 75%. Edinburgh Crystal's seconds stock is clearly marked with decanters reduced from £95 to £66.50; vases from £50 to £37.99; bowls from £65 to £45; blue glass vases from £9.95 to £4.99. Some items were marked down by 50%. The village also has two restaurants, a small children's play area and free parking. The telephone number given here is for the village.

## ENGLISH COUNTRY POTTERY

STATION ROAD, WICKWAR, WOTTON-UNDER-EDGE,
GLOUCESTERSHIRE GL12 8NB
☎ (01454) 299100. OPEN 9 - 4.30 MON - FRI.

English Country Pottery has two venues, a showroom and a shop,
where it sells seconds and discontinued ranges from its handpainted,
brightly coloured pottery with art deco influences, at half price or less.
The range includes mugs, cups and saucers, lamps, egg cups, ash
trays, vases, tea pots, condiments and candlesticks and is guaranteed
for use in microwave, dishwasher and oven. The showroom is next to
the pottery in Wickwar; the shop is called Crafts, at 16 Cheap St,
Bath; 0225 464397. Open 9.30 - 5.30 Mon - Sat.

## GAYLINE LTD

LLWYNYPIA ROAD, TONYPANDY, MID-GLAMORGAN CF40 2ET
☎ (01443) 433232. OPEN 9 - 5 MON - FRI, CLOSED 1 - 1.30 DAILY,
9 - 12.30 SAT.

Specialise in blinds of all types - venetian, roller, vertical and Austrian
- which are sold by mail order and to high street department stores,
as well as some curtains and netting. Made to measure vertical blinds
are available at 50% less than normal retail prices, as are venetian
blinds. Other styles cost 20% less than normal retail prices, with a
further 10% discount for orders placed within a certain time period.
Catalogue returns are also sometimes available. Operates a home visit
and fitting service.

## GOODSON LIGHTING FACTORY SHOP

CHURCH LANE, HIXON, STAFFORDSHIRE
☎ (01889) 270161. OPEN 9 - 5 MON - SAT.

Sells a wide range of lamps, bases, lampshades and covered hat boxes,
all of which are made in their factory for top department stores. The
company is one of the largest independent manufacturers of lampshades and table lamps in the UK and the factory shop stocks more
than 10,000 lampshades and 2,000 table lamp bases, some of which
are one-offs, some ends of lines and yet others samples. The lamps
cover a wide spectrum from ceramics ones in a variety of colours and
finishes to metal stands, and prices range from £5.99. Lampshades
can be pleated, floral, plain or leopardskin design - the range is as
great as you would find in some of the famous lighting department

stores. There is also a giftware range of glass and pottery, candlesticks and vases, dishes and planters, jugs and bowls, as well as silk and dried flower arrangements, table linens and fabrics and braids. Hat boxes are covered in pretty floral fabric, have wipeable interiors and cost from £10.99. They also sell a special, moire-covered wedding box for £89. There is a coffee shop on site, free car parking and wheelchair access.

## ISIS CERAMICS

THE OLD TOFFEE FACTORY, 120A MARLBOROUGH RD, OXFORD OX1 4LS
☎ (01865) 722729. OPEN 10 - 4 MON - FRI.
Makers of beautiful Delftwear, Isis has a range of cut-price seconds on sale at its workshop and showroom set in an old toffee factory in Oxford. Their most popular seller is the flower brick (£15 usually, compared with £28 retail) followed by lamps and colander bowls, all painted in traditional seventeenth centry colours - blue, green and plum. They also do complete dinner services, platters with tulips, birds and farmyard animals, dessert plates with scalloped edges, teapots and cream jugs, vases and cachepots. Seconds range from £10, high quality seconds in candlestick, flower bricks and colander bowls are half price. There are twice-yearly clearance sales in January and July.

## JANE AND STEPHEN BAUGHAN

THE STABLE, KINGSWAY FARM, ASTON, OXFORDSHIRE OX18 2BT
☎ (01993) 850960. PHONE FOR OPENING TIMES.
Scheduled to open in November 1995, in a converted barn next to their workshop, Jane and Stephen Baughan's factory shop will sell seconds and overmakes of their hand decorated pottery. The pottery is made using traditional methods of slip-casting and jollying before being decorated by hand using a combination of fresh colours and a wide variety of surface designs. They have also developed their own specialised technique of hand stencilling on pottery. Designs range from Sunflower and Blue Wild Clematis to birds and animals and all products are microwave and dishwasher safe.

## JOHN JENKINS

BICESTER OUTLET SHOPPING VILLAGE, PINGLE DRIVE, BICESTER,
JUNCTION 9 OF M40, OXFORDSHIRE OX6 7WD
☎ (01869) 323200. OPEN 10 - 6 MON - SAT AND BANK HOLIDAYS,
11 - 5 SUN.

One of 48 shops, with more planned, in this factory shopping village
which opened in June 1995. Billed as Bond Street comes to Bicester,
the shops are very smart indeed, beautifully designed and stocked
with end-of-season designer fashions, mens and childrenswear, tableware, shoes and more, all on permanent sale at prices reduced from
25%-50%, with some reductions up to 75%. This shop sells crystal
and porcelain such as flower ashtrays, £5.95 reduced from £11.95;
strawberry design painted plates, £3.95, and mugs, £3.50; Oxford
vases, £8.95 from £11.95; fish butter dishes, £14.95 from £26.95;
decanters, glasses, tumblers, coloured glass bowls, Russian lacquer
boxes and jewellery chests. The village also has two restaurants, a
small children's play area and free parking. The telephone number
given here is for the village.

## MINTON BONE CHINA & ROYAL DOULTON

MINTON HOUSE, LONDON ROAD, STOKE-ON-TRENT,
STAFFORDSHIRE ST4 7QD
☎ (0782) 229292. OPEN 9 - 5.30 MON - SAT.

Large shop selling seconds of Royal Crown Derby, Minton and Royal
Doulton Crystal at promotion prices.

## MOORLAND POTTERY

CHELSEA WORKS, 72A MOORLAND ROAD, BURSLEM, STOKE-ON-
TRENT, STAFFORDSHIRE ST6 1DY
☎ (01782) 834631. OPEN 9 - 5 MON - FRI.

Small factory shop selling tableware, giftware, Staffordshire dogs and
figurines in hand decorated spongeware at reasonable prices. Mugs,
£4.40; candlesticks, £15; sugar bowls, £5.50; large fruit bowls, £17;
Staffordshire dogs, £24 for a large pair or £12.50 for a small pair.

## MOULINEX SWAN LTD

THORNS ROAD, BRIERLEY HILL, WEST MIDLANDS DY5 2LB
☎ (01384) 892400. OPEN 9 - 4 MON - FRI, 9 - 1 SAT, CLOSED 1.30 - 2.

Saucepans, cookware and some electrical items, from these well-known ranges at discounted prices. Some are slight seconds, but most are firsts and the prices are about one-third off the full retail price. For example, two-slice toaster, £10.99-£14.75; food processors from £21.99-£88; teasmaids, £31.50; kettles, £9.99 to £19.99; saucepans, £12.99-£42.99 a set; deep-fat fryers, £17.75-£50; coffee makers, £15.99-£24.99; irons, £9.99; juice extractors, £8.99-£31.99.

## ONEIDA

BICESTER OUTLET SHOPPING VILLAGE, PINGLE DRIVE, BICESTER, JUNCTION 9 OF M40, OXFORDSHIRE OX6 7WD
☎ (01869) 323200. OPEN 10 - 6 MON - SAT AND BANK HOLIDAYS, 11 - 5 SUN.

One of 48 shops, with more planned, in this factory shopping village which opened in June 1995. Billed as Bond Street comes to Bicester, the shops are very smart indeed, beautifully designed and stocked with end-of-season designer fashions, mens and childrenswear, tableware, shoes and more, all on permanent sale at prices reduced from 25%-50%, with some reductions up to 75%. Oneida is the world's largest cutlery company and originates from the United States of America. It sells silver and silver plate at discounts of between 30% and 50%, plus frames, candlesticks and trays. The village also has two restaurants, a small children's play area and free parking. The telephone number given here is for the village.

## PORTMEIRION

SILVAN WORKS, NORMACOTT ROAD, LONGTON, STOKE-ON-TRENT, STAFFORDSHIRE ST3 1PW
☎ (01782) 326412. OPEN 9.30 - 5 MON - FRI, 9.30 - 3 SAT.
25 GEORGE STREET, NEWCASTLE-UNDER-LYME, STAFFORDSHIRE
☎ (01782) 615192. OPEN 9 - 4.30 MON - WED, 9.30 - 4.45 FRI, SAT.
LONDON ROAD, STOKE, STAFFORDSHIRE
☎ (01782) 411756. OPEN 9.30 - 5 MON - SAT.

Factory shops selling Portmeirion seconds in all patterns. The selection includes tableware (tea, coffee and dinner set); giftware (vases, planters, mugs, candlesticks, salad and fruit bowls) and co-ordinating accessories (placemats, cookware, textiles, tumblers). Discounts are approximatley one third but vary from item to item.

## PRICE AND KENSINGTON POTTERIES

TRUBSHAW CROSS, LONGPORT, STOKE-ON-TRENT, STAFFORDSHIRE ST6 4LR
☎ (01782) 838631. OPEN 9.45 - 5 MON - SAT.
Seconds in pottery and ceramics from teapots and novelty teapots to cups and flatware at discounts of 40%. Nearly all are handpainted and include biscuit barrels, from £7; post boxes; pigs, £8.45; rabbits, £11; and half a dozen different designs in dinnerware.

## PRICE'S CANDLES

BICESTER OUTLET SHOPPING VILLAGE, PINGLE DRIVE, BICESTER, JUNCTION 9 OF M40, OXFORDSHIRE OX6 7WD
☎ (01869) 323200. OPEN 10 - 6 MON - SAT AND BANK HOLIDAYS, 11 - 5 SUN.
One of 48 shops, with more planned, in this factory shopping village which opened in June 1995. Billed as Bond Street comes to Bicester, the shops are very smart indeed, beautifully designed and stocked with end-of-season designer fashions, mens and childrenswear, tableware, shoes and more, all on permanent sale at prices reduced from 25%-50%, with some reductions up to 75%. Everything sold in this shop are seconds. Church candles were £3.95 for a 6"x3" in June 1995 and £4.79 for a 9"x3"; lawn spikes were £7.69; there are also lanterns, candles in pots and glass jars, star-shaped candles, floating candles, candlestick holders, serviettes, patio lights, scented candles and garden torches. Discounts are about 30%. The village also has two restaurants, a small children's play area and free parking. The telephone number given here is for the village. Price's also has a factory shop in London (see Household, London).

## ROYAL BRIERLEY CRYSTAL

MOOR STREET, BRIERLEY HILL, WEST MIDLANDS DY5 3SJ
☎ (01384) 573580. OPEN 9.30 - 5.30 MON - FRI, 9 - 5 SAT, 10 - 4.30 SUN.
Sells seconds of Royal Brierley crystal at 30% off retail price, with two special sales. Also Royal Worcester porcelain available at seconds prices.

## ROYAL GRAFTON CHINA

MARLBOROUGH ROAD, LONGTON, STOKE-ON-TRENT,
STAFFORDSHIRE ST3 1ED
☎ (01782) 599667. OPEN 9 - 4.30 MON - FRI, 9 - 3 SAT.
Discounted prices for seconds and discontinued lines. Factory shop
has discounts of up to 50%-75% off chinaware. Thirty-seven piece
dinner services from £240; tea services from £80; coffee services from
£80. Giftware - vases from £3.50; bowls and figurines from £25 for
seconds, £49.95 for perfects which would cost £80 in normal retail
outlets.

## ROYAL WINTON

COPELAND STREET, STOKE, STOKE-ON-TRENT, STAFFORDSHIRE
ST4 1PU
☎ (01782) 745464. OPEN 10 - 5 MON - SAT. MAIL ORDER.
Discounts on seconds from the Royal Winton range. The shop sells
hand decorated china, earthenware, glass, ceramics, hand-decorated
spongeware, dinnerware collectibles, lamps and lampshades and gifts,
but only the seconds are discounted. Savings can amount to 45%
with bigger discounts on large dinner sets.

## ROYAL WORCESTER PORCELAIN

SEVERN STREET, WORCESTER, WORCESTERSHIRE WR1 2NE
☎ (01905) 23221. OPEN 9 - 5.30 MON - SAT.
Infinitesimally flawed porcelain seconds at 25% less than "perfect"
prices. Also sells Royal Brierley, Dartington, Caithness and Stuart
Crystal as well as Arthur Price cutlery. There is a vast range with
special offers throughout the year on anything from crystal decanters
and bowls to figurines, cookware and dinner sets. Shipping arrangements worldwide can be organised.

## SALISBURY CHINA

45 UTTOXETER ROAD, LONGTON, STOKE-ON-TRENT,
STAFFORDSHIRE ST3 1NY
☎ (01782) 333466. OPEN 10.30 - 4 MON - SAT.
Small factory shop selling dinner services with six settings for less than
£90 up to £300; half the price of the same items in normal retail
outlets. All the stock is seconds from mugs to fruit bowls, jugs to
coffee sets and teapots.

## SCHOTT ZWIESEL

DRUMMOND ROAD, ASTONFIELDS INDUSTRIAL ESTATE, STAFFORD, STAFFORDSHIRE ST16 3EL
☎ (01785) 223166. OPEN 10 - 4.30 MON - FRI, 10 - 3 SAT. MAIL ORDER.

Europe's largest manufacturer of blown crystal glassware, Schott Zwiesel has been established for more than 100 years. They make fine cut crystal stemware, plain crystal sstemware, crystal giftware and blown decorative crystal. The factory shop sells a variety of glassware including stemware, glass bowls, heat resistant glass, vases, rosebowls, sets of handmade crystal, boxed presentation sets with matching decanters, tankards, fruit bowls.

## SPODE LTD

CHURCH STREET, STOKE-ON-TRENT, STAFFORDSHIRE ST4 1BX
☎ (01782) 744011. OPEN 9 - 5 MON - SAT, 10 - 4 SUN.

Factory shop selling Spode china, earthenware and stoneware at about 35% below the normal retail price, as well as holding regular sales at which discounts of 75% are available on some discontinued lines. All the stock, including seconds, are current patterns and include tableware, wall plaques, fine bone china dinner sets, tea and coffee sets and giftware. There's also a museum and factory tours can be arranged.

## STEWART SECONDS

12 PIER STREET, ABERSTWYTH, DYFED, WALES
☎ (01970) 611437. OPEN 9 - 5.30 MON - SAT, 11 - 5 SUN IN SUMMER.
14 NOTT SQUARE, CARMARTHEN, DYFED, WALES
☎ (01267) 222294. OPEN 9 - 5.30 MON - SAT.
HARFORD SQUARE, LAMPETER, DYFED, WALES
☎ (01570) 422205. OPEN 9.30 - 5.30 MON - SAT.
52 STEPNEY STREET, LLANELLI, DYFED, WALES
☎ (01554) 776957. OPEN 9 - 5.30 MON - SAT.
Y MAES, PWLLHELI, GWYNEDD, NORTH WALES
☎ (01758) 701130. OPEN 9 - 5.30 MON - SAT.

Branded merchandise from most of the major UK chain stores, all well-known high street department store names. It stocks mainly family fashion but also household textiles, such as bedding and towels at reduced prices and crockery, glasses and cutlery, all at reduced prices. The Carmarthen store does not sell bedding, china, cutlery or glass. Check Pier St is open on Sundays. 01834 844621

## STUART CRYSTAL

RED HOUSE GLASSWORKS, WORDSLEY, STOURBRIDGE, WEST
MIDLANDS DY8 4AA
☎ (01384) 828282. OPEN 9 - 5 SEVEN DAYS A WEEK AND BANK
HOLIDAYS.
Seconds of Stuart Crystal at about 30% discount. The selection
includes wine glasses, flower holders, perfume holders, everyday
tableware, salt and pepper sets, ice buckets, wine coolers, and candle
lamps. Also seasonal special offers. First quality is also for sale at the
appropriate price.

## THE FACTORY SHOP

WESTWARD ROAD, CAINSCROSS, STROUD, GLOUCESTERSHIRE
GL5 4JE
☎ (01453) 756655. OPEN 9 - 5 MON - THUR, SAT, 9 - 6 FRI, 11 - 5 SUN
AND BANK HOLIDAYS.
115 HIGH STREET, NEWCASTLE-UNDER-LYME, STAFFORDSHIRE
ST5 1PS
☎ (01782) 717364. OPEN 9 - 5.30 MON - SAT.
NEW ROAD, PERSHORE, WORCESTERSHIRE WR10 1BY
☎ (0386) 556467. OPEN 9 - 5 MON - SAT, 10.30 - 4.30 SUN AND BANK
HOLIDAYS.
Wide range on sale includes men's, ladies and children's clothing and
footwear; household textiles, toiletries, hardware, luggage, lighting
and bedding, most of which are chainstore and high street brands at
discounts of approximately 30%-50%. There are weekly deliveries
and brands include all the major stars: Coloroll, Wrangler and
Dartington to name just three. Lines are continually changing and
few factory shops offer such a variety under one roof.

## VILLEROY & BOCH (UK) LIMITED

BICESTER OUTLET SHOPPING VILLAGE, PINGLE DRIVE, BICESTER,
JUNCTION 9 OF M40, OXFORDSHIRE
☎ (01869) 323200. OPEN 10 - 6 MON - SAT, 11 - 5 SUN AND BANK
HOLIDAYS.
One of 48 shops, with more planned, in this factory shopping village.
The UK's second factory outlet for Villeroy & Boch (see London for
main outlet) carries an exclusive range of tableware, crystal and
cutlery from Europe's largest tableware manufacturer. Convenient
parking and pleasant surroundings make for a pleasurable and unhur-

ried shopping experience. A varied and constantly changing stock, including seconds, hotelware and discontinued lines, on sale at excellent reductions, always makes for a worthwhile visit.

## WEDGWOOD GROUP FACTORY SHOP

KING STREET, FENTON, STOKE-ON-TRENT, STAFFORDSHIRE
☎ (01782) 316161. OPEN 9 - 5 MON - SAT, 10 - 4 SUN AND BANK HOLIDAYS.
Now incorporating ranges from Wedgwood, Johnson Brothers, Masons Ironstone and Coalport. Masons' decorative tableware and giftware at factory shop prices with seconds at about 40% off the first quality prices. At Wedgwood, seconds are sold at the normal retail price minus 40%. There's a nursery range of Wedgwood Peter Rabbit, Thomas the Tank Engine and Rupert Bear wall clocks, £15.95 usual price about £27, plus Coalport figurines, jugs, vases. The Johnson Brothers department has some imperfect china, while others are ends of lines or discontinued patterns. There is a wide variety on sale.

# EAST ANGLIA AND EAST MIDLANDS

## *Permanent Discount Outlets*

## RUTLAND LIGHTING

THISTLETON ROAD INDUSTRIAL ESTATE, MARKET OVERTON, OAKHAM, LEICESTERSHIRE LE15 7PP
☎ (01572) 767587. OPEN 9 - 4 MON - FRI, 9 - 3 SAT.
10-12 WATERGATE, GRANTHAM, LINCOLNSHIRE
☎ (01476) 591049. OPEN 9 - 5 MON - SAT.
Sells outdoor and indoor lights, from light bulbs to lampshades, from lamps to chandeliers, at factory shop prices, which usually mounts to a discount of one third to one half. Lampshades cost from £1.50 to £30; lampstands from £32-£45. Some stock is made by Rutland, some bought in from other manufacturers' ends of lines and chain-store seconds.

# SPOILS

UNIT LS2, CASTLE MALL, ST JOHN'S WALK, NORWICH, NORFOLK
☎ (01603) 762052. OPEN 9 - 5.30 MON - FRI, UNTIL 8 ON THUR,
9 - 6 SAT.
UNITS 10 AND 11, THE SHIRES, HIGH STREET, LEICESTER LE1 4FR
☎ (01533) 624002. OPEN 9 - 5.30 MON - FRI, UNTIL 8 ON WED, 9 - 6 SAT.
2B HIGH STREET, NOTTINGHAM NG1 2ET
☎ (0115) 9581210. OPEN 9 - 5.30 MON - SAT.
57 SUSSEX STREET, CAMBRIDGE CB1 1PA 01223 316518. OPEN 9 - 5.30
MON - SAT.
24 ST MATTHEW'S STREET, IPSWICH, SUFFOLK IP1 3EU
☎ (01473) 252020. OPEN 9 - 5.30 MON - SAT.
22 NORFOLK STREET, KINGS LYNN, NORFOLK
☎ (01553) 763870. OPEN 9 - 5.30 MON - SAT.
12 GUILDHALL STREET, LINCOLN
☎ (01522) 537183. OPEN 9 - 5.30 MON - SAT.
21A MARKET SQUARE, NORTHAMPTON
☎ (01604) 36382. OPEN 9 - 5.30 MON - SAT.
2B HIGH STREET, NOTTINGHAM NG1 2ET
☎ (0115) 9581210. OPEN 9 - 5.30 MON - SAT.

General domestic glassware, non-stick bakeware, kitchen gadgets,
ceramic oven-to-tableware, textiles, cutting boards, aluminium non-
stick cookware, bakeware, plastic kitchenware, plastic storage,
woodware, coffee pots/makers, furniture, mirrors and picture frames.
Rather than being discounted, all the merchandise is very competitively priced - in fact, the company carry out competitors' checks frequently in order to monitor pricing. With 29 branches, the company
is able to buy in bulk and thus negotiate very good prices.

# STAGE TWO

SAVILLE ROAD, WESTWOOD, PETERBOROUGH, CAMBRIDGESHIRE
PE3 7PR
☎ (01733) 263308. OPEN 10 - 8 MON - FRI, 9 - 6 SAT, AND BANK
HOLIDAYS.
UNIT 3, TRITTON RETAIL PARK, CENTURION ROAD, LINCOLN LN1
☎ (01522) 560303. OPEN 10 - 8 MON - FRI, 9 - 6 SAT, 10 - 4  BANK
HOLIDAYS.

The name of the stores which sell discontinued lines from Freeman's
catalogues. The full range is carried, but stock depends on what has
not been sold at full price from the catalogue itself, or has been
returned or the packaging is damaged or soiled. Clothing discounts

range from about 50% - 65%. There are also household items and electrical equipment. There are branches in Nottingham, Lincoln and Peterborough.

## Factory Shops

### CAITHNESS CRYSTAL

11 PAXMAN ROAD, HARDWICK INDUSTRIAL ESTATE, KINGS LYNN, NORFOLK PE30 4NE
☎ (01553) 765111. OPEN 9 - 5 MON - SAT, 11 - 4.30 SUN.
Coloured and cut glass, crystal glass including vases, wine and sherry glasses, goblets and flutes, bowls, atomisers, and paperweights sold at seasonal discounts of about 25% off. There is usually a sale from October to Christmas with good bargains. Free glass-making demonstration, tea room. Special engraving service available.

### COPPICE SIDE POTTERY

NORTH STREET, LANGLEY MILL, NOTTINGHAM, NOTTINGHAMSHIRE NG16 4EU
☎ (01773) 716854. OPEN 9 - 5 MON - FRI, 10 - 2 SAT, SUN.
Specialists in quality terracotta pots for the home and garden, the factory shop sells overstocks and seconds in wall planters, jardinieres, patio pots, window boxes, Ali Baba urns and small stencilled pots at prices which are lower than retail. Prices range from 50p.

### DENBY POTTERY

DERBY ROAD, DENBY, NR RIPLEY, DERBYSHIRE DE5 8NX
☎ (01773) 570684. OPEN 9 - 5 MON - SAT, 10 - 5 SUN.
Famous Denby pottery perfects and seconds in tableware, cookware, mugs, informal dining sets, cutlery, pans, lamps and vases as well as seconds in Dartington Crystal. Seconds are sold at 25% less than the normal retail price, with even greater discounts at sale times. Also bargain baskets with pottery which costs up to 75% less than its original price. Sales twice a year in January and June.

## DERWENT CRYSTAL

SHAWCROFT, ASHBOURNE, DERBYSHIRE DE6 1GH
☎ (01335) 345219. OPEN 9 - 5 MON - SAT.
LITTLE BRIDGE STREET, DERBY, DERBYSHIRE, DE1 3LA
☎ (01332) 360186. OPEN 9 - 5 MON - SAT.

A wide selection of glassware and fancy items at factory shop prices. Full English lead crystal from liqueur glasses to vases and bowls, ring-stands and dressing-table novelties. More than 200 different items on sale. Gift wrap service available.

## LADY CLARE LTD

LEICESTER ROAD, LUTTERWORTH, LEICESTERSHIRE LE17 4HF
☎ (01455) 552101. OPEN 9 - 4.45 MON - THUR, 9 - 3.45 FRI.

Lady Clare supplies high class gift shops and top department stores with table mats, trays, coasters, wastepaper bins, picture frames and paper weights. Most of the stock in this small shop adjacent to the factory is seconds, cancelled orders or ends of lines with one third to one half off the normal price. Trays, bins and table mats are all hand lacquered, hand gilded and felt-backed with central designs.

## ROYAL CROWN DERBY

194 OSMASTON ROAD, DERBY, DERBYSHIRE DE23 8JZ
☎ (01332) 712833. OPEN 9 - 5 MON - FRI, 9 - 4 SAT, 10 - 4 SUN.
OPENING TIMES CHANGE DURING WINTER.

One third of the stock in this small shop is made up of seconds of bone china at discount prices of about one third off normal retail. This includes giftware, tableware and paperweights. Seconds sell for one third less than the original price. Tours can be booked and cream teas arranged.

## STANDARD SOAP COMPANY LTD

DERBY RD, ASHBY-DE-LA-ZOUCH, LEICESTERSHIRE LE65 2HG
☎ (01530) 414281. OPEN 10.30 - 5.30 MON, 9.30 - 5.30 TUE - THUR,
9.30 - 3 FRI.

Manufacturers to brand name retailers, they have a small factory shop selling seconds and ends of lines of well known soaps. You buy a basket for 99p and fill them with products from a range which includes soap (10 for £1.50), shampoo, foam bath, talcum powder (35p) and face cloths; there are also gift sets in glass bowls, for less than £5.

## SUZANNE KATKHUDA

HOLDENBY DESIGNS, HOLCOT ROAD, BRIXWORTH,
NORTHAMPTON NN6 9BS
☎ (01604) 880800. OPEN 9.30 - 5 MON - FRI.

Suzanne makes wonderful, colourful, hand-painted ceramics for the kitchen, and has recently opened a factory shop in Northampton. If you like pretty florals or farmyard animal designs, You can find seconds and ends of lines there at about half the normal price. Suzanne first made her name with her striking flower designs from the simplicity of Blue Daisy to the exotic splendour of Sunburst. She then was inspired by the primitive pottery of Africa and the dream symbolism of Australia to bring out an earthy range. Other designs include dots and dashes, fishes, grapes, English landscapes and shells. The outlet is called Suzanne Katkhuda's factory shop.

## TARLETON MILLS FACTORY SHOP

C/O KWIKSAVE, 540-570 SHEFFIELD ROAD, WHITTINGTON MOOR,
CHESTERFIELD, DERBYSHIRE S41 8LX
☎ (01246) 456726. OPEN 8.30 - 5.30 MON, TUE, SAT, 8.30 - 8 WED, THUR,
FRI.

Owned by the Tarleton Mill Factory, there are three factory shops (see Soft Furnishings, North West) which only sell merchandise which is manufactured by Tarleton. They operate as completely separate concessions within Kwik Save stores in order to keep costs and therefore prices down. Tarleton Mill make household textiles for major high street stores and uses only top quality fabrics. The shops sell duvet sets, throwovers, curtains (cotton, velvet, moire), pelmets, tie-backs, Austrian blinds, cushion covers and pads, seat pads, bean bags, top-up beans, floor cushions, conservatory cushion and patchwork pieces. All stock is either quality seconds or discontinued lines, so in some cases it is possible to purchase a whole matching range for a fraction of the high street price. Examples of prices include: single duvet set, £11; cotton curtain from £7.50 to £50; piped cushion cover, £2.

## THE FACTORY SHOP

SOUTH GREEN, EAST DEREHAM, NORFOLK NR19 1PY
☎ (01362) 691868. OPEN 9 - 5 MON - SAT, 10 - 4 SOME BANK HOLIDAYS.
THE FACTORY SHOP, NEWBOLD FOOTWEAR, BROOK STREET, SILEBY,
LEICESTERSHIRE LE12 7RF
☎ (01509) 813514. OPEN 9 - 5 MON - SAT.

Wide range on sale includes men's, ladies and children's clothing and
footwear; household textiles, toiletries, hardware, luggage, lighting
and bedding, most of which are chainstore and high street brands at
discounts of approximately 30%-50%. There are weekly deliveries
and brands include all the major stars: Coloroll, Wrangler and
Dartington to name just three. Lines are continually changing and
few factory shops offer such a variety under one roof.

## THE WORKSOP FACTORY SHOP

RAYMOTH LANE, WORKSOP, NOTTINGHAMSHIRE
☎ (01909) 472841. OPEN 9 - 5 MON - SAT, 10 - 4 SUN.

Manufacturers for top chainstores, the factory shop sells over-runs
and returns in household textiles, bedding, fashion for all the family,
including knitwear and underwear at discount of 20%-40%. The
factory shop is 10,000 sq ft and most of the stock is clothing with
good availability on colours and sizes.

# NORTH WEST, YORKSHIRE AND HUMBERSIDE

## *Permanent Discount Outlets*

## BARGAIN STREET

BUY WELL SHOPPING CENTRE, THORPE ARCH TRADING ESTATE,
WETHERBY, WEST YORKSHIRE
☎ (01937) 845650. OPEN 9 - 5 MON - FRI, 9.30 - 5.30 SAT,
10.30 - 4.30 SUN.

A wide range of ex-catalogue items from men's, women's and
children's clothes to leisure wear, sports gear, underwear, household
goods, linen, electrical equipment such as tvs, music centres and

vacuum cleaners, and toys. Prices are usually about 50%-70% off the catalogue prices with extra discounts on certain days. Quality is variable and stock changes constantly.

## BOUNDARY MILL STORES

BURNLEY ROAD, COLNE, LANCASHIRE BB8 8LS
☎ (01282) 865229. OPEN 10 - 6 MON - FRI, 10 - 5 SAT AND BANK
HOLIDAYS, 11 - 5 SUNS.

One of the largest clearance stores in Britain, it covers more than 60,000 square feet. As well as a department selling household textiles at discount prices, some of the top end of the high street designer labels are on sale here for both women and men. The section where household textiles and bedlinen are sold has many well-known brand names among the stock. Four times a year, there are special sales at which prices are discounted still further. Most of the stock is perfect clearance and ends of lines with the occasional marked seconds. There is a coffee shop and restaurant.

## FLORAKITS LIMITED

WORRAL STREET, CONGLETON, CHESHIRE CW12 1DT
☎ (01260) 271371. OPEN 8 - 5 MON - FRI, UNTIL 9 ON THUR,
9 - 12 SAT, SUN.

Importers and distributors of dried flowers and silk and artificial flowers, trees, plants, baskets and pot pourri, they have available a constant stock of dried flower arrangements at virtually wholesale prices, as well as everything flower arrangers need from baskets and ribbons to wires. Examples of prices include basket arrangements from £5 to £35 , straw hats with flowers, from £2.95 to £4.95, terracota arrangements from £3.65 to £9.85; headresses from £1-£12; hair combs, £1.49 for 12; Alice bands, £3.99 for 10; posies, from £1.23. VAT must be added to all prices.

## FOSC (FACTORY OUTLET SHOPPING CENTRE)

HULL ROAD, YORK, YORKSHIRE YO1 3JA
☎ (01904) 430481. OPEN 10 - 6 SEVEN DAYS A WEEK.

Branded merchandise from more than 50 manufacturers which initially consisted of ends of lines, surplus stock, cancelled orders and slight seconds but is more likely now to be firsts. Some of the best-known high street names are here, including clothing from

Courtaulds, selling everything from bedding, towels, small electrical kitchen equipment such as kettles, stereos, batteries and toys at discounts of between 30%-70%. There is also a cafe, free car parking, disabled facilities and no membership is necessary.

## READMANS LTD

ALFRED HOUSE, SPENCE LANE, HOLBECK, LEEDS, WEST YORKSHIRE LS12 1EF
☎ (0113) 2444960 DRAPERY. ☎ (0113) 2436355 CASH AND CARRY.
Mainly women's, men's and children's clothing as well as bedding, textiles, footwear, towels at prices which are cheaper than the high street.

## SECOND CHANCE

8 PORTLAND STREET, SOUTHPORT, LANCASHIRE PR8 1JU
☎ (01704) 538329. OPEN 9.30 - 5.30 MON - SAT.
Sells mostly good quality seconds in English bone china. For example, Queens cups and saucers, £3.99, list price approx £8.99; Queens mugs, £2.99, list price £5.99; Royal Stafford china 10" plate, £2.75, list price £7.26; teapot, £10, list price £30.70. There is also a large range of Ben Thomas English hand-sponged porcelain at discounts of 40%; Burgess & Leigh seconds at 30% discounts; and a large range of Italian best quality fancies at half price or less - for example, jug £12.99, list price £28. The Kendal branch (see Household, North and Scotland) also stocks Hinchcliffe & Barber seconds at 40% discount and a wide range of table lamps by Saville at 40% off the list price.

## SPOILS

UNIT LG9, PRINCES QUAY, HULL
☎ (01482) 327102. OPEN 9 - 5.30 MON - SAT.
1 HIGH STREET, SHEFFIELD S1 2ER
☎ (0114) 2728402. OPEN 9 - 5.30 MON - SAT.
UNITS 10/17 VOYAGER'S WALK, ARNDALE CENTRE MANCHESTER
☎ (0161) 839 1101. OPEN 9 - 5.30 MON - FRI, 9 - 5.30 SAT, 11 - 5 SUN, UNTIL 8 ON THUR.
48-50 UPPER MALL, MARKET PLACE, BOLTON BL1 2AL
☎ (01204) 528860. OPEN 9 - 5.30 MON - SAT, UNTIL 9 ON THUR.

UNIT MSU4, THE PYRAMIDS CENTRE, BIRKENHEAD L41 2RA
☎ (0151) 647 5753. OPEN 9 - 5.30 MON - SAT.
General domestic glassware, non-stick bakeware, non-electrical
kitchen gadgets, ceramic oven-to-tableware, textiles, cutting boards,
aluminium non-stick cookware, bakeware, plastic kitchenware,
plastic storage, woodware, coffee pots/makers, furniture, mirrors and
picture frames. Rather than being discounted, all the merchandise is
very competitively priced - in fact, the company carry out competitors' checks frequently in order to monitor pricing. With 29
branches, the company is able to buy in bulk and thus negotiate very
good prices.

## TK MAXX

15 PARKER ST, OFF CLAYTON SQUARE, LIVERPOOL, MERSEYSIDE
☎ (0151) 708 9919. OPEN 9 - 6 MON - SAT.
Based on an American concept, TK Maxx is the first British retailer
to practise "off-price" retailing. This means a centrally located store
which offers famous label goods with up to 60% savings off recommended retail prices. TK Maxx has fashion for the whole family -
women's, men's and childrenswear - accessories, shoes, gifts, kitchenware and home goods. Everything in the store is branded with a
choice of well-known high street names to designer labels, and while
a small percentage mightly be clearly marked past season, the great
majority of items in store are current season, current stock and still
with phenomenal savings. There is a huge choice with 50,000 pieces
in store with 5,000 new items arriving a week, so it's worth keeping
abreast of the latest deliveries as turnaround is very fast. One of the
ways in which TK Maxx is able to offer such low prices is by running
a very low-cost operation, so the stores are simple and unfussy with
wide aisles, shopping trolleys and baskets, and a spacious, functional
feel to them. Service is not compromised, however: there are individual changing rooms, ramps for buggies and wheelchairs, plenty of
staff on the shop floor and all the branches accept all major credit and
debit cards.

# *Factory Shops*

## ASTBURY LIGHTING FACTORY SHOP

FOUNDRY BANK, CONGLETON, CHESHIRE
☎ (01260) 298176. OPEN 10 - 5 MON - SAT AND BANK HOLIDAYS.
Factory shop situated in an old mill selling lamp shades, while in
another part of the building, bedding, curtains and clothes are sold
including Dorma, Sheridan, Fogarty and Horrick's. Double quilt
covers, £52.50; double bedspreads, £85; festoon pelmets, £37.50;
double box pleated valance sheets, £42.50. Towels sets at 10% discounts.

## BROOKS MILL

SOUTH LANE, ELLAND, NEAR HALIFAX, WEST YORKSHIRE
☎ (01422) 377337. OPEN 9.30 - 5.30 MON - SAT, 11 - 5.30 SUN.
The clearance outlet for Ponden Mills merchandise - from tablelinen
and quilts, duvets and sheets to bedding and pillowcases, all at appropriately reduced prices. Also clothes for men, half of which is designer
wear including such names as Jac Dale and Maggie of London.

## COURTAULDS BEDLINEN

WIGAN PIER COMPLEX, TRENCHERFIELD MILL, THE PIER, WIGAN,
LANCASHIRE WN3 4ES
☎ (01942) 239531. OPEN 9.15 - 4.30 MON - FRI, 10 - 3.30 SAT - SUN.
Factory shop in Wigan selling bedlinen made for Habitat and Marks
& Spencer, as well as baby linen, Christie and Ashton towels,
curtains, place mats, padded seat cushions and tablecloths. All are
made on the premises, are seconds or discontinued lines and are sold
at discounts of about 50%. Pillowcases sell for £4.50, hand-stitched
single duvets, £23.99.

## DAMART FACTORY CLEARANCE SHOP

UNIT 6A, ALSTON ROAD RETAIL PARK, BYPASS ROUNDABOUT,
BRADFORD ROAD, KEIGHLEY BD21 3NG
☎ (01535) 690648. OPEN 9 - 5.30 MON - SAT, 10 - 4 SUN AND BANK
HOLIDAYS.
Discontinued branded chainstore fashion, some of which is branded
Damart, as well as household items: kitchen utensils, glassware,
towels, tablecloths, brushes, mops but no electrical equipment. Most

of the stock is bought in from other manufacturers and consists of overmakes and discontinued lines at discounts of 50%. Coffee shop on site.

## EDINBURGH CRYSTAL

HORNSEA FREEPORT SHOPPING VILLAGE, HORNSEA, EAST YORK-SHIRE, HU18 1UT
☎ (01964) 534260. OPEN 10 - 5 MON - FRI, 10 - 6 SAT, SUN, BANK HOLIDAYS.
Wide range of crystalware from glasses and vases to tumblers and bowls at discounts of between 33% - 40%. The shop sells firsts and seconds of crystal from one third off the normal price. There are also special promotional lines at discount prices up to 70% off seconds. The Shopping Village has plenty to entertain the family with an adventure playground, an indoor play centre, restaurants, a vintage car collection and butterfly world.

## EDINBURGH CRYSTAL

CHESHIRE OAKS OUTLET VILLAGE, KINSEY ROAD, NEAR ELLESMERE PORT, SOUTH WIRRAL L65 9JJ
☎ (0151) 357 3661. OPEN 10 - 6 MON - SAT, 10 - 4 SUN.
Wide range of crystalware from glasses and vases to tumblers and bowls at discounts of between 33% - 40%. There is also an outlet at Hornsea Freeport Shopping Village.

## FREEPORT SHOPPING VILLAGE

ANCHORAGE ROAD, FLEETWOOD, LANCASHIRE
☎ (01253) 877377. OPEN 10 - 6 SEVEN DAYS A WEEK.
Up to 40 shops, a marina, and lots of activities for the family. Household shops include: Edinburgh Crystal and Acorns (dried flowers).

## HIRAM WILD

SOLLY STREET, SHEFFIELD, SOUTH YORKSHIRE
☎ (0114) 2723568. OPEN 8 - 5 MON - THUR, 8 - 2 FRI, 9 - 12 SAT.
Cutlers and silversmiths since 1864, the factory shop sells discontin-ued lines and slight seconds in silver plate and stainless steel. Brand names include Mutual, Bear in Kind and High Toned and can be found in homes, hotels and restaurants worldwide. There is a stag-

handled range, also available in imitation pearl, imitation horn, white acetate, white acrylic and rosewood; silver plated accessories such as soup tureen spoons, cheese knives and pastry cutters, as well as grained handle knives, boxes sets and old English stainless steel.

## LIGHTWATER VILLAGE AND FACTORY SHOPPING

NORTH STAINLEY, RIPON, NORTH YORKSHIRE HG4 3HT
☎ (01765) 635321. OPEN 10 - 5 SEVEN DAYS A WEEK. OPENING TIMES VARY SEASONALLY.

Lightwater valley theme park is the biggest leisure park in the North of England; now, some of the property has been converted to factory shop retailing. You can visit the shopping village free, without the theme park which makes a charge. There are various factory shops on site selling brand names such as Windsmoor, Planet, James Barry, Tula, Jane Shilton, Edinburgh Crystal, Hornsea pottery. The pottery shop has plenty of ceramics and kitchen utensils to choose from, while the crystal shop has glasses, decanters, giftware and bowls. There are two enormous "warehouses" with masses of fashion for women and men, bedlinen, duvets, shoes, perfume, cookware, suitcases and cosmetics. there will eventually be parking for 4,000 cars and 120 coaches, a market square, coffee shops, food shops, a wine bar, covered garden centre, visitors farm and trout pond. Lightwater is 3 miles off the A1

## OSBORNE SILVERSMITHS LTD

WESTWICK WORKS, SOLLY STREET, WEST BAR, SHEFFIELD S1 4BA
☎ (0114) 2724929. OPEN 9 - 4 MON - FRI, SAT BY PRIOR ARRANGEMENT; CLOSED END JULY/BEGINNING AUGUST.

For almost 300 years, the Osborne family have been Sheffield craftsmen, and now is one of Britain's leading cutlery manufacturers, supplying most of the top stores in London's West End. The factory shop sells slightly blemished or surplus perfect items of cutlery at special prices direct to the public. Their extensive ranges cover both English and Continental patterns in sterling silver, silver plate and stainless steel. In addition to canteens, place sets or individual pieces, they also manufacture an extensive selection of servicing and accessory items often difficult to find elsewhere.

## OSWALDTWISTLE MILLS

MOSCOW MILL, COLLIER ST, OSWALDTWISTLE, LANCASHIRE
BB5 3DF
☎ (01254) 871025. OPEN 9 - 5 MON - SAT, 11 - 5 SUN, UNTIL 8 ON
THUR.

A working mill which manufactures for top hotels and restaurants
within the UK, with lots of attractions for families, apart from the
bargains on offer. There are landscaped grounds, fishing, mini golf,
croquet, a disabled equipment centre, coffee shop, wildfowl and of
course, shopping. The bubble factory and Calico Shop offers slight
seconds and perfects at highly competitive prices in everything from
pottery, glass and ceramics to table cloths, bedlinen and upholstery
fabrics. There is locally woven fabric as well bedding, sheets, towels.
It is part of a retail outlet.

## TARLETON MILLS FACTORY SHOP

PLOXBROW, TARLETON, LANCASHIRE
☎ (01772) 814041. MONTHLY SALES. C/O KWIKSAVE, 177 TOWNGATE,
LEYLAND, NEAR PRESTON, LANCASHIRE PR5 1TE
☎ (01772) 457696. OPEN 8.30 - 6 MON, TUE, SAT, 8.30 - 8 WED, THUR,
FRI, 10 - 4 SUN.

Owned by the Tarleton Mill Factory, there are three factory shops (see
Soft Furnishings, East Anglia) which only sell merchandise which is
manufactured by Tarleton. They operate as compeletely separate concessions within Kwik Save stores in order to keep costs and therefore
prices down. Tarleton Mill make household textiles for major high
street stores and uses only top quality fabrics. The shops sell duvet
sets, throwovers, curtains (cotton, velvet, moire), pelmets, tie-backs,
Austrian blinds, cushion covers and pads, seat pads, bean bags, top-
up beans, floor cushions, conservatory cushion and patchwork pieces.
All stock is either quality seconds or discontinued lines, so in some
cases it is possible to purchase a whole matching range for a fraction
of the high street price. Examples of prices include: single duvet set,
£11; cotton curtain from £6 to £50; piped cushion cover, £2. The
main mill at Tarleton holds monthly sales - phone to get your name
on the mailing list.

## THE BUBBLE FACTORY

MOSCOW MILL, COLLIER STREET, OSWALD TWISTLE,
NR ACCRINGTON, LANCASHIRE BB5 3DF
☎ (01254) 871025. OPEN 9 - 5 MON - SAT, 10 - 5 SUN.
Sells everything you need to keep the house clean, including brand-names such as JIF, Comfort and Flash. And you don't have to bulk buy. There is also a separate shop in the complex selling textiles, including bedding and towels, at factory prices.

## THE DAVID MELLOR FACTORY SHOP

THE ROUND BUILDING, HATHERSAGE, SHEFFIELD S30 1BA
☎ (01433) 650220. OPEN 10 - 5 MON - SAT, 11- 5 SUN.
David Mellor's classic cutlery at discounts of 15%. The shop, situated in a former industrial workshop at an old gasworks in the Peak District, also sells handthrown pottery with which David Mellor has been involved in design or development at normal prices, as well as kitchen racks, cutlery boxes and small gift boxes. Lots of wooden utensils and good quality kitchenware.

## THE FACTORY SHOP

LAWKHOLME LANE, KEIGHLEY, WEST YORKSHIRE BD21 3HW
☎ (01535) 611703. OPEN 9.30 - 5 MON - SAT, 10 - 4 BANK HOLIDAYS.
LANCASTER LEISURE PARK, WYRESDALE ROAD, LANCASTER,
LANCASHIRE LA1 3LA
☎ (01524) 846079. OPEN 10 - 5 MON - SAT, 11 - 5 SUN AND BANK HOLIDAYS.
5 NORTH STREET, RIPON, NORTH YORKSHIRE HG4 1JY
☎ (01765) 601156. OPEN 9 - 5 MON - SAT, 11 - 4 BANK HOLIDAYS.
HORNSEA FREEPORT SHOPPING VILLAGE, HORNSEA, EAST
YORKSHIRE
☎ (01964) 534211. OPEN 10 - 5 MON - FRI, 10 - 6 SAT, SUN.
COMMERCIAL STREET, MORLEY, WEST YORKSHIRE LS1 6EX
☎ (0113) 2381240. OPEN 9.30 - 5 MON - FRI, 9 - 5 SAT.
Wide range on sale includes men's, ladies and children's clothing and footwear; household textiles, toiletries, hardware, luggage, lighting and bedding, most of which are chainstore and high street brands at discounts of approximately 30%-50%. There are weekly deliveries and brands include all the major stars: Coloroll, Wrangler and Dartington to name just three (the Morley branch does not stock

Wrangler). Lines are continually changing and few factory shops offer such a variety under one roof. The Hornsea branch stock special buys bought specifically for the Freeport outlet.

## THE TEA POTTERY

LEYBURN BUSINESS PARK, HARMBY ROAD, LEYBURN,
NORTH YORKSHIRE DL8 5QA
☎ (01969) 623839. OPEN 9 - 5 SEVEN DAYS A WEEK.

A boon for collectors of novelty teapots, all of which are manufactured on site in up to 40 different designs and in sizes from one cup to five cups. Designs include Welsh dressers, wheelbarrows, chests of drawers, Agas, cookers, bellboys with luggage, and a host of others, many of which are collectors' items. Prices start from £18-£45 for perfects, which represents a 10%-20% savings on retail prices, and up to 50% discounts on seconds. Refreshments available. There is a smaller factory shop in Cumbria.

## *Designer Sales*

## HOMES & GARDENS SUMMER GRAND SALE

ORGANISER: ROBERT TORRANCE, PO BOX 427, LONDON SW10 9XE
☎ 0171-351 3088. OPEN 9.30 - 5.30 MON - FRI.

The annual Homes & Gardens Summer Grand Sale takes place at Ripley Castle, near Harrogate, with about 80 different small companies selling their merchandise to the public. Quality is high and covers everything from dried flowers to bath accessories, Amish quilts to silverware, wooden toys to hand-painted kitchenware, often at discount because they are ends of lines. Book tickets in advance through a coupon in Homes & Gardens magazine in the months running up to the sale, with a proportion of the revenue going to charity. There is also a Homes & Gardens Christmas Grand Sale held in London every November and in 1996 a Spring Grand Sale is to be held in Edinburgh.

## *Secondhand Shops*

### CHINA CHASE

DAISYBANK, OSCROFT, CHESTER, CHESHIRE CH3 8NQ
☎ (01829) 741095.
Rather like marriage agency, China Chase matches up those who've lost or broken an item of china with those who've got one to sell. They also search for china at auctions, car boot sales and antique shops. There is a regestration fee of £6 but no commission on matching pieces as buyers and sellers work that out for themselves.

# NORTH AND SCOTLAND

## *Permanent Discount Outlets*

### SECOND CHANCE

27 ALL HALLOWS LANE, KENDAL, CUMBRIA LA9 4JH
☎ (01539) 740414. OPEN 9 - 5.30 MON - SAT. MAIL ORDER.
Sells mostly good quality seconds in English bone china. For example, Queens cups and saucers, £3.99, list price approx £8.99; Queens mugs, £2.99, list price £5.99; Royal Stafford china 10" plate, £2.75, list price £7.26; teapot, £10, list price £30.70. There is also a large range of Ben Thomas English hand-sponged porcelain at discounts of 40%; Burgess & Leigh seconds at 30% discounts; and a large range of Italian best quality fancies at half price or less - for example, jug £12.99, list price £28. This branch also stocks Hinchcliffe & Barber seconds at 40% discount and a wide range of table lamps by Saville at 40% off the list price (see Household, North West for other branch).

### SEYMOUR'S WAREHOUSE

1 EAST ROW, DARLINGTON DL1 5PZ
☎ (01325) 355272. OPEN 9 - 5 MON - SAT.
Trading in Darlington for more than 30 years, this warehouse sells the best makes of household linens, including Sheridan, Fogarty, Christy and Snuggledown, at discounted prices as well as clearance lines in towel, pillows and duvets.

## TK MAXX

LOWER GROUND FLOOR, MONUMENT MALL,
NORTHUMBERLAND STREET, NEWCASTLE-UPON-TYNE, TYNE &
WEAR.
☎ (0191) 233 2323. OPEN 9.30 - 5.30 MON - FRI, UNTIL 8 ON THURS,
9 - 6 ON SAT.

Based on an American concept, TK Maxx is the first British retailer
to practise "off-price" retailing. This means a centrally located store
which offers famous label goods with up to 60% savings off recommended retail prices. TK Maxx has fashion for the whole family -
women's, men's and childrenswear - accessories, shoes, gifts, kitchenware and home goods. Everything in the store is branded with a
choice of well-known high street names to designer labels, and while
a small percentage mightly be clearly marked past season, the great
majority of items in store are current season, current stock and still
with phenomenal savings. There is a huge choice with 50,000 pieces
in store with 5,000 new items arriving a week, so it's worth keeping
abreast of the latest deliveries as turnaround is very fast. One of the
ways in which TK Maxx is able to offer such low prices is by running
a very low-cost operation, so the stores are simple and unfussy with
wide aisles, shopping trolleys and baskets, and a spacious, functional
feel to them. Service is not compromised, however: there are individual changing rooms, ramps for buggies and wheelchairs, plenty of
staff on the shop floor and all the branches accept all major credit and
debit cards.

# Factory Shops

## BAIRDWEAR RACKE

6-8 COLVILLES PLACE, EAST KILBRIDE, GLASGOW, SCOTLAND
G75 OQS
☎ (01355) 236441. OPEN 10 - 4 MON - THUR, 10 - 12 FRI.
24 ROSYTH ROAD, POLMADIE, GLASGOW
☎ (0141) 429 6611. OPEN 11 - 4 MON - THUR, 9.30 - 12.30 FRI, CLOSED
2.30 - 3.
INCHINNEN INDUSTRIAL ESTATE, ABBOTSBURN, RENFREWSHIRE
☎ (0141) 812 6388. OPEN 9.30 - 4.30 MON - WED, 9.30 - 2.15 THUR,
9.30 - 12.30 FRI.

Manufacturers for a major high street chainstore for more than 20 years, Bairdwear has a wide selection of seconds and overmakes in its factory shops. The East Kilbride shop makes men's shirts and sells them as well as women's and children's clothes, with some babywear, as well as towels, sheets and duvets covers. The Abbotsburn shop sells mainly womenswear with some menswear and lots of babywear. The Polmadie shop sells women's and children's clothes, some men's, and household linen and towels, but no duvets.

## EDINBURGH CRYSTAL

JACKSONS LANDING, HARTLEPOOL FACTORY OUTLET SHOPPING MALL, HARTLEPOOL MARINA, HARTLEPOOL, CLEVELAND TS24 OXN
☎ (01429) 234335. OPEN 10 - 6 MON - FRI, 11 - 5 SUN AND BANK HOLIDAYS.
Indoor factory shopping centre with twenty-four outlets selling brand name items including cut-glass crystal. This shop has displays all round packed with glasses, decanters, gifts, glass picture frames, coloured glass, vases, bowls and jugs. Examples of prices include decanters reduced from £80 to £55.99; large tumblers from £14 to £9.75 for perfects; seconds wine glasses from £21 to £10.50; seconds decanters from £84.95 to £42.50; glass bowls from £50 to £19.99; and Caithness handmade glass vases from £9.95 to £5.99. Also when we visited, there were Royal Worcester special offer table mats and oven gloves, 20% off Arthur Price cutlery and 50% off George Butler cutlery. Hartlepool Marina hosts a recreated historic quay and harbours HMS Trincomalee, the oldest British warship still afloat, and is also the site of the new Hartlepool Museum with its interactive fighting ships section and a replica seventeenth century children's play area. There is free parking adjacent to the centre, a coffee shop, restaurant overlooking the Marina, and baby changing and disabled facilities.

## FACTORY BEDDING SHOP

ATLAS HOUSE, NELSON STREET, DENTON HOLME, CARLISLE CA2 5NB
☎ (01228) 514703. OPEN 10 - 5.30 MON - FRI, 9 - 5 SAT, 10 - 4 BANK HOLIDAYS.
Bedding, curtains, duvets, duvet covers, pillows, towels, cushions, and curtain fabrics bought in direct from the manufacturer at factory shop

prices. No brand names, but all sold in high street department stores. Pillows from £1.99; quilts from £5.99; curtains from £10.99; double fitted sheet from £6.49; double duvet cover, £12.99; double valances, £8.99. Wide range of furnishing fabrics from £1.30 a metre, a curtain making service, and co-ordinating kitchen textiles. Also dress fabrics.

## HIGHLAND CHINA LTD

OLD STATION YARD, KINGUSSIE, INVERESSHIRE PH21 1HP
☎ (01540) 661576. OPEN 9 - 5 MON - FRI.

Seconds of bone china and porcelain at up to 50% off. Teapot, £16, porcelain animals, £3-£32.

## JACKSONS LANDING

HARTLEPOOL FACTORY OUTLET SHOPPING MALL, HARTLEPOOL MARINA, HARTLEPOOL, CLEVELAND TS24 0XN
☎ (01429) 866989 INFORMATION LINE. OPEN 10 - 6 MON - FRI, 11 - 5 SUN AND BANK HOLIDAYS.

Indoor factory shopping centre with twenty-four outlets selling a range of brand name items from companies such as Edinburgh Crystal, Royal Brierley. Hartlepool Marina hosts a recreated historic quay and harbours HMS Trincomalee, the oldest British warship still afloat, and is also the site of the new Hartlepool Museum with its interactive fighting ships section and a replica seventeenth century children's play area. There is free parking adjacent to the centre, a coffee shop, restaurant overlooking the Marina, and baby changing and disabled facilities.

## JOCKEY UNDERWEAR FACTORY SHOP

EASTERN AVENUE, TEAM VALLEY TRADING ESTATE, GATESHEAD, TYNE & WEAR
☎ (0191) 491 0088. OPEN 10 - 4 MON, TUE, THUR, 10 - 2.30 FRI, CLOSED WED.

Although this factory makes underwear, because it is part of the Courtaulds group, the factory shop also sells Wolsey socks, Cristy towels, Zorbit babywear, pillows and duvets.

# K VILLAGE FACTORY SHOPPING

KENDAL, NEAR JUNCTION 36 OF M6, CUMBRIA
☎ (01539) 721892. OPEN 9.30 - 7 MON - FRI, 9 - 6 SAT AND BANK
HOLIDAYS, 11 - 5 SUN.

Eight outlets including Crabtree & Evelyn, Denby Pottery,
Dartington Crystal and The Baggage Factory, selling a wide range of
labels from Laura Ashley, Delsey, Cica, and Antler. There is also a
heritage centre, a 150-seater restaurant, a coffee shop and free
parking.

# KILNCRAIGS MILL

PATON & BADLWINS LTD, ALLOA, SCOTLAND
☎ (01259) 723431. OPEN 10 - 4.30 MON - FRI, 10 - 4 SAT.

Sells a range of knitwear from Angora jumpers to tapestries and kits,
as well as Patons wool and discontinued yarns. It also sells garments
from the Coats Viyella group, silk skirts, blouses and ties and
swimwear, nightwear, bedding and towels. Many have been used for
photography for patterns; some are former display garments. The vast
majority, though, are seconds and discontinued lines and are sold at
about half the normal retail price. Tapestries and kits range from £5-
£30; mohair from £6-£10 instead of its normal retail price of £27.50.
Kilncraigs is a working mill with an on-site factory shop.

# LONHRO TEXTILES

NELSON WAY, NELSON INDUSTRIAL ESTATE, CRAMLINGTON,
NORTHUMBERLAND NE23 9JT
☎ (01670) 713434. OPEN 9 - 5 MON - FRI, 9.30 - 4 SAT.

Perfect seconds and reject bedlinen, curtains (perfect) and towels,
bath sets, blankets, bedspreads, duvets and pillows. Full range of
Brentfords and Accord bedlinen in both perfects and seconds at
savings of 10%-30%.

# MCINTOSH'S FACTORY SHOP

UNIT 1, THE FACTORY SHOP CENTRE, TUNDRY WAY, CHAINBRIDGE
INDUSTRIAL ESTATE, BLAYDON ON TYNE NE21 5SJ
☎ (0191) 414 8598.

Quilts, duvet covers, towels, pram covers, beach towels, small
babywear, bedlinen, dusters and bath mat sets at bargain prices. Most
of the household textiles are perfect with some seconds. Parking is
easy and there is a coffee shop.

## NEWALL COMPANY SHOP

WEAR WORKS, OFF TRINDON STREET, MILLFIELD, SUNDERLAND
SR4 6EJ
☎ (0191) 567 6222. OPEN 10 - 4 SAT.
Factory shop which as well as selling current perfect lines at full price,
also sells end of line ranges, as well as surplus orders, of its heat-resis-
tant dishes for the kitchen including Pyrex (cookware, bakeware and
oven to tableware) and Pyroflam - white casserole dishes which are
safe to use in the microwave, dishwasher, freezer or oven top.

## ROYAL BRIERLEY CRYSTAL

JACKSONS LANDING, HARTLEPOOL FACTORY OUTLET SHOPPING
MALL, HARTLEPOOL MARINA, HARTLEPOOL,
CLEVELAND
☎ (01429) 865600. OPEN 10 - 6 MON - SAT, 11 - 5 SUN.
Royal Brierley crystal seconds and Poole Pottery at very good prices,
with up to 50% off retail sold in this indoor factory shopping centre
with twenty-four outlets selling brand name items. Hartlepool
Marina hosts a recreated historic quay and harbours HMS
Trincomalee, the oldest British warship still afloat, and is also the site
of the new museum of Hartlepool with its interactive fighting ships
section and a replica seventeenth century children's play area. There is
free parking adjacent to the centre, a coffee shop, restaurant overlooking the Marina, and baby changing and disabled facilities.

## THE COUNTRY STORE

THE COLONY GIFT CORPORATION LTD, LINDAL BUSINESS PARK,
LINDAL-IN-FURNESS, CUMBRIA LA12 OLL
☎ (01229) 465099. OPEN 9 - 5 MON - SAT, 12 - 5 SUN.
This is one of the biggest outlets for factory price candles, scented
candles, candle holders and lamps in Britain, with stock selling at
between 10% and 50% of the normal retail price. There are normally
3,000 candles on display, both perfect and seconds. The store also
sells dining room textiles, oven gloves, napkins, aprons, tea cosies, tea
towels, placemats, tablecloths, coffee mugs, pot pourri and gift soaps.
There is a special Christmas shop on site.

## THE FACTORY SHOP

EMPIRE BUILDING, MAIN STREET, EGREMONT, CUMBRIA CA22 2BD
☎ (01946) 820434. OPEN 9.30 - 5 MON - SAT, 10 - 4 BANK HOLIDAYS.
Wide range on sale includes men's, ladies and children's clothing and
footwear; household textiles, toiletries, hardware, luggage, lighting
and bedding, most of which are chainstore and high street brands at
discounts of approximately 30%-50%. There are weekly deliveries
and brands include all the major stars: Coloroll, Wrangler and
Dartington to name just three. Lines are continually changing and
few factory shops offer such a variety under one roof.

## THE TEA POTTERY

CENTRAL CAR PARK ROAD, KESWICK, CUMBRIA CA12 5DE
☎ (017687) 73983. OPEN 9 - 5 SEVEN DAYS A WEEK.
A boon for collectors of novelty teapots, all of which are manufactured on site in up to 40 different designs and in sizes from one cup
to five cups. Designs include Welsh dressers, wheelbarrows, chests of
drawers, Agas, cookers, bellboys with luggage, and a host of others,
many of which are collectors' items. Prices start from £18-£45 for
perfects, which represents a 10%-20% savings on retail prices, and up
to 50% discounts on seconds. There is a larger factory shop in
Leyburn, North Yorkshire.

# NORTHERN IRELAND

## *Permanent Discount Outlets*

## SPOILS

UNITS 55, 56, 57, CASTLE COURT, BELFAST
☎ (01232) 328512. OPEN 9 - 5.30 MON - SAT, UNTIL 8 ON FRI,
UNTIL 9 ON THUR.
General domestic glassware, non-stick bakeware, kitchen gadgets,
ceramic oven-to-tableware, textiles, cutting boards, aluminium non-
stick cookware, bakeware, plastic kitchenware, plastic storage,
woodware, coffee pots/makers, furniture, mirrors and picture frames.
Rather than being discounted, all the merchandise is very competi-

tively priced - in fact, the company carry out competitors' checks frequently in order to monitor pricing. With 29 branches, the company is able to buy in bulk and thus negotiate very good prices.

## TK MAXX

FIRST FLOOR, CASTLE COURT SHOPPING CENTRE, BELFAST, NORTHERN IRELAND OPEN 9 - 5.30 MON - WED, 9 - 9 THUR, 9 - 8 FRI, 9 - 6 SAT.

Based on an American concept, TK Maxx is the first British retailer to practise "off-price" retailing. This means a centrally located store which offers famous label goods with up to 60% savings off recommended retail prices. TK Maxx has fashion for the whole family - women's, men's and childrenswear - accessories, shoes, gifts, kitchenware and home goods. Everything in the store is branded with a choice of well-known high street names to designer labels, and while a small percentage might be clearly marked past season, the great majority of items in store are current season, current stock and still with phenomenal savings. There is a huge choice with 50,000 pieces in store with 5,000 new items arriving a week, so it's worth keeping abreast of the latest deliveries as turnaround is very fast. One of the ways in which TK Maxx is able to offer such low prices is by running a very low-cost operation, so the stores are simple and unfussy with wide aisles, shopping trolleys and baskets, and a spacious, functional feel to them. Service is not compromised, however: there are individual changing rooms, ramps for buggies and wheelchairs, plenty of staff on the shop floor and all the branches accept all major credit and debit cards.

## *Factory Shops*

## DESMOND & SONS LTD

THE MAIN STREET, CLAUDY, LONDONDERRY BT47 3SD
☎ (01504) 338441. OPEN 10 - 5 MON - SAT.
KEVLIN ROAD, OMAGH
☎ (01662) 241560. OPEN 10 - 5 MON - SAT.
MILL STREET, ENNISKILLEN
☎ (01365) 325467. OPEN 10 - 5 MON - SAT.

BALLYQUINN ROAD, DUNGIVEN
☎ (01504) 742068. OPEN 10 - 5 MON - SAT.
31 GARVAGH ROAD, SWATRAGH
☎ (01648) 401639. OPEN 10 - 5 MON - SAT.
Large range of clothes, most of which is seconds and is sold at discounts of one third. They also buy in some imperfects of household items such as handtowels and bath towels which are sold at competitive prices.

## TYRONE CRYSTAL LTD

KILLYBRACKEY, DUNGANNON, COUNTRY TYRONE BT71 6BN
☎ (01868) 725335. OPEN 9 - 5 MON - SAT. MAIL ORDER.
Factory shop selling first and second quality Tyrone crystal, all of which are mouth blown, handcut and polished, Irish linen, Irish Heritage and jewellery. On sale are paperweights, crystal bowls, stemware, decanters, vases, letter openers, tankards, candlesticks and mantel clocks. Only the seconds quality products are cheaper at about one third of the normal price.

## ULSTER WEAVERS

44 MONTGOMERY ROAD, CASTLEREAGH, BELFAST BT6
☎ (01232) 313700. OPEN 10 - 4 MON - FRI.
Linen and damask tablecloths, napkins, lace doilies, PVC aprons, linen tea towels and dish cloths, towel gift sets, placemats, napkins, and tablecloths all at factory prices with reductions of about 30%.

# ELECTRICAL EQUIPMENT

From Washing Machines to Hairdryers

*Permanent Discount Outlets,*

*Factory Shops*

# LONDON

## *Permanent Discount Outlets*

### BUYERS & SELLERS

120-122 LADBROKE GROVE, LONDON W10 5NE
☎ 0171- 229 1947/8468. OPEN 9 - 5 MON - SAT, CLOSED 2.30 ON THUR.
Buyers & Sellers has been in business for more than 40 years, selling brand name domestic equipment at bargain prices. Everything from fridges and freezers, ovens and microwaves, hobs and vacuum cleaners, washing machines and dishwashers, tumble dryers and cookers, all new and guaranteed and in perfect working order. They also sell many ends of lines at bargain prices and can obtain almost any make and model. Nationwide delivery service. Telephone orders taken. Advice line and free leaflets are part of the service.

### HOT & COLD INC

13 GOLBORNE ROAD, LONDON W10 5NY
☎ 0181-960 1200. OPEN 10 - 6 MON - SAT.
Supplies all the products of nearly one hundred brands of large electrical kitchen equipment - a total of about 10,000 different items - at prices which they claim will beat any genuine competitor's. In fact, they are so sure of this that they promise to refund the difference if you find you could have bought the same product elsewhere at the same time for a lower price, provided you give them proof of that within two weeks. All goods are brand new, perfect and guaranteed. Their strength is in built-in equipment, but they can also supply free-standing appliances. Prices include VAT. Delivery can be arranged countrywide.

## Secondhand Shops

### AUDIO GOLD

31 PARK ROAD, CROUCH END, LONDON N8 8TE
☎ 0181-341 9007. OPEN 11 - 6 MON - SAT, CLOSED THUR.

Small shop with friendly, unintimidating atmosphere where old, loved music machines get a second life. Catering for the run-of-the-mill end of the secondhand hi-fi market as well as the esoteric and expensive end. There aren't a lot of CD players as they are expensive to repair, but particular bargains can be found in the imposing speaker areas as most people trading in equipment tend to trade down, not up, in size. Most equipment is guaranteed for three months. One of the few places left in London where you can still get a good range of turntables.

# SOUTH EAST

## Permanent Discount Outlets

### GD EVANS

331-333 HIGH STREET, SLOUGH, BERKSHIRE SL1 1TX
☎ (01753) 524188/535138. OPEN 9 - 5.30 MON - SAT, 10 - 1 SUN.

Great discounts on former exhibition AEG, Neff and Siemens appliances. Phone for free brochure.

### HOME AND MOTORING SERVICE

1 ETON COURT, ETON, WINDSOR, BERKSHIRE SL4 6BY
☎ (01753) 621162. BY TELEPHONE ONLY.

A members-only organisation which offers preferential prices on more than 25,000 top brand-name products from fridges to lawnmowers, hi-fis and videos, to office equipment and luggage, furniture and cars. The large membership means the organisation can negotiate discounts on goods and pass the rates onto members. Prices are only preferred once you are a member, but you can join temporarily for only £1 (for three months), converting to the full fee of £39 a year if you think it's worth it. Phone the telephone number above for full membership details.

## RDO KITCHEN APPLIANCES

BANCROFT ROAD, REIGATE, SURREY RH2 7RP
☎ (01737) 240403. OPEN 9 - 5.30 MON - FRI, 9 - 4 SAT.

Specialises in British, French and German brand names at trade prices. There are continuous special offers - phone for details. Delivery nationwide. Range of more than 150 appliances constantly on show, including built-in and freestanding appliances. Access/Visa phone orders accepted.

## *Secondhand Shops*

## REFRIGERATION SERVICES

116 SOUTH STREET, DORKING, SURREY RH4 2E2
☎ (01306) 742199. OPEN 9 - 5.30 MON - SAT.

Retail outlet selling brand new fridges, but also some which have been revamped from the 1950s. Also sells washing machines, cookers, dishwasher and dryers from a wide range of manufacturers at competitive prices.

# SOUTH WEST

## *Factory Shops*

## REMINGTON

UNIT 33, CLARKS VILLAGE, FARM ROAD, STREET, SOMERSET
BA16 OBB
☎ (01458) 840209. OPEN 9 - 6 MON - SAT AND BANK HOLIDAYS,
11 - 5 SUN.

Lots of famous names here from Oneida and Monogram cutlery to Braun, Philips, Remington, Clairol, Wahl, Krups, Swan and Kenwood. There is also a Remington shop at Cheshire Oaks Outlet Village (see Electrical, North West).

# WALES AND WEST MIDLANDS

## *Permanent Discount Outlets*

### M C HITCHEN & SONS LTD

299 COVENTRY ROAD, BIRMINGHAM, WEST MIDLANDS B10 ORA
☎ (0121) 772 1637. OPEN 9 - 5.30 MON - SAT.
236 HAWTHORN ROAD, KINGSTANDING, BIRMINGHAM, WEST
MIDLANDS B44 8PP
☎ (0121) 373 1276.OPEN 9.15 - 5.30 MON - SAT.
14-16 NORTH STREET, RUGBY, WARWICKSHIRE CV21 2AF
☎ (01788) 565116. OPEN 9.30 - 5.30 MON - WED, 9 - 5.30 THUR - SAT.
Littlewoods sell off their overstocks in a network of shops called M C
Hitchen & Sons Ltd. Most of them are in the North of England and
offer up to 40% off the catalogue price for clothing and between 50%
and 60% off for electrical goods. Littlewoods also run a mobile shop
which operates in cities where they don't have a sale shop. For details
of further venues for the sales, which usually take place once a month,
contact Jean Banks, c/o Crosby DC, Kershaw Avenue, Endbutt Lane,
Crosby, Merseyside L70 1AH.

## *Factory Shops*

### A E CLUTTERBUCK LTD

CRANMORE DRIVE, SHIRLEY TRADING ESTATE, SHIRLEY, SOLIHULL,
WEST MIDLANDS B90 4PG
☎ (0121) 704 3134. OPEN 8 - 4 MON - FRI, 8 - 12 SAT.
One of the largest manufacturers of quality domestic lighting from
wall lights to table lamps has a factory shop selling seconds, ends of
lines and ex-display goods. All are fully tested for safety. Savings can
be as much as 50% off normal retail prices.

### PIFCO GROUP

SHEFFORD ROAD, ASTON, BIRMINGHAM
☎ (0121) 359 8691. OPEN 9 - 4.30 MON - FRI.
Discontinued lines and seconds of Pifco, Carmen, Salton, Russell
Hobbs and Tower, as well as some perfect lines. For example, travel

kettles £12; travel hairdryers, from £9; travel irons, £10; toasters, from £10; saucepan sets, from £40; trouser presses, £60; slow cookers, mini ovens, steam cuisines, electrical tool equipment, tea and coffee makers. Also Christmas tree lights, including electronic remote control ones, at discount.

## RUSSELL HOBBS FACTORY SHOP

BRIDGE NORTH ROAD, WOMBOURNE, WOLVERHAMPTON, WEST MIDLANDS WV5 8AQ
☎ (01902) 324123. OPEN 9 - 4.30 TUE- FRI, 9 - 12.30 SAT.
Seconds and overstocks from the Pifco, Salton, Carmen, Russell Hobbs and Tower ranges. On sale are toasters, kettles, pressure cookers, deep fat fryers, beard trimmers, heated rollers, hairdriers, sun lamps and Christmas tree lights at factory shop prices.

## THE SWAN FACTORY SHOP

POPE STREET, HOCKLEY, BIRMINGHAM B1 3 DL
☎ (0121) 200 1313. OPEN 9 - 4 MON - FRI, 9 - 1 SAT.
Moulinex, Swan and Krupps kitchen appliances as well as microwaves, kettles, toasters, electric knives, irons, saucepans and frying pans. All are seconds or discontinued items with some slightly imperfect but electrically sound. A top of the range food processor which would cost £150 in department stores would sell for £100 here; kettles, from £9.99; toasters from £10.99. all come with a one-year guarantee.

# EAST ANGLIA AND EAST MIDLANDS

*Permanent Discount Outlets*

## APPLIANCE WAREHOUSE

BUNNY TRADING ESTATE, GOTHAM LANE, BUNNY, NOTTINGHAM NG11 6QJ
☎ (0115) 9844357. OPEN 10 - 5 MON - FRI, 10 - 4 SAT AND SUN.
Large warehouse with 10,000 fitted kitchen appliances. They specialise in built-in kitchen appliances, stocking all leading brands from

AEG to Zanussi at up to 60% discounts. For example, Bosch/Siemens inteintegrated washer/dryers with a recommended retail price of £949 are sold by Appliance Warehouse for £439. There is a large showroom /warehouse displaying 90 single/double ovens in gas and electric , and 800 ceramic, halogen, gas and electric hobs are always in stock.

## M C HITCHEN & SONS LTD

7 HIGH STREET, GRANTHAM, LINCOLNSHIRE NG31 6PN
☎ (01476) 590552. OPEN 9.30 - 5.30 MON, 9 - 5.30 TUE - SAT.

Littlewoods sell off their overstocks in a network of shops called M C Hitchen & Sons Ltd. Most of them are in the North of England and offer up to 40% off the catalogue price for clothing and between 50% and 60% off for electrical goods. Littlewoods also run a mobile shop which operates in cities where they don't have a sale shop. For details of further venues for the sales, which useually take place once a month, contact Jean Banks, c/o Crosby DC, Kershaw Avenue, Endbutt Lane, Crosby, Merseyside L70 1AH.

## STAGE TWO

SAVILLE ROAD, WESTWOOD, PETERBOROUGH, CAMBRIDGESHIRE PE3 7PR
☎ (01733) 263308. OPEN 10 - 8 MON - FRI, 9 - 6 SAT, AND BANK HOLIDAYS.
UNIT 3, TRITTON RETAIL PARK, CENTURION ROAD, LINCOLN LN1
☎ (01522) 560303. OPEN 10 - 8 MON - FRI, 9 - 6 SAT, 10 - 4  BANK HOLIDAYS.

The names of the stores which sell discontinued lines from Freeman's catalogues. The full range is carried, but stock depends on what has not been sold at full price from the catalogue itself, or has been returned or the packaging is damaged or soiled. Clothing discounts range from about 50% - 65%. There are also household items and electrical equipment. There are branches in Nottingham, Lincoln and Peterborough.

## *Secondhand Shops*
### SECONDHAND LAND

115-117 MAGDALEN STREET, NORWICH, NORFOLK NR3 1LN
☎ (01603) 613606. OPEN 9 - 6 WED - SAT.

Sells tvs, videos, computers, hi-fi systems, washing machines, dish-washers, recording equipment - all of which are, as the name suggests, second-hand. Some are reconditioned, all come with a six or twelve month guarantee. A two-year-old 26" standard tv set with remote control and Teletext costs between £165-£250.

# NORTH WEST, YORKSHIRE AND HUMBERSIDE

## *Permanent Discount Outlets*

### GORSE MILL LIGHTING

GORSE ST, BROADWAY, CHADDERTON, GREATER MANCHESTER
OL9 9RL
☎ (0161) 628 4202. OPEN 9 - 4.30 MON - FRI, 10 - 4 SAT, SUN.

Makes decorative lamps, ceiling lights and wall lights and sells end of lines at discounts of 50%. A gothic light with 5 bulbs, £49.99, Pleated lamp shades start at as little as £3 and also come in a variety of sizes, paterns and colours. Gorse Mill supplies major chain stores and has vast ranges of decorative lighting, outdoor lighting, crystal chandeliers, as well as Chinese and Portuguese pottery. Alongside the lighting factory warehouse is a 4,000 sq ft warehouse selling clothes at half price: leisure and casual wear, children's outfits and some schoolwear.

# M C HITCHEN & SONS LTD

C/O CROSBY DC, KERSHAW AVENUE, ENDBUTT LANE, CROSBY,
MERSEYSIDE L70 1AH
☎ (0151) 928 6611.
116 ST JAMES STREET, BURNLEY, LANCASHIRE BB11 1NL
☎ (01282) 425615. OPEN 9.30 - 5.30 MON, WED - FRI, 9.30 - 4.30 TUE,
9 - 5.30 SAT.
602-608 ATTERCLIFFE ROAD, SHEFFIELD, SOUTH YORKSHIRE S9 3QS
☎ (0114) 2441611. OPEN 9.30 - 5.30 MON - SAT.
102 DEANSGATE, BOLTON, GREATER MANCHESTER BL1 1 BD
☎ (01204) 384969. OPEN 9.30 - 5.30 MON - WED, 9 - 5.30 THUR - SAT.
185 STAMFORD STREET, ASHTON-UNDER-LYME, GREATER
MANCHESTER OL6 7PY
☎ (0161) 339 0966. OPEN 9 - 5.30 MON - SAT, UNTIL 5.15 ON THUR.
160 MARINE ROAD, CENTRAL MORECAMBE, LANCASHIRE LA4 4BU
☎ (01524) 412074. OPEN 9.30 - 5.30 MON, 9 - 5.30 TUE - SAT.
C/O LITTLEWOODS SHOPPING CITY, RUNCORN, CHESHIRE
☎ (01928) 717777. OPEN 9 - 5 MON - SAT.
69 - 74 LORD STREET, FLEETWOOD, LANCASHIRE FY7 6DS
☎ (01253) 773418. OPEN 9 - 5.30 MON - SAT.
UNIT 3, MONUMENT BUILDINGS, LONDON ROAD, LIVERPOOL
L3 8JY
☎ (0151) 708 6118. OPEN 9 - 5.30 MON - SAT.

Littlewoods sell off their overstocks in a network of shops called M C
Hitchen & Sons Ltd. Most of them are in the North of England and
offer up to 40% off the catalogue price for clothing and between 50%
and 60% off for electrical goods. Littlewoods also run a mobile shop
which operates in cities where they don't have a sale shop. For details
of further venues for the sales, which usually take place once a month,
contact Jean Banks, c/o Crosby DC, Kershaw Avenue, Endbutt Lane,
Crosby, Merseyside L70 1AH.

# METRO DOMESTIC APPLIANCES

WAREHOUSE: FALMOUTH WORKS, OFF COPSTER HILL ROAD,
OLDHAM, LANCASHIRE OL8 1QD
☎ (0161) 626 6240. OPEN 9 - 4.30 MON - FRI.

This cut-price warehouse specialises in ends of lines or slightly blemished ovens, hobs, hoods, fridges, freezers - everything for the kitchen
except for the furniture. Goods are branded names such as Zanussi,
Hoover, Tricity, Fagor, and New World, and a full warranty is
provided.

## WHOLESALE KITCHEN APPLIANCES

144 BUXTON ROAD, HEAVILEY, STOCKPORT, LANCASHIRE SK2 6PL
☎ (0161) 456 1187. OPEN 9.30 - 5.30 MON - FRI, 9 - 5 SAT, 11 - 2 SUN.
Specialists in Bosch, AEG, Neff and German appliances, there are discounts particularly for cash purchasers.

# *Factory Shops*

## ASTBURY LIGHTING FACTORY SHOP

FOUNDRY BANK, CONGLETON, CHESHIRE
☎ (01260) 298176. OPEN 10 - 5 MON - SAT AND BANK
HOLIDAYS.
Factory shop situated in an old mill selling lamp shades - patterned and plain bases and shades and wall lighting from £10 - £100. Most of the stock is seconds and are reduced by about one-third. In another part of the building, bedding, curtains and clothes are sold including Dorma, Sheridan, Fogarty and Horrick's. On the ground floor is a new furniture department which although not part of the factory shop, has settees, beds, suites and cabinet furniture at competitive prices.

## PIFCO GROUP

PRINCESS STREET, FAILSWORTH, MANCHESTER M35 OHF
☎ (0161) 681 8321. OPEN 9 - 5.30 MON - FRI, SAT, 9 - 1, CLOSED TUE.
Discontinued lines and seconds of Pifco, Carmen, Salton, Russell Hobbs and Tower. Discontinued lines and seconds of Pifco, Carmen, Salton, Russell Hobbs and Tower, as well as some perfect lines. For example, travel kettles £12; travel hairdryers, from £9; travel irons, £10; toasters, from £10; saucepan sets, from £40; trouser presses, £60; slow cookers, mini ovens, steam cuisines, electrical tool equipment, tea and coffee makers. Also Christmas tree lights, including electronic remote control ones, at discount.

## REMINGTON

CHESHIRE OAKS OUTLET VILLAGE, KINSEY ROAD, NEAR ELLESMERE
PORT, SOUTH WIRRAL L65 9JJ
☎ (0151) 357 2477. OPEN 10 - 6 MON - SAT, 10 - 4 SUN.

Lots of famous names here from Oneida and Monogram cutlery to
Braun, Philips, Remington, Clairol, Wahl, Krups, Swan and
Kenwood. Examples of prices include: Clairol hairdryer, £7.49,
Remington foot spa, £24.99, Monogram 24-piece cutlery set,
£37.99, Philishave, £24.99; 44-piece silver plated cutlery canteen,
£119; Oneida 24-piece stainless steel cutlery set, £44.99; Krups
Espresso Uno, £149.99. There is also a Remington shop at Clarks
Village (see Electrical, South West).

# NORTH AND SCOTLAND

## Factory Shops

## M C HITCHEN & SONS LTD

19 FAWCETT STREET, SUNDERLAND, TYNE & WEAR SR1 RRH
☎ (0191) 564 0684. OPEN 8.45 - 5.30 MON - SAT.
RAWLINSON STREET, BARROW-IN-FURNESS, CUMBRIA LA14 ABS
☎ (01229) 870668. OPEN 8.45 - 5.15 MON - SAT.

Littlewoods sell off their overstocks in a network of shops called M C
Hitchen & Sons Ltd. Most of them are in the North of England and
offer up to 40% off the catalogue price for clothing and between 50%
and 60% off for electrical goods. Littlewoods also run a mobile shop
which operates in cities where they don't have a sale shop. For details
of further venues for the sales, which usually take place once a month,
contact Jean Banks, c/o Crosby DC, Kershaw Avenue, Endbutt Lane,
Crosby, Merseyside L70 1AH.

# DIY/RENOVATION

Including
Tools, Tiles, Wallpaper,
Paint, Bathrooms,
*Permanent Discount Outlets,*
*Factory Shops,*
*Architectural Salvage*

# LONDON

## Permanent Discount Outlets

### BERNARD ALLEN

29 HIGH STREET NORTH, EAST HAM, LONDON E6
☎ 081-471 9015. OPEN 9 - 5.30 MON - SAT.
597 ROMAN ROAD, BOW, LONDON E3
☎ 0181-983 3464. OPEN 9 - 5.30 MON - SAT.
74 EAST STREET, WALWORTH, LONDON SE17
☎ 0171-703 9629. OPEN 9 - 5.30 MON - SAT.

Family-run business selling wallpaper and paint at very competitive prices and what they claim are cheaper than most department and diy stores. Wallpaper from £2.49 to £7.99; choice of 200 colours in vinyl matt paint, £7.99 for five litres.

### COLOURWASH

165 CHAMBERLAYNE ROAD, LONDON NW10 3NU
☎ 0181-459 8918. OPEN 9 - 5.30 MON - FRI, 10 - 5 SAT.

Colourwash, the bathroom specialist, has a discount shop above its showroom in North London selling major brand names such as Imperial and Majestic. Most of the stock is ex-display, cancelled orders from other branches, seconds, clearance items and some items bought in in large quantities at competitive prices. You can save about 40% off normal retail prices, choosing from up to 30 suites on display together with accessories such as showers and cabinets.

### DAVE'S DIY

296 FIRS LANE, LONDON N13
☎ 0181-807 3539. OPEN 9 - 6 MON - FRI
4 ENFIELD ROAD, ENFIELD, MIDDLESEX
☎ 0181-363 1680. OPEN 8.30 - 5 MON - FRI, 9 - 5 SAT.

Aimed at the trade, it will cater for members of the public who benefit from the discounts. Carries wallpaper brands from Kingfisher, Mayfair, Crown and Vyimura among others from a range of 300 wallpaper books at discounts of up to 40%. Next day ordering for wallpapers. Also carries a large stock of paint, with a computerised mixing machine that offers thousands of combinations of colours.

## DISCOUNT DECORATING

157-159 RYE LANE, PECKHAM, LONDON SE15 4TL
☎ 0171-732 3986. OPEN 8 - 5.30 MON - FRI, 9 - 5.30 SAT.
Three thousand square foot warehouse selling top of the range wall-papers including Contour, Crown, Sanderson, Vymura, Hill & Knowles at between 10% and 50% discount. Also mainly Dulux paints and decorating equipment at low prices. All current, last season's or discontinued stock - no seconds sold.

## G THORNFIELD

321 GRAY'S INN ROAD, LONDON WC1 8PX
☎ 0171-837 2996. OPEN 7.50 - 2 MON - SAT.
Offers from 20%-50% off wallcovering brands such as Sanderson and Kingfisher. The more you buy, the greater your discount. Also one-third off co-ordinating fabrics. Don't hold stocks of wallpapers and fabrics but you can order from their books.

## JUST TILES

142 KENTON ROAD, HARROW, MIDDLESEX
☎ 0181-907 3020. OPEN 9 - 5.30 MON - SAT, 10 - 4 SUN.
Specialise in discount tiles for both floor and wall. Trends are towards larger tiles and design printing can be carried out in house. Many continental tiles.

## LESLUX

148 HIGH ROAD, EAST FINCHLEY, LONDON N2 9ED
☎ 0181-883 9522. OPEN 8.15 - 5.30 MON - FRI, 9 - 5.30 SAT.
Wallpaper, fabrics, tiles ( floor and wall) and paint at competitive or discount prices. For example, competitively priced Dulux and Crown paint discounted Osborne & Little, Monkwell, Hill & Knowles and Sanderson fabrics. No stock of tiles, wallpaper or fabrics carried - you look through the books and choose what you want and they will then order it for you. Or you can look at the real thing elsewhere, take all the details and order it from Leslux. They are able to offer discounts because they take a lower profit margin.

# LEYLAND

371-373 EDGWARE ROAD, LONDON W2 1BS
☎ 0171-723 8048. OPEN 7 - 7 MON - SAT.
6 TACHBROOK STREET, LONDON SW1
☎ 0171-828 8695. 7 - 7 MON - SAT.
683 FINCHLEY ROAD, LONDON NW2
☎ 0171-794 5927. 7 - 7 MON - SAT.
43-45 FARRINGDON ROAD, LONDON EC1
☎ 0171-242 5791. 7 - 6 MON - SAT.
111-113 THE BROADWAY, WEST EALING, LONDON W13
☎ 0181-810 0126. OPEN 7 - 6 MON - SAT.
335-337 KINGS ROAD, LONDON SW3 5EU
☎ 0171-352 4772. OPEN 7 - 6 MON - SAT.

Everything the enthusiastic diy-er could require from tools and equip-ment to wallpapers, cornicing, moulding, brace fittings and paint. In fact, there are four thousand colours from which to choose which can be mixed to match fabric or carpets, all at discounts of nearly 40%.

# THE REJECT TILE SHOP

178 WANDSWORTH BRIDGE ROAD, LONDON SW6 2UQ
☎ 0171-731 6098. OPEN 9.30 - 5.30 MON - FRI, 9.30 - 5 SAT.
2A F GLANDS LANE, LONDON NW3 4TG
☎ 0171-483 2608. OPEN 10 - 6 MON - FRI, 10 - 5 SAT.

Sells anything from floor tiles and quarry tiles to Victorian-style dec-orated tiles, fireplace tiles and dado tiles at discount prices. Most are seconds, but quality control is so tight nowadays that the label "second" might be due to barely perceptible pinholes in the glazing or slight colour mismatching. There is also a selection of discontinued lines.

# TILE CITY

NORTH CIRCULAR (NEAR HEATHER PARK DRIVE JUNCTION)
LONDON NW10
☎ 0181-965 8062. OPEN 9 - 6 MON - FRI, 9 - 5 SAT, 10 - 4 SUN.

Sells seconds in mainly ceramic tiles for the bathroom and kitchen walls and floors as well as quarry tiles for about half the normal retail price. Kitchen and bathroom accessories are also very competitively priced.

## TILES GALORE

GRACEFIELD GARDENS, STREATHAM, LONDON SW16 2ST
☎ 0181-677 6068. OPEN 8 - 5.30 MON - SAT.
1 CROSS WAYS PARADE, SELSDON PARK ROAD, ADDINGTON
☎ 0181-651 3782. OPEN 8 - 5.30 MON - SAT.

Sells perfect tiles from round the world at discount prices by buying direct from the factories, unlike the large department stores which buy from distributors. There are hundreds of designs to choose from. The Addington Shop is small, whereas the Streatham shop has 10,000 sq ft of tiles.

## WALL TO WALL

549 BATTERSEA PARK ROAD, BATTERSEA, LONDON SW11 3BL
☎ 0171-585 3335. OPEN 10 - 6 MON - SAT, 11 - 4 SUN.

Top name designer brand wallpaper, all at £6.95 a roll, with 450 different designs from which to choose. Discontinued patterns and job lots. Order when you see as there won't be any more stock in.

## WARD & STEVENS

248 HIGH STREET NORTH, MANOR PARK, LONDON E12 6SB
☎ 0181-472 4067. OPEN 9 - 5.30 MON - SAT.

Seconds of bathroom and kitchen tiles, plus discounts on perfects if paid with cash. Brands include Pilkington's, Candy and Cristal. Tiles from £1.98 a sq yard, with the average price about £5; up to 40% off wallpapers and tiles, with wallpapers starting at £1.99 a roll; pre-production run borders only £1 a roll. Deliver locally.

## *Architectural Salvage*

## CROWTHER OF SYON LODGE

BUSCH CORNER, LONDON ROAD, ISLEWORTH, MIDDLESEX
TW7 5BH
☎ 0181-560 7978. OPEN 9 - 5 MON - FRI, 11 - 4.30 SAT, SUN.

Architectural antiques, garden ornaments, wrought iron gates, sculpture, panelled rooms and chimney pieces, statuary, fountains, seats.

## FENS RESTORATION

46 LOTS ROAD, CHELSEA, LONDON SW10 0QF
☎ 0171-352 9883. OPEN 9 - 5 MON - FRI, 9 - 1 SAT.

Reclaimed doors, bathroom fittings and mouldings. Furniture including pine. Repairs, French polishing and metal cleaning. Also (caustic) pine stripping.

## HARDWOOD FLOORING CO LTD

146-152 WEST END LANE, LONDON NW6 1SD
☎ 0171-328 8481. OPEN 9 - 5 MON - FRI.

Large warehouse with showrooms and car parks, stocking over 200 different types of timber, both reclaimed and new, from blocks, strips and parquet to tongue and groove; they can also supply and lay floors.

## LAZDAN

218 BOW COMMON LANE, LONDON E3 4HH
☎ 0181-981 4632. OPEN 8 - 5 MON - FRI, 8 - 12.30 SAT.

Secondhand bricks, slates, sash weights and chimney pots.

## PECO

72 STATION ROAD, HAMPTON, MIDDLESEX TW12 2BT
☎ 0181-979 8310. OPEN 8 - 5.15 MON - SAT.

One of the largest door and fireplace warehouses in the country with two floors of display area and two additional shops. Stocks period doors up to 1930s fireplaces. Wooden beds and pot stoves from France. Stained glass studio on site which takes orders.

## THE ANTIQUE FIREPLACE WAREHOUSE

194-202 BATTERSEA PARK ROAD, LONDON SW11 4ND
☎ 0171-627 1410. OPEN 9 - 5.30 MON - FRI, 9.30 - 5 SAT.

Antique and reproduction fireplaces with at least 100 in stock at any one time. Full fitting service. Marble fireplaces range from £250 to thousands of pounds; stone from £350 to £2,500; pine from £290 to £725.

## THE HOUSE HOSPITAL

68 BATTERSEA HIGH STREET, LONDON SW11 3HX
☎ 0171-223 3179. 10 - 5 MON - SAT, 1 - 2 CLOSED.

Fireplaces, doors, cast iron radiators, wooden and marble flooring, bathroom fittings, brass mixer taps, door handles and tiles.

## THE LONDON ARCHITECTURAL SALVAGE AND SUPPLY COMPANY

MARK STREET, OFF PAUL STREET, LONDON EC2A 4ER
☎ 0171-739 0448. OPEN 9.30 - 5.30 MON - FRI, 10 - 5 SAT, SUN.

Enormous collection of architectural salvage including wooden flooring, tiles, doors, garden furniture, marble, fireplaces, stained glass, lighting, shop interiors and panelled rooms.

## THE ORIGINAL DOOR SPECIALIST

298 BROCKLEY ROAD, LONDON SE4 2RA
☎ 0181-691 7162. OPEN 9 - 6 MON - SAT.

Welsh dressers, cupboards, doors, stair spindles, handrails, French doors, room dividers and window shutters, all size doors.

## TOWNSENDS

81 ABBEY ROAD, LONDON NW8 0AE
☎ 0171-625 6762. OPEN 10 - 6 MON - FRI, 10 - 5.30 SAT.

Antique fireplaces and related items, and antique stained glass at the Boundary Road branch just down the road.

## VICTORIAN PINE

298 BROCKLEY ROAD, BROCKLEY, LONDON SE24 2RA
☎ 0181-691 7162. OPEN 9 - 6 MON - SAT, BY APPOINTMENT SUN.

Dressers, flooring, chests of drawers, newel posts, handrails, spindles, shutters, room dividers, cupboard doors, and all sizes of internal doors in hard or soft wood, all of which are original.

## WHITEWAY & WALDRON

305 MUNSTER ROAD, LONDON SW6 6BJ
☎ 0171-381 3195. OPEN 10 - 6 MON - FRI, 11 - 4 SAT.

Ecclesiastical stained glass, Gothic antiques and religious statues, candlesticks, plaster statues, stained glass, carved masonry.

# Secondhand Shops

## RENUBATH SERVICES

248 LILLIE ROAD, LONDON SW6 7QA
☎ 0171-381 8337. OPEN 9 - 5.30 MON - FRI.
If you've got a good quality bath that looks a bit tatty and chipped, why not have it resurfaced, polished or cleaned by the experts? They also sell cast iron baths from £525 plus VAT.

## THE WATER MONOPOLY

16-18 LONSDALE ROAD, LONDON NW6 6RD
☎ 0171-624 2636. OPEN 9 - 6 MON - FRI.
While freestanding restored cast iron baths cost from £1,500, they also sell some unrestored suites or will restore yours. Also make up bathroom suites from Victorian to Edwardian, Deco and Art Nouveau with appropriate brassware.

# SOUTH EAST

## Permanent Discount Outlets

## DISCOUNT DECORATING

6 THE BROADWAY, CRAWLEY, SUSSEX
☎ (01293) 404243. OPEN 9 - 5.30 MON - SAT.
53 QUEEN'S ROAD, WATFORD, HERTFORDSHIRE WD1 2QN
☎ (01923) 250663. OPEN 9 - 5.30 MON - SAT, 10.30 - 4 SUN,
UNTIL 8 ON THUR.
Sells top of the range wallpapers including Contour, Crown, Sanderson, Vymura, Hill & Knowles at between 10% and 50% discount. Also mainly Dulux paints and decorating equipment at low prices. All current, last season's or discontinued stock - no seconds sold. The Watford branch also offers a wide range of bathrooms: Ideal Standard, Heritage, Qualitas, with up to 15 suites on display at any one time. Suites start at £175 and there are discounts of 25%, for example, on Heritage suites. Bathrooms accessories are also discounted. Free parking.

## SIESTA CORK TILES

UNIT 21, TAIT ROAD, CROYDON, SURREY CRO 2DP
☎ 0181- 683 4055. OPEN 9 - 5 MON - FRI. MAIL ORDER.
This is primarily a mail order company. It usually has some items on special offer - for example, one third off PVC surface tiles, with both a clear varnish and hard wax finish, and coloured cork tiles. Orders can be be faxed on 0181-683 4480.

## THE BATHROOM WAREHOUSE GROUP

UNIT 23, ARUN BUSINESS PARK, SHRIPNEY ROAD, BOGNOR REGIS, SUSSEX PO22 9SX
☎ (01243) 841345. OPEN 9 - 6 MON - SAT.
4 CHAPEL STREET, GUILDFORD, SURREY GU1 3UH
☎ (01483) 573434. OPEN 9 - 5.30 MON - SAT.
37 QUEEN STREET, MAIDENHEAD, BERKSHIRE SL6 1NB.
☎ (01628) 32622. OPEN 8.30 - 5.30 MON - SAT.
UNIT 3, WYKEHAM ESTATE, MOORSIDE ROAD, WINNALL, NEAR WINCHESTER SO23 7RX
☎ (01962) 862554. OPEN 8.30 - 5.30 MON - FRI, 9 - 5.30 SAT.
Dedicated bathroom specialists in the middle to upper range offers bathroom suites at competitive or discounted prices. The Winchester and Bognor Regis branches are display warehouses. The Guildford branch is known as The Bathroom Shop

## THE WILKY GROUP

STAKE WORKS, INVINCIBLE ROAD, FARNBOROUGH, HAMPSHIRE GU14 7QT
☎ (01252) 377177. OPEN 8 - 5.30 MON - FRI, 8 - 5 SAT.
PEMBROKE HOUSE, MARY ROAD, GUILDFORD, SURREY GU1 4QA
☎ (01483) 37131. OPEN 9 - 5.30 MON - FRI, 9 - 5 SAT.
Discontinued bathroom suites by Twyford and Doulton at one-third to one half of the current list price. Current Twyford bathrooms at discounted prices. Army surplus items from desks to jerseys, ammunitions boxes to filing cabinets.

# *Architectural Salvage*

## ALFRED G. CAWLEY

HAVERING FARM, GUILDFORD ROAD, WORPLESDON, SURREY
GU4 7QA
☎ (01483) 232398. OPEN 8 - 5 MON - FRI, 8 - 1 SAT.
Bathroom fittings, floorboards, roof tiles, bricks and beams.

## ANTIQUE BUILDINGS LTD

DUNSFOLD, SURREY GU8 4NP
☎ (01483) 200477. OPEN WEEK DAY HOURS, BUT REQUEST
TELEPHONE CALL PRIOR TO ARRIVAL.
Specialise in ancient timber framed buildings, they have over thirty-five barn, cartshed, hovel, granary and house frames available for re-erection, each of which has been measured, drawn and photographed before being dismantled. They also stock an immense number of ancient oak beams, ceiling joists, bressumes, handmade clay tiles, bricks and walling stone, reclaimed handmade bricks and peg tiles.

## ARCHITECTURAL ANTIQUES

70 PEMBROKE STREET, BEDFORD, BEDFORDSHIRE
☎ (01234) 343421. OPEN 12 - 5 MON - SAT. MORNING APPOINTMENTS
AVAILABLE.
Buy and sell antiques, good quality furniture, original fireplaces and all architectural salvage. They have a large selection of original Georgian, Victorian and Edwardian fireplaces in marble, slate, cast iron, mahogany, oak and pine. All types and sizes of internal and external doors and cupboards, glazed doors and bookshelves; rolltop baths, basins, glazed and stone sinks, brass taps, radiators and towel rails, stone flooring, tiles, bricks, floorboards, moulded skirting and architrave. Balustrades, chimney pots, garden edging, grates and timber; good quality antique chests of drawers, wardrobes, dressing tables, dining chairs, dressers, bookcases, mirrors, clocks, lamps radios and other unusual items at 70 Pembroke Street, Bedford.

## BATH SHIELD

BLENHEIM STUDIO, LONDON ROAD, FOREST ROW, SUSSEX
RH18 5EZ
☎ (01342) 823243. OPEN 8.30 - 5.30 MON - FRI; PHONE FIRST FOR AN
APPOINTMENT.
If you've got a good quality bath which is looking a bit tatty, have it
re-enamelled in situ. Also provides traditional and victorian
bathroom equipment, taps, shower roses and fittings and old-fashioned bathrooms. Up to 100 different baths on display at any one
time. Delivers in the London area and abroad.

## BRIGHTON ARCHITECTURAL SALVAGE

33-34 GLOUCESTER ROAD, BRIGHTON, SUSSEX BN1 4AQ
☎ (01273) 681656. OPEN 9 - 5 MON - SAT.
Lots of pine furniture, marble fire surrounds, cast iron inserts from
Regency and Art Nouveau. Doors, columns, stained and etched glass.

## BROMLEY DEMOLITION

75 SIWARD ROAD, BROMLEY, KENT
☎ 0181-464 3610. OPEN 9 - 5 MON - FRI, 9 - 12 SAT.
Bromley Demolition reclaim whatever is usable from demolished
properties including doors, old bricks, assorted sizes of timbers, fireplaces.

## D.S.& A.G. PRIGMORE

MILL COTTAGE, MILL ROAD, COLMWORTH, BEDFORDSHIRE
MK44 2NU
☎ (01234) 376264. OPEN 8 - 5 MON - FRI, 8 - 12 SAT.
Reclaimed building materials, oak and pine beams, slates, tiles, bricks,
woodblock flooring, doors and other quality items including a good
selection of 2-inch Tudor-style bricks. Also RSJs.

## DRUMMONDS

BIRTLEY FARM, HORSHAM ROAD, BRAMLEY, GUILDFORD, SURREY
GU5 0LA
☎ (01483) 898997. OPEN 9 - 6 MON - FRI, 9.30 - 5 SAT, 10 - 5 SUN.
Bathroom fittings feature heavily. Also fireplaces, all kinds of interior
and exterior architectural items, bricks, slates, tiles, garden items and
statuary.

# IN DOORS

INVICTA WORKS, MILL STREET, EAST MALLING, KENT ME19 6BP
☎ (01732) 841606. 9 - 5 MON - FRI, 9 - 12.30 SAT.

Reclaimed pine and some oak doors and new doors made from reclaimed wood for the kitchen, wardrobe or door frames.

# OLD COTTAGE THINGS

BROXMORE PARK, OFF BUNNY LANE, SHERFIELD ENGLISH,
NR ROMSEY, HAMPSHIRE
☎ (01794) 884538. OPEN 9 - 5 MON - SAT.

Antique architectural materials. Approximately 1,000 pine doors in stock. Oak beams, architrave, bathroom furniture, pine furniture, Victorian and Georgian fire inserts and surrounds, spindles and chimney pots. Pine-stripping service.

# PEW CORNER

ARTINGTON MANOR FARM OLD PORTSMOUTH ROAD,
ARTINGTON, GUILDFORD, SURREY GU3 1LP
☎ (01483) 301428. OPEN 10 - 5 FRI, SAT OR BY APPOINTMENT.

Showroom with over 10,000 sq ft of floor space filled with scores of styles of church pew in pine, oak, elm, chestnut and mahogany. Also pulpits, lecterns, fonts and panelling. Phone for brochure, map and/or appointment.

# ROMSEY RECLAMATION

STATION APPROACH, RAILWAY STATION, ROMSEY, HAMPSHIRE
SO51 8DU
☎ (01794) 524174. OPEN 8 - 5 MON - FRI, 8.30 - 12.30 SAT.

Reclaimed slates, bricks, tiles and oak beams, Yorkshire flags, quarry tiles, railway sleepers.

# SALVAGE

83-89 BELGRAVE ROAD, PORTSWOOD, HAMPSHIRE SO17 3AN
☎ (0170) 3671120. OPEN 8- 5.45 MON - FRI, CLOSED AT 4.30 IN
WINTER, 8 - 4 SAT.

Literally anything that can be salvaged from architectural demolition, including sheds, barns, gates and railings.

## SILVERLAND STONE

HOLLOWAY HILL, CHERTSEY, SURREY KT16 0AE
☎ (01932) 569277. OPEN 8 - 5 MON - FRI, 9 - 1 SAT, 9 - 1 SUN IN
SUMMER ONLY.
Natural stone floors for both interior and exterior and fireplaces.

## THE TAP FACTORY

RENDALLS NURSERY, LYNE LANE, LYNE, SURREY KT 16 0AW
☎ (01932) 566106. OPEN 9 - 6.30 MON - FRI, 9 - 5 SAT.
Specialises in the supply and restoration of original period bathroom
fittings in a variety of finishes including brass, chrome and nickel.

## THE WEST SUSSEX ANTIQUE TIMBER
## COMPANY LTD

RELIANCE WORKS, NEWPOUND, WISBOROUGH GREEN, WEST
SUSSEX RH14 0AZ
☎ (01403) 700139. FAX (01403) 700936. OPEN 8.30 - 5.30 MON - FRI,
9 - 1 SAT.
Specialists in old pine, oak beams, flooring and mouldings. Also sells
pine and oak doors and old timber furniture.

# SOUTH WEST

## *Architectural Salvage*

## ARCHITECTURAL ANTIQUES OF SOUTH
## MOLTON

WEST LEY, ALSWEAR ROAD, SOUTH MOLTON, DEVON EX36 4LE
☎ (01769) 573342. FAX 0769 574363. OPEN 9 - 5 TUE - SAT.
Bar and shop-fittings and larger items. Also doors, fireplaces and
stained glass.

## ASHBURTON MARBLES

GREAT HALL, NORTH STREET, ASHBURTON, DEVON TQ13 7DU
☎ (01364) 653189. OPEN 8 - 5 MON - SAT.
Period marble and wood fireplace surrounds, cast iron inserts,
fenders, guards, overmantel mirrors, chandeliers and some furniture
including Bergere suites.

## AU TEMPS PERDU

5 STAPLETON ROAD, EASTON, BRISTOL BS5 OQR
☎ (0117) 9555223. OPEN 10 - 5.30 MON - SAT.

General architectural salvage with French and English stock: bathroom fittings, fire surrounds, cooking ranges, Chateau gates, spiral staircases.

## BRIDGEWATER RECLAMATION

THE OLD CO-OP DAIRY, MONMOUTH STREET, BRIDGEWATER, SOMERSET TA6 5EQ
☎ (01278) 424636. OPEN 8 - 5 MON - FRI, 8 - 12 SAT.

Reclaimed bricks, tiles, flagstones, chimney pots, doors, baths, fireplaces, reproduction furniture, purpose-made joinery from the on-site workshop - in fact everything!

## COLIN BAKER

CROWN HILL, HALBERTON, TIVERTON, DEVON EX16 7AY
☎ (01884) 820152. 01884 821007 (EVENINGS) BY APPOINTMENT ONLY.

Reclaimed oak beams and joists, oak and pine floorboards.

## DORSET RESTORATION

COW DROVE, BERE REGIS, DORSET BH20 7JZ
☎ (01929) 472200. OPEN 8 - 5 MON - FRI, 9 - 4 SAT.

Bathroom fittings, fireplaces, stained glass, Dorset bricks, flagstones, quarry tiles, clay Peg and ridge tiles, beams, floorboards, doors, oak beams, reclaimed wood flooring, garden ornaments, chimney pots, and lead garden figures. Take business park exit off A31 roundabout at Bere Regis.

## H & R CONTRACTORS

FAIRWATER YARD, STAPLEGROVE ROAD, TAUNTON, SOMERSET TA1 1DP
☎ (01823) 337035. OPEN 9.5.30 MON - FRI, 10 - 12 SAT.

Tiles, slates, bricks, recycled timber, floorboards, fireplaces, sanitaryware, staircases and interesting curios discovered during demolition.

## ROBERT MILLS

NARROWSWAY ROAD, EAST VILLE, BRISTOL, AVON BS2 9XB
☎ (0117) 9556542. OPEN 9.30 - 5.30 MON - FRI.
Specialists in Gothic fixtures and fittings reclaimed from Victorian churches. Shop interiors with counters and glass display cabinets also available.

## TOBYS (THE OLD BUILDERS YARD AND STORE)

HENNOCK ROAD, MARSH BARTON INDUSTRIAL ESTATE, EXETER, DEVON
☎ (01392) 422711. OPEN 8.30 - 4.30 MON - FRI, 9.30 - 4 SAT.
BRUNEL ROAD, NEWTON ABBOT, DEVON
☎ (01626) 51767. OPEN 8.30 - 4.30 MON - FRI, 9.30 - 4 SAT.
Ten thousand square feet of reclaimed doors, fireplaces, timber, sanitaryware, bricks, furniture, windows and stained glass; seconds in slates.

## WALCOT RECLAMATION

108 WALCOT STREET, BATH, AVON BA1 5BG
☎ (01225) 444404. OPEN 9 - 5.30 MON - FRI, 9 - 5.30 SAT.
Fireplaces, chimney pots, doors, bathroom furniture, garden statuary, floor boards, roofing, door furniture, column radiators, gates and railings.

## WELLS RECLAMATION COMPANY

THE OLD CIDER FARM, COXLEY, NR WELLS, SOMERSET BA5 1RQ
☎ (01749) 677087. OPEN 8.30 - 5.30 MON - SAT.
Reclaimed timber: pine and oak beams, pine doors, flooring, bathroom accessories, quarry tiles and flagstones (pennent and blue lias), fireplaces and bricks. Three and a half acres in all.

## WINKLEIGH TIMBER

SECKINGTON CROSS, INDUSTRIAL ESTATE, WINKLEIGH, DEVON EX19 8DQ
☎ (01837) 83573. OPEN 8 - 5 MON - FRI, 8 - 12.30 SAT.
Pitch pine floorboards, oak beams and joists and joinery grade timber.

# WALES AND WEST MIDLANDS

## *Permanent Discount Outlets*

### PEARCE & CUTLER

ELECTRIC AVENUE, WITTON, BIRMINGHAM, WEST MIDLANDS
☎ (0121) 328 2442. OPEN 8 - 5 MON - FRI, 8 - 12 SAT.
A double glazing company, they sell window frames, mirrors, PVC windows and wardrobe doors at prices which are usually much cheaper than retail.

### REJECT TILES

16 HIGH STREET, MARLBOROUGH, WILTSHIRE
☎ (01672) 512422. OPEN 9 -5 MON - SAT, CLOSED 1 - 2.
13 MILFORD STREET, SALISBURY, WILTSHIRE
☎ (01722) 328010. OPEN 9.30 - 5 MON - SAT.
Sells mainly wall tiles for the kitchen and bathroom at discounts of up to 50%. Most of the stock is rejects or seconds from the Marlborough Tiles factory, which makes top quality tiles for retail. Prices start at £3.60 a sq yd; tiles that cost up to £41.03 a sq yd in department stores are sold at £7.20 a sq yd.

## *Factory Shops*

### FIRED EARTH

MIDDLE ASTON, ON THE MAIN ROAD FROM STEEPLE ASTON, OXFORDSHIRE OX5 3PX
☎ (01869) 347599. OPEN 9.30 - 5.30 TUE - SAT.
As a result of the success of the Battersea, London, outlet which sells imperfect and discontinued lines from Fired Earth's spectacular designs at discounts of up to 50%, and the merger with The Merchant Tiler, the company has now set up a factory shop. There is a large, ever-changing stock in what is the company's original warehouse and showroom. Examples include intricately decorated traditional delft tiles for the fireplace; hand decorated kitchen tiles; Country Kitchen six-inch bathroom tiles; reclaimed 100-year-old

French terracotta tiles. This half-acre site with its three buildings also houses a reasonably priced Persian rug warehouse and a selection of tribal curios and bric a brac from Nomadic Persian tribes including fabrick, crewel work and tapestries. There are also paints in 18th and 19th century colours and fabrics based on V & A originals.

## Architectural Salvage

### ADFERIAD GWENT OF MONMOUTHSHIRE

MONMOUTHSHIRE
☎ (01291) 690709.
☎ (0600) 85406. RING FOR APPOINTMENT.
Ancient oak timbers and floorboards. Victorian pitch pine, panelling and beams. Other fine old period flooring and doors. Also pews and antique country tables. There isn't really a showroom and the barns are hard to find so it's best to ring up first to get directions and make sure someone will be there. The outlet is near Monmouth.

### BAILEYS ARCHITECTURAL ANTIQUES

THE ENGINE SHED, ASHBURTON INDUSTRIAL ESTATE, ROSS-ON-WYE, HEREFORDSHIRE HR9 7BW
☎ (01989) 563015. OPEN 9 - 5 MON - SAT.
Bathroom fittings, fireplaces, statuary, stonework, garden furniture, gates ironwork, lighting, Belfast sinks and dressers.

### CARDIFF RECLAMATION ARCHITECTURAL SALVAGE

SITE 7, TREMORSE INDUSTRIAL ESTATE, CARDIFF, SOUTH GLAMORGAN.
☎ (01222) 458995. OPEN 9 - 5.30 MON - SAT, 10 - 1 SUN.
Flagstones, Victorian fireplaces, pine doors, church pews, handrails, chimney pots, quarry tiles, oak beams and lots more.

### CAWARDEN BRICK COMPANY

CAWARDEN SPRINGS FARM, RUGELEY, STAFFORD, STAFFORDSHIRE WS15 3HL
☎ (01889) 574066, 01831 355012. OPEN 9 - 5 MON - FRI, 9 - 4 SAT.

Large quantities of reclaimed handmade bricks; also tiles, flagstone and block stone. Oak flooring, doors and cupboards.

## CONSERVATION BUILDING PRODUCTS

FORGE WORKS, FORGE LANE, CRADLEY HEATH, WARLEY, WEST MIDLANDS B64 5AL

☎ (01384) 564219. 8 - 4.30 MON - FRI, 8 - 12.30 SAT.

Bricks, roof tiles, slates, quarry tiles, flooring beams, decorative ironwork, staircase parts, complete oak-framed buildings, garden statuary and interesting artifacts.

## DICKINSONS ARCHITECTURAL ANTIQUES

140 CORVE STREET, LUDLOW, SHROPSHIRE

☎ (01584) 876207. 10 - 5 MON - SAT.

Specialise in genuine period bathrooms, fireplaces, architectural fittings, doors, lighting and fenders.

## DYFED ANTIQUES & ARCHITECTURAL SALVAGE

WESLEYAN CHAPEL, PERROTS ROAD, HAVERFORDWEST, DYFED, WEST WALES

☎ (01437) 760496. OPEN 9.30 - 5.30 MON - FRI, 10 - 5 SAT.

Slate slabs, quarry tiles, oak beams and flooring, doors, Victorian fireplaces, tiled insets, surrounds in wood, marble and cast iron, antique furniture, many huge dressers and curios, gardenware including urns. Furniture and fire surrounds made to measure in new or old wood.

## IJP BUILDING CONSERVATION

HOLLOW TREE COTTAGE, BINFIELD HEATH, HENLEY ON THAMES, OXFORDSHIRE RG9 4LR

☎ (01734) 462697. GENERALLY OPEN 8 - 5 MON - FRI, CHECK TIMES FOR SAT.

Sells traditional building materials including lime mortar and plasters, lime putty and limewash, riven laths and oak pegs, wattle and daub, horse hair and goat hair, rosehead nails, hand-forged hinges and latches and oak ledged and planked doors.

## RECLAMATION TRADING COMPANY

22 ELLIOT ROAD, CIRENCESTER, GLOUCESTERSHIRE GL7 1YS
☎ (01285) 653532. OPEN 9 - 5 TUE - FRI, 9 - 4 SAT.
Internal architectural reclamation including fireplaces and doors,
floor tiles. Also gardenware, including stone troughs and flagstones.

## ROBERTSONS

JODRELL STREET, NUNEATON, WARWICKSHIRE CV11 5EH
☎ (01203) 384110. OPEN 9 - 5 MON - FRI, 8 - 1 SAT.
Doors, chimney pots, staircase parts, reclaimed timber, reinforced
steel joists, roof tiles and slates.

## THE ORIGINAL CHOICE

56 THE TYTHING, WORCESTER, WORCESTERSHIRE WR1 1JT
☎ (01905) 613330. OPEN 10 - 6 MON - SAT, 1 - 5.30 SUN.
1340 STRATFORD ROAD, HALL GREEN, BIRMINGHAM B28 9EH
☎ (0121) 778 3821. OPEN 11 - 6 MON - SAT, CLOSED TUE & WED.
Fireplaces and stained glass windows from 1750 to 1930.

# EAST ANGLIA AND EAST MIDLANDS

*Permanent Discount Outlets*

## AYLSHAM BATH & DOOR

BURGH ROAD, AYLSHAM, NORFOLK NR11 6AR
☎ (01263) 735396. OPEN 8.30 - 5 MON - FRI, 9 - 5 SAT. 10 - 4 SUN.
Bathroom equipment, kitchen displays, bedroom fittings, all at
reduced prices of at least 20%- 25% less than normal retail prices.
Top brands such as Dalton, Ideal Standard, Armitage, Shires and
Shanks are some of the 70 bathrooms displayed here; and there are 30
display kitchens with appliances by Neff, Philips, Whirlpool and
Zanussi.

# *Architectural Salvage*

## ARCHITECTURAL HERITAGE

THE WOODYARD, NR WEEDON, NORTHAMPTONSHIRE NN7 4LB
☎ (01327) 349249. OPEN 9 - 5 TUE - SAT, 11 - 5 SUN.

Converted farmyard dealing in architectural antiques and reclamations- everything from a belltower to a doorknob. Also handpainted furniture, bric a brac and baths including re-enamelling and tiles. There is a tea room and gift shop on site. On A5, two miles north of Weedon.

## BATHCRAFT

82 ALFRED STREET, KETTERING, NORTHAMPTONSHIRE
☎ (01536) 81298. OPEN 10 - 5.30 WED, FRI, 10 - 4.30 SAT.

Old fashioned rolltop baths, taps bath fittings, reproduction shower roses, re-enamelling.

## NOTTINGHAM ARCHITECTURAL ANTIQUES

531 WOODBOROUGH ROAD, NOTTINGHAM, NOTTINGHAMSHIRE
NG3 5FS
☎ (0115) 9605665. 10 - 5 MON- SAT.

Garden ornaments, bathroom fittings, Victorian fireplaces, doors, stained and etched glass.

## ORWELL PINE CO LTD

HALIFAX MILL, 427 WHERSTEAD ROAD, IPSWICH, SUFFOLK IP2 8LH
☎ (01473) 680091. OPEN 8.30 - 5.30 MON - FRI, 8 - 4 SAT.

Knocks down condemned buildings and removes the old pine floorboards, joists and architravings to make new "old" pine furniture, including kitchens. It usually has 1,000 doors in stock in old pine. As its name suggests it also strips doors for £12 plus VAT a door, as well as making bedroom furniture, and selling fireplaces and restored house clearance furniture. 100-year-old pine doors cost from £35-£65.

## SOLOPARK LTD

THE OLD RAILWAY STATION, STATION ROAD, NR PAMPISFORD,
CAMBRIDGESHIRE CB2 4HB
☎ (01223) 834663. OPEN 8 - 5 MON - THUR, 8 - 4 FRI, 8 - 1 SAT.
CLOSED 1 - 2 DAILY.
Reclaimed bricks including soft reds, Suffolk whites, Cambridge
stocks and two-inch Tudors. Also oak and pine beams and flooring,
oak barrels, railway sleepers, chimney pots, York flagstones, granite
sets, stained glass, windows, gates and garden furniture.

## TONY HODGSON & PARTNERS

THE FORGE, 2 WESLEY ROAD, TERRINGTON ST CLEMENT,
NR KING'S LYNN, NORFOLK PE34 4NG
☎ (01553) 828637. OPEN 8 - 6 MON - FRI, WEEKENDS BY
APPOINTMENT.
Hand-forged wrought iron work, including restoration. Anything
from fenders and fire irons to finials and gates.

# NORTH WEST, YORKSHIRE AND HUMBERSIDE

## Factory Shops

### PILKINGTON'S TILES

RAKE LANE, CLIFTON JUNCTION, MANCHESTER M27 8LP
☎ (0161) 727 1000. OPEN 8.30 - 5.30 MON - FRI, 9 - 5 SAT, UNTIL 8 ON
THUR, 10 - 3 SUN.
Sells seconds of the well-known Pilkington's wall tiles and diy tiling
equipment at discount prices. Two hundred and fifty ranges of wall
and floor tiles from which to choose.

# *Architectural Salvage*

## AGRICULTURAL BYGONES

ASHTON'S FIELD FARM, WINDMILL ROAD, WALKDEN, WORSLEY,
MANCHESTER M28 5RP
☎ (0161) 702 8604. RING FOR APPOINTMENT.
Original doors, baths, radiators, sinks, sash windows, Victorian stable
fittings, cart wheels, troughs.

## ANDY THORNTON ARCHITECTURAL ANTIQUES

VICTORIA MILLS, GREETLAND, HALIFAX, WEST YORKSHIRE HX4 8AD
☎ (01422) 377314. OPEN 8.30 - 5.30 MON - FRI, 9 - 5 SAT, 10 - 5 SUN.
Fireplaces, stained glass, panelled rooms, church interiors, bathroom
fittings, radiators, balustrades, chandeliers, stained glass, marble, pews
and light-fittings all situated in an enormous converted mill. If you
can't find the original piece you want, they will make you a reproduction. One of the five floors is devoted to reproductions with a
huge range of Tiffany lamps. The top floor houses Americana and
outside are plenty of garden urns, statuary and cast-iron gates.

## CHAPEL HOUSE FIREPLACES

ST GEORGE'S ROAD, SCHOLES, HOLMFIRTH, HUDDERSFIELD,
WEST YORKSHIRE HD7 1UH
☎ (01484) 682275. OPEN TUE - SAT BY APPOINTMENT ONLY.
Period fireplaces with correct grates, baskets and inserts, including
French fireplaces dating from 1750-1910.

## CHESHIRE BRICK & SLATE COMPANY

BROOK HOUSE FARM, SALTERS BRIDGE, TARVIN SANDS,
NR CHESTER, CHESHIRE CH3 8HL
☎ (01829) 740883. FAX (01829) 740481. OPEN 8 - 5.30 MON - FRI, 8 - 4.30
SAT, 10 - 4 SUN.
Reclaimed bricks, slates, setts, tiles, lamposts, doors, Victorian
bathroom suites, fireplaces, ranges, garden ornaments, beams,
Yorkshire paving and brass door furniture.

## CHESHIRE HERITAGE

ESTATE OFFICE, TRAFFORD PARK ROAD, TRAFFORD PARK, MANCHESTER
☎ (0161) 872 1352. OPEN 8.30 - 5 MON - FRI, 9 - 11.30 SAT.
Reclaimed bricks, natural stone flagstones, tiles and cast stone.

## DOLMENS

107 LATHAM LARNE, GOMERSAL, CLECKHEATON, WEST YORKSHIRE BD19 4AP
☎ (01274) 872368. FAX (01274) 869953. BY APPOINTMENT ONLY.
Old and new York stone paving flags. Various prices and quality. Worldwide delivery.

## GREAT NORTHERN ARCHITECTURAL ANTIQUES

NEW RUSSIA HALL, CHESTER ROAD, TATTENHALL, CHESHIRE CH3 9AH
☎ (01829) 70796. FAX (01829) 70971. OPEN 9.30 - 4.30 MON - FRI, 9.30 - 5 SAT, SUN.
Doors, panelled rooms, sanitary fittings, stained glass, garden furniture, York stone sets and pews, gates, railings, curios, bric a brac.

## HAVENPLAN LTD

THE OLD STATION, STATION ROAD, KILLARMARSH, SHEFFIELD, SOUTH YORKSHIRE S31 8EN
☎ (0114) 2489972. OPEN 10 - 4 TUE - SAT.
Period doors, pine and oak planking, church pews, sanitary and garden furniture, fireplaces, inserts and surrounds.

## IN SITU

607 STRETFORD ROAD, OLD TRAFFORD, MANCHESTER M16 OJS
☎ (0161) 848 7454. OPEN 9 - 5.30 MON - SAT, 10 - 4 SUN.
Period fireplaces, doors, joinery, leaded glass and French polishing, antique bathrooms, garden ware, staircases, chimney pots, furniture, flooring. Deliver anywhere.

## KITCHENALIA

36 INGLEWHITE ROAD, LONGRIDGE, NEAR PRESTON, LANCASHIRE
PR3 3JS
☎ (01772) 785411. OPEN 10 - 4 MON - SAT, CLOSED WED.
Freestanding furniture for the kitchen; sets of shelves made from the
Bible rests on the back of old church pews; dressers made from old
wood; tables, old pottery; old church pews also for sale.

## NOSTALGIA ARCHITECTURAL ANTIQUES

61 SHAW HEATH, STOCKPORT, CHESHIRE FK3 8BH
☎ (0161) 477 7706. OPEN 10 - 6 TUE - FRI, 10 - 5 SAT.
At any given time there are one and a half thousand original Victorian
fireplaces and 100-150 basins and 30-40 toilets from the 19th
century. Also a few Georgian pieces including fireplaces.

## RECLAIMED MATERIALS

NORTHGATE, WHITE LUND INDUSTRIAL ESTATE, MORECAMBE,
LANCASHIRE LA3 3AY
☎ (01524) 69094. 8 - 5 MON - FRI, 8 - 2 SAT.
Timber, roof tiles, pitch pine, hardwood flooring, chimney pots and
flagstones.

## REDDISH DEMOLITION LTD

ALBION HOUSE, UNDER LANE, CHADDERTON, NEAR OLDHAM,
LANCASHIRE
☎ (0161) 682 6660. OPEN 7.30 - 5 MON - FRI, 7.30 - 12 SAT.
Reclaimed bricks, slates, beams and Yorkshire flags.

## W MACHELL & SONS LTD

LOW MILLS, GUISELEY, LEEDS, WEST YORKSHIRE LS20 9LT
☎ (0113) 2505043. OPEN 8 - 5 MON - FRI, 8 - 12 SAT.
Stocks recycled building materials and architectural stone, hardwood
flooring and virtually anything that can be taken away from demolished buildings.

## YORK HANDMADE BRICK CO

FOREST LANE, ALNE, YORK, NORTH YORKSHIRE YO6 2LU
☎ (01347) 838881. OPEN 8.30 - 4.30 MON - FRI, 9 - 12 SAT.
One of the few businesses still producing handmade bricks, as well as
pavers and terracotta floor tiles. They can provide bricks for archways,
slopes, edges, ledges and corners and do all the British Standards
specials as well as taking special orders.

# NORTH AND SCOTLAND

## *Factory Shops*

### BLACK & DECKER

SERVICE STATION, GREEN LANE, SPENNYMOOR, CO DURHAM
DL16 6JG
☎ (01388) 422429. OPEN 8.30 - 5 MON, TUE, THUR, FRI, 9.30 - 5 WED,
8.30 - 12.30 SAT.
Reconditioned tools and acccessories from the famous Black &
Decker range, all with full B&D warranty. This is essentially an after-
sales service with a retail outlet. All the reconditioned tools come
under the Gold Seal label. Often, stock consists of goods returned
from the shops because of damaged packaging or are part of a line
which is being discontinued. Lots of seasonal special offers.
Reconditioned lawnmowers from £27-£150; drills, £37; jigsaws,
£22.99.

## *Architectural Salvage*

### BURNTHILL DEMOLITION LTD

FLOORS STREET, JOHNSTONE, RENFREWSHIRE PA5 8QS
☎ (01505) 329644. OPEN 9 - 5 MON - FRI, 9 - 12 SAT.
Secondhand timber, roofing tiles, slates, steel and wooden beams and
a selection of other reclaimed items.

## DEMOLITION RECOVERIES LTD

31-41 WESTERBURN STREET, CARNTYNE, GLASGOW, SCOTLAND
G32 9AT
☎ (0141) 778 3602. OPEN 8 - 4.30 MON - FRI.
Dealers in slate and accessories.

## EDINBURGH ARCHITECTURAL SALVAGE YARD (E.A.S.Y.)

UNIT 6, COUPER STREET, OFF COBURG STREET, LEITH, EDINBURGH
☎ (0131) 554 7077. OPEN 9 - 5 MON - FRI, 12 - 5 SAT.
85 COLVEND STREET, GLASGOW G40 4DU
☎ (0141) 556 7772. OPEN 9 - 5 MON - FRI, 12 - 5 SAT.
Wooden doors, cast iron spiral staircases, original fixtures and fittings, and general architectural salvage. The Glasgow outlet is a warehouse.

## OLD MILL ANTIQUES

OLD MURRAYFIELD, 1A MAIN STREET, BANNOCKBURN, STIRLING,
SCOTLAND FK7 8LZ
☎ (01786) 817130. OPEN 9 - 5 MON - FRI, 10 - 4 SAT.
Fireplaces and stained glass. Specialise in installation of Victorian fireplaces, of which they have over one hundred in stock. Also antique and reproduction furniture, upholstery and polishing.

## WILSON RECLAMATION SERVICES AND ARCHITECTURAL ANTIQUES

YEW TREE BARN, NEWTON IN CARTMEL, NEAR GRANGE OVER-
SANDS, CUMBRIA LA11 6JP
☎ (01539) 531498. OPEN 10 - 5 MON - SAT, 12 - 6 SUN IN SUMMER.
Fireplaces, oak beams, doors, bathroom fittings, flagstones, chimney pots, quoins and antiques. There's also a cafe.

# NORTHERN IRELAND

## *Architectural Salvage*

### ALEXANDER THE GRATE

126-128 DONEGAL PASS, BELFAST, NORTHERN IRELAND BT7 1BZ
☎ (01232) 232041. OPEN 10 - 5 MON - SAT.
A specialist in antique fireplaces, as well as leaded windows, doors and general architectural salvage. There is also garden furniture in the spring and summer. The owner also runs an antiques market on the first floor of the same premises every Saturday from 9.30-5 with 16 different stallholders.

### WILSONS CONSERVATION PRODUCTS IRELAND

123 HILLSBOROUGH ROAD, DROMORE, COUNTY DOWN BT25 1QW
☎ (01846) 692304. OPEN 8 - 5 MON - FRI, 8 - 12 SAT.
Reclaimed timber, slates, pine beams, radiators, cast iron fireplaces with pine and marble surrounds, chimney pots, quarry tiles and bricks.

# FURNITURE/SOFT FURNISHINGS

Including
Fabrics, Curtains, Beds, Sofas, Tables,
Chairs, Carpets
*Permanent Discount Outlets,*
*Factory Shops,*
*Designer Sales,*
*Secondhand Shops*

# LONDON

*Permanent Discount Outlets*

## ALEXANDER FURNISHINGS

51-61 WIGMORE STREET, LONDON W1H 9LF
☎ 0171-935 7806. OPEN 9 - 6 MON - SAT, UNTIL 7 ON THUR.

The largest independent curtain retailer in the UK, Alexander Furnishings has been operating from the same base for more than 40 years. Famous for curtaining, they also sell upholstery fabric, wallpapers and carpets. There's usually a discount on all fabrics - for example Sanderson cotton chintz at just over one quarter of the original price. The biggest bargains are the discontinued lines. There is also a trimming shop on the premises and sofas and sofabeds are on sale. Fabrics start at £1.99 and there is a vast selection below £10.

## BICKENSTAFF & KNOWLES

6 THE ARCADE, THURLOE STREET, LONDON SW7 2NA
☎ 0171-589 7971. OPEN 9.30 - 6 SEVEN DAYS A WEEK.

Even a recession offers good news for some people. Goods sold under pressure can offer great buying opportunities for the dedicated bargain hunter. Auctioneers Bickenstaff & Knowles run regular countrywide public clearance auctions of contemporary (ie up to 30 years old) Persian rugs. The goods are top quality, but may have to be sold because of financial difficulties, insurance problems, or because they have been used as collateral against a loan. Phone for details of forthcoming auctions.

## BY THE YARD

8-12 WINDMILL HILL, ENFIELD, MIDDLESEX EN2 6SA
☎ 0181-363 7768. OPEN 9 - 5.30 MON - SAT.

Soft furnishings and upholstery fabrics, which are imported, as well as wallpaper and blinds at discount. Sanderson, Warner and Monkwell are just some of the fabric names on offer. Some stock is carried, but usually you order after looking through the order books. Small purchases - say one metre of fabric - won't be heavily discounted as the cost of transporting the item from the manufacturer to the shop will wipe out most of the profit. So the larger your order, the bigger the discount.

## CARPET TILE CENTRE

227-229 WOODHOUSE ROAD, LONDON N12 9BD
☎ 0181-361 1261. OPEN 9 - 5 MON - SAT.

Offers a wide range of Heuga seconds as well as end of line carpet tiles, specials and seconds. Prices start at £1.75-£2.95 for tiles which normally cost £5. Even the perfect tiles are competitively priced.

## CIDMAR

10 SPRINGBRIDGE ROAD, LONDON W5 2AA
☎ 0181-567 8188. OPEN 9 - 5.15 MON - SAT.

Cidmar holds large stocks of both plain and printed fabric, net curtain, curtain tracks, and poles - all at discounted prices. Most leading brand names are sold here. Ready to hang net curtains are marked down by 20%, glazed cotton at about half-price, and there is a standard 15% discount off curtain tracking. From time to time, they also have a free curtain-making-up special offer.

## CORCORAN & MAY

11 THE GREEN, HIGH STREET, EALING, LONDON W5 5DA
☎ 0181-567 4324. OPEN 10 - 5.30 MON - SAT. MAIL ORDER.
157 & 161 LOWER RICHMOND ROAD, LONDON SW15 1HH
☎ 0181-788 9556. OPEN 10 - 5.30 MON - SAT.

Corcoran & May sell seconds, overstocks and clearance from top designers including Monkwell, Colefax & Fowler and G P & J Baker. You will also find many of the best designs from some of the brightest newcomers. Their stock includes simple cream damask from Lancashire, checks and stripes from India, brightly coloured brocades from Italy, plus intricate floral prints in the great English tradition. It is possible to have made to measure every type of curtain and blind, swags and tails, pelmets (shaped or straight), covered bedheads and all manner of bedspreads, valances, tiebacks and tablecloths.

## DIRECT BARGAIN CENTRE

69-79 MILE END ROAD, LONDON E1
☎ 0171-790 1094. OPEN 9 - 6 MON - FRI, 8 - 8 THUR, 10 - 4 SUN,
CLOSED SATURDAYS.

DBG sells bankrupt and salvaged good quality carpets, some with branded Axminster and Wilton labels. Fitting can be arranged. Also sells cut-price materials such as Dulux paint and tiles, as well as some furniture, lighting and ceramics.

# EDWARD SYMMONS & PARTNERS

2 SOUTHWARK STREET, LONDON BRIDGE, LONDON SE1 1RQ
☎ 0171-407 8454. OPEN 9.30 - 5.30 MON - FRI.

Deals mainly in plant and machine tools for liquidated companies but they have also sold equipment from offices and restaurants. Some equipment is sold by private treaty or tender. Prices depend on how long they have available to market the sale; the shorter the time, the more your chances of picking up a bargain.

# FORREST & CO

17-31 GIBBINS ROAD, STRATFORD, LONDON E15
☎ 0181-534 2931. OPEN 9 - 5 MON - FRI.

General auction selling household furniture, office equipment, domestic electrical equipment, china, glassware and vehicles, rugs and carpets, held every 2 weeks on Thursdays. Auction rooms open at 10, auction starts at 11. Viewing the previous day from 10 - 5. Catalogue £1.50 by post, £1 at the door.

# HENRY BUTCHER & CO

BROWNLOW HOUSE, 50-51 HIGH HOLBORN, LONDON WC1V 6EG
☎ 0171-405 8411.

Eastablished more than 100 years ago, Henry Butcher & Co are international auctioneers and valuers, dealing with all types of industrial plant, machinery and equipment. They have a mailing list of some 30,000 names under the categories of equipment which they are looking for from heavy engineering to office furniture and computers. They sell anything from boardroom tables to typists' chairs, computers to manufacturing plants. Put your name on their mailing list for a colour flysheet of sales which you might be interested in.

# P N JONES

18 HOLLY GROVE, LONDON SE15 5DG
☎ 0171-639 2113. OPEN 9.30 - 5 MON - FRI, BY APPOINTMENT ON SAT, SUN. MAIL ORDER.

Packed with natural-fibre fabrics, all hand-woven Indian cotton and silks, at trade prices. Twenty-eight different colours in checks and stripes, voiles and cheesecloths as well as curtaining and upholstery fabrics. VAT extra.

## PAUL SIMON FACTORY SHOP

KEMPTON MEWS, KEMPTON ROAD, EAST HAM, LONDON E6 2LD
☎ 0181-472 2333. OPEN 9 - 6 MON - SAT, 10 - 4 SUN.
Discount designer furnishing fabrics, nets, tracks, roller blinds at up
to 20% below normal retail price. Also nine mobile showrooms to
brings samples to your home.

## POSNERS CARPETS

35A-37 FAIRFAX ROAD, SWISS COTTAGE, LONDON NW6 4EW
☎ 0171-625 8899. OPEN 9 - 6 MON - FRI, 10   3 SAT.
Eastablished in 1946, Posners is an independent family business specialising in fitted carpets. First quality rolls of carpet are bought in
bulk together with overmakes and ends of ranges for selling at up to
one third or half of the high street price, giving the best possible value
for money from this large showroom. Customers get professional
advice, more than 40 rolls of stock or 550 ranges to choose from,
immediate response, fitting within 48 hours, free cuttings, and an in-
house team of skilled carpet layers to give peace of mind. All major
brands of carpet and vinyl are carried as well as special lines. Bespoke
carpets and special designs are also available together with a continual
sale of constantly changing roll ends. They have recently introduced
a revolutionary flooring from Sweden, a resilient wood look-alike
called Pergo laminated flooring. It's available in more than 40 designs
from stencilled, coloured, or stripwood flooring. It's non scratchable.

## R F GREASBY LTD

211 LONGLEY ROAD, TOOTING, LONDON SW17 9LG
☎ 0181-672 1100 (RECORDED MESSAGE);
☎ 0181-672 2972/0181-682 4564. OPEN 9 - 5 MON - THUR, 9 - 4 FRI,
VIEWING 10 - 4 SAT.
Want to buy a computer for £30, a leather briefcase for £20, a dozen
umbrellas for the price of one good one? R F Greasby Ltd (Public
Auctioneers) deal in goods from London Transport's and British
Airways lost property offices, Customs & Excise, among others, plus
those obtained because of outstanding debt. Merchandise includes
office equipment, clothing, computers, furniture, coffins, garden and
agricultural equipment. This is the place where dealers get great
bargains, but there's still some left for members of the public. Regular
buyers are admitted first, then entry is on a first-come, first-served

basis every second Monday. The catalogue can only be obtained by annual subscription of £55.

## RUSSELL & CHAPPLE

23 MONMOUTH STREET, LONDON WC2H 9DE
☎ 0171-836 7521. OPEN 8.30 - 5 MON - FRI.
Specialists in artists' supplies, they also sell natural upholstery fabrics at rock bottom prices for hessians, calicos and muslins. Prices from 99p per metre for muslin to £18.62 a metre for linen. The more you buy, the bigger the discount.

## S & M MYERS LTD

100-106 MACKENZIE ROAD, HOLLOWAY, LONDON N7
☎ 0171-609 0091. OPEN 10 - 5.30 MON, WED, FRI, 9.30 - 2 SAT.
Specialists in plain carpets, they offer end of range carpets at discount prices, as well as value-for-money perfect quality carpets by buying direct from the manufacturer or selling liquidated stock. Mainly 80% wool twist carpets with some ranges of wool blends and manmade velvet piles.

## SOFA TO BED

UNIT 1, BAYFORD STREET INDUSTRIAL CENTRE, LONDON E8 3SE
☎ 0181-533 0915. OPEN 7 DAYS A WEEK.
1A CLEVELAND WAY, MILE END ROAD, LONDON E1 4TZ
☎ 0171-790 4233. OPEN 10-2.30 MON - THUR.
Ex-display model sofas and sofabeds at greatly reduced prices, as well as made to order, using Sanderson, Liberty and Parkertex fabric. Also Ottomans, stools, armchairs.

## THE CURTAIN MILL

46-52 FAIRFIELD ROAD, LONDON E3 2QB
☎ 0181-980 9000. OPEN 9 - 5.30 SEVEN DAYS A WEEK.
207-211 THE VALE, ACTON, LONDON W3 7QS
☎ 0181-743 2299. OPEN 9 - 5.30 SEVEN DAYS A WEEK.
Huge choice of top quality fabrics at really low prices - from 99p a yard and including excellent discounts on many designer labels. A large warehouse, it stocks Wilson Wilcox, Ashley Wilde, Gordon Richmond, Blendworth, among other leading names at discount prices.

## THE FABRIC PHONELINE

THE ONE-OFF SOFA COMPANY, 545 OLD YORK ROAD,
WANDSWORTH, LONDON SW18 1TQ
☎ 0181-875 9561. OPEN 10.30 - 5 MON - SAT. MAIL ORDER.
Top quality named fabrics and wallpapers at the best prices with
delivery to your door. There is no set discount as that depends on the
supplier. Post and packaging costs £9.25 per supplier. The showroom
also sells fabric and makes furniture to order to customers' own
design.

## VICTOR OF ROMFORD

1A WESTERHAM ROAD, LEYTON, LONDON E10 7AE
☎ 0181-532 8636. OPEN 10 - 6 MON - SAT. 10 - 3 SUN.
MAIL ORDER.
Sheeting, curtain fabrics, lining, wadding and patchwork at discount
prices. Most of the sheeting and curtaining is clearance lines and
seconds, although some stock is the result of buying in bulk and
selling at very competitive prices. Brand names include Coloroll,
Dorma and the occasional Designers Guild. They also operate a mail
order service.

## *Factory Shops*

## ADAM RICHWOOD LTD

5 GARDEN WALK, LONDON EC2A 3EQ
☎ 0171-729 0976. OPEN 8-4.30 MON - FRI.
Makers of fine period furniture, Adam Richwood Ltd operates a
factory shop selling their top quality pieces at savings of between 75%
and 100% on shop prices. (VAT is extra and delivery can be arranged
at a nominal cost.) A Queen Anne walnut kneehole desk with 8
drawers with solid brass fittings costs £571; 4-drawer yew Colonial
Bureau, £535; 30" high, 3-drawer mahogany Georgian desk with 9
drawers, £637; wall hanging solid mahogany corner cabinet with
glazed or inlaid panel door, £110; 2-drawer walnut file cabinet,
£327, £250 in mahogany, £284 in yew. Prices change in January of
each year.

## CRUCIAL TRADING LTD

174 TOWER BRIDGE ROAD, LONDON SE1
☎ 0171-234 0000. OPEN 10 - 6 TUE - FRI, 10 - 4 SAT.

Crucial Trading has two London showrooms - 77 Westbourne Park Road, W2 and 4 St Barnabas Street, Pimlico Green, SW1 - as well as the factory shops at Craven Arms and Tower Bridge Road (see Furniture/Soft Furnishings, Wales and West Midlands) which sell natural floor coverings and natural rugs at half price or thereabouts. They offer the widest, and wildest, collection of natural floor coverings including about 120 designs in sisal, seagrass, coir, jute, wool, sisal and medieval matting in Europe. There are also natural rugs with 18,000 possible combinations of natural material and borders.

## *Designer Sales*

## THE DESIGNER WAREHOUSE FABRICS SALE

ROGER DACK LTD, STUDIO 2, SHEPPERTON HOUSE,
83 SHEPPERTON ROAD, LONDON N1 3DF
☎ 0171-704 1064. 10 - 8 FRI, 10 - 6 SAT, 11 - 5 SUN.

The Designer Warehouse Fabric Sale is the sister sale to the Warehouse Sale for Women and Men and usually takes place at The Worx, Balfe St, London N1, over a weekend. Offcuts and ends of rolls from designer fabrics are sold at prices which are normally about one third of the shop price. Admission is £2. Phone for more details and dates.

## *Secondhand Shops*

## SEERS ANTIQUES

THE CONSERVATORY, 238A BATTERSEA PARK ROAD, LONDON
SW11 4NG
☎ 0171-720 0263. OPEN 10 - 6 TUE - SAT, 10 - 4SUN, CLOSED MON.
THE BANK, 213 TRAFALGAR ROAD, GREENWICH SE10 9EQ
☎ 0181-293 0293.

Brimming with largely undiscovered bargains that you would never imagine were available in today's well-trodden market. The furniture is a mixture of antique and reproduction intermingling with a vast array of frames and mirrors and a selection of gifts all at bargain prices. Original bedroom fireplaces are priced around £125 with reproduction dining tables varying between £75 and £175 and low-priced antiques such as Pembrokes starting at £95. Prices are competitive because they have a policy of quick turnover and low profit margins. All the prices are clearly displayed and the friendly atmosphere, along with the bustle and bargains is in stark contrast to the hush usually associated with antique shops.

## THE CURTAIN EXCHANGE

133 STEPHENDALE ROAD, LONDON SW6 2PG
☎ 0171-731 8316/7. OPEN 10 - 5 MON - SAT.
40 LEDBURY ROAD, LONDON W11
☎ 0171-229 4923. OPEN 10 - 5 MON - SAT.

The Curtain Exchange is a countrywide network of shops selling top quality, nearly-new curtains, blinds, pelmets, etc at between one-third and one half of the brand new price. Their stock comes from a variety of sources: people who are moving house and hate the drapes in their new home; people who are moving house and want to sell their old curtains to help with the bills; show houses, where the builder wants to recoup some of his outgoings; interior designers' mistakes. Stock changes constantly and ranges from rich brocades, damasks and velvets to chintzes, linens and cottons. Designer names include Colefax & Fowler, Designers Guild, Laura Ashley, Warner, Sanderson, Osborne & Little and Fortuny and Bennison.

## THE CURTAIN SHOP

54 ABBEY GARDENS, LONDON NW8 9AT
☎ 0171-372 1044. OPEN 10 - 6 MON - SAT.

Formerly part of The Curtain Exchange groups of franchised businesses, it is now operating independently selling quality secondhand curtains. The ground floor and basement rooms house dozens of pairs of curtains, many of which are lined and interlined and come with matching tie-backs. Lots of neutral fabrics as well as Colefax & Fowler and Laura Ashley. Fitting and alteration service available.

## THE OLD CINEMA

157 TOWER BRIDGE ROAD, LONDON SE1 3LW
☎ 0171-407 5371. OPEN 9.30 - 6 MON - SAT, 12 - 5 SUN.
Thirty thousand square foot warehouse with antique furniture, some from pub fittings, garden furniture, and pine furniture. Periods include art deco, art nouveau, Victoriana and Americana. There's everything from kitchen sinks to veteran cars. Chairs start at £20, art deco dining room suites from £400 to £2,000, Victorian dining tables from £900.

## THE OLD CINEMA

160 CHISWICK HIGH ROAD, LONDON W4 1PR
☎ 0181-995 4166. OPEN 10 - 6 MON - SAT, 12 - 5 SUN.
Ten thousand square feet of antique furniture, some in complete room settings. Wide range of Victorian, Georgian, Edwardian and art nouveau. Items range from light fittings and mirrors to dining tables and room panelling.

## TULLEY'S OF CHELSEA

289-297 FULHAM ROAD, LONDON SW10 9PZ
☎ 0171-352 1078. OPEN 9 - 5.30 MON - SAT.
Recommended by more than one GDD reader, who says that their furniture is very competitively priced, with sofas from £425, beds, reproduction furniture and two sales every year.

## WELL HUNG

137 NORTHCOTE ROAD, LONDON SW11 6PX
☎ 0171-924 4468. OPEN 9.30 - 5.30 MON - FRI, 10 - 5 SAT.
A secondhand curtain agency which opened in July 1994 in South London. Run by two sisters, Catherine Robson and Liz Pryor, Well Hung stocks more than 300 pairs of curtains and blinds at any one time, many of which are hand made from designer fabrics. They also sell headboards, cushions, tablecloths and bed valences. Well Hung also makes up a range of plain cream curtains, made to the customer's measurements and still at incredibly reasonable prices. Fabrics range from calico to cream damask. The turnover of stock in this shop is very high so the stock quantities vary - more than one visit may be necessary.

# SOUTH EAST

## *Permanent Discount Outlets*

### ALLDERS

CLEARANCE CENTRE, 78-82 HIGH STREET, SUTTON, SURREY M1 1EF
☎ 0181-770 9770. OPEN 9 - 5.30 MON - FRI, 9 - 6 SAT.
Allders department store has a special clearance centre in its old shop
just down the road from Sutton station. Operating under the name
of Clearance Centre, rather than Allders, the centre sells carpets, rugs,
beds, sofas and a host of other products, all at the sort of discounts
you'd expect from end-of-line stock. Don't confuse the discount
centre with the Allders store in the St. Nicholas Shopping Centre.

### BELL HOUSE FABRICS

HIGH STREET, CRANBROOK, KENT TN17 3DN
☎ (01580) 712555. OPEN 9 - 5.30 MON - SAT.
Two-storey shop which is a pleasure to browse in and to buy.
Sanderson specialist, they also operate an ordering service for other
manufacturers, too, at competitive prices. They carry current, seconds
and discontinued lines, priced appropriately. Most printed cottons
cost from £4.99 to £9.99; brocades from £9.99 - £11.99. There are
also tapestries, damasks and dress fabrics from £1.25 a metre for dress
nets and £8 a metre for silks. They also sell new upholstered furniture
and operate a full interior design service.

### CHELFORD HOUSE

STATION ROAD, GAMLINGAY, SANDY, BEDFORDSHIRE SG19 3HQ
☎ (01767) 651888. OPEN 9.30 - 5.30 MON - SAT.
Large warehouse selling discounted fabric from £2.99 a yard to
£11.99 a yard and including everything from glazed cotton chintzes
to tapestries and damasks from leading manufacturers. You can
choose from more than 4,000 rolls, order from the manufacturer's
books or buy own-brand fabric which is one third cheaper than
branded material. Curtain accessories - rails, hooks, tape - are also on
sale and there are also 40-50 wallpaper books, towels, cushions, pillow
inners, and duvets.

## CORCORAN & MAY

1 ST BOTOLPH'S ROAD, SEVENOAKS, KENT TN13 3AJ
☎ (01732) 741851. OPEN 10 - 5.30 MON - SAT.

Corcoran & May sell seconds, overstocks and clearance from top designers including Monkwell, Colefax & Fowler and G P & J Baker. You will also find many of the best designs from some of the brightest newcomers. Their stock includes simple cream damask from Lancashire, checks and stripes from India, brightly coloured brocades from Italy, plus intricate floral prints in the great English tradition. It is possible to have made to measure every type of curtain and blind, swags and tails, pelmets (shaped or straight), covered bedheads and all manner of bedspreads, valances, tiebacks and tablecloths.

## FABRIC WORLD

287 HIGH STREET, SUTTON, SURREY SM1 1LL
☎ 0181-643 5127. OPEN 9 - 5.30 MON - SAT.
6 BRIGHTON ROAD, SOUTH CROYDON, SURREY CR2 6AA
☎ 0181-688 6282. OPEN 9 - 5.30 MON - SAT.

A family business which claims to be the largest factory warehouse of designer curtain and upholstery fabrics in England. It stocks at least 2,000 rolls of material, most selling at between £2.99 and £12.99 a yard for fabric which would normally cost between £20 and £50 a yard. Designer names on sale include Warners and Sandersons, and stock is all perfect and includes current lines. The company imports from all over the world: tapestries, damasks, natural fabrics, checks, stripes, linens, cottons and satins. There is a making-up service.

## G P & J BAKER AND PARKERTEX

WEST END ROAD, OFF DESBOROUGH ROAD, HIGH WYCOMBE,
BUCKINGHAMSHIRE HP11 2QD
☎ (01494) 467400. OPEN 9 - 1 SAT.

Normally a wholesaler to the top department stores, on Saturday this outlet serves as a clearance shop for discontinued lines of these famous-name furnishing fabrics and curtaining. There are also lining fabrics, wallpapers, velours and silks, with some co-ordinated furnishing and curtaining fabrics available. Prices range from £3.95 to £16.95 a metre, with the normal retail price marked on a board nearby so you can see what you're saving. Twice a year, after stocktaking, there are annual sales.

# KNICKERBEAN

11 HOLYWELL HILL, ST ALBANS, HERTFORDSHIRE AL1 1EZ
☎ (01727) 866662. OPEN 9 - 5.30 MON - SAT.
87 HIGH STREET, TUNBRIDGE WELLS, KENT TN1 1XZ
☎ (01892) 520883. OPEN 9 - 5.30 MON - SAT.
8 BARTHOLOMEW STREET, NEWBURY, BERKSHIRE RG14 5LL
☎ (01635) 529016. OPEN 9 - 5.30 MON - SAT.

Knickerbean have a fabulous range of top designer curtain and upholstery fabrics assembled from many different sources. On my last visit,
I saw selections from Designers Guild, Anna French, Jane Churchill,
Colefax & Fowler, and Osborne & Little, among the hundreds of different fabrics. While some of these are discontinued lines, ends of
ranges, or off-shade lots, a growing number are now coming in
directly from mills and manufacturers overseas - most recently some
new designs from Collier Campbell. Because they buy in such large
lots, they can usually obtain fabrics at less than the usual wholesale
price, with many of their fabrics sold at about half of the original recommended retail price. Their fast-moving selection of more than
100,000 yards from £5.95 a yard includes glazed chintzes, cotton
prints, stripes and checks, and a huge selection of luxurious upholstery fabrics including a large range of Italian damasks and tapestries.
Customers are encouraged to pop in regularly to browse through the
latest arrivals and there's the added benefit of being able to see entire
rolls rather than just a small sample book of swatches. They also offer
a complete making-up service for curtains, blinds, loose covers and
other soft furnishings. Overall, their discounted fabrics coupled with
low making-up charges work out at about half to one third less than
normal made to measure soft furnishings. They hold twice-yearly
sales in January and June with even greater reductions on their ranges
of fabrics.

# PAT CHANDLER

CLOVELLY, MARTIN, NEAR FORDINGBRIDGE, HAMPSHIRE SP6 3LD
☎ (01725) 519345. OPEN WEEKENDS ONLY AND WEEKDAYS BY
APPOINTMENT.

Pat Chandler sells teak and painted furniture and decorative accessories from a huge barn next to her home in Hampshire. She visits
Bali once or twice a year for four or five weeks at a time and hand
picks vast amounts of furniture which are then shipped back here.

The painted furniture is similiar to that found in the best Fulham showrooms but about half of the price. For example, small semi-circular verdigris painted side tables, less than £100; matching display cabinets, about £250. There are also lots of painted accessories such as animals. The heavier teak furniture is also priced to sell. For example, 4ft 6in coffee table, about £440. Definitely well worth a visit, but telephone beforehand.

## SUE FOSTER FABRICS

57 HIGH STREET, EMSWORTH, HAMPSHIRE PO10 7YA
☎ (01243) 378831. OPEN 9.30 - 5 MON - FRI, 9.30 - 1 WED, SAT.
MAIL ORDER.
Supplies top name furnishing fabrics at discounts. Her showroom has one of the widest range of pattern books outside London, where customers can choose perfect fabrics and wallpapers, usually 15-20% below retail price and where they can also find trimmings, cushions and some lighting. Also takes orders over the phone and sends out samples and undertakes sample searches - send for the questionnaire.

## THE CURTAIN MILL

21 GREYCAINE ROAD, WATFORD, HERTFORDSHIRE WD3 4PS
☎ (01923) 220339. OPEN 9 - 5.30 SEVEN DAYS A WEEK.
Huge choice of top quality fabrics at really low prices - from 99p a yard and including excellent discounts on many designer labels. A large warehouse, it stocks Wilson Wilcox, Gordon Richmond, Ashley Wilde, Blendworth, among other leading names at discount prices.

## TRACKS AND TRIMMINGS

50 THE PANTILES, TUNBRIDGE WELLS, KENT TN2 5TN
☎ (01892) 515288. OPEN 9 - 5.30 MON - SAT, 9 - 1 WED.
Tracks and trimmings, upholstery and curtains, cushions, tie-backs, £2.65 a pair, compared with £15 in the high street; string-type tie backs, £14, compared with £25 in department stores; plaited and rope tie-backs, from £8.85; cushion covers, £3.95; braids from 50p a metre for discontinued ranges; pelmet boards and handmade lamp-shades.

# *Factory Shops*

## BOYNETT FABRICS CO LTD

2 ASTON ROAD, CAMBRIDGE ROAD, BEDFORD, BEDFORDSHIRE
MK42 OJN
☎ (01234) 217788. OPEN 9 - 5.30 MON - FRI.
Curtain fabrics manufactured by Boynett, who are wholesalers, for
top London department stores, are sold in this small factory shop at
discount prices for seconds and over-runs. Also a curtain-making
service.

## COLLINS AND HAYES

PONSWOOD INDUSTRIAL ESTATE, ST LEONARDS, HASTINGS, EAST
SUSSEX
☎ (01424) 720027. OPEN 9 - 5 MON - SAT.
Manufacturers of upholstered furniture and with their own collection
of fabrics, Collins and Hayes have recently opened their first factory
shop. Here, they will be selling ends of lines, discontinued models
and cancelled orders of sofas and chairs, as well as fabrics, at half price
or less. Upholstered furniture is a fashion industry and accordingly
new collections are brought out once or twice a year, so there is a
steady supply of ends of lines.

## GRANDFORD CARPET MILLS

UNIT 11, BRIDGE INDUSTRIES, BROAD CUT, FAREHAM, HAMPSHIRE
PO16 8ST
☎ (01329) 289612. OPEN 9 - 5 MON - FRI, 10 - 4 SAT.
Family-run factory shop which sells the majority of their carpets
direct to the consumer. Good quality carpets at half the price you
would pay in high street shops. The top price is £15.95 a square yard
for carpet which you would pay at least £30 for in the high street.
Seconds, which may be due to uneven dyeing, are £6.50 per square
yard.

## HUBBINET REPRODUCTION FACTORY SHOP

UNIT 7, HUBBINET INDUSTRIAL ESTATE, EASTERN AVENUE WEST,
HAINAULT ROAD, ROMFORD, ESSEX
☎ (01708) 762212/757511. OPEN 9 - 5 MON - FRI, 10 - 4 SAT.
Manufacturers of reproduction furniture in mahogany and yew, all of

which are sold in the factory shop at discounts of about 20%. Seconds in dining room suites, bookcases, video cabinets, display cabinets and cupboards at factory shop prices.

## Secondhand Shops

### A BARN FULL OF SOFAS AND CHAIRS

FURNACE MILL, LAMBERHURST, KENT TN3 8LH
☎ (01892) 890285. OPEN 10 - 5 TUE - SAT.
Three storeys of pre-1950s sofas and chairs, some antique, ranging from £200-£400. Can restore back to their original state using all the traditional fabrics or sell in un-restored condition. Also new range of sofas based on old models from £1,600 upwards.

### CURTAIN CALL

52 FRIARS STILE ROAD, RICHMOND, SURREY RG14 2QG
☎ 0181-332 6250. OPEN 9 - 4 MON - SAT, CLOSED WED.
Stocks a wide range of nearly-new curtains from sill length to a 9 ft drop. Simple lined curtains range from about £40, while you can find full-length interlined curtains to fit a large bay window for as little as £300 or at least half their original cost. Stock has also included cushions, quilts, coronet sets and even a hand-painted four-poster single child's bed complete with antique lace drapes. Curtain Call offers an alteration and track fitting service.

### CURTAIN CALL

UNIT 1A, HAMBRIDGE FARM, HAMBRIDGE ROAD, NEWBURY, BERKSHIRE TW10 6QN
☎ (01635) 41544. OPEN 9 - 5 MON - FRI.
Top quality lined and interlined secondhand curtains and pelmets, as well as soft furnishings, cushions, poles, designer mistakes, left-over fabrics, and trimmings. Curtains range from Marks & Spencer to designer label and there are sometimes matching headboards, lampshades and bed covers. Three-inch rufflette tape, continuous zip and piping cord is also sold, as are tie backs. Leftover curtain and upholstery fabric costs from £2 to £6 a metre, cushion covers are from £4 to £20.

## CURTAIN UP

STONEFIELD PARK, MARTINS LANE, CHILBOLTON, STOCKBRIDGE, HAMPSHIRE SO20 6BL
☎ (01264) 781244. OPEN 2 - 5 MON, WED, THUR, 10 - 1 SAT, AND BY APPOINTMENT.

Now in its fourth year and recently moved to larger premises, this shops stocks an even larger choice of top quality secondhand curtains in fabric names such as Colefax & Fowler, Charles Hammond, Designers Guild, Bakers, Warners and Sandersons. Stock changes constantly and there is a huge range of sizes. Also available are bedspreads, bedheads, cushions, cloths, lamps, stools and tie-backs. Just off the A30, close to the village of Stockbridge, do phone for directions. Out of town small but packed shop selling top quality and designer secondhand curtains and accessories at a fraction of their original cost. Stock changes constantly and there are always more than 75 sets of curtains in fabric names such as Colefax & Fowler, Osborne & Little, Designers Guild, Bakers, Warners, Laura Ashley and Crowsons. Many curtains are new and range from a small pair for £20 to large grand ones for £400. The setting is delightful in a building adjacent to a lovely hotel which can offer tea, coffee, lunch, etc, for those making a longer journey.

## FINISHING TOUCHES

1 HIGH STREET, HYTHE, KENT SO45 6AG
☎ (01703) 841967. OPEN 9.30 - 4.30 MON - SAT.

As-new curtains, lampshades, furniture, wall lampshades, bedspreads, duvet covers, rolls of furnishing and curtain fabric. For example, small wall lampshades cost from £2.50-£3.50; a set of Ercol dining table seats, £220; cushions from £6-£8; teak wall unit, £25; Lloyd Loom bedroom cabinet, £65.

## GREEN OAK BUILDERS

THE YARD OFFICE, ST CHRISTOPHER'S COTTAGE, NEWNEY GREEN, WRITTLE, CHELMSFORD, ESSEX
☎ (01245) 420627. PHONE FOR APPOINTMENT.

A distributor for Country Cookers, who sell reconditioned Rayburn cookers and sometimes also Agas and Nobel reconditioned models. These are considerably cheaper than the brand new version. They can incorporate a domestic heating system for hot water and radiators.

## LONDON CURTAIN AGENCY

298 SANDYCOMBE ROAD, KEW, SURREY TW9 3NG
☎ 0181-940 5959. OPEN 10 - 4 TUE - SAT.

A mixture of new and secondhand curtains. Reflecting the fact that the owner is the former Sales and Marketing Director of a top London hotel, some of the curtains are refurbishment stock from London's five-star hotels, others designer samples and former display stock from fabric houses and interior designers. Stock ranges from curtains for small windows for £50 up to £800 for drapes for huge bay windows with swags and tails. There are also curtain rails, cushions, bedheads, lamps, blinds, tie-backs and pelmets. All the curtains are lined or interlined. Fantastic bargains at approximately one third of the original cost.

## MORLEY MARKETING

MARSH LANE, WARE, HERTS SG12 9QB
☎ (01920) 468002. FAX (01920) 463893. OPEN 9 - 5 MON-FRI, 9 - 4 SAT.

A distributor for Country Cookers, who sell reconditioned Rayburn cookers and sometimes also reconditioned Agas. These are considerably cheaper than the brand new version. They can incorporate a domestic heating system for hot water and radiators. They also sell new Nobels, which are considerably cheaper than their better-known competitor.

## NEWBURY FIREPLACE CENTRE

SHERBOURNE HOUSE, SHAWHILL, NEWBURY, BERKSHIRE
RG14 2EQ
☎ (0163)5 40480. FAX (01635) 40405. OPEN 8.30 - 4.30 MON - FRI, 9 - 1 SAT.

A distributor for Country Cookers, who sell reconditioned Rayburn cookers and sometimes also Agas and Nobel reconditioned models. These are considerably cheaper than the brand new version. They can incorporate a domestic heating system for hot water and radiators.

## THE CURTAIN AGENCY

231 LONDON ROAD, CAMBERLEY, SURREY
☎ (01276) 671672. OPEN 9.30 - 4.30 MON - SAT.

Period shop on a corner site of the A30 in Camberley, with a wide range of all sizes and types of curtains, blinds (Roman, festoon and

Austrian), tassels, cushions, headboards and antique lighting and antique curtain poles. Most are designer curtains, though there is a small area where cheaper curtains are displayed. Alteration service, as well as a new curtain-making service and track fitting.

## THE CURTAIN CONNECTION LTD

108A LONDON ROAD, ST ALBANS, HERTFORDSHIRE AL2 2PE
☎ (01727) 868368. OPEN 10 - 2.30 TUE - FRI, 9.30 - 5 SAT.
A wide range of quality secondhand and former display curtains, cushions, blinds, headboards and other soft furnishings. There are usually more than 300 pairs of curtains in all shapes and sizes, most of which are lined with many also interlined. The majority come with valances and tie-backs. Many designer fabrics are represented including Crowson, Osborne & Little, Warners, Designers Guild, Sanderson and Laura Ashley. The shop also sells light fittings, many of which are antique; plates and vases from the turn of this century to the 1950s; lampshades and many other home accessories. Also stocked are some upmarket surplus lamp bases and cushions from large department stores which are sold at greatly reduced prices. You are advised to measure up before you come and bring a sample of material, carpet, etc, from each room where curtains are required.

## THE CURTAIN EXCHANGE

SHOP 3, 194 MAXWELL ROAD, BEACONSFIELD, BUCKINGHAMSHIRE HP9 1QX
☎ (01494) 680662. OPEN 9.30 - 4.30 MON - SAT.
NAGS CORNER (A134), WISTON ROAD, NAYLAND, NR COLCHESTER, ESSEX CO6 4LT
☎ (01206) 263660. OPEN 10 - 4 MON - SAT.
45 HIGH STREET, CUCKFIELD, WEST SUSSEX RH17 5JU
☎ (01444) 417000. OPEN 10 - 4 TUE - SAT.
The Curtain Exchange is a countrywide network of shops selling top quality, nearly-new curtains, blinds, pelmets, etc at between one-third and one half of the brand new price. Their stock comes from a variety of sources: people who are moving house and hate the drapes in their new home; people who are moving house and want to sell their old curtains to help with the bills; show houses, where the builder wants to recoup some of his outgoings; interior designers' mistakes. Stock changes constantly and ranges from rich brocades, damasks and

velvets to chintzes, linens and cottons. Designer names include Colefax & Fowler, Designers Guild, Laura Ashley, Warner, Sanderson, Osborne & Little

## THE CURTAIN SHOP

12 GOODS STATION ROAD, TUNBRIDGE WELLS, KENT TN1 2BL
☎ (01892) 522682. OPEN 9.30 - 5.30 MON - SAT.

A former public house, the walls are festoooned with good quality nearly-new curtains of all colours and sizes. Some may have been on display in an interior designer's showroom or a show house, some are mistakes. Some are ideal for small cottages, others for lofty rooms or patio windows. There is also an alteration service and pelmets can be specially designed and made to match or contrast. A selection of material on the roll is also stocked. Accessories include silk and silver tassels and a range of cords. A professional track-fitting service is operated independently by a member of this family-run business.

## THE CURTAIN TRACK

103 WEST STREET, FARNHAM, SURREY GU19 7EN
☎ (01252) 714711. OPEN 9.30 - 4.30 MON -SAT.

Good quality lined and interlined curtains both full-length and shorter with prices ranging from £25 to £500 a pair. They also sell padded headboards, bedspreads and cushions as well as a large and varied range of chandeliers, table lamps and wall lights, antique curtain poles French gilt tie backs and tassels. They offer an alteration and track fitting service.

# SOUTH WEST

## Permanent Discount Outlets

## CAVE INTERIORS

MOUSEPLATT, SIDBURY, SIDMOUTH, DEVON EX10 OQE
☎ (01395) 597384. BY APPOINTMENT ONLY.

Specialists in discontinued and seconds designer fabrics, Cave Interiors sells everything from florals to stripes and checks, chintzes, printed cottons and kilims from quality designers. The majority of fabric, which normally sells for in excess of £15 a metre, will cost from £8-£10 a metre for fabric which normally retails at £20-£35 a metre; nothing is priced at more than £15.

## EXETER SURPLUS

BAKERS YARD, ALPHIN BROOK, MARSH BARTON, EXETER PL15 7YZ
☎ (01392) 496731. OPEN 8.30 - 5 MON - SAT, 10 - 4 SUN.

Operates from a 16,000 square foot warehouse, buying good quality, used goods from government departments, schools and the armed forces , among others. Their merchandise includes anything from camping equipment, Irish linen and woollen blankets to office furniture, shelving, nuts and bolts, leather and bolts of cloth. There are usually more than 20,000 different lines in stock; examples of prices includes brand new Irish linen sheets for £6.99; down and feather sleeping bags, from £15, usually about £100; marquees for £400, usual price £2,500.

## JUST FABRICS

THE BRIDEWELL, DOCKACRE ROAD, LAUNCESTON, CORNWALL
☎ (01566) 776279. OPEN 9 - 5 MON - SAT. AND MAIL ORDER.

Based in a large showroom in a former warehouse approached through an open courtyard, Just Fabrics hold the largest sample library in the country for all types of furnishing fabrics and wallpapers. All the top brand names are represented and there is a discount of between 20%-25% off the recommended retail prices of most items. The company undertakes to despatch the goods to customers on receipt of the order, and says that distance is no object. They also have a mail order catalogue of their bedlinen and patchwork quilts.

## KNICKERBEAN

5 WALCOT STREET, BATH, AVON BA1 5BN
☎ (01225) 445741. OPEN 9 - 5.30 MON - SAT.

Knickerbean have a fabulous range of top designer curtain and upholstery fabrics assembled from many different sources. On my last visit, I saw selections from Designers Guild, Anna French, Jane Churchill, Colefax & Fowler, and Osborne & Little, among the hundreds of different fabrics. While some of these are discontinued lines, ends of ranges, or off-shade lots, a growing number are now coming in directly from mills and manufacturers overseas - most recently some new designs from Collier Campbell. Because they buy in such large lots, they can usually obtain fabrics at less than the usual wholesale price, with many of their fabrics sold at about half of the original recommended retail price. Their fast-moving selection of more than 100,000 yards from £5.95 a yard includes glazed chintzes, cotton prints, stripes and checks, and a huge selection of luxurious upholstery fabrics including a large range of Italian damasks and tapestries. Customers are encouraged to pop in regularly to browse through the latest arrivals and there's the added benefit of being able to see entire rolls rather than just a small sample book of swatches. They also offer a complete making-up service for curtains, blinds, loose covers and other soft furnishings. Overall, their discounted fabrics coupled with low making-up charges work out at about half to one third less than normal made to measure soft furnishings. They hold twice-yearly sales in January and June with even greater reductions on their ranges of fabrics.

## LOOSE ENDS

GILES GREEN, BRINKWORTH, CHIPPENHAM, WILTSHIRE SN15 5DQ
☎ (01666) 510685. OPEN 9 - 1 MON - FRI OR BY APPOINTMENT.
Operating from two large converted barns in the grounds of the proprietor's house, Loose Ends offers top quality discontinued lines of fabric and textured and plain upholstery fabrics which they obtain from the best houses in London and New York and sell at about one third of the normal price. They hold very large stocks of all types of furnishing fabrics including lining, interlining and wallpapers which you can buy on the spot.

## THE FACTORY SHOP

7 - 9 FARADAY MILL, PRINCE ROCK, PLYMOUTH, DEVON
☎ (01752) 253351.OPEN 9 - 5 MON - SAT, 10 - 4 SUN.
Shop sells material, foam, re-upholstery nets, curtain-making equipment and bean bags. There are more than 2,000 rolls of fabric in stock, both curtain weight and upholstery weight, as well as bedding,

sheeting and nets. There are also accessories: zips, brass hooks, curtain tracks, Velcro, pillow and cushion covering and pelmets, as well as a curtain making service. Fabric costs from £2.99 to £12.99 a square yard.

## THE MAGNIFICENT MATERIAL COMPANY

188 TYTHERINGTON, NR WARMINSTER, WILTSHIRE BA12 7AD
☎ (01985) 840870. 0985 850501. OPEN 9.30 - 12.30 MON AND THUR AND BY APPOINTMENT.

Sells fabric seconds, discontinued and ends of lines, as well as a few firsts from a converted barn in Wiltshire. Designer labels include Fischbacher, Monkwell, GP & J Baker, Thorpe & May, Wemyss, Charles Hammond and many more.

## *Factory Shops*

## BALMAIN & BALMAIN

DORSET
☎ (01963) 220247.

Buying a sofa is one of the biggest home purchases you make, particularly for good quality. Balmain & Balmain offer traditional handmade furniture which is custom made and can be delivered throughout the country at workshop direct prices. The sofas, sofa beds and chairs are built on best beechwood frames, with coil-sprung seats and feather cushions and carry a ten-year guarantee. Prices are 20%-30% less than the equivalent quality in the high street.

## FELL FABRICATION

UNIT 5, CAREY DEVELOPMENT, TWEED ROAD, CLEVEDON, AVON BS21 6RR
☎ (01275) 879956. OPEN 9 - 5 MON - THUR, 9 - 4 FRI.

Manufacturers of gas coal-effect burners and convector boxes, and supplier to more than 100 retailers countrywide, Fell Fabrications has a factory shop near Bristol. You don't need a chimney, just an outside wall to enjoy the effect of a real fire. A made-to-measure service is also available.

## LAURA ASHLEY

UNIT 5, CLARKS VILLAGE, FARM ROAD, STREET, SOMERSET
BA16 OBB
☎ (01458) 840405. OPEN 9 - 6 MON - SAT AND BANK HOLIDAYS,
11 - 5 SUN.
UNIT 32, GREEN LANES SHOPPING CENTRE, BARNSTAPLE, DEVON
☎ (01271) 329072. OPEN 9 - 5.30 MON - SAT.
Laura Ashley home furnishings and fashion. Most of the merchandise
is made up of perfect carry-overs from the high street shops around
the country, though there are also some discontinued lines. Stock
reflects the normal high street variety, though at least one season later
and with less choice in colours and sizes.


# Secondhand Shops

## AYRES HEATING SYSTEMS

1 CEDAR UNITS, WEBBERS YARD, DARTINGTON, NR TOTNES,
SOUTH DEVON TQ9 6JY
☎ (01803) 865555. OPEN 9 - 4.30 MON - FRI, 8.15 - 12.30 SAT,
CLOSED 1 - 2.
Plumbers and heating engineers, they sell reconditioned Agas and
Rayburn cookers at prices considerably lower than the brand new
versions, and brand new Nobels at prices considerably less than their
more famous rivals.

## SANDPITS HEATING CENTRE

SANDPITS HILL, CURRY RIVEL, LANGPORT, SOMERSET
☎ (01458) 251476. OPEN 8 - 5.30 MON - FRI, 8 - 4.30 SAT.
A distributor for Country Cookers, who sell reconditioned Rayburn
cookers and sometimes also Agas and Nobel reconditioned models.
These are considerably cheaper than the brand new version. They can
incorporate a domestic heating system for hot water and radiators.

# THE CURTAIN EXCHANGE

1ST FLOOR, 123 HIGH STREET, MARLBOROUGH, WILTSHIRE SN8 1LZ
☎ (01672) 516994, OPEN 10 - 4.30 MON - SAT.
LONGALLER MILL, BISHOP'S HULL, TAUNTON, SOMERSET TA4 1AD
☎ (01823) 326071. OPEN 10 - 4 WED - SAT.
The Curtain Exchange is a countrywide network of shops selling top quality, nearly-new curtains, blinds, pelmets, etc at between one-third and one half of the brand new price. Their stock comes from a variety of sources: people who are moving house and hate the drapes in their new home; people who are moving house and want to sell their old curtains to help with the bills; show houses, where the builder wants to recoup some of his outgoings; interior designers' mistakes. Stock changes constantly and ranges from rich brocades, damasks and velvets to chintzes, linens and cottons. Designer names include Colefax & Fowler, Designers Guild, Laura Ashley, Warner, Sanderson, Osborne & Little.

# THE CURTAIN RING

5 PERRY ROAD, (PARK ROW), BRISTOL, AVON BS1 5BQ
☎ (0117) 929 2844. OPEN 10 - 6 TUE - FRI, 10 - 5 SAT.
Fine quality secondhand curtains and soft furnishings. Mainly curtains but also bedspreads, bedheads, lampshades and cushions. Age doesn't matter if the design is classic and the quality is good. Some brand new "mistakes" or display items. Prices range from £5 for tiebacks to £700 for magnificent interlined and Italian strung designer curtains in mint condition. Requests can be entered on a database and contact made when something suitable comes in. The showroom is between the Broadmead Shopping Area and the Clifton Triangle, close to St Michael's Hill and Christmas Steps. Items accepted for sale, on commission, at any time during opening hours.

# THE CURTAIN TRADING COMPANY,

ROUNDWAY FARM, DEVIZES, WILTSHIRE SN10 2HU
☎ (01380) 723113. OPEN 9.30 - 2.30 TUE, THUR, 9.30 - 1 SAT, AND BY APPOINTMENT ONLY.
The Curtain Trading Company sells top quality and designer sec-ondhand curtains and blinds. There are usually at least 75 pairs of curtains in stock in fabrics such as Osborne & Little, Hill & Knowles, Parkertex and Laura Ashley. Some of the curtains are brand new samples or designer mistakes.

## WENDRON WOODSTOVES

MALLOW COURT, WENDRON, HELSTON, CORNWALL TR13 0NA
☎ (01326) 572878. OPEN 9 - 5 MON - FRI, 9.30 - 4.30 SAT.
A distributor for Country Cookers, who sell reconditioned Rayburn
cookers and sometimes also Agas and Nobel reconditioned models.
These are considerably cheaper than the brand new version. They can
incorporate a domestic heating system for hot water and radiators.

# WALES AND WEST MIDLANDS

## *Permanent Discount Outlets*

## CLASSIC CHOICE FURNISHINGS LIMITED

BRYNMENYN INDUSTRIAL ESTATE, BRYNMENYN, BRIDGEND,
GLAMORGAN CF32 9TD
☎ (01656) 725111. MAIL ORDER.
Save money on high quality furniture by purchasing direct. Choose
from modern and traditional designs in suites or separates - all fully
guaranteed for quality and supplied with a twenty-one day no-quible
guarantee. There is an excellent choice of fabric and leather furniture
in a wide choice of covers.

## CURTAIN WORLD

3 SOUTH PARADE, OXFORD, OXFORDSHIRE OX2 3TX
☎ (01865) 516181. OPEN 9 - 5 MON - SAT.
Brand name fabrics at bargain prices including Jonelle, Osborne &
Little, Next, Ametex, Sanderson and Monkwell. The average discount
is between 40%-50% and they also sell a wide range of chintzes from
£4.99 a yard, curtain poles and accessories. The company has been in
operation for more than 20 years and can offer lots of helpful advice.
Up to 500 rolls of fabric at any one time sold at about half price
including lots of natural and Indian fabrics.

## JUST FABRICS

BURFORD ANTIQUES CENTRE, CHELTENHAM ROAD, BURFORD,
OXFORDSHIRE OX18 4JA
☎ (01993) 823391. OPEN 9.30 - 5.30 MON - SAT, 2 - 5 SUN.

Just Fabrics sells quality furnishing fabrics, mostly designer clearance,
some regular and some their own range which is woven and dyed for
them exclusively. There is a huge range in stock at very competitive
prices.

## LAURA ASHLEY SALE SHOP

BEAR LANE, NEWTOWN, POWYS, WALES
☎ (01686) 626549. OPEN 9.30 - 5.30 MON, 9 - 5.30 TUE - SAT.

Laura Ashley home furnishings and fashion. Most of the merchandise
is made up of perfect carry-overs from the high street shops around
the country, though there are also some discontinued lines. Stock
reflects the normal high street variety, though at least one season later
and with less choice in colours and sizes.

## LOOSE ENDS

78 HIGH STREET, WITNEY, OXFORDSHIRE
☎ (01993) 773508. OPEN 9.30 - 5 MON - SAT, CLOSED 1 - 2 FRI.

Selected seconds in furnishing fabrics from well-known designers.
Budget ranges of first quality fabrics in cotton prints and natural
fabrics. Damasks, Madras checks and moire taffeta all under £10 a
metre. Medium-sized shop in busy high street with double yellow
lines outside.

## TOP SERVICE

CHURCH END HOUSE, WHICHFORD, SHIPSTON ON STOUR,
WARWICKSHIRE CV36 5PG
☎ (01608) 684829. OPEN 9 - 5 MON - FRI.

Offer both a discounted service and a showroom which you can visit.
They usually hold about 150 manufacturer's products including
fabrics, wallpapers and curtains, selling them at about 25%-30% less
than the high street retail price. The larger the order, the bigger the
discount.

## WARWICKS FABRICS CLEARANCE SHOP

HACKLING HOUSE, BOURTON-ON-THE-WATER INDUSTRIAL PARK,
JUST OFF A429 STOW TO CIRENCESTER ROAD, GLOUCESTERSHIRE
GL54 2EN
☎ (01451) 820772. OPEN 10 - 5 MON - SAT.
They stock there own label fabric for curtains and upholstery from
£2.95 a metre up to £17.50, as well as brand name fabrics, linings,
heading tapes, threads, tracks and poles. Also sell some braiding, trim,
fringes and curtain tracks.

## *Factory Shops*

## CARPETS OF WORTH LTD

SEVERN VALLEY MILLS, SEVERN ROAD, STOURPORT-ON-SEVERN,
WORCERSTERSHIRE DY13 9HA
☎ (01299) 827222. OPEN 8.30 - 5 MON - FRI, 8 - 12 SAT.
Sells Axminster carpets and rugs, both patterned or plain. These are
usually seconds or overmakes, discontinued lines or end of contract
rolls. Patterned Axminsters are half price.

## CRUCIAL TRADING LTD

THE MARKET HALL, CRAVEN ARMS, SHROPSHIRE SY7 9NY
☎ (01588) 673666. OPEN 10 - 5 MON - FRI. MAIL ORDER.
Crucial Trading has two London showrooms - 77 Westbourne Park
Road, W2 and 4 St Barnabas Street, Pimlico Green, SW1 - as well as
the factory shops at Craven Arms and Tower Bridge Road (see
Furniture/Soft Furnishings, London) which sell natural floor coverings and natural rugs at half price or thereabouts. They offer the
widest, and wildest, collection of natural floor coverings including
about 120 designs in sisal, seagrass, coir, jute, wool, sisal and medieval
matting in Europe. There are also natural rugs with 18,000 possible
combinations of natural material and borders.

# HICO

BICESTER OUTLET SHOPPING VILLAGE, PINGLE DRIVE, BICESTER,
JUNCTION 9 OF M40, OXFORDSHIRE OX6 7WD
☎ (01869) 323200. OPEN 10 - 6 MON - SAT AND BANK HOLIDAYS,
11 - 5 SUN.

One of 48 shops, with more planned, in this factory shopping village
which opened in June 1995. Billed as Bond Street comes to Bicester,
the shops are very smart indeed, beautifully designed and stocked
with end-of-season designer fashions, mens and childrenswear, tableware, shoes and more, all on permanent sale at prices reduced from
25%-50%, with some reductions up to 75%. Owned by Tarleton
Mills who manufacture quality home furnishings, bed linen and
sheets for a range of department stores, this shop stocks their seconds
and overmakes at discounts of 25%-30%. The village also has two
restaurants, a small children's play area and free parking. The telephone number given here is for the village.

# MUSEUM MERCHANDISE

BICESTER OUTLET SHOPPING VILLAGE, PINGLE DRIVE, BICESTER,
JUNCTION 9 OF M40, OXFORDSHIRE OX6 7WD
☎ (01869) 323200. OPEN 10 - 6 MON - SAT AND BANK HOLIDAYS,
11 - 5 SUN.

One of 48 shops, with more planned, in this factory shopping village
which opened in June 1995. Billed as Bond Street comes to Bicester,
the shops are very smart indeed, beautifully designed and stocked
with end-of-season designer fashions, mens and childrenswear, tableware, shoes and more, all on permanent sale at prices reduced from
25%-50%, with some reductions up to 75%. This shop houses a collection of overstocks and unsold gift items from the shops at the Tate
Gallery, the National Gallery and the British Museum. There are lots
of lovely cards at 60p each instead of the usual £1; rugs, £12.00;
throws, £13.99; parchment photo albums, £8.99; decorated trays,
£24.99; wrapping paper, 50p; bistro tables and 4 chairs, £150;
painted CD holders, £15.99; painted frogs, £24.99, and lots of beautiful books. The village also has two restaurants, a small children's play
area and free parking. The telephone number given here is for the
village.

## RMJ (ALLOYS) LTD

46-48 BAYTON ROAD, COVENTRY, WEST MIDLANDS CV7 9EJ
☎ (01203) 367508. OPEN 9 - 4.30 MON - THUR, 9 - 3.30 FRI.
Made to measure staircases in metal or wood for indoors or outdoors
- spiral, straight or fire escapes - at factory prices.

## ROGER OATES DESIGN ARTS

THE LONG BARN EASTNOR, LEDBURY, HEREFORDSHIRE HR8 1EL
☎ (01531) 631611.
Manufacturer of a range of English woven floor coverings, shawls and
wraps, the factory shop sells seconds and ends of rolls. Runners are
£10 per square foot instead of £15; 100% wool small rugs in plaids
and herringbone patterns are £20-£25; wood wraps from £25.

## SKOPOS DESIGN

CHELTENHAM, GLOUCESTERSHIRE
☎ (01242) 584344. OPEN 9.30 - 5 MON - FRI, 9 - 5.30 SAT.
Not as much stock as in the parent mill shop in Yorkshire, where they
design and manufacture flame retardant fabrics for leading international hotel groups and interior designers. They offer end of contract
runs, specials and quality seconds direct to the public. Ends of rolls
are half price, plus there are 100% cotton furnishing fabrics, sheers,
voiles and linings, discontinued and imperfect fabrics, ex-display
curtains, quilted pieces, cushions, haberdashery and remnants.

## SOFAS & CO

NEWLAND COURT, 10 NEWLAND, WITNEY, OXFORDSHIRE
☎ (01993) 708228. OPEN 9 - 5.30 SEVEN DAYS A WEEK.
Small workshop where sofas are made up, with very friendly staff.
Offers two different types of sofa - plywood or chipboard - and three
different types of cushion fillings: warman fibre, qualifill or feather.
The basic cost works out at £150 per seat (thus, £450 for a three-
seater sofa), plus £100 if you choose ply as opposed to chipboard, plus
the fabric. It's about an extra £100 for a sofabed. Most of their sofas
are made up with Qualifill cushions. Staff claim they're not trying to
compete with Wesley Barrell or Parker Knowle, but are a mid-price
range good deal sofa company.

## TREFIW WOOLLEN MILL SHOP

TREFIW, NEAR CONWAY, GWYNEDD LL27 ONQ
☎ (01492) 640462. OPEN 9 - 5 MON - FRI, 10 - 5 SAT.
Sells products manufactured on the premises: Welsh tapestry bedspreads, £70; tweed travel rugs, £16.50 per yard; coats £70; wool, £24.50 a kilo; tweed fabrics from £11.95; tapestries and tweed coats £88.95; mohair coats, £86.70.

## VICTORIA CARPET WEAVERS SHOP

GREEN STREET, KIDDERMINSTER, WORCESTERSHIRE DY10 1HL
☎ (01562) 754055. OPEN 10 - 5.30 MON - FRI, 9 - 5 SAT.
Large range of Axminsters and Wilton manufactured in own factories, as well as tufted carpets. Roll ends and slight seconds are 25-30% cheaper than normal retail prices. Twelve to fourteen tufted ranges; four Axminster ranges; and two Wilton ranges. The factory shop does not stock carpets on the roll or large quantities of any one carpet.

## VOGUE CARPETS

11 BRUNSWICK STREET, NEWCASTLE-UNDER-LYME, STAFFORDSHIRE ST5 1HF
☎ (01782) 630569. OPEN 9 - 5 SEVEN DAYS A WEEK, 9 - 12 THUR.
All types and styles of carpets including Axminsters and Wilton at very competitive prices. Vogue work on small margins and buy direct as part of a large group from the manufacturers, thereby getting good prices.

# Secondhand Shops

## COUNTRY COOKERS

5 SHERFORD STREET, BROMYARD, WORCESTERSHIRE HR7 4DL
☎ (01885) 488918. OPEN 9 - 5 MON, WED - FRI, 9 - 1 TUE, 10 - 4.30 SAT, CLOSED 1 - 1.30 DAILY.
Offers Aga and Rayburns at considerably less than the original price by selling carefully reconditioned models. All ranges are guaranteed and there's a nationwide delivery and installation service. There are modern or traditional cookers, available for oil, gas and a few solid fuel. Also manufactures Nobel cooker which sells at about £1,000 less than its more famous competitor.

## GANDOLFI HOUSE INTERIORS

211-213 WELLS ROAD, MALVERN WELLS, WORCESTER WR14 4HF
☎ (01684) 569747. OPEN 10 - 5.30 TUE - SAT.

Victorian Gothic house built into the Malvern Hills, even the con-
vervatory and the terrace are used to display and sell antiques. There
are 12 rooms of room settings containing quality antiques, repro furniture, Victorian watercolours, painting, rocking horses, garden furniture, and one room specialising in dolls houses. Prices are variable
but tend to be reasonable compared with competitors. For example,
a dolls house selling in rival outlets for £445 would cost £245 here.

## GERALD LLEWELYN

DRYSLYN, GOWER VALLEY DRIVE, CLYNDERWEN, DYFED CF7 8XU
☎ (01437) 563589. BY APPOINTMENT ONLY.

A distributor for Country Cookers, who sell reconditioned Rayburn
cookers and sometimes also reconditioned Agas. These are considerably cheaper than the brand new version. They can incorporate a
domestic heating system for hot water and radiators. Nobel only on
display.

## LEEKS

COWBRIDGE ROAD, PONTYCLUN, LLANTRISANT
☎ (01443) 237700. OPEN 9 - 5.30 SEVEN DAYS A WEEK, UNTIL 8 ON FRI.

A distributor for Country Cookers, who sell reconditioned Rayburn
cookers and sometimes also reconditioned Agas. These are considerably cheaper than the brand new version. They can incorporate a
domestic heating system for hot water and radiators.

## THE CURTAIN BROKERS

THE GREY HOUSE, BURFORD ROAD, FILKINS, NEAR LECHLADE,
GLOUCESTERSHIRE GL7 3JW
☎ (01367) 860362. BY APPOINTMENT ONLY, VERY FLEXIBLE.

The Curtain Brokers is an independently-owned and operated
business which sells top quality and designer secondhand curtains,
bedspreads and blinds. There are usually at least 100 pairs of curtains
in stock in fabrics such as Osborne & Little, Hill & Knowles,
Sanderson and Laura Ashley. Some of the curtains are brand new
samples or designer mistakes.

# THE CURTAIN EXCHANGE

SHIPTON SOLLARS MANOR, SHIPTON SOLLARS, NR. CHELTENHAM, GLOUCESTERSHIRE GL54 4HU

☎ (01242) 820100. OPEN 10 - 3 WED - SAT OR BY APPOINTMENT.

The Curtain Exchange is a countrywide network of shops selling top quality, nearly-new curtains, blinds, pelmets, etc at between one-third and one half of the brand new price. Their stock comes from a variety of sources: people who are moving house and hate the drapes in their new home; people who are moving house and want to sell their old curtains to help with the bills; show houses, where the builder wants to recoup some of his outgoings; interior designers' mistakes. Stock changes constantly and ranges from rich brocades, damasks and velvets to chintzes, linens and cottons. Designer names include Colefax & Fowler, Designers Guild, Laura Ashley, Warner, Sanderson, Osborne & Little

# THE CURTAIN RACK

25 HIGH STREET, PERSHORE, WORCESTERSHIRE WR10 1AA

☎ (01386) 556105. OPEN 10 - 4.30 MON - FRI, 9.30 - 5.30 SAT.

Three large showrooms, including a Designer Showroom, packed with full-length designer curtains, many from London, for about one third of the original cost. The enormous selection caters for all budgets from low cost curtains ideal for rented accommodation through to magnificent curtains fit for a palace. There is also a wide selection of fabrics at competitive prices and a made to measure service. Customers can take curtains home on approval.

# WHITCHURCH MULTI-FUEL HEATING

1 FLETCHER COURT, DEERMOSS LANE, WHITCHURCH, SHROPSHIRE SY13 1AD

☎ (01948) 663954. OPEN 9 - 5 MON - SAT, CLOSED WED.

A distributor for Country Cookers, who sell reconditioned Rayburn cookers and sometimes also reconditioned Agas. These are considerably cheaper than the brand new version. They can incorporate a domestic heating system for hot water and radiators.

# EAST ANGLIA AND EAST MIDLANDS

## *Permanent Discount Outlets*

### CLOTH MARKET

STAMFORD WALK, ST MARY'S STREET, STAMFORD,
LINCOLNSHIRE
☎ (01780) 64715. 01780 53409. OPEN 9.30 - 5.30 MON - SAT, CLOSED 1
ON THUR.

Well-loved little shop selling upholstery and furnishing fabric by
Liberty, Sanderson, G P & J Baker, Monkwell and other good quality
makes. Here, customers can see it all in stock, check out the good
prices and walk away with it. Some even borrow a roll to look at
against their home colours. There is also a marvellous stock of dress
fabrics, thanks to the sure eye and buying talent of Jeannie Barr, the
proprietor. Friendly, personal service.

### ESSENTIAL ITEMS

CHURCH HOUSE, PLUNGAR, NOTTINGHAM NG13 0JA
☎ (0194) 9861172. FAX 0115 9456252. OPEN 8 - 8 SEVEN DAYS A WEEK.
MAIL ORDER.

Essential Items is one of the country's most established companies
manufacturing and designing stools and Ottomans. Because of their
low overheads, their mail order service offers much more competitive
prices than similar items bought in department stores. A new
brochure and price list was produced in April, 1994, with many new
ideas and designs for the home. Although items can be covered in
calico, most lines are covered in customers' own material at no extra
charge. Examples of prices include a PM103 style stool, 30"x20"x13"
with Queen Anne legs, £145; SPO 200 filing cabinet Ottoman,
£195. Add £15 for carriage and packing.

### FABRIC CORNER

MARKET STREET CENTRE, MARKET STREET, SOUTH NORMANTON,
DERBYSHIRE DE55 2AB
☎ (01773) 863700. OPEN 10 - 5 MON - SAT, 10 - 2 SUN, CLOSED WED.

Top quality curtain fabrics from £1.99 a yard, as well as designer
name roll ends, cottons, chintzes from £2.50 a yard, linings from
£1.20 a yard, nets, voiles, and muslins. There are also poles, rails and

tapes. Choose from more than 700 rolls from £1.99 a yard to £9.99. Children's play area, car parking, wheelchair access.

## FABRIC DESIGN

10-12 NORTH PARADE, MATLOCK BATH, DERBYSHIRE DE4 3NS
☎ (01629) 584747. 10 - 4.45 MON, 10 - 5 TUE & WED, 1 - 5 THUR, 10 - 5 FRI, SAT, 1.30 - 5 SUN.

Situated in a beautiful spa town, the Matlock Bath outlet is a busy, exciting Victorian shop on the parade by the river, which carries a huge range of designer clearance fabrics from £3.75 per yd, heavy linens from £4.99 per yd and an ever-changing range of bargain one-off buys such as £42 per metre fabric reduced to £9.99 per metre. Fabrics sold in the shop include such names as Sanderson, Monkwell, Warner, Anna French and Liberty, but there is also available a range of natural fabrics - calico, twills and cream weaves. Those looking for good quality fabric for upholstery and curtaining should be prepared to buy on the day as the good deals don't stay in the shop for long.

## JUST A SECOND FABRICS

7 KIRKSTALL LODGE, HIGH ST, EDWINSTOWE, NEAR MANSFIELD, NOTTINGHAMSHIRE
☎ (01623) 825156. OPEN 10.30 - 4.30 MON - SAT, CLOSED WED.

Stocks some of the top designer names in fents of about 2 yards and in longer measurements. Labels seen in this outlet have included Anna French, Jane Churchill, Osborne & Little and Designers Guild. Fent cost £8, fabric which would normally cost £18 costs £6.95, 48" wide chintz costs £1.85 a yard and they also sell Victoriana white bedlinen, lace and table linen. Bullion fring and braids from as little as £2 a yard. There is a curtain making up service.

## KNICKERBEAN

4 OUT NORTHGATE STREET, BURY ST EDMUNDS, SUFFOLK IP33 1JQ
☎ (01284) 704055. OPEN 9 - 5.30 MON - SAT.

Knickerbean have a fabulous range of top designer curtain and uphol-stery fabrics assembled from many different sources. On my last visit, I saw selections from Designers Guild, Anna French, Jane Churchill, Colefax & Fowler, and Osborne & Little, among the hundreds of dif-ferent fabrics. While some of these are discontinued lines, ends of ranges, or off-shade lots, a growing number are now coming in directly from mills and manufacturers overseas - most recently some new designs from Collier Campbell. Because they buy in such large lots, they can usually obtain fabrics at less than the usual wholesale price, with many of their fabrics sold at about half of the original recommended retail price. Their fast-moving selection of more than 100,000 yards from £5.95 a yard includes glazed chintzes, cotton prints, stripes and checks, and a huge selection of luxurious upholstery fabrics including a large range of Italian damasks and tapestries. Customers are encouraged to pop in regularly to browse through the latest arrivals and there's the added benefit of being able to see entire rolls rather than just a small sample book of swatches. They also offer a complete making-up service for curtains, blinds, loose covers and other soft furnishings. Overall, their discounted fabrics coupled with low making-up charges work out at about half to one third less than normal made to measure soft furnishings. They hold twice-yearly sales in January and June with even greater reductions on their ranges of fabrics.

## LINCOLN CLOTH MARKET

83 BAILGATE, LINCOLN, LINCOLNSHIRE LN1 3AR
☎ (01522) 529872. OPEN 9.30 - 5.30 MON - SAT.
Stocks Liberty, Jane Churchill, Ramm son & Crocker, Christian Fischbacher and Harlequin wallpaper, and a range of discounted fabric. It also sells dress fabrics, boarder wallpaper, cottons and silks. There are usually seconds in various fabrics at one third to one half of the original price, and a catalogue of wedding dress fabrics.

## LLOYD LOOM DIRECT LTD

PO BOX 75, SPALDING, LINCOLNSHIRE PE12 6NB
☎ (01775) 725876. MAIL ORDER.
Traditional Lloyd Loom furniture made from beechwood direct by mail, so fewer overheads as no retail outlet.

## OLDWOOD PINE FURNITURE

51-53 HIGH STREET EAST, UPPINGHAM, RUTLAND LE15 9PY
☎ (01572) 823607. OPEN 9 - 5.30 MON - SAT, BY APPOINTMENT ON SUN.
Pine furniture constructed from old wood pine which has been recovered from old buildings and halls. It is dipped twice to regain its

original state and then polished by hand in a mellow wax. This gives the products a warm, rustic look and the quality portrays the individual handcrafting which goes into each peice. Most pieces are custom built to the customer's specifications and design. There are also standard sizes of beds, tables and wardrobes. Prices include a bedside table, £85; six foot refectory table, £225; five foot farmhouse table, from £130; large two-drawer coffee table, £115; six foot provincial dresser, £650; swivel top round dining table, £120.

## PARTRIDGE AND PEAR TREE

6 PARK LANE, NEWMARKET, SUFFOLK CB8 8AX
☎ (01638) 560438. OPEN 9.30 - 5.30 MON - SAT, CLOSED THUR, OR BY APPOINTMENT AT OTHER TIMES.

Three storey shop full to the brim with designer and furnishing fabrics and trimmings at up to one fifth of their normal retail prices. Stock - which mostly consists of bankrupt merchandise, seconds, ends of lines and clearance - is constantly changing. Fabrics usually include chintz, damasks, linen unions, weaves and silks by top designer names. Designer names include Colefax & Fowler, Monkwell, Warners, Bakers, Design Archives and Osborne & Little, as well as many other Continental and American names. They also sell top quality secondhand curtains, blinds, headboards, valances and pelmets.

## SILK SHADES INTERIORS SHOWROOM

12 MARKET PLACE, LAVENHAM, SUFFOLK CO10 9QZ
☎ (01787) 247029. BY APPOINTMENT ONLY. MAIL ORDER.

Although primarily in the mail order business, they do sell from the showroom - but by appointment only. Dupion silk sells for £10.95 a metre - department store price is £13; Duchess silk sells for £46.90 a metre, department store price, £86. They also sell lace for brides from £1 for narrow edging to £180 a metre; silks from £7 a metre to £130 and offer discounts of 10% on orders over £300. On the whole, though, they are cheaper than the same fabrics in well-known department stores.

## THE CURTAIN MILL

ST GEORGE'S MILLS, HUMBERSTONE ROAD, LEICESTER,
LEICESTERSHIRE LE1 1SN
☎ (01533) 620264. OPEN 9 - 5.30 MON - SAT. HOTLINE
☎ 0171-375 1000.
Huge choice of top quality fabrics at really low prices - from 99p a
yard and including excellent discounts on many designer labels. A
large warehouse, it stocks Wilson Wilcox, Ashley Wilde, Gordon
Richmond, Blendworth, among other leading names at discount
prices.

## THE REMNANT SHOP

3-5 HAMILTON ROAD, FELIXSTOWE, SUFFOLK
☎ (01394) 283186. OPEN 9 -5.30 MON - SAT.
Although not strictly a discount fabric shop they sell cut-price ends of
rolls and remnants in curtain materials, dressmaking fabrics (satins,
silks, dupions, polyesters) and patterns. They always have a good
range of curtain fabrics and hold thousands of rolls of fabric in stock.
But lines change constantly so you might not always find something
to suit.

# *Factory Shops*

## CREATIVE CARPETS LTD

UNIT 8, MILL HILL INDUSTRIAL ESTATE, QUARRY LANE, ENDERBY,
LEICESTERSHIRE LE9 5AU
☎ (0116) 2841455. OPEN 9 - 3 SAT ONLY, WEEKDAYS BY APPOINTMENT
ONLY. CLOSED FIRST TWO WEEKS JULY AND CHRISTMAS.
Genuine factory shop where all the goods are made on the premises.
All carpets are quality heavy domestic, 80/20 wool/nylon, hessian
backed. There is a large choice of colour including plain dyed,
Berbers and heather tweeds. Savings of 50% can be made by buying
direct from the factory. Prices for the perfects start at about £8.75 a
sq yd; seconds from £5.85 a sq yd.

## FILIGREE

CARTER LANE EAST, SOUTH NORMANTON, DERBYSHIRE DE55 2EG
☎ (01773) 811619 EXT 296. OPEN 9 - 4 MON - THUR, 9 - 6.30 FRI,
9 - 1.30 SAT.
Makes net curtains on the premises for well-known high street
department stores and sells them at half the price you would pay in
the high street. Nets range from £1 a metre to £8 with fabric from
£1.99 a yard to £5.99 a yard and remnants from 50p.

## FILIGREE

THE CURTAIN FACTORY SHOP, 279 HIGH STREET, LINCOLN,
LINCOLNSHIRE LN2 1JG
☎ (01522) 522740. OPEN 9 - 5.30 MON - SAT.
makes net curtains on the premises for well-known high street department stores and sells them at half the price you would pay in the high
street. Eighty percent of the stock is net curtaining from basic net to
French voiles; 20% is printed cotton curtaining. Nets range from £1
a metre to £8 with fabric from £1.99 a yard to £5.99 a yard and
remnants from 50p.

## HOMES IN WOOD

22 DUKES CLOSE, EARLS WAY, THURMASTON, LEICESTER,
LEICESTERSHIRE LE4 8EY
☎ (0116) 2697165. OPEN 6 - 4 MON - FRI, 6 - 12 SAT.
Manufacturers of rabbit hutches, dog kennels, aviary panels, nest
boxes, sheds, Wendy houses. They supply the pet trade and garden
centres, but you can buy direct at trade price, which is half the normal
retail price.

## LINCOLNSHIRE CRAFT WORKSHOPS LTD

4 HOLLIS ROAD, GRANTHAM, LINCOLNSHIRE NG31 7QH
☎ (01476) 79728. OPEN 9.30 - 4.30 MON - FRI, 8.30 - 12 SAT.
Supply leather goods, pine furniture and cold cast bronze to outlets
in London, using the very best quality materials. Individual shoppers
can visit their workshop in Grantham and buy goods at factory direct
prices which usually means discounts of 5%-15%. For example, a
Victorian bed, £400; carved bed, £280; Malvern bed, £196; four-

poster, £656; farmhouse table, £156, and chairs, from £41 each; doube tower CD holder for 80 CDs, £25. The leather goods include a wallet holding eight credit cards, money clips, writing sets, manicure sets. In cold cast bronze are hedgehogs, kingfishers, blue tit key hooks, tawny owl wall motifs in bronze and 3-D fish plaques. (Please phone before visiting as opening times were changing as we went to press.)

## STUART BUGLASS

THE GALLERY, CLIFFORD MILL HOUSE, LITTLE HOUGHTON, NORTHAMPTONSHIRE NN7 1AL
☎ (01604) 890366. PHONE FOR OPENING HOURS.
Hand-crafted candleholders, candle wall sconces, wine racks, chandeliers, curtain poles, finials, shelves and other metalwork in a variety of designs on sale in this converted barn at direct to the public prices.

## WATERSIDE MILL SHOP

359 SHEFFIELD ROAD, WHITTINGTON MOOR, CHESTERFIELD, DERBYSHIRE S41 8LQ
☎ (01246) 456886. FAX 01246 456752. OPEN 9.30 - 5 MON - SAT, 10 - 4 SUN.
Very large outlet selling soft furnishing fabrics - some on complete rolls, others as remnants - and also bedding fabrics from names such as Dorma and rose and Hubble, bedding, dress fabrics, curtaining and haberdashery. Thousands of yards of top quality designs and chainstore seconds, all at unbeatable prices. Full making up service on the premises. Also available: various dress fabrics, towelling, leatherette, PVC, damask, corduroy, fleece, muslin, waddings, woollens, blanketing and haberdashery. Parking is easy.

# Secondhand Shops

## CURTAINS COMPLETE

THE STABLES, EAST FARNDON HALL, MARKET HARBOROUGH,
LEICESTERSHIRE LE16 9SE
☎ (01858) 466671. OPEN 9.30 - 3 TUE, OTHER TIMES BY
APPOINTMENT.

Owner Caroline Everard spent five years in London working for most
of the top interior decorators and twenty years making top quality
hand-made curtains and soft furnishings for private clients. Now, the
stables at her home house a formidable array of nearly-new curtains
in top quality fabrics such as Colefax & Fowler, Jane Churchill and
Designers Guild. Many are in almost perfect condition, but for those
needing repairs or alterations, these can be easily organised. Linings,
interlinings, hooks and tapes are also available for those wishing to do
their own alterations. There is also a range of "almost ready to hang"
new curtains made from designer fabrics with only the heading to
finish. Customers choose the style of heading they want and this can
then be sewn on while they wait. Curtains can also be taken home on
approval.

## REMARK

103 WALGRAVE, ORTAON MALVORNE, PETERBOROUGH,
CAMBRIDGESHIRE PE3 ONS
☎ (01832) 274900. OPEN 9 - 5 MON - FRI.

Acts on behalf of liquidators, selling repossessed office furniture and
equipment from fax machines and computers to telephones and pho-
tocopiers. Faxes have been sold for about £200, telephones for £8, but
the normal price is at least half the as-new price. Can instal equipment and service.

## THE CURTAIN EXCHANGE

69 ELTHAM ROAD, WEST BRIDGFORD, NOTTINGHAM,
NOTTINGHAMSHIRE NG2 5JP
☎ (0115) 9455092. OPEN 11 - 4 TUE - SAT.
56 ST JOHN'S STREET, BURY ST EDMUNDS, SUFFOLK IP33 1SN
☎ (01284) 760059. OPEN 9 - 5 MON - SAT.

The Curtain Exchange is a countrywide network of shops selling top
quality, nearly-new curtains, blinds, pelmets, etc at between one-third

and one half of the brand new price. Their stock comes from a variety of sources: people who are moving house and hate the drapes in their new home; people who are moving house and want to sell their old curtains to help with the bills; show houses, where the builder wants to recoup some of his outgoings; interior designers' mistakes. Stock changes constantly and ranges from rich brocades, damasks and velvets to chintzes, linens and cottons. Designer names include Colefax & Fowler, Designers Guild, Laura Ashley, Warner, Sanderson, Osborne & Little.

# NORTH WEST, YORKSHIRE AND HUMBERSIDE

## *Permanent Discount Outlets*

## BARNTEX FABRICS

9 THE ARCHES, VIADUCT STREET, HUDDERSFIELD, WEST YORKSHIRE
☎ (01484) 450509.
Curtain and upholstery own brand fabrics and those from many well-known high street brands such as Laura Ashley, Next and Marks & Spencer. Because they buy job lots from the USA, Europe and the UK, prices range from 99p a yard to £12.99 a yard although the normal recommended retail price of many items ranges from £16 to £25 a yard. Most goods are first quality. There are more than 12,000 yards always in stock and the majority of goods are priced in the range of £3.99 to £5.00 a yard. Stock is continually changing and brands include Crowson, Blendworth (to order), and Matthew Stevens.

## E G INTERIOR FABRICS

226 HARROGATE ROAD, CHAPEL ALLERTON, LEEDS LS7 4QD
☎ (0113) 2370447. OPEN 9.30 - 5 MON - SAT, CLOSED WED.
89 BRADFORD ROAD, EAST ARDSLEY, WAKEFIELD WF3 JQD
☎ (01924) 820593. OPEN 9.30 - 5 MON - SAT, CLOSED TUE.
Sell curtaining and sheeting fabrics and curtain linings, specialising in wider widths. They also sell ends of lines and seconds of well-known

chain store designs at savings of up to 50% and have a small haberdashery section at competitive prices. Both shops offer a making up service. The East Ardsley branch also has household textiles.

## FACTORY FABRICS FROM THE MILL SHOP

102 PIONEER HOUSE, NORTHGATE, DEWSBURY, WEST YORKSHIRE
☎ (01924) 459740. OPEN 9.30 - 5.30 MON - FRI, 9.30 - 4.30 SAT.
High street outlet measuring 800 sq ft selling curtain and upholstery own brand fabrics and those from many well-known high street brands such as Laura Ashley, Next and Marks & Spencer. Because they buy job lots from the USA, Europe and the UK, prices range from 99p a yard to £12.99 a yard although the normal recommended retail price of many items ranges from £16 to £25 a yard. Most goods are first quality. There are more than 12,000 yards always in stock and the majority of goods are priced in the range of £3.99 to £5.00 a yard. Stock is continually changing and brands include Crowson, Blendworth (to order) and Matthew Stevens.

## LOOSE ENDS

LAWKLAND GREEN, AUSTWICK, NEAR SETTLE, NORTH YORKSHIRE
LA2 8AT
☎ (01729) 823250. OPEN 10 - 1 TUE - FRI OR BY APPOINTMENT.
Situated in a converted barn in the beautiful Yorkshire Dales, Loose Ends sells top of the range furnishing fabrics made by well-known names in England and America. Stock consists of ends of ranges, discontinued lines and occasionally slight seconds of chintzes, cottons, linens, plain and woven upholstery fabrics all on the roll. Lining also available. Prices are approximately one third of retail price. Easy parking, children welcome. Enjoy browsing in a friendly atmosphere with helpful advice.

## MATERIAL THINGS

38 CHARLOTTE STREET, MACCLESFIELD, CHESHIRE SK11 6JB
☎ (01625) 428923. OPEN 9.30 - 5 MON, TUE, 10 - 5 WED,
9.30 - 5.30 THUR, FRI, SAT.
Sells seconds, fents (small sections of 2 yards in length), roll stock and perfect ends of lines of furnishing and upholstery fabrics from top designers at very cheap prices. The material from which the fents come would normally cost about £15-£25 a metre; here, fents are sold

at £7.50 each. Upholstery fabric costs £10 a yard, about one third of the normal price. Heavy cotton Italian damask is sold at £14.50 instead of £25-£30 per yard. Also seconds of lace bedspread panels, muslins, calico and top designer trimmings from £2.50 a metre. Making-up service available.

## STAPLES

UNIT 11B, JUNCTION STREET, CROWN POINT RETAIL PARK, HUNSLET LANE, LEEDS, YORKSHIRE LS10 1ET
☎ (0113) 2421061. OPEN 8 - 8 MON - FRI, 9 - 6 SAT, 11 - 5 SUN.

Office equipment and furniture supplier which is aimed at businesses, but is also open to the public. The owner buys in bulk and so is able to sell at very competitive prices a range of goods from paper clips to personal computers. Customers do not have to buy in bulk to make savings. Becoming a member entitles you to extra discounts of about 10%-15% on more than 300 items. A mail order catalogue is available and delivery is free on purchases over £50 (area permitting).

## THE FABRIC SHOP

82 MAIN STREET, ADDINGHAM, NEAR ILKLEY, YORKSHIRE LS29 0PL
☎ (01943) 830982. OPEN 10 - 6 MON, 9 - 1 TUE, WED, FRI, 12 - 4 THUR AND 10 - 4 SAT.

Great fabric bargains in this rabbit warren of interconnecting rooms, stacked high to the ceiling with bolts of perfects and seconds of furnishing fabrics. Brands include Osborne & Little, Moygashel and Harmony. Most of the fabric, tapestries and damasks are from Italian and US manufacturers and even book orders can be discounted. Fabrics range from £2-£10 a yard, curtain linging from £2 a yard, tapes from 40p a yard and interlining from £2.30 a yard. No making up service; telephone orders taken. They also stock seconds of basics such as lining fabrics, muslin and 90" wide sheeting. The staff are very helpful and knowledgeable and there is parking directly outside or in the next side street at the village car park. You can also find the merchandise at York market on a Tuesday and Ripon market on a Thursday.

## THE SHUTTLE FABRIC SHOP

BAILDON BRIDGE, OTLEY ROAD, SHIPLEY, YORKSHIRE BD17 7AA
☎ (01274) 587171. OPEN 9 - 5.30 MON - SAT.
Sells discounted dress fabrics and some furnishing fabrics from well-known designers as well as furnishing sheeting, quilting, curtain lining, plastic fabrics for tablecloths, wadding, patterns and general haberdashery. Many are ends of lines and there are always special offers.

## WALTONS MILL SHOP

41 TOWER STREET, HARROGATE, NORTH YORKSHIRE HG1 1HS
☎ (01423) 520980. OPEN 10 - 5 MON - SAT.
High street retail outlet which sells international designer fabrics with the emphasis on high class designs with a difference. More unusually, they also stock a vast range of quality trimmings, cords, bullions, tassels, tie-backs, etc. Regular customers really do describe the shop as an Aladdin's Cave, with its tapestries, handmade quilts, Egyptian cotton bedding, throws, cushions and traditional household textiles. Those who have tried the famous Knaresborough linen dishcloth vow never to use anything else again. Most of the stock is overmakes, bankrupt merchandise, bought from the US or imported from all over the world. Tucked away, you have to take the A61 Leeds road into Harrogate, and take the first right hand turn after the Prince of Wales roundabout at the longterm car park sign. The shop is 200 yards up on the left hand side.

# *FactoryShops*

## ABAKHAN FABRICS

LLANERCH-Y-MOR, COAST ROAD, MOSTYN, CLWYD CH8 9DX
☎ (01745) 560312. OPEN 9 - 5 SEVEN DAYS A WEEK UNTIL 8 ON THUR.
111-115 OLDHAM STREET, MANCHESTER
☎ (0161) 839 3229. OPEN 9.30 - 5 MON - SAT, UNTIL 7.30 ON THUR.
34-44 STAFFORD STREET, LIVERPOOL
☎ (0151) 207 4029. OPEN 9.30 - 5 MON - SAT
8-12 GREENWAY ROAD, BIRKENHEAD, LANCASHIRE
☎ (0151) 652 5195. OPEN 9 - 5 MON - SAT, UNTIL 8 ON THUR AND FRI.

65-67 CHURCH ROAD, BIRKENHEAD, LANCASHIRE
☎ (0151) 647 6983. OPEN 9 - 5 MON - SAT.

With six outlets in the North West, Abakhan Fabrics are as well known for the emphasis they put on value for money as they are for the huge variety of fabrics, needlecrafts, haberdashery, gifts and knitting yarns that they have gathered from all around the world. The large mill shop complex in Clwyd has baskets of remnant fabrics, wools, yarns and unrivalled selections of fabrics sold by the metre from evening wear, bridal wear and crepe de Chine to curtaining, nets and velvets. Here in this historic building, there are more than ten tonnes of remnant fabrics and 10,000 rolls, all at mill shop prices. Abakhan is able to offer such bargains through bulk buying, or selling clearance lines, job lots and seconds. There is a coffee shop and free parking at the Clwyd outlet and coach parties are welcome provided they pre-book. The Manchester and Liverpool outlets do not have free parking facilities. The Greenway Road, Birkenhead, outlet has a bridal fabric and accessories shop, and the Church Road branch also supplies craft fabrics.

## ACRE MILL CARPETS LTD

UNIT F2, TOLLBAR BUSINESS PARK, NEW CHURCH ROAD,
STACKSTEADS, BACUP, LANCASHIRE OL13 ONA
☎ (01706) 875709. OPEN 9 - 5 MON - FRI, 9 - 4.30 SAT, 10 - 4 SUN.

Carpet cash and carry. Ten percent discount on any orders over £100; 80/20 twists and 50/50 wool twists from £4.99-£8.99, free delivery. Usually carried Axminster, Wilton and Saxony in a wide range from shag piles to berbers. Some Axminster remnants are usually available in various sizes. The more you spend, the bigger the discounts.

## ASTBURY LIGHTING FACTORY SHOP

FOUNDRY BANK, CONGLETON, CHESHIRE
☎ (01260) 298176. OPEN 10 - 5 MON - SAT AND BANK HOLIDAYS.

Factory shop situated in an old mill selling lamp shades - patterned and plain bases and shades and wall lighting from £10 - £100. Most of the stock is seconds and are reduced by about one-third. In another part of the building, bedding, curtains and clothes are sold including Dorma, Sheridan, Fogarty and Horrick's. On the ground floor is a new furniture department which although not part of the factory shop, has settees, beds,suites and cabinet furniture at competitive prices.

## FREEPORT SHOPPING VILLAGE

ANCHORAGE ROAD, FLEETWOOD, LANCASHIRE
☎ (01253) 877377. OPEN 10 - 6 SEVEN DAYS A WEEK.

Up to 40 shops, a marina, and lots of activities for the family. Shops which sell items for the home include: Ponden Mill (home furnishings) and Acorns (dried flowers).

## HORNSEA FREEPORT SHOPPING VILLAGE

HORNSEA, EAST YORKSHIRE HU18 1UT
☎ (01964) 534211. OPEN 10 - 5 MON - FRI, 10 - 6 SAT, SUN, BANK HOLIDAYS.

The original British factory shopping village on the east coast of Yorkshire comes complete with masses of family entertainment including Butterfly World, adventure playground, vintage cars, water games, plus about two dozen shops where you can buy brand name discounted goods. Labels for men include Daks Simpson, Wrangler, Aquascutum, Tom Sayers menswear, Tog 24 and Sports Unlimited.

## LAURA ASHLEY

HORNSEA FREEPORT SHOPPING VILLAGE, HORNSEA, EAST YORKSHIRE HU18 1UT
☎ (01964) 536503. OPEN 10 - 5 MON - FRI, 10 - 6 SAT, SUN.
BOUNDARY MILL STORES, BURNLEY ROAD, COLNE, LANCASHIRE BB8 8LS
☎ (01282) 860166. OPEN 10 - 6 MON - FRI, 10 - 5 SAT AND BANK HOLIDAYS, 11 - 5 SUN.

At Hornsea, Laura Ashley fashion is on the ground floor and home furnishings on the first floor. Most of the merchandise is made up of perfect carry-overs from the high street shops around the country, though there are also some discontinued lines. Stock reflects the normal high street variety, though at least one season later and with less choice in colours and sizes. The shopping village has restaurants, play centres, a vintage car collection, water games, and plenty for the family to do and see. At Boundary Mill Stores, Laura Ashley is one department in this huge high quality clearance warehouse for men and women's clothes and home furnishings.

# RED ROSE

KILBANE ST, FLEETWOOD, LANCASHIRE FY7 7PF
☎ (01253) 878888. OPEN 9 - 5 MON - FRI, 9 - 1 SAT.
Carpet manufacturer's who make good quality carpets and sell
perfects in their factory at least £5 a square yard cheaper than you
could buy it in the shops. Top quality 42 oz carpets cost £11.95 a
square yard; 50 oz carpets cost £15.95 a square yard. Carpets come in
a range of 18 different colours, all in 80% wool. Will colour match
to your requirements. Free local delivery; charged for petrol outside
local area.

# SANDERSON CLEARANCE OUTLET SHOP

2 POLLARD STREET, ANCOATS, MANCHESTER M4 7DS
☎ (0161) 272 8501. OPEN 10 - 6 TUE - SAT, UNTIL 7.30 ON THUR,
10 - 4 SUN.
Seconds in furnishing fabrics from discontinued patterns, lines and
end of ranges; wallpapers and ready made curtains, duvet covers, and
carpets, most of which cost less than half price. Lots of room-sized
carpets cut-offs and ends of ranges and slight seconds of bedding.

# SKOPOS DESIGN LTD

COLBECK HOUSE, CHEAPSIDE MILLS, BRADFORD ROAD, BATLEY,
YORKSHIRE WF17 6LZ
☎ (01924) 475756. OPEN 9.30 - 5.30 MON - FRI, 9 - 5.30 SAT,
10 - 4.30 SUN.
SALTS MILL, VICTORIA ROAD, SALTAIRE, SHIPLEY, WEST YORKSHIRE
BD18 3LB
☎ (01274) 581121. OPEN 10 - 6 SEVEN DAYS A WEEK.
FIRST FLOOR, NORTH WING, DAISY MILL, STOCKPORT ROAD,
LONG SIGHT, MANCHESTER M13 OLF
☎ (0161) 273 7123. OPEN 9.30 - 5 MON - FRI, 9.30 - 6 SAT, 9 - 4 SUN.
One of the world's leading designers and manufacturers of furnishing
fabrics, you can now buy many of these superb ranges at substantial
savings. At their Yorkshire mill, they design and manufacture flame
retardant fabrics for leading international hotel groups and interior
designers. They now offer end of contract runs, specials and quality
seconds direct to the public. Ends of rolls are half price, plus there are
100% cotton furnishing fabrics, sheers, voiles and linings, ex-contract
and ex-display curtains, quilted bedspreads, quilted pieces, polycotton duvets and sheets, cushions, haberdashery and remnants. There is

also a wide range of gifts including lamps, candlesticks, bowls, vases, mirrors and pictures, some at normal retail price, some reduced. The furniture showroom on the ground floor of the Batley outlet, as well as offering a wide range of sofas and chairs, also sells ex-display and prototype models at greatly reduced prices. There is also ex-display furniture at the Shipley and Manchester branches.

## STANDFAST FACTORY FABRIC SHOP

CATON ROAD, LANCASTER, LANCASHIRE LA1 3PA
☎ (01524) 64334. OPEN 9.30 - 1 MON - FRI, 10 - 12.30 SAT.
Genuine factory shop selling a very wide range of well-known designer named fabrics, which are suitable for all soft furnishings, at discounted prices. Stocks vary according to factory production and all fabrics are seconds. Prices range from £5 to £8 per metre. They always stock plenty of pieces for cushion covers and patchwork from 15p each to £3 for small sackful. Usually they also have some fabrics on special offer, ranging from £1.50 per metre to £7 a metre. None of the fabric is flame retardant but once treated, can be used for upholstery.

## THOMAS WITTOR

PO BOX 16, FROOM STREET, CHORLEY, LANCASHIRE PR6 NAP
☎ (01257) 263031. OPEN 9 - 4.30 MON - FRI, 10 - 4 SAT.
Middle of the range carpets from £1.85 a sq yard up to £14.50.

## WATERSIDE MILL SHOP

CLARENCE MILL, CANAL SIDE, CLARENCE ROAD, BOLLINGTON, CHESHIRE SK10 5JZ
☎ (01625) 576443. OPEN 9.30 - 5 MON - SAT, 10 - 4 SUN AND BANK HOLIDAYS.
Very large outlet selling soft furnishing fabrics - some on complete rolls, others as remnants - and also bedding fabrics from names such as Dorma and rose and Hubble. Thousands of yards of top quality designs and chainstore seconds, all at unbeatable prices. Full making up service on the premises. Also available: various dress fabrics, including wedding dress fabrics (silk, lace, brocade, taffeta) some leatherette, PVC, damask, corduroy, fleece, muslin, waddings, woollens, blanketing, curtain rails, hooks, cottons, patchwork fabrics and haberdashery. Parking is easy .

# Secondhand Shops

## NORTH WALES OFFICE SUPPLIES

CURZON STREET, SALTNEY, CHESTER CH4 8BP
☎ (01244) 677053. OPEN 9 - 4 MON - FRI, CLOSED 12 - 2 EACH DAY.
Office furniture up to 6 years old which the company strips and
reconditions. Desks, chairs, executive chairs, boardroom tables. Desks
sell from £40-£170. The owner also makes Tudor, Georgian and
Victorian-style dolls houses to a scale of one-twelfth.

## SWIFT & SONS

BERRY LANE, LONGRIDGE, PRESTON, LANCASHIRE PR3 3NH
☎ (01772) 782324. OPEN 9 - 5.30 MON - TUE & THUR - FRI,
9 - 4.30 WED & SAT.
A distributor for Country Cookers, who sell reconditioned Rayburn
cookers and sometimes also Agas and new Nobel cookers. These are
considerably cheaper than the brand new version. They can incorporate a domestic heating system for hot water and radiators.

## THE CURTAIN EXCHANGE

3 HAWTHORN LANE, WILMSLOW, CHESHIRE SK9 1AQ
☎ (01625) 536060 OPEN 10 - 5 MON - SAT.
The Curtain Exchange is a countrywide network of shops selling top
quality, nearly-new curtains, blinds, pelmets, etc at between one-third
and one half of the brand new price. Their stock comes from a variety
of sources: people who are moving house and hate the drapes in their
new home; people who are moving house and want to sell their old
curtains to help with the bills; show houses, where the builder wants
to recoup some of his outgoings; interior designers' mistakes. Stock
changes constantly and ranges from rich brocades, damasks and
velvets to chintzes, linens and cottons. Designer names include
Colefax & Fowler, Designers Guild, Laura Ashley, Warner,
Sanderson, Osborne & Little

## THE CURTAIN TRANSFER LIMITED

BACK TEWIT WELL ROAD, OFF SOUTH DRIVE, HARROGATE, NORTH
YORKSHIRE HG2 8JF
☎ (01423) 505520. OPEN 10 - 5 TUES, THUR, FRI, SAT, BY
APPOINTMENT ON MON AND WED.

Curtain Transfer has recently moved to just off the A61 Leeds Road
St Georges Roundabout, close to the famous Tewit Well near the
town centre. This erstwhile stable in a courtyard opposite the owner's
home is a treasure trove of secondhand curtains, blinds, bedcovers
and all kinds of upmarket furnishing accessories - pictures, lamps and
lampshades, cushions, rugs and small furniture. Goods are taken in
on sale-or-return agency terms. There is always a good selection of
long lined or interlined curtains - from Liberty, Sanderson, G P & J
Baker and Laura Ashley, as well as current designer names. Buyers can
take goods home overnight on approval. A computerised stocklist can
be mailed on request. Parking is in the courtyard and children are
welcome.

# NORTH AND SCOTLAND

## *Permanent Discount Outlets*

### J & W CARPETS

22 GREENHILL ROAD, PAISLEY, SCOTLAND PA3 1RN
☎ (0141) 848 5502. OPEN 9 - 8 MON - FRI, 9 - 5.30 SAT, 12 - 5 SUN.
24 BACK MAIN STREET, AYR, SCOTLAND KA8 8BZ
☎ (01292) 265539. OPEN 9 - 8 MON - FRI, 9 - 5.30 SAT, 12 - 5 SUN.
UNIT 1, FORGE INDUSTRIAL ESTATE, BONNYTON ROAD,
KILMARNOCK
☎ (01563) 535397. OPEN 9 - 8 MON - FRI, 9.30 - 5.30 SAT, 12 - 5 SUN.
9 PORTLAND AVENUE, IRVINE, SCOTLAND KA12 8HY
☎ (01294) 274724. OPEN 9 - 8 MON - FRI, 9 - 5.30 SAT, 12 - 5 SUN.

The largest carpet retailer in Scotland, they sell carpets from
polypropylene and wool twists to Axminsters at discounts of up to
50%. They also sell Chinese rugs from £20-£175, representing discounts of 20%-30% on the high street. Carpets range from £1.50 a
square yard to £16.

## JENNY CLARKE FABRICS

CHURCH STREET, WINDERMERE, CUMBRIA LA23 1AQ
☎ (01539) 444686. OPEN 9 - 5 MON - FRI.

Fabric discounters, curtaining and upholstery only, at the top end of the market. Usually about 20%-25% discount and starting from £4 a metre. Studio shop with lots of sample books available and will also try and source any fabric including foreign ones. Orders taken over the phone.

# Factory Shops

## ANTA

FEARN, TAIN, ROSS-SHIRE, SCOTLAND IV20 1TL
☎ (0186) 283 2477. MAIL ORDER.

Anta make everything on site, using tartan check designs in traditional Scottish landscape colours and there are usually seconds and ends of lines available at discounted prices. There are jazzy check woollen rugs, carpets, luggage, fabric, salad bowls, throws, blankets and ceramics on sale at discounts of about 25%.

## FACTORY BEDDING SHOP

ATLAS HOUSE, NELSON STREET, DENTON HOLME, CARLISLE CA2 5NB
☎ (01228) 514703. OPEN 10 - 5.30 MON - FRI, 9 - 5 SAT, 10 - 4 BANK HOLIDAYS.

Mostly bedding bought in direct from the manufacturer at factory shop prices. But also stocks a wide range of furnishing fabrics from £1.30 a metre, curtains and a curtain making service.

## GARDINER OF SELKIRK

TWEED MILLS, SELKIRK, SCOTLAND TD7 5DZ
☎ (01750) 20283. OPEN 9 - 5 MON - SAT IN SUMMER, 10 - 4 IN WINTER.

Factory shop making textiles: mixed tweeds at £8 a yard, Shetland wool at 35p an ounce, tartan rugs at £19.50, woollen rugs, £8.95-£14.95. Best buys are the tweeds and rugs.

# McAPLIN & CO LTD

CUMMERSDALE PRINT WORKS, CARLISLE, CUMBRIA CA2 6BT
☎ (01228) 25224. OPEN 9 - 4.30 MON - FRI AND EVERY SAT.
Factory shop selling seconds in linen, cotton, satin and upholstery
fabric as well as cushions. Some of the fabric is slightly faulty.
Everything is at least half the normal retail price. Free car parking.

# SEKERS FABRICS

HENSINGHAM, WHITEHAVEN, CUMBRIA CA28 8TR
☎ (01946) 692691. OPEN 9 - 7 THUR, 9 - 3 FRI, 9 - 1 SAT.
Discontinued curtain and upholstery fabrics sold off at monthly sales,
usually held on the second Thursday, Friday and Saturday of each
month. There is 5,000-6,000 metres to choose from at discounts of
up to 75% off normal retail prices.

# THE COTTON PRINT FACTORY SHOP

58 ADMIRAL STREET, GLASGOW G41 1HU
☎ (0141) 420 1855. OPEN 9.30 - 4.30 MON - SAT.
Large outlet selling cotton fabric, up to 6,000 rolls of curtaining
fabric, heading tapes, tie-backs, curtain pulls, cushion pads, track
fabrics at anything from 95p to £5.95 a yard.

# VALLEY TEXTILES

1 CAMPBELL STREET, DARVEL, NEAR KILMARNOCK, SCOTLAND
KA17 0BZ
☎ (01560) 320140. OPEN 8 - 5 MON - THUR, 8 - 1 FRI.
All types of curtaining materials from lace and cotton to voiles, satins
and Terylene, as well as a making-up service on site. Fabric costs from
£2 - £5 a yard, at least half the normal retail price. They also sell table
linens, bedcovers and bed canopies from £25-£50.

# Secondhand Shops

## BONK & CO

7 TOMNAHURICH STREET, INVERNESS IV3 5DA
☎ (01463) 233968. OPEN 9.30 - 5 MON - FRI, 9.30 - 1 SAT.
A distributor for Country Cookers, who sell reconditioned Rayburn
cookers and sometimes also Agas and Nobel reconditioned models.
These are considerably cheaper than the brand new version. They can
incorporate a domestic heating system for hot water and radiators.

## GREENFIELDS LTD

31 HAWKSHILL, DUNDEE DD1 5DH
☎ (01382) 2244540. OPEN 9 - 5.30 MON - FRI, 11 - 4 SAT, SUN.
A distributor for Country Cookers, who sell reconditioned Rayburn
cookers and sometimes also Agas and Nobel reconditioned models.
These are considerably cheaper than the brand new version. They can
incorporate a domestic heating system for hot water and radiators.

## THE BURNING QUESTION

19B HOWE STREET, EDINBURGH EH3 6TE
☎ (031) 557 4262. OPEN 10 - 6 MON - FRI, 10 - 5 SAT.
A distributor for Country Cookers, who sell reconditioned Rayburn
cookers and sometimes also Agas and Nobel reconditioned models.
These are considerably cheaper than the brand new version. They can
incorporate a domestic heating system for hot water and radiators in
Rayburns.

## THE CURTAIN EXCHANGE

30 JAMAICA STREET, GLASGOW G1 4QD
☎ (0141) 221 1070. OPEN 10 - 5 TUE - SAT.
The Curtain Exchange is a countrywide network of shops selling top
quality, nearly-new curtains, blinds, pelmets, etc at between one-third
and one half of the brand new price. Their stock comes from a variety
of sources: people who are moving house and hate the drapes in their
new home; people who are moving house and want to sell their old
curtains to help with the bills; show houses, where the builder wants
to recoup some of his outgoings; interior designers' mistakes. Stock
changes constantly and ranges from rich brocades, damasks and

velvets to chintzes, linens and cottons. Designer names include Colefax & Fowler, Designers Guild, Laura Ashley, Warner, Sanderson, Osborne & Little

# NORTHERN IRELAND

## *Secondhand Shops*

### JOHN CATHCART & SONS LTD

DUBLIN ROAD, ENNISKILLEN, COUNTY FERMANAGH BT74 6DE
☎ (01365) 322677. OPEN 8.30 - 5.30 MON - FRI, 10 - 1 SAT.
A distributor for Country Cookers, who sell reconditioned Rayburn cookers and sometimes also Agas and Nobel reconditioned models. These are considerably cheaper than the brand new version. They can incorporate a domestic heating system for hot water and radiators.

# FOOD AND LEISURE

Including

Food and Drink, Gardening, Bycycles, Travel

*Permanent Discount Outlets,*

*Food and Drink Discounters,*

*Hire Shops*

# LONDON

## *Permanent Discount Outlets*

### BCP AIRPORT CAR PARKING

CHARLWOOD ROAD, LOWFIELD HEATH, CRAWLEY, WEST SUSSEX
RH11 OQB
☎ (01293) 561066. 24-HOUR SERVICE.

Recommended by most leading travel agents and direct sell tourist
operators, BCP Airport Car Parking is considered the UK's market
leader. BCP provides secure and competitively priced car parking
from £2.80 a day for the top ten UK airports: Heathrow, Gatwick,
Manchester, Luton, Birmingham, East Midlands, Newcastle, Leeds-
Bradford, Edinburgh and Glasgow. All car parks are situated within
minutes of the airport terminals and are served by efficient courtesy
transport. As a GDD reader, when booking, you can claim a 10%
discount by simply telephoning the reservation line above, quoting
reference Good Deal Directory. You will receive a written confirmation of your booking, together with a map showing directions to your
chosen car park.

### BIBLIOPHILE BOOKS

5 THOMAS ROAD, LONDON E14 7BN
☎ 0171-515 9222. MAIL ORDER ONLY.

Mail order books from biographies and art, to literature and general
tomes at half price or less. Stock is brand new, remaindered.

### BUSINESS & FIRST CLASS AIR FAIR GUIDE

221 WESTBOURNE PARK ROAD, LONDON W11 1EA
☎ 0171-221 6095. FAX 071-229 3595. OPEN 10 - 6 MON - SAT.
MAIL ORDER.

A 28 page booklet published by Riaz Dooley, so-called king of cut-
price travel and founder of the Travel Bazaar agencies, outlining the
enormous savings to be made at the top end of the travel market. It
cites examples such as a first-class return ticket from London to LA,
usual cost £4,358, now £1,790 - a saving of £2,578. Or London to
Tokyo, first class, usual price £5,185, now £1,180 - saving £4,005.
The guide is available by post (send a SAE).

## C & T EYEWEAR LTD

PO BOX 41, TEDDINGTON, MIDDLESEX TW11 0SZ
☎ 0181-943 4815. MAIL ORDER.

Sell sunglasses by mail order at prices which are about 30% cheaper
than the recommended retail price. Examples include Wayfarer's at
£44 instead of £69; Wayfarer's 11s at £48 instead of £79; Baloramas
at £61 instead of £89; and Wayfarer Max 11s at £79 instead of £109.
VAT is included, but an additional charge of £1.50 is made for post
and packing. Delivery takes 72 hours if you pay by credit card, 10
days if by cheque.

## ENTERTAINMENT PUBLICATIONS LTD

MEMBERSHIP DEPT, SPRING GARDENS, 4 CITADEL PLACE,
TINWORTH STREET, LONDON SE11 5EG
☎ 0171-793 1510.

A Directory of hundreds of restaurants, sports events, and days out,
Entertainment 95/96 promises that you need never again pay full
price for days or nights out as members take advantage of specially
negotiated discounts. Restaurant bills at 630 designated venues are
usually reduced by 25% for up to four people including soft drinks;
Channel crossings and hotel rooms can save you 50%; and there are
also savings to be made at MGM/Canon cinemas, Stoll Moss West
End theatres, and shows from Crufts to the Royal Tournament. There
are also potential savings to be made at more than 650 British,
European and American hotels. Membership costs £52, including
£2.50 p&p. There are similar publications for more than 120
American cities and other European cities. (The company plans to
move premises at the end of 1995, but the telephone number should
remain the same. )

## FIRST SPORT

456-458 THE STRAND, LONDON WC2R 0RG
☎ 071-839 5161. OPEN 9.30 - 6 MON - SAT, UNTIL 7 ON THUR.

They are so certain that their prices for top brand-name sports shoes
are the lowest you will find that they guarantee that if you buy from
them and then see the same shoes cheaper elsewhere, they will refund
the difference. Brand names on sale at discounts of up to 50% include
Nike, Reebok, Puma and Adidas. The shop also sells clothing, bags,
T-shirts, skiwear, skis, ski boots and a full range of back packing

equipment such as tents, camping tools and accessories. With 60 shops to buy for, they can purchase in bulk and get good deals.

## LONDON FOR LESS

☎ 0181-964 4242.

Anyone who likes visiting London or who lives in London may like to take advantage of London for Less. Usually promoted to American visitors, it is now being launched to the domestic British market. For £12.95, you get a package which includes a "credit" card providing discounts at over 200 places in central London, plus a 23-page guide-book and map. Discounts are applicable for up to five people with one card and you can use it as often as you like. Examples of discounts include: 20%-25% off more than 20 attractions and museums; 25%-75% off ticket prices to 20 shows, concerts, operas and ballets; 20%-25% off food and drink at 75 restaurants; and 10%-20% off all goods at 75 shops. Restaurants include Langham's Brasserie, Smollensky's Balloon and Borshtch 'n' Tears. Shops include Georgina Von Etzdorf and Trumper's.

## MONEY £ACTS

☎ (01692) 500765.

Very little in this life comes free and often saving money involves spending some first. This is true in the case of Money £acts, the guide to savings, investment and mortgage rates, guaranteed income bonds, national savings and annuities, which operates an update by fax. Whether you want to find out what the interest rates are on mortgates or where to open your Tessa account to get the best rates, you simply dial the relevant fax number and wait for the information to appear at your end. Commercial and residential mortgage information is updated daily, as is savings information. Cost is about 49p per minute at daytime rates.

## POSTSCRIPT

DEPT GDD95, 24 LANGROYD ROAD, LONDON SW17 7PL
☎ 0181-767 7421. FAX 0181-682 0280. MAIL ORDER ONLY FROM 9 - 5.30 MON - FRI.

A family run-business specialising in high quality books by mail at greatly reduced prices. Unlike the big book clubs, you are under no obligation to buy any books at any time. The selection covers a huge range of interests from art, gardening, cookery, biography, travel and reference to history, philosophy, psychology and literature - from classic works to the frankly esoteric - many of which cannot be found in bookshops and all priced at a fraction of publishers' latest prices. For example Dictionary of Idioms and Their Origins, £5.99, originally £14.99; Family Roots: How to Trace Your Family History, £7.95, originally £15.99; Cassell's Colloquial French, £1.99, originally £3.99; County Guide to English Churches, £4.99, originally £9.95. Telephone for free catalogue.

## RUNNING HEADS

82 EAST DULWICH GROVE, LONDON SE22 8TW
☎ 0171-738 4096.
Publishes a number of books from buying by mail order around the world (The Global Shopper) which gives details of items such as CDs, hi-fi equipment, golf gear etc which can be cheaper to buy across the Atlantic, to The Good Telecoms Guide, which tells you how to save money on your phone bills.

## WISEMAN ORIGINALS

34 WEST SQUARE, LAMBETH, LONDON SE22 8TW
☎ 0171-587 0747. PHONE FOR AN APPOINTMENT.
Offers a comprehensive range of original prints by artists such as Picasso, Hocknee, Elizabeth Frink, Peter Blake, John Piper, Marc Chagall and Matisse at prices which are less than would be paid in a West End gallery. All the works are limited edition prints. They comprise images produced from a lithograph stone, etching plate or silkscreen and are usually signed and numbered by the artist. Every work is old with a certificate of authentication. Prices range from £50 to £5,000 with the majority costing from £200 to £600. Members of the Modern Art Collectors Club, which costs £10 to join, are entitled to a discount of 5% off all stock, as well as quarterly catalogue sheets, invitations to viewings and special offers. The gallery is at the Wiseman's Georgian house, so phone first.

## *Hire Shops*

### BLACK & EDGINGTON HIRE LTD

30 MARSH GATE LANE, LONDON E15 2NH
☎ 0181-534 8085. OPEN 8 - 5 MON - FRI.

Offers everything the discerning summer wedding or garden fete organiser could want from marquees and tables to flags and banners. With three depots, they can supply equipment anywhere in the country and abroad.

## *Secondhand Shops*

### VERMILLION BOOKS

57 RED LION STREET, LONDON WC1 4PD
☎ 0171-242 5822. OPEN 12 - 6 MON - FRI, CLOSED SATS.

Sells brand new books bought from reviewers at approximately one third off the published price. All subjects are covered except for science, law and economics. Many of the books, both hardback and paperback, are art, literature, history, music, cinema and biographies and are sold on publication date. All are in mint condition and if you are looking for a particular book, staff will reserve it for you if they can.

# SOUTH EAST

## *Permanent Discount Outlets*

### AIRFARES GUIDE

FORUM HOUSE, CHICHESTER, SUSSEX PO19 2EN
MAIL ORDER.

Find out how to travel without paying the full fare by subscribing to the Airfares Guide. Updated monthly and published quarterly, it lists thousands of cheap air fares for hundreds of destinations, with details of how to buy the tickets. How it works is that consolidators ("wholesalers") approach airlines and offer to bulk buy tickets to particular destinations at favourable prices. The airline only appoints a few consolidators, who then sell on to the travel agent trade, who sell the tickets to you, with appropriate mark-ups along the way. The Airfares Guide enables you to bypass the travel agent and go directly to the consolidator and buy the tickets at "wholesale" prices. Or if you feel uncomfortable with that, you can ask your travel agent to buy from a named consolidator and charge you a handling fee. The Guide lists destinations with one-way and return fairs (including their restrictions) and the seasons they're valid for. Then it lists the code of the agent or consolidator offering that fare, which you can look up in the back of the Guide to find the telephone number and book the ticket yourself. The Guide costs £49.50 a year or £15 a quarter. Good Deal Directory readers can get a special discount, paying just £9.95 for an issue of the Guide if they quote reference no. 26 and state they are a GDD reader.

## BCP AIRPORT CAR PARKING

CHARLWOOD ROAD, LOWFIELD HEATH, CRAWLEY, WEST SUSSEX RH11 OQB
☎ (01293) 561066. 24-HOUR SERVICE.
Recommended by most leading travel agents and direct sell tourist operators, BCP Airport Car Parking is considered the UK's market leader. BCP provides secure and competitively priced car parking from £2.80 a day for the top ten UK airports: Heathrow, Gatwick, Manchester, Luton, Birmingham, East Midlands, Newcastle, Leeds-Bradford, Edinburgh and Glasgow. All car parks are situated within minutes of the airport terminals and are served by efficient courtesy transport. As a GDD reader, when booking, you can claim a 10% discount by simply telephoning the reservation line above, quoting reference Good Deal Directory. You will receive a written confirmation of your booking, together with a map showing directions to your chosen car park.

# *Hire Shops*

## TAYLOR'S HIRE SERVICE

THE OLD BARN, GREEN END, BARAUGHING, NEAR WARE,
HERTFORDSHIRE SG11 2PG
☎ (0920) 821523. BY APPOINTMENT ONLY.
Marquees and associated accessories such as chairs and tables for hire.
Marquees for weddings cost from £1,000-£4,000.

# *Food and Drink Discounters*

## EDGCUMBE TEA AND COFFEE

WICKS HOUSE, FORD LANE, FORD, ARUNDEL, WEST SUSSEX
BN18 0DF
☎ (01243) 555775. OPEN 9 - 6 MONDAY TO FRIDAY. MAIL ORDER.
Primarily trade suppliers, Edgcumbe do sell direct to the public to
personal shoppers and have some very good bargains in ends of lines.
They offer top quality tea blends in tea bag or loose form and a "roast
and post" coffee service by mail order - within 24 hours of ordering,
you will find fresh coffee on your doorstep. They roast and blend
their own coffee on site to order, and you can enjoy a range of
flavoured coffee from amaretto to choc-mint. Because of their low
overheads, the prices are very competitive. For example, £19 for
3,000 tea bags of English Breakfast blend or £25 for a special fine tea
box.

## NEW HALL VINEYARDS

CHELMSFORD ROAD, PURLEIGH, CHELMSFORD, ESSEX CM3 6PN
☎ (0621) 828343. OPEN 10 - 6 MON - FRI, 10 - 1.30 SAT, SUN.
Specialises in white wine - Muller, Bacchus and Huxelrebe - on which
it offers discounts of up to 8% depending on the quantities you buy.
A case of 12 bottles costs £1 less per bottle. There is an annual
weekend wine festival and tours.

# THE CHILTERN BREWERY

NASH LEED ROAD, TERRICK, AYLESBURY, BUCKINGHAMSHIRE
HP17 OTQ
☎ (01296) 613647. OPEN 9 - 5 MON - SAT.

Three different types of bitter are manufactured here: Chiltern and Beechwood bitters, and Three Hundreds Old Ale. Also stocks mustards and chutney with beer, marmalade with malt, pickled onions with hops and fruit cake with barley wine.

## *Secondhand Shops*

## BAGGINS BOOK BAZAAR

19 HIGH STREET, ROCHESTER, KENT ME1 1QB
☎ (01634) 811651. OPEN 10 - 6 SEVEN DAYS A WEEK.

Secondhand book shop which mainly deals in rare and secondhand books, but also sells some brand new review copies at substantial discounts. Prices of the older books depend on their condition.

# SOUTH WEST

## *Permanent Discount Outlets*

## BCP AIRPORT CAR PARKING

CHARLWOOD ROAD, LOWFIELD HEATH, CRAWLEY, WEST SUSSEX
RH11 OQB
☎ (01293) 561066. 24-HOUR SERVICE.

Recommended by most leading travel agents and direct sell tourist operators, BCP Airport Car Parking is considered the UK's market leader. BCP provides secure and competitively priced car parking from £2.80 a day for the top ten UK airports: Heathrow, Gatwick, Manchester, Luton, Birmingham, East Midlands, Newcastle, Leeds-Bradford, Edinburgh and Glasgow. All car parks are situated within minutes of the airport terminals and are served by efficient courtesy transport. As a GDD reader, when booking, you can claim a 10%

discount by simply telephoning the reservation line above, quoting reference Good Deal Directory. You will receive a written confirmation of your booking, together with a map showing directions to your chosen car park.

## CD SELECTION

DORCHESTER, DORSET DT2 7YG
☎ (01305) 848725. MAIL ORDER ONLY.
CD Selection publishes its bargain selection of CDs, tapes, books and videos five times a year. Two editions are 60 or more pages; three editions are sale supplements. These full-colour guides offer a remarkable range of classical, opera, jazz, easy listening and popular CDs with prices starting at 99p. Overstocks, deletions and ongoing titles are selected for value for money. All sales are backed by a full refund guarantee. CD Selections also sells audio books, ballet and opera videos, popular and general interest videos, and bargain books.

## *Factory Shops*

## CLAUDE GILL BOOKS

CLARKS VILLAGE FACTORY SHOPPING, FARM ROAD, STREET, SOMERSET BA16 OBB
☎ (01458) 840064. OPEN 9 - 6 MON - SAT, 11 - 5 SUN. TIMES CHANGE WINTER AND SUMMER.
Wide range of books across a large subject area for sale at discount prices. Phone number is general number for the Village.

## *Hire Shops*

## YEO PAULL

NORTH STREET, MARTOCK, SOMERSET TA12 6DJ
☎ (01935) 824391. OPEN 8 - 5 MON - FRI. 8 - 12 SAT IN SUMMER.
Family-run business in operation for more than 100 years, hiring out tents, tubular pavilions, marquees, furniture, dance floors, trestles, lighting, staging and coconut matting - everything you need for a summer shindig or an outdoor wedding. available countrywide.

## Food and Drink Discounters

### HANCOCK'S DEVON CIDER SHOP

CLAPWORTHY MILL, SOUTH MOLTON, DEVON EX36 4HU
☎ (01769) 572678. OPEN 9 - 5 MON - SAT, CLOSED 1 - 2 DAILY.
Top quality cider, recommended in the Good Cider Guide, at 20% less than local prices for the draught cider. You can bring your own container.

### MOORES BISCUITS

FACTORY SHOP, MORCOMBELAKE, NEAR BRIDPORT, DORSET DT6 6ES
☎ (01297) 489253. OPEN 9 - 5 MON - FRI, 9 - 1 SAT.
Broken biscuits including shortbreads, walnut crunch, chocolate chip and ginger biscuits sold in 800 gram bags at 30% saving. Tend to sell out very early in the day, so don't leave your visit until late in the afternoon.

# WALES AND WEST MIDLANDS

## Permanent Discount Outlets

### BCP AIRPORT CAR PARKING

CHARLWOOD ROAD, LOWFIELD HEATH, CRAWLEY, WEST SUSSEX RH11 0QB
☎ (01293) 561066. 24-HOUR SERVICE.
Recommended by most leading travel agents and direct sell tourist operators, BCP Airport Car Parking is considered the UK's market leader. BCP provides secure and competitively priced car parking from £2.80 a day for the top ten UK airports: Heathrow, Gatwick, Manchester, Luton, Birmingham, East Midlands, Newcastle, Leeds-Bradford, Edinburgh and Glasgow. All car parks are situated within minutes of the airport terminals and are served by efficient courtesy transport. As a GDD reader, when booking, you can claim a 10% discount by simply telephoning the reservation line above, quoting

reference Good Deal Directory. You will receive a written confirmation of your booking, together with a map showing directions to your chosen car park.

## RENAHALL LTD

61 LIMETREE AVENUE, BILTON, RUGBY, WARWICKSHIRE CV22 7QT
☎ (01788) 811454. MAIL ORDER ONLY.

Vitamins and similar products such as evening primrose oil, fish oil are sold by mail order only (post paid) usually within 48 hours of receipt of order. Vitamin C is sold in powder form (also as Calcium Ascorbate) to avoid unwanted fillers and binders (and the cost of tabletting) in packs of 240 grams. It is pure ascorbic acid and costs £7 compared with £2.69 for 60 grams at a high street chemist chain. Vitamin E is sold in both powder and capsule form, from d-alpha tocopheryl ex soya beans. Beta-carotene from dunaliella salina, the carotene .ch sea plant, has just been introduced. Send for price list by return. Telephone orders are accepted from established customers.

## *Factory Shops*

## EQUATOR LUGGAGE

BICESTER OUTLET SHOPPING VILLAGE, PINGLE DRIVE, BICESTER, JUNCTION 9 OF M40, OXFORDSHIRE OX6 7WD
☎ (01869) 323200. OPEN 10 - 6 MON - SAT AND BANK HOLIDAYS, 11 - 5 SUN.

One of 48 shops, with more planned, in this factory shopping village which opened in June 1995. Billed as Bond Street comes to Bicester, the shops are very smart indeed, beautifully designed and stocked with end-of-season designer fashions, mens and childrenswear, tableware, shoes and more, all on permanent sale at prices reduced from 25%-50%, with some reductions up to 75%. Well known brand name suitcases, vanity cases, cabin luggage, haversacks, travel accessories, wallets, handbags from Samsonite, Delsey and Hugo Boss at discounts of 30% and more. The village also has two restaurants, a small children's play area and free parking. The telephone number given here is for the village.

## HAWK CYCLES LIQUIDATIONS

FORGE LANE, CRADLEY HEATH, WEST MIDLANDS B64 5AL
☎ (01384) 636535. OPEN 9 - 6 MON - SAT, 9 - 4.30 SUN.
Sells all types of adults and childrens' bikes direct to the public at
factory prices. Children's trikes start at £24, adult mountain bikes at
£88, normally £150.

## SAPPHIRE BOOKS

BICESTER OUTLET SHOPPING VILLAGE, PINGLE DRIVE, BICESTER,
JUNCTION 9 OF M40, OXFORDSHIRE OX6 7WD
☎ (01869) 323200. OPEN 10 - 6 MON - SAT AND BANK HOLIDAYS,
11 - 5 SUN.
One of 48 shops, with more planned, in this factory shopping village
which opened in June 1995. Billed as Bond Street comes to Bicester,
the shops are very smart indeed, beautifully designed and stocked
with end-of-season designer fashions, mens and childrenswear, tableware, shoes and more, all on permanent sale at prices reduced from
25%-50%, with some reductions up to 75%. Familiar fiction writers,
holiday reading novels, classics, cooking, children's books and educational tomes, all at reduced prices. Some come in packs of two or
three. The more you buy, the greater the saving. The village also has
two restaurants, a small children's play area and free parking. The telephone number given here is for the village.

## WOODS OF WINDSOR

BICESTER OUTLET SHOPPING VILLAGE, PINGLE DRIVE, BICESTER,
JUNCTION 9 OF M40, OXFORDSHIRE OX6 7WD
☎ (01869) 323200. OPEN 10 - 6 MON - SAT AND BANK HOLIDAYS,
11 - 5 SUN.
One of 48 shops, with more planned, in this factory shopping village
which opened in June 1995. Billed as Bond Street comes to Bicester,
the shops are very smart indeed, beautifully designed and stocked
with end-of-season designer fashions, mens and childrenswear, tableware, shoes and more, all on permanent sale at prices reduced from
25%-50%, with some reductions up to 75%. This shop sells gift sets,
soaps, perfume, and talc at discounts of 25% for standard ranges and
70% for discounted ranges. The village also has two restaurants, a
small children's play area and free parking. The telephone number
given here is for the village.

# Food and Drink Discounters

## THE IVY BUSH BREWERY

BREWERS WORLD LTD, 226 MONUMENT ROAD, EDGBASTON,
BIRMINGHAM, BIRMINGHAM, WEST MIDLANDS B16 8UZ
☎ (0121) 454 7447. PHONE FOR BOOKING AND OPENING HOURS.

Britain's first brewery where you are allowed to brew it yourself. It is
not a pub or a shop where you can buy a home brew kit; rather it an
alternative to home brewing. Traditional equipment assures good
results each time and the staff do all the messy clearing up. You can
brew beer and lager to your own taste, free of preservatives. Ten
gallons of beer (80-90 bottles) costs between £35-£65 depending on
the type of brew. This works out at around one quarter of the retail
price, though normally you could pretty well guarantee to save 50%
as long as you brew a minimum of 80 bottles. The whole process
takes just under two hours. You are advised to book membership well
in advance. Hours of opening change but mainly run from Tuesday
through to Saturday from Midday onwards. Day membership available at £2.50.

## THE WELSH WHISKY DISTILLERY

2 PARCMENTER, BRECON LD3 1XX
☎ (01874) 622926. OPEN 9 - 5 MON - FRI, 10 - 5 SAT, 12 - 3 SUN.
MAIL ORDER.

Factory shops selling the products which they distil - whisky, gin,
vodka, wine and cream liqueurs including Welsh Special Reserve,
Merlin Welsh Cream Liqueur, Canydelyn Whisky Liqueur and
Dewisant Welsh Mead.

# Secondhand Shops

## THE BOOKSHOP

THE PAVEMENT, HAY ON WYE, HEREFORDSHIRE HR3 5BU
☎ (01497) 821341. OPEN 9 - 8 MON - SAT, 11 - 5 SUN.

Secondhand and remaindered books, as well as new and review
copies, are sold in this huge shop, including recently published books,
usually one-third off and sometimes half price.

# EAST ANGLIA AND EAST MIDLANDS

## *Permanent Discount Outlets*

## BCP AIRPORT CAR PARKING

CHARLWOOD ROAD, LOWFIELD HEATH, CRAWLEY, WEST SUSSEX
RH11 OQB
☎ (01293) 561066. 24-HOUR SERVICE.

Recommended by most leading travel agents and direct sell tourist operators, BCP Airport Car Parking is considered the UK's market leader. BCP provides secure and competitively priced car parking from £2.80 a day for the top ten UK airports: Heathrow, Gatwick, Manchester, Luton, Birmingham, East Midlands, Newcastle, Leeds-Bradford, Edinburgh and Glasgow. All car parks are situated within minutes of the airport terminals and are served by efficient courtesy transport. As a GDD reader, when booking, you can claim a 10% discount by simply telephoning the reservation line above, quoting reference Good Deal Directory. You will receive a written confirmation of your booking, together with a map showing directions to your chosen car park.

## GALLOWAY & PORTER

THE PADDOCKS, CHERRYHINTON ROAD, CAMBRIDGE
☎ (01223) 67876.

Holds regular book warehouse sales about once a month on a Saturday from 9 - 5 at which most books cost £1 or £2, regardless of the original price. There are new hardback copies in the huge variety of tomes, covering many subjects including children's. Free parking.

## PAPWORTH TRAVEL GOODS LTD

PAPWORTH EVERARD, CAMBRIDGE CB3 8RG
☎ (01480) 830345. OPEN 8.30 - 5 MON - THUR, 8.30 - 11.30 FRI,
CLOSED 12.30 - 1.30.

Ends of lines and seconds of leather and hard luggage. VAT must be added to all prices. Suitcases from £15; canvas and leather trim bags, £100, usually £200. Orders taken on the phone.

# *Hire Shops*

## TOP TABLE

MOORS FARM, WEST FARNDON, DAVENTRY, NORTHAMPTONSHIRE
NN11 3TX
☎ (01327) 260575. FAX (01372) 261843. OPEN 9 - 5.30 MON - FRI,
9 - 1 SAT.
Hires out unusual patterned tableware, coloured glass and patterned
table cloths, unlike a lot of companies who stick to plain white. Also
offers French white china and stainless steel cutlery with coloured
handles, and delivers anywhere in England. Local delivery is free, elsewhere is negotiable. They aren't necessarily cheaper than their competitors, but they do offer an unusual range for special occasions
including glass plates, gold lustre china and silver cutlery.

# *Food and Drink Discounters*

## ASHFORD HALL LTD

HEMPSTEAD ROAD, INDUSTRIAL ESTATE, HOLT, NORFOLK NR25 6EC
☎ (01263) 711447. OPEN 9 - 5 MON - FRI, 10- 4 SAT, AND SPECIAL
SUNDAYS.
Sell overstocks of preserves, pickles, jams, biscuits and salts which
they make for well known stores and under their own label. Also
make gift baskets, food hampers and sell cookshop items and
aromatic herbs.

## EDWARDIAN CONFECTIONERY LTD

HUTHWAITE, BARKER STREET, NOTTINGHAMSHIRE NG17 2LG
☎ (01623) 554712. OPEN 9 - 6 MON - FRI, 9 - 1 SAT.
Sweets and rock made on the premises and sold at two-thirds of the
shop price. Range includes rock and boiled sweets, peanut brittle,
treacle slab, caramel slab and chocolate, peanut and raisin slab, all of
which can be bought either whole or broken up.

## GILCHRIST CONFECTIONERY LTD

UNITS 1 & 2, OXBOROUGH LANE, FAKENHAM, NORFOLK NR21 8AF
☎ (01328) 862632. OPEN 8 - 3 THUR.
Factory shop underneath the offices sells all sorts of chocolate items -
walnut whips, petit fours, mints, Thomas the Tank Engine chocolates, Christmas chocolate tree decorations - to well known department stores. Seconds and misshapes are sold in bags for £1; overmakes at half price. Stock varies from week to week.

## PIC A CHIC

FACTORY SHOP, NOTTINGHAM ROAD INDUSTRIAL ESTATE,
ASHBY DE LA ZOUCH, LEICESTERSHIRE LE6 5DR
☎ (01530) 413077. OPEN 9 - 4 MON - FRI, 9 - 12 SAT.
Frozen chicken pieces sold in packets of 40 (either legs, breasts or a
mixture of both) at savings of 20%. Also 10% savings on steak and
kidney pies sold in packs of 12. Frozen gateaux sells for an average of
£5 a cake and had 18 portions.

## THE BEER CELLAR & CO LTD

31 NORWICH ROAD, STRUMPSHAW, NORWICH, NORFOLK NR13 4AG
☎ (01603) 714884. MAIL ORDER.
From time to time, the Beer Cellar finds a few of the beers they hold
in stock are either approaching or past their quoted "Best Before"
date. More often than not, there is absolutely nothing wrong with the
beer. Rather than throwing it away, they make it into a special offer
to Beer Cellar members as part of a "Lucky Dip Bin End". All the
beers are tasted before being sent out. Lucky Dips are not always
available. Contact the company for further details. Quote Reference
BR002.

## THE COLSTON BASSETT AND DISTRICT DAIRY LTD

HARBY LANE, COLSTON BASSETT, NOTTINGHAMSHIRE NG12 3FN
☎ (01949) 81322. OPEN 9.30 - 4 MON - FRI, CLOSED 12.30 - 1.30,
9.30 - 11 SAT. MAIL ORDER.
Own Blue Stilton cut for you from the round - the smallest amount
is 1 kilo at £6.04.

## THORNTONS

38 KING STREET BELPER, DERBYSHIRE DE5 1PL
☎ (01773) 827222. OPEN 9 - 5.30 MON - SAT.

Although the factory shop has now closed, Thorntons shop in the nearby high street has a "quality clearance" corner which sells, as well as lollipops and bars, mis-shapes at half price, sent fresh from the factory for Monday morning. Some of the good deals on offer include half-price Continental chocolates, Thorntons luxury selection and half-pound pack bars.

# NORTH WEST, YORKSHIRE AND HUMBERSIDE

*Permanent Discount Outlets*

## BCP AIRPORT CAR PARKING

CHARLWOOD ROAD, LOWFIELD HEATH, CRAWLEY, WEST SUSSEX RH11 OQB
☎ (01293) 561066. 24-HOUR SERVICE.

Recommended by most leading travel agents and direct sell tourist operators, BCP Airport Car Parking is considered the UK's market leader. BCP provides secure and competitively priced car parking from £2.80 a day for the top ten UK airports: Heathrow, Gatwick, Manchester, Luton, Birmingham, East Midlands, Newcastle, Leeds-Bradford, Edinburgh and Glasgow. All car parks are situated within minutes of the airport terminals and are served by efficient courtesy transport. As a GDD reader, when booking, you can claim a 10% discount by simply telephoning the reservation line above, quoting reference Good Deal Directory. You will receive a written confirmation of your booking, together with a map showing directions to your chosen car park.

# EQUATOR LUGGAGE

CHESHIRE OAKS OUTLET VILLAGE, KINSEY ROAD, NEAR ELLESMERE
PORT, SOUTH WIRRAL L65 9JJ
☎ (0151) 357 3248. OPEN 10 - 6 MON - SAT, 10 - 4 SUN.

Range of well-known brand names such as Delsey, Tula, Hugo Boss
and Samsonite, as well as a keenly-priced Equator range. The shop
sells backpacks, vanity cases, cabin luggage, suitcases, handbags,
leather accessories, sunglasses and umbrellas. Hugo Boss accessories
range included leather wallets reduced from £55 to £45 and key rings
from £25.99 to £18.20. Tula bags started at £13.99. There was 20%
off Samsonite cases with a small range of discontinued colours which
had bigger discounts. The Delsey range was reduced by between 20%
and 50%.

# HORNSEA FREEPORT SHOPPING VILLAGE

HORNSEA, EAST YORKSHIRE HU18 1UT
☎ (01964) 534211. OPEN 10 - 5 MON - FRI, 10 - 6 SAT, SUN, BANK
HOLIDAYS.

The original British factory shopping village on the east coast of
Yorkshire comes complete with masses of family entertainment
including Butterfly World, adventure playground, vintage cars, water
games, plus about two dozen shops where you can buy brand name
discounted goods. Labels for men include Daks Simpson, Wrangler,
Aquascutum, Tom Sayers menswear, Tog 24 and Sports Unlimited.

# SAPPHIRE BOOKS

CHESHIRE OAKS OUTLET VILLAGE, KINSEY ROAD, NEAR ELLESMERE
PORT, SOUTH WIRRAL L65 9JJ
☎ (0151) 357 3889. OPEN 10 - 6 MON - FRI, 11 - 5 SUN AND BANK
HOLIDAYS.
☎ (01326) 373800 (MAIL ORDER)

This bookshop at Cheshire Oaks offers a wide range of books from
popular fiction titles to cookery, gardening and classics. Examples of
some titles include Delia Smith's Complete Illustrated Cookery
Course, Winnie the Pooh and Little Women. Contemporary fiction
from authors such as Tom Clancy, Stephen King and Jeffrey Archer is
usually sold in two or threes. You can save between 30% and 50% on
the publisher's price, depending on whether you are a gold or
platinum member of the Sapphire Book Club. Membership status

depends on how many books you have purchased. You can join on the spot, buying books at the 30% discount and receiving the Sapphire magazine each month with scores more book bargain opportunities. You have to buy from at least three of the 12 magazines over your one-year free membership. If you're not planning a trip to Cheshire Oaks but want to join the Club, write to 1 Book Mews, Flitcroft Street, London WC2H 8DJ or phone the telephone number above.

## *Hire Shops*

### TENT VISION LTD

14 CASTLE ROAD, LOWER WORTLEY, LEEDS, YORKSHIRE LS12 4RX
☎ (01234) 712639. OPEN 9 - 5.30 MON - FRI.
Deliver and set up marquees with a dance floor, if required, seating, lining, chandeliers. Estimates are subject to a survey of your site, but a clear span structure would cost at least £2,500.

## *Food and Drink Discounters*

### HI-LIFE DINERS CLUB

44A COOKSON STREET, BLACKPOOL, LANCASHIRE FY1 3ED
☎ (01253) 20319. 24-HOUR MEMBERSHIP LINE.
The Hi-Life Club has been operating for more than 10 years in the north-west of England and is the biggest diners club of its type, with more than 10,000 members. Members can choose from among 250 Lancashire restaurants, many of which now give a complimentary three-course meal when two people dine. The club literature says that most people save over £100 per year and offers a no-quibbble money back guarantee if you're not delighted with your membership. Membership costs £23.95 per annum.

## KIPPAX BISCUITS LTD

FACTORY SHOP, KING STREET, COLNE, LANCASHIRE BB8 9HU
☎ (01282) 864 198. OPEN 10 - 3.45 WED, FRI, SAT, CLOSED 1 - 1.15.
More than 100 different types of biscuits from ginger wafers and
shortbread to plain assorted and chocolate sold in packets, tins or
loose. The top 15 products sell at 90p per pound, while misshapes
cost 60p per pound with chocolate misshapes costing £1 per pound.
Tins and boxes of biscuits from £2. Coach parties welcome by prior
appointment only.

## LEWIS REGENCY FOOD LTD

FACTORY SHOP, MIDDLEGATE, WHITE LUND INDUSTRIAL ESTATE,
MORECAMBE, LANCASHIRE LA3 3BN
☎ (01524) 61616. OPEN 9 - 5 MON - FRI, 9 - 12 SAT, SUN.
Ice creams, gateaux and frozen foods such as pizzas and pies from
Norpark, Homefarm and Bird's Eye which are sold at prices lower
than in the shops. Own brand ice cream sells at 30-40p less on the 2-
litre quantity, and Black Forest Gateau costs about £1 less than in the
shops. You do not have to bulk buy, but orders are only delivered
(locally only) if the total is more than £30.

## THORNTON'S

ST JOHN'S SHOPPING CENTRE, LANCASTER WAY, PRESTON,
LANCASHIRE
☎ (01772) 202421. OPEN 9 - 5.30 MON - SAT.
Sells misshapes at bargain prices. Continental misshapes cost £1.49
for a half pound, Select misshapes cost £1.69 a half pound; assorted
misshapes, 99p for 200 gram bag.

# NORTH AND SCOTLAND

*Permanent Discount Outlets*

## BCP AIRPORT CAR PARKING

CHARLWOOD ROAD, LOWFIELD HEATH, CRAWLEY, WEST SUSSEX
RH11 OQB
☎ (01293) 561066. 24-HOUR SERVICE.
Recommended by most leading travel agents and direct sell tourist
operators, BCP Airport Car Parking is considered the UK's market
leader. BCP provides secure and competitively priced car parking
from £2.80 a day for the top ten UK airports: Heathrow, Gatwick,
Manchester, Luton, Birmingham, East Midlands, Newcastle, Leeds-
Bradford, Edinburgh and Glasgow. All car parks are situated within
minutes of the airport terminals and are served by efficient courtesy
transport. As a GDD reader, when booking, you can claim a 10%
discount by simply telephoning the reservation line above, quoting
reference Good Deal Directory. You will receive a written confirmation of your booking, together with a map showing directions to your
chosen car park.

*Factory Outlets*

## BOOKSCENE

JACKSONS LANDING, HARTLEPOOL FACTORY OUTLET SHOPPING
MALL, HARTLEPOOL MARINA, HARTLEPOOL, CLEVELAND TS24 OXN
☎ (01429) 861223. OPEN 10 - 6 MON - FRI, 11 - 5 SUN AND BANK
HOLIDAYS.
Indoor factory shopping centre with twenty-four outlets selling brand
name items including a wide range of books from fiction to health,
sport to children, cookbooks to biographies. There are also jigsaws,
posters and some secondhand fiction. Price reductions include cookbooks reduced from £16.99 to £6.99. Hartlepool Marina hosts a
recreated historic quay and harbours HMS Trincomalee, the oldest
British warship still afloat, and is also the site of the new Hartlepool
Museum with its interactive fighting ships section and a replica sev-

enteenth century children's play area. There is free parking adjacent to the centre, a coffee shop, restaurant overlooking the Marina, and baby changing and disabled facilities.

## EQUATOR LUGGAGE

JACKSONS LANDING, HARTLEPOOL FACTORY OUTLET SHOPPING MALL, HARTLEPOOL MARINA, HARTLEPOOL, CLEVELAND TS24 0XN ☎ (01429) 235998. OPEN 10 - 6 MON - FRI, 11 - 5 SUN AND BANK HOLIDAYS.

Indoor factory shopping centre with twenty-four outlets selling brand name items including travel goods and accessories. The window of this shop shows the manager's special offer of the week. Inside are briefcases, suitcases, handbags, wallets, purses, rucksacks, vanity cases and chromatic sunglasses. A notice states the company policy on factory shops: all stock is the result of production over-runs which means that they have produced too much of this type of product to service all their outlets and for this reason they need to clear the product at substantially reduced prices. Examples of prices include cabin baggage with integral wheels and handle, £27.99 reduced from £39.99; handbags reduced from £69.99 to £42.99; large Samsonite case, £56.99 from £75. At the time of our visit in May 1995, there was 20% off Samsonite and Delsey luggage. Hartlepool Marina hosts a recreated historic quay and harbours HMS Trincomalee, the oldest British warship still afloat, and is also the site of the new Hartlepool Museum with its interactive fighting ships section and a replica seventeenth century children's play area. There is free parking adjacent to the centre, a coffee shop, restaurant overlooking the Marina, and baby changing and disabled facilities.

## HALLMARK

JACKSONS LANDING, HARTLEPOOL FACTORY OUTLET SHOPPING MALL, HARTLEPOOL MARINA, HARTLEPOOL, CLEVELAND TS24 0XN ☎ (01429) 275680. OPEN 10 - 6 MON - FRI, 11 - 5 SUN AND BANK HOLIDAYS.

Indoor factory shopping centre with twenty-four outlets selling brand name items including everything you need for celebrations. Most of the stock here is discounted by 50% including Noddy party packs, stuffed toys, cards, wrapping paper, gift rosettes, Sellotape, crepe paper, souvenir mugs. Gift wrap was 35p or four sheets for £1;

rosettes, 15p or five for 50p; wedding day albums, £2.99 reduced from £6.99; Christmas cards in boxed sets of 10 with enveloples, £1.99 reduced from £3.99; 20 napkins, 50p reduced from 90p. All the cards are half price and include the usual range of celebratory valedictions. Hartlepool Marina hosts a recreated historic quay and harbours HMS Trincomalee, the oldest British warship still afloat, and is also the site of the new Hartlepool Museum with its interactive fighting ships section and a replica seventeenth century children's play area. There is free parking adjacent to the centre, a coffee shop, restaurant overlooking the Marina, and baby changing and disabled facilities.

## HOUSE OF HARDY

WILLOW BURN, ALNWICK, NORTHUMBERLAND NE66 2PF
☎ (01665) 602771. OPEN 9 - 5 MON - FRI, 10 - 5 SAT, 1.30 - 5 SUN FROM APRIL - OCTOBER.
Sells ends of lines for the outdoor type, especially fishermen and women, including waxed jackets, jumpers, fly vests, tops and trousers, countrywear bags, fishing rods, reels, and lines. There is also a bargain basement with own brand items on sale at discounts of about 50%.

## K VILLAGE FACTORY SHOPPING

KENDAL, NEAR JUNCTION 36 OF M6, CUMBRIA
☎ (01539) 721892. OPEN 9.30 - 7 MON - FRI, 9 - 6 SAT AND BANK HOLIDAYS, 11 - 5 SUN.
Eight outlets including The Baggage Factory selling a wide range of labels comprising Delsey, Cica, and Antler. There is also a heritage centre, a 150-seater restaurant, a coffee shop and free parking.

# Food and Drink Discounters

## BRADLEY GARDENS NURSERY

SLED LANE, WYLAM, NORTHUMBERLAND NE41 8JL
☎ (01661) 852176. OPEN 9 - 5 SEVEN DAYS A WEEK. MAIL ORDER.

Sells fresh-cut herbs by post at prices about two-thirds less than the supermarkets. All year round, they offer a range of about 13 different herbs, with more unusual varieties added to the selection in the summer months up to 80 different types. A 50 gram pack, which is in self-sealing plastic bags, casts £1.90 including post and packaging, about one-third less than in supermarkets. There are punnets of flowers in the summer and edible flowers for salads. The Nursery is closed to visitors between October and March, but the mail order service still operates.

## HIGHLAND FINE CHEESES LTD

BLURLEITH, TAIN, ROSS AND CROMARTY 1V, SCOTLAND 19 1EH
☎ (01862) 892034. OPEN 9 - 5 MON - FRI.

Specialised cheeses sold, with plans to expand the range and the premises. There are no discounts, but the selection at the factory is usually less expensive than the same cheeses in shops. All the cheese are soft cream and low fat, each with their own distinctive flavours and made in the traditional way.

## NORTHUMBRIAN FINE FOOD PLC

DUKESWAY, TEAM VALLEY INDUSTRIAL ESTATE, GATESHEAD, TYNE & WEAR NE11 OQP
☎ (0191) 487 0070. OPEN 9.30 - 1.30 MON - FRI.

Value for money cakes, biscuits and snack foods from this north-east based company which manufactures biscuits and cakes under its own brand name, such as Dunkers, Country Fitness Foods, Sunwheel, Knightsbridge, Bronte, and Cakes for the Connoisseur. They also produce a selection of private label goods for many of the high street supermarkets. The factory shop sells overruns of its entire range at very reasonable prices. Availability varies but typically includes plain and chocolate biscuits, flapjacks, cookies, confectionery and cakes.

# ROYAL LOCHNAGAR DISTILLERY

CRATHIE, BALLATER, ABERDEENSHIRE AB35 5TB
☎ (01339) 742273. OPEN 10 - 5 MON - SAT, 10 - 4 SUN IN SUMMER.
MAIL ORDER.

Spend £2 on a factory tour and you get a £3 voucher to spend at the shop attached to the distillery. While prices for these classic malts aren't rock bottom, they are likely to be cheaper than you'll find elsewhere - for example, a case of six bottles attracts a 10% discount. The shop also sells hip flasks with the distillery logo, leather items and tea towels.

# SHAW'S DUNDEE SWEET FACTORY

THE KEILLERS BUILDING, MAINS LOAN, DUNDEE DD2 4SW
☎ (01382) 461435. OPEN 11.30 - 4 MON - FRI IN SUMMER, TIMES VARY IN WINTER.

Specialises in fudge and boiled sweets, tablet and tray toffee and nougat. Discounts and special offers always available.

# REPORT FORMS

Please use the report forms on the following pages to endorse or criticise an existing entry or to nominate an outlet that you feel deserves inclusion in next year's Guide. Please nominate only outlets you have visited in the last twelve months. If as a result of your information your entry is published in The Good Deal Directory newsletter or book, you will receive a cheque for £10. So please always send us your name and address.

# REPORT FORM
# EARN £10

Write and tell us about a Good Deal shop you have visited and if we publish it, we'll send you a cheque for £10.

TO:   **The Good Deal Directory,
PO Box 4, Lechlade, Glos GL7 3YB**

**Name of Outlet** ...................................................................................

...........................................................................................................

**Address** ...........................................................................................

...........................................................................................................

...........................................................................................................

**Telephone number** ........................................................................

**Type of Merchandise** ...................................................................

...........................................................................................................

...........................................................................................................

**Comments**

*Please continue overleaf*

**Signed** ....................................................................................

**Name** (capitals please) ..........................................................

**Address** ..............................................................................

.................................................................................................

**Tel No.** ...............................................................................

**Date** ...................................................................................

# REPORT FORM
# EARN £10

Write and tell us about a Good Deal shop you have visited and if we
publish it, we'll send you a cheque for £10.

TO:  **The Good Deal Directory,
PO Box 4, Lechlade, Glos GL7 3YB**

**Name of Outlet** ........................................................................

........................................................................................................

**Address** ...................................................................................

........................................................................................................

........................................................................................................

**Telephone number** ..............................................................

**Type of Merchandise** ..........................................................

........................................................................................................

........................................................................................................

**Comments**

*Please continue overleaf*

**Signed** .................................................................................

**Name** (capitals please) ................................................................

**Address** ..............................................................................

.....................................................................................................

**Tel No.** ...............................................................................

**Date** ..................................................................................

# REPORT FORM
# EARN £10

Write and tell us about a Good Deal shop you have visited and if we publish it, we'll send you a cheque for £10.

TO: **The Good Deal Directory,
PO Box 4, Lechlade, Glos GL7 3YB**

**Name of Outlet** ...................................................................................

...........................................................................................................

**Address** ...............................................................................................

...........................................................................................................

...........................................................................................................

**Telephone number** .............................................................................

**Type of Merchandise** .........................................................................

...........................................................................................................

...........................................................................................................

**Comments**

*Please continue overleaf*

**Signed** ..................................................................................................

**Name** (capitals please) ..........................................................

**Address** ..........................................................................................

................................................................................................................

**Tel No.** ..........................................................................................

**Date** ..............................................................................................

## REPORT FORM
# EARN £10

Write and tell us about a Good Deal shop you have visited and if we
publish it, we'll send you a cheque for £10.

TO:     **The Good Deal Directory,
        PO Box 4, Lechlade, Glos GL7 3YB**

**Name of Outlet** .............................................................................

..............................................................................................

**Address** .......................................................................................

..............................................................................................

..............................................................................................

**Telephone number** .......................................................................

**Type of Merchandise** ...................................................................

..............................................................................................

..............................................................................................

**Comments**

*Please continue overleaf*

# REPORT FORM
# EARN £10

Write and tell us about a Good Deal shop you have visited and if we
publish it, we'll send you a cheque for £10.

TO:     **The Good Deal Directory,
        PO Box 4, Lechlade, Glos GL7 3YB**

**Name of Outlet** ............................................................................

............................................................................................................

**Address** ........................................................................................

............................................................................................................

............................................................................................................

**Telephone number** ....................................................................

**Type of Merchandise** ................................................................

............................................................................................................

............................................................................................................

**Comments**

*Please continue overleaf*

**Signed** .................................................................................................

**Name** (capitals please) ...........................................................

**Address** ...............................................................................................

.................................................................................................................

.................................................................................................................

**Date** .......................................................................................................

# THE GOOD DEAL DIRECTORY NEWSLETTER

The Good Deal Directory newsletter
keeps you up to date with showroom
and designer sales and new openings
of discount outlets. It appears monthly
(except for January and August).
An annual subscription costs just £15.
Write now to The Good Deal Directory,
Freepost SW 6037, London SW10 9YY
for your free sample copy.
(No stamp required)